THE HUMAN PERSON:
ANIMAL AND SPIRIT

The Human Person:
ANIMAL AND SPIRIT

David Braine

UNIVERSITY OF NOTRE DAME PRESS
NOTRE DAME, INDIANA

Library of Congress Cataloging-in-Publication Data

Braine, David.
    The human person : animal and spirit / David Braine.
      p. cm.
    ISBN 0-268-01098-6
    1. Philosophical anthropology. 2. Mind and body.
3. Mechanism (Philosophy)—Controversial literature.
I. Title.
BD450.86465 1992
128—dc20   92-53754
                                        CIP

In love to the memory of
MY MOTHER AND FATHER
that their honour may remain upon earth—
their souls lie in the hand of God

When I look up at your heavens, the work of your fingers,
At the moon and the stars you set in their place—
Ah, what are human beings that you should remember them,
Their children that you should care for them?

Psalm 8:3–4

Contents

Preface

A preface is personal, while a book is presented impersonally.

For some, the human being is primarily a spirit, a being with intellect and choice, and only secondarily a being tied up with the body and living in the world with other animals.

In this book I approach things from the opposite perspective. The first need is to understand the human being's character as an animal living in the world, and it is only at a second stage that one can go on to understand what is special to human beings, what is involved in their intellectuality and their capacity for reflection and choice. (It is for this reason that, except for the sake of literary convenience, I do not speak of the human person as a 'person' in Part One of the book but only as a 'being' or 'animal'. For that is the question of Part Two, whether this particular kind of being is indeed a 'person', a being whose thought and action is moved through the intellect rather than merely by chance or material causation.)

Accordingly, Part One of this book is directed towards systematically closing off each and every avenue to the reconstruction of dualistic or materialist positions reducing animals and human beings to their parts and their interrelations, and to setting forth the resulting holism in a positive light. This establishes the human being as truly an animal. The question then remains as to whether and how this animal can also be a spirit, a spiritual or intellectual being whose existence transcends the body. Part Two makes it intelligible how this can be so and indeed demonstrates that it is so, basing its principal arguments on the nature of language—on the generality and openness of its basic structures and concepts and its flexibility, all within the context of an intrinsic self-reflexiveness. This is crucial since it is language in its integral development (a development which reveals each element and aspect as integrated with others in an organic whole) which is above all the peculiarity, the specific defining feature of human nature.

Elizabeth Anscombe was once challenged with the remark 'But you said in your book. . .', and in response expostulated 'We're not interested in what I said in my book. We are trying to get to the truth of the matter'. The vocation of the philosopher is to make no compromise. Others may rest satisfied with their thoughts, but the philosopher may remain dissatisfied. Such as philosopher is liable to be his or her own most severe critic.

And at all times, both here and in my previous work on *The Reality of Time and Existence of God* I have found this the situation. In that work I was occupied in the task of proving, rendering unmistakable the existence of God, the furnace causing the existence and continuance in existence of all things. In this work I am occupied in the more bizarre and difficult task of proving the existence of Man—the human person as truly animal and bodily and yet also truly intellectual and free.

In respect of the present work, an earlier draft was criticized for a neglect of more recent discussions of perception and of action by 'analytical' philosophers. However, upon examination, I found that these discussions raised no new issue, no argument of any quality, only fresh illustrations of how academics can fail to see the point and substitute a mere fudge, a pretence of argument in place of real understanding. True, behind some of the points made were issues about the status of states and events made explicit by Davidson, the *eminence grise* behind much recent writing: these issues, important also in the philosophy of science, presented a deeper problem. Again, the behaviourist idea expressed in Kenny's remark that, if human behaviour remained the same, the same ways of speaking would be appropriate even if the brain was made of sawdust, suggested to me that Aristotle's notion of the human animal as a 'body with organs' is vital to the concept of the human being—as at once a member of the physical universe and an intellectual or reflective being—it is part of human nature that the mental should be underpinned by physical function, and this is something which the behaviourist has failed to register.

But my main fight was quite different, a matter of comparative unconcern to contemporary analytical philosophers who are mostly firmly set in a physicalistic or materialistic bent. I have already indicated the need to avoid any truck with dualistic ideas, whether disguised in contemporary brain/body materialism or in the traditional mind/body form. In this context, the primary motive for introducing the idea of 'soul' was to express the repudiation of dualistic ideas in favour of a more holistic view. However, in using the same word "soul" in connection with the special character of the operation of intellect, whose peculiar human mode of exhibition is seen in language, it was vital to avoid smuggling the soul back in such a way as to become again a distinct substance from the body. In this fight I was kept faithful above all by the earthy realism of one of my student helpers, Paul Murray—to whom the common uncritical talk of soul seemed like a delving back into pre-Wittengensteinian and pre-modern superstition. Yet at the same time I had to avoid the farce whereby the idea of the soul is represented as redundant to religion, as if a mere qualitative identity would suffice to make the person that dies the same as the person that will enjoy resurrection. This makes talk of soul a mere manner of speech—and suggests that as such the notion of immaterial intellect is nonsense, so that all talk of God can be dismissed without further thought. Yet it is quite evident that the ideas of the human soul and of God cannot be expurgated from Christian teaching, or from that of other religions.

Yet, how to produce an account which allows the human person to continue existing after death, and even to have body restored to it, while remaining completely faithful to the insight that it belongs to human nature to be bodily, bodily in the material underpinning of the ensemble of its operations and bodily in its expressions! This was the real challenge, to do this and yet avoid re-erecting the soul into a complete substance, a challenge with which most analytical philosophers, mesmerized by the idea that mental processes are essentially brain processes, have no preoccupation. Yet, does all pass to nothing at death?—only a memory, a meaning or a message, being possibly left, and this only if chance allows—but no substantial being or person? no being or person even to hope or pray for restoration and interactive communion with others, let alone to enjoy it?

With this the normal run of analytical philosophers have no concern, self-lumbered with an at root dualistic brain/body preconception of the relation of the mental and the behavioural. As a result, if compelled to consider the matter at all, they conceive the claimed transcendence of the human being and the human capacity to survive death only according to patterns set by dualism and their own dualistic analysis—pretending that they would prefer to reinstate the soul as a separate substance correlated with the brain rather than experiment with any more holistic way of viewing the human being. And here lies their superficiality: to ignore what has been most alive in modern philosophy, the singular freshness of its revitalized critique of dualism, with the effect merely of making themselves little more than uncritical underservants of the most modern form of materialism, that presented by Artificial Intelligence theorists; and this is capped by their complete lack of concern with the existential problems of freedom and death which belong to the human lot.

The roots of my coming to view things in the order I have indicated—with the unity of human kind with the animals and the physical universe first, and the peculiarities of the human only second —lie back in the period of my first encounter with academic philosophy, in 1962. At that time I was introduced to that whole historical tradition, inspired by Descartes and the British empiricists, which creates a logical gulf between mind and body, the tradition which begins by thinking of human beings as minds, and only afterwards inquires about their knowledge of the world and relation to it. At the very same time, I met in Ryle, Wittgenstein, and Austin the beginnings of an antidote to this false way of viewing the human situation and began to discover some of the clues to an approach which would restore a perception of the unity of the human being—the beginnings indeed of a restoration to respectability of our ordinary ways of thinking about perception, emotion, and action, as it were before the philosophers had corrupted them. And I began to see these philosophers and some of those influenced by them as beginning to provide the analytic framework required if one was to escape the seeming madnesses of the dualistic tradition.

Then, over the years, first in Maritain's little book *The Dream of Descartes*, then in Aristotle and Aquinas, and later in Marcel and Merleau-Ponty, I found that this perception of man as by nature a bodily being—not indeed simply material, but a psychophysical unity, an incarnate consciousness—was not new in philosophy, but itself represented a longstanding tradition running counter to the dualism, severing mind and body, which stemmed from Plato and Descartes. I also found that, far from being the enemy of religion, this holistic perception of the human being as a unity was integral to Jewish, Christian, and much other religious tradition.

In the meantime, I discovered that in recent 'Anglo-Saxon' or 'analytical' philosophy the insights of Ryle, Wittgenstein, and Austin and the structure of their critique of dualism had been almost completely abandoned. But this critique had not been answered; it had been simply lost sight of. It was as if Copernicus and Galileo had written, but the philosophers were still constructing epicycles to explain how despite it all the sun and the planets still went round the earth. And of course the elaborations of analytical philosophy are bottomless.

Yet then, worse still, I realized that the whole modern materialist theory of mind depended on a simple reduplication of the dualist picture: you have to make the mental into something inner before you can even suggest that it is identical to a state or event in the brain. As a companion student about 1963 confessed to me 'I would be ashamed to be found saying that thoughts were anything else than brain processes'—his subject was psychology and his presumption the same uncritical presumption which has governed psychologists from the eighteenth century to the present with little new in the way of systematic supporting evidence (after all, ought one not first to understand what it is to think, which may not be just one thing? and, in order to understand the peculiar character of human thinking, perhaps first to examine what it is to speak?—but this is to anticipate the argument of this book). And the further I went the more it was confirmed that this kind of materialist approach, relying upon its own system of epicycles or specially contrived explanation, depended upon the same myopia of reliance on the principle of turning the blind eye—as if Aristotle, Ryle, Wittgenstein, and Austin need never have existed.

Descartes makes no distinction between self-consciousness and consciousness and rests his argument against materialism on consciousness, something we seem to share with the higher animals, and only makes human beings unique by turning the other animals into automata. The insights I have spoken of show that it is as mistaken to treat perception, emotion, and pain mechanistically in the animal as in the human case: if the doctrine of 'compatibilism', the idea that our common understanding of these things is compatible with a mechanistic explanation of behaviour is wrong in the human case, then it is wrong in the higher animal case also.

However, all this was only the first stage of my thinking.

I said that Descartes rests his argument against materialism on consciousness. But the older argument for the special nature of personal beings turned not on consciousness but on intellect, something whose most evident human expressions are not in perception, emotion and the experience of pain, but in speech and writing—in brief in the works of language.

Meantime, the Artificial Intelligence theorists work on the principle 'Softly, softly, catchee monkey', discovering ways of simulating this or that piece of end-directed behaviour, this or that aspect of phonetics and the work of translation, and then latching on to the mathematically proven results that certain parts of logic and grammar allow a mechanical decision procedure. On this meagre basis they expect that the whole explanation of human linguistic and other behaviour will fall like an apple into their hands. And here is their weak point. They have grasped at superficial aspects of structure while ignoring the central elements of what is involved in human linguistic understanding and thinking in the medium of words. And they make this error yet more flagrant by also ignoring mathematically proven results as to the impossibility of formalizing natural language or even something so limited as the modes of proof accessible to us in natural arithmetic—now ignoring Tarski and Gödel in addition to a multitude of philosophers from Aristotle to Wittgenstein.

For the obstacles which language presents are obstacles in principle. The things I present in Chapter XII, first the way in which thinking in the medium of words is composed of parts in its expression but not in itself, second, the fact that judgement cannot be explained in terms of modelling, third, the distinction between *langue* and *parole* and this as the root of the extensibility and flexibility of language, and fourth the structures of self-reflectivity internal to natural language and implicit in every utterance, are not new discoveries but open to common view. And the idea that they make material simulation impossible is not modern but ancient, not the secret of some special science but the common opinion of most reflecting persons of all times. What is new in this century is that developments in linguistics and the mathematical theory of systems of proof allow us to *demonstrate* the points concerned. (And, since it is mathematically demonstrable that, if a task cannot be performed by a Turing machine, then it will not be performable by any other mechanism however much its efficiency or speed had been increased by such devices as parallel processing, this recent suggestion makes no difference to the argument.)

But the belief in mechanism owes nothing of its strength to reason, and so the result of such demonstrations has been only a yet further elaboration of epicycles.

One favoured idea is that the 'brain/mind' is to be compared with a system of 'computers/unintelligent minds' working together like a committee, with the Ego as a kind of public relations officer giving the supposedly relevant gloss to any actions performed. In this analogy, the thinking is entirely undisciplined: the chance workings of a committee and public relations officer, supposedly unreasoned, have been substituted for any mechanical system of parallel processing.[1] But this cheap analogy misses the main point: the given structures of human life, presupposed to thinking, experience, and action (including the thinking and judgement of those putting forward the theories concerned) have been entirely ignored—and even the structures which we share with the higher animals. Here, I have contented myself with using a few authors, Dennett, Allport, and suchlike, as representative, rather than attempting a global review of writing in the field—just as in treating perception and action, I consider only a few authors, some six or seven, sufficient to show how the main lines of counter-argument are to be dealt with, but not attempting a survey designed to deal with every footling variation on what turn out to be the same basic moves.

For here we return to the earlier difficulty, since if the AI theorists cannot account for the unitariness of human operation it will turn out that they cannot account for the unitariness of operation in the higher animals. For the basic structures of human life include these, first that the subject of experience (including perception) is the same as the subject of thought and judgement, and second that the subject of experience (above all perception) is the same as the subject of intentional action. And it was the second of these evident features of human life, the feature shared with animals, which was questioned in Plato and throughout the tradition inaugurated by Descartes. It is the task of the first Part of this book to restore the initial vision and thus dispel the cloud of dust raised by philosophers—restore the vision of a living being whose nature is to have operations whose mental and physical aspects are inextricable from each other, indeed parts and members of the physical or natural universe but living and

---

[1]True, modularization and the suggestion of distinct elements within mental functioning being simulated by distinct parallelly processed subsystems may be helpful in understanding some mental functions. But they still do nothing to explain the unitariness of intellectual function as expressed in language.

in the human case unmistakably reflective and responsible on behalf of themselves and the whole.

In my use of quotation marks, I have followed the following rule. Wherever a logician would wish to distinguish between using a name or other expression (as in saying that Socrates taught Plato) and speaking about this name or other expression (as in saying that "Socrates" has eight letters), and wherever a logician or philosopher would want to mark out statements or propositions or forms of statement or proposition for the purposes of marking out how certain inferences work or are supposed to work, I have used double quotes for the singling out of the relevant names, expressions, statements, etc. And for the logical purposes mentioned I have kept to this even when it involves putting double quotes inside double quotes. But, where no such formal purpose is served, I have in all other circumstances kept to single quotation marks as in simply quoting other authors or in (e.g.) saying informally that John was called 'John'.

I have also kept rigidly to the rule that no foreign punctuation or other matter should appear within quotation marks of either kind which does not belong to what is cited or singled out (except for indications of incompleteness in one's citation or explanatory matter in square brackets).

The origin of this work lay in my second series of Gifford Investigations presented in 1984 as Gifford Fellow at the University of Aberdeen. In its continuance since 1988, I have been especially upheld by the constant faith and support of Professor Alvin Plantinga and the Notre Dame Center for the Philosophy of Religion, including the assistance of the Center in publication. I must also thank Anthony Schmitz, David Alston, and Dr Ingolf Ebel for their patience in reading the whole script at different stages of its development, and the particular advice of Professor Angus McIntyre and Dr Ebel in regard to particular points.

In the Preface of my earlier book *The Reality of Time and the Existence of God*, composed between late 1983 and 1987, which itself began as the first series of Gifford Investigations, I recorded the names of twenty-one people who had been involved secretarially in helping me. However, the preparation of this second work has extended from 1984 into 1992, and perhaps sixty people have helped me as the work passed through different transformations in the extraordinary system of help which has supported me in the exigencies, physical and psychological, arising out of my spinal injury. I cannot name them all, but before any others I must pick out those who were involved in helping me when I was at my weakest at the very start, Professor Kamil Ettinger and Patsy Henderson, even as the conception of the work first took form. In 1987 as my work on this project resumed, I had the advantage that all the foreworkings had been put onto disk by Barbara Rae relying upon the system Keith Whitefield had set up for me. For the next two years I was supported above all by the help and belief in my work of Dr Sean Wilkie and Paul Murray, with Rob Scott and others introduced through him. The personal support not only of these but of Ashley Gaskin, Simon Saunders, John Reid, William Pickard, and Kevin Forbes was of special importance but without the help and faithfulness of many others the work would never have been brought to completion—amongst them Phillipa, Jane Dobbie, David Flannagan, Judith and Gavin, Donald Meston, Jonathan Brocklebank, Martin Waterson, Terry Durkin, Matthew Grant, Graham Bell, Daibhidh Grannd, Graeme Herd, Janet, Maria, Donald, Stephen, and Mark, Barbara, Louise, Meryl, and Alison, Lars, Kirsty, Ally, and Giles, Marion, Alasdair, Colin, Alison, Alan, Graeme, Sonja, Ruth, Kenny, Dawné, and Eric.

From this record, itself leaving the most key help unrecorded, it may be seen that, if Empedocles was right that the world is the field of operation of love and strife, then this book is the work of love.

Prologue: What It Is for the Human Being to Be an Animal and for This Animal to Be a Spirit

To be a human being is, I shall demonstrate in this book, to be at the same time an animal and also a spirit.

What do I mean by these things? In this Prologue let me sketch this out in a few broad strokes, in this way announcing beforehand the main theses of the book and some of their context.

Our Meaning in Saying That Human Beings Are Animals: Animals Are Not Physical Mechanisms

As my argument unfolds, we shall see ever more clearly how deeply materialism betrays what is distinctive in human beings as animals and bodily living things. Materialism proposes that the physical behaviour which exhibits life or consciousness can ultimately be explained without bringing in non-physical principles. For the materialists the only ultimate or fundamental laws of the universe are physical. For them, living things are only transitory nodes of stability, more long-lived than waves or vortices, things whose stability and modes of functioning are determined by underlying physical law, so that the fundamental laws of the universe do not need to include any which refer specifically to life or consciousness.

The dualist differs from the materialist by asserting that there are other, non-physical, entities called souls alongside a physical universe considered to be made up only of purely physical entities—souls external to this universe and not parts of it. These souls are supposed to interact with the physical universe, so that the fundamental laws of the universe include, besides purely physical laws, other laws governing the life of these souls, their interference in the physical world, and the side-effects of physical things upon them. Except for

1

these latter laws, governing the interference of these souls with the world of bodies, the reign of physical law within the physical universe remains complete. Dualism sets aside the Aristotelian conception that the physical universe embraces a spread of different types of thing, each successive type liable to be marked by different kinds of principle of activity, a world within which there is a pluralism of radically varied kinds of bodily thing apart from any pluralism of kinds of immaterial substance. In its place we are presented with a world of homogeneous entities conforming to one uniform pattern of explanation in purely physical terms, a monism of purely material things, or else a dualism in which these are interfered with as if from the outside by supposed spirits conceived of as purely immaterial.

In this way neither the materialist nor the dualist allow for the existence of things which are essentially biophysical in character, bodily things which are integral parts of the physical universe but of such a kind that their principles of behaviour involve life and consciousness in ways not reducible to physical terms. That is, neither allow for the existence of entities which are indeed parts of the physical universe but whose behaviour can only be understood in terms of biological or psychophysical, not purely physical, law—parts which have to be considered as wholes ('holistically'), because their behaviour cannot be analysed by considering them as interacting combines of a soul external to the physical universe with a physical body within it. Neither allow for the possibility that some of the ultimate or fundamental laws of the physical universe cannot escape reference to the phenomena of life and consciousness. By "the physical universe" I mean the spatial world in which bodily things move: it is to this that the 'souls' of dualist doctrine are external but to which human beings and other animals, as psychophysical unities, themselves bodily things, are internal.

By the terms "animal" and "living thing", I mean to indicate precisely those bodily beings the principles of whose behaviour, even bodily behaviour, involve such things as life and consciousness in a way which is not merely derivative but fundamental, reference to which is not capable of being eliminated. The whole of what is involved will only become clear in Chapter IX.

How, if the material is real, can there be any alternative to materialism and dualism?

In order to see how this is possible, we need to grasp the peculiar sameness of materialism and dualism. Both view the human being as an aggregate of parts in certain relations, the behaviour of the whole being the resultant of the interactions of these parts. In materialism, we have the brain and the rest of the body. In dualism, we have just the same material parts as in materialism and, in addition, a non-material part, the soul.

But the sameness is more intimate than this.

Destroy the unity of the human being and you destroy the unity of the biography of this human being. Perception is dissolved into, first, a 'perceptual experience' conceived of as something entirely 'inner' to the mind (whether it be a going-on in the brain or a going-on in the soul); second, 'external' goings-on and states of affairs in the sense organs and the physical world; and third, together with these, a causal relation between them. Intentional action is likewise dissolved into an 'inner' act of will and an 'outer' bodily movement, together with a causal relation between them. And so it is with every state or going-on involving consciousness: it is dissolved into an inner part which is an element in the history of the soul or brain and an outer part which is purely physical and an element in the history of the 'outer man' and the rest of the physical world.

It is no longer the human being as such who enjoys direct perception of the world in a situation of exploratory relation to it and who acts within the world. There are no direct human relations of knowledge of or of causal action upon the world. On analysis, it is not that the human being as such is in direct and real relations of these kinds to the world but that states or goings-on in the human soul, mind, or brain are in indirect, mediated, and contingent relation to states and goings on in the world. For the mind to be directed towards an object is, in this analysis, for it to be directed towards an 'intentional' object, for things to be 'as if' they are as they are believed or assumed to be, for them to be 'as if' this object were real, without any implication that things are in fact as they are believed or assumed to be or that the object is in fact real.

In all this the materialist has exactly the same picture as the dualist. Indeed, unless the mental can first be represented as inner, logically independent of anything in the 'outer man' and the 'world', there is no way in which it can be identified with a brain-process or state. And once the mind is identified with the brain, instead of being the notional prey of deceiving demons as in Descartes' dualism, it becomes with more seeming realism the possible prey of supposed neurosurgeons; and in this way the origins and status of its private world can be just as obscure as they were in Descartes.

As against all this, I insist that the human being is not an aggregate of parts in certain relations, but a being who has to be treated as a subject of life and consciousness if one is to describe and explain even his or her bodily behaviour. Human beings like other higher animals are essential unities: the physical cannot be extricated from a proper account of what is logically involved in the mental in human life. Conversely concepts such as life and consciousness cannot be extricated from an account of the nature of human bodily behaviour—any proper account of the mental involves the physical and any proper account of the physical involves the mental.

We must not envisage the holistic view of human beings and the other higher animals simply in terms of a different kind of integratedness which they might possess if they were 'material entities' ('machines' in Ryle's terms)—i.e., some special kind of integratedness in how their physical parts act together. Rather it is an integratedness whereby they are focalized—whereby they are centres of consciousness in such a way that bodily behaviour is attributed to this centre of consciousness and in such a way that consciousness enters into, not only the description, but also the explanation of the behaviour. As I shall show, there is no self-sufficiency in the physical: it is not just that the physical may require God to explain its existence and continuance in existence, but that (quite aside from this) the fullest explanation and prediction of the behaviour of the physical depend on bringing in the mental—not the mental as an outside influence, but the mental as involved inextricably in psychophysical concepts. In Aristotelian terms, it is not primarily that form or soul depends on matter, but that matter depends for its existence and determinate nature, the nature which is the principle of its behaviour, upon form or soul.

What we have to insist upon is an integratedness whereby it is the human being or animal as such which is the centre of this consciousness and of these consciousness-involving bodily activities, and not merely some special inner part of this 'he or she' such as the mind or brain. The 'inner' perceptual experiences and acts of will, believed in by dualist and materialist alike as elements within normal perception and action, are myths. There are here no such elements, and therefore no such inner mental candidates to be identical with some events or processes in the brain. Perception and intentional action each involve aspects and parts but cannot be analysed into these parts. Each of them involves direct cognitive and causal relations between the human being as a perceptually active exploring agent and the world. In this way, it is the bodily animal being as such, not just its mind, which is an 'I', a 'he or she', a focalized subject in relation to the world. The primary reason why human behaviour cannot be simulated by a computer does not lie in things special to human beings, but in the fact that this focalized psychophysical structure which they share with the higher animals cannot be thus simulated. And we shall find that the only viable conceptions of soul are not the dualistic ones but older conceptions in which the idea of soul expressed not dualism but an holistic understanding of human existence and functioning, conceptions whereby other animals also have souls.

This then is what I mean by saying that the human being is an animal. It is as Ryle told us: 'Man need not be degraded to a machine by being denied to be a ghost in a machine. He might, after all, be a sort of animal, namely, a higher mammal. There has yet to be ventured the hazardous leap to the hypothesis that perhaps he is a man.'[1]

To restore this conception of the unity of the human being and the community of human kind with the higher animals, their essentially psychosomatic or psychophysical character, and to paint its significance will be the work of the first nine chapters of this book. Always we should follow the principle of treating what belongs to the human being as an animal first, and then allow this to shape our way of viewing the things peculiar to human beings.

Language as the Animal Form of Intellectuality

We now have to introduce the perspective of Part Two of this book, Chapters X to XV.

What differentiates human beings from the other animals is language in that full sense of the word which is made plain in Chapter X, along with what is inseparable from such language, namely linguistic understanding and thinking in the medium of words. It is this which differentiates human or animal intellectuality from any other possible

---

[1] *The Concept of Mind*, p. 328 (Hutchinson), p. 310 (Penguin).

form of intellectuality—whether of God, of angels, or any other kind of being whose existence might be envisaged. For, just as when life figures within the physical world, it figures in the form of biological life, and when consciousness figures in the world it figures in the form of the life of higher animals, so also when intellectuality figures in the world it figures in the form of language—and, in human nature unimpaired, in the form of language in the medium of vocal sounds.

Here it is vital to recognize that in regarding language in this full sense as what is peculiar to human nature, we pick on something which is itself inseparably animal as well as intellectual. That is, we pick on something which involves not only understanding and thinking but also expression in some particular medium. Linguistic understanding and thinking in the medium of words belong to the same biography as hearing and speech, and along with them to perceptual, emotional, and action-involving relation to the environment and other people in general. For it belongs to human nature unimpaired to have all the structures of brain, nervous organization, anatomy, and musculature required for expression in vocal sounds—where this whole physical apparatus is adequate to serve as a vehicle of overt linguistic activity of the structure concerned.

In brief, it is the human being, the animal, who is a 'spirit', an intellectual being or substance. If anything human is open to God, it is the human being as such, the animal, not just the human soul.

These privileges belong primarily to the human animal as such, to the human primate, something genuinely part or member of the natural universe. They are not reserved to some inner component—soul or mind—within the human being, some immaterial entity, as if this alone was the spirit, the intellectual substance, the self-reflective being open to God. If we can speak of soul or mind at all as spirit or as intellectual substance or as open to God, it is only in some secondary way of speaking, derived from the primary idiom, according to which we say these things unqualifiedly of the man or woman, the animal, the real part or member of the physical universe.

And because of this, it is not primarily a soul, but primarily the human being or person which, if anything, might continue after death—to borrow Shakespeare's words, 'sans teeth, sans eyes, sans taste, sans everything'—perhaps waiting upon a restoration or resurrection, but apart from this in privation, without body and whatever depends on it. The human being is not a pure soul which might wait a new incarnation, beginning again from the womb or taking different form, to have a new history unrelated to the old. Rather he or she would await something which would constitute a meaningful continuation, restored in bodily faculty and memory, of his or her already lived history. Human beings like other animals have their being and identity anchored in their original beginnings in the womb, and continue like other animals to require bodily faculties for the living of their lives according to their natures. This is the elemental fact, so that the primary question is of the character of the human being in this life; the question of survival after death is secondary, being determined by one's answer to the first.

Against this background, the whole existential question confronting human beings is the question, applying to them in this life which we know of, as to whether in their thought and in their values—their preferences and their choices—they are enclosed and determined by the material. But this is only a real question for beings who are fully in the natural or physical world. What matters is whether there exists or can exist a genuine member of the physical world which or who is also self-reflective, 'intellectual', or even conceivably in some sense able to represent the world in relating to God. But this question concerns the human being as such, as indeed a member of this physical world, not some immaterial soul or mind somehow adjoined to a physical body.

To consider this question, we need to consider more closely the character of this thing, 'language'—language in the primary sense of that word—which specifically differentiates human beings from the other animals. Amongst the highest animals lower than *homo sapiens* there can certainly be developed systems of communication which deserve the name 'language' because of their partial resemblance to human language. However, language in the full sense (exemplified in the human language whose semantics, grammar, and phonetics linguists are concerned with) is distinguished by a certain many-faceted unitary structure whose facets are not separable from one another. To demonstrate this fully belongs to a separate work on language,[2] but I explain in Chapter X the main lines of what is involved, since my later argument turns upon it.

---

[2]To be published as *The Expressiveness of Words: the key to the nature of language* (forthcoming).

Language in this full sense is the specifically animal kind of intellectuality. And as such it has the characteristics which belong to 'intellectuality' or 'understanding'. Understanding is indeed in itself something which enables us to proceed according to rule or intelligible reason, but without this being by a mechanically representable or formal rule because of the generality and informality involved, and so without benefit of 'mechanisms'. This is exemplified in the linguistic case by the way in which understanding of *langue* determines the understanding of speech or *parole* without this being by a formalizable or mechanically simulable rule.

What we have to escape is the fiction that there is no alternative besides those of a rigidly rule-governed mechanical system and a system not properly rule-governed at all. It is a fiction which would force us to view any understanding, whether by God or other immaterial spirit or by human beings, as proceeding according to mechanical rules, and which would thereby abolish any understanding whatsoever—whereas in fact it is only understanding operating non-mechanically (restricted to accordance with mechanical rule would in any case exclude reflectiveness and self-criticism) which can judge of the virtue of any mechanism.

The idea that within linguistic utterance there are meaning-determining components from which utterance-meaning can be calculated is commonplace amongst contemporary philosophers of language. It follows from this idea that what is involved in linguistic understanding and communication is ultimately the resultant of what can be represented as a sequence of digitally distinguishable operations analysable according to the combinatorial approach of 'Artificial Intelligence'. In this way this idea has been made the basis of the most ambitious modern form of materialism, the form which proposes a programme allowing a completely mechanistic treatment of language. It is a consequence of the unformalizability of natural language and of the relationship of *langue* and *parole* implied by it that no such calculation is possible. And in this way it is not some isolated proofs but certain of the most general features of natural language which exhibit how materialism must be false.

Just as in demonstrating our general holistic view of the human being and the other higher animals, in this case we demonstrate the absurdity of something which is universally and fashionably assumed. For it is a corollary of the unformalizability of natural language (something which has been demonstrated in many ways) that the understanding of *langue* cannot be a brain-state and that thinking in the medium of words cannot be a brain-process—nor, of course, state or process in some immaterial apparatus. This we shall demonstrate in Chapter XII in four converging lines of argument, drawing upon the features of linguistic understanding and thinking made clear in Chapters X and XI.

The Question of the Transcendence of Human Existence

The question then arises as to whether we can argue further that the human being has not only states and activities which transcend the body but also an existence which transcends the body.

Two approaches suggest themselves, one in terms of the transcendence of the existence of the human soul over the existence of the material, and the other in terms of the transcendence of the existence of the human being as such. In Chapter XIII I explain two non-dualistic ways of speaking of souls, both of which require one to speak of souls in the case of other higher animals as well as in the case of human beings, and make clear that any dualistic conception of soul is incoherent. Then in Chapter XIV, I explain how human transcendence can be expressed in terms of a transcendence of the human soul without a return to dualism. However, in Chapter XV, I go further and show how the relevant kind of transcendence can be expressed more directly in terms simply of the transcendence of the existence of the human being as such without bringing in soul, and this will be the primary way of speaking. In both approaches, the transcendence of the human being follows straightway from the fact that linguistic understanding and thinking are not bodily operations of any kind, transcendence in operation showing some transcendence in existence.

What we have achieved in this line of argument running right through from Chapter X to Chapter XV is the opening out of a non-dualistic account of human transcendence.

Since the time of Galileo it has been assumed that the sphere of the material or physical is explanatorily self-sufficient, effects caused from outside that sphere being interferences upon a world of bodies with existence in their own right, independent substances in their own right. And within this framework the only way to salvage the capacity of the human being to survive death—even to be available to be raised up, the same person, in a resurrection—is to suppose the mind or the soul to be another independent substance interfering and interacting with the body as independently established. That is, once one has embraced the superstition of the self-sufficiency of the material, the only way of salvaging the transcendence of the human being is by embracing a second superstition, the one called dualism. And Descartes embraced this way out, offered to him by a long established tradition rooted in Plato.

But our way is different. We know from Part One of the book that the material or physical lacks the self-sufficiency or substantial independence which, ever since Galileo, it has been assumed to have—that no proper account or explanation can be given of the living body and its behaviour in purely material or physical terms, that the psychophysical or mental has to be brought in even for the understanding and prediction of bodily behaviour. Therefore, what we have to insist upon is not that the human being or the human soul can have no existence not dependent on the body, but only that the human body in its nature has no existence independent of the human being or (if we speak of souls) of the human soul—a thing's nature is the principle of its behaviour and key to its identity.

And this is the context of our argument from the nature of language in Part Two of this book demonstrating the transcendence of the human being and (if we speak of souls) of the human soul. And in taking language as the starting-point of our demonstration we begin, not from something supposedly purely spiritual or immaterial, but from something, language, which is in itself unmistakably psychophysical, something unmistakably characteristic not of angels or so-called 'pure spirits' but of human beings—and it is from this starting-point that we proceed to consider the character of the kind of understanding and thought which language expresses. And in demonstrating the transcendence of the existence of the human being and the human soul over the material, we are concerned not just with the possibility of continuance after death but more generally with the status and significance of the human being and of his or her thought and freedom in this life—as something not determined by, enclosed within, or limited to the material and what is set by the material.

In this way, we show human beings to have a nature commensurate with their situation.

Language in the full sense with which we are concerned exhibits that human beings are animals whose situation is being laid bare, not only to the objects of their natural environment, which they perceive or can imagine and to the emotions which these give rise to, but also to an indefinitely wider range of objects—indeed to whatever human beings may, through language, be laid bare. By their situation, as language makes it present to them, human beings are animals with a peculiar character and role. For they are thus made open to being alert to the values of personhood, life, order, and existence as such. As a result of the human being's being in this way alive to his or her community, to his or her environment, to the cosmos, and to God, his or her life has a dimension not shared with the other animals, albeit one which he or she may be regarded as having on their behalf.

In this last aspect, as a member of the community of nature, the human being may be regarded as guardian of respect for it, guardian against the adoption of a technological mentality in regard to it. As animal becomes conscious of itself, the human being is able to be aware that he or she is not in the position of a mind administering machines, but in the position of a member of Nature to exercise reverence towards it and, if it has a Maker, towards its Maker.

This is the human situation in its many aspects, defined by the preoccupations which come with the understanding and thought expressed by language. In showing that human beings have a nature commensurate with this situation and preoccupations, we show that the significance they set upon the issues with which they find themselves presented and upon their responses to these issues is not mere self-deception—as if the preoccupations which come to human beings with language had the status of mere invention, figments of cultures which they cannot escape, their judgements being by-products of a merely material nature, determined in ways ultimately set by physical parameters, so that the conclusions they reach, the decisions they make, which things they decide to stand for, their seeming value to themselves or to other people, were all ultimately of no importance or significance. On the contrary, the preoccupations we have indicated are appropriate to human nature and human beings are not deceived in thinking these things have importance and significance.

Observations on the Wider Context of Our Enquiries

I now come to the wider context in which our discussions are set, topics not dealt with in this book, but the approach to which is transformed by the perspectives we put forward. I have in view here the question of the possibility and shape of ethics and the place of the environment within it, and the question of the possibility of relationship with God and the continuance of this relationship after death.

As to the latter question, Jewish religious tradition—and with it orthodox Christian tradition with its sense of the value of the sacramental, of the liturgical, and of art, and with its emphasis on the resurrection of the body—are deeply imbued with the holistic point of view which this book espouses, and so have never sat happily with Platonist or Cartesian dualism.

For these traditions the problem as to how life after death is possible is an old difficulty. The idea of soul and body as independent realities so that the soul can even pre-exist a particular incarnation in the body and once incarnated can readily be reincarnated is excluded as a dualist conception. Rather, the human being, with any human 'soul' which is spoken of, can only take its origin with the body and is conceived of as possessing only a deprived existence after death, an existence without a body, waiting to be resurrected. Indeed there has always been a problem for these traditions as to how the human being or the human soul can have any existence apart from the body so as to be available to await resurrection, the problem we address in Chapters XIV and XV. But the gulf between the conceptions of resurrection and reincarnation is not often fully realized. The conception of reincarnation involves the supposedly independently existing soul in a process of passing through several separate biographies or personal life-histories, each involving a passage from egg and larva or embryo through infancy to various states of more mature knowledge and behavioural formation, virtue or vice—a supposed continuity of spirit in the absence of any continuity of psychological, cognitive or appetitive state. By contrast, the concept of resurrection involves a single life-history or biography in which there is only one non-metaphorical passage from embryo through infancy to the process of maturing in many stages; the developed personal ties, intellectual virtues of wisdom and understanding with their particular character and direction of interest, and yet more important, the moral virtues with their particular physiognomy as developed on the individual person, reflected in different emphases—seen in this life in such terms as care of people, or poverty and detachment, or contemplation and love of wisdom—will not then be lost in the resurrection but brought to fulfilment. That is to say that, according to the concept of resurrection, grace may perfect nature but never does away with it, so that the process of natural development from infancy to adulthood and death is never done away with so as to be open to repetition, but only brought to completion.

However, it is upon the first problem that I now wish to concentrate attention—the problem of the possibility and shape of ethics and of the place of respect for nature within ethics, a problem of which we have only become properly aware in more recent times.

In this regard, materialism and dualism have exactly the same effect. Both engender the concept of the human being as a mind administering a machine, whether the mind be conceived of as a separate entity or as identical to a certain particular part of the machine, viz., the brain. In this way, both views introduce a strange alienation between human beings and their own bodies and between human beings and their environment of which their bodies are part: in so far as they think, deliberate and choose they are in the position of minds administering physical machines with which, as minds, they have nothing in common, no community.

The same way of thinking, which isolates the individual mind within the human constitution (whether or not this mind is identified with the brain), also isolates this same mind within the community of other minds and within the environment. In these ways of thinking, the mind in its deliberations and choices stands above the body, uncommitted to the community of other human beings, and external to its environment. Whatever the way in which the mind's deliberations and choices are determined, whether by some supposed reason or mechanistically, we are put in a position of regarding the person in deliberating and choosing as operating as a mind administering a machine, a mind with no natural at-homeness in its body, in the human community, or in its environment—we might say, a mind *alienated* from its body, community and environment. We have here a perspective within which at root human beings as deliberators or even as contemplators are external to what they administer so that they can regard it in a purely technical way, whether the ends they seek are pleasurable sensations or pleasurable inner biographies or some subjectively chosen external end or complex of ends. We may call this the technological mentality. This becomes the mentality which subordinates human beings' environment and even their own bodies to whatever some ideology may project as in the human interest and which relegates the theoretical and contemplative aspect of human nature to the area of play and recreation except in so far as they may have some utilitarian by-product geared to human beings' temporarily imagined interests.

The predominant approach of modern moral philosophers has been held in the steel grip of a framework set by Descartes. This is a framework within which the individual deliberating mind has no given reason for respecting the calls of human community, let alone what is called for by respect for and non-abuse of the body and natural environment or by acceptance of the human being's rootedness in and community with it. This predicament as presented by Hume has come to be regarded as a datum of thought by most English philosophical writers. But it is exhibited more dramatically in Sartre—his conception of freedom shaped by Descartes—so that the supposed lack of reason for choosing any one course of action over others is a root of existential anxiety.

In place of this whole blind alley, we need to grasp the rationale of a perspective which will allow rein to the natural feelings which accord with this general sense of the 'at-homeness' or belonging of the human being to his or her body, community and environment. That is, we want a rationale for the perspective whereby seeing what is appropriate to the human being as an animal, and acting accordingly, is a part of the human being's being rational. Being rational involves that human beings freely choose in a way appropriate to their being animals and that they violate or abuse their humanity when they violate or abuse what belongs to their animalhood—as well as conversely violating their animalhood when they violate what belongs to their particular form of animalhood, a form which involves the understanding, concern for truth, and reflective regard for the good, incorporating a reflective respect for the good of others and even a recognition of how it is part of his or her own good.

We need to get into a position to see the human being *qua* animal as thereby part of the community of the family, of mankind, of animals, and of nature. In this way, the good of parents, siblings, and children is given as part of each individual's good. And likewise the good of whatever belongs to the individual's roots and home, including the good of every member of the human race as a fellow 'sibling' within the framework of nature, and including the good of the environment according to its different aspects, are given as parts of the individual's good, so that each individual has reason to be unhappy, is unfortunate, is injured in any injury within such community. In this way, we have to grasp the structured relevance to human satisfaction and deliberation of widening circles of community, community established in the first place through the human being's animalhood and psychosomatic nature.[3]

It must become a datum to us that the norm for every human good desirable for its own sake is for such a good to be something psychophysical, psychosomatic, embracing the body inseparably from the psyche and embracing the community and the environment with both of these. To take typical examples, the intrinsic goods of the pleasures of landscape or of music embrace body, psyche, and environment. The intrinsic goods of the architecture of a cathedral embrace the community in its worship also. The good in mathematical pleasure has a double gearing, to the architecture of language and to our understanding of the world, while the objects of play always derive their meaning from some other context, albeit that play (of which some mathematics is an example) is an intrinsic good in human life. Creativity involves the body, the senses, the capacity for appreciation, and typically the community also. Meanwhile, the relationships involved in the many forms of friendship and family relationship exhibit other dimensions of this complex web, these forms of relationship standing at the focus of human good. In sum, none of the intrinsic human goods which shape human life attach purely to the isolated psyche.

This way of viewing human goods, seeing their interrelations, and grasping the way in which human goods are structured—so that the individual good includes the common good as part of itself and vice versa—puts one in a position to deal with the problem as to how an 'ought' may be derived from an 'is'. But one will approach this, not within the context of a preoccupation with laws or principles bearing directly upon actions, but within the context of a recognition of gen-

---

[3]The resulting perspective upon ethics, emphasizing the different levels of community and insisting on the psychophysical nature of the human being exemplified in the human goods which embrace the body and community, traceable in Aristotle and Aquinas, requires another book to open out fully. This perspective is opened out in 'Human Animality: its Relevance to the Shape of Ethics' and 'Human Life: its Secular Sacrosanctness', my two essays in *Ethics, Technology, and Medicine*, ed. David Braine and Harry Lesser, together with 'The Human and the Inhuman in Medicine: Review of Issues concerning Reproductive Technology' (forthcoming). These essays may later be joined with others, including earlier papers on community, the shape of human good, and objectivity in ethics, in a collection to be published when time allows.

eral human goods. These general human goods will include what belongs to community with intellectual beings as such, to the sharing of knowledge and of intention so that others may rely upon my testimony and upon my prospective action as promised as if it had been their own. They will, at the same time, include attention to human goods which are fundamental in a different way because they have to do with truth, knowledge, and the reasonableness which is directed towards truth and the good. For in all one's thinking one should have already recognized that 'evaluative facts' are not 'extra' or 'non-natural' facts, but 'facts' nonetheless, inasmuch as one will have recognized "true", "valid", "reasonable", and even "knowledge" as evaluative terms. But these general human goods will also include whatever arises from human kind's community with nature, so that its good is a part of his good, both as a wonder to enjoy and as an end to seek.

One will find that the main obstacle to accepting 'objectivity' in ethics is not that supporting argument for conclusions is systematically impossible but that it is too easy, so that one seems to be able to prove contradictions: the way to escape these contradictions is through a correct description of the structuredness of human good and happiness and of the communities into which every man and woman is knit—and here again the role of the human being's being an animal will come in.

All these are themes for another book and other discussions, opening out an Aristotelian perspective on ethics, and are not themes for the present work. But it is vital to see the full context of any metaphysical discussion of the natures of the human being and of other animals, and vital to the significance of the uncovering of the irrationality of materialism along with the irrationality of the dualism which preceded it. Such discussion has to be seen not just against the background of the question of the possibility of the human being's having some real openness to God or to religion, but in the context of the question of the human being's capacity to serve even as an honourable member of the community of the animals and of nature. The spiritual good of the human being may indeed be incommensurable with other goods, but is inseparable from virtue—and the virtue required for spiritual health includes respect for the whole of human nature and therefore respect for, indeed the embracing of, the community with animals and nature which belongs to this nature.

For, in the end, it is the underlying belief which men and women hold about human nature which calls the tune for aesthetic and moral, political and environmental values.

PART ONE

The Human Being as an Animal:
The Nature of Psychophysical Unity

I. Overview of Part One: The Sameness of Materialism and Dualism and the Need for a Holistic View Opposed to Both

My aim in Part One of this book is to open out a vision of the unity of the human being, the kind of unity which human beings share with other higher animals. This is a kind of unity whose special character is particularly well exhibited in perception and intentional action. Any account of what is peculiar to human nature, such as I give in Part Two, will be distorted unless it is seen in this context of a realization of the unity of the human being.

There have grown up two kinds of philosophical world. In the one, the universe is viewed according to the perspectives suggested by language, by the phenomenology of experience or by each person's existential situation, and there is no preoccupation with bringing the human into compatibility with a science conceived in purely physical terms and quasi-mechanistically. In the other, it is a primary datum that physical science is to be regarded as self-sufficient within its own sphere and to be allowed entirely free rein so that one must hold open the possibility that everything physical—the physical aspects of animal behaviour and human activity included—is a product and reflection of material process, capable of being brought within a scheme of explanation in physical and quasi-mechanistic terms.[1] Between these two philosophical worlds there has been little sympathy or contact.

It is no use ignoring the kind of scientific viewpoint here concerned, e.g., on the ground that it stems from an approach which is out of date even in physics, because it remains true that it is

---

[1]Such quasi-mechanistic science, an 'indeterministic mechanism', is well described in David Bohm's *Causality and Chance in Modern Physics*, pp. 101–103 and *passim*, along with the compulsion even in physics to get beyond it (especially his Chapter V).

still this viewpoint which dominates orthodox medicine, psychology, and cognitive science and which shapes the technological thinking which western man disseminates through the world. If it is said that a philosophy adapted to this kind of scientific viewpoint does not answer to human needs, it may be answered or felt that no truth-respecting philosophy will answer to human needs and that the human lot is an ultimate despair. The extraordinary scale of the physical universe, and its extraordinary degree of order at many different physically describable levels, constitutes the setting of human and other biological life, and appears to dwarf the phenomena of life. Within this perspective it has come to many to seem rationally simpler to view the human and biological either as a mere local epiphenomenon or as something, perhaps recurrent in the universe, the roots of whose order lie in the physical. The universe then appears, as it were, uninterested in the particular lot of the individual human being, the human race or even the earth as a whole. Against this background, the tendency towards materialism or physicalism stems not just from the strength of the position of mechanism within physics in the past, but from the force of the impression made by physical scale and physical order on the mind and imagination.

To ignore the cultural drive towards making the kind of science we have mentioned the stable point which determines the role of any account of the human and the biological, and not to vindicate the credentials of a more human-orientated philosophy against it, is to leave such human-orientated philosophy with the appearance of a private game in which some individuals or groups of individuals withdraw into a private world of their own. The drive to accept the materialistic perspective has never, of course, been intellectually compelling—there has always been an alternative perspective which would view the whole physical universe as designed to be the womb of beings whose existence and behaviour is not to be explained in purely physical terms, and indeed would regard this as the crowning aspect of the richness of physical order. But what we now require is to set such an alternative perspective on a firm footing.[2]

---

[2]It is this firm footing which the impressionistic presentation of an holistic perspective by Teilhard de Chardin in *The Phenomenon of Man* fails to provide, the coherence of what he says and his remarks about different kinds of energy being quite obscure.

The importance of contemporary Anglo-Saxon or 'analytical' philosophy arises from the fact that, in its attempt to bring together the philosophy of language with the sorts of science within which the only kinds of causation reckoned on are physical, it stands almost alone in seeming to take seriously the need to bring human-orientated philosophy and the perspectives of a quasi-mechanistic physical science into relation with one another. But, alas, what we are confronted with within this Anglo-Saxon setting is only a lamentable failure. Current 'analytical' philosophy has not merely reinforced the alienation between human-orientated philosophy and the philosophy determined to preserve quasi-mechanistic science intact, but also simply repeated the mistakes made in the dualism of Descartes. Yet this dualism, the theory which presents minds as only externally related to merely physical bodies, is the one thing that both the human-orientated philosophies we have spoken of and the kind of science referred to agree in rejecting as totally alien.

Our task, therefore, is to bring these two worlds into connection in a quite different way. This will require two things.

Firstly, we need a positive insight into the way in which human beings and other higher animals can be viewed as psychophysical wholes. In this way, we will get to see the rejection of materialism and dualism, not in a purely negative way in terms of the incoherences they involve, but in the context of a holistic perspective to which they are blind.

But secondly, we have to observe that the task of setting this holistic perspective on a firm footing is constantly subverted by approaches which make the mental essentially inner, and therefore end up making it localizable in soul or brain—analysing the human being into parts, whether into a soul and a body or into the brain and then his other bodily parts. In order to avoid this subversion, we have to pursue a task of relentless analysis, in this taking advantage of the attempts at precision in the Anglo-Saxon tradition. We need to trace all the different kinds of argument and preconception which support the idea of the mental as inner, and painstakingly trace them right back to their roots. This is indeed the pain of this book, for if we relent in this task of analysis in all the detail it requires, it is inevitable that on some excuse the dualistic perspective, dividing the inner and the outer, will creep back again. And this analysis must be carried through to a consideration of explanation and causation, neglect of which has been the main weakness of earlier twentieth century critiques of dualism. It will need to be made clear first that causation cannot be reduced to a relation between events but essentially involves agents, whether inanimate or animate, and second that not all causation is physical causation. Rather, some causation can be understood only in psychophysical terms. But without painstaking analysis and argument none of this can be established in a way which will hold up against the person who dissolves human being or animal into mind and body or brain and body.

The human-orientated philosophy—existentialist, phenomenologist or whatever—which relies on our day-to-day holistic categories of thinking about human beings and animals but ignores the question of the relation of these categories to physical science is ostrich-like, burying its head in the sand. It is a philosophy which lives in a world of its own, as if the idea of the human being as a physical machine or as a mind in a machine had never been conceived, as if there were no puzzle as to how the explanation of human behaviour in the ordinary terms we meet with in history, biography, and literature relates to the explanation of the physical aspects of this behaviour in physical terms. On the contrary, the puzzle, the intellectual and existential problem is real—it would still be there even if materialism and dualism with all their queer consequences had never arisen—these mis-shapen philosophies are merely responses to it.

Therefore, if we are to maintain our ordinary human and holistic way of viewing things, we cannot dispense with the kind of argument and analysis with which this book is occupied. Each mistake we diagnose will be found incipient in common ways of popularizing physical science, neurology and computer theory, in the common acceptance of the association of all mental function with the brain, and in common over-simplified ways of speaking of cases of illusion, delusion and failure to carry through one's intention. For centuries we have been indoctrinated with dualistic ways of thinking, making the mental inner, a matter of the state of a person's mind independently of any carry through in ways of behaving, and this has softened us up for the ready acceptance of materialist ways of thinking making these inner states internal to the brain. Against this we shall re-establish the holistic perspective which views human being and animal, notably revealed in perception and action, not as assemblages of parts, inner and outer, but as wholes—psychophysical wholes—wholes in whose operations the mental cannot be extricated from the physical and the physical cannot be understood apart from the mental.

In this way, we will find that our primordial, pre-critical ways of thinking, and the kinds of philosophy which rely on their categories, stand vindicated. We do not need to take up the ostrich-like posture of ignoring the development of the physical sciences, but can envisage these sciences as abstracting only certain integral aspects of bodily existence for separate consideration, not as capturing all that is fundamental to it or as offering the basis of a global explanation of the phenomena of bodily life. And it is this measured holism—a holism which admits but delimits the role of physical explanation—which reason and the data of experience require.

1. The Sameness of Structure of Materialism and Dualism: The Inner/Outer Divide

What we need to grasp is how the primordial insight into the unity of the human being is betrayed as much by materialism as by dualism, and not by dualism alone.

It has long been conventional to attack dualism—indeed to regard it as some kind of superstition. But it is little realized that the principal objections to dualism apply equally to the kind of materialism which for some is now philosophical or scientific orthodoxy. And it is this sameness of dualism and materialism and the sameness of the problems to which they give rise which give us the clue to what is wrong with both and the clue to the understanding of the special character of the higher animals, and therefore to what is involved in the character of the human being as an animal.

The basis for considering dualism and materialism together is easily seen: for materialism to get going at all in its main contemporary form it is an absolute condition that one should have established a dualistic pattern of analysis of what goes on in human life. That is, before mental states and events can be identified with brain-states or events, or regarded as 'realized in the brain', these mental states and events have to be conceived in a way which makes them purely 'inner', logically segregated from the 'outer world' and the 'outer man' with his behaviour in the way which is characteristic of dualism. But it is precisely this dualistic analysis which is open to philosophical objection.

It is vital to be absolutely clear about this sameness of structure between contemporary materialism and the dualism which preceded it. It is not just that both involve regarding the human being as a composite or aggregate of parts in certain relations, material parts or material parts plus a supposed immaterial part (the mind or soul). Rather what needs to be grasped is the sameness of the analysis of mind-involving states and goings-on in general—even where these seem to involve the body—the sameness in the analysis which for both materialist and dualist goes before the reduction of human being and animal to their supposed parts.

Both positions equally require one to suppose that, within any mind-involving state or going-on, we can separate out the mental, conscious or experiential element—separate this element out as something causally and ontologically distinct from any of the states of the perceived world and sense-organs and from any of the behaviour and behaviour-patterns normally associated with this element in the case of the man or animal concerned—and separate it out as a state or going-on conceivable in mentalistic terms so as to be logically independent of physical state and goings-on. In line with this, materialist and dualist are equally committed to an analysis of every mind-involving state or going-on which also involves the body into (1) this purely mental and inner element (which the materialist may regard as realized in or identical with a brain state or process), (2) the various physical states and goings-on referred to above as normally interconnected with this mental element, together with (3) causal or coordinative relations between these mental and physical elements. And it is this analysis of perception, sensation, emotion and action which requires to be nailed as objectionable—whether it be put forward by dualist, materialist or anyone else.

It is striking to see the exactness of the parallelism between the arguments of the dualist Descartes, arguing towards a division between a thinking substance (the mind or soul) and a physical substance (the body) within the human composition, and the arguments of modern materialists. In Descartes we have the 'thoughts' or 'perceptions of the mind' involved in sensory perception and sensation, and we are to be persuaded that they might have other causes than we naturally suppose: they might be illusions, naturally caused delusions or even the results of the operations of a deceiving demon. And amongst modern materialists we find a return to the same way of thinking. In Armstrong, to take a representative example, we are to be persuaded again that the 'experiences' involved in perception might have other cause than we naturally suppose, in the extreme case because they might be the results of the operations of a cunning neurosurgeon.[3] Indeed, amongst some philosophers, in discussions of personal identity and moral theory, we meet the idea of brains in vats sustained by neurosurgeons with elaborate provision in order to supply the simulation of a whole lifeful of 'experiences', including pleasures and pains, generating a full spectrum of beliefs, attitudes, and emotions.

But amongst quite sober philosophers who would eschew any such extravagant hypotheses about demons or neurosurgeons, it has nonetheless become the norm to treat perception in the same Cartesian way. Each perception of some public object or situation is supposed to have its experiential element limited to something which is 'as of X' or 'as if P' in such a way that this element would remain the same even if X did not exist or P were false. This idea is often expressed in terms of there being 'perceptual experiences' with a certain 'intentional' or 'experiential' content or directed towards certain 'intentional objects' (we shall discuss this treacherous vocabulary of 'intentionality' later). 'Perceptual experiences' are thus supposed to be 'logically distinct existences', logically independent of any physical state of the sense-organs or world, and in this way in a parallel situation to sensations, e.g. the pain which seems to be located in a certain place and be caused in a certain way but is not so.

We have to realize that the same way of thinking often persists even when philosophers appear to be distancing themselves from such straightforwardly dualistic and Cartesian analysis. Thus, it has often been suggested that perceptual experiences, sensations such as pain, and beliefs are logically connected with patterns of behaviour. And many other classes of so-called 'mental' state have been thought of as being or involving 'dispositions' or 'aptnesses' to behave in certain ways: desires, intentions, supposed 'acts of trying', and even beliefs in general. However, when it is materialists or those who want to

---

[3]David Armstrong, *A Materialist Theory of the Mind*, p. 39 and p. 217, cf. pp. 211–212, has this argument that the same experience can be differently caused. The same argument reappears in John Searle's *Mind, Brains and Science*, pp. 18–19, and in Howard Robinson's 'The General Form of the Argument for Berkeleian Idealism', pp. 172–177.

leave it open that materialism might be true who say such things, it always turns out on inspection that they still think that the mental state or event concerned is strictly speaking logically independent of any complex of physical behaviour and physical states of the sense-organs and perceived world. The magic trick is to say that it is a logical matter that the behaviour would follow in 'normal' conditions, but then regard what constitutes 'normal' conditions as ultimately defined in terms of empirical causal law. Thus they still think that, for instance, the supposed 'trying' involved in any intentional action logically could have occurred without the action, and the perceptual belief revealed in a certain behavioural aptitude could have been present without this aptitude.[4] And, with this, we again have on our hands a 'mental' or 'psychological' state or event which is eligible to be the cause of, correspond with, be realized in, or be identical with some brain-state or event—the 'inner' element required by all these dualist or materialist theories in order to get going at all.

Again, all those who envisage the possible truth of physiological determinism, the doctrine whereby outward behaviour is determined by physical states, turn out to imply the same picture of the mental as something inner, at least if they insist upon free-will and insist that wants affect actions. For, to hold on to the view that wants affect actions, they have to say that my physical state would have to be different from what it is now if I wanted something different, and they envisage here physical states of the brain (albeit perhaps of a quite global or highly structured kind).[5] In this perspective, there have to be brain-states correlated with wants in such a way that what is explained by the want is caused by the brain-state. They may then, of course, say with the dualists that this is because the want causes the brain-state. However, they are more likely today to adopt the materialist option: even if they refuse to say that the want is *identical with* the relevant brain-state, they may still say that it is *realized in* the brain-state—the

---

[4]In this form of argument, based on the idea that the relevant experiential element in intention action '(logically) could' have been present without its typical physical accompaniment, we see an almost exact revival of the Cartesian argument that because the mental can be clearly and distinctly conceived without the physical so that there is no contradiction in supposing the first without the second, it must be possible [for Descartes, like Duns Scotus and Ockham, only because of God's omnipotence] for the first to occur without the second.

[5]Cf. A. Kenny, *The Metaphysics of Mind*, pp. 148–149.

place in reality where it finds expression or realization and because
of which it has causal effect, is not in a soul but in the brain. But
whichever view they adopt, they have returned to the conception of
the mental as inner.

Along with the conception of the mental as 'inner'—as in its
reality perhaps a state or going-on in the soul or brain, and logically independent of states of the 'outer' man or perceived world—
comes some conception of 'immediate awareness'. For, of course,
the main things conceived of as thus mental and inner—perceptual
experiences, beliefs, intentions, experiences of acting, tryings, emotions, sensations—are all alike conceived of as typically, if not always,
objects of 'immediate awareness'.[6] In this way, materialism brings with
it the same conception of consciousness or introspection as dualism,
the materialist often comparing introspection with the supposed 'self-
scanning' capacities of computers.

These ways of thinking do not require a belief in the mind or
the 'I' or self as a substance, some being or entity distinct from the
human being as a whole. It may very well be insisted that the self
is nothing else than the human being as such, and that the mind is
simply a capacity, faculty, or set of faculties of the human being as
a whole. Rather all that is required for this way of thinking to get
going is firstly the acceptance of the existence of what may be called
an experiential, conscious or 'mental' element within our perceptions,
sensations, emotions, and intentional actions; and secondly the acceptance of the idea that the whole of this experiential or mental element
within any particular perception, sensation, emotion, or intentional
action could be the same even if the state of the perceived world and
the person's sense-organs and behaviour were quite different. All that
is required for the dualistic way of thinking to get going is a belief that
the conscious element in key mental phenomena—what is often called
the 'experience' or 'state of consciousness' involved—is something (it
might be said, some event or state), which is logically independent of
facts about the perceived world and the 'outer man'.

---

[6] I say "if not always" to allow for the supposedly unconscious or subconscious
or cases of self-deception or incomplete self-knowledge, in the case of which we still
speak in the same mentalistic terms of beliefs, emotions, intentions, etc. because these
things enter into the explanation of other features of our life in some of the same ways
as ordinary beliefs, emotions, intentions, etc.

But it is precisely this way of thinking which materialist and dualist share.[7] And, as we have seen, the reasons given by the materialist for conceiving of the mental as inner in this way are just the same as those given by Descartes: firstly, these experiences, wants, intentions, 'tryings', and beliefs could have been the same even if we had been mistaken about their truthfulness or their relation to behaviour; secondly, those which involve belief in facts about the 'outer man' or about the world could have been caused in a different way not involving these facts.

Now it is this conception of the mental as inner, shared equally by the materialist and the dualist, which is objectionable.

It is often imagined that the main difficulties in dualism have to do with the problem as to how the mental can act causally upon the physical and vice versa. As a result, materialism is preferred because it involves no such complications, all causation being physical—supposedly, it is only because mental states and goings-on are realized in or identical with brain-states and goings-on that they can have any effect on what goes on in the physical world.

However, for a long line of philosophers the primary difficulties in dualism were quite different. For Aristotle and Aquinas, Merleau-Ponty and Heidegger, and in the modern Anglo-Saxon context for the later Wittgenstein, Ryle and Austin, the founders of so-called 'ordinary language philosophy',[8] the real trouble lay in the way the dualists conceived the mental—the fault was with the whole conception of the

---

[7]True, one can meet with the suggestion that (in some or all cases) mental states are realized, not in states of the brain, but in states of the whole bodily system of a person, e.g., in Thomas Nagel's 'Physicalism' where it appears (in section II) that the still separately describable mental states may correspond to or be identical with states of the whole body rather than with states of the brain. But in reply one should say firstly that this has never been followed up in the analytical Anglo-American context within which materialism has seemed so attractive (one finds no trace of it in Grice, Searle, Davidson, O'Shaughnessy, Hornsby and the like), secondly that the only way of putting explanatory meat on the bones of a materialistic theory of the mental seems to be by returning to a mind-realized-in-brain form of such theory, and thirdly that, once one has conceded the need for a holistic understanding of the functioning of the human body, it seems stupid not to go whole hog and accept the necessity of drawing on teleology- and mind-involving concepts in the explanation of this functioning and thus abandoning materialism.

[8]This is the most convenient name to give to the kind of philosophy associated with these philosophers and their followers. The reason for grouping them together

mental as inner or as self-contained and having an existence isolable from the perceived world and states of the 'outer man'. Indeed, for these philosophers, this false way of conceiving the mental results in the questions of the relation of the physical and mental being entirely wrongly posed.

In this, I believe, these philosophers were right, and it is this shared holistic perspective which I want to open out in this book.

2. The Psychophysical Integration of the Human Being

The truth that we have to bring out is that the events and goings-on which we refer to as perceptions, sensations, emotions, and intentional actions are irreducibly hybrid, the mental inextricable from

---

can be seen from the way they form a family standing in striking contrast with a rival tradition within Anglo-Saxon philosophy.

For Quine and what we might regard as an American line of tradition, Carnap and not the later Wittgenstein is the master or exemplar philosopher, following Russell and marking the line which studies in philosophy ought to take. This advertizes a divorce inside what is described as 'analytical philosophy' between two quite different types of approach: the one emerging from the background of the Vienna circle and marked by a concern for the precision of formal logic, crystallized in Carnap and developed in Quine and his disciples; and the other British based school for whom the later Wittgenstein, Ryle (writing contemporaneously or in advance of the spread of Wittgenstein's influence) and Austin, despite the gross divergencies of attitude between them, were the exemplars of the right philosophical approach. This contrast is made vivid by Quine in 'Homage to Rudolf Carnap' and by Dummett in *Truth and Other Enigmas*, pp. 431–441.

It is this contrast which makes it legitimate to speak of 'ordinary language philosophy', with 'ordinary language' being allowed to provide a norm or base, and never an object of disrespect. (The term "Oxford philosophy" was never appropriate since the approach was never limited to Oxford and indeed Wittgenstein and Moore were Cambridge figures, and the term "linguistic philosophy" is too ambiguous, on the one hand seeming to embrace Ayer, never an 'ordinary language' philosopher, and on the other hand suggesting interest in linguistic theory.) A few authors before 1970, e.g., Geach, truly bestraddle the divide.

What one has seen since around 1970 has been a merging of the American Carnap-Quine influenced tradition with some of the elements of the 'ordinary language' tradition under the influence of Davidson and Dummett. Meantime the steady extension of the influence of the mind-brain identity theory (in the 60s a minority phenomenon amongst academic philosophers, but now almost predominant) has eroded the anti-Cartesianism intrinsic to the 'ordinary language' tradition, reinstating a presumption that mental states and activity correspond to or exist as brain states and activities.

the physical. We cannot extricate the mental or experiential element from the physical, seeing it as something independent of facts about the perceived world and the 'outer man'. And therefore we are in no position to go on to analyse all features of human life in the way we described, that is into (1) such a supposed purely mental element, (2) physical facts about this perceived world and 'outer man', and (3) causal or other co-ordinative relations between them. This analysis cannot be got off the ground—there simply does not exist any such isolable experiential or mental element as both presuppose. The quarrel as to whether such a supposed mental or inner element is identical with or realized in some brain state or going-on, as the materialists suppose, or whether it is only (as in Descartes' view) in external causal relations with this brain-state or going-on is a quarrel about an inner element which does not exist, and this rules out both dualism and contemporary materialism equally. We cannot get into a position even to pose this question between various forms of materialism and dualism, simply because we cannot abstract the mental or experiential element from the physical in this way.

An alternative view of these phenomena in the life of the animal or human being is not far to seek. We need to envisage each of these key phenomena in a quite different way. In perception, sensation, emotion, and intentional action, mental and physical aspects have to be seen as intertwined, neither capable of being analysed away into the other, nor of being understood in abstraction from the other. In short, all these phenomena have to be understood holistically, as involving the human being or animal as such, and not regarded as consisting in elements, inner and outer (along with causal or co-ordinative relations between them).

To make this intertwining of the mental and physical vivid, we need to begin with perception. Perceptual experience, the experiencing itself, is a real relation with things in the world—the cognitive relation is itself also a behavioural relation, a state of behavioural adaptedness to the things about us—a kind of cognitive relation appropriate to one of the higher animals.

Perceptual experience is not something purely inner, an experience *as if* things looked or seemed in a certain way but which could have remained the same experience even if this appearance or seeming had been quite false and the causation of the experience had been quite other than that which we commonly suppose. Rather perceptual experience is something which is of its very nature integrated with actions, actions which involve the sense-organs, e.g., changing the vantage-point from which they are used by shifting one's position, looking about, exploring with the fingers and such like. It is therefore something which of its very nature has real and not 'merely intentional' objects—real objects, the very same objects as those around which behaviour is orientated and in regard to which behaviour becomes adapted by perception. If we have an experience which is not caused and integrated with behaviour in this way—perhaps because the way it is caused is not integrated with behaviour in the normal way or because things do not look or seem as they are—it is not and should not be counted as the 'same experience'.

We come now to intentional action—by which I mean action springing from emotion and directed towards an end, i.e., perceptually guided action such as we ascribe to the higher animals as well as to human beings.[9] This does not consist in some inner movement of mind causing some bodily movement external to it. The act's being intentional is not a matter of its being preceded by a separate existence, the intention, which causes it. Rather it is a matter of the human being or animal as a unitary or focalized psychophysical agent exercising direct causal agency within and upon the world—according to a mode of action, intentional and voluntary, distinct from the kind of agency exercised by inanimate bodies. The intention involved in my performing my act intentionally is not a previous state such as the intention I had when I might yet change my mind, but something internal to the act—not just the intention of doing something, but the intention I have in doing it. And the intending which is thus internal to the action is an intending which has as its object the things actually involved in the action, not a model of them—has as its object the actual outcome as it occurs according to intention, not a model of this outcome. (And in the performance of the action I do not know the intention with which I perform the action separately from my acting or separately from my knowing my action; rather, when I act intentionally, I have a knowledge of my intention in acting, a knowledge that I am acting and a knowledge of what I am doing, all of

---

[9] I discuss intentional action in this wider sense more fully in Chapter IX, Section 2(b), below.

which arise together, and I have these, not just observationally or after the event, but in the act simply in virtue of its being intentional—this is what we may conveniently call 'practical knowledge'.)

As perception has the setting of action, dispositions towards action and sensation, so action and non-observational knowledge of what we are doing has the setting of perception, sensation, and the non-observational knowledge of such things as the position of our limbs. Each arises and exists only in the dynamic setting which also involves the others. The consciousness exemplified in these mental phenomena is what Merleau-Ponty called 'incarnate consciousness'.

This 'incarnate consciousness', already apparent in the inseparability of perceptual knowledge and behavioural aptitude, is peculiarly exhibited in sensation, in the emotions and in the kinds of non-observational knowledge I have spoken of. Our bodies and bodily movements are familiar to us, not just in the sense that we observe them in perception and observe correlations between experience and bodily state, but in much more intimate ways. In the case of sensations and emotions, I have non-observational knowledge of the behaviour they engender and know non-observationally that this or that behaviour is from this or that sensation or emotion. And it belongs to our experience of the emotions that some sensations should be associated with them, e.g., the sensation of a generalized bodily agitation associated with excitement or a sinking sensation in the stomach with apprehension of evil to come, so that there is a non-observational knowledge of the sensation being caused by the emotion—caused, not as if the emotion and the sensation were separate existences, the emotion earlier causing the sensation later, but in such a way that the experiencing of the sensation is part of the experiencing of the emotion, the sensation being because of the emotion (in Aristotelian terms the sensation having the emotion as its formal cause).

The unity of mind and body of which I speak is seen in a further way, not just in knowledge of the world, my actions, and the body, but in the internality of the interrelation of the mental and the bodily to our knowledge of either of them.

When we writhe in pain, sob with grief, smile with pleasure, snap with irritation, or scream in terror, or when desire or fear move us to action, we should not think of the sensations and emotions concerned as external to the behaviour, any more than we should think of a person's intention in acting as external to his intentional action—or perceptual experience (e.g., seeing the table and its position) as external to the change in behavioural aptitude (being able to touch the table's edge or walk round it). It is not just that these things are associated with a non-observational knowledge of the behaviour involved and its roots in the sensation or emotion, but that it is a part of what it is to have this pain or to experience these emotions that one's behaviour should be affected by them in the way that it is. The physiognomy or quality and direction of concern in the particular sensation or emotion being considered is of such a kind as to be expressed in a certain physiognomy or change of physiognomy in our behaviour—the shape of the way it affects our behaviour and dispositions to behave. Wittgenstein remarks that 'The human body is the best picture of the human soul'[10] and the most perfect example of this is in the relation of behaviour to sensation and emotion.[11]

In brief, the world in which we mentally live is not a world presented to us in representation only, in experiences which are *as if* the world were thus and thus but which could have been the same even if the world had been otherwise. Rather we live in real and direct cognitive relation with the world so that the world in which we live is the same as the world in which we act. Our relationship with the world in experience and engagement with it is never that of observers and knowers only, a cognitive relationship only, as if we were centres of consciousness observing the world independently of behavioural adaptation to it. Rather our forms of engagement and experience are always at once cognitive and behavioural, and this means that they are never purely mental, but always psychophysical—the mental and the physical inextricably intertwined, both logically in the way each is to be described, and from the standpoint of explanation in the way each is to be explained.

---

[10] *Philosophical Investigations*, II, iv.

[11] One could think in Aristotelian terms of the emotion or sensation, that which shapes or gives sense to the behaviour, as the form, and of the associated pattern of behaviour as the matter. For, as the soul of one of the higher animals requires expression, not in just any kind of matter, but flesh and bones and the type of life characteristic of this type of animal, so the emotion or sensation as form requires expression, not just in any kind of behaviour, but in behaviour or pattern of behaviour with this or that physiognomy, the physiognomy appropriate to this emotion or sensation. And emotion or sensation and pattern of behaviour will be inseparable as form and matter are inseparable, neither capable of being understood except as in relation to the other. Cf. Aristotle's *De Anima*, I.1 (cf. *Metaphysics*, Eta, 2).

3. Hybrid Facts and Propositions:
The Logical Aspect of Holism

What I have been saying may seem obvious to commonsense. Yet it precisely exhibits each of the types of mind-involving phenomenon I have mentioned—perception, sensation, emotion and intentional action, along with our awareness of links between them—as incompatible with the dualistic analysis. None of these features of human life can be analysed in the way which is required equally by dualism and contemporary materialism, because none allows the isolation of a 'pure' mental element.

What the examples I have mentioned make clear is the existence, at a basic level of analysis, of hybrid states and goings-on, and hybrid propositions or statements—hybrid of mental and physical aspects or hybrid in their mix of mental and physical implications. When I say 'at a basic level', I mean that there is no way of representing the states and goings-on concerned as consisting of some other more basic states or goings-on, some mental and some physical, together with a superstructure of causal or co-ordinative relations; and no way of analysing the propositions concerned into implications or truth-conditions of two basic kinds, mental and physical, along with higher level propositions co-ordinating them in some way.

In insisting upon the existence of such irreducibly hybrid realities or propositions, we break out of the long standard map of possible views in the philosophy of mind. In describing this standard map, I shall leave causal and co-ordinative relations and propositions on one side because they are supposed to be non-basic, always presupposing the realities or propositions co-ordinated.[12] Both dualists and materialists offer many different accounts of these second-level relations and propositions, but in their ideas as to the possible views as to what kinds of basic reality and proposition there might be they seem to be in singular agreement.

If we consider views as to what kind of basic reality there are, firstly, evidently enough, the materialist presumes that ultimately all

---

[12] Thus, these thinkers envisage causal and temporal propositions asserting external relations between the mental and the physical, but they conceive these as precisely not basic, but rather presupposing already established purely mental and purely physical propositions as alone basic and proposing special kinds of non-truth-functional connection between them.

states and goings-on will be found to be physical, while the dualist insists that there are also mental ones. The idealist fits easily enough into the picture as holding that there are only mental ones. In this way, all these thinkers agree that, amongst basic states of affairs or goings-on, there are none of a mixed or hybrid kind.

If we bring in a consideration of kinds of basic proposition, the picture becomes more complex, but in the end we find the underlying dualistic framework yet more firmly entrenched. Most thinkers assume two types of basic contentful proposition about persons, one mental or 'intentional' and the other expressible in terms of the concepts of physics.

Of course, it is at this stage that important further divergences arise. Thus some contemporary materialists who suppose that all states and goings-on are ultimately physical may simply make out that what we have are two sets of specification of these states and goings-on, i.e., they may make out that experiences, beliefs, intentions, and so forth are simply identical to certain brain states and goings-on; or they may rather say that these are 'realized in' such brain states and goings-on. Yet it remains that whichever option they adopt, and however they explain the notion of 'being realized in', they are still in the position of agreeing with the dualist that there are two logically independent kinds of basic proposition about people. And in this both still discount the possibility of there being some third kind of basic proposition, as it were hybrid, involving the mental and physical inextricably, with implications both for the mental and for the physical but not analysable into them.[13]

Various rather queer views fit into this picture very straight-forwardly, simply as offering degenerate versions of the same basic classification. The so-called 'logical behaviourists' simply propose that seemingly mind-concerning propositions have a meaning completely expressible in physically specifiable events and patterns of physically describable behaviour—thus reducing the mental to the physical—while the phenomenalists imagine that all physical concepts can be defined by reference to possible experience in such a way that all

---

[13]Of course, Descartes seems to say that there is such a third kind of hybrid proposition, but the trouble for him and all the rationalists and empiricists who followed him was that he at the same time suggested a way in which these might be analysed away.

propositions about the world are mental.[14] But none leave any place for any irreducibly hybrid statements.

Of course, it is fashionable for those who accept the existence of purely 'intentional' statements, non-committal as to anything about the external world, and who presume that our normal states of experience might have been caused without involving the external world in the normal way, to insist that these statements or the descriptions of these experiences should be made in terms of the public, material-world concepts which we ordinarily use. It is also fashionable to assume that these states of experience are normally caused and may be presumed to be normally caused in a way which makes them veridical—corresponding with the facts. But neither of these concessions makes any difference to the dualistic character of the positions being adopted. The states are still inner and the statements still purely mental in character.

Within this whole context the fashionable view attempts to regain plausibility by offering an explanation of why most or all of our ordinary statements of experience are not of either of the basic kinds described. Indeed, it even leads us to expect this. We do not normally, and see no need to, specify our experiences in statements neutral as to implications about the perceived external world. Nor do we break down our account of the part action plays in our biography into separate itemizations of, firstly, a supposed intentional element of willing and, secondly, the bodily upshot. However, it remains that the same fashionable view continues to insist that the experiences themselves are 'distinct existences' (possibly caused by or identical with events in the brain) and it normally presumes that we can give a description of the experiential element in our engagements with the external world, a description which is neutral as to any determinate

---

[14]These views, phenomenalist and behaviourist, seem peculiar, but the tendency towards them is ever-present so long as this basic map of possibilities of thought is present. Thus, amongst those, materialists or dualists, who prefer to speak of mental states as correlated with or realized in physical states rather than identical to them, the criteria for identity of the person may become blurred, and the 'self' reappear as some kind of construction. And amongst those who insist upon the idea of mental states as involving being apt to behave in certain ways, albeit that the connection is not one of unconditional logical implication but of such-and-such patterns of behaviour following *if* the conditions are 'normal', the possibility of a degeneration to logical behaviourism, whereby the mental states consist in a certain physically definable tendency to behave in certain ways, always remains.

physical facts about us or the world—even being willing to suggest definite ways in which such a non-committal description might be given. The connections allowed between life as experienced and reality are conceived of as always loose and in such a way that they might be at root causal rather than logical.

In these ways fashion has constructed what is only an elaborate facade, a facade which leaves the original dualistic analysis unaffected.

And what is left out of account in all these presentations, contemporary or traditional, is the possibility that there might exist a surd, something which does not fit into the categories they provide, something describable or explicable neither in purely mental (or 'intentional') nor in purely physical terms, but only in terms uneliminably involving both the mental and the physical. For instance, to give an example out of our later discussion in Chapter IV, when we have something like pain, which might seem more purely mental, we not only discover on consideration that the very notion of it involves relation to various emotions and to various characteristic kinds of behaviour, but also find that there are the associated complex phenomena we have indicated such as writhing in pain, which compel us to recognize that the supposed 'experiential' or conscious element in the complex extends not just to the pain but to its relation to the writhing. And what is thus characteristic of pain and its expressions is also characteristic of sensations[15] and emotions in general, and at a further stage, within action, also characteristic of the agent's intention in acting.

Thus what first appears a 'cloud no bigger than a man's hand' affecting only the consideration of sensations soon seems to envelop the emotions, intention, and above all, perception. In this way, this same difficulty can be seen to require a re-drawing of the whole original map of possible views as to the basic kinds of state and going-on or of proposition. There is no prospect of eliminating irreducibly hybrid states and goings-on and propositions from our account of human beings.

To complete this section, we need to clarify some of the logical aspects of what is involved in the notion of 'hybrid proposition'.

---

[15] This is seen even in the simplest type of case, as in the relation of itching to scratching.

In the philosophy of mind, one has to be constantly wary of the surreptitious influence of a tendency towards a logical atomist pattern of analysis. Being 'not yet married' and being 'male' are distinct ideas, and one can construct the idea of being a bachelor from a combination of these more elementary ideas. Such cases attract one to think that our pattern of thought is like this: discovering that someone is a bachelor, one registers as an aspect of this that he is male and then enquires what else is required for him to count as a bachelor, and then further anticipates that this something else will be something logically independent of being male. Thus in general one may be attracted to a pattern of analysis whereby whenever one finds some proposition or state "P" which has as a truth condition or element the proposition or state "Q", one presumes that there will be some remainder proposition or state "R" independent of "Q" such that the conjunction of "Q" and "R" is equivalent to or amounts to "P".

The influence of this way of thinking and the attractive simplifications it suggests are beguiling. They will lead one, on meeting with a perception which as a total state of affairs involves a certain state of the world perceived and some relevant alteration in the sense-organs, to anticipate that there will be some remainder element to do with the mind or brain which will have some mentalistic or 'intentional' description logically independent of the state and alteration mentioned, and then one will think that these elements, together of course with causal relations, constitute the total event of the perception. And one will think that the conjunction of the statements about the world perceived and the mentalistic specification of the remainder element, together again with an appropriate causal statement, is equivalent to the perceptual statement. Likewise, on meeting with an intentional action which as a total state of affairs involves a certain bodily movement, one will anticipate some remainder element, again to do with the mind or brain, supposedly some act of will logically independent of the bodily movement, such that the bodily movement and this mental element, together with their causal relation, constitute the total event of the intentional action. And also likewise one will think that the conjunction of appropriate statements about the bodily movement and this mental element (these statements logically independent of one another), together with the appropriate causal statement, is equivalent to the intentional action statement.

It might be thought that the causal and other co-ordinative relations and statements involved themselves constituted a violation of the atomistic patterns of analysis concerned. But every version of atomism has always reckoned on causal and other co-ordinative relations or statements as constituting a special exception to general atomistic theory, one indeed of the large range of groups of special exception which have to be taken into account.[16] The reality of causal and other connections with the physical is not supposed to enter directly into our experience, even if our experience is 'as if' there were such connections; and causal or other connections with the mental do not enter the physical descriptions of behaviour, the states of the sense-organs or the perceived world.

What we have here is a coming together of a metaphysical atomism with a logical atomism. The metaphysical atomism considers states and goings-on (realities) involving both mental and physical aspects as made up of inner mental and outer physical components in causal or other co-ordinative relations. The logical atomism considers statements reporting these states and goings-on as equivalent to conjunctions of logically independent mental and physical statements together with causal or co-ordinative statements. The metaphysical atomism requires the existence of inner mental components and these must be considered describable in mentalistic terms in some way (whether they are also describable in physical terms as the believer in mind-brain identity supposes is a separate question).

Now it would be open in principle to a philosopher to hold that these mentalistic statements all had implications of a physical kind, holding a metaphysically atomist position without the logical atomist accompaniment, e.g., holding that the perceptual experience was in the perceiver but that it could not be specified mentalistically without implications for physical behaviour, the sense-organs and the perceived external world. However, in practice neither contemporary materialists nor dualists show any great interest in this option because they tend to begin by assuming the possibility of the logical atomist analysis. Thus Descartes began with the logical atomist move of supposing that the mental could be conceived to exist without the physical, and derived his metaphysically atomist analysis from it on the ground

---

[16]Wittgenstein's *Tractatus* might be considered as providing the beginnings of an inventory of such groups of exception, contingent existential statement, statements of assignment to logical types, modal statements in general, causal statements and natural laws, evaluative statements, etc.

that God could cause anything which could be conceived without contradiction. And as we shall see in later chapters, contemporary materialists and associated thinkers agree or even think it obvious that the mental or experiential element or aspect of mind-involving phenomena can be specified in purely 'intentional' terms—and by this they mean without any implications as to alterations in the sense-organs, states of the perceived world, or the physical behaviour of the person concerned.[17]

Such atomism inspires the most extraordinary misrepresentations of thinkers who in fact reject it. Thus, when in Wittgenstein and Ryle we meet with the conception that there might be logically necessary connections between pain and behaviour, or between other mental states and behaviour, we find them dismissed as logical behaviourists.[18] The assumption that there can be no logical connections between distinct existences is thought so obvious and unquestionable that the only alternative to the dualistic analysis which makes mental statements logically independent of the physical is imagined to be the behaviourism which reduces mind-involving statements to very complex physical ones. In this way the many thinkers concerned show themselves blind to the possibility of holding that the mental is logically inextricable from the physical, in particular from behaviour, without reducing the mental to the physical, which is precisely the possibility which Wittgenstein and Ryle are insisting upon. These thinkers are simply relying upon the map of possible views in the philosophy of mind described earlier, a map which leaves no room for the views of Wittgenstein or Ryle simply because it does not allow of the existence of irreducibly hybrid states and goings-on and irreducibly hybrid statements—hybrid in involving each of the mental and the physical uneliminably, each inextricably from the other. They also show themselves blind to the existence of a whole theory of the meaning of personalistic or mind-involving statements about human beings and animals, a theory opposed equally to the introspectionism associated with dualism and to behaviourism, the theory we try to clarify in Chapter V.

----

[17]Whether they are supposed to imply general facts about the person concerned such as the possession of a body, or at some time of sense-organs, or of language, or to imply the existence of an external or objective world is not to the point here.

[18]*A Materialist Theory of Mind*, pp. 54–55, echoing the normal view of cognitive psychologists.

The same atomistic simplification which we find in regard to the relation of the mental and the physical we find also within the sphere of the mental itself. The relations between pain and awareness of pain and between pain and associated emotions, or between fear and the belief that there is danger and between fear and aversion from its object, or in many cases between different beliefs are represented as logically contingent, all these being 'distinct existences'.

However, although it is true that pain and awareness of pain appear to be in some sense 'logically distinct', they do not seem to be in purely 'logically contingent' relation. To the common mortal, it would seem that it was part of the notion of pain that we should be aware of it (subject to the qualification that we can be distracted from lower degrees of pain and inattentive to pain to which we have become accustomed). And pain (whether physical pain or other) does not seem logically unconnected with distress and aversion. Feelings of fear, beliefs that there is danger, emotions of aversion from the object of fear, do not seem to be in logically haphazard relation. It does not seem 'logically contingent' that the combination of beliefs that P and that if P, then Q should be accompanied by the belief that Q or the absence of belief that not-Q. In this way, it becomes less obvious that 'there are no logical connections between logically distinct existences' within the mental field, and indeed it has been part of the phenomenologists' task in describing 'essences' (e.g., the essence of fear) to describe the logically necessary or 'synthetic a priori' connections between such mental phenomena. And the same logically non-accidental connections have been noticed by so-called ordinary language philosophers. What is important is that these connections— although not 'logical' or 'analytic' in the sense of belonging to formal logic as a subject-matter independent science bestraddling all subject-matters indifferently, abstract or concrete—are nonetheless 'conceptual' or 'a priori' so that it does not wait upon experiment or observation after the event to discover them. What we require is not a scientific theory explaining why such 'distinct' phenomena should arise in such regular interconnections, but an appropriate theory of meaning, again a theory of meaning which will allow the existence of conceptual connections between things which are in some sense logically distinct, not reducible to each other.

Once we recognise the existence of such connections of 'mental' facts or existences amongst themselves, we have even less reason to be doctrinaire and deny the possibility of such connections between the so-called 'mental' and the physical—the possibility of statements irreducibly hybrid in meaning and making reference to irreducibly hybrid states and goings-on.

4. The Effects of the Inner/Outer Divide: (I) The False Chasm between the Knower and the Known

We have described how materialists and dualists alike remain blind to the existence of such irreducibly hybrid statements in the way we have indicated, blind to the impossibility of purging our descriptions of human experience and engagement with the world so as to rid it of psychophysical holism. Materialist and dualist alike persist in decomposing human biography into logically independent inner and outer elements external to each other. What we now have to grasp is the mess which this engenders, first within accounts of knowledge, the concern of this section, and then within accounts of action, the concern of Section 5 below.

In this section I shall describe the four classical problems in the theory of knowledge, problems emerging in Descartes, Locke and Hume, inescapably generated by this inner/outer divide. I do so because it is vital that the reader should realize that these problems are not just the academic concern of historians of philosophy, but provide standing refutations of any account of human nature which accepts this same inner/outer partition. And in Chapter III I shall make clear that the accounts of perception offered by Grice, Searle and their fellows and embraced by materialists lie open to the same refutations.

(a) The predicament of explaining knowledge of the external world

Firstly there is the problem of 'our' knowledge of the external world, supposing that 'we' are (so far as the data of consciousness give us to know) essentially 'minds'.

That true states of belief should be caused may be explicable on dualist and materialist theories but for both there is a problem as to how this can ever, even in the case of perception, rate as knowledge. If all we ever immediately know is our own states of consciousness, our experiences and beliefs, both conceived of as 'inner', by what means do we infer to anything of a quite different nature beyond them?

As we shall make clear in Chapter III, recent approaches do nothing to ease the situation. In brief, there can be no real presentation of an object sensorily to a disembodied mind, and the Cartesian mind and the brain, as things inner, are no better off than a disembodied mind would be.

And the reason why these approaches fall foul of the same Cartesian problems is clear. They have each set up a structure in which there are two sets of propositions, the first declarative of what we experience in a way non-committal as to the causation of the experiences and the public existence of their objects as external to us, and the second implying this existence and the normality of the causation of the experiences. The first set state all we know from experiences as they are given, even if they present themselves 'as if' more were given, while the second set go beyond this. And at this stage all these philosophers are ineluctably trapped. As Chapter III will make plain, they have removed the possibility of saying that we have direct knowledge of the second set. And once having removed this possibility, they can give no satisfactory account of how we have knowledge of this second set.

It has been supposed that our 'experiences' have to be described not in a vocabulary of their own but in the vocabulary in which we are accustomed to describe the public world, to be described as (e.g.) 'the experience as if so-and-so', so that their description at every point presupposes the 'pre-theoretical' or 'commonsense' view of the world.[19] And it has been imagined that, somehow because of this, the sceptical problem is resolved: there is supposedly no inner world of special inner objects (e.g., sense-data) from which inference has to be made to outer objects of quite different and more substantial character, but only an inner world which is always *as if* it were of just such an outer world. This would make it certain that the truth of ordinary perceptual beliefs cannot be conceived of as a 'theory' in terms of special 'theoretical entities' (so-called physical substances) brought in to explain our experiences since the notions of these kinds of entity are already internal to the understanding or reception of the experiences themselves.[20] Yet just because the hypothesis that the general way in which things appear (the way our experience is as if they were) is the general way they actually are is not in a refined modern

---

[19] P.F. Strawson, 'Perception and Its Objects', pp. 96–105.
[20] *Ibid.*

sense 'a theory', it does not follow that the sceptical problem is solved. Rather, this hypothesis remains a presumption, or a presupposition of common discourse and of science without which neither could proceed, in terms of modern ways of speaking a 'convention' rather than an immediately given datum of experience.

The description of the object presented intentionally or in an 'as if it were so' manner may be the same as the description of the object which, in an appropriate manner, caused the experience concerned. And the associated pre-critically given beliefs may include the existence of the object and its appropriate causation of the experience. But it remains that, according to these views, such existence and causation are still never intrinsic to any 'experience'.

Since there is never any direct experience of the presumed world, there can be no observation of any correlation between our experience conceived of in this Cartesian way and the world, and so no reasoning by induction from such experience to the world according to the canons of Hume. If reasoning is possible from such experience to the world, it must be by kinds of reasoning not allowed for by Hume, reasoning in terms of coherence and suchlike. A good example of such an approach is provided by the recent author Mackie: his reasoning does not presume the necessity of a cause in the general case, but only presumes that, if the supposition of a certain causal framework introduces simplicity and coherence into one's view of certain experiences, it should be accepted.[21] The game is not to offer a way in which, from the piecemeal experience of the individual, such a total framework might be discovered,[22] but to take advantage of already possessing such a framework (thanks to a shared language and a vast heritage of knowledge upon testimony) and as it were retrospectively to explain how the individual might justify to himself his acceptance of this framework.[23]

---

[21]J.L. Mackie, *Problems from Locke*, pp. 62–67.

[22]The way the piecemeal character of 'experience', as Cartesian and empiricist conceive it, make such reconstruction hopeless is made particularly clear by Price in *Hume's Theory of the External World*, expounding Hume's *Treatise*, Bk. I, Pt. IV, Sect. II, and is also the background of Price's insistence (*Perception*, Ch. VII) that sense-data could only provide corroboration, not justification, of our perceptual judgements. Mackie's approach circumvents these difficulties.

[23]An alternative gambit has been to suggest that the belief that the general way in which things appear is the general way in which they actually are is a belief apart from which we not only could not find any way of describing our experience,

However, the whole problem of justifying the acceptance of the supposed framework only arises because the human situation has been misdescribed in the first place. As a result, there is an inconsistency built into the description of the 'commonsense view of the world' for which vindication is sought: on the one hand, it is part of this view that perception involves direct cognitive relation with its objects, and, on the other hand, acceptance of the framework of justification being offered removes the possibility of giving any proper account of this 'immediacy' or 'directness'. As will become ever more starkly clear in the next two chapters, the world within which the thinkers postulated by Descartes and Mackie deliberate and initiate their action remains essentially inner and private. Once let it be recognized that real relation with its object is internal to perceptual experience and that the arena of perception is the same as the arena of action, namely the world itself, and the 'problem of perception' is removed.

The elemental character of the madness of doubting the existence of the external world (and the madness even of supposing there to be room for a doubt here) has made many question the value either of philosophy or of reason itself. But, as we shall make clear, the defect is rather in the ways of thinking which generate the problem, in the madness of the atomism segregating the mental from the physical to which I have referred.

---

but also apart from which we could not have the experience we do. But we must nail an ambiguity here. We may be told that 'our sensible experience could not have the character it does have unless—at least before philosophical reflection sets in— we unquestioningly *took* that general view of the world to be true [the general view which our perceptual judgements reflect]' (Strawson, *op. cit.*, p. 96). But this does not show that this sensible experience requires that this view is actually true but only that it requires that the experiencer take this view to be true. If none of the particular experiences, nor any ensemble of experiences (apparent memories included) requires more than the *belief* that things generally are as they generally appear, it is difficult to see how it can be proved that we *could* not have such experience without this belief's being true.

Kant takes empirical experience of the empirically real as a datum. Either he can be interpreted as, at heart, a metaphysical realist committed here to a holistic view of the relation of perception to what is objectively perceived, or as, at root, a Berkeleian idealist in which case experience neither depends on nor carries with it any commitment to the transcendentally real. Neither way does his argument support the idea that experiences, *if* understood in the Cartesian way, would presuppose not only the belief in some independent reality apart from appearances but also the truth of this belief.

Absurdities are like festering sores, one disease providing a breeding ground for others. Feeding upon the initial opening out of a room for doubt as to the existence of the external world are yet more radical doubts. There is the problem of the nature of the self or subject of experience to which we shall come later. But first there is the problem, not merely as to how we can get knowledge of the external world, but as to how propositions purporting to be about the external world can even be intelligible.

On the views we are dealing with, some typical propositions about the external world arrive before us 'as if' directly verified, and 'as if' they were propositions the possibility of whose direct verification was part of their meaning. They are therefore propositions of which one would not expect that their meaning and meaningfulness would be independent of their mode of verification and verifiablity. But precisely the accounts being offered remove the possibility of the relevant kind of 'direct' verification, the possibility which the meaning of these propositions seems to require. A billiard ball is as such a material substance with active and passive powers, powers of pushing and being pushed, and *qua* red object of suitable size, is an object for vision: we therefore don't know what it would be for there to be a red billiard ball before us and yet for its presence not to be directly verifiable by us as freely exploring agents exercising touch and sight. Therefore, if the sort of 'direct' knowledge which (e.g.) sight and touch are pre-theoretically supposed to give us is denied, there is a problem not only as to our knowledge of the external world, but also as to the meaningfulness of our statements about it.[24,25]

---

[24]This is the problem first raised by Berkeley who supposed that we might have a notion of agent or substance from our own self-knowledge, but that the only things we know directly by perception are essentially passive ideas, with the implication that the notion of a material or perceivable substance is incoherent.

[25]J.L. Mackie in *Problems from Locke*, pp. 55–62, supposes that the idea that the meaningfulness of a statement might, in some cases, involve their verifiability to be incoherent on the ground that something has to be already meaningful in order for us to be in a position to discuss whether or how it might be verified. But it is easy for there to be things that are linguistically expressed with sufficient determinateness of meaning for us to discuss their verification, even while their full meaningfulness or coherence is in doubt; and it is plainly reasonable to hold that there is a necessary connection between meaningfulness and verifiability in the case of perceptual judgements.

(b) How to get from knowledge of the external world to knowledge of other minds

Secondly there is the converse problem: supposing that we have once achieved the feat of crossing from our knowledge of the data of consciousness to reach knowledge of the external world, how we can cross back again from knowledge of physical facts about the bodies we describe as 'other people's' to knowledge of their 'minds'? How, in brief, do we know that such bodies are not mere automata?

In handling this second problem we commonly meet with a simple-minded approach usually referred to as the 'argument from analogy'. In this it is supposed that first we observe other bodies' behaviour as exhibiting structural parallels to our own behaviour and then, knowing that in our own case our mental states are correlated with and in key ways explanatory of such behaviour and its structures, we infer that the behaviour of other bodies is accompanied and explained in similar ways by parallel mental states.

Just as in the case of the first problem, it is normal to render its solution even more hopeless by adopting the Humean model of explanation, the model which reduces explanation to exhibiting the particular instance as an example of a consistent regularity or the less wide regularity as an exemplification of a wider regularity. It is then a matter of making an inference from the supposed observation of regular correlations between mental and bodily events to the conclusion that the same correlations must arise in the case of other bodies behaving similarly to our own. In this form, the argument becomes exceedingly weak, because although it draws on instances of many varied structural types it nonetheless draws on instances limited to one case only (one's own).[26]

Again, once the problem has been raised in the form set by the dualist, the only beginnings of hope of resolving it lie in abandoning Humean presumptions about explanation. In fact, the argument draws most of its force and plausibility from the suggestion that mental states are *explanatory of* behaviour and of sequences in which the

---

[26]The difficulties are well brought out in Ayer, *Philosophical Essays*, Chapter 8; Ryle, *The Concept of Mind*, Chapter 2, sec. 9, pp. 50–55; and Malcolm, *Problems of Mind*, pp. 16–23.

bodily events entering into perception precede mental states and these issue in behaviour, and not just *correlated with* this behaviour and these sequences, a suggestion strongly present in Mill,[27] and very obvious when we think of the way in which desire enters into the explanation of behaviour and thought into that of speech. And, in closer analogy with Mackie's approach to the problem of the existence of the external world, it might seem that in a more general way coherence is brought to our understanding of a mass of behaviour on the part of other bodies on the supposition that they are persons like ourselves.[28]

However, just as the sceptical move in respect of the external world seems to falsify a key part of our knowledge of ourselves by making perceptual experience something purely inner, so the sceptical move in regard to other minds seems almost equally bizarre. Humanly, the madness of imagining all other 'people' to be automata, might seem to have more the character of a literary *jeu d'esprit* than of a serious view. In the one case, we are invited to 'bracket' the world as if it were not intrinsic to our experience of ourselves to be in it, and, in the other case, we are invited to bracket the minds of other people and animals as if it was not intrinsic to our experience of them that they are indeed people and animals. Against the first bracketing we have to insist that our knowledge of ourselves includes our seeing this or that material thing in this or that dynamic situation of our own exploration and movement, rather than merely apprehending that we are enjoying a perceptual experience as if such and such were so. And now against the second bracketing we have to insist that our knowledge of what we see and hear includes our appreciation of people and cats as walking intentionally, with their shape as something dynamic rather than static, and our appreciation of speech according to its meaning and not just as a series of noises.

---

[27]J.S. Mill, *An Examination of Sir William Hamilton's Philosophy*, pp. 243–244.

[28]It has been pointed out that this would be closely parallel to the way in which belief in God seems to bring coherence to a mass of data about the world (Alvin Plantinga, *God and Other Minds*, cf. Basil Mitchell, *The Justification of Religious Belief* for a general consideration of the way the kind of argument concerned works with its analogies with the way in which one paradigm in science is succeeded by another one which gives some more comprehensive coherence).

(c) The problem of how words referring
to the mental have meaning

This second problem of our knowledge of other minds, even of their very existence, is associated with a third, the problem of how we ascribe meaning to 'mental' words, a problem less striking to the ordinary man but made evident in the discussions of modern philosophers.

In raising the question of 'our knowledge of other minds', we can distinguish between the question as to how we know that the 'body' in front of us has a mind at all and how we know that this 'mind' is in this or that state.

Now in relation to this latter question it might seem that some states of mind, e.g. desire and intention, were so related to the structures of behaviour which they explained as to be identifiable from them. In a different way knowledge and belief, choice and intention, and certain other mental states are explanatory of their expression in speech so that from speech in appropriate context the presence of these states may be known. Thinking in this way, of course, depends upon rejecting the atomism of Hume whereby states of mind and pieces of behaviour, because they are 'distinct existences', have only contingent connection, merely 'happening' to arise in regular or constant conjunction, and upon rejecting the associated Humean view of explanation: but the Humean view on these matters in regard to the relation of the mental and the physical has never seemed very plausible.

However, in the case of, for instance, 'seeing red' and seeing other colours, what seems determined by its relation to speech and other behaviour showing colour-discrimination appears to be a certain discriminatory structure involving a structured spread of colours and shades, not the supposed 'quality' of each colour and shade, what each is 'experienced as like': but, if this be so, how, for a given colour, can we know that the state of mind, the 'experience', of one person is the same as that of another? It has also been held that in the case of pain the sensation has a distinct introspectible quality in addition to and not defined by the structure of the behaviour associated with it, a quality which belongs to the meaning of the word "pain" as it is used in speech, and similarly in the case of other sensations: again, if this be so in the case of pain or any other sensation, how can we know that what one person means by the word "pain" or other such words is the same as what another person means, and how can we know that the state of mind rightly described by one person as his being in pain is the same as the state of mind so described by another? And, if 'pleasure', 'desire', or 'will', likewise have an introspectible quality not defined by the structures of the associated behaviour, then the same problem will arise with them.

Thus this problem of the meaning of 'mental' words appears to arise whenever, as commonly happens, we apply a term or predicate to ourselves without having to use or advert to behavioural criteria for the application of the term but apply it to others on the basis of such behavioural criteria, yet do not doubt that we are ascribing to others the same 'mental' state (not a 'structure of behaviour') which we ascribe to ourselves by the use of the same term or predicate.[29]

The problem is as to how this can be possible. Any view which 'internalizes' the 'mental', making the essential meanings of mental terms something known only by introspection or immediate awareness and logically only accidentally related to behaviour is debarred from explaining how we apply the terms in the same sense to others. On the other hand, the logical behaviourist view which defines the meaning of mental terms in terms of behaviour and patterns of behaviour, might seem to explain how we apply the terms to others, but fails to explain how we apply them to ourselves without reference to behaviour. The solution to the problem requires an account which avoids both introspectionism and logical behaviourism and reveals our capacities to apply the terms to ourselves and to others as logically interdependent, so that there are inevitably logical connections between the mental and behaviour. Wittgenstein and Ryle laid the basis for such an account, and in developing an account on this basis in Chapter V, I am developing what is precisely a theory of the meaning of hybrid concepts—the concepts which determine the character of what I called hybrid propositions, concepts such as see, hear, pain, fear, anger, to give only a few samples from a very long list.

Once, of course, the character of these hybrid concepts has been realized, the character whereby the positions from which we can know that they apply to ourselves are quite discrepant from the positions

---

[29]In this use of the word "state" I diverge from Wittgenstein in a way discussed in Chapter V.

from which we can know that they apply to others, the problem of
how we can have knowledge of other minds fades away as a pseudo-
problem. We perceive and understand the behaviour of others in terms
of the same psychophysical concepts according to which we know and
understand our own life and behaviour, and if this were not warranted
these concepts would have no sense. If doubts arise in the application
of these concepts, e.g., as to whether certain behaviour is drilled
or mechanical in character (so as to suggest that such concepts are
inapplicable), at each stage such doubts can be resolved, but at each
stage the presumption remains that the concepts apply until they are
shown not to.[30] But we do not remain in ignorance as to whether
the bodily being before us has a mind, or is in a state of pain, anger,
or fear, or is intentionally acting in a certain way, or is saying this or
that, until we have removed all the possible grounds for doubt which
might arise in certain extravagant hypothetical cases.[31]

(d) The problem of personal identity
and knowledge by memory

Fourthly, once some divorce, in our knowledge or in its place
or way of existence, has been introduced between the mental and the
rest of nature, the philosophers have made it plain that there can be
no viable account of personal identity.

Descartes saw the logic whereby there has to be an 'I', a 'that
which thinks', in order for there to be a thinking or experiencing,
a point well seized by Berkeley and Kant: the very notion of an
experience presupposes the notion of an experiencer. But how can
a person be certain of anything in the past of this 'I', certain that
something which presents itself to him as a memory of his past is
indeed such a memory? Once having conceived there to be a set
of goings-on described mentalistically, whether they be goings-on in
the soul or in the brain, what is it that unifies them so as to make
them the experiences of one 'person'? This question was the one
made fresh to modern discussion by Strawson in the first part of his
book *Individuals*.

In the context of modern discussion, these difficulties reappear
in two more specialized forms.

---

[30]Cf. Chapter V, Section 2 (b), below.
[31]Cf. David Braine, 'The Nature of Knowledge', Section 1.

In the first place, it has been suggested that it is just the causal relation of these mental goings-on to a certain body which makes them experiences of the same 'person'. Yet this relation to a particular body seems to be, on the dualistic view of the mental, a mere accident of the experiences concerned, rather than something essential to them.[32] And, even if they are in an appropriate causal relation to a certain body, this does not give the status of knowledge to our supposed awareness that various different experiences which we are now having are experiences of the same person as various experiences we suppose we have had in the past.[33,34]

In the second place, it is possible to imagine or describe the performance of brain operations which involve the exchanging of parts of brains or otherwise affect memory, character, behaviour, and bodily continuity in such a way as to bring personal identity into doubt. If these performances were possible, then this would introduce arbitrariness into our judgements of identity of a kind which seems inconsistent with our conception of personhood. Yet we can imagine or describe experiences which would suggest that time-travel had occurred, but this in no way proves that time-travel is possible, even conceptually coherent. And both the dualist and the holist will hold that such performances bringing personal identity into doubt are simply impossible, albeit for different reasons.[35] By contrast, on

---

[32]This is the problem highlighted by Strawson in *Individuals*, Chapter 3.

[33]The necessity of recognising a 'knowledge not by the application of criteria' of the sameness of subject of different mental states of one's own is well shown by Sydney Shoemaker in *Self-Knowledge and Self-Identity*, Chapter 1.

[34]The philosophers who explain personal identity in this way might try to explain the existence of this kind of knowledge by making appeal to the so-called 'causal theory of knowledge'. One would then make out that the beliefs which mark such awareness of one's previous states count as knowledge because they have been causally generated in an appropriate way. But this seems to make all examples of knowledge of personal identity, such as that two thoughts or pieces of reasoning are thoughts or pieces of reasoning within the same mind (namely my own, as the person currently thinking) into things whose title to be called knowledge depends upon elaborate chains of reasoning—whereas some knowledge of this kind, and its status as knowledge and not just belief, must be presupposed to any knowledge whatsoever.

[35]The dualist holds these performances impossible on the ground that personal identity is something in principle independent of anything physical, e.g., because it is a matter of the identity of a spiritual substance. In our holistic view, such performances are impossible for the quite different reason, that personal identity is a matter of the identity of a complete human animal. In this view, a piece of brain tissue with a certain level of function could not be determinative of personal identity unless this level of function was already the level of function of a complete human animal with

materialist views, which see the mental as identical with or realized in brain states and goings-on, such performances would seem to be in principle possible. Hence it appears that, if such materialist views are adopted, judgements of personal identity will again have become infected with arbitrariness.

But our holistic view is affected by none of these difficulties, neither those which arose with the older dualism, nor those which arise from defining personal identity in terms of causal relation to the body, nor those which arise from fantasies involving brain operations. Rather, as Chapter V will make clear, the same theory of meaning which requires acceptance at once of knowledge of others on the basis of their behaviour and of knowledge of our own present, also gives the presumption of truth to memories of our own past, and thereby gives content or 'body' to our knowledge of our own identity.

Awareness of these four problems is not particularly novel. Berkeley and Hume, following Descartes, identified the difficulty of knowledge of the external world. Descartes' conception of bodies as perceivable as automata and Berkeley's simplistic coherentist account of our knowledge of other minds provide the backcloth for the modern discussions of the 'problem of other minds', extended by Wittgenstein into a general problematic of the possibility of 'mental' words having meaning. Locke identified the difficulty about personal identity, the difficulty popularized by Hume.

What was novel amongst the 'ordinary language philosophers', those whose ways of thinking were formed by Wittgenstein, Ryle, and Austin, was the diagnosis of the problem. The 'perceptual experiences' and 'volitions' imagined in the dualistic analyses proposed appeared to them purely mythological, and what they saw in the dualist accounts—unveeringly followed by the materialists—was a systematic misdescription of perception, action, sensation, and the emotions.

---

its charateristic integrated holistic mode of functioning within a certain appropriate life-history. A piece of brain tissue could not have this level of function outside the context of appropriate integrated relation with the rest of the body: for, as the rest of our holistic argument shows, the level of function involved in the mental aspects of perception, sensation, emotion and intentional action is one which involves the body or 'outer man', and therefore not at all a level of function which could be associated with a brain or mass of brain tissue in isolation. This is not because it is coherent to suppose the animal or human being functioning without the brain, but because the relevant level of brain function is only describable or explicable in a way which makes the total functioning of the animal or human being as such fundamental.

Encapsulated in this misdescription was a belief in the physical or metaphysical 'inner' (within the brain or within the soul) supposedly present to awareness as a datum of consciousness. It was this belief in the essentially 'inner' character of the mental which they saw as a grand mistake.

As will be confirmed in Chapter III, in whatever way this belief arises, it generates the epistemological problems we have outlined. Today the main root of this belief in the 'inner' lies not in the Cartesian or empiricist idea that we have infallible knowledge of our own states of consciousness or experiences, but in the ideas that human beings and other higher animals can be compartmentalized into brain and body and that the mind has all the innerness of the brain—so that the person is still conceived of as, in his immediate consciousness, connected only indirectly with the world.

Strangely, in recent times these initial four problems have even been compounded with a fifth. It is not just that the atomistic kind of analysis we have been considering has a problem with knowledge by memory with its presuppositions about self-identity, but there is a difficulty in regard to any self-knowledge whatsoever. We have referred to our knowledge, not by observation, of the position of our limbs and our own intentional bodily movements. But our knowledge not by observation is far more extensive: we know not only what we have visual experience of, but that we have visual experience of it, and this latter is not by visual observation; we have a knowledge, as it were beforehand rather than by observation, of our intentional actions not only in the case of our bodily actions but also in the case of our 'mental' actions, as when we draw out a picture not with our pencil but in our imagination; and we have a knowledge not by observation both of our pains and of our beliefs and desires (all very different cases). And in the Humean way of thinking, it is not just the mental and the physical which are held to be distinct existences in logical independence of each other, but each and every psychological state— the thinking or imagining, the pain, desire or belief—independent of the knowledge (or belief) in our being engaged in or having them. And this casts doubt on how any case of self-consciousness or introspection is to be explained.

Some materialists assume that self-consciousness or awareness of one's own mental states is achieved by a self-scanning mechanism analogous to those found in computers. It has even been presumed that, in a spiritual substance, awareness of its own mental states would have the same logical structure as such self-scanning material mechanisms (i.e., would work by a mechanism showing the same logical structure in its operation).[36] Since one of the principal arguments against mechanism is the impossibility of any mechanism exercising self-consciousness, and to speak of a computer as self-scanning is a mere convenience of speech ignoring the role of the computer users, this approach seems naive.

(e) The causal theory of knowledge generalized

The most favoured recent approach to all these problems is to adopt what is called the 'causal theory of knowledge'. The causal theory of knowledge makes all knowledge consist in a causal generation of beliefs in settings which are such as to make it normal (i.e., in accord with normal causal patterns) that beliefs thus generated will be true. The theory thus does away with all 'direct knowledge', whether 'without observation' of one's own mental states and (in virtue of their being intended) of one's own actions when done intentionally, or whether by perception.

Everywhere we are put into the situation of supposing that we have no direct knowledge of the world and things in the world, but only beliefs about the world and things in it including beliefs about how our beliefs are caused, in general, beliefs to the effect that our beliefs are caused in such a way as to be true and not by accident. In this way we are represented as being in a situation in which all we ever have is beliefs to support beliefs: as a result, either we are never in a position of knowledge in regard to any of them, or else there is nothing more to knowledge than appropriately related beliefs 'supporting' other beliefs.

It will be replied that we are simply setting up too demanding a criterion of knowledge. The suggestion is that, if we have a thoroughly coherent set of beliefs and believe them to be all caused in such a way as to be non-accidentally true, then we should demand nothing more in order to count as having knowledge. But this reply misses the point: it is not that we are being too demanding in what we require for a person's mental state to count as one of knowledge, as if we

---

[36]D.M. Armstrong, *A Materialist Theory of the Mind*, p. 107.

had already been provided with lots of evidence and what we were demanding was simply a bit more; rather what we are saying is that what is being offered is simply not of a sort to count as the justification of a claim to knowledge. What justifies a claim to knowledge is not having some set of beliefs, however ramified, but *being in a position to have knowledge*, being in a position which gives knowledge: what constitutes knowledge is not any set of beliefs but some relationship to the world of what is known.[37]

It will be said that it is not legitimate to call all beliefs into question at once, and that this is what I am supposing the dualistic analysis to make possible. That is, the people I oppose will assume that in the consideration of the justification of any particular beliefs, the truth of some other beliefs which people hold must be taken for granted. To this I reply that when other beliefs are taken for granted in such a consideration, they are taken for granted, not just as things presumed true, but as things in regard to which one is in some position of knowledge (or, as they would say, to which one is justified in believing, although what justification one has does not come within the particular consideration concerned). That is, within a genuine, serious, or truth-directed consideration of the justifiedness of believing another proposition, one cannot put forward just any proposition, whether a guess, a common prejudice, or even something of which one feels particularly sure, but only things which one could, within an objective or public context, take to have the status of knowledge or well-grounded judgement. Now for those who have made the mental inner, no belief about the outer or external world is given with this epistemological status. Once concede some perceptual knowledge of the external world, or some knowledge in virtue of their being intended of one's actions in this world, or even some knowledge of one's own states of consciousness—then one may have something to go on in justifying other claims to knowledge. But, concede no knowledge of any such kind, or concede it as knowledge only in the sense of mentally specially situated belief, and then there will be no knowledge.

---

[37]This is a key part of the point of Austin's distinction between the answers given to questions "How do you know?" as distinct from those given to questions "Why do you believe?" ('Other Minds', pp. 44–65, esp. 44–51), cf. David Braine, 'The Nature of Knowledge', pp. 51–53 (reading "as" for "is" in p. 52, l. 31).

We are offered two alternatives, either to accept the conventionalist view whereby all that is required for knowledge is the supporting of beliefs upon appropriate related prior beliefs,[38] or else to grasp at Mackie's Lockean suggestion that we can recognize, i.e., *know*, that our having the beliefs we do is properly explained in the way scientific realism suggests. But still both conventionalism and the Lockean view involve a revision of a key element in our ordinary belief-system, namely the idea that we have direct knowledge by perception of the public world (they will also involve the rejection of direct knowledge, not by perception, of our own mental states and what we do intentionally). But this revision involves a rejection of belief in such direct knowledge, belief on which one might have supposed that acceptance of the proposed causal or scientific framework was based.[39]

5. The Effects of the Inner/Outer Divide: (II) The False Chasm between the Agent and the World

We must now see agency presents both materialist and dualist a quite parallel problem to the one presented by knowledge.

For, as we have just seen, the dualist has set the ego in cognitive isolation from the world, having the world as an object of belief but not of direct engagement in his experience—and even in isolation from his fellow egos and in doubt as to his own past and as to his own identity. And, whatever problems as to knowledge arise for the dualist, the same problems arise in just as evil a form for the materialist.

---

[38]We may be familiar with the idea that the decision as to which paradigms we should accept for scientific explanation is a matter of convention, of what is accepted in the 'scientific community'. What we now have is the more radical conventionalism whereby which statements are to be accepted as basic data of perception is again a matter of which statements are actually accepted by some community.

[39]Wittgenstein's Remark 289 in *Remarks on the Philosophy and Psychology*, Vol. II, is apposite: 'Some will say that my talk about the concept of knowledge is irrelevant, since this concept as understood by philosophers, while indeed it does not agree with the concept as it is used in everyday speech, still is an important and interesting one, created by a kind of sublimation from the ordinary, rather uninteresting one. But the philosophical concept was derived from the ordinary one through all sorts of misunderstandings, and it strengthens these misunderstandings. It is in no way interesting, except as a warning.' These remarks are exactly applicable to the conventionalist causal conception of knowledge, indeed the fruit of misunderstandings and reinforcing these misunderstandings.

But now we must see how the dualist and materialist have isolated the ego from the world not only as a knower but as an agent.
For any atomist for whom the mental and the physical are logically
distinct existences as they are for Hume, it must be that 'The world
is independent of my will'[40] in the words of Wittgenstein's *Tractatus*.
And this problem arises just as much for the person who identifies the
mind with the brain: for from this view also it follows that whatever is
mental or psychological, in its aspect of being mental or psychological,
can only be contingently related with the bodily movements or actions
which are supposed to be willed; it cannot under that aspect include
the willed event, and therefore *qua* mental or psychological it cannot
be the direct causing by an agent of an event in the world.

And this brings to light a new aspect of the predicament in which
dualist and materialist alike are set. There may be some dualists who
keep some direct causal action by agents; but within the sphere of
ordinary or created agents, this is limited to a causing by the agent
of an inner event of brain or soul, what is often now called an act
of trying.[41] This still leaves the gulf or gap between the supposed
inner event and the outer event of the bodily action or movement. In
this way, the understanding of human action as a case of direct causal
action within the physical world is broken. But further, what might
have seemed the paradigm instance of direct causal agency within the
world now has to be analysed entirely in terms of events or states
causing other events or states, substance or agent causation in this
key case now being reduced to, explained in terms of, causation by
events and states.

Of course, the materialist may still envisage that there exists some
direct causal action of a physical sort, as when one billiard ball pushes
another. But this is of no relevance in considering the influence of
human desires and intentions on human bodily movements. In this
sphere, both mind-brain identity materialist and dualist alike require
a model whereby an inner event or state (e.g., an act of trying or
an intention) causes a bodily movement. The materialist most especially requires this analysis in terms of events or states because he

---

[40] *Tractatus*, 6.373.
[41] Chisholm calls it an undertaking and O'Shaughnessy speaks of strivings and
'having a go' as part-events within complexes involving the willed action (cf. Chapter
IV below).

requires that some inner event or state should be describable in two ways, mental and physical: for him, the mental event, mentalistically described, is able physically to cause a bodily movement only because it is identical with, or realized in, a brain event which is the physical cause of this bodily movement.

In this way, dualist and materialist alike are committed not only to a mythology of inner experiences and 'acts of will' as things we must, in their view, attribute to or predicate of human beings. But also they are committed to this mythology as a part of a more general mythology of 'events', 'states', and 'processes', as objects to be the terms of causal relations—it always being one real object (say, an event) which causes another real object (a different event).

Of course, they were already committed to this mythology of events being objects and to the doctrine that 'event-causation' is fundamental in the relation of mind and body by their account of perception. In that case it was not inner events which caused outer ones, but outer ones which caused inner ones. However, in the case of perception the causal relation does not enter into the description of the object of knowledge as such, except perhaps in the case of the perception of pressure by touch, and therefore it does not enter essentially into the statement of the epistemological problems to which a dualistic analysis gives rise. But, in the case of intentional action, we are confronted by the mythology of events and the idea that event-causation is primary head on.

In this way, they propose, for instance, that a causal action by a bodily being or 'substance', i.e., its causing of an effect, as when 'Smith carries the dog Rex across the river' requires to be understood in terms of causal relations between events, e.g., between some series of events in Smith's mind or brain and the event or process of Rex's body moving across the water.

But an event or state cannot push or exercise force, support, carry, or move anything. It is a mystery how an event located at one time can have any effect at another time, as to how it could have any links with other events at intermediate times so as to reach forward to the time of the supposed effect. Certainly, it would seem, it cannot have logical links. Therefore inescapably, once we reduce substance-causation to event-causation, we are drawn into ways of thinking about causation in terms of regularity, of things occurring in conformity with law so that causation can be explained in terms of necessary or sufficient conditions.

It is at this stage that the question can reasonably be raised as to whether we are suffering the results of a conspiracy. There seems to be a clear distinction between the meaning of the word "cause" as referring to a causal agent such as a person, an animal, a billiard ball, a rock, or a river, and its meaning as referring to states or events which we might mention in answer to a 'Why'-question or state within a 'because'-clause. But regularity theories of causation conspire together with the requirements of the dualist/materialist account of man and animals to make one regard states and events as objects in a metaphysical sense and the only real causes, if real causes exist—reducing agent-causation to event-causation in the way made popular in recent times by Davidson.

And in order to restore a proper conception of agency, including the kinds of agency exercised by animals and human beings, we need to expose this underlying mythology of events—a task we undertake in Chapter VI. A conception of substances, inanimate bodies, animals or human beings, as causes or agents is required as the proper background of any understanding of the role of teleology and intention in causation.

6. The Hybrid Nature of the Human Being: Mechanistic Explanation Not Fundamental

We have seen how the type of atomism we have described is fuelled by the causal consideration that our experiences or tendencies to believe must be capable of being caused, not only in some normal way, which involves the external and real existence of the things experienced or believed to exist, but also in other ways not requiring this—at the extreme, by some manipulation by demon or neurosurgeon of soul or brain. It is very convenient to feel able to suppose that there are such inner 'experiences' to correspond to or be identifiable with certain brain processes. It greatly simplifies the patterns of explanation we offer. For, if the materialist option of regarding these 'experiences' as realized in or identical with the brain processes concerned is adopted, it enables us not only to regard everything physical in human life as explicable causally in physical terms but even to regard the mental, so far as it is to be explained causally at all, as explicable in these terms.

This causal approach does not itself explain the notion of 'experience' here involved, but simply presumes that epistemology will be able to explain it in some way or other. We have indicated how this presumption is doomed to disappointment and will seal our demonstration of this in Chapters II and III. The description of human and animal experience, as it is experienced, is irreducibly holistic or hybrid, reference to the mental and the physical inextricable from each other within it.

However, there is an alternative avenue of approach which materialists and dualists may yet try to follow.

For, even if the logical atomism we described is rejected and the irreducibly hybrid character of mind-involving statements is acknowledged, it is still open to a philosopher to say that, even though such hybrid statements cannot be eliminated from our descriptions of our experience or from the explanations we give of them at an *ad hominem* level, the underlying realities are not thus hybrid. In this way the philosopher is making a distinction between things as they appear to us and things as they are in themselves. And today the most common reason for making this distinction will not be a Kantian one, as if the level of things as they are in themselves was inaccessible to our knowledge, but a belief that the fundamental level of reality is physical and capable of explanation in terms of physical causation. It is common to suppose that the ultimately explanatory is always something 'behind' the phenomena—explanation being in abstract or theoretical terms, or consisting in a bringing within the range of generalizations—but usually it turns out that the terms or generalizations concerned are supposed to belong to physical science.

To show what is wrong with this move, one has to demonstrate (this is the task of Chapter VIII) that the level of description whereby one describes human and animal experience and engagement with the world in irreducibly psychophysical terms also provides a fundamental level of explanation, even in respect of the physical itself. And a key mark of this is that our ordinary accounts of animal and human behaviour in mind-involving terms do not just make what happens intelligible retrospectively without having any predictive power beforehand, but that, besides explaining the phenomena they explain, they often allow us to predict them in cases in which no other mode of prediction would be possible: in this respect these accounts can be predictively more powerful than physical ones, even in regard to physical states and events.

Philosophers impose false restrictions on the notion of 'causal explanation' as if this always had to be in physical, non-intentional,

non-teleological terms, and by reference to universal laws, and as if
'explanation' in mind-involving terms was explanation only in some
quite different sense. On the contrary, within any field in which
consideration of smaller units and relations among them leave the
behaviour of larger units indeterminate, there is no reason beforehand
for supposing that there cannot be relations and laws in respect of
these larger units which determine some upshots both in the behaviour
of these larger units and, consequentially, in the behaviour of some of
their subordinate parts, which would not be determined if the only
relevant relations and laws were those governing the smaller units.
Holism cannot be excluded a priori.

This is a lesson insisted upon by such writers as Whitehead
and Bohm even in respect of the merely physical. Mechanism, even
if backed up by theories of chaos, is inadequate to deal even with
the phenomena of electromagnetism, let alone quantum phenomena,
cosmological theory, and nuclear forces. Moreover, it is not just that
it fails at the level of our capacity to perform calculations depending
upon detailed knowledge of initial states or because of our ignorance
of some initial conditions in themselves determinate. Rather, what
we find is that the behaviour or characteristics of parts of things or
of local aspects of phenomena can only be considered determined in
virtue of relation to the behaviour and characteristics of the wholes
containing them. More is determined, if we take into account forms
of explanation involving larger wholes as well as forms of explanation
involving smaller wholes, than would have been determined if only
the latter were to be taken into account.

Holism within the sphere of predictive causal explanation has,
therefore, to be accepted into our system of thought even at the
physical level. But what we are concerned with is its importance in
the predictive causal understanding of mind-involving phenomena in
the lives of animals and human beings. And here what we shall make
clear and insist upon in Chapters VII and VIII is that reference to these
mind-involving phenomena with their uneliminably hybrid character
is indispensable to the predictive causal explanation of much animal
and human behaviour even in its physical aspects. True, there can be
systems of whose behaviour we can give a teleological account, but in
the case of which the conformity of the behaviour with a teleological
pattern can be explained mechanistically or physically. But we shall
demonstrate that, where the reason why teleology comes in is because
of the applicability of mind-involving descriptions, no such reduction
to the mechanistic or physical is possible.

At a previous stage it seemed open to a philosopher to argue that the types of statement we make do not reflect the types of reality which exist on the ground that we never in our statements get beyond the level of 'appearance' or 'how we speak' to a level of 'how things are in themselves', so that the view that there are basic statements of the hybrid kind which I have described did not at once compel one to the conclusion that there are hybrid realities. It dovetailed with such a view, but did not require it. However, with the consideration of explanation itself in Chapter VIII, I demonstrate that we can speak more definitely and say the holism established in earlier chapters obtains not just at the level of experience and description but at the level of ultimate explanation and reality.

In brief, the facts commit us to a radical rejection of the self-sufficiency of the physical even for the purposes just of the explanation and prediction of the physical. The principle that more is determined if we take into account higher orders of causes as well as lower ones than we would have realized to be determined if we had taken into account only lower orders of causes has here its most important application.

But more follows from this.

Each of these mind-involving phenomena is focalized upon a subject as a kind of hub from which they radiate in a way made plain in Chapter IX. This subject who perceives, feels, or acts is not an inner self, nor a mind realized in a brain, but an animal or human being. But, since some of the fundamental principles governing the behaviour of this bodily being are essentially mind-involving, and since they therefore carry with them the need to accept criteria of identity through time of a kind distinctively appropriate to an animal with consciousness or a human being, it is quite wrong to speak of this bodily being, animal or human, as essentially a 'material entity' or 'material body'. To say such things would be to imply, quite falsely, that the bodily being concerned was an entity the explanation of whose physical behaviour is ultimately in physical terms. Rather, they are integrated natural unities of a kind which is *sui generis*, at once mental and physical in character.

Since the mind as realized in perception, sensation, emotion, and intentional action is not a separate entity interacting with a material body or machine, what we have to do with is a bodily being, a whole which is by nature bodily, i.e., possessed of bodily properties and relations, albeit animal or human. Therefore we do not have on our hands any form of dualism. That is, we do not hold that the natural universe comprises two interacting kinds of whole or substance, minds and material bodies: if there be a God creating and upholding this universe, he does not have to create a material world and, separately, to create minds to interact with parts of it. However, we are committed to something which is, in its way, equally striking, namely that the natural universe comprises bodily things of many kinds, some of which have a nature or principles of behaviour which essentially involve the mental and cannot be in any sense explained by or reduced to the physical: if there be a God creating and upholding such a universe, then what is involved is his creating and upholding not just a physical system or system of material bodies, but a system including wholes of this kind whose principles of behaviour transcend the physical.

7. Recovering the Vision of the Human Being as a Unity: The Scale of the Task

The holistic way of viewing human beings and animals I have outlined is deeply set in our ordinary-life ways of speaking and thinking. This holism is central to the Aristotelian tradition and implicitly reverted to by all those existentialists and phenomenologists who reject dualism and dualistic analyses of human life. But existentialism and phenomenology have not been preoccupied with leaving an absolutely free rein to physical science, with leaving it absolutely open how much it might in the end explain. By contrast, the preconception that philosophy will in no way obtrude upon the domain of science set the context within which 'ordinary language philosophy' developed. Therefore, the revival of holistic ways of thinking and the spurning of dualistic analyses within this 'ordinary language philosophy'— dominant within the Anglo-Saxon setting from the 1950s into the 1970s—was particularly striking. These philosophers were glaringly aware of the gross inappropriateness of the analyses of perception and action, of sensations and the emotions, which the dualists proposed only to be followed by the materialists later. And accordingly these philosophers occupied themselves in a therapy—a therapy which would free people from dualism or any such dualistic belief in the 'inner', and *ipso facto* free them from the epistemological problems we sketched.

Why was this therapy so unsuccessful? How is it that, in the very Anglo-Saxon regions where this kind of philosophy predominated, belief in 'sensations', 'perceptual experiences', 'experiences of acting', and other 'inner' states or goings-on—so 'inner' as to be identifiable with brain states or goings-on—should be now rampant. Why was it that the apparent consensus in the rejection of the 'inner' represented in Austin, Ryle and Wittgenstein alike should have been so easily set aside—almost as though their arguments had never been?

To this question the answer seems to be threefold.

Firstly, for the most part the 'ordinary language philosophers' provided negative reasons, rather than positive ones, for the holistic perspective which their rejection of dualistic analyses entailed. They offered a therapy intended to remove the attractiveness of these analyses by exhibiting the misunderstandings from which these analyses resulted and the absurdities to which they led. But they seemed to give no positive insight into any alternative way of viewing the phenomena with which they had to deal.

Secondly, to take the example of perception, the detailed criticism of various arguments for 'sense-data' and the diagnosis that many of these arguments depended on, assuming that judgements about immediate experience must be infallible or incorrigible, did little to remove the initial plausibility of the dualistic analysis in terms of an inner experience caused by changes in the sense-organs in the context of a previous history. The case for inner 'perceptual experiences' had not been proved, but neither had it been decisively or convincingly disproved. And parallel remarks apply in the case of action and other key features of psychophysical life.

Thirdly, and perhaps most importantly, they ignored the importance of considerations of explanation and causation in thinking about the philosophy of mind and the nature of human beings. They treated the philosophy of mind and the philosophy of language as constituting a part or parts of philosophy separate from anything to do with causal explanation and the philosophy of science. But it has been, above all, causal considerations—of the apparent ease with which it may be supposed that mental states, identical with or realized in states of the brain, may cause or be caused by physical states of the rest of the body—which have given the dualistic picture its appearance of simplicity.

What we have is a syndrome. The ancient analyses of perception, action, etc. which have become commonplace since the time of Plato are supported not only by certain ways of thinking in epistemology, but also by the way of thinking whereby events are distinct existences which cause one another. And they are also supported by the apparent simplicity of compartmentalizing human beings into the brain with the mind and, on the other hand, the rest of the body with its relations with the world.

Against this background, we find any number of ways of being led up the garden path into a vision of the human being as composed of an inner part or aspect (the mind or brain) and an outer part or aspect (outward form and behaviour)—any one of which lands one with the whole dualistic mind/body or brain/body package. In this situation, it is no use tackling the arguments with which one is presented piecemeal, cutting off one head of the hydra at a time. Nor is it any use just trying to deal with the arguments presented by an obscurantist resort to authority, even the authority of 'ordinary language'.[42] The 'ordinary language philosophers' made implicit or explicit appeal to our ordinary ways of talking and thinking, but they failed to show the rationale of these ways of talking and thinking.

Our need is to supply the defects of the 'ordinary language approach', defects which it has sometimes shared with the 'phenomenological approach', by providing a critical articulation of what it is for the human being to be an animal—or, if you prefer it, an irreducibly psychosomatic, psychophysical, being.

What we require is, firstly, a positive perspective exhibiting the systematic integration of the mental and the physical both at the level of experience and description and at that of causation and explanation. But secondly we require some systematization—what the 'ordinary language philosophers' were terrified of—that minimum of systematization which is required to prevent the subversion of our basic insights in respect of the unity of man. We have to pursue each of the lines of thought which lend plausibility to the dualistic analysis back to its root, showing the basic structures of the relations between mind and object, mind and behaviour, and how these are violated in the dualistic presentations—in particular in common accounts of intentionality. We have to provide the systematizations in the theory of meaning which will enable us to steer between behaviourism and introspectionism. Chapters II to V achieve what is required at the level of description

---

[42]This appearance of obscurantism presents itself, for instance, when Malcolm in *Problems of Mind* (pp. 73–77) regards it as obvious nonsense to speak of brains as thinking or Geach in *God and the Soul* (p. 40) sees the suggestion that machines think in the same light without either of them giving any full rationale of the 'ordinary language' seemings indicated.

and experience, but all remains insecure until we have established the same holism at the level of explanation and causation in Chapters VI to VIII. There we show what is wrong in trying to reduce agent-causality to event-causality, and then, having thus restored the focal position of the agent in causation, we unravel each of the mistakes which have made philosophers and scientists reject the autonomy of teleological and mentalistic explanations.

But then, having demonstrated how human beings and other higher animals transcend the material, we have to prevent this from being understood in ways which subvert the original grasp, the grasp only just recovered, of the unity of the mental and the physical in both human being and animal. For it is very easy for the ideas of the community between human beings and other animals and of the unity of the human being to get subverted. We have to identify the structures which the other higher animals share with human beings and show how the 'less intellectual' features involved in these structures provide a necessary bridge between the 'intellectual' and the bodily without which the assertion of the unity of the human being would become a legal fiction. Finally we have to recognize the internality of bodily function to mental function within these bridging 'less intellectual' features as likewise necessary if unity of human being or animal is not to become a legal fiction.

Conclusion

The upshot of our presentation will be to restore the respectability of the notions of direct cognitive relation and of the direct operation of the will in the world: to restore the logical possibility of envisaging perception and action, formative cases for our way of thinking of the rest of human life, as unitary or, according to the way of thinking introduced in this book, indeed 'animal' or irreducibly psychophysical.

What we are concerned with is the immediacy and directness of human and animal presence and action in the world.

Instead of conceiving there to be a number of modes of causal agency in the world, none reducible to the others, there has come to be conceived to be only one mode, the physical, so that all others have to be thought of according to this model. In this way, intentional action is dissolved into an intention or volition in the mind or brain acting physically (or conceived of in a way modelled on bodily action in its physical aspects) upon the body within which, as a result, further physical causal actions take place, physically engendering a bodily movement. Likewise, instead of conceiving there to be a number of modes of relation according to which fields of bodily things can affect a bodily being set in their midst, again none reducible to the others, amongst these the mode of relation whereby a field of bodily things can cognitively affect a human being or animal, there are conceived to be only 'physical' modes of relation.

Therefore, in place of this, our discussion will restore the insights that the mode of relation in virtue of which, e.g., various kinds of physical force are exercised is only one of the modes of relation between bodily beings exemplified in the world; and that the physical mode of causal action is only one of the modes of causal action or 'modes of causality'[43] exercised in the world. Intention is not the extrinsic cause of certain physical bodily movements, but is the mode of the exercise of causality involved where an animal or human being executes a bodily action intentionally. It is not that a spirit or brain performs some operation called a volition, and that by some mechanism secured by God or nature this volition causally brings about some bodily movement whereby some end is achieved in the world. Rather the human being or animal, acting according to its nature in the mode of causal agency proper to it, him or herself acts bodily in the world.

In a parallel way, the possible modes of relatedness between a bodily being and the field in which it is set whereby that field influences the bodily being are different for different types of bodily beings. In the case of animals and human beings there is a mode of relatedness which consists in an openness to a cognitive relation. We need to rediscover cognitive relatedness as a mode of real relatedness, redrawing the notion of intentionality. It is to this task that we now turn in our next two chapters, on perception.

---

[43]On the spread of types of 'mode' of causality, causal action, or causal agency exemplified in the world, see my *The Reality of Time and the Existence of God*, pp. 76–81, 289–293.

II. Perception (I): The Shape of a Holistic View

1. The Inseparability of Perception and Behaviour

(a) Perception as in internal retrospective and prospective relation to behavioural disposition

In order to understand perception we have to see each perceptual experience in relation to the behaviour or patterns of behaviour which precede and follow it. The custom in considering perception in the past has been to take each supposed perceptual experience and consider it in isolation from its context of behaviour and other perceptions, and then only in this context of isolation to ask whether the perceptual experience is of outer public or inner private objects, whether of real or 'intentional' objects. It is only by breaking with this custom and instead considering perceptual experience in its full context of activity that we can recover a true grasp of its nature. Once we do this, we shall find the idea of perception as a direct cognitive relation with the world restored to us, but it will be the idea of a direct cognitive relation, not of an observing mind to experiences presented to it, but of an active exploring animal to a world perceived as a field of action.[1] Later discussion will show that there is nothing naive about the realism involved.

---

[1] Schopenhauer thought that it is only in action that we come to know the self as noumenon, as a thing as it is in itself rather than just something as it appears to us (cf. *The World as Will and Idea*, Vol. II, Ch. 29). What I demonstrate is that perception and action are so inextricable from one another that perception cannot be conceived of except as an act (in a generalized sense of "act") of a being which is active in a causative way in the world, inextricable from action in the ordinary sense. As a result, perception itself, carrying this essential integration with action with it as an internal feature, brings with it knowledge of the self as noumenon—not in any elevated intellectualist sense, but simply in the sense that perception, no less than action, brings knowledge of ourselves as we are and not just as we appear. In either case the knowledge is not of the object of perception or action but only, by reflective

Let us begin by considering a simple example.

Suppose that Smith is conscious of seeing a table in front of him, and of seeing *where* it is in relation to himself and the room—*not* in the sense that he could *judge accurately* that it was 1 foot $3\frac{1}{2}$ inches from his right knee, *but* in the sense that he could *behave accurately* towards it, e.g., touch it exactly on the edge (to within half an inch) or avoid walking into it.

Some event involving Smith's mind, some experience, has taken place here. Many accounts have been given of what the experience is or consists in, and of what kind of object it is an experience of, and of what its relation to these objects is. But whatever this experience is, whether merely the gaining of beliefs and aptitudes or whether the being presented with some object, and whatever kind of object the experience is an experience of, whether of some inner mental image of a table or of the table itself, and in whatever sense it is 'of' these objects, it still remains true that *this experience* has some relation to *that table*, in *that position*, within *that room*. Now the question is: what things make it so that *this experience* has the relation it does to *that object*?

It cannot be just that the *content* of the experience corresponds to reality, i.e., that the experience is *as if* there were some table, placed thus and thus, within a room, before his eyes, and that *in fact* this is just how things were. And it cannot be just that *the table*, and so forth, were amongst the causes on which Smith's having the experience depended. No, because two other things seem required, things which are usually left out.

Firstly, it is not just that the table *causes* the experience: it has to cause it in a *natural manner*, e.g., not by a television camera being set up, and cunningly contrived so as to feed signals into my optic nerve, but *by my using my eyes and looking across the room*; i.e., it has to cause the experience in a way which fits into my life in a normal way; the seeing of the table and of where it is, takes place in a context in which my vantage point (the position of my body and my head) either is, or could naturally have been, the result of intentional movement, *and* in a context in which it is conceivable for me to move again in order to get a different view of the situation.

---

awareness of the acts of perceiving and doing things, an awareness which is always in a larger context of awareness of a spirit of experience and action, and an awareness always involving self-awareness.

It is within this context, in which it is natural for me to have some awareness of my vantage-point, that it is possible for me to have an experience (as if of a table) as the result of a natural exercise of the sense, using my eyes and looking, and therefore possible for *the table* to cause the experience in a manner which is in the relevant way natural, i.e., to cause it in a way which *dovetails with* and *depends on* what we might refer to as 'behavioural preparedness[2] or behaviour focused towards perception', i.e., preparedness and behaviour whose natural consequence is perception or better perception (like opening one's eyes, or turning one's head, or going up closer).

Secondly, the experience itself affects Smith's behaviour towards the table: that is, it is part of the sense of saying that he sees where it is in relation to himself and the room, that he is now able (or better able) to touch its edge, or to avoid walking into it. And these behavioural aptitudes are internal to the experience Smith has when he sees where the table is [since this cannot be explained in terms of judgements], just as in a yet more evident way some behavioural aptitudes must be internal to any experience of one thing as being *above* another one in my visual field.[3]

Now, it is perhaps *these behavioural aptitudes* above all which make it so that *this experience* is related to, or directed towards, *this table*, rather than just towards a mental picture of some table or other. For, it might have been thought that *the experience itself*, although (as it happens) *caused by* this table, was not itself an *experience of this table*, but merely an experience *as of* a table (a table with this appearance), an experience consisting as it were of the presentation of a picture to the mind's eye, a picture not bearing any internal sign of whether it was a picture of *this table and room*, or of another one exactly like it. But now it appears plain that the *object* of the experience, i.e., what the experience is of, is the same as *the object towards which these behavioural aptitudes are directed*—and there is no economy in supposing the experience to be *as if* of this table and room *but not as such* of this table and room, or to be of *an inner mental picture*

---

[2]This preparedness is a disposition or state in an Aristotelian sense, not a disposition in the currently accepted restricted sense, a contrast which I amplify later in the book. In Rylean terms, it is a many-track, not a single-track, disposition.

[3]'Up' and 'down' carry necessary semantic connotations connecting them with the natural vertical posture assumed by all land animals in standing, walking and running.

looking like this table and room, since it is just as good to look at a thing, as to look at a picture of it.

And, of course, Smith is aware of this object, the table, which he is conscious of seeing, not only as the *object* or *focus* of these behavioural aptitudes, something he is now better able to touch or avoid walking into, but also *as being that which he sees by looking at,* i.e., as (in a sense) focus of *behaviour directed towards perception*—in the case of *attending to a thing* or *watching it,* the *intended focus*; and in other cases, the *unintended focus.*

In this way we have picked out as internal to any perception, in paradigm cases, both anticipatory or background behavioural dispositions and consequent behavioural dispositions. These aspects of perception, fitfully taken account of in the epicycles of the theories of such thinkers as Price, Armstrong and Searle,[4] and central in the thought of Merleau-Ponty and Hampshire amongst philosophers and Gibson,[5] call for the explicitness I have given them. We need to recognize that a perceptual experience at a time is a reality with logical links across time, logical links with behavioural dispositions before and after it. The human being is a reality, not only immersed in and enmeshed with the world, but also immersed in and enmeshed with time.

(b) The depth and contours of our rejection of atomism in respect of perception

Now, there is (I suppose) in any perception such as I have described, even granted these links with prior and subsequent behavioural dispositions, a physical effect or stimulus on the retina, and

---

[4]Price introduces a backcloth of perceptual acceptances to do the jobs of what he refers to as the Bodily Adjustment Theory and the Emotion Theory (*Perception,* Chapter VI). Armstrong explains perception in terms of changes in sensorily caused comings to believe (*A Materialist Theory of the Mind,* Chapter 10), and belief for him is dispositionally related to behaviour or sorts of behaviour (albeit not in such a way that there can be a logical connection between the mental state and a physical law of behaviour). Searle (weaker in allowing only for the prior setting of perception and not for its effects on subsequent behavioural aptitudes, in giving an account of what is internal to perception) produces a Network and a Background determinative of visual Intentional states (*Intentionality,* pp. 54–57).

[5]James J. Gibson, 'The Concept of Stimulus in Psychology'; *The Senses Considered as Perceptual Systems; The Ecological Approach to Visual Perception.* The first mentioned article shows the turning point in his thought. It is to the last that I mostly refer in this book.

also a physical effect upon parts of the brain which have to do with my skills and aptitudes in behaviour, and a whole lot of other changes and goings-on *in the brain* intermediate between these. And the central-state materialist *postulates* that the *mental* or *conscious* element in perception (its *experiential* content, or what I am *directly or immediately aware of*) is identical to or realized in one of these intermediate events or processes, in particular to some pivotally placed event or process in the brain affected by my past history and causally influential on my behaviour. And the dualist differs from the materialist only in saying that the mental element in perception is something *caused by* or *corresponding with* such a pivotally placed brain state or process, rather than simply *identical* to it.

But why tie *the mental or conscious element* in perception to this, entirely inner, intermediate event or process, within the brain?

There is a confusion between the cause of a perception, conceived of as an event taken place at a particular time, which might be or include something physiological taking place at that time (e.g., a change of state in the retina, or a change in state of some more inner part of the brain) as well as a spread of elements in the biography of the perceiving animal setting a context and, as some would say, determining the processing of this change of state (conceived of theoretically as a change of 'informational state'), and the object of the perception. This confusion has led philosophers to identify the object of a perception with some supposedly immediate cause of this perception. They believe that there is some 'experience' which could be had, one and the same in utterly different external circumstances, circumstances of a normal 'veridical kind', circumstances of illusion, or delusion, circumstances of having one's soul or brain meddled with by a demon or a brain technician;[6] and they believe that this could be or correspond to a state of the brain—but need there be any such 'same experience'? The belief that there must be such a thing is largely founded on the mistaken thought that the 'experience' or 'object' in a perception must be or correspond to some physiological cause of the perception.

Rather, one should say that the 'conscious' or 'mental' or 'mind-involving' element in perception is something which is of a piece with our awareness of our behaviour both before and after the perception,

---

[6]See Chapter I, n. 1.

and that the content of any statement describing or referring to what we are conscious of in perception will overlap with the content of statements expressing our awareness of our behaviour. So, the mental or conscious element in perception is to be tied, or related, not just to some supposedly privileged state in the brain, nor even just to this *plus* events in my eye or in my retina, *but also* to a mass of facts relating to my awareness of my behaviour before and after the perception!

What one has to beware of is the surreptitious introduction of two conscious stages in perception, or two 'mentalistically' describable (even if one is pre-conscious) stages. This is the normal upshot of distinguishing 'sensations' or 'experiences' (still conceived of as mental data) and 'perceptions' (in some cases no longer conceived of as mental or psychological data but as constructions).

One has to recognize that there is no inference from the atomizability of physical stimuli or effects in the sense-organ or in relevant parts of the brain to the atomizability of what is to be conceived of as mentally or psychologically given. In particular the atomizability of physical effects in respect of time and the limitedness of their implications for the past and future have no implications for the atomizability of perceptual states and the limitedness of their implications for the past and future. That is, the 'data' for the human being or other animal are not, or need not be the stimuli to the sense-organs or any effects in the physical sensory apparatus taken as a whole (from the sense-organ to the relevant parts of the brain).

Likewise there is no inference from any logical independence between physical structures in the sensory apparatus of an animal and its behaviour to a logical independence between perception and behaviour.

Finally there is no inference from the uncategorized, or in some relevant respect unformed, character of physical stimuli or effects at some stage in the chain of effects in the sense-organ and the brain to the uncategorized or unformed character of some primary, conscious or unconscious, mental or psychological datum. That is: suppose one accepts the fact that any supposed data of 'perception' must be conceptualized according to some set of categories or conceptual scheme or, as I have argued, that they must be integrated into some structures of behaviour; then it remains that there is no inference whatsoever to the prior existence, possibly pre-conscious, of some more atomic sensations or experiences, unconceptualized or not thus integrated, waiting for mental processing ('construction', 'synthesis' or 'inference').

(c) The mistaken 'cinematograph' model of perception

What is involved here is the achieving of a complete escape from what I shall call the 'cinematograph model' of perception—whereby, as Gibson would put it, snapshot vision is made the model for all vision. In this conception the experience of seeing is conceived of as like having a series of pictures presented to one, while sight is treated, as by Hume, as the paradigm case for all perception, and, following Berkeley,[7] sight is treated as separable from touch. This approach, in sum, involves three main features.

(i) There is the feature of the attempt to consider sight in isolation from touch, and, in general, the separation of observation from any exploration, head movement, and suchlike, i.e., from our intentional knowledge (that is, as we explained earlier, knowledge in virtue of these things' being intended) of all the intentional activities germane to observation, knowledge most obvious in the case of moving in order to touch things but also exemplified in the case of sight by what we call 'looking'. We have already commented as to how this is to ignore the cooperation of sight, touch, kinaesthetic sensation, intentional movement in exploration, etc. involved in all typical nondefective cases of perception.

It is not that depth is appreciated first by touch and then taught to sight—this seems contrary to the evidence.[8] Rather the point is that the world within which we appreciate things as being at different distances from us is the world within which we move, turn our heads, change our position, and explore—within which, when I see where the table is, that I have done this is confirmed when I reach out and touch it, touching it at just the point at which, guided by sight, I mean to touch it. For perception, neither the visual world nor the tactile world is a thing previously given to which the other is an extra. Rather there is one world within which I move, see, and feel. The organism which moves develops so as to perceive, its perception integrated with its movement and dispositions to move.

---

[7]Berkeley insists on the distinction between objects of sight and touch in his *New Theory of Vision*.

[8]Both the young baby and the young chick, unschooled by variety of experience, stall at a visual cliff (in an experiment of the Gibsons)—a cliff suggested by sight alone as when a firm transparent piece of glass apt for crawling or walking upon reaches beyond a visually appreciated firm surface to where there is nothing beneath the glass except the bottom of some apparent precipice.

(ii) There is the related supposition that there is no knowledge given or involved in perception except knowledge reflected in differences of description of the objects of perception. This is particularly mad in the case of the sense of touch as if knowledge by touch of the object could be separable from knowledge of the touching organ.

(iii) Thirdly, intimately connected with and perhaps resulting from these first two defects, this model invites us to treat experiences as isolable from each other, each 'a distinct existence', whether the experiences under one sense or experiences arising from different senses. (We have already remarked that the logical independence of physiological data from each other is irrelevant, although if experiences were isolable the physiological data might be peculiar to each experience—but in fact what I am conscious of, and what I know as the immediate result of perception, need not be the result merely of this isolated stimulus).

The second point, (ii), presupposes the distinction between perceiving and the object of perception, e.g., between seeing and what is seen. In the cinematograph model whereby the experience of seeing is conceived of as like having a series of pictures presented to one, it is presumed that all knowledge of differences in seeing or sensing is got from knowledge of differences in description of what is sensed or seen. So we need to raise the question of how we should describe what is seen.

It is clear that on any view we will need to distinguish between descriptions true of 'what is seen' and descriptions of 'what is seen as it is seen': plainly we can see a man who had been born in Jerusalem without this fact about him entering into how we see him,[9] and on a beach we can have a front view of a woman with a mole on her back without the mole entering into how we see her.[10] The question thus becomes that of what is the right principle for distinguishing descriptions of 'what is seen as it is seen' from amongst other descriptions of what is seen.

And here the cinematograph model suggests that the picture of a tomato looks just the same as a picture of a well-simulated plastic model of a tomato and even a picture of a carefully placed

---

[9]Cf. n. 12.

[10]G.E.M. Anscombe gives this example in 'The Intentionality of Sensation', *Collected Philosophical Papers II.*

skin (plastic or otherwise, without anything corresponding to the inside or back of a tomato).[11] Therefore, if, as point (i) suggests, what governs the description of what we see as we see it has nothing to do with exploratory behaviour, looking or changing place to get a different look, or any coordination of sight with possible touch, then the temptation to suppose that what we see as we see it is most appropriately described in terms determined by 'what a camera picture would show up' becomes almost irresistible. Indeed, if all we got in seeing a tomato were a single isolated glance, surely, the model suggests, the presentation to our senses would be no different from the cases of appropriately contrived models or skins?—so the rhetoric inspired by this model proceeds.

And, if what we see is never seen 'as a tomato', then certainly by parallel arguments nothing we ever see is seen 'as a material thing', 'as a substance' and certainly nothing ever 'as a man' or 'as an animal', let alone 'as a man being shaved'[12] or 'as a dog walking'. Nor will there be any hope of perceptually envisaging two objects or states as in a causal relation.[13]

The plausibility of such a model of perception depends, not only on selectivity in considering the sense of sight in isolation from the use of any other senses and from knowledge of intentional exploratory or perception-directed behaviour and related kinaesthetic and other sensations, but also on selectivity in considering only the sense of sight or (occasionally) hearing—studiously avoiding consideration of the sense of touch (or the, for human beings, minor senses, taste and smell, which involve touch or involve some parallel cognizance of the sense-organ). Touch cannot be handled in this way: it is ridiculous to say that there is no knowledge of touching apart from knowledge of what is touched, as if there could be knowledge of what it touched independently of any knowledge of the touching organ. All this leads

---

[11]These remarks are inspired by Price's example of a tomato on p. 3, *Perception*.

[12]Austin anticipates a contrast in the senses in which "a man being shaved" and "a man who was born in Jerusalem" are descriptions of 'objects' of perception (p. 98, *Sense and Sensibilia*).

[13]Hume takes it to be impossible for us to have an impression of outer sense of any causal relation, and this is the basis of one of his two key arguments against supposing a causal relation to have any reality 'in the objects' (*Treatise*, Bk. I, pt. III, sect. XIV). The general point that being in a causal relation is not something recorded in a picture is well brought out by Anscombe, "'Whatever has a Beginning of Existence must have a Cause': Hume's Argument Exposed', *Collected Philosophical Papers I* in connection with Hume's earlier argument in *Treatise*, Bk. I, pt. III, sect. III.

us to look for a different model and a different criterion for the appropriate description of what is seen as it is seen.

(d) The proper description of 'what is seen as it is seen'

What we have to do is set the discussion of the proper description of 'what is seen as it is seen' in the right context. There is indeed no seeing without seeing as, not in the sense that the specialized idiom of 'seeing as' always has application, but in the sense that there is always a distinction amongst descriptions of what is seen as to whether or not they are descriptions of how it is seen.

What we have to fight against are two key mistaken tendencies.

In the first place there is a tendency to suppose that the 'how we see it' must correspond to 'what is presented to the eyes'. As we remarked earlier, it is vital to distinguish psychological data from physiological data and not to invent a second set of fictitious psychological data to marry with the physiological data, as if there were two conscious, or at any rate, mental, stages in perception, the one the having of sense-data and the other corresponding to Price's perceptual acceptance. We have to escape any idea of a construction, whether by the mind or by the brain, of a 'perception' out of prior unformed data or sensory stimuli, and we may note that it was the key to the start of Gibson's advances towards thinking of 'ambient and ambulatory' perception to reject any such notion of two stages and a construction.

Once we have grasped that there does not have to be any psychological or mental 'object' of a perception (whether conscious or unconscious) corresponding to the isolable change in pattern of stimulation, physiologically describable, i.e., no 'object' corresponding to this key element in the 'cause' or causal background of the perception, the temptation to espouse this cinematograph model should die. There need not be any 'sensing' whether of camera-simulable presentations or of sense-data prior to, or internal to, the event or experience of 'perceiving', or (in the most usually considered case) 'seeing'.

Further, it has to be realized that, even thinking in terms of 'what is presented to the eyes', what is presented is not e.g., in the case of a coin presented sideways, something which looks elliptical,[14] or in the case of a table 'a brown trapeziform sense-datum',[15] since physically

---

[14]Cf. Ayer in *Foundations of Empirical Knowledge*, p. 3.
[15]Price, *Perception*, p. 156.

light does not come to the eyes as coming from any particular distance, nor even as Leonardo da Vinci contrived to imagine, as if fixed in one plane[16] as it were in the glass of a window. Rather, the appearance of things 'in perspective' or, to be more precise, in the skillfully perspectived way in which they are actually experienced, is not as such 'deceptive'. Indeed we see a coin as round, presented sideways, not as elliptical, and a table as rectangular or square, not trapeziform (and railway lines going away from us as parallel, and portrayals of railway lines going into the distance as portrayals of lines which do not merge). And there opens out a way of viewing perception according to which the appropriate ways of describing things 'as we see them' is in terms appropriate to them as objects in regard to which we might act, in respect of which we might change our position, etc.— so that a 'visual field' without visual depth is as Gibson realized a fiction in normal perception (depth is not given by cues, but, in his conception, the whole world is given in its layout, within or against a three-dimensionally structured background).[17]

In the second place, we meet with the supposition that, if I can recognize that things might have looked the same without it being a tomato, I ought not to describe what I see in terms committed to there being a tomato, i.e., I ought only to use descriptions which, simply from the experience taken in isolation, I know cannot fail. The supposition, of course, derives from the view that any judgements as to what we 'directly perceive', 'directly apprehend', or 'intuit' must be infallible, a foreign doctrine derived from a mistaken epistemology, consideration of which I reserve to Section 2. For the purposes of this section all that we need to observe is that this supposition simply assumes the legitimacy, in considering the knowledge we get from experience, of taking experiences individually in isolation from one another and from their context of behavioural stance and from resultant behavioural aptitudes. And we have already shown such isolating of experiences to be entirely misguided.

Once we avoid the mistakes of trying to make the description of 'what we perceive as we perceive it' conform to some imagined

---

[16]I owe this reference to lectures given by G.E.M. Anscombe on Locke and Berkeley in Oxford in 1964.

[17]Rare instances of perception arising by special contrivance in the laboratory or within the context of very special training, so that a person might like da Vinci contrive to imagine that all the light coming to him came from the same distance, may be such that depth can only present itself 'by cues'.

physical or physiological datum, associated with the experience taken
in isolation, or to some judgements about which we could not conceivably be mistaken arising from such notionally isolated experience,
we can go forward to identify the primary field of objects of perception
with the field in relation to which action takes place.

That is, we can now envisage the right context for considering
what would count as a description of 'what is seen as it is seen'
as that of what we might call the 'percepto-behavioural stance' of
the human being or other animal. This is well-exhibited by a reflection upon which of a person's 'takings for granted' are relevant
to Price's perceptual 'takings for granted'. For Price, every case of
perception involves 'takings for granted', examples of 'perceptual assent' or 'perceptual acceptance'.[18] These express what one might call
a 'percepto-behavioural attitude', that which is changed in perception.
This attitude is admirably described by Price except that the infallibilism we shall examine later led him to regard it as merely 'pseudo-
intuitive', so that a 'bodily adjustment' could figure only as an external
extra to 'sensing' and 'acceptances'.[19]

Of course, once let it be granted that we see things 'as', or in
the way that we relate to them in action, so that we see them, not as
colour patches or spreads or distributions of colour in a visual field
as if it might just as well (for instance) be a cunningly contrived skin
or surface as a billiard ball or a tomato in front of us, and not as
snap-moment states of affairs, but as balls, tomatoes, and suchlike,
and as substances such as these in dynamic causal relation, pushing
and being pushed, or resting, their weight supported in a dish, and so
forth—and then the results will be far-reaching. For, not only will it
now be reasonable to say that we see material substances and stuffs as
material objects and stuffs (e.g., water) of their various more specific
kinds, acting and interacting in their characteristic ways, but also it
will be reasonable to say that we see sheep, cats and dogs, and even
men and women, and, more than this, that we see them walking
and eating, and, in the human case, hear them speaking and saying
particular things: and all these will be examples of 'how' we perceive
them—even our hearing them as saying this particular thing in this
particular meaning. Thus it will be natural to the point of view which

---

[18] See Price's account of perceptual acceptance, *Perception*, Chapter VI, pp. 139–
142, 150–165.
[19] *Op.cit.*, p. 157.

we are expounding to regard the behaviour of animals and human beings which we perceive, not as 'merely physical' or 'merely bodily movements', but as intentional and meaning-loaded: this will belong to the description of 'what is perceived as it is perceived', 'what is given in perception as it is given'.

All this lends a new aspect to the significance of Austin's contempt for the modern 'scholasticism' in which all 'veridical' perception is presumed to be of 'material objects'.[20]

2. The Privilege of the Normal Case

It fits with the perspective we have set that one should always begin by considering the normal case and only then at a second stage go on to consider abnormal cases, describing them in ways dictated by their way of deviating from the norm. One will then find that the normal case is departed from in a multiplicity of different ways, different in the case of optical illusions from the case of hallucination and this is but the short beginning of a much longer list. The insistence upon such an Aristotelian approach has, in recent times, been most evident in writers such as Ryle, Austin, and Hamlyn, and was one of the marks of so-called 'ordinary language philosophy'.

In fact, this approach in this area, of beginning by taking what I have called the normal case, is but an example of what is exemplified in other parts of science. The status of the law of inertia in Newtonian mechanics is special. One does not need explanation in terms of special forces but explanation of a cosmological kind for the continuance of

---

[20]That Austin was aware of this aspect of its being mad to consider all 'veridical' perception to be of 'material objects' is exhibited in his examples in *Sense and Sensibilia*, e.g., of the shape of cats (when walking?) or of a man being shaved.

On the other hand, care has to be taken not to be too cavalier in giving specimen lists of the 'objects' of perception, as if seeing tomatoes, animals, men being shaved, shadows, reflections, and mirages were all to be understood according to the same pattern. On the contrary, just as when one dreams a dream one does not dream of dreaming but dreams (e.g.) of a man attacking one or of oneself struggling up a mountain or something else particular, so in seeing a mirage (whether it be optical illusion or possible delusion that is involved) what one sees, described as one sees it, is not a mirage as such but (e.g.) an oasis with palm trees, sand and sunlight, so that the description "mirage" borrows something from the verb "see" just as the description "dream" of what one dreams borrows something from the verb "dream". Both involve a description of what is seen/dreamt, not as it is seen/dreamt, but according to the form of mental directedness (seeing/dreaming) towards it.

a body with constant mass in a straight line with constant velocity. Special forces are brought in within Newtonian mechanics to explain deviations from this so-called norm of constant momentum, just as within Aristotelian mechanics there was conceived to be a norm of staying in the same place except in so far as a thing was out of its natural place so that special forces had to be brought in to explain change of place as such where it was not a case of a thing's moving towards its 'natural' place.

And so it is here also, with the cases of perception and action, that we should begin with the normal case and only at a later stage turn to consider cases in which deviations of different kinds arise for different types of cause or reason. We do not have to find some element common to all the deviant cases and shared by them with the normal case, and then build up a definition of the normal case in terms of this shared element together with extra features, such as 'veridicalness' and 'causedness by the fact perceived' in the case of perception, or 'realization of intention' and 'causedness by intention' in the case of action. There need not be, and indeed is not, a single definition of what is common to all 'non-normal' or 'defective' cases. What we have here is an example of the general Aristotelian point that we should define privations or states of privation in terms of positive states ('havings'), never vice versa, or in terms of later philosophy define 'harms' (*mala*, evils) in terms of the goods which they represent injuries to or deprivations of; and the related general point that privations and evils being accidents, not 'essences' or natures, we should not expect anything positively or non-disjunctively definable about them. Just as the Aristotelian does not expect one kind of failure in the reproductive process, but many discrepant types arising at many different stages and with no one kind of effect—the failure to achieve fertilization, meaning that there is no progeny at all, not even a 'monster', but the results of failure at later stages not being uniformly definable, being of many discrepant kinds—so it is with failures in perception and action. (I reserve consideration of the case of action to Chapter IV and here concentrate upon the case of perception.)

(a) Mistakes arising from misconception of the 'standard' case: the need for a 'critical realist' account of perception

In the rhetoric of scepticism, the roots of doubt as to the existence of 'direct cognitive relation' between the human being and the physical, 'material', 'external' world often lie, not in the rejection of the idea that 'standard' cases or cases conforming to 'the norm' play a leading role in the acquisition of knowledge or the shaping of our critical assessment of what is known, but in a false conception of what is 'standard' or 'the norm'.

"Directly perceive" has often been understood, not as meaning 'directly see, hear, etc.', but as meaning 'directly get to know'. As a result the reason for thinking that the perception of so-called material objects is indirect has often been that it is in some way not in conformity with some ideal or standard pattern supposed to be appropriate to 'direct knowledge'. It is supposed that in direct knowledge, 'genuine knowledge' in some sense approvable by Plato, there must be no possibility of error in judgement and that, therefore, perception cannot be a direct apprehension of material objects since in perceptual judgements about material objects we can make mistakes. It is argued that, in cases when it would be true in an ordinary sense that someone, x, saw A, there is something we can call the 'experience', the ultimate cognitive datum, which could perfectly well be qualitatively no different from what it would be in other cases in which there was nothing there at all (hallucination) or in which there was something there but it was not rightly described as 'A' (illusion). And the reason for saying that the 'experience' was the same in the different cases would be that I could be mistaken as to which of the situations I was in. In this way, what we normally speak of as perceiving (seeing, hearing, etc.) ceases to count as direct knowledge because it does not conform to a Platonic ideal, and these 'experiences' (neutral as to how the external world is) are offered as the substitute objects of infallible or authoritative judgement and knowledge.

In addition, there is a deep-rooted preconception that, if error occurs in a particular case, then this shows that a method of procedure is being relied upon which is unreliable or insecure so that, relying upon it, mistakes will be endemic and all judgements will be uncertain. As a result, it is presumed that, wherever error in judgement can enter in, we do not have an example of genuine or direct experience, and none of the things ordinarily called 'perceptions' will count as direct knowledge.

It is these epistemological prejudices, a priori and second-order in nature, which inspire the idea that perceptual experience must be an infallible mode of apprehension.

Let us consider more precisely how the common attack on so-called 'naive realism' proceeds.

The naive realist is represented as holding that "x thinks that he or she (x) *sees* A" (where "A" is some material object) implies "A exists", and in a parallel way that "x thinks that he or she (x) *sees* that P" (where "P" is a proposition about material objects, e.g., that A is larger than B or that A is round) implies "P is the case". However, in many cases when x thinks that he or she sees a material object A, there is no such material object in his or her physical field of vision, and in many cases when x thinks that he or she sees that P, P is in fact false. As a result, the direct realist view appears obviously false and some alternative is sought.

In the common alternatives, the inferences proposed by the naive realist are accepted but in a specialized interpretation of "see" (or of some other word brought in for the purpose such as "perceive", or "apprehend", or "intuit", perhaps with the qualification "directly" or "immediately" brought in to quiet commonsense objections).[21] Thus, we may be told that "x thinks that he or she (x) *directly perceives* (or '*directly apprehends*') A" implies "A (a sense-datum or 'intentional object') exists [in whatever sense, sense-data or 'intentional objects' exist or are]", and that in a parallel way "x thinks that he or she (x) *directly perceives* (or '*directly apprehends*') P" implies "P (sense-datum statement or statement of visual experience) is the case".

The original sense-datum theories, on the model of the 'naive realism' which they tended to caricature, had some epistemological attractions, most obviously in proposing at least some things as infallibly known, albeit only certain states of consciousness, but more importantly, in conforming to an apparent requirement of the logic of 'direct' perception. But some of its later versions lacked even these advantages, proposing not that anything 'empirical' was infallibly known, which might seem something of an asset, but that certain things were

---

21'Directly perceiving' appears in Price and Ayer. 'Direct apprehension' is Moore's favoured term, cf. *Some Main Problems of Philosophy*. Price uses the terms "intuit" and "apprehend", as notably on p. 156 of *Perception*, where our relation to material and public objects expressed in our perceptual acceptances or takings for granted are represented as 'pseudo-intuitive' because our judgements in regard to them are not infallible. The use of the word "immediately" is suggested by Berkeley's example of (supposedly) only 'immediately' hearing a sound when, in common speech, one would say that one heard a coach (Berkeley in *The Three Dialogues*).

such that one could not be corrected in regard to them,[22] which, as such, might seem nothing but a liability. The sell-out whereby infallibilism was exchanged for incorrigibilism should present itself as amongst the more humorous ventures in philosophy.

But our question should not be of what might belong to what is considered, a priori, to be an ideal of knowledge, but of what we should say about seeing, hearing, etc. In other words, we should simply take "perceiving" as a blanket term to cover these different sensory modalities.

And in this setting there is a commonsense form of direct realism which is quite free from the type of objection to naive realism which I have just outlined.

In this commonsense realist approach there is no inference from the making of a perceptual judgement, e.g., a judgement to the effect that x *thinks* that he or she (x) sees (directly perceives or apprehends) this or that, to his or her actually seeing (directly perceiving or apprehending) the thing or state of affairs concerned, let alone to this thing's existing or this state of affairs being so. What x *thinks* or *judges* that he or she perceives is beside the point for the purposes of describing the logic of realism. There is no infallibity of judgement in perception, but only a distinction between actually being in the psychophysical relation of perceiving (i.e., seeing, hearing, etc.) and not being so. What matters is not an imagined inference from "x *thinks* (or '*judges*') that he or she perceives A [or 'that P']" but the inferences to be drawn from "x *does* perceive A [or 'that P']" in cases in which the verb "perceive" is being used in a case of 'normal' sensory perception, some case of a sort paradigm for the sense concerned—the verb "perceive" merely serving as a stand-in for "see", "hear", etc.[23]

---

[22]This resort to incorrigibility was one of the supposed advances made by Ayer in his *The Problem of Knowledge*, supposedly improving upon the earlier *Foundations of Empirical Knowledge*.

[23]It is not even that thinking or judging that P establishes a probability that P, and that judgement on the real is founded on a mass of judgements of the kind "Probably, P", as if still we had an a priori intellectual calculus deducing judgements as to the real and extra-mental from judgements about states of belief. Rather it is only the fact that the perceptual judgement is made in the appropriate context of psychophysically direct relation which marks it as an expression of knowledge.

What commonsense realists will, therefore, insist upon is that there is a certain paradigm and primary use of perceptual verbs, such as "see" and "hear", according to which "x sees A" does indeed imply "A exists [A being a public thing, whether a material object, an animal or human being, a plant, or the Sun, the sky, or a shadow]", and "x sees that P" does indeed imply that "P is the case". They are not occupied in epistemology, or in picking out some infallible or even merely 'incorrigible' judgements, but occupied in giving an account of perception, i.e., in a certain first-order study belonging to what we might call phenomenology or a general zoology and anthropology.

This commonsense view of perception does not go up the cul-de-sac which results from allowing second-order considerations to determine one's view of a first-order relation, the relation of perceiving. It is not that there is no interplay between first-order and second-order discussions, but that it is never second-order study that provides the concepts primary in first-order study.[24] It is 'critical' because it repudiates an infallible faculty for making 'experiential' judgements and allows some of the interplay mentioned, but 'realist' because it makes the natural environment the direct object of perceptual experience.

(b) The pre-requisites of 'critical realism' as an account of perception

The method of argument which sceptical or 'indirect realist' approaches almost invariably make use of involves the introduction or identification of some special sense of the verb "to perceive" and other perceptual verbs to express or report 'perceptual experience' in a way non-committal as to the 'veridical character' of the 'experience' in question, or introduction of some new verb or set of verbs which have the same function.

Thus, we are led to suppose that within every 'visual experience' there is an element, the only properly 'experiential' or 'cognitively direct' element, which is typically expressible in statements of the forms "x directly perceived . . ." or "x directly apprehended . . ." or "x intuited . . ." or "x (immediately) saw . . ." or "x (immediately)

---

[24] I explained this primacy of the first order over the second order within the structure of critical thought in 'The Nature of Knowledge', especially pp. 44–50, and *The Reality of Time and the Existence of God*, Chapter 7, pp. 234–248, 256–257.

heard . . ." and so forth—statements which are supposed to encapsulate infallible (or at least 'incorrigible') judgements.

[Alternatively it is insinuated that no logical error is likely to be introduced if one substitutes for the form of locution "A seems to see$_1$ an X" a novel locution "A sees$_2$ a seeming-X", 'seeming-objects' or 'looks'[25] being treated logically as a new species of 'object' in the logicians' sense (i.e., member of a set of things, a domain, over which one may quantify or generalize).[26] Under this excuse, there is smuggled in a new verb "see$_2$" to do the work of "directly see" or "immediately see" or suchlike. However, this presentation would justify a conception whereby Pegasus, Black Beauty, Bucephalus, and Foxhunter (a modern Olympic show-jumper) were brought together as 'believed-in-objects' or 'story-objects'—involving the violation of logic in Meinong and his imitators which Russell and Quine rightly repudiate.][27]

As against any such views, Austin wished to protest against the success of any supposed identification of a pre-existing perceptual verb behaving in this way, so as to imply either infallibility or incorrigibility in the related perceptual judgements as to what has been perceived, and against the success of any manoeuvre designed to introduce or define a perceptual verb with these properties.[28] And he wished to pour contempt on the idea that there existed or epistemologically needed to exist a class of propositions stating what was fundamentally 'given' in 'experience' or 'empirically' or as a 'fact', such as might be supposed to be the content of such judgements or statements of the form, "x perceived. . . ."[29]

That is, in his view, there are verbs such as the verb "to see", whose use in different contexts gives the statements made in those contexts different types of implication, and no 'form of statement' (i.e., syntactically distinctive sentential form) encapsulating some privileged, distinctively 'experiential', element in every so-called 'perceptual experience'. Rather than there being any such privileged form of

---

[25]Cf. Frank Jackson on 'looks' as objects in 'The Existence of Mental Objects'.

[26]See A.J. Ayer, *The Problem of Knowledge*, III (iii), pp. 96 ff. on seeming objects.

[27]Russell, 'On Denoting', and Quine, 'On What Exists'.

[28]Austin argues against any special 'directly perceive' sense of perceptual verbs in *Sense and Sensibilia*, IX–X.

[29]See Austin, *Sense and Sensibilia*, pp. 107–124, on the falseness of the idea of a syntactically identifiable class of epistemologically fundamental statements.

statement, giving rise when true to a set of epistemologically fundamental statements, there are, in his understanding, a multiplicity of
statements, none privileged by their form, none even given determinate truth-conditions by their form independent of context, which
cover the range of types of case involved in the indirect realist's
'veridical' and 'non-veridical' 'perceptions'.

That is, what Austin is here expressing is precisely the anti-
empiricist (and, we shall find, anti-Gricean) view that one cannot identify or formulate some single class of statement which will encapsulate
the 'experiential element' in all so-called 'perceptions' in some way
which is non-committal as to whether the case is one of perception
proper, illusion or hallucination. It is good to highlight this view
because the Cartesian perspective whereby, even in perception proper,
the experience or state of consciousness is something inner which
might have been caused in quite different ways depends on precisely
the opposite idea that one *can* formulate such a class of statement—
the idea that the 'experiential content' of a perceptual experience is
something neutral as between the cases of perception proper, illusion and hallucination. This Cartesian perspective has revived because
the materialist, just as much as the Cartesian, conceives perceptual
experience (the experiential element in perception) to be something
which might have been caused in different ways and therefore possibly
non-veridical. The materialist's motives may be metaphysical or causal
rather than epistemological but they have exactly the same upshot.
Thus, in examining and developing the rival Austinian point of view
which encapsulated orthodoxy for British philosophy thirty years ago,
we come to see afresh how it is possible and, indeed, necessary to open
out a holistic perspective which is as much opposed to this materialism
as to dualism.

In his attempt to make his position clear, Austin declared his
opposition to the idea that such verbs as "see" had linguistically
many meanings.[30] He regarded this idea as merely an excuse softening
people up for the acceptance that such verbs might be given a quite
new special meaning to serve the purposes of some alternative to
direct realism, albeit a special meaning to be grasped intuitively, not

---

[30]Austin, *Sense and Sensibilia*, pp. 84–102, against "see" having many meanings.

introduced by explicit definition. His war was with new-fangled uses of such verbs as "see" introduced on what he regarded as specious grounds, or any theory which operated by supposing that such verbs, considered as parts of the language, had a spread of meanings prior to use and prior to context.

For my own part, for reasons which will become apparent in Chapter X, I consider that one has to distinguish differences in meaning which belong to *langue* (i.e., roughly speaking, differences which should be distinctly itemized in a dictionary or lexicon) and differences which consist in and which are only identifiable by reference to the semantic differences between complete statement-forms, statement-forms being things typically differentiated only with the help of considerations of context in the case concerned. The differences we are concerned with appear in the logical implications or presuppositions of the sentence-factor " . . . see——" in its different species of use, species which are in part context-differentiated. That is, there is a use of the words "meaning" and "sense"—to pick out what I later call *parole*-meaning or speech-meaning—according to which one will say that there are two 'meanings' or 'senses' of "see" whenever there are two logically differentiable uses of " . . . see——".

Against the background of this way of speaking of 'meanings', or of the 'senses' or 'uses' of words, and of applying it to the case of "see" and other perceptual verbs, we need to consider in the case of each perceptual verb the rationale underlying the spread of uses which speech[31] presents to us. In each case, we will find that there is a primary use of the verb concerned that do not deviate from some paradigm conditions, and alongside it a spread of other uses, some of them 'deviating' from the norm in ways which in no way involve defect in perception, but others deviating in a scatter of quite disparate ways (not reducible to any single definition or account, not even all 'non-veridical')[32] each involving some 'defectiveness' in respect of perception.

Thus, let us consider the case of the verb "to see".

Here, the primary use of the verb is represented in cases in which there is full integration between the behavioural approach to

---

[31] Like Gardiner in *The Theory of Speech and Language*, I treat writing as a form of speech.

[32] See Austin, *Sense and Sensibilia*, III cf. pp. 10–14, on the disparate character of illusion and delusion.

perception, the perception itself, and the resulting behavioural aptitudes, and in which there is full freedom for exploratory behaviour,
including such things as change of vantage-point and collaboration
between sight and touch, and in which there is nothing which counts
as a discrepancy between appearance (looks) and reality, no false belief
or invitations to it, and nothing inviting hesitation in judgement.

Against the background of these requirements there are obviously cases, themselves varied in kind and forming an open-ended list,
such as seeing the Sun, seeing the Evening Star, seeing the sky, seeing
stars in the sky, seeing a sunset, seeing a rainbow, seeing shadows,
seeing reflections in a mirror,..., which do not conform to the
'paradigm' just stated but yet which involve no defect in perception. It
was the existence of these cases which made the idea that all 'veridical'
perceptions are of 'material objects' so peculiarly contemptible to
Austin.[33] Yet that these cases do not altogether conform to what ought
to be called the norm can be seen from some of the anomalies to
which they give rise, e.g., in astronomical cases discrepancies between
the time of the state of affairs as seen and the time of the seeing, or
(a very different case) when we describe the Moon as 'looking the
size of a sixpence'.[34] That there is room for such anomalies to arise
is precisely because of the breakdown of some of the features of the
'paradigm' we described, in particular the absence of the possibility
of immediate collaboration between vision and exploration including
collaboration with touch.

Then there are other cases associated with various kinds of optical
illusion: e.g., at the optician's, as a pencil is held vertically between the
eyes and brought closer, there is the 'illusion' signalled by the client
saying "I see two pencils"; then there are the commonplace examples
of straight or crooked sticks looking bent in water or of mistakes as
to depth of water, examples of colour-judgements made in peculiar

---

[33]Austin, *Sense and Sensibilia*: this is the point of Austin's rhetoric against
supposing that what we see is always a 'material object'.

[34]Sean Wilkie instructs me that the Sun has been variously judged to look the
size of a large coin or to look one or two feet across. Judgements of this kind are not
as arbitrary as judgements like "Wednesday is sad", but need to be set in the context
of perspectival judgements of the kind that allow us to say that railway lines as they
recede into the distance look closer, but not as if they are not parallel or become
actually closer: the peculiarity of the cited judgements about the Sun and the Moon
is that their perspectival context has been left either unclear or arbitrary.

light conditions, or misjudgements as to the length of sticks due to differences in geometrical presentation (the Muller-Lyer illusion). All these in varying ways involve defects, not in our sensory 'apparatus' or 'psychology', but nonetheless in the perceptual situation.[35] But, besides these, we find there is a multiple spread of other types of case which can arise quite separately from any of the above, or be mixed in with some of their features, cases of visions in which nothing open to touch is present despite its appropriateness to the object of perception but which, nonetheless, is in some measure public,[36] cases of straight hallucination to the individual, some of them without false belief but many of them with false belief, and so on: besides the case of 'seeing stars' after having been knocked on the head. In some cases there can be uncertainty as to what is going on as in the seeing of a speck in the case of which one is uncertain whether it is an astronomical object or a fleck in the lens of the telescope, a piece of dirt in the basin or something due to *muscae volitantes* in the eye, and so forth: in all these cases it remains that there is a defect in the 'perceptual situation'.

If, in any of these cases a judgement of the form "I see...", or afterwards "I saw...", is made, the question arises (granted that the judgement has some linguistic meaning) first of its truth, and second of its meaning, in that sense of the word "meaning" in which 'meaning' is differentiated according to logically differentiable use. What becomes apparent upon examination is that, on the one hand if in the speaker-hearer context it is presumable that the speaker presupposes a non-defective perceptual situation, then if things are not as the speaker says that they are seen, the speaker's perceptual statement is false. But on the other hand, if it is an open question in the public discourse context whether or not the perceptual situation was defective, then in a secondary use of the perceptual verb concerned the

---

[35]It is sometimes obscure whether what is involved in a 'delusion' (i.e., where false belief is integral) is an optical phenomenon (e.g., the explanation of the experience of mirages in terms of refraction, the hot air appropriately layered making a distant oasis appear nearby) or whether it is an hallucination (i.e., so that 'seeing a mirage' will be the result of a confused state caused by lack of water and high body temperature). Austin seems to have conceived all delusions to have been hallucinatory and vice versa, and thus to have oversimplified the situation.

[36]The 'apparitions' of the Virgin Mary at Fatima, and elsewhere seem to have been of this character, and the phenomena in the sky seen by so many associated with one of the appearances at Fatima may have been of this kind, or may in part have been more 'objective'.

perceptual statement made may, depending on other considerations, yet be true.

If asked "Did you see a bus in the High Street?", I answer "Yes", and yet there was no bus in the High Street, then my judgement that "I saw a bus" is rejected as untrue just as unequivocally as my judgement "There was a bus". Similarly, my judgement is also rejected if asked "Did you see two pencils on the table?" and I answer "Yes" but there was only one. But, if speaker and hearer know beforehand that by deliberate contrivance the conditions of perception are peculiar, e.g., at the opticians, then from the judgement "I see two pencils" no inference can be made to "There are two pencils before me", and from the absence of two pencils before my nose no inference can be made to the falsity of "I see two pencils". What this makes plain is that we have here a distinct use of the word "to see" logically differentiable from the way the implications of statements of the form " . . . see——" in this case differ from their implications in other cases.

Since in direct reports in the form "I see . . . ", no peculiarity of psychological state being in question, the normal presumption is that the context is normal, when looks deceive the result is that the report is rejected: "You did not see . . . ; but what you saw looked . . . ". By contrast, when a peculiar psychological state is anticipated to have had a key influence on what is reported in this form, the normal presumption is absent and as a result the report is accepted, the use of the verb "to see" being automatically, in virtue of the absence of the presumption, not the primary one with its characteristic implications, but a secondary use in which these implications (e.g., of the existence or publicity of the 'object' of 'perception') are absent.[37]

All the cases of 'seeing' which are not in accord with the paradigm case invite some inquiry. In all those cases in which there is 'defect' the inquiry will extend to the conditions of 'perception' and the explanation of the 'defect'. In considering perception, the method of explaining 'defects' will always take one into a second level or level of explanation which presumes that the 'normal' needs no special explanation, somewhat as in Newtonian mechanics conservation of momentum within a system is considered to need no special explanation

---

[37]This discrepancy whereby there is a greater tendency to attribute falsity to statements of the form "I saw . . ." in the more objective-seeming cases is noted in many authors, e.g., Anscombe, 'The Intentionality of Sensation', *Collected Papers II*.

in terms of external or alien forces, whereas failure in such conservation (deviation from this norm) requires such explanation in terms of special forces—of which, historically, the first to be considered, after the simple case of pushing, was gravitation. The extent to which this 'normative' approach has penetrated scientific psychology has been well illustrated by David Hamlyn,[38] but what is at issue here is not just a scientific but also a philosophical point, a point in the very logic of perceptual verbs, without which no rounded empirical science of perception can get off the ground.

---

[38]David Hamlyn, *Psychology of Perception*.

III. Perception (II): Clarifying the Notion of Real Cognitive Relation and Assessing Contemporary Discussion

1. Contemporary Accounts of Perception Remain Bankrupt because They Still Sever It from Behaviour

(a) State of the problem: the revival of a non-realist conception of perceptual experience despite standing objections

In Chapter II I opened out a realist view of perception and showed what was wrong with the main traditional lines of argument for non-realist views.

In the refutation of these traditional arguments, I drew upon what was commonplace amongst 'ordinary language philosophers' at least until the late 1960s. Sealing each of these traditional arguments, these philosophers tended to see one grand mistake. This was the mistake of imagining that the experiential element in any episode in human life was something—in the perceptual case called a sense-datum, a sense-impression, a perceptual experience, a sensation (the labels make little difference and have not changed in more recent discussions[1])—about which we could not be mistaken or about which one could speak with authority without being open to correction. And once having rejected the idea that one's experiences must be things of which one has authoritative knowledge, these philosophers saw no reason to have any truck with any notions of sense-datum and sense-datum statement as objects of such knowledge. They did

---

[1]Grice speaks of 'sense-impressions', Strawson and Searle of 'perceptual experiences', while Jackson and Swinburne speak of 'sensations' ignoring the preference in Ryle and Armstrong for restricting the term "sensation" to bodily sensations.

not meet with any definition of sense-datum or sense-datum statement independent of this Cartesian idea, and did not expect any, since the whole idea of such notions seemed to be inspired by it. And, led by Austin for the reasons we saw in our last chapter, they were at war with the view that there exists a class of what might be called 'sense-datum statements' or 'propositions' which capture the whole experiential content of perceptions without any commitment in respect of states or goings-on in the sense-organs or the perceived world.

They also regarded the doctrine of sense-datum statements as engendering the problems of our knowledge of the external world, of the meaning of statements about the material, and of the nature of the self which we sketched in Chapter I. But for them, the existence of these problems was merely the symptom of a diseased conception of perception or perceptual experience.

However, what those earlier 'ordinary language philosophers' rejected is now commonplace. The belief in 'experiences' as inner events and in statements encapsulating them—that is, statements which capture the whole experiential content of perceptions without any commitment in respect of states or goings-on in the sense-organs or the perceived world—had never been abandoned by Ayer or by mind-brain identity theorists and had never died amongst psychologists. But in 1961 Grice restored this belief to respectability even amongst the circles schooled in 'ordinary language philosophy'.[2]

Grice suggested that in every case of a perception, if one could say "X sees that. . .", it would also be true (if misleading) to say "It looks to X as if. . .". This suggestion, taken by itself, might be harmless. But Grice put it forward as part of something counting as a causal theory of perception, and it will only serve this role if it is taken that facts of the sort stated in this guarded way encapsulate the *whole* experiential content of the perception, and indeed of any experience which is in some sense apparently perceptual. That is, the key move is to suppose that there exists a certain class of facts, e.g., (if one followed Grice) facts such as things looking to X in a certain way, such as might be expressed by a certain class of statement, "It looks to X as if. . .", which encapsulate the *whole* experiential content of a

---

[2]Grice, 'The Causal Theory of Perception'.

perception. These will then be such as taken together with physical facts about the sense-organ and world and a causal relation between these physical facts and the inner experiential fact are necessary and sufficient conditions of the perception.

Grice had no attachment to his particular formulation of such facts or statements in terms of how things look—and indeed for reasons we have noted such dependence on the notion of 'how things look' has weaknesses of its own. Strawson suggests the formulation "I had a visual experience such as it would have been natural to describe by saying that I saw . . .", with the proviso that it is to be understood that commitment to propositions about independently existing objects is to be excluded. Here we have the advantage that the specification of the content of the supposed experiences is to be entirely in the natural terms which we would ordinarily use in a philosophically uncritical mood and does not give any privilege to verbal formulations in terms of 'looking' or 'seeming'. The same advantage is preserved in Searle's account, what he calls allowing the 'Intentional content' of any experience to be expounded in quite ordinary terms, although his associated use of the notion of 'Intentional object' is objectionable for reasons which will become plain in Section 2.

But still we have in these authors, quite undiluted, the conception of an 'experience' (typically a 'visual experience') which is specifiable without commitment to any propositions about the sense-organs or perceived world, which together with its being caused in an appropriate way, makes up a perception.

The key move in Grice and all these authors is not the discovery or invention of some non-committal form of statement, but the supposition that this form of statement (or the type of fact it states) captures the *whole* of the experiential content of whatever perceptual experience is under consideration. And it is this supposition which these authors never justify.

(b) The incoherence of the conception of experience as inner

And this is our main objection against any such position, that no reason has been given for saying that the *whole* experiential content of perception is captured in these non-committal statements, although we can no doubt devise them. The expectation that it might be thus captured depends upon a conception of experience which considers it logically separable from behavioural preparedness and aptitude. And against any such conception, the argument of Chapter II stands firm: such a conception severs the position of the human being or animal as an observer from his position as a wanderer, explorer, and agent. That this is a capital mistake should have been evident from the approaches of Merleau-Ponty and Hampshire,[3] but in any case was our starting point in Chapter II.

The primary point is that in the paradigm cases of perceptual experience the intentional object of the experience or perception is a real object, not just in the sense that it is describable in the same terms as some real object, but in the sense that what the mind in perception is directed towards is the very same as that to which behaviour is adapted. In consequence, there is no way of logically separating the 'experience' in perception from its nestedness within a behavioural situation or from its relation to behavioural aptitude. The second and associated point is that there is no way of logically segregating or isolating knowledge of the 'experience' in perception from knowledge of this nestedness or from knowledge of this relation—this is the importance of our emphasis on the impossibility of encapsulating the *whole* of the experiential content of experiences in any of the proposed kinds of non-committal statement, 'bracketing' the world.[4]

---

[3]It is also apparent from reflection on Ryle and Austin. For Ryle, perception in the sense of observation (typically for him in a context of watching) will always be in a behavioural context, in a way which sets it in contrast with mere 'sensation' (*Concept of Mind*, Ch. 7). The behavioural will also be key to the consideration of the concomitants of a perception referred to by Austin in *Sense and Sensibilia*, pp. 53–54.

[4]Some philosophers have been deceived by the word "similar". We do not build up our description of the case of normal sight out of a statement of what it has in common with blurred or dazzled vision of objects described in some respects in the same way together with statements of extra features additional to and independent of these shared features. Likewise, we do not build up our conception of what it is to be a pig in terms of what it is to be piglike together with some extra features making a thing actually a pig. So, in general, if a deviant case A is similar to a paradigm case B, this does not have to be analysed in terms of there being something common, C, to both cases so that A and B are to be analysed respectively as C + A' and C + B'.

This gives us the proper background for considering the similarity of various experiences (in dreams, hallucinations, or illusions) to normal cases of perception in virtue of which they are described in parallel terms. This does not consist in the presence in each case of an element, 'the experience', which is the same in both the 'veridical' and the 'non-veridical' situations, albeit that other non-experiential features of the context differ—as if the 'experience' was something inner and neutral as to how the world is and our behavioural position within it. Rather the deviant cases count as perceptual experiences only in a secondary sense, in virtue of a range of different kinds of likeness to non-deviant cases.

We have identified the failure to grasp the internality of behavioural posture or preparedness and behavioural aptitude to perceptual experience as such, the internality which makes it absurd to
think that the object of experience is only intentional whereas the
focus of behavioural preoccupation is real. Out of this failure there
arises a key weakness in the accounts offered of the supposed causal
relation between the outer world and the postulated inner experience.

Grice supposes that we should specify the mode of causal connection by an open-ended list of examples.[5] This is equivalent to saying
that it is the mode of causal connection exemplified in cases which are
normal in the relevant way. But it is no use stipulating that perceptual
experience has to be caused in the 'normal' way by what is perceived
if, in the end, the explanation one gives of being 'normal' (whether
by examples or otherwise) amounts only to this: that the experience
arises within such a behavioural framework as to make the object of
experience the same as that in regard to which one behaves appropriately. For, as we have seen, for a case of perceptual experience to be
normal in the relevant way is precisely for it to arise in a way which
is integrated with what we described as 'behavioural preparedness or
behaviour focused towards perception'. However, what this kind of
integratedness requires is precisely a logical or 'internal' connection
between the previous lead-up or context of posture and behaviour and
the perceptual experience or perception itself. That is, it is not just that
the knowledge of the experience is not separable from knowledge of
the lead-up to the experience,[6] but that the experience itself is not
separable from this lead-up or context.

But in the background of this problem as to what it is for the
supposed 'experiences' to be caused normally lies the deeper problem
as to what these things called 'experiences' are anyway. We have some
knowledge of what a perception is but a perception involves the sense-
organs and the public world, whereas the 'experiences' being spoken
of are meant to be 'inner', logically independent of sense-organs and
world, and we still don't know what they are, or indeed whether there
are any such things.

Grice made it plausible that some non-committal statements can
be made, true both in so-called 'veridical' and in so-called 'non-
veridical' cases, but, as we have said, this is nothing to the point:

---

[5]*Op. cit.*, p. 143.
[6]Cf. Strawson, 'Perception and its Objects', p. 104.

it does nothing to give reason to suppose that these were of a sort to capture the whole experiential content of a perceptual experience.

Our task in this chapter is to confirm that there is no avenue of approach by means of which we can capture the whole experiential content of perceptual experiences in a way which is non-committal as to facts about the real world within which and in relation to which experiences take place or are likely to take place. In Section 2 we shall confirm that Austin was absolutely right in rejecting explanations of what the supposed inner experiences are in terms of inner objects, and right in supposing that explanations in terms of how things look or seem will not work. And we shall see that the conception of intentional object as being as such debarred from being a real object, and of relations of mental directedness towards intentional objects being debarred from being real relations, are simply ill-founded. There is, we shall find, no reason why an intentional object cannot be a real object and the mind directed towards it precisely in its reality—and so the technical language of intentionality helps not a wit in explaining the supposed notion of experience as inner. But what we have now shown in this section is that Grice's approaches, proposing to dispense with the device of introducing reference to 'inner' objects or 'intentional' objects, do no better.

The old reason for believing in 'experiences' as things inner, logically independent of sense-organs and world, lay in epistemology—in the idea that judgements of experience had to be infallible or authoritative *qua* judgements of experience, an infallibility or authority we plainly do not have in individual perceptual judgements about the physical world, and which therefore could only concern 'experiences' as things inner. But this old reason is baseless, no reply having been given to Austin's arguments, the arguments reiterated in Chapter II.

After this, the only reasons left to us for embracing these old-hat dualistic ideas of 'experiences' as essentially inner are metaphysical or causal, whether these ideas are inspired by a mind-body dualism or whether by a preconception that everything mental is embodied in the brain. That is, the only argument left is the argument that the experiential element in human life must be inner in order to be identical with or realized in states and goings-on in the brain, states and goings-on caused physiologically and physically, or even to correspond with them as the dualist thinks. We are presented with the hypothesis that the mental or experiential is something inner, and this hypothesis is supported on the ground that *if* it were thus inner we could regard it as corresponding with, realized in or identical with a brain-state or going-on, and could adopt causal theories fitting with this.

But this is poor use as a reason. Everything about it is promissory: we have nothing in hand which brings us anywhere near an explanation of human speech and behaviour in what would be mechanistic terms. And this mere promissory note is all that is being offered as excuse for dismissing the opposite view, that the experiential element in human life is not thus inner, but that it involves the sense-organs, the perceived world, and relation to behaviour not just externally but essentially. What is to be proved is just assumed, and the whole question begged.

But this new reason is especially poor because the supposed inner experiential element in human life has to be already there and well-known to us in order to serve its role, whether as something which someone might associate with a brain-state or process, or as something which might help provide foundations for knowledge. But the emperor has no clothes. It is not just that the dualistic analysis is unproven, and open to the capital objection we have put forward, that it creates a false divide between perception and action, observation and behaviour. But, what is worse, this inner experiential element in human life, inner in the particular sense concerned, has still not been identified to us—we still don't know what it is, even despite the fact that it is understood to be 'experiential', the most evident of all. Our perceptions we know, our pains we know, all in their connections with the rest of our life and behaviour. Yet these supposed 'inner experiences' (experiences within the context of perception and sensation, not of imagination), logically unconnected with the rest of life and behaviour and not directed towards the real objects about which our behaviour circulates—what are they?

(c) The sameness in the epistemological impasse

However, not only is the underlying conception of 'experience' or 'sense-impression' such as we find in Grice, Strawson, and Searle, without viable explanation; and not only does it fail to account for the logical integration of experience with behaviour; but also their positions fall foul of the same classical epistemological problems we sketched in Chapter I.

And the reason why they fall foul of these same epistemological problems is clear. They have each set up a structure in which there are two sets of propositions: the first set declarative of what we experience in a way non-committal as to the causation of the experiences and the public existence of their objects as external to us; and the second set, stating that we see (hear, feel, etc.) so and so, implying this existence and the normality of the causation of the experiences. The first set are supposed to state all we know from experiences as they are given, even if they present themselves 'as if' more was given, and therefore the second set must be supposed to go beyond this.

It is at this stage that all these philosophers are ineluctably trapped. They are in the same predicament as Descartes and Hume, and so cannot escape the logic of the structure we described in Chapter I. They have no new magic to deal with the problem. And therefore they are in the position of denying that perception (seeing, hearing, feeling, etc.) is a cognitively direct relation, and in this way they belie the ordinary understanding of perceptual verbs.

The best way of seeing this is by looking at their explanations.

Always the question we ought to ask is: what is the character of perceptual relation? Is it some relation to the actual objects and the world of actual objects to which our behaviour is adapted? or is it only some relation to objects only 'purely' intentional, 'mental objects', such as a dream might present, objects towards which on waking we might reach out and find them absent?

Grice and his company suppose that they are not at risk from sceptical questions, that their positions put the human being in the position of direct and immediate consciousness of enduring physical objects. But the question is as to what is required for such perception or consciousness to count as 'direct'. On the one hand, the perception has to be as such of something which is objective, public or real, and, on the other hand, the fact of perception in the individual case has to be something which puts us in the individual case in a position of knowledge. The epistemological role of perception is not to provide an experience which should be the ground of knowledge by fitting as 'evidence' within the framework of some more general pattern of reasoning,[7] but to constitute in itself in each individual case an

---

[7] By contrast, Grice is willing to accept that "perceptual consciousness is fundamentally an inference from effect to cause" if what is meant is that the fundamental form of such justification must be an exhibition of the material object as cause of the relevant beliefs (op. cit., the argument (3) on pp. 146–147). In this way, in place of accepting the more ordinary role of individual statements that (e.g.) one saw it happen before one's eyes as answers to individual "How do you know it?" questions, he has

example of knowledge, according to a mode special to animal beings with senses, amongst them human beings. (There are of course cases when we think we have perceived this or that when in fact we haven't: these cases do not present examples of knowledge.)

For a perceptual experience to be immediately and really of an object it is not enough for it to be caused by that object, nor even for it to be caused in an appropriate way. But it ought to be clear that for a material object to cause a sense-impression (even in a way appropriate for its being veridical) no more makes it the case that the material object is perceived, i.e., is the real object of a cognitive relation of seeing or feeling, than if it were to cause a dream or a vision in which it figured.[8] To be the object of a perception is to be internally integral to the perception, not merely to be in external causal relation to it. It is not that some infallibility in judgements as to perception and what is perceived is required (we showed in Chapter I that this is a quite false requirement to lay upon perception).[9] Perception proper,[10] when it occurs, is a example of knowledge, but we are not infallible as to whether or not it has occurred. Rather, what is essential is that the focus of perceptual experience, its object, should be the same as the focus of behavioural posture and aptitude, and therefore as such a real object—not a mental object, an object of mind, to whose presentation to the mind in experience it is indifferent whether it is real or not. That is, it is not that the experience is of a mental object which *qua* mental object might just as well have been merely mental while the behaviour is centred round some real object, but that the two are focussed upon one and the same real object.

Strawson lays heavy emphasis on the fact that 'we take ourselves to be immediately aware of real—enduring physical things in space—things endowed with visual and tactile properties; and we take it for granted that these enduring things are causally responsible for our

---

invested in a theory grounding perceptual judgements in a general theory as to the causation of sense-impressions by material objects.

[8]This makes Grice's first suggestion as to what might be at issue in asking whether material objects are 'incapable of being perceived' (*op. cit.*, the argument (1) on p. 146) miss the point.

[9]In this way, Grice's second surmise as to what might be intended by requiring that perception be 'direct' (*op. cit.*, the argument (2) on p. 146) is also beside the point.

[10]We made plain in Chapter II, 2 that in the case of each perceptual verb (see, hear, etc.) there is a paradigm use of the verb concerned according to which the inferences hold, e.g., from "x sees A" to "A exists" and from "x sees that P" to "It is the case that P".

interrupted perceptions of them'.[11] And he evidently thinks this not only in the sense that this view is an element in our ordinary pre-theoretical commonsense view of the world, but in the sense that within the setting of each particular perceptual experience we take ourselves to be enjoying immediate consciousness of physical things causative of this consciousness: that is how our experience presents itself in each individual case, not just in general. The immediacy, he says, is 'something given with the given'.[12]

However, all this insistence and eloquence serves for nothing. For Strawson has already conceded that the essential experiential content of each individual experience can be described in terms non-committal to the reality of things external to us. It remains that the experience is only *as if* it were immediate, and *as if* it were caused in the specified way. There is nothing essential to or about the experience which makes it, not just as if immediate and as if caused by physical things, but actually immediate and actually of the physical things which caused it. Experience, to have the character it has, has to be believed to be immediate and believed to be caused by physical things, but on Strawson's account this character does not require that these beliefs to be true. This character also requires such general beliefs as that experiences are generally caused in an appropriate way so as to be veridical or that our concepts belong to an actually public language, shared by body-possessing human beings, but Strawson has not shown that it requires even that these general beliefs are actually true.

Searle may boldly declare that 'perception is an Intentional and causal transaction between mind and the world',[13] and that 'action, like perception, is a causal Intentional transaction between mind and the world',[14] but it emerges that in each case we have two components, an Intentional component (the visual experience or experience of acting) and a physical component between which there is to be a causal relation, and, a distinct matter from this, the Intentional component is to be as if of a causing. There is, he tells us, 'direct awareness of causation in perception'[15] but it turns out that all he

---

[11]Strawson, *op. cit.*, p. 105.

[12]*Op. cit.*, p. 99.

[13]*Intentionality*, p. 49. Searle is aware that the word "intentional" has been used in more than one way and therefore puts a capital for his own use of the word. I have kept his capitalization in my references to his particular use of the word.

[14]*Op. cit.*, p. 88.

[15]*Op. cit.*, p. 125.

is saying is that the causal nexus is part of the content of the experience, not that the experiencing is itself a causal transaction. Visual experience has an Intentional content which may extend to its being presented as if caused in a certain way; and, if it is veridical, it will have been appropriately caused by the world. But perception, and likewise action, remain composites. There is nothing unitary which both includes causation as a real aspect and is at the same time Intentional, no causal transaction which is at the same time Intentional and cognitive.

Searle is also very disingenuous in another way: the whole plausibility of what he says depends on not querying what he means by the phrase "content of an experience". Thus he disarmingly tells us:

> 'I no more infer that the car is the cause of my visual experience than I infer that it is yellow. When I see the car I can see that it is yellow and when I see the car I have an experience, part of whose content [by which he must mean 'Intentional content'] is that it is caused by the car. The knowledge that the car caused my visual experience derives from the knowledge that I see the car, and not conversely. Since I do not infer that there is a car there but rather simply see it, and since I do not infer that the car caused my visual experience, but rather it is part of the content ['Intentional'] of the experience that it is caused by the car, it is not correct to say that the visual experience is the 'basis' in the sense of *evidence* or *ground* for knowing that there is a car there. The 'basis' rather is that I see the car, and my seeing the car has no prior basis in that sense. I just do it. One of the components of the event of seeing the car is the visual experience, but one does not make a causal inference from the visual experience to the existence of the car.'[16]

I say 'disarmingly' because, as we have seen, for Searle the 'content of an experience' is always an 'Intentional content' so that to say that an experience has this or that content implies nothing actual about the causation of the experience or about the physical reality of its objects. For the content of an experience to be 'Intentional' is again only for the experience to be *as if* the propositions specifying this content to be true, and carries no implication that they are actually true. The experience of the car presents itself *as if* it were caused by an actual car and indeed *as if* it were of such an actual car, but *qua* experience

---

[16]*Op. cit.*, p. 73.

with this content involves nothing actual either as to its causation or as to the presence of a car.

Thus in this way of thinking one has "I see a car" as an epistemologically basic proposition, without yet having any account of 'basic propositions' and in a context in which one already has another set of propositions on one's hands, namely those that express what Searle calls 'the Intentional content' of visual and other sensory experience. But this second set is understood to capture the whole experiential content of our sensory experiences. And so, whatever Searle may say, he has not escaped the trap into which his many predecessors have fallen.[17] Ayer had material object statements and sense-datum statements and could not escape giving primacy to the latter as par excellence encapsulating the 'empirical facts',[18] while logic of Searle's position leaves him in the same predicament, albeit that his sense-datum statements (statements of the having of a visual or other sensory experience with a certain Intentional content) are stated in a much more sophisticated way.[19]

These positions are direct realist in name only. Armstrong disowned a presentational aspect to perception, reducing it to a set of acquirings of belief,[20] but the addition by Grice, Searle, etc. of

---

[17]He may say 'Experience has to determine what counts as succeeding [i.e., actually perceiving]', *op. cit.*, p. 38, as if he meant that previous actual cognitive perceptual relation with actual objects enabled us to judge what counted as actually perceiving, but he has debarred experience from telling us anything about the actual: in his official view it extends only to telling us how it is as if things are.

[18]This is well brought out by Austin, *Sense and Sensibilia*, pp. 105–107.

[19]When Searle represents the existence of 'visual experiences' as an empirical, not a notational, matter, it turns out that this has nothing to do with the existence of the experiences concerned, but only with whether or not they are 'visual' in the sense of involving appropriate stimulation of the optic nerve, i.e., with the causation, not with the having of the experiences whose existence might have seemed to be in question, nor with their Intentional content or Intentional object (*op. cit.*, pp. 46–47). A person may perfectly well have a belief that P without the condition of satisfaction of the belief, viz., that P should be true, being satisfied. In a parallel way, for a person to have an experience with a certain Intentional content is not at all for the 'conditions of satisfaction' of that Intentional content to be satisfied: therefore, the Intentional content of a visual experience may be said, if one follows Searle's account, to require visual experience, but only in the sense that it requires this as part of its conditions of satisfaction, not in the sense that to have an experience with this Intentional content implies that the conditions of satisfaction of the Intentional content are satisfied. Therefore, the appearance of realism on p. 48 is entirely deceptive.

[20]His *A Materialist Theory of the Mind*, Chapter 10, in this way shows up the splendid apparent realism of *Perception and the Physical World* as a mere facade.

a presentational aspect whereby the experience is *as if* directly and immediately of something real, enduring, and independent without necessarily being actually directly and immediately of any such thing does not alter the situation.[21]

These philosophers are therefore in no different situation from Price with his knowledge of sense-data alongside knowledge of perceptual acceptances (for others, 'perceptual beliefs'). They have committed themselves to avoiding making knowledge of the external world rest upon knowledge of visual and other 'sensory' experience as something inner, and even (if they hold consistently to their official positions) forgone the luxury of Price's theory of 'corroboration'. Therefore, like Armstrong, they have no appeal to direct experience left to them at all. Accordingly, they will have no choice but to fall back on some general theory whereby, in virtue of convention or otherwise, experiences give some probability to beliefs, but no particular experience constitutes knowledge.

2. The Value of the Notion of Intentional Object

The notion of 'intentional object' has a vital role in enabling us to clarify many features of perception and, in particular, to avoid the conception of inner objects.[22]

---

[21]It is unsurprising that Searle should feel the need to give some further explanation of the presentational immediacy of the object within perceptual experience. So he tells us that a visual experience should be described as a presentation rather than a representation because 'the experience has a kind of directness, immediacy and involuntariness which is not shared by a belief I might have about the object in its absence' (*op. cit.*, pp. 45–46). But the only immediacy and directness which Searle makes apparent is the presence of a referring expression for an Intentional object *qua* Intentional object within the description of the Intentional content (just as "a cow" might occur within the description of the Intentional content of a case of imagining), and not any immediacy or directness of the object of perception *qua* real object, i.e., not any immediacy or directness to the perceiving *qua* perceiving. In this way he has only produced a cloud of words to present again the same quandary which Locke found himself in: he, like Locke, has a general doctrine which belies the immediacy and forcefulness of which he thinks he is aware. As to involuntariness, this seems another hark back to Locke and Berkeley, and to do nothing to save the day. So we are left with an entirely empty use of the word "presentation", as well as no real transaction between mind and the world.

[22]Anscombe introduced this theme into English philosophy in 'The Intentionality of Sensation', *Collected Papers*, Vol. II.

However, our first task is to reintroduce the concept in a way free from the Cartesian presuppositions evident in Brentano and Husserl. Unfortunately, 'intentionality' has come to connote uncommittedness in respect of reality rather than simply being an object of mind—whether by being an object of perceptual knowledge or in some other way. As implying such uncommittedness it has seemed to provide a refinement on the earlier positions of Ayer and Grice—convenient for allowing the mental to be regarded as realized in the brain.[23] Therefore, to achieve clarity, let us consider the matter from scratch.

(a) The need for the notion of 'intentional object'

The word "object" is radically ambiguous.

On the one hand, we have the use of the word "object" consecrated by modern logicians whereby it means a thing appropriate to be referred to by a singular 'subject'-term, commonly called 'a referring expression'. Objects in this sense are 'entities' or 'things' with identity, falling within the scope of some set or species of generalizations, i.e., in logicians' ways of speaking 'values of bound variables', 'objects' in the sense meant by Frege, founder of our modern extensional logic—a sense whereby the word "object" means much the same as "logical subject". This use of the word "object" we shall refer to as its use to mean 'object (in the logicians' sense)' or (we shall sometimes say) 'real object'.[24] (There is, as has often been observed, not one pool of objects or logical subjects: rather these are of many different logical types—stones, people, numbers, colours, *et al.*, each kind of 'logical subject' having different kinds of predication or question appropriate to it.)

On the other hand, we have the older use of the word "object" to mean 'that which something is directed towards in some way'—for brevity, in our future discussion, 'intentional object'.[25] In this way, we

---

[23]Thus it is because both Dennett (e.g., in *Brainstorms*) and Searle (in *Mind, Brains and Science*) use intentionality in this misguided sense as definitory of the mental that they are both able to regard it as realized in the brain, despite their quite opposite attitudes to the theory of Artificial Intelligence.

[24]Anscombe uses the phrase "material object" where we speak of 'object in the logicians' sense' or 'real object', and Descartes speaks of 'formal reality' (as opposed to 'objective reality') in expression of the same distinction with which we are concerned.

[25]The directedness with which we are here concerned is normally a mental directedness such as we associate with consciousness but there is no a priori reason

can speak of the object of a person's aim or of their action, the object of their thought or of their worship, the object of their hope or of their fear, the object of their imagining or of their attention, and not only the object of their perception or of their physical action or relation.

The motivation for introducing this notion of intentional object is to describe the logic of what we might call semantically transitive verb-expressions. What we have to register is not just a grammatical point about certain verbs, but a semantic point about a whole range of often more complex expressions—applying as much to "see in a dream . . ." as to the simple "see . . .".

We need this idea of semantically transitive verb-expressions, wider than the modern notion of relation, because the concern of the modern logic of relations is much narrower. This limited logic is extensional: that is, before something counts as a relation, it is required that the objects between which the relation holds are implied or presupposed to exist, that descriptions true of such objects should be intersubstitutable without affecting the truth or falsity of statements of the relation, and that it should be determinate what descriptions hold of the objects. This is because it is only of relations in this restricted sense that a full symbolic logic has so far been developed. But, although such restrictions may be satisfied in individual types of case, no such requirements can be laid upon semantically transitive verb-expressions in general, especially not when we are concerned with the kind of directedness instanced in the wide variety of cases we have just indicated.

It might be asked what these two uses of the word "object" have in common. The answer is that these uses are related only grammatically or syntactically, namely by their parallel connections with two uses of such expressions as "there is . . .", uses whereby it serves as an operator to pick out a noun or noun-phrase immediately subordinate to a predicate within a sentence of syntactically transitive form.[26] In

---

why cases of teleology not involving consciousness should not show intentionality in the sense here delimited.

[26]These two uses of "there is" are parallel to a third use whereby it picks out a complement to the verb "to be", as when we say "There is a colour which is the colour which this wall is (is the colour of this wall)" or "There is a number which is the number which the Apostles were (is the number of the Apostles)". Wherever we have complements of a verb, whether the complement "Jill" in "Jack hit Jill", the complement "a cow" in "James imagined a cow", the complement "red" in "The sky was red", or "that Simon was bigoted" in "John said that Simon was bigoted",

brief, one can say that every act of wanting is an act of wanting something, every act of imagining is an act of imagining something, every act of worshipping is an act of worshipping something, so that in each case 'there is' something wanted, something imagined, something worshipped, without its following uniformly that 'there is' or 'there exists' an entity or 'object' (in the logicians' sense) which is wanted, imagined, or worshipped. That is, one can distinguish between two ways in which reference to objects of the relation or directedness arise: (a) one way whereby it is implied or presupposed that there would be some answer to the question "what is the true completion of the statement of the form 'X wanted (imagined, worshipped)...'?" and (b) another whereby the object is being spoken of in such a way that it is implied or presupposed that the laws of extensional logic apply.

What is important is not mere syntactic transitivity which can arise in secondary ways, as (e.g.) when we speak of dreaming dreams or feeling pains, but rather what I have called semantic transitivity. I mean by this the feature present not only when verbal expressions take only real objects, true descriptions of which are freely intersubstitutable in the context of the verbal expression, such as the verb "to kick", but also when verbal expressions take as object-expressions terms of the same syntactic kinds as the first set of verbs, but without one or other of these implications. As we shall make clear below, intentional objects are always things which either are real objects or are of the same syntactic kinds: as we can kick or see a football or a tomato, so also we can imagine or want a football or a tomato.

(b) Fallacious arguments drawing on the ambiguity of the term "object"

The danger of confusing the two different senses of the word "object" can be dramatized by considering a fallacious argument which had become commonplace in arguing for the existence of sense-data.

---

we have uses for the expression "there is" as is instanced even in the last case since we could say "There is one remark which John made about Simon which I thought unfair". What the cases we have picked out as involving an 'object (intentional object)' have in common is that the complement expression is primitively a genuine noun or noun phrase, not quasi-sentential as in the last case where, it needs to be noted, we do not have a syntactically transitive verbal construction in the relevant way, let alone a semantically transitive one. The precise separating off of this last case is dealt with in Chapter XI.

Consider the parallelism between the following pair of arguments, the first adapted from *The Foundations of Empirical Knowledge* by A. J. Ayer and the second suggested by considering conventional Anglo-Saxon criticisms of Meinong.

(i) Every perception has an object;

> The objects of veridical perceptions and of non-veridical perceptions are not (or need not be) qualitatively different, i.e., do not differ in description or in the type of description appropriate to them;

> Therefore the objects of veridical perception and non-veridical perception are entities (things) of the same kind (both material or both non-material and inner)—they are of the same general type or category.

> Accordingly, since the objects of non-veridical perception are not material or outer, but inner, the objects of veridical perception are not material or outer, but inner.

(ii) Every assertion of existence or non-existence has a subject;

> These subjects are not (or need not be) qualitatively different, i.e., do not differ in description or in the type of description appropriate to them;

> Therefore these subjects are entities (things) of the same kind (are of the same general type or category).

> Accordingly, since the things which do not exist are not material things, the things which do exist are not material things.

We could present the fallacy involved in a slightly different way by posing the following for comparison. (1) The objects of veridical and non-veridical perception are similar, therefore they are the same in kind; in the case of non-veridical perception, they are not material or public; therefore, in the case of veridical perception, they are not material or public. (2) The objects of imagination are similar to the objects of sense, and therefore the same in kind; the objects of imagination are not material or public; therefore the objects of sense are not material or public. (3) Non-existent objects are similar to existent objects, and therefore the same in kind; non-existent objects are not material or public; therefore existent objects are not material or public.

What these parallels bring out is that to be described by a noun phrase of a kind syntactically appropriate to a real object—in the way that (e.g.) the subjects of denials of existence, the objects of 'perception' understood in a smudged sense to cover so-called 'veridical' and 'non-veridical' cases alike, and the objects of imagination are described—is not as such to exist, not as such to be a 'real' object, not as such to be an object (entity or subject of predication), i.e., not to be an 'object' in the logicians' sense. And further, for two things (syntactic subjects or objects) to be described in the same terms is not for them to be existent objects (entities, *Gegenstande* in Frege), let alone for them to exist in the same way: in the arguments set forth above, in faithful caricature, 'being described in the same terms' is being confused with 'being similar (i.e., an entity which is similar)' or 'being an entity of the same kind'.[27]

In each group of arguments only the first had any kind of plausibility and one can reasonably ask why.

Why, for instance, was one ever inclined to accept the suggestion that non-veridical perceptions had objects (entities with no extramental existence) which were not material things? Presumably it was because, having been softened up into supposing that imagination had

---

[27]Against this background, one of Austin's objections to Ayer's argument seems rather superficial, namely the objection that it was assumed that, if the objects of 'veridical' perceptions were similar to the objects of 'non-veridical' perceptions, they would be of the same kind, whereas the qualitative sensory similarities of lemons to certain possible pieces of soap would not imply sameness of kind, so that there was no inference from qualitative sensory similarity to sameness of kind (*Sense and Sensibilia*, pp. 50 f.). To concentrate attention on things like similarity and sameness of kind, which presuppose existence, might have relevance to the discussion to which we refered earlier as to whether (e.g.) 'what is seen as it is seen' corresponds to some physical or physiological datum such as the pattern of light coming towards the eyes or whether it is to be described less neutrally in terms of a perspectively-seen field of people, other animals, and other bodily things, moving in their characteristic ways, shadows, Sun, sky and clouds, and so forth. But to concentrate on these things in a context in which what is at issue is the similarity or sameness of kind of the existent and the non-existent is to distract attention from the root fallacy being committed.

Some sense of the real problem is shown by drawing attention to the poor credentials of terms like "veridical perception" and "non-veridical perception": after all, when I see a stick in water looking bent, or water looking less deep than it is, I am seeing things looking just as they ought to look and the sense in which the perception is 'non-veridical' is quite different from the sense in which an hallucination is 'non-veridical' (and preferably not counted as a 'perception' at all). And, in general, there is no plausibility (unless the way of thinking under dispute is already being drawn upon) in such a statement as "The objects of optical illusions are not material or public". But observations such as these in Austin, *Sense and Sensibilia*, especially I–III, IV–VI, merely draw attention to the symptoms of the underlying malaise without achieving diagnosis.

entities as objects, namely 'images', which were not material things, one had already accepted the point most requiring proof, namely that even (e.g.) hallucinations had real objects which would be 'ideas' or something like that, additional non-material 'mental' or 'inner' entities somewhat analogous to these 'images'. Having conceded the existence of such inner entities, it can seem quite economical to suppose that so-called 'veridical' perception consists in some relation to similar objects, perhaps called 'sense-data', caused by or identical with similar brain-states, but differing in their relations to the 'external' world, the relations which make them 'veridical'.

In other words, the first cause of the plausibility of the argument about perception lay in the fact that the thinkers who were considering it already accepted the way of thinking which it was the object of the argument to justify: 'ideas' or 'sense-data' were being assumed to exist in the very argument being offered to prove their existence. It is a question of the interpretation of the very first premiss: "Every perception, veridical or non-veridical, has an object (in the same sense, whatever that is, of 'having an object')". For by treating 'veridical' and 'non-veridical' as 'having an object' in the same sense, and by interpreting this as fulfilled in the case of hallucinations by the 'perceiving' of a real 'inner' object (real entity) called an 'idea' or 'appearance' or some such, the way is opened for treating (for the sake of economy in describing experience) 'veridical' perceptions as having similar kinds of object.

This whole way of thinking is bolstered by thinking of imagination as consisting in having inner objects called 'images' presented to the mind's eye, an equally misconceived point of view.[28] If I want a cow, what I want is not an 'idea' of a cow but a cow: a cow is the object of my wanting, even if there is no particular cow I want by preference, or no cows available or still in existence. Similarly (from a logical or syntactic perspective), if I imagine a cow, what I imagine is not a picture (e.g., on a wall or on a cinema screen) of a cow, but a cow, even though I do not imagine a black cow with five areas of white coat on the side from which I am picturing it rather than a black cow with eight such areas, and even though it is clear that since I am

---

[28]Gilbert Ryle in *The Concept of Mind*, Chapter VIII, recognizes the need to repudiate explaining imagining as the inner visualizing of images as inner real objects, but tries to do this oversimply by reducing imagining to supposing.

imagining (rather than dreaming) of a cow, there is no particular cow I am imagining.[29] Likewise, if I hallucinate a cow, I do not therein hallucinate a picture of a cow, but a cow. The syntactic resemblances between imagining, hallucinating and seeing include the 'semantically transitive' structure whereby there has to be an 'object (intentional object)' of the activity in question, but not the resemblance that there has to be an 'object (logical subject)', i.e., in this case a real entity to be inner or outer object of the activity.

(Thus, in the primary idiom, what we say is that we imagine cows, fields, hedges, people, shadows, rainbows, etc., just as we see objects such as cows, fields, hedges, people, shadows, rainbows, etc. Of course, it is accurate to say syntactically that we could speak of imagining images of cows, just as we could speak of seeing sights of cows. But to regard this idiom of imagining images as the primary idiom is just as mad as regarding the idiom of seeing sights as primary.)[30]

The other root of the plausibility of the argument which began "Every perception has an object" lies in the already mentioned supposition that the 'object' ought to be referred to in ways not going beyond what one could not be mistaken about. This supposition comes in under the cover of the undefined conception of the 'qualities of an experience' involved in estimating two experiences to be 'qualitatively indistinguishable' (so that I could mistake the one for the other). But the word "experience" is ambiguous: is it the *experiencings* or is it the *objects experienced* which are supposed to be qualitatively indistinguishable? and are we concerned with qualitative distinctions between intentional objects of experiences (even hallucinations), i.e., with how descriptions of how we experience things are to be further spelled out, or with differences in the qualities of real objects? So it is totally obscure which things are being said to be indistinguishable so that one could be mistaken about them. But in any case, as we have already seen, the idea that either our experiencings or their objects are things of which we have an infallible knowledge is baseless as we made clear in Section 2 of the last chapter.[31]

---

[29]If I imagined an identified existent cow as doing this or that, I would not be rightly described as imagining this cow or imagining a cow, but only as imagining this cow doing this or that.

[30]Cf. Chapter II, n. 20.

[31]Against this background some other quite valid objections to various popular presentations of the argument from illusion seem quite superficial. For instance, it is

(c) Rejecting any explanation of perception
      in terms of inner objects, and clarifying the
      contrast between perception and sensation

      Grice looked for 'sense-datum statements' rather than an identifi-
cation of 'sense-data' as a type of inner object. Almost always in recent
discussion, it has been anticipated that the facts about the inner life
of human beings (their experiences) of concern in perception will be
ones stated or reported, not in statements about some special kind
of inner private object, but in reserved forms of statement in which
the description of the content of experience is entirely in what we
may call 'public world' concepts—we are to describe our experience
as being 'as of this or that,'[32] or 'as if so-and-so'.[33] The description
or 'thinking' of the content of experience show a framework and an
integration exhibited in public language and presupposing an objective
time, and so, whether or not we accept the whole of the accounts
offered by Wittgenstein and Kant as to why a private language or why
the subjective is parasitic on the objective, it remains that the practical
consequences of their views for identifying the content of the experience we actually have are little doubted and the belief in inner objects

---

rightly said that 'it does not follow' from the proposition that "Of each perception,
it is true that we cannot be certain that it is not a perception of an inner object or
sense-datum, rather than of a material object" that "We cannot be certain that it is not
true that every perception is a perception of an inner object or sense-datum, rather
than of a material object". But to present an objection in this form is to presuppose
the good sense of the idea of 'perceiving inner objects or sense-data' and already to
entertain the possibility that a person's judgements of the form "I perceive . . . " may
be in general determinative for our judgements as to whether and what he or she
perceives. It is true that 'the primary purpose of the argument from illusion is to
induce people to accept 'sense-data' as the proper and correct answer to what they
perceive on certain *abnormal, exceptional* occasions', and this is 'usually followed up
by another bit of argument intended to establish that they *always* perceive sense-data'.
These quotations are from *Sense and Sensibilia*, p. 20. But this further bit of argument
does not normally draw upon the straightforward formal fallacy, of going from "Of
every perception, x, (it is possible that x is a sense-datum)" to "It is possible that (every
perception, x, is a sense-datum", but rather draws upon the mode of description of
sense-experience in general supposedly established at the first stage of argument. So,
as Austin wished to insist, we must resist the misdescription of the abnormal case
purportedly established at the first stage.

[32] E.g., in Christopher Peacocke, *Holistic Explanation*, p. 7.

[33] Possibly the best explanation of how this is to be done is given by Strawson
in 'Perception and its Objects', pp. 94–96.

has mostly been abandoned.[34] Anscombe's explanation whereby the objects of the mind's directedness are primarily 'intentional' and not necessarily 'real' or 'material' makes general belief in inner objects (images or sense-data) seem like a misunderstanding.

It is important to get a proper grasp of the notion of 'intentional object'. It is not merely a grammatical notion, registering the fact that certain verbs take a grammatical object without needing to express 'relations' in the sense in which this term is used in the modern logic of relations. Rather it is a semantic notion expressing the fact that various, often complex, verb-expressions require an object of the same semantic and syntactic category as other much simpler expressions whose objects are real. Thus, all such expressions as "He was under the impresssion that he saw . . .", "He had an hallucination of . . .", "He saw in his dream . . .", "He imagined . . .", "It looked like . . .", "His vision was of. . ." and suchlike require a nominal complement (an 'object-expression') of the same categorial type as "He saw . . .". Although what we see in a dream or imagine need not exist, it has to be a would-be existent, something the expression for which is of the same type as expressions for the existent things we actually see.

Likewise, even when what we fear or worship does not exist, it still has to be of the same category as things it would be appropriate to fear or worship, and what we desire or aim at has to be something of the sort the possession of which would count as a satisfaction of the desire or the hitting of which would count as the hitting of the target aimed at. These latter, like things it would be appropriate to fear or worship and things we actually see, are things which exist, things public or objective, external or independent of us. Therefore, the specification of the intentional object has in these cases to be in terms appropriate to something likewise external or public.

This brings 'intentional objects' into striking contrast with sensations such as pains.

It is not that we cannot speak of inner objects at all, but that such talk is likely to be misunderstood. We only speak of having or feeling a pain somewhat as we speak of having or dreaming a dream—dreams and pains are alike in being denoted by what we may call internal or cognate accusatives of such verbs as have, feel and dream.

---

[34]D. M. Armstrong, *Perception and the Physical World,* is helpful in marshalling the arguments against 'sense-data' as objects.

We do not have to deny the existence of pains and dreams, and could call them inner objects inasmuch as they have no existence outside the experiencer. But they are objects in the very limited logicians' sense, i.e., we can ask a limited range of questions directly about them (e.g., we may ask of a pain whether it was stabbing or dull, whether in the foot or in some other location) and ask questions about the experiencing of them (e.g., when and by whom); yet we understand what pains and dreams are only from understanding what it is to have, feel or dream them, not vice versa.[35]

By contrast, the pink rats which I hallucinate or about which I dream are not inner objects: they do not enter the list of actual rats or of any kind of object in the logicians' sense at all; it is not just that they have no existence outside the speaker but that they have no existence whatsoever. The intentional objects of perception or of emotion come into speech, not as things with mental existence, but as would-be external or public objects. It may happen that they are not actual at all, but it is in the terms appropriate to external and public objects that they are described, not in terms appropriate to sensations or any other so-called inner objects. And this is what is distinctive of perception, along with the emotions and in contrast with sensations,[36] that what it is directed towards is conceived of and described in the terms appropriate to external and public objects.

(d) Looking as parasitic on the intentionality of seeing

In seeking notions of pure experience and of 'sense-datum statements' expressing it, once having abandoned explanation in terms of inner objects, the second move is to represent how things look as prior to what is seen.

In order to understand the wrongness of this move, we need to grasp the typical features of intentional objects in general. For, indeed,

---

[35]Pains, dreams and hallucinations will each be objects of different logical types (i.e., with different ranges of question appropriate to them—the nature of each type to be understood from how it comes at a secondary stage into discourse. Thus likewise we have to understand the noun "look" from the verb, not vice versa. So Frank Jackson has been misled by an uninteresting logical fact into giving pains and looks a quite false prominence in the treatment of perception and sensation, *Perception*, Ch. 3, and 'The Existence of Mental Objects'.

[36]This is the point on which Merleau-Ponty so rightly insisted, *The Phenomenology of Perception*, Introduction.

it is one of the most characteristic features of intentional objects that they should be the objects of directedness under certain aspects and not others.

Not aware that the man at whom I am pointing my gun is my cousin, I intend to shoot the man at whom I am pointing my gun (a person whom I thought was a terrorist), but I do not intend to shoot my cousin. That is, we might invent this way of speaking: "I aimed at what I was aiming at as a man, but not as my cousin". In a parallel way, we might redescribe Austin's example by saying that we see a person *as* a man being shaved, not *as* a man who had been born in Jerusalem, or (to take Anscombe's example) that we see a person *as* a woman standing on a beach, not *as* a woman with a mole on her back.[37] In effect, in these cases where the intentional object of a mental act is a real or public object, we are introducing, on top of the basic semantically transitive locutions "x saw A" and "x aimed at A", the specially contrived philosophers' ways of speaking,[38] "x saw B as C" and "x aimed at B as C".[39]

But precisely also in cases of this type, i.e., when the intentional object is real or public, there can arise cases where things are not as

---

[37]Our use of the expression "seeing as" corresponds with 'how' things are seen in an appropriate sense of "how".

This use, thus explained, in a certain key way coincides with the use described by Wittgenstein in *Philosophical Investigations*, II, xi, but not in all (see next footnote). I see that which is in front of me at one time as a duck and at another time as a rabbit (never as both at the same time), and this is the psychological datum. It is a mistake to suppose that there is another psychological datum which is present in both cases but indeterminate as to how it is seen such as might correspond to something physiological and be explained in what are commonly called 'causal' terms—meaning 'causal' in a sense excluding teleology. There is no psychological datum thus corresponding and thus to be explained. The only psychological datum in either case can be historically or causally explained but only in a wider sense of the word "causal".

[38]The point that these ways of speaking are indeed artificially contrived and specially invented philosophers' ways of speaking needs to be emphasized. As such, they are to be understood only in the way I explain in this subsection. In particular, it especially needs to be emphasized that this way of speaking works in one important way quite differently from the normal way of using the expression "seeing as". In this normal well-established way of speaking, the way of speaking on which Wittgenstein drew, we can only talk at all of seeing B as C (e.g., as a rabbit) when there is some other contrary expression, D (e.g., a duck), such that we could also see B as D, but could not see B as C and as D at the same time.

[39]These expressions can be used in the case of animals which do not have the use of language—as I indicate in Chapter IX.

they are seen: in such cases, although there is a relation between "B" and "C" which is adequate within the context for B to be seen as C, nonetheless the public object B is not C. To cater for the possibility of such cases we develop the locutions "look" or (in Latin-based idioms) "appear", leaving it open that in some cases a thing may be as it is seen, so that we say that it is straight and that it looks straight, while in other cases the thing may not be as it is seen so that we say that it is straight but looks bent.

I explain the matter in this careful way in order to make plain that what is involved in all cases even when things look as they are. In all cases, when we see a thing B, there are some descriptions C, D, E, etc. such that we see B as C, D, E, etc. and other descriptions F, G, H, etc. which truly apply to B but which are not such that we see B as F, G, H, etc. Thus, we see a woman as a woman, but although she has a mole on her back we don't see her as a woman with a mole on her back, or we see a man being shaved as a man being shaved, but although he was born in Jerusalem we don't see him as a man born in Jerusalem. For things to look as they are is just this, that there is no description "C" such that we see B as C even though B is in fact not C.

The purpose of this explanation has been to allow us to make the following crucial point: *it is not that the idioms of seeing are constructed from idioms of looking but that they involve a structure from which the idioms of looking can be generated.*

We can now see what is wrong with any attempt to explain what it is for something to be red in terms of what it is for it to look red.[40] The fundamental judgements, e.g., in respect of a colour such as red, are of such forms as " . . . is red" and "x sees a red . . .", and judgements like " . . . looks red" and " . . . looks red to x" are parasitic upon them. To judge that something looks red is to judge that something looks in the way in which something that is red properly looks—that is, that it looks in the way in which something which is red looks when we see it as it is.

It is therefore quite wrong to explain what it is to be red as 'to look red when seen under normal conditions'.[41] What it is for

---

[40] I derive this second line of objection from G.E.M. Anscombe, *op. cit.*

[41] It is only because Frank Jackson (*Perception*, Ch. 2) imagines that the ordinary (non-epistemic) use of the verb "look" in order to refer to 'objective' or public

the conditions of vision to be normal is for them to be apt for what is of a colour/shape/size/visual depth/etc. to look as of the colour/shape/size/visual depth/etc. it is, whereas what it is for the conditions of vision to be abnormal is for them not to be thus apt. The normality here does not have to do with the normality of causal conditions but is teleological, having to do with aptitude for right judgement and behaviour (one might say, right discrimination, thus allowing for other animals as well as man). Just as what it is for grounds for belief to be good is for them to be apt for knowledge,[42] so what it is for conditions of vision to be good, normal or 'OK' is for them to be apt for in varying degrees satisfactory sight: there is no property separately identifiable from aptness for knowledge or sight which grounds of belief or conditions of vision have and in virtue of which they are apt for knowledge or sight.

But there is a further fundamental fault in any analysis of seeing in terms of things looking in a certain way as a result of being caused to look in this way. Already the use of the word "look" shows that we are dealing with a case of seeing a public object. That is, Grice's original tentative suggestion, that we should give an account of seeing in terms of things looking to us in a certain way, is not adapted to his purpose because it is adapted only to cases where, if mistaken judgement occurs, it is due to 'illusion', not to 'hallucination' or non-physical 'vision'. It is only by introducing two qualifiers, e.g., by asking that one consider 'how it seems that things look', that one could have hope of satisfying what seems to be Grice's desire, namely to achieve what Austin regarded as impossible, viz., the encompassing within one formula of all would-be perceptual experiences.

But the consideration of this second qualifier, "seems", on examination introduces parallel difficulties, albeit of a very different kind. In general, what is primary for the use of the verb "seem" is the conditions of judgement as to what is the case, and to say that

---

appearances (instanced when one says, in the case of the Muller-Lyer illusion, that the one line looks shorter than the other) has to be explained with reference to the 'normal' person in 'normal' conditions, and so regards it as implicitly 'comparative', that he fabricates the idea of a third, 'phenomenological' or 'phenomenal', use of the word "look" (understood to be neither epistemic nor comparative). But the ordinary objective use of "look" should never have been understood comparatively in the first place.

[42]David Braine, 'The Nature of Knowledge', pp. 44–50, 52–53.

something 'seems to the case' is merely to register that in one of a spread of disparate ways arising with the type of judgement these conditions have only deficiently been filled. In sum, we can say that the sense and conditions of a type of judgement of the form "It seems that it is the case that. . . " are derivative on the sense of the corresponding types of judgement "It is the case that. . . ."

It seems then that no form of language provided by ordinary speech is likely to serve Grice's purpose. We have seen that Ayer's proposal of secondary specially contrived sense of such verbs as "see" to mean supposedly "seem to see" works no better—it would, in any case, need some explanation anchoring it in ordinary speech. What we now have to look at is the proposal that the technical philosophers' idioms of 'intentionality' will serve the purpose all these proponents of causal theories of perception, Descartes, Grice and the mind-brain identity theorists alike.

(e) The fundamental mistake in contemporary treatments of intentionality

In considering the notion of intentional object, it is important to begin with an adequate spread of examples.

When one is angry at a person's action, or wants an apple (but not this one rather than that one) or to get to Edinburgh, or imagines a green field, or promises one's nephew a horse (a certain particular horse which he has always wanted), or sees a car, or worships the Sun, it is the person's action, an apple, getting to Edinburgh, a green field, the horse, the car, and the Sun which are in the respective cases the objects of one's anger, desire, imagining, promise, perception, and worship.

It is a mistake to be doctrinaire and insist that all the objects of 'mental directedness' must have a real existence. *But it is also equally a mistake to be doctrinaire and insist that none of the objects of mental directedness is a real object or presents itself in its reality.* On the one hand, a man may worship Apollo without its being true that Apollo exists, but, on the other hand, a man's worship of the Sun may be expressed or realized in ways which involve facing or bowing before the Sun. If my nephew is promised a horse, the case described thus loosely may be a case in which any reasonable horse will do, but it may be the case referred to in which there exists (and was implied to exist) an identified determinate horse which has been promised.[43]

We have already made the point that the modern logic of relations is not designed to deal with the significance of the transitive form of verbal expression in general, but only with relations in a narrow sense conforming to the requirements of an extensional logic. The notion of relation in the logic of the school books represents a specialization, not an explanation, of the general notion of what is expressed by a transitive verbal expression. Being directed towards a so-called 'intentional object' is not to be treated as a deviant or deficient case of being in a relation, a deviant case taking just one form to be defined negatively according to the features whereby it deviates from an extensional 'norm'. That is, it is not the case that all examples of 'directedness' involving intentionality have to deviate in just one way from the extensional case: none of them implying or presupposing the existence of their objects, none of them allowing or inviting the intersubstitutability of different descriptions of the same object, and all leaving an open class of descriptions of the object indeterminate. On the contrary, in many cases and, indeed, the fundamental or paradigm cases, the intentional object is a real object or (as we say) exists, and many though not all descriptions applying to it are intersubstitutable without the truth of what is said being affected.

Wherever we have 'semantically transitive' verbs, it is endemic, in the first place, that there should arise cases in which the object of the verb does not exist, or is not implied or presupposed to exist. We may say that the Egyptians worshipped the Sun; but we may also say that the Greeks worshipped Apollo. In the second place, it is endemic that when the mind is directed towards an object according to a certain range of descriptions there will be other descriptions true of the same object according to which the mind is

---

[43] It is a mistake to try to analyse all these examples of 'directedness' as if, for instance, all the objects of certain of the relevant mental attitudes were propositional (as W. Kneale suggested in 'Intentionality and Intensionality'), so that my wanting would either be (that I have some apple) or (that I possess the apple identified thus and thus), and that my promising should either be (that, you, my nephew possess some horse) or (that you, my nephew, possess that particular horse). For the 'objects' of the forms of mental directedness concerned are not the propositions or propositional contents but certain 'objects', and it is what it is to be an 'object' in the relevant sense, not the means used to disambiguate certain examples, which we are concerned with.

not directed towards it. Thus seeing a man being shaved need not be seeing him as having been born in Jerusalem, even though he was indeed born in Jerusalem. In the third place, it is endemic that when there is mental directedness there can be an indeterminacy as to what descriptions apply to the intentional objects towards which the mind is directed. Thus, there can readily arise indeterminacy as to how exactly I saw something or as to what descriptions apply to what I wanted, imagined or remembered: I may see a thing without seeing whether it was ten or twelve millimetres wide, remember a real object without remembering many even of its obvious properties, imagine a potted plant without imagining it as of one species rather than another; and the indeterminacies concerned may have different roots—uncertainty in respect of what I do not know but which is already determinate being very different from uncertainty in respect of what I have yet to draw.

All these features arise in the case of intentional action, in that descriptions under which you intend to do what you do may or may not come true, in that only under certain descriptions will what you do be intentional, and in that the descriptions under which you intend what you do can be vague or indeterminate. This has encouraged the tendency to consider the cases of intending and wanting, along with the case of imagining, as setting the pattern for describing 're-lations' which do not conform to the extensional case. In this way, types of directedness whose non-extensional features are associated with the openness of the future, or with the unrestrictedness of the supposable, are quite wrongly taken as the pattern for treatment of cases where the non-extensional features have a clearly quite different origin, associated with imprecision of sense or lack of knowledge.

And this is the fundamental mistake.

It is quite wrong to treat all cases of directedness as a single class and say that, uniformly, in their case the existence of the 'intentional' object is never implied. That is, it is wrong to 'define' such a class, or to 'define' such a type of 'object', negatively, in terms of the absence of such implications—as if there were just two simple cases, the one of a purely extensional object with all the features defining extensionality, and the other of a purely intentional (or as earlier philosophers would have said 'mental') object exhibiting not just one but all the features whereby extensionality may be deviated from. On the contrary, there are not two cases but many and there is no one way of being an 'intentional object'.

Modern philosophers are in the position of having mostly resisted two temptations, firstly the temptation of denying that perception and aiming have any objects at all (e.g., the idea that the apparent specifications of objects are to be understood adverbially),[44] secondly the temptation of supposing that their objects are real but inner (sense-data being put alongside pains and other sensations). But they are now tempted to succumb to a third more subtle temptation: to accept a distinction between being a real object and being an intentional object, but then to fall into the trap of separating two classes of statements, the one reporting 'real' relations to 'real objects', the relations being understood according to the lines of interpretation suggested in expositions of extensional logic, and the other reporting 'intentional' directedness towards 'intentional objects', these latter statements being understood according to patterns of interpretation suggested by post-Cartesian treatments of 'non-veridical perception' and united by the logical criteria which mark the cases concerned as 'defective'.

This last temptation has a constant tendency to reappear in subtly varied guises. It appeared at an early date in G.E.M. Anscombe's remarks in which, after characterising intentionality in logical terms, she goes on to entertain an analysis of seeing's having a normal ('material') object in terms of its having an intentional object plus certain causal relations.[45]

This is precisely how Searle conceives the relation of experience to object in perception: the object involved in the Intentional content of the visual experience causes the experience and its existence satisfies the Intentional content of the experience.[46] But, for him, what he calls 'the Intentional object' is only given according to the way it is involved in the Intentional content of the (e.g.) visual experience, and therefore, as we have remarked, given in a way indifferent to whether it exists or not and indifferent to how the experience is actually caused. Therefore in his account of the 'intentionality' of perception, there is still no direct presentation of the object as existing to the perceiver, no cognitive relation which is a real relation.

And it is only because Searle's account has thus still—despite all its nuances and qualifications—made the mental and intentional inner

---

[44]An idea suggested by Hirst in his book, *Perception*.
[45]Anscombe, *op. cit.*
[46]*Op. cit.*, p. 57.

that he is able to regard the mental and intentional as a property of or realized in the structures of the brain. If the mind is something inner, such that it even might be identical to the brain, there can be no real sensory presentation of an object to it: if the mind or person is not an animal, perception is emasculated. The views of Searle, just as much as those of Armstrong, serve to confirm this.

The effect of separating statements of directedness to intentional objects from statements of real relation to real objects so as to put them in two mutually exclusive classes is to put the intentional objects of perceptual experience in the same logical situation as the objects of imagining or of desire and hope for the future. According to this way of thinking an intentional object, simply *qua* intentional object, cannot be real.

We can dramatize what is involved by considering an example. If I picture a golden mountain in my mind's eye, and then set to the building of such a mountain, ever comparing the actual construction with what I imagine or desire (somewhat as I might compare the actual construction in front of me with a visualized drawing over on my left), there would still be no sense in identifying the real object with the object of my imagination or the object of my desire.

Non-historical or not yet actual objects brought into historical novels or science-fiction or into accounts of the future of any kind may correspond in description with objects actual at the time spoken of. But, if it does not enter into our way of referring to them that they are already identified historical or actual objects (e.g., because their existence is wholly future), then the only question that can arise is as to whether what did exist or what later comes to exist corresponds in kind or description to what has been imagined or conceived.[47] There

---

[47]In more technical terms, we have to distinguish between cases in which a quantifier or singular term is prenex or occurs outside, as it were governing, a predicative context (or, as is said, so that the predicative context is within the scope of the quantifier or singular term rather than vice versa), and cases in which the opposite is true: thus we can distinguish "There exists something, x, such that it is possible that F(x)" from "It is possible that there exists something, x, such that F(x)", or distinguish "Of the thing, a, it is possible for it(a) to F" from "It is possible that there is something, x, such that A(x) and F(x)" (where A is a property which would identify a), e.g., as we distinguish "Of Cheops, I imagined that he had built a unique golden sarcophagus" from "I imagined that whoever built the Great Pyramid of Gizeh had built a unique golden sarcophagus". Just as quantifiers must either have the scope

is no question of what has thus been conceived of only in imagination or as possible or future having any numerical or physical identity with any past or future existents—the two do not come into the scope of the same generalizations.

Note on the vocabulary of intentionality

Historically, the notion of intentionality was applied first to the subjects of experience and action, and to their acts with the principles of these acts, and only at a later time to the objects of these acts.

In Aquinas' conception a sensible *species* or form had a double role: the first as being a kind of imprint left upon the sense-organ in the way appropriate to the sense concerned, the role in virtue of which it was described as a *species* or likeness of the object sensed; and the second whereby it was that in virtue of which the perceiver was mentally directed towards the object sensed in the appropriate way, the role in virtue of which it was described as intentional. In some cases the likeness is spoken of as a material likeness (the likeness in the case of touch is supposed to be like this, as is an imprint on the sand, and this might be true of the image on the retina) and in other cases it is spoken of as a non-material likeness, intentional because of its function, as in the case of the alteration in the pupil.[48]

In order to understand Aquinas' conception of this species or alteration in the pupil, the so-called sensible species in the case of the sense of sight, we need to understand the setting of his theory. In the theory of vision to be found in Aristotle as interpreted by Aquinas, light from the object of vision has an existence in the air or the empty space between us and the object, and makes no material difference to any matter present such as air. This existence in the air is a sort of passing through or *en route* existence (*esse viale* in

---

only of the modal or intentional clause or other context within which they appear or have the scope of the whole statement containing them, so that the quantification is into the modal or intentional context rather than within it, so likewise an apparent referring expression (name or description) may either have only the scope of the modal or intentional context or have the scope of the whole statement containing them.

[48]Searle says that 'Intentional states represent objects and states of affairs in the same sense that speech acts represent objects and states of affairs' (*Intentionality*, p. 4) and explains that the notion of representation is apposite because some notion of 'fit' is appropriate such that the object or state of affairs fits or does not fit a corresponding Intentional state or vice versa (*op. cit.*, pp. 7–13). This has no similarity to Aquinas' reasons for speaking of likeness, which have to do (e.g.) with the skin being heated when touching the hot (material likeness) or there being an appropriate configuration of light in the pupil (intentional likeness).

Aquinas), or (because of its function) 'intentional' existence, not a material one (as if the air became coloured by the light).

In a parallel way, the light from the object in its structured configuration has existence in the pupil of the eye through which we see, making no material alteration and giving no colour to the pupil any more than it does to the air. We could think of it as a kind of ideal direction-from-which-the-light-came-registering 'photographic positive'. The alteration in the pupil is non-material in a way analogous to that in which the configuration of light in an ideal window-pane as it passes through towards the eye is non-material, involving no change in the colour of the window—it again has what Aquinas calls an *esse viale*, an *en route* existence. (In this way what is in the pupil of the eye is a kind of microcosm of the world presented to vision, somewhat as in the dramatic presentation of David Bohm, in 'Quantum Theory as an Indication of a New Order in Physics', what is present within a cubic metre of 'empty' physical space is, if one considers the patterns of radiation passing through it, a kind of microcosm of the whole universe.) Because it is this *species* in the pupil, and not any supposed image on the retina, which is the principle of vision, this theory makes vision the most purely 'spiritual' of the senses, the sense-organ receiving only non-material or 'spiritual' *immutationes*, impressions, or changes relevant to perception. By contrast, the sense of touch receives material as well as spiritual modifications.

The point that it is the alteration in the pupil, thus thought of as *en route*, immaterial and intentional, involving no material alteration in the pupil (no change of sensible quality, that is no change in the causal properties of the sort which are affected by contact, such as moist and dry, hot and cold, and no change in colour), which is for Aquinas the principle in virtue of which we see what we see, and not any alteration to the retina, requires special emphasis. It reinforces the point that the intentionality spoken of is in what has or gives the directedness towards the object in question, and is not the property of any object towards which the directedness is had, nor the property of any supposed image of any kind.

In modern times the characteristic use of the term "intentionality" has been in respect not of the person or animal, state of mind or imprint whereby the mind is directed towards an object or kind of object, but in respect of the object towards which the person, animal or mind is thus 'mentally directed'. This usage of the term originated with Brentano and became characteristic of the whole phenomenological tradition represented by Husserl and Merleau-Ponty, and is the usage picked up by the Anglo-Saxon tradition in Anscombe, Searle and others, but is utterly different in the way we have explained from that of Aquinas.

3. Perception as a Real Cognitive Relation: The Flouting of Logical Atomism

The suggestion that there might be direct cognitive relations between man and the world involves a head-on collision with the incipient tendency in almost all 'philosophical analysis' towards a 'logical atomism', that is to supposing that, whenever a proposition "P" implies a proposition "Q" but not vice versa, there is some remainder "R" such that in the ideal case "P" can be analysed into a conjunction of "Q" and "R", and "Q" and "R" are logically independent.

The working out of this tendency is seen most simply in the case of perception. There it seems obvious that a perception-statement "P" will imply a certain statement or statements about the physical world "Q" (having to do with the existence of the object seen and its optical relations to the perceiver's eyes), and we have seen how it is presumed that there will be some remainder-statement "R" (taken to refer to the 'mental element' of 'experiencing'), independent of "Q", which together with "Q", will be equivalent to "P". The only difficulty is imagined to be that of accommodating the supposed causal and other co-ordinative relations between the physical (stated in "Q") and the mental (stated in "R"), but it is standard for all atomistic theories that causal and other such co-ordinative relations should be reckoned to be exceptions, whether to be accommodated along Humean lines or some other.

Perception is, in fact, just a particular case of knowledge of external matters of fact.

Accordingly, it is unsurprising to find that all cases of knowledge of external matters of fact are commonly analysed along the same structural lines. "x knows that Q" is analysed into a statement "Q" as to the external matter of fact concerned (sometimes expressed "It is true that Q"), together with a mental state of sure belief, together with a related mental state of being justified in this sure belief. That this analysis is inadequate is well-known, since it must not be accidental that x got it right;[49] and it has been shown that 'justifiedness' cannot be described or understood independently of applications of the concept of knowledge itself;[50] it therefore cannot

---

[49]Edmund L. Gettier, 'Is Justified True Belief Knowledge?'
[50]Braine, 'The Nature of Knowledge'.

be a mental state in the non-external-fact-involving sense required for the proposed analysis.

This failure in atomistic analysis in the case of knowledge of external matter of fact, considered in general, does not augur well for its appropriateness in the case of perception.

However, all cases of so-called 'conscious states', not only the case of perception, involve the concept of knowledge. We have the knowledge a person has of his or her own pain, emotion, and intention, and we have the knowledge that he or she has of the expression of pain or emotion that it is what it is (e.g., a groaning with pain or a sobbing with grief) or of his or her utterance or action that it was uttered or done with the meaning or intention which it was uttered or done with. In none of these cases does the relation of the assent given to the relevant statement of what is known to what is known seem to be a contingent relation to an 'external matter of fact'. Nor does knowledge of mathematics seem readily to fall under this heading. It is a matter of some awkwardness that the proposed atomistic definition of knowledge of external matter of fact in the case of perception should show so little of what this knowledge has in common with other knowledge, not of 'external matters'.

The involvement of logical atomism in the case of the consideration of knowledge of 'external matters of fact' is nicely highlighted by its unannounced appearance in Professor Ayer's eloquent discussions. His discussion comes to its climax as follows:

> ' "The effect", he [Hume] says, "is totally different from the cause, and consequently can never be discovered in it." Or again, "there is no object, which implies the existence of any other if we consider these objects in themselves, and never look beyond the idea which we form of them". As Hume puts them, these statements are not obviously tautological; but they become so when it is seen what he is saying is that when two objects are distinct, they are distinct; and consequently to assert the existence of either one of them is not necessarily to assert the existence of the other.'[51]

On this basis Ayer is arguing that, if in any particular case knowledge were a mental state, because *qua* mental state it is a distinct existence from the external state known, it could not imply that external state;

---

[51]Ayer, *The Problem of Knowledge*, p. 29.

and that therefore a state of knowledge must in general be a composite of a mental state and a matter of fact external to it. Thus he presumes an atomistic or compositional theory whereby 'states' such as knowledge, because they cannot be conceived of as purely internal mental states without violating the principles of logical atomism, must be composites of internal mental states and independent (we say 'external', because it fits with the way of thinking here concerned) states of affairs. This is borne out by what he insists on earlier:

> There cannot be a mental state which, being as it were directed towards a fact, is such that it guarantees that the fact is so.[52]

Or, as he goes on to say:

> The most that it [the mental state] could reveal would be that the subjects were having certain experiences and that they were convinced of the truth of whatever it was that these experiences led them to assert. But this would not prove that they knew anything at all, except, possibly, that they were having the experiences in question. It would still have to be established by an independent argument that the experiences disclosed the existence of anything beyond themselves.[53]

From a logical point of view, it is irrelevant to the validity of his argument that he imagines that the only candidate mental states are states of extreme conviction or sureness of belief. Of course, if these were the only candidate mental states, and if they could be proved to be so, his additional remarks[54] drawing upon Austin[55] to the effect that knowledge was not the performance of a particularly striking feat in the same scale as believing and being quite sure would close this formal gap in his argument. But neither Plato nor any believer that common cases of perception are cases of knowledge ever held or holds that knowledge is a mental state in this scale, and such philosophers will object to the slovenly way of speaking amongst philosophers whereby a term such as "cognition" is made to bestraddle knowledge and belief. And one is under no compulsion to suppose that all mental states are to be conceived of as Descartes conceived *cogitationes* or *pensees*, to be compared only in respect of their objects

---

[52] *Op. cit.*, p. 19.
[53] *Op. cit.*, p. 24.
[54] *Op. cit.*, p. 16.
[55] 'Other Minds', J.L. Austin, *Philosophical Papers*.

or in Hume's manner in respect of their forcefulness, steadiness and vivacity. To restrict mental states in this way is precisely to exclude cognitive states of the whole person in relation to his environment from being considered to be 'mental states'.

A key part of the inspiration of this idea lies in the presumption that all the states of a thing have to be non-relational, but this presumption is quite unfounded. The opposite to 'state' is 'episode', not 'relation'. And there is no reason to suppose that relational states can be reduced to non-relational ones.

What we have in Ayer is a logical atomism, with its presumption that, if "P" implies "Q" but not conversely, the other conditions of "P" will be statable in a way independent of "Q". In treating the mental in this way Ayer, along with Hume before him, simply stands inheritor of the idea in Descartes that the mental can be conceived without the physical without contradiction—along with what seems an almost Leibnizian conception of minds as monads with no essentially relational states.

In this way we have traced the almost universal philosophical prejudice against the common-sense presumption that the human being is in direct cognitive relation to the world to its origins. Against this prejudice we must insist upon the presence of direct cognitive relation to the world both in perception and in the kinds of knowledge which arise, not by perception or observation after the event, but as it were beforehand or in the act, internally to intentional action and the expressions of emotion and sensation.

What we must at all costs avoid in opposing the more common philosophical standpoint is any way of thinking whereby mental states, or the propositions affirming their presence, are or affirm metaphysical or logical simples, without implications for the physical—or intelligible independently of such implications. Rather mental states, such as knowledge, are states of a person viewed in a wider context of relations incorporating these implications. In this way, the consideration of the logic of perception and the logic of knowledge bring us face to face with the need to recognize the existence—indeed the pre-eminence— and irreducibility of hybrid mental/physical propositions in the case of human beings. What we must next see is how the consideration of action, emotion and sensation force upon us the same recognition.

IV. Action, Emotion, and Sensation

In the case of perception it is obvious that the whole activity is focalized in a subject of experience. This focus, this subject, is not a mind or a brain but a complete animal or human being. The whole character of the act of perception was not that of a pure observer, a mind in abstraction from physical activity, but that of a wandering, exploring, active agent.

In the case of intentional action it likewise appears obvious that it has a focus or centre, a point of origin—namely, the agent, the logical subject of the action. And our argument in this chapter is again directed towards establishing that this focus, this subject, that which acts, is not the mind or the brain, but the animal or human being as such—and that again the activity is to be conceived in an holistic psychophysical way, the mental and the outer physical behaviour not to be separated either logically or in their ontological realizations.[1]

Our starting point here must be to grasp that intentional action is one particular form or mode of *causal action*.[2] To understand what is meant by "causal action" we need to appreciate the distinction between a cause in the sense of *a causal agent*, that which pushes or pulls things, hits, cuts, carries, burns, wets, or makes noises, or, in general, achieves effects in the world, and a cause in the sense of *something because of which so-and-so*, i.e., something which we would specify in answer to a question 'Why so-and-so?' The events, states, and facts which we specify in answering 'Why'-questions do not themselves move, push, pull, carry, burn or wet anything. According to our ordinary modes of description and explanation events, states, and facts do nothing, achieve nothing, in no way act causally, but rather it is only agents (whether deliberately, moved by emotion,

---

[1]Our concern here is always with the character of human and animal action, not with that of God or of pure spirits, whether angels or devils.

[2]Cf. P.T. Geach, *Three Philosophers*, p. 107.

under their own impetus or subject to force from other agents) which act causally. (Conversely, agents explain nothing: a cause in the sense of a causal agent may be mentioned in an explanation of why so-and-so, but naming it apart from its role in action does not by itself provide such an explanation.)[3]

Later on, in Chapter VI, we shall deal with the mistake of trying to eliminate this focalization of action upon agents by trying to explain the notion of causal action by causal agents entirely in terms of causal relations between events and states—the logicians' mistake of reducing agent-causality to event-causality. But in this chapter we are concerned to eliminate the earlier dualist mistake, that of reducing all causal agency to either agency by minds or agency by bodies, instead of allowing for the existence of another irreducible kind of agency, a kind characteristic of animals and human beings with the mental and physical integrated and inseparable—encapsulated in what we referred to as irreducibly hybrid facts and propositions.

But first we must discount a fable—the fable that the only agents are persons and possibly animals. On the contrary, causal agents are of many kinds—people, animals, rivers, rocks, planets, and billiard balls amongst them—each main kind exercising a different mode of causality. Or, we might say, each main kind 'causes' or 'is an agent' and 'acts' in a different way, to be judged of according to different criteria, just as people, rivers, and rocks are 'substances' or 'things' each in a different way, not conformable to any single proper definition. In the primary sense of the verb "cause", causing is a genus which includes cases of pushing, kicking and carrying (making to move), heating and wetting (causing to be hotter or wetter), etc.; and it is only in a secondary use of the verb "cause" that it expresses a relation between states and events, a relation primarily expressed using sentential connectives such as "because".

It is a huge mistake to suppose that we should only use the word "agent" of persons and animals. If people push things to make them move, so also billiard balls push other billiard balls with this effect. It is because bodily things as such act and have the capacity to act

---

[3]E.g., an event does not break my leg, although it may explain why I broke my leg. If there was an agent that broke my leg it would be something like an axe or a man using an axe.

causally, independently of whether or not they are animate, that we need the conception of different modes of causal action, not reserving the notion of agent to animals, let alone just to persons.[4]

The recognition of bodies as agents is part of the core of the concept of body itself, also shaping one aspect of our concept of space. The very concept of a body as occupying a volume and having boundaries depends upon an appreciation of types of relation involving causal interaction at these boundaries, an interaction involving being acted upon at these boundaries ('passion'), being pushed as well as pushing. Solidity, which is what differentiates bodies from more ethereal or purely visual occupants of space, involves the idea of some resistance and impermeability to some other comparable things at the surfaces of bodies. And without a concept of the surface of a body formed in this way we would not have the conception of the place of that body which we do have. Our conception of space as a field of causal interaction, and not just as a field of entities observed from a distance (observed as it were neutrally as to their powers of causal interaction), depends upon this appreciation of bodies as the subjects of such interaction. (Or, to take an example different from that of a body with an ordinarily defined volume and surface: we would not have the concept of something with electric charge apart from the conception of action by a thing at one place upon other things with electric charge at other places.)

But, once having re-grasped the concept of agency and realized again that it applies also to physical and inanimate agents, not only to people and animals, we need to avoid the converse mistake of thinking of physical agency as the only kind of agency. We have to recover the idea of human and animal agency as modes of causal action in their own right, and envisage a spread of 'modes' of causal action.

---

[4]People, animals, rivers, winds, and billiard balls are all agents, all subjects of active power. But there are differences among the cases. The concepts of person, animal, river, and wind, all imply a propensity to exercise active powers to move other things. But, although a billiard ball when stationary has some power to resist the motion of other balls, it has no power *qua* billiard ball to move other things, only *qua* billiard ball in motion relative to such other things—the concepts of river and wind imply motion relative to things presumed stationary apart from their action, but the concept of billiard ball does not imply this. By contrast, the active power of people and animals does not depend on being thus already in motion.

In order thus to see human agency as a mode of causal action, we have to restore a grasp of the unity of the human act. That is, we have to undo the effects of viewing it as an intention, a volition, or an act of trying in causal relation to a bodily movement. This dualistic way of viewing it is the result of an atomizing of human biography into supposed elements. Within any person's life there are many distinguishable aspects or facets—different facts or actualities between which 'because'-relations obtain as when we say 'he ran away because he was afraid and wanted to get away from the bull' or 'he hit me because he was angry' or 'he was afraid because he saw the bull' or 'he was angry because I had shown him up as a fool'. The mistake of the atomizer is to transmute these facts or actualities[5] into logically independent 'distinct existences' (to use Hume's famous phrase found in the tag 'there can be no logical connection between distinct existences'). The atomizer thus makes events, states, and processes into objects, and breaks human biography into separable elements.

We met the same mistake in the case of perception. There we had the person's knowledge of his or her own position and his or her looking about in advance of the perception and various patterns of behaviour (being able to touch the edge of a table or avoid knocking it over) after it, and the mistake of the atomizer in trying to make 'the perceptual experience' a discrete existence in between. In the case of action, we have a background of beliefs, desires, and intentions and as the upshot a bodily movement, and the atomizer tries to make a 'volition' or 'act of trying' into a discrete existence in between.

From the point of view of logical analysis, a parallel problem arises with emotions such as anger and fear, where we have the belief or experience presupposed by the emotion beforehand (e.g., that I have been insulted or that there is danger), the feeling of the emotion concerned and of other related emotions (desire to injure, desire to withdraw, distress, confusion . . .), and the tendencies to the behaviours realizing or expressing these emotions, there again a temptation is to make the feeling of fear or anger into a discrete state or event. No one doubts the existence of experiences, attempts or

---

[5] I use the phrase "facts or actualities" because events, states, and processes cannot be straightforwardly identified with facts, if by "fact" we mean just anything stated by a true proposition, and I use the term "actualities" as the most convenient blanket term to cover them. The importance of this will appear more clearly later, both in this chapter and in Chapter VI.

tryings to do things, feelings of various emotions, and of sensations. The mistake is to require them to be each, and the behaviour associated with them, a 'logically distinct existence'. Emotion and sensation are not discrete atoms within the life of an inner psyche or brain exercising only external causal effects on the public world. Rather, alongside intentional action, they can only be understood as facets integrated together within the life of a complete human being, bodily and animal, as we shall illustrate in Section 3.

But first let us consider the nature of intentional action.

1. The Unitary Character of Intentional Action

Intentional action does not at all consist in a bodily movement proceding from a previous mental act. Indeed, I may come into some unexpected situation, and just act, without having had the previous intention or desire so to act, and without formulating any decision to myself; I don't first observe a 'volition', whatever that might be, and then observe the action; rather, what happens in such a case is just that I act and am conscious of the action precisely as being done intentionally; e.g., I know why I did it, and that it was not, for example, like an involuntary twitch or spasm.

Suppose that acting intentionally did involve a volition, or act of will, to act in that way. This would not be a matter of my having previously intended or decided to act in this way, nor of my now saying to myself "I will do this, and do it now", but of my putting this decision into effect, or making it operative. Suppose that I am aware of having some previous settled intention to do a certain thing now—or aware of having made or of now making some conscious decision to do this and do it now—so that the thing is, as it were, formulated in my mind, there are still three possibilities:

(i) I may act in accord with my intention or decision, and do this intentionally (in this case the supposed volition would have taken place),

(ii) I may fail to act because I find suddenly that, for some mysterious reason, I am unable to move my legs or arms or other parts of my body in the requisite way (in this case again it would be supposed that some mental act of volition had taken place),

(iii) I may fail to act in accord with my intention or decision because I changed my mind or because in the event I was unwilling to do the thing (in this case, it would be supposed that the volition supposedly present in the previous two cases was absent).

But now, it is not that I experienced something special, something called a volition, in the first two cases, but not in the third; so far as introspectible feelings are concerned, the mind may seem empty in all the cases; but that in the first case I am conscious of the action as resulting from or issuing from my state of intending, or my decision; while in the second case, I am conscious of the failure of this action to take place as being the result of things outside my power, and not the result or issue of anything in the sphere of intention, decision, and such-like; while in the third case I am conscious of the absence of the action as having been the result of a change of mind or of an unwillingness to act. So the supposed 'volition' seems to be, if anything, a theoretical entity rather than something I am conscious of or experience.

That is, while there is a mental aspect to intentional bodily action, this is not known by means of an introspection of inner events by themselves, and nothing has suggested that it consists in anything 'purely' mental or 'inner'. Rather, the knowledge of it is inseparable from, and internal to, the knowledge we have of our bodily actions. For it to be 'intentional' or 'voluntary' is for it to be a human or animal action in the sense paradigm for human beings and animals, and for certain kinds of 'because' statement to be true in respect of it. We will deal more fully with the way this presumption of normality or paradigm character works later on.

What we are occupied in is the analysis of what lawyers call *mens rea*. In brief, we might say that, in their action, agents are minded to do what they do and, inseparably from this, that they 'attempt' to do what it is in their minds to do. Inseparably from these, there would be also a knowledge of what they are doing, and that they are doing it in those respects in which it is intentional: it is this knowledge which people have of what they are doing simply in virtue of the fact that they are doing it intentionally that I call 'practical knowledge'.

In the normal case, these facts or actualities are all distinct aspects of the total situation and there is no compulsion to regard them as distinct contingently related elements within it which together with the bodily movements involved 'compose' it. If we want to insist that they are not just 'facts' or 'truths', but events, states or goings-on in the world (we might call them 'actualities'), we must still insist that the primary way of referring to them is by sentential expressions, not noun ones, and that they are like statements in being aspectual in character, and not 'objects'. The actualities are not less real for that, inasmuch as reality is comprised of them, but reality is a seamless web within which the actualities (events, states, etc.) which interweave are not discrete each from all others.[6]

The tendency to view actions and 'willed events' as objects distorts the consideration of the nature of practical knowledge. For it is a mistake to think of what I know in knowing what I am doing in the act of doing it as an object, e.g., an object called an event or an action. If it was an object it would have to stand as a goal not yet existing, any direct knowledge of which could only be an occult knowledge of something future,[7] or else as something already past to be known by observation. Nor is it propositional knowledge, e.g., that a certain event or action will occur or has occurred.

Rather, practical knowledge is a knowledge arising from familiarity with one's own past and present dispositions and actions. It does not fit with either of these other ways of thinking but perfectly exemplifies the need to consider the different facets of human biography as interwoven and interdependent, and not in any way discrete, logically independent existences.

For, in order to understand practical knowledge and the kind of familiarity it exemplifies, we need to bring into play analogies and connections with knowing how to do things, or knowing the position of objects round about one, e.g., the sort of knowledge of where a table is which is exercised in touching the edge of it or walking round it. These analogies and connections are apparent from the inseparability of the practical knowing of an action from, on the one hand, prior states of intention and prior stages in the practical knowing of the action up to the stage to which it has reached and, on the other hand, behavioural aptitudes appropriate to that stage. It

---

[6]For events and states to be subjects of discourse in regard to which some questions of identity arise in the way explained in Chapter VI is not at all for them to be 'objects' in any metaphysical sense. Events and states have metaphysical status but only as actualities, not objects, cf. David Braine, *The Reality of Time and the Existence of God*, pp. 149–161, and, although, if God exists, His existence is discrete, all other actualities interweave.

[7]Cf. Brian O'Shaughnessy, in *The Will*, Vol. I, where he objects to the idea of the agent as in immediate contact with the effect he or she wills (p. 120), and objects to the idea of an occult knowing of the effect arising from such immediate contact (p. 99).

is also inseparable from the relevant knowledge of one's own body, e.g., the position and power of one's limbs,[8] the knowledge which one has to have in order to use it in physical action,[9] but which is no more propositional than one's knowledge of the position of objects round about one.

In the cases of success, failure, and illusion, we have different global situations. All these are the same in certain respects and different in others, and for this reason the same temptation arises as arose in the case of perception. There we found that two experiences can be similar or even the same in a certain respect, and there we found that the right way of thinking was not to suppose that the similarities arose from common elements in a composite in a situation composed of elements and the differences from differences in the elements present, but simply from its being the case that certain things can be said in all the similar cases (literally or by analogy) but not all. A hallucination is like a veridical experience in that certain things are said in both cases and unlike it in that certain things are not said in both cases.

In the case of action we have the same tendency to mythologize, in this case creating a mythology not of 'perceptual experiences' but of 'intentions to act now', 'acts of trying', and 'experiences of acting'. It is not, of course, that it is not *true* in the case of an intentional action that the person 'intends to act now', 'tries', and 'has an experience as if of acting', but that the intentional action is not *composed* of these together with bodily movements.

Let us get a grasp of the problems which result from regarding intentional action as a composite thing, *made up of* 'intentions to act now',[10] tryings to act, experiences as if of acting, and bodily movements in sundry causal relations. Consider the case of the intentional action wherein I leap into a swimming pool.

Let us consider the intention first. On the face of it, it would seem that I can intend to leap now but in fact just hesitate a bit longer. But this is not the main problem as to how the arrival of an intention

---

[8]This also is a knowledge that one has without observation, as is made clear by G.E.M. Anscombe, *Intention*, pp. 13–14.

[9]This knowing of one's own body is presupposed both to action and to trying. But the behaviour exhibited in action and in trying to act are criterial for its presence.

[10]O'Shaughnessy, *The Will*, Vol. II, p. 263, 266–267, cf. 330–344.

to act now can make my acting when it occurs intentional. The deeper problem is that an intention, even an intention to act now, is directed towards a sort of action at a time which is not identified retrospectively as 'when the act happened' but prospectively in terms of some general concept such as 'when the seconds hand of the swimming pool clock reaches the 12 o'clock position' or 'the immediate future'. That is, no intention was directed towards the historical act of which we know later that it did occur and which was performed intentionally, but only to a goal conceived of as a 'possible' within my power.

The problem is the obverse of the problem we met with in the case of visual perception.

The mystery in that case lay in the problem as to how experiences conceived of as orientated towards objects identified to the mind indifferently to whether or not they were actual could be married to behavioural aptitudes orientated around actual objects *qua* actual.[11] That is, once the experiencing is conceived of as directed towards 'mental' or 'intentional' objects or 'possibles' rather than as such towards real objects, it has become out of joint with the behavioural aptitudes which we normally associate with perception, e.g., in the case of knowing the position of the table, being ready to look in the right direction in order to see it (this will involve appropriate head movements) or being able to touch its edge or avoid walking into it.

Once having thus disjoined the mental and the behavioural, the philosopher's only remedy was to paste them together with the glue of causation, making out that by some magic of metaphysical or brain technology a model in the mind's eye is kept in correspondence with the conduct of behaviour. In place of this in Chapter II we sought to restore the primordial Gestalt of an experiencing whose objects are the same as the objects around which relevant behavioural aptitudes are orientated, and which is not discrete from these aptitudes. In this way we restored the conception of a direct cognitive relation with the world.

---

[11] In the case of vision, we were confronted with the problem of the relation between, on the one hand, supposed havings of visual experiences which were as if of certain objects (characterized according to certain descriptions, identified without the implication of existence, and in this sense as 'possibles') and, on the other hand, a system of behavioural aptitudes orientated around various actual objects in the physical world.

Now, in the case of intentional action, we are confronted with a quite parallel disjoining of a mental aspect or element, variously described as an 'intention-now' or a 'trying', directed towards an object conceived of abstractly or in a way not involving its existence, that is conceived of as a goal or 'possible', from behaviour which is supposed to result causally from this mental element—so that again we have a pasting together of a mental state directed towards an object in the mind's eye with what occurs in history, the bodily movement or willed event involving actual objects, again with the glue of causation. And again what we have to do is to restore the original human conception of intentional behaviour, a conception which makes being intentional internal to the kind of action concerned, not something causally prior to it.

Thus, the first main obstacle to the dualistic atomizing which transmuted the different aspects of intentional action into 'logically distinct existences' lies in the chasm it creates between the objects of any 'intention to act now' or trying and the focuses of the bodily movement concerned. I turn now to the second obstacle, its awkwardness in treating what I have called practical knowledge.

The appearance of the case is that, when I do something intentionally, I *ipso facto* know what I am doing and that I am doing it, so that this knowledge does not wait upon observation after the event. Nor does my knowledge of what I did and that I did it, as I have this knowledge in memory later, need to derive from observation after the event. And the situation is striking in another respect, namely that, in this kind of knowledge, it is not just that I know of something in the physical world and that I separately know of mental states or facts which are *de facto* associated with it, but I know the first as because of the second. It should be quite unsurprising that, in this *ipso facto* knowing of a certain happening (namely my action), I also know that it is happening because I intended it—but what it involves flies in the face of common models of the sort which contrast and separate our knowledge of the 'inner' and our knowledge of the 'outer'.

The appearance of absurdity in separating the knowledge we have of the conscious bodily movement concerned and the knowledge we have of the mental state in question arises not only in the case of intentional action but also in the case of all the conscious bodily movements expressive of emotions and sensations. Just as there is strangeness in separating my knowledge of my action from my knowledge of it as intentional, so there is strangeness in separating my knowledge of my groaning from my knowledge of it as groaning from pain.

In considering cases of my acting intentionally, my doing something because I wanted to, or my groaning with pain, or quivering with anger, it is useless for the materialists or dualists merely to internalize the intention, the wanting, the pain, or the anger. They need to deal with the whole of the conscious or mental element in these events, and this involves dealing with my consciousness of the act as being the result of the intention (or want), of the groan as being the result of the pain, of my bodily excitement as being because of my anger. It is not just that I have a special introspectively distinguished feeling called a want or an intention or pain, and that then (as it happens) I observe that this is followed by a bodily action or a groan, and that, since I have often observed that such feelings are followed by such bodily movements, I infer that the feelings must be the cause of the bodily movements. On the contrary, I am aware of the bodily movements precisely as being out of intention or out of pain.

The problem is that, not only in the case of intentional action, but also in the other cases mentioned, it is not just that we have a non-observational knowledge of mental aspects of the phenomena in question and some non-observational knowledge of their physical aspects, but that we have a non-observational knowledge of the second as being because of the first. That is, the phenomena themselves make it awkward to deny the presence of some immediate, non-inductive knowledge of causal or quasi-causal connection in cases of these types.[12]

We have already remarked[13] on how modern authors who keep to the dualistic pattern of analysis of action deal with the problem here, namely by bringing in their 'causal theory of knowledge' whereby all knowledge consists in a causal generation of beliefs in settings which are such as to make it usual that beliefs thus generated will be true. In the case of intentional action the knowledge of what one is doing and that one is doing it is supposed to be caused by the 'intention to act now' combined with the belief that the conditions of action are normal. The ordinary person confronted with this analysis would say

---

[12]There is nothing new in this: Berkeley refers to knowledge of one's own causal agency in a non-inductive way (cf. Hume's attempted reply in his first Enquiry).

[13]Chapter I above, end of Section 4.

that it represented agents as being in a position of believing that they were doing such and such, rather than of directly knowing it. But, of course, on the causal theory of knowledge no one directly knows anything or is familiar with anything. All that happens in regard to any kind of knowledge is that people get things right and there is a cause for their getting things right: their beliefs are reliable, but they never have any reason for reckoning that they will be since there is no kind of state or event, inner or outer, with which they are directly familiar; people think all the appropriate thoughts, have the whole conceptual framework of 'the common sense view of the world', but without direct cognitive linkage with the world.[14]

This internality of intention to the intentional action has sometimes been expressed by saying that the being intentional is adverbial to the action concerned. And this might be regarded as a particular case of the action concerned being done 'appetitively', with the type of appetition characteristic of the higher animals and human beings—and, by an extension of the normal application of the word "trying", the modern writer might describe it as the particular case in which the category of action concerned is the category of actions done 'tryingly' (unlike the actions of plants and inanimate things). There is a logical parallel here with seeing: all seeing is, one might say, a seeing lookingly. That is, one cannot see without there being a looking as it were within the act of seeing, and it is by this looking that one sees. There is no place for a theory which makes this looking, which is internal to seeing, into something external and causally prior to it, and similarly there is no place for a theory which makes trying into something external and causally prior to action.

This parallelism with the case of looking offers a lesson. Because the bodily movement may be described piecemeal in its physical aspects without bringing in reference to a supposed trying or to intention, one is tempted to erect this 'trying' which is only one facet of a single unity (the intentional action itself) into a distinct event or part-event—in regard to which one may then later raise the question as to whether it is identical with some going on in the brain. Yet

---

[14]I reject this analysis, not only because it conflicts with our ordinary understanding of intentional action, but also because it renders coherent understanding of perception impossible.

the fact that this is indeed a mere temptation, a move in thought to be resisted, is shown by considering the parallel case of looking. We can oscillate when we speak of 'an action' between referring to the intentional action as a whole and referring to the bodily movement involved in abstraction from its intentional context; as a result, we easily pass to thinking of the action as the outer element of a whole of which trying would be the inner part. But there is no parallel way of coming to think of the perception in seeing as the outer part of something of which looking would be the inner part. However, the difference only arises from the ready abstractability of the bodily movement in the case of action: it does not arise from 'trying' being any better established as a separate reality than 'looking'—it is not, but rather we are aware of each of them as aspects respectively of our acting and our seeing, and neither is discrete.

By regarding that which makes the action intentional as internal to it, rather than causally prior, we make its being intentional into a matter of the *mode* of causality being exercised. This will be a mode of causality distinct from the physical agency exercised by inanimate objects such as billiard balls, and peculiar to animals and human beings. This point of view is sometimes expressed by saying that in acting intentionally the being intentional is adverbial to the acting. This way of expressing what is involved tends to meet with the trite objection that "intentionally" is not an adverb of manner like "clumsily" or "slowly".[15] But this objection merely misconstrues the role of the adverb.

The point being made is simple: acting causally[16] is no more one sort of thing than existing, living, or knowing. In each case, we have an unparaphrasable primitive term which is used analogously in different cases. Animal living and plant living are not two manners of doing one thing, but two modes of living. Knowing that and knowing by sensory acquaintance are not two manners of doing one thing, but two modes of knowing. But neither the word "living"

---

[15]Donald Davidson, *Essays on Actions and Events*, p. 121 f., and O'Shaughnessy, *The Will*, II, pp. 46–48.

[16]One might say that all action, whether on the part of animate or of inanimate beings, is an 'acting causally', but there is a useful distinction in philosophical tradition between immanent acts such as knowing and loving and *transeunt* acts in which the acting is a causing.

nor the word "knowing" is used equivocally as if different words or paraphrases would serve equally well. Likewise, there is not one way of being a concrete thing or substance, shared equally by planets, stones, ions, bacteria, plants, animals, and persons, but different ways—not different manners distinguished accidentally, but ways of being concrete, and, what is pertinent here, ways distinguished according to the different modes of acting of the substances concerned and their different logical types of relation towards other things.

Each kind of causal action has its own unity. The kind we have been especially concerned with is that of human and animal action. When Smith punches Brown upon the nose, this is a paradigm case of human action, voluntary and intentional, constituting a unity in itself. It is not voluntary because it possesses a special introspectible quality called 'voluntariness', as if being voluntary were something private, and not because it proceeds from some previous inner action of 'trying' or 'undertaking'. Rather it is voluntary in itself because of the way it proceeds from its subject, a way shown by the grammatical character of the predication in the cases concerned: this grammatical character might be marked by linguists by saying that such predications are causative. Causativity is internal to the sense of the verb phrase in such predications at an even deeper level than aspect and tense. What is embraced within the action, the kind of unity it has, is characteristic of the mode of action concerned. This mode is not a matter of variation in external relation between action and subject, but a matter of the kind of predication involved, the kind of causativity indicated by grammar and context.[17]

Unless people have been trained in special techniques, such as those which yoga or biomedical feedback make possible, they do not have direct control over their muscles. I do not choose to contract my muscles and thereby, as an effect, bring about the clenching of my fist. Rather, if I wish to contract the relevant muscles in the relevant way,

---

[17]I note that the notion of the 'voluntary' (using the word to identify a particular mode of causal action), just like the notion of causal action in general (causal or *transeunt* action being contrasted with immanent action), belongs to logical grammar, i.e., is a grammatical notion in Wittgenstein's sense, belonging to semantics rather than to syntactics in a formal linguist's sense. Such notions cannot be defined in purely formal syntactic terms, but the need within syntactic theory to mark certain distinctions by terms such as causativity, which are only explicable in semantic terms, i.e., in these cases precisely in terms of these semantic notions from so-called 'logical grammar', is a mark of the indispensability of this kind of notion.

I bring this about by deliberately clenching my fist.[18] Someone may say that people clench their fists by contracting their muscles, but they do not mean that what they primarily intend is to contract their muscles and that their plan is to use this as a means to clench their fist. The intentional bodily action of human beings and persons is a unitary whole within which the effect which defines the action, e.g., that which has the social significance of clenching the fist, comes about by means of the contraction of relevant muscles: this is the way nature works. But the whole, that is the intentional bodily action considered as such, is not caused by the contraction of muscles:[19] this is in no way a cause of the intending internal to the whole being considered, but is only an element in the overall functioning of the human being or animal as such in the type of case concerned.

These remarks may serve to highlight what is involved in considering a human action, and, more generally, an animal action, as a unity. The action is not to be identified with the outward physical movement, as if this, the action, might be caused by something in the muscles, and this by something in the nerves, and this by something in the brain, and this perhaps by something in the soul. Rather the action is a whole which proceeds, not from the brain or from the soul, but from the person, human being or animal.

Note on the privilege of the normal case in the description of action

In the case of perception, there was a normal or paradigm case from which there were many discrepant modes of deviation, some involving defect and some not. The case of action presents a parallel structure. Again there is no kernel common to all cases from which the others are differentiated by different additional features.

Thus, one set of kinds of deviation is represented in the cases where the action does not occur so that we speak of trying and such like, but for reasons we began to see above it is quite wrong to think of 'trying' as

---

[18]In this sense, I do contract my muscles by clenching my fist, contrary to the opinion of Jennifer Hornsby, *Actions*, p. 94.

[19]In this way, it is wrong to say that I clench my fist by contracting my muscles, if one means by this that the contracting is the cause of the action of clenching, although it is the cause of clenching as a physical effect (as in *rigor mortis*) as opposed to as an action. Contrast Hornsby, *Actions*, p. 94.

a kernel element shared by cases in which the intended action is done as intended and cases in which the action does not occur.[20] Rather, as we shall see in Section 2, tryings are to be conceived only as incomplete or incipient actions, not as primary elements from which action proceeds, and the way we describe tryings is shaped by the way we describe actions.

Another spread of kinds of deviation from the paradigm case is represented in the cases where some 'action' does occur and is for a variety of reasons 'not free', 'not intentional', or 'involuntary'. Here again the different kinds of case are described according to their different ways of deviating from the paradigm, not according to supposed additional features they exhibit on top of some kernel.

However, this second class of case requires some further remark because of the common presumption that the word "action" and attributions of action do not in themselves imply intention or refer to some whole which includes whatever makes the action intentional. This presumption is quite erroneous. The ungilded statements that someone was walking along a road or that one saw him or her walking, or that he or she was speaking or that one heard him or her speaking, imply intention, and it is only special contexts of utterance which provide the gilding necessary to remove such implication.

In general, as we remarked earlier, for an action to be 'intentional' (or in Aristotle's or Ryle's terms 'voluntary') is for it to be a human or animal action in the paradigm sense, the sense which does not require further qualification because it is not defective or incomplete in any way which requires to be noted. In the human case, it is to be what we might regard as a properly 'human action' and not just an 'act of a human being'.[21]

---

[20]The position I am explaining in regard to action is comparable with the Aristotelian position in regard to moral virtue. In Aristotelian ethics, moral virtue is described in terms implying achievement, i.e., in terms wherein action and emotion in accord with disposition are included without separating disposition from its exercise, not in terms of intention, will, or disposition alone. Analogously, I regard the paradigm of human action, the paradigm presumed in the absence of counter-indications, as one which implies the following of achievement upon intention (achievement following according to plan, and not accidentally). And, if we speak of acts of will or volitions at all, these should likewise be described in terms implying achievement—so that trying is as much a deviant case of an act of will as goodwill without action is a deviant case of virtue.

[21]We may trace this way of thinking in Aquinas, for instance, when he contrasts the workings of (e.g.) the digestive system (indeed still realizations of aspects of human nature) with 'human acts'. A key reference is *Commentary on the Nic. Eth.*, Book 1, Lectio 1; other relevant passages include *S. Th.* Ia IIae, Q. 17, Art. 8, ad 2, and *Q. D. De An.*, Art. 11 and Art. 13, resp. and ad 14.

In regard to each kind of agent, a certain kind of action is characteristic. In the human case, the presumption is that the action will be 'free', 'deliberate', 'intentional', 'voluntary' and not in varied ways 'unfree', 'unintentional', 'not intended', 'involuntary', 'by accident', 'by mistake',[22] each positive term importing a certain somewhat different range of contrasts—so that, somewhat as Hart would have it, in this echoing Austin's understanding, the positive terms enshrine 'defeasible' concepts,[23] and it is the negative terms which in one way 'wear the trousers,' as Austin put it.[24] In the case of human action, the paradigm case is that of an acting for reasons, the reasons 'why' the action was done being such as would have appeared in a deliberation beforehand as reasons why the action should be done. In the case of higher animals lower than the human, the presumption will be that the action is 'intentional' and 'voluntary' in a somewhat weaker sense, but the same type of structure will be present.

When we speak of human beings, e.g., in general propositions with such subject-terms as "man", "woman", "artist", "cobbler", "politician", "judge", "player", and so forth, or in singular propositions with such subject-terms as "Napoleon", "Catherine the Great", "the man who assassinated the Duke of Buckingham", "the next man in the queue", "the boy who painted that rude picture", "the painter we employed last year", and so forth, we presuppose the applicability to them, not just of the predicates applicable to bodily things in general (relating, for instance, to position, size, and weight), but also of personal predicates.

When we attribute action to such subjects, spoken of with these pre-suppositions, in the typical case the action-predicate will have a paradigm use in which it is implied that the action was what we referred to earlier as a properly or fully human action, not just an 'act of a human being'.

Just as in the case of perception there were cases of non-defective perception which departed from the paradigm, so in the case of action there are cases which depart from the paradigm without any defect being implied. For instance, people laugh (which is voluntary, at least to some extent, in

---

[22]Austin, in 'A Plea for Excuses', *Philosophical Papers*, on the contrast between 'accidental' and 'by chance'.

[23]H.L.A. Hart, 'The Ascription of Responsibility and Rights'. To imply like him that such words as "true", "full", and "voluntary" have no positive sense is misleading: the point is that they imply that the term they are used to qualify, e.g. "action", is used in the full unrestricted sense characteristic of the type of agent involved rather than differentiating a supposed wider genus of 'actions'.

[24]Austin, *Sense and Sensibilia*, VII, esp. p. 70.

that commonly people can control themselves and avoid laughing), breathe
(which is voluntary to a more limited extent, since there are limits to how
long one can hold one's breath), and sit (which is, in a certain sense, a case
of non-activity).

The lack of deliberation in the case of anger, and the interference with
it in the case of sensible desire, produce other structures of deviation from the
paradigm, generating features of which some have been already instanced and
some not. But the fullness of human 'freedom' in respect of an action has
many other aspects of which phrases like 'slavery to ideology' and 'slavery
to the passions' remind us. And many human actions, although not trivial
in the sense that scratching one's ear is trivial (not involving intentions or
motives at all, although not unconscious or unintentional or involuntary),
are nonetheless slight, not engaging the 'heart': the man or woman is not
'fully' *involved*, as people say, in them, or, although they are the fruit of
deliberation, this deliberation has not reached back to or does not express
the person's whole 'heart', value-system or perspective upon life.[25]

Each of these classes of case introduce deviations from the paradigm
case of 'doing' in structurally different ways. But in each of these types of case,
we certainly will not say that the person did not do the action concerned,

---

[25]The realization of this is reflected in the ideas of 'incontinence' (in Aristotle's
sense) and of 'venial' sin.

It seems that for Aristotle, if one acts from weakness of will, it is as if one has
two contrary principles in one's mind and desire has made one's grasp and assent to
one of them, even though it be the principle more rooted in one's choice, merely
notional or verbal like the words of Empedocles cited by a drunk.

As to venial sin, Aquinas takes it that human beings in a state of grace refer
themselves and all that they have to God habitually, i.e., in the virtue of 'charity';
what happens in venial sin is that actual reference of the particular human act to
God is omitted, but without destroying the habitual reference to God (*S. Th.* Ia IIae,
Q. 88, Art. 1, ad 2). This can arise because the human mind, unlike the angelic mind,
can be subject to inordinateness in respect to the means without being subject to
inordinateness in respect to the end, i.e., it can be directed towards 'means' otherwise
than according to the way they stand under their order towards 'the end' (*S. Th.* Ia
IIae, Q. 89, Art. 4, resp.). It is evident that Aquinas is here conceiving 'the end', not
as one of the ends commonly named in particular limited pieces of deliberation, but
as the general end, perfect good or structure of happiness towards which a human
life with its whole network of habits in deliberation is orientated, i.e. in the way he
conceives 'the end' in considering happiness in *S. Th.* Ia IIae, Q. 1, Arts. 5–7. In
respect of this 'ultimate end', Aquinas says 'the force of the first intention, which is in
view of the ultimate end, remains in the desiring of anything even though one is not
actually considering the ultimate end, just as when going somewhere we do not have
to think of the end at every step' (Q. 1, Art. 6, ad 3).

even if in a certain sense the action lacked the completeness as an action which actions can have so that the agent was less completely 'behind' his or her action than agents can be.

By contrast, just as in the case of perception, there are cases in which defect enters in, and these are again of quite disparate kinds.

In the case when I do something 'by mistake', there is something determinate which I do which I do intentionally, e.g., I intend to turn the left hand tap on and I do turn the left hand tap on, mistakenly thinking that it is the hot tap, but I turn on the cold tap which the left one happens to be. In the case when I do something 'by accident', there is nothing determinate which I do which I do intentionally: e.g., I meant to turn the left tap on rightly thinking that it was the hot tap, but in abstraction of mind turned on the right tap, the cold one. The case of doing something 'by accident' is a more defective case of action than that of doing something 'by mistake', but still in either case I did intend to turn some tap on, although in neither was it a case of intending to turn on some tap or other, no matter which: so both cases were defective ones.

In the case when I am pushed against a table and the table falls, or when I am drunk and fall against the table and again it falls, again I knock the table over by accident, and in a certain sense it is something I do, but in another sense, whereas turning the tap on was certainly something I did, and even turning the cold tap on, in these other cases one is able to say that 'knocking the table over' was not something I did at all. In both cases 'it happened' although, in the case when I was drunk, one could not say 'it just happened' since I was in a way responsible, and, if I was deliberately pushed, then again one could not say 'it just happened' because in a stronger sense someone else was responsible, whether or not he intended such a dramatic effect. In the extreme case, when I fall through gravity alone, the only sense in which 'I do' what happens is that the event can be described using a verb in the active mood predicated of me as subject. Likewise, if I give an involuntary twitch, the same seems to be true.

Quite a different dimension of deviation from the paradigms of 'a person's doing so and so' are provided by cases where everything 'directly' intended is done as intended, and the question arises of the 'doing' of (e.g.) things which are foreknown consequences of what is 'aimedly' done (as when food-servers in armaments factories are killed in the bombing of the factories), some reluctantly and some not, or things which are likely, 'natural' or anticipable consequences of this; and here the question is made more complex by the fact that, in some cases, the foreknowledge or the likelihood depends on the knowledge and fixedness of other people's wills, so that evils which follow would seem to be their responsibility, rather than that of the initial agent; and yet again we make distinctions between foreknown consequences which, although no part of the aim and even abhorred by the agent, will still count amongst things he 'did voluntarily' (e.g., Smith murders Jones for his money and thereby deprives Mrs Jones of her husband), and other foreknown consequences which we will not so describe. We are here in the area of 'what was not intended', although we hesitate to use this expression when we would still ascribe moral responsibility or where the consequence concerned is something not just 'consented to' but something in regard to which there is 'willingness' on the part of the doer.

The cases here overlap with cases when my action is 'not voluntary' and 'not free' for reasons which have nothing to do with defects in deliberation or psychosomatic disorder, but are so because they are done under duress although still with full knowledge. In these cases, it is not only the foreknown but unwanted consequences of my action, but also the very thing aimedly done of which I am not the ultimate author or the doer. But these are not cases of the involuntary, the unintentional, or even the 'not intended'.

Other dimensions of deviation from the normal case are provided by the case of 'the involuntary'. This can cover some of a wide range of types of example in which the procedures of deliberation are disturbed, whether by one of various kinds of ignorance or misinformation, or by one of various kinds of disorder or confusion of mind. But it can also cover cases where one would hardly say that there was deliberateness at all, or where there was clearly none and clearly no case for speaking of voluntariness or responsibility: I have in mind cases ranging from kleptomania to involuntary fidgets and twitches— an 'involuntary' twitch betrays less of human character and classifies less as a 'human action', than an 'involuntary' smile or shudder.

If, therefore, an action is attributed to a human being, there are thus many disparate reasons for denying or qualifying this claim, and these display the spread of significances in the use of the active mood of verbs in respect of human subjects, and the spread of logically differentiable 'uses' in related verbs like "do" and "act", reflected in the different implications of statements of such forms as "X laughed" or "X killed Y". These do not merely form a heterogenous heap but are unified by there being a certain paradigm of fully human action to which they are all structurally related in disparate ways. In so far as they deviate from the paradigm, some explanation of this deviation is appropriate; of cases that conform to the paradigm, no such explanation is needed.

2. The Attempt to Break Up the Holistic Picture

The conception which I am presenting is the conception of human intentional action as a unity or unitary whole with many aspects or facets. How, one may ask, does this natural way of thinking get subverted, so that each different aspect or facet is elevated into a separable element within a conglomerate of elements?

The first motivations for this atomization of action stem from within the philosophy of mind itself. It will turn out that the key arguments all involve making psychological states and events, not persons or animals, the causes of external voluntary action. The grand mistake here concerned, of substituting states and events for substances as causes, needs to be dealt with separately as a general question in logic and the philosophy of science, in no way local to the philosophy of mind: this I do in Chapter VI. But first we need to look at the arguments separating psychological and physical elements within action as these arise locally within the philosophy of mind itself. And the first of these turns out to be that all too familiar friend which we met in discussing perception, the argument from failure or illusion.

Thus we can be told: "One can simply and crudely be mistaken in thinking one is actively moving a limb that is there and then moving. This is a basic and enormously important point in the philosophy of action. It proves that in physical action there can be no such thing as an immediate experience of a causal nexus immediately linking internal phenomenon with its outer phenomenal object."[26] Again, with the same assurance, we are told that everything can be just the same experientially so that we are aware of the intention to act now and the trying both in the case when we succeed and in the case when we knowingly fail; and the same experientially so that we are aware of intending to act now, trying, and believing that we have succeeded both in the case when we do succeed and in the case when we unknowingly fail.[27]

From this it is inferred that there are events or states, intending to act now, trying, believing that we have succeeded, and moving bodily in the relevant ways which all occur in the case of non-accidental

---

[26] O'Shaughnessy, *The Will*, I, p. 116.
[27] *Op. cit.*, II, pp. 266–267.

success but which are, one or both of the last two, missing in the defective cases. So it is being presumed without argument that where different global situations arise, the difference will arise from the presence or absence of this or that component of the situation, rather than simply from certain things being true in all cases and certain other things not being true in some of them. The presence or absence of certain aspects of situations is being viewed as the presence or absence of certain discrete elements.

What one has to insist is that such an inference is simply quite unsubstantiated. It seems to rest upon the theory that such facets of situations as intending to act now and trying should be thought of as entities or objects which seems to be a carry-over from the ontologizing of events and states which I shall discuss in Chapter VI.

This first type of argument appealing to the cases of failure and illusion is sometimes supported by another, namely the theory that our method of distinguishing between the different global situations spoken of is by introspecting particular elements within, as it were, the psychological scene. A trying, for instance, we are told, is an event distinguished by a particular introspectible quality called voluntariness.[28] In this way, we find a modern revival of the view of Hume according to whom 'by the will, I mean nothing but the internal impression we feel and are conscious of, when we knowingly give rise to [or, in Geach's gloss, not 'on occasions immediately preceding'][29] any new motion of the body, or new perception of the mind'.

But in our review of the three main types of situation which need to be distinguished, the paradigm case of action according to intention, the case of failure in action whether or not I am aware of failure, and the case in which action does not occur because of

---

[28] *Op. cit.*, II, pp. 250–251. For O'Shaughnessy being voluntary marks out a genus of psychological event and he insists that this is quite different from the case of a sensation, where the quality which is supposedly introspected does not distinguish the genus (sensation) but only the species (e.g., pain). Of course, to those who, for reasons in the theory of meaning made vivid by the problem of other minds, object to introspection as a means of getting at the quality of anything mental, it matters not a whit whether the supposed introspectible *quale* is one which defines a genus or one which differentiates a species.

[29] *Three Philosophers*, p. 107.

a change of mind or unwillingness to do the thing concerned, we showed that the most natural way of viewing the position did not turn upon the introspection of a special event (perhaps called a 'trying') in the paradigm case. Rather, each type of situation is known globally, and in our awareness of it different aspects are picked out—notably we know the paradigm case itself as a whole, as an intentional action, and are not aware of its being intentional or (except where difficulty has entered in) of its being a case of trying separately from knowing it unitarily as an intentional action. Accordingly, the theory which explains our knowledge of what is common to the paradigm case and the case of unintended non-action in terms of the introspection of a distinct element does not seem right—besides that it engenders all the difficulties in the theory of meaning which we mentioned in Chapter I in connection with the problem of how we know other minds, the difficulties we deal with in Chapter V.

However, the root attractiveness of the atomistic conception for contemporary thinking lies in the consideration that there must exist such discrete entities as these supposed 'tryings', 'willings', or 'undertakings', in order to correspond with or be identical to brain processes, on the presumption that the roots of our actions are inner, either simply in the brain itself, or in a soul acting through the brain. The preoccupation with the possibility of identifying an introspectively known 'event of willing' or 'act of will' with an inner brain event pervades the discussion, e.g., when it is said of the supposed 'event of willing' that it 'spreads developmentally out from the brain' so as to 'encompass' the physical bodily movement willed.[30] Thus, even in the context of a discussion aimed at exhibiting the action as a unity, we find that 'the event of willing' is said to 'causally develop so as to bring' the physical bodily movement 'into being', and that a 'part event of striving precedes and causes' this physical movement.[31] And it would seem that the main design of recent authors dealing with action has been to open the way to a causal theory of action parallel

---

[30] *Op. cit.*, II, p. 286.

[31] *Ibid*. On p. 287, repeating the message of p. 259, O'Shaughnessy tells us that in all voluntary acts the event of the physical bodily movement is preceded by an event e/v, which is psychological, of the sort 'act of will', and suitably causes the physical bodily movement.

to Grice's causal theory of perception, and to do this with an eye to the possibility of conceiving mental or psychological states as being realized in the brain.[32]

Let us see what is wrong with the way of thinking of trying which is here involved.

Just as a perceptual experience (that which makes one of Grice's sense-datum statements true) is supposed to be that which is in common between cases of veridical perception and non-veridical cases, so a 'trying' is postulated as something which is the same both in cases in which action is carried through to completion in the normal way and in cases of failure or non-action. It is regarded as essential to the mental or psychological that it should show 'intentionality', containing no guarantee of its object; we refuted this conception of the intentionality of the psychological in Chapter II, and what we find here is the extension of the same false conception from 'experiences' to 'tryings'.[33]

This parallelism between 'experiences' and 'tryings' suggests lines of criticism of contemporary conceptions of 'trying' parallel to our earlier criticisms of the conception of 'experiences'. When we are confronted with statements of such forms as "x seems to perceive y", "it looks to x as if y", or "x has a perceptual experience as of y", the first line of objection commonly tried is to say that such reserved statements are only made in, and imply that one is dealing with, an already problematic case, doubtfully veridical or definitely non-veridical. Similarly, it is implied that the word trying implies some difficulty, a success not yet complete, or a failure. In the case of 'experiences' this objection was unsound: as followers of Grice would point out, what we have is a suggestion rather than an implication, and it is unsound in the same way in the case of 'trying'.

This suggests that the more appropriate objections would be: (a) that, as the description of the looking is determined by and parasitic upon the modes of description of the seeing, so the description of the trying is adapted to the description of successful action; and (b) that, cases of success being the norm, the ways of deviating from a normal

---

[32]Note O'Shaughnessy, *op. cit.*, pp. 224–225. Hornsby and Searle fit the same picture.
[33]*Op. cit.*, pp. 351 ff.

case are varied so that there is no one idiom especially calculated to capture what is shared by the normal case and an abnormal case in each and every case of the abnormal.

It also suggests a much deeper line of complaint, presumed in the way of conceiving 'perceptual experiences' and 'acts of trying' in the first place. We are supposed to understand these things which have been thus picked out as including the whole experiential content of the act of perceiving and of the intentional acting respectively. And to this we must make a parallel response in both cases. In the case of perception what is experienced cannot be limited to a sensory impression isolated either from what led up to it or from the behaviour or behavioural attitudes which flowed from it. So, likewise, what is experienced in acting cannot be separated or conceptually isolated from the life-setting of the action, including its place in the working out of our intentions and our familiarity with the posture and our powers of our own body, it also cannot be separated from the normal kinaesthetic feedback during the action. We have to realize that kinaesthetic feedback does not serve by providing discrete psychological experiences, sensory information to be synthesized with other information as to intentions and the supposed tryings—rather it comes within the context which action gives it and is experienced according to the way it fits into this context.

On the supposition that the cases of experiencing and trying are indeed analogous in the way supposed in the approach being considered in which the phenomena of failure and illusion are treated in the same way in the two cases, then these objections do indeed hold.

However, it is in fact a mistake to treat these cases as thus analogous. Knowing, seeing, and judging are in the knower, the see-er, and judger, rather than in the object known, seen, or judged about. Modulations in how things look are modulations in how things are seen and modulations in how things seem are modulations in assessment of the judgements warranted by perception. So both still relate to the cognitive and judgemental position of the see-er or experiencer. The principles according to which cases of trying are grouped together are quite different, being governed by considerations of relation to the action projected, not of relation to the cognitive and judgemental position of the subject. If we think of perceiving and experiencing as in the subject, not in the arena known, we should think of trying as, like action, in the arena of action and in this sense outer to the deliberating and experiencing subject.

What trying consists in is different in different cases. If I crouch poised at the top of the ski run, and hesitate for lack of confidence, what is the difference between the times I flex all the relevant muscles and seem to be about to go but don't, and the time when at last I go? I make to go but do not go (nor do I try, and fail) all the earlier times. The difference when I do go is not that then at last I try, but only that then I do actually go: I have indeed in this case used my will, but my use of the will is in acting, not in some presupposed trying; if I push off, and my ski sticks break so that after all the skis fail to move, then I have tried, and my trying consists in what I did towards action germane to the action intended.

In the case of difficulty or failure, 'trying' is no answer to the question 'What did you do in trying to do so-and-so?'. In every case trying consists in some activity, different types of activity in different types of case. In the case of a paralysis which one discovers precisely in the act of failing to achieve movement, the mental struggling to get one's arm to move counts as a trying, not because it is an 'effort of will' made conscious, but because it is an attempt to use special means (saying things forcefully to oneself, etc.) to achieve one's end. The possibility of struggling is parasitic upon a presumption of some power, direct or indirect, over one's movements. When this sense of presumption is lost (e.g., after an extended period of paralysis) there comes to be no possibility of struggling and therefore no possibility of trying—as it were, a supposed trying to move one's legs then becomes as vacuous (just as much mere fancy) as one's trying to move an external object simply by 'willing it to move'.[34]

The peculiar case has been suggested in which a person has the intention of moving his arm but, because his arm is hidden from him and has been anaesthetized, does not know that he has failed.[35] In order to understand this case it is useful to consider the difference

---

[34]One can say to oneself "Let it move", "May it move", or "Move", but the willing here is not the willing integral to action but more analogous to wishing: one might try by energetically and feelingly 'wishing' to cause something to move, but if one succeeded it would not be true that one had performed an action of moving it, but only that one had performed an action which caused it to move. Moving a thing is a certain kind of bodily action which has not taken place in the supposed case. Rather one has done something else in the hope or expectation of having the effect that the thing moves.

[35]O'Shaughnessy, *The Will*, Vol. II, p. 266 f., cf. 265–266.

between two cases in which we would say that 'I see nothing', one in which I am blind and there is no seeing taking place let alone a seeing of nothing, and the other in which I am not blind but it is utterly dark so that I am seeing and what I see is 'nothing'. In the case of action, there are likewise two cases, the one of doing nothing in which there is no doing and no intending, and the other of doing nothing where there is an intending (we are speaking here of the sort of intending which is internal to the normal case of action, not of a state of intention) but what is done (what is achieved) is precisely 'nothing'—and this latter is exemplified in the situation of intending to move my arm but in fact doing nothing, not even struggling, trying, or attempting to move my arm, because I don't know that it hasn't moved. The intending is not an acting, nor a trying, nor an attempting.

In order to understand this intending, which is internal to an action (and which might still occur in the case of paralysis even without there being any action, nor any trying or attempting), we should consider the common and quite normal case when the choosing is in the action, as when I act without having chosen the course of action and formed the relevant intention previously. In such a case there is no distinction between the intending, which is within the action, and the choosing. But now we should reflect that, in cases when we had made a previous choice and therefore did have a previous intention, it remains that, whatever our previous choice and intention, we are still free when it comes to the act to change our mind and in the act itself to choose differently. Therefore, that intending which is internal to an action should be considered as having the character of choice, whether what is concerned is the consummation of an already made choice in the act of acting or whether the exercise of choice in the act of acting.[36] Accordingly, this intending has no more the character of a first movement within action in accord with intention than does choice in general: the choice to act, to try, to have a go, is not itself

---

[36]It is this case, rather than the other, in which I might yet change my mind, which shows the nature of choice as an election whose primary expression is action.

In all this, the perspective we suggest fits with the idea of divine action whereby it is not that within each divine action there is a primary element which is a divine choice made in eternity as a result of which, by some automatic process, something happens in time. Rather, in the case of divine as well as of human action, the primary realization of will is in the doing, which is within time.

an action, trying, or having a go, even when it is a choice in the act.[37] And we must add this: although this intending which is internal to action has the character of choice, this does not in the least re-erect it into a distinctly experienced event which causes or fails to cause the body's movement—in the case when the choice is made earlier and there is no change of mind, the maintenance of the choice is not an act separate either from the preceding state or, if it occurs, from the action, and in the case when the choice is only made in the act itself again there is no separation from the action. For, as we saw earlier, maintenance of choice or choice is not known except in knowing a whole context, and is not a 'logically distinct existence'. And it is only a cause in the sense that we say things like 'She did it because she chose'—which we do in order to exclude explanations incompatible with the action's being free, not in order to identify an external cause.

Accordingly, words like "trying" and "attempt" refer to whatever activity in execution of choice which is towards the accomplishment of the action, and not to some inner event or component of activity, some first movement in the realization of choice which all the different cases of success, difficulty, and failure include. Tryings and attempts, just as much as actions, are things which proceed from the will— things willed, not the willing of them. In this sense, one could say

---

[37]When we read Aquinas on the topics of intention, choice, consent, etc., we should not think of him as dealing sequentially with a sequence of acts prior to action: after all, there is no fixed intention prior to choice and choice and intention can be more or less determinate in their object (we decide to go to Perth but this leaves it still to be decided whether we go via Dundee). At any stage, choice involves, not only a settling of the intention, but also a judgement of the intellect whereby, determined by choice, it says "Let this be done", what Aquinas calls the act of command (*imperium*). None of these, of course, is a 'logically distinct existence', and none is an action: to be an act in the relevant sense requires only some positive description so as to be intelligible as the exercise of a capacity.

Aquinas speaks of 'use' as a distinct act of will so that, following logically after choice and after the action's being commanded, there has to be a 'use of powers'. But what he has in mind is the use of powers subordinate to the will as, for instance, in moving one's limbs. E.g., one wills the relevant movement and firm holding of one's hands in willing the action of moulding of clay. If the willing to use one's powers included first of all a willing to use the power of the will, one would be landed with an infinite regress of willings to will. (When Aquinas speaks of *usus* he does not mean simply 'an exercise of will' but a willed use of subordinate powers: the *usus* is an act of will in the sense that the *usus* is willed, not in the sense that it is the will that is used since this is in no way distinctive: in the ordinary way of speaking, the state of intention, the act of choice, and the action itself along with tryings and attemptings would all count as exercises or 'uses' of the power called the will, but are not what is referred to as *usus*.)

that they belong to what is external or posterior in intentional action, as it were outer or posterior in aspect to the judging and experiencing subject who acts and tries. Being appetitive, voluntary or intentional are things adverbial to the action, the attempting, the trying, and do not provide an idiom for describing some act which takes place in all types of case and captures the experiential element in them.

It has been thought that trying, imagined to be mediate between a person and his action, is in some way a clue to the immediate link of a person with his body. But this is a mistake because trying is no more immediate than doing itself. Philosophers have sometimes had the picture of trying as being tied up with body-image, knowledge of body position and powers, and bodily sensation feedback enabling it to keep its bearing on the goal. But these things are not more internal to trying than they are to doing. The relevant knowing of one's body and of knowing how to use it are necessary to trying only because they are necessary to doing; they are prior to trying because they are prior to doing, and as much prior to trying as they are to doing—trying is in no way a clue to their nature.[38]

It is only because the philosophers have set the agent at a distance from his or her action that they resort to something like trying as a supposed bridge between agent and action. But the things which make it possible to try to do something do this only because they are precisely the things which make it possible actually to do it. What puts us into such a relation to our bodies as to be able to try to do something does this precisely because it is of the sort which puts us into such a relation to our bodies as to be able to do it.

Note on some recent views

We are now in a position to comment on some rather convoluted recent accounts of action and of trying—by considering representative examples,

---

[38]Thus it may be noted, although it is aside from our present argument, that trying provides no clue to the familiarity with the arena of action upon which action depends. In the human case, one may do something feeling one's way forward towards doing the next thing, regathering appreciation of one's environment and bodily powers or gathering fuller appreciation, but any action and therefore any trying to act presupposes some familiarity or presumption of familiarity with the arena of action. In the case of divine action, this familiarity with the arena of action comes directly from the fact that the existence of each and every part and facet of this arena depends upon the willing divine giving and upholding of the existence of things in their order.

exhibiting the poverty of contemporary Anglo-Saxon discussion in raising any new issue.

These accounts take as their starting point something which ought to be uncontroversial. In the cases where action succeeds, it seems a mistake to say there was no trying, just as in the case when one unproblematically sees and recognizes an X it is a mistake to say that it did not look as if an X was there. In each case to say I tried, or it looked as if. . ., suggests non-success or failure in perception, but does not imply it. In general, when an action succeeds and there is no difficulty and no indirectness in the means adopted, the trying seems nothing other than the action itself.

But this truth is put to quite implausible use, albeit in two very different ways, by Hornsby and O'Shaughnessy in their recent accounts.

Jennifer Hornsby's account in her book, *Actions*, is the simpler. She takes it that when we speak of an action we are speaking, not of a totality which would include both an act of trying and the intended upshot (the upshot consisting of the intended bodily movement and its intended sequel), but only of that which caused the intended upshot: a movement in the transitive sense ("He moved his body") is an event inside his body causative of a movement in the intransitive sense ("His body moved"), p. 13. She argues that in all cases this inner cause is the relevant act of trying, so that actions are simply identical to certain acts of trying, viz., those acts of trying which are successful in the anticipated way (*Actions*, Chapter 3). The effect of her account is to make actions into inner events of a sort called tryings. Some acts of trying will achieve non-accidental success, and these will be called actions, and the others will be cases of failure in action, failure to do what was intended.

One might be puzzled as to how she arrives at such a peculiar view. On the face of it, if I try to telephone friends and fail to get them, my trying consists in various pertinent outward activities such as dialling a certain number and waiting for an answer. On examination, her view turns out to arise from a subtle shift from saying that the action is the causing of something to happen to saying that it is the thing (agent or event) which does the causing. One might naturally think that, in action, it is the agent which makes or causes something to happen. But, for her, the protagonist of this view is Chisholm, according to whom the agent only causes something to happen externally by causing an inner event, an undertaking (or endeavouring, *Person and Object, passim*) which then causes the external happening. But Chisholm has here already conceded the main point, viz., that we will always find an inner event of some sort which is the cause of the external happening.

Against her view, one must insist that an action is a totality which includes the relevant bodily movement and its intended sequel, not just its inner cause whether this be a trying or 'undertaking' or an agent acting inwardly to cause a trying or 'undertaking'. This is the position which Brian O'Shaughnessy takes as his starting point in his book, *The Will: A Dual Aspect Theory*. The action or the trying is the whole development which proceeds from intention. For O'Shaughnessy the event of trying or 'having a go' (*op. cit.*, Vol. II, p. 286n.), which is supposed to occur in cases both of action and of failure in action, is, in the cases of success, identical with what we refer to as the action, embracing within one whole the willed event or external action with what it proceeds from (*op. cit.*, Chapter 14, cf. Vol. I, p. 111).

So far O'Shaughnessy's account accords with our own. But at this stage he attempts a reinstatement of 'trying' or 'striving' as a component 'part-event' within the whole development which proceeds from intention. In conformity with the holistic conception being proposed, it is insisted that this part-event is 'non-autonomous' (*op. cit.*, Vol. II, pp. 259, 287), neither identical with nor distinct from the willed event or intended bodily movement (*op. cit.*, p. 347). O'Shaughnessy's idea is to introduce a quasi-Aristotelian element into his account: the action when it comes off is a totality to which this inner 'part event' of striving and the outer 'willed event' are, as it were, material parts of something conceived of as a whole.

However, these inner 'part-events' are imagined to be candidates for being identical with certain brain-events and to have a nature whereby they could exist even if the action did not follow, whereas Aristotelian material parts in their functional nature within natural wholes have no possibility of existence with this nature apart from these wholes.

O'Shaughnessy's conception of this inner psychological part-event of trying represents an elaboration of the idea that 'trying' as a mental or psychological state will be in Armstrong's terms 'a state apt for bringing about a certain sort of behaviour'. He holds that, when an event is referred to as 'a trying', it is logically implied by the use of the word 'trying' that this event occurs within a framework of contingent causal laws whereby in causally normal circumstances the event will be followed by the anticipated bodily behaviour, stating the causal connection in this way: 'given a human body in a normally whole and healthy state that at that moment both permits arm rise and does not interfere with the normal working of the body, then trying to raise an arm is a logically sufficient condition of an event of arm rise'—in brief, granted normal physiological circumstances and settings of physical liberty, trying both explains and is a sufficient condition of arm rise (*op. cit.*, p. 348). It will be noted that this does nothing to make a connection with behaviour part of the intrinsic nature of this event as it occurs in Nature or physically; rather it simply makes this connection something implied by the description of the event as a 'trying'.

However, O'Shaughnessy is very insistent that the connection with behaviour belongs to the 'real essence' of this part-event of trying. He tells us that trying to raise an arm 'is and is essentially: an x which in a physically normal human, world permitting (etc.), is a causally sufficient condition of arm rise' (*op. cit.*, p. 352), and earlier (*op. cit.*, p. 351f.) that 'this psi [psychological] event [of bodily trying], though a directed psi item and therefore lacking absolute guarantee of its object in the outer world, has no other existence than as a putative causally sufficient condition, in determinate circumstances, of a determinate bodily event. That characterization uniquely and exhaustively defined its being. Were the act of trying and otherwise independently specifiable . . . then whereas that act would putatively relate to items in the outer world and also putatively be a causally sufficient condition of arm rise, it would retain its identity as a distinctive act of a certain kind. We would then merely re-describe the act as 'trying to raise the arm', and its causal efficacy would be a contingent property akin to that of a steak to cause watering of the mouth.' He summarizes his position by saying 'Because trying is psychological, there can be no guarantee of its object [here we have his Cartesianism and acceptance of arguments from illusion]; that is, of success. But because it is in essence nothing but a causally sufficient condition in normal circumstances of its physical objective, its causal power cannot be an external property like the power of a thought to cause goose pimples [here we have his Aristotelianism and concession to phenomenology]' (*op. cit.*, p. 352f.).

This position depends on making 'trying' into something whose phenomological real essence involves logically that it be of a nature to have a causally non-accidental connection with its bodily outcome. But this is in tension with regarding this 'trying' as possibly identical with a brain-event whose real essence could be stated in physical terms and would not logically involve the causal connections with the outer behaviour which, as we remarked earlier, he says arises by a causal development 'spreading out from the brain' reaching to the physical movement willed (*op. cit.*, p. 286): the connections between a brain-event with its context and the outer behaviour are supposedly matters of contingent empirical law.

In brief, O'Shaughnessy is struggling to do justice to the fact that the 'trying' which he is speaking of is something which we experience precisely as in certain non-accidental connections with behaviour. But from this it follows, not that these things belong to its 'real essence' as an element in the make-up of the universe (whether this element be conceived of in a materialist, dualist, or Aristotelian way), but that they belong to its 'essence' as a psychological phenomenon, that is to its 'essence' in a phenomenological sense. But 'trying' as a psychological phenomenon does not have to be conceived of as an element of reality, an element belonging to a certain natural kind with a real essence as such, but only as an aspect or facet of reality as it presents itself to us. [O'Shaughnessy wants to conceive key psychological phenomena, such as experiences, intentions (*op. cit.*, p. 305), and tryings, as 'entities' with 'real essences' according to the natural kind defined by their psychological character. In this, he lacks the sophistication of Christopher Peacocke who shows how such kinds of phenomena should not be considered natural kinds, even if they were kinds of entity (*Holistic Explanation*, pp. 99-102).]

In this way we see how the technical vocabulary of 'real essences' becomes in this context merely a device for papering over the divorce between two quite different conceptions, one the conception of events as objects, elements of reality, each a 'genuine ontologically significant reality' (I take this phrase from *The Will*, Vol. I, p. 15.), with law-bound relations between them, and the other the conception of events as interlocking facets or aspects of reality—in the case of mind-involving facets or aspects, facets or aspects picked out according to the way we experience them and experienced as having conceptual interconnections.

---

3. Emotion and Sensation

In intentional action, the intention is internal to the action as a psychophysical reality, and the desire and motivation internal to the intention are likewise internal to the action. If I can see an apple on the table, and have no reason for not taking it, then it follows logically, that, if I don't make to take the apple, it can't be true that I really want an apple, and, if I do really want the apple, then I will make to take it. That is, it seems wrong to say that wanting is something purely internal to the mind in the strong sense which dualist and materialist require, of being without any kind of logical connection, strict or non-strict, simple or complex, with physical behaviour and dispositions to behave—and, of course, all wanting and intending will involve some beliefs internally, so that without these beliefs there would not be this wanting or intending and would not be the behaviour to which this wanting and intending was internal. Likewise, speaking involves some linguistic understanding and one's meaning what one says, besides many beliefs (this will be especially important in our consideration of language in Chapter X). Thus, it is a quite general characteristic of human behaviour, properly thought of, as Ryle and others thought of it, not in purely physical terms but as it occurs and as we perceive it, that it involves a multiplicity of mental 'states' internally—and this is typical of higher animal behaviour in general.

But now we must make clear the especially intimate connections of the emotions and sensation with behaviour, and the effect of the intimate connections between various sensations and emotions on their behavioural expression.

(a) The character of pain

Wittgenstein has been understood to make it plain that pain, far from being simply identifiable as a 'distinct introspectible sensation' was not and could not be recognized to self or referred to in public language apart from its being characteristically expressed in overt behaviour, groaning, grimacing, writhing, and wincing amongst such expressions alongside the use of language (since man is a language-using animal). Others have emphasized a connection with evil or harm, so that the connection with behaviour most essential to pain is that it tends to engender aversion-behaviour, aversion both from the pain as such and from the evil or damage presumed to be the cause of pain. For it is characteristic of pain to be caused by harm or damage. This causal relation, like other causal relations, is commonly regarded as a contingent, 'merely' empirically known, fact. But, although this is less commonly recognized, there is a stronger connection: it is part of the nature of pain that, whether or not it is actually caused by damage, it should tend to be believed to be caused by damage. More precisely, if an activity generates pain, we suspect the activity of increasing damage, and that this is so is shown by the way in which, if reasons for thinking 'the pain-message' to be 'false' are brought in to doubt, a pain which a person has grown accustomed not to attend to becomes impossible to ignore.

Two ideas have over recent times become fashionable, the one that pain is indeed a 'distinct introspectible sensation' so that in peculiar circumstances people may have pain without any of the normal accompanying emotions of aversion and distress, and the other that pain is something whose essence is physical so that it may be present and even achieve its influence on behaviour independently of any consciousness of it on the part of the person in pain.

Let us consider the second idea first. It has been suggested that individual pains are to be identified with individual events of the stimulation of C-fibres. But it is wrong thus to identify the pain with some event in the brain or spinal cord which supposedly explains the bodily movement involved in a withdrawal of the hand or a wince for this reason: describing the experience as a pain situates it in a cognitional and emotional context, key to the explanation of the behaviour. A withdrawal of the hand on touching a hot object, or a wince in response to a sharp pain, are both attitudinal realities (neither "withdrawal" nor "wince", as normally understood, are purely physical descriptions). The fact that what is experienced is a pain explains the attitudinal aspects of the withdrawal and the wince as well as the physical movements involved, and it must be wrong to explain the physical movements in a way which would make them independent of these attitudinal aspects, unless indeed our ordinary presumption that they are not thus independent is false.[39] It is this which makes it wrong to identify the pain with any physical event in the brain or spinal cord. To identify the pain which causes me to withdraw my hand or to wince with some event in the brain or spinal cord does not explain the way in which this effect upon my behaviour depends upon a coming together of features of which the event in the C-fibres is only one, and does not explain how it is that this concatenation is relevant to whether what results is appropriately described as a withdrawal or a wince; nor does it explain the unity of the whole phenomenon of pain understood psychophysically explaining behaviour understood psychophysically.

As to the first idea, those who dwell upon pathological cases in which patients report pain without aversion or distress make a mistake in thinking this abnormal case a good guide to the general nature of pain, as if it by itself sufficed to prove that pain is a 'distinct introspectible sensation' (this is a further example of the mistake of considering the abnormal the guide to the normal, rather than the normal the guide to the understanding of the abnormal). Rather we should regard the use of the word "pain" in these cases as itself a

---

[39]Peacocke argues for the token identity of each physical pain with some particular stimulation of C-fibres on the ground that each is the one and only cause of withdrawal from painful objects in certain cases (*Holistic Explanation*, p. 136f.), and in this way presumes this independence of the explanation of physical behaviour from any psychological or attitudinal accompaniment—as is confirmed by his argument against double causation (p. 137).

puzzle, no more a guide to the general meaning of the word than the case of the 'seeing stars' because of a blow on the head is a guide to the general meaning either of "see" or of "star".

The trouble with both ideas, both the idea of pain as something essentially inner and introspectible and the idea of pain as primarily and essentially only something physical, is not only that they consider pain in isolation from directed behaviour of any kind, but also that they consider pain and pain-behaviour in isolation from related emotions.

That this is a mistake becomes evident if we consider the complexity of pain-behaviour: this arises from the intimate logical links between pain and a spread of interrelated other emotions so that the kinds of behaviour which might seem accidental in relation to the function of expressing pain do not appear thus accidental in relation to these other emotions. Thus some pain-behaviour seems expressive of withdrawal or aversion; some seems expressive of anger and aggression; these kinds of behaviour are also associated with fear; both pain and fear involve 'distress', one symptom of which is the withdrawal which is not from a particular object but an expression of wanting to escape 'crowding', the desire for a world in which one will be at least temporarily free from pressures, decision-making, etc., a world in limited respects 'under one's control', and 'in which one can think' or at least pause—these things are reflective of reaction to confusion: confusion in behaviour as well as in mind is characteristic of pain as well as of fear. And the link between pain and 'sorrow' (in the most generalized sense indicated below), perhaps the most profound of all, engenders close links between pain-behaviour and 'sorrow'-behaviour. Perhaps one can say that physical pain is unlike other bodily sensations in that it has no behaviour peculiar to itself, but only behaviour shared with anger, distress, fear, aversion, sense of evil, pleas for help, or sorrow.[40]

Therefore it seems a mistake to consider the relation of pain to behaviour as if it were as simple as the relation of itching to scratching. Rather the tendency of pain to be elevated into the opposite of pleasure arises from its connection with such fundamental emotions as I

---

[40]As to the 'qualities' attributed to pains, as for instance throbbing, searing, stabbing, stinging, they seem to mark connections with time, associated or comparable sensations, or, in respect to our reactions to or experience of them, comparisons with the pains experienced or which might be imagined to be experienced within a global context involving, for instance, heat or attack with a dagger.

have instanced, and its most fundamental connections with behaviour arise from its connections with aversion, aggression, and distress, and most important of all, for reasons which I shall make clear, with 'sorrow' as the generic counterpart to pleasure.

(b) The emotions in general

The view that pleasure is a sensation has never had the same plausibility as the view that pain is a sensation. As G.E.M. Anscombe has it 'Pleasure could not be a sensation: no sensation could have the consequences of pleasure'.[41] We can consider bodily pain as the non-metaphorical case of pain, as seeing with the eyes and grasping with the hands are non-metaphorical cases of seeing and grasping, and regard all other cases of 'pain' as thus called in virtue of parallelisms in the emotions, such as aversion, fear, anxiety, and distress, with which they are linked, somewhat as other cases of 'seeing' and 'grasping' are thus called in virtue of parallelisms in their links with knowledge. By contrast, the concept of pleasure arises from connections with the verb "to please", with being pleased and what pleases. There appears to be a notion of 'value' ('love' or *amor* in Aquinas) which embraces both, but apart from this desire and pleasure stand as the two conceptually fundamental emotions, they or their opposites (aversion and 'pain' or *tristitia*) underlying or presupposed by all other emotions—desire or wanting standing as our relation to the good we do not have and pleasure, enjoyment or satisfaction as our relation to the good which we do have.

This way of thinking helps make intelligible the Aristotelian position whereby, rather than pleasure being a distinct introspectible sensation consequent upon some activity yielding pleasure, pleasure is distinguishable only in aspect from what pleases, i.e., from the activity or fulfillment of potentiality in which pleasure is taken or which is enjoyed.[42]

Pleasure, then, let us summarize, is related to the structures of human motivation and action no less essentially than desire. The way in which the end desired or aimed at is good or worthwhile is the

---

[41]Anscombe, *Intention*, p. 77.

[42]Aristotle, *Nicomachean Ethics*, Book X. For modern imitations of this approach, see Ryle on pleasure in *The Concept of Mind*, Ch. 4, and in 'Pleasure', *Collected Papers II*; and Kenny in *Action, Emotion and Will*.

basis of its being an object of pleasure and the rationale of its being an object of desire. And pleasure's being good to have is the rationale of its being appropriate to desire. In sum, for the good to be the object of pleasure is more fundamental to its nature than its being desirable, which is merely derivative from its prospective pleasurability.[43]

In the case of a pleasure of sense it is what makes it to be pleased at or to be pleased in and enjoyed which makes it desirable. Its role in respect of human life as a whole is as a part, not just a cause, of happiness. Quite certainly it is what makes a thing the object of pleasure which makes it desirable, not vice versa. A thing's being experienced as pleasurable is its being experienced as part of a more general well-being: the person who enjoys or has enjoyed their game of golf shows it in their good humour during and after, the sense of freedom exuded in their breathing, their sitting down, their limb movements, their lack of acerbity and their accepting manner in conversation, and the full rein given to whatever enthusiasm comes naturally to them. What is true in the case of these lesser pleasures is more obviously true in the case of pleasures of more strategic importance for the general direction of life.

Thus, in judging that one is or was pleased in one's own case, one does not in general use considerations about one's own behaviour in order to make the judgement. But it remains that the meaning of a judgement that one is or was pleased has to do with the role of the object and cause (in the case of pleasure the two are the same) of pleasure in one's general well-being or sense of well-being. As such, a judgement of this sort is related to the general structures of behaviour. It is the things which are generically pleasurable which constitute the candidates for desire and aim, inspiring intention and choice.

In parallel with the case of pleasure we ought to consider the case of sorrow.

As pleasure is in the good we have (while desire is towards the good we do not have), so 'sorrow' is in respect of the evils we have (while aversion is in respect of the evils we do not have). In this way sorrow is one of the most general of human emotions. And its parallelism with pleasure makes it unsurprising that there should be

---

[43]See Braine in 'Human Animality: Its Relevance to the Shape of Ethics', Section 3, in *Ethics, Technology and Medicine* (ed. Braine and Lesser).

parallel difficulties in distinguishing sorrow from its object to those much discussed in distinguishing pleasure from the object of pleasure. (In the case of sensory pleasures there seems to be no intrinsic good in them such as might make us pleased or glad at them considered as objects independent of our feelings, but only intrinsic good as pleasures according to the natural role they play in our human animal life and in its 'happiness'. In the case of physical pains they present no object to be grieved at after they are passed, and again the evil in them arises from our inextricable involvement in them while they continue; when chronic, it is in their nature to constitute an element in 'misery'. The cases of physical pain and physical pleasure are parallel.)

The residual element in the concept of pain not explained by our earlier analysis and remarks arises from this connection with sorrow. One could express this by saying that every pain is a grief.[44] Pain is an evil, not just for its effects in interfering with activities and with pleasure in them, associated with the distress it engenders as something internal to it, and not just because of its connections with harm and damage or with anticipation of these, but because in itself it constitutes a sorrow or a grief. And the basis of the metaphorical extension in the use of the word "pain" seems to lie in the human tendency to call every sorrow or grief a 'pain'. Crying is primarily an expression of grief or sorrow, although also a symptom of distress or confusion, as well as, incidentally, of many physical conditions bringing on effects, sometimes purely physical, sometimes psychosomatic. That crying should be an expression of grief, not just of physical pain, is a striking example of the human being's unitary, animal, psychosomatic, nature: he or she who laments a great evil does so in a physical way, even if the evil is spiritual.

In these ways and others, the sensations and emotions strikingly exhibit the essentially psychophysical, psychosomatic nature of human beings and other higher animals. This theme could be developed much

---

[44]It has been said that pain is a mystery because nothing comes between a person and his pain. In respect of cases when we can be distracted from the pain, this seems inaccurate, but at root it contains the truth because some distraction is false as in the case of false avoidance of mourning.

The problem of the doctrine of the heavenly city where there is no more pain, no more weeping, etc., is as to how there can be no more objects of grief or of how it can come to be as Lady Julian of Norwich said "All will be well, and all manner of things will be well".

more amply by considering other, less generic, emotions and attitudes, such as anger, fear, hope and anxiety, respect, admiration, wonder, contempt, disgust and dread, which still presuppose desire, aversion, pleasure or sorrow—as well as more specific forms of any emotions, differentiated according to special kinds of object and perhaps also special kinds of relation to these objects. Considering these, we will find the inextricability of the mental and the biological or physical yet more intimately demonstrated. But for our argument it suffices to have demonstrated this in regard to those most general emotions and attitudes, desire and aversion, pleasure and 'pain', on which Anglo-Saxon analysis with its atomism has so much concentrated.

V. A Non-Dualistic Account of the Meaning of Statements Involving Mind

We have highlighted the importance in speaking about human beings and the other higher animals of what we have called irreducibly hybrid facts and propositions—hybrid in that they straddle the mental and the physical, and irreducibly hybrid in that there is no analysing them into separate mental and physical components together with co-ordinative relations.

To get a grasp of the full character of these hybrid facts and propositions, we need first to see the shape of the theory of meaning required to accommodate them and second to register their role in explanation.

1. Charting a Way Which Avoids Both Introspectionism and Behaviourism

The theory of meaning cannot be isolated from epistemology.

We have a knowledge of our perceptions, sensations, moods, emotions, beliefs and intentions, even in advance of any checking upon its consistency with the rest of our experience and behaviour. And others learn of what we see, feel, believe, and intend, simply from our telling them, and not only from our behaviour. Yet equally it was a key virtue in the 'ordinary language philosophy' formed by Wittgenstein and Ryle that it recognized logical connections between, on the one hand, pain, anger, fear, desire, intention, belief, and suchlike and, on the other hand, behaviour: patterns of behaviour are not just symptomatic of mental states but intrinsic to the character of these states in such a way that we can learn of people's sensations and emotions, intentions in acting, perceptions and beliefs not only from what they tell us, but also directly from their behaviour—and even know of the sensations, emotions, intentions, and perceptions of animals in the same way. The connections between pain and pain-behaviour, highlighted by Wittgenstein, represented only one instance out of a much wider range.

It rightly seemed vital to the 'ordinary language philosophers' that one and the same mind-involving state or event should be ascribable on the basis of observation of behaviour to others and without observation to ourselves, since otherwise we shall have *either* an idea of the state concerned which is based on introspection alone so that everything physical or behavioural seems accidental *or else* an idea which is purely behavioural and leaves out the possibility of knowledge without observation in one's own case. In this way, it became a crux in the theory of meaning that one should avoid, on the one hand, the introspectionist theories of meaning suggested by the dualistic division of types of basic proposition into mental and physical, and on the other hand the logical behaviourist theory of meaning which implausibly makes mental statements into dispositional statements (albeit very complex ones) about physical behaviour.

In short, those types of statement which we make about ourselves and about others, which are simplest in sense, in terms of which we explain the meanings of other statements, which we make in regard to ourselves without checking by reference to other supposedly more fundamental statements, and which, for these reasons, deserve to be counted as logically basic, typically have implications both for the mental and for the physical. Typically, they have a sense which allows us to make them about ourselves without checking and about others merely upon their testimony, and yet also can be verified by observation of behaviour.

Our task is to refine this intrinsic double-aspect meaning of mental terms, preserving the quasi-autonomy of the mental against the behaviourist and also against those who put forward the 'causal theory of knowledge', and preserving the essential connection between the mental and behaviour against the introspectionist.

(a) Strawson's attempt at systematization

This appreciation of what a theory of the meaning of what I have called irreducibly hybrid statements requires, implicit in many earlier authors, was first clearly set forth by Strawson.[1] It is convenient to use his account as a basis for later refinement.

---

[1] I make Strawson my starting point because of the schematic generality of his remarks, combined with the presence in them of the germs of a limited systematization

Strawson offers an account of the logic of a 'key class' of what he calls 'P-predicates', meaning personalistic or mind-involving predicates. He distinguishes two kinds of predicate which we ascribe to human beings, 'M-predicates', which are those which apply also to material bodies of sorts to which we 'would not dream of ascribing states of consciousness', and 'P-predicates', which are 'all the other predicates which we apply to persons . . . [and which] imply the possession of consciousness in that to which they are ascribed'.[2] But this key sub-class of mind-involving predicates which he next attempts to characterize is precisely the class of predicates which our understanding of irreducibly hybrid facts and propositions requires. Indeed it is the class of all mind-involving predicates, not only as applied to human beings but also to other animals—because, although it is only we human beings as language-users who apply these predicates to anything, whether ourselves or others, we rightly apply them not only to ourselves but also to many other animals.

As an aside, important for our later discussion in Chapter XV, we must, of course, recognize that in his use of the word "person", Strawson is restricting its use in the convenient way common amongst modern Anglo-Saxon philosophers, limiting it to beings of a bodily nature which happen to be personal (i.e., whatever would have counted traditionally as 'rational animals'), principally human beings but also any other beings of a bodily nature (dolphins have been suggested) which may also turn out to be personal.[3] This notion of "person", as a personal bodily being, would seem to be a specialization of the most general meaning of the word in English and older philosophical usage, according to which it seems to mark the range of appropriate joint application of such predicates as "know", "understand", and "judge", and with them, "desire", "prefer", "rejoice in", "intend",

---

whose absence makes the grasp of the positions of such precursors as Ryle and Wittgenstein so precarious. It is striking that Strawson's *Individuals* (1959), Anscombe's *Intention* (1957), Hampshire's *Thought and Action* and Shoemaker's doctoral thesis (1958) (developed into *Self-Knowledge and Self-Identity*, 1961) all appeared within such a short interval.

[2] *Individuals*, pp. 104–105.

[3] This conception of "person" as a trans-generic concept but still limited to bodily beings is well explained by David Wiggins, pp. 171–173, *Sameness and Substance*, thus embedding the definition he finds in Locke (Locke's *Essay*, II, XVII, 2) within his own nuanced account of peculiarly human identity (cf. Chapter VIII below, n. 6). It is the one made vivid by C.S. Lewis and J.R.R. Tolkien and now commonplace in science-fiction.

and "choose", together with (if these may be taken metaphorically) "speak" and "hear", all of which are predicates which have been applied to God and to angels.[4] But it is only the personal in the convenient modern restricted sense with which we are concerned in this chapter and this part of this book.

What then is Strawson's characterization of this 'key class of P-predicates', i.e., this key sub-class of 'person-predicates', the ones which are most evidently body-involving or behaviour-connected?

It is the class of those P-predicates in the case of which one can have 'an entirely adequate basis for ascribing the P-predicate concerned to oneself, and yet this basis be quite distinct from the bases on which one ascribes the predicate to another person.' In such cases, 'one ascribes P-predicates to others on the strength of observation of their behaviour', and 'the behaviour-criteria one goes on are not just signs of the presence of what is meant by the P-predicate, but are criteria of a logically adequate kind for the ascription of the P-predicate.'[5] That is, the behavioural criteria used to base the ascription of the predicate to other people are internal to its meaning, and yet are not what one needs to go on in applying the predicate to oneself.

In these cases 'just as there is not in general one primary process of learning, or teaching oneself, an inner private meaning of predicates

---

[4]Cf. my first book, *The Reality of Time and the Existence of God*, p. 268. This account makes the term "person" into a term marking what one might regard as the 'range of significance' of certain predicates, using the notion of 'range of significance' (used by Russell to explain the notion of logical type) in a way which accords with natural ways of talking. Such range concepts always indicate the subjects, not just of one predicate, but of a family of interrelated predicates, a family united by a role in a mass of discourse, in the case of "person" a role in statements with a certain place in schemes of historical explanation, the role whose importance appears in Chapter VIII. It is primarily this which explains the kinship of the term "person" to natural kind terms, a kinship emphasized by Wiggins, *op. cit.* pp. 170–173, a kinship which it shares with certain other 'range' concepts such as those of "animal", "living thing", and "body". [It is this more general, unrestricted notion of "person" which is traditionally marked by the aspects of intellect, will, other-relatedness, and a certain creativity (capacity for originality) mentioned in my first book pp. 268–272.]

There are, of course, arguments that there are no persons in this more general formal sense except bodily ones, i.e., except persons in this modern more restricted sense, but this does not seem to be a matter of the fixed ordinary meaning of the word but of supposed necessary consequences of this meaning, consequences whose necessity we will question in Chapter XV.

[5]*Individuals*, pp. 105–107.

of this class, then another process of learning to apply such predicates to others on the strength of a correlation, noted in one's own case, with certain forms of behaviour, so—and equally—there is not, in general, one primary process of learning to apply such predicates to others on the strength of behaviour-criteria, and then another process of acquiring the secondary technique of acquiring a new form of behaviour, viz., first-person P-utterances.' Rather 'to learn their use is to learn both aspects of their use. In order to *have* this type of concept, one must be both a self-ascriber and an other-ascriber of such predicates and must see every other as a self-ascriber. In order to *understand* this type of concept, one must acknowledge that there is a kind of predicate which is unambiguously and adequately ascribable *both* on the basis of observation of [the behaviour of] the subject of the predicate *and* not on this basis, i.e., independently of observation of [the behaviour of] the subject.' Thus, 'we have to do with a class of predicates to the meaning of which it is essential that they should be both self-ascribable and other-ascribable to the same individual, where self-ascriptions are not made on the observational basis on which other-ascriptions are made, but on another basis. It is not that these predicates have two kinds of meaning. Rather, it is essential to the single kind of meaning that they do have, that both ways of ascribing them should be perfectly in order.'[6]

In order to accept this we have to avoid two mistakes, the one of confusing ascribing or stating with describing, and the other of confusing the sense of an utterance with its situational or pragmatic meaning[7] so far as this goes beyond its sense. The main trouble is that the moment we think of an utterance like "I believe P" to describe a state rather than merely to predicate it ('ascribe it' or 'state it about a subject'), we begin to think of this state which is thus being 'described' as being experienced inwardly so that its ascription must have a sense corresponding to this inner experience and different from the sense of "believe" as we use it of others on the basis of their

---

[6] *Individuals*, pp. 108–110.

[7] As Chapter X will make evident, this distinction (in linguists' terms, between semantics and pragmatics) is not easy to make because many things belonging to sense have to be gauged from the context of utterance so that the distinction cannot be made in terms of what is context-neutral and what is not. Its treatment belongs to the theory of language, not anthropology, and I deal with it fully in my The *Expressiveness of Words: the key to the nature of language* (forthcoming).

behaviour.[8] In order to avoid this mistake we have to develop a conception of statement correlative with notions such as truth and falsity, rather than epistemological ideas associated with a word like "description", and develop a conception of 'state' correlative with predicates in such statements when they are of subject-predicate form, as what is ascribed to or stated about a subject.

In his remarks Strawson describes exactly the tight-rope which has to be walked to avoid the pitfalls of behaviourism and introspectionism on either side. He sets forth the data from which any right account of the meaning of mind-involving predicates as applied to human beings or other animals must not swerve, whatever further questions these data may suggest.

When I speak of further questions, I have in mind, for instance, that whenever we have propositions of a kind to whose meaning it belongs that they can be verified in two different ways, or in regard to which what puts us in a position of knowledge can be of two different kinds, philosophers are liable to ask the question "How is it possible for there to be concepts of this kind?"[9] It may be said— according to what is called a transcendental argument—that the existence and meaningfulness of such concepts, with a unitary meaning, but a double mode of verification, is a condition of the possibility of empirical knowledge, or of our having the concept of person we do, or of the existence of language. But this does not explain how it is possible for such concepts to exist; it merely makes plain that it is a datum that they do exist—that it would be mad or impossible to doubt it.

The datum that such concepts do exist, and the need to hold fast to the tight-rope set by faithfulness to the recognition of this, are things in regard to which vacillation comes easily to philosophers.

---

[8]It is as a result of such mistake that we find Wittgenstein speaking in *Philosophical Investigations*, II, x, as if it meant nothing to say that "—1" meant the same in relation to—1 as "1" means in relation to 1, and implying that it is in a similar way meaningless to say that "I believed" means the same in relation to the past as "I believe" means in relation to the present.

[9]This is the kind of question which Dummett introduces in 'The Justification of Deduction' (reprinted in *Truth and Other Enigmas*), and raised earlier by Kant— answered by the latter in terms of what we are able to know being conformed to the forms set by our faculty of knowledge.

Thus, for instance, Thomas Nagel[10] has had a recurrent preoccupation with the subjective as something which cannot be expressed or identified in objective terms, although insisting that objective study may register that such a thing as this subjective element must exist. But this whole way of thinking is based on the idea that the description of a form of life in objective terms will be in purely behavioural terms (in the narrow purely physical sense) in such a way that the subjective will escape it—and this supposition arises from exactly the kind of separation of first person meaning and second and third person meaning which, in the way I have shown, Strawson and Wittgenstein show the necessity of avoiding. That is, what they realized and what we have explained and insisted upon is the inseparability of the meaning of first person mind-involving statements from the meaning of second and third person ones, so that neither could have the meanings which they do have if they were not understood in their inseparability from the others. (And, as we shall see, the same inseparability was exhibited by Shoemaker between first person present tense statements and second

---

[10]In 'Physicalism', section V, in 'The Limits of Objectivity', and in 'What it is like to be a bat'. The special mistake in which Nagel imitates others is in supposing there to be something special, not identified in objective terms, about the meaning or reference of "I".

I deal with the special mistakes of the bat case in Chapter IX, but where human beings are concerned the problems of the quality of experience (as distinct from the meaning or reference of the word "I", used of the experiencer) tend to be concentrated on two types of case, one the case of pain and other bodily sensations. The first case is a case in which, for reasons apparent in Chapter III and later in this chapter, there is no private meaning (though for the individual there may be a quite peculiar import within his personal life), and the second the case of colours (with parallels in the case of the other senses), in regard to which I would like to make some comment here.

In regard to a colour—let us have in mind a particular seemingly distinct shade—in one way it seems almost as mad to suppose that we express what the shade is like in using words written or spoken as to suppose that when we use the name of a person in writing or speaking, e.g., the name "Alexander", the person himself stalks our page or issues from our mouth. But in another way, not only is it possible for us to express (poetically or otherwise, or by whatever comparisons) the starkness or dullness and other character of the colour, but also there is for us no separation between what we experience when we publicly identify something as of a certain colour and what we mean by the colour-word concerned (with the result that, even if we have occasion to explain that we see things with our right eye as being of a browner hue than we see them with our left eye, we still draw upon the same vocabulary given sense in its shared use with other people).

and third or other tense statements in respect of their implications in regard to personal or psychological identity.)

My view is that how it is possible for such concepts to exist cannot be explained, but only shown: it is exhibited by putting the shape of human life, in intentional action, in sensation, in perception, and in their integration, up to view. And this has been part of the purpose of our earlier chapters. Moreover, as we meet human life, as it presents itself in intentional action, sensation, and perception and as much in the experience of others as in our own self-knowledge, we meet it not simply as a given of experience but as a given within which experience and explanatory role are inseparable—as Chapters VI-VIII will make plain. Explanatory role has this importance in this connection: although we do not gain knowledge of other people's minds by causal reasoning from their behaviour, as if we knew only their bodies and physical facts about them directly and anything else only indirectly, nonetheless, *when* doubt is raised in regard to a particular kind of case, it is resolved when the experience or *prima facie* knowledge is put in its place within the context of the general patterns of explanation appropriate to human and animal life.

However, for our present purpose all that matters is the fact that such concepts exist possessing meaning in the way that they do; what matters is this fact, independently of any further explanation of it. This fact alone is full of embarassing consequences for some philosophical positions. For it follows at once that the assumptions of logical atomism are violated. There will be propositions ascribing pain and a multitude of other mind-involving predicates or 'conscious states' which imply propositions of a complex hypothetical form about behaviour, but in which the meaning of the proposition ascribing the 'conscious state' cannot be reduced to the propositions about behaviour conjoined with some other independent ones—and there will be propositions about behaviour which imply propositions about 'conscious states', but in the case of which this second set cannot be understood as if they did not go beyond the first set about behaviour. As a result, there will be propositions belonging to a special subject-matter, with some content in regard to that subject-matter, not reducible to logical tautologies by the method of substituting synonyms for synonyms (or by using definitions of kinds in a certain way trivial), but which are true in virtue of the meanings of their terms and knowable as such, good candidates for being called synthetic a priori—since, for a thing to be counted as epistemologically a priori amounts to no more than this, that it is known but should not be classed as empirically known. But this presents itself as a simple consequence of the datum that meaningful concepts of this kind exist, not as an extraordinary mystery requiring separate explanation.

Strawson's presentation avoids the implausibilities of Ryle when he tries to model the means of self-knowledge on the means of knowledge of others, and also the implausibilities of the tendency in Wittgenstein and the early Malcolm[11] to represent assertions like "I am in pain" as pieces of behaviour of a different kind from statements, and not as expressing knowledge, a view from which Malcolm later turned away.[12] Wittgenstein represented assertions such as "I am in pain" in this non-cognitive way because of what he supposed to be false parallels dangerously deceptive for the theory of meaning, the philosophy of mind and epistemology. But, as we have seen, these mistakes spring from confusing ascribing to or stating something about a subject with describing that subject. We must not be led, because of the existence of such mistakes, to deny that the first person, present tense utterances are ascriptions of 'states' in a logician's sense and statements about a subject in a logician's sense. As such they can be true or false, and so are assertions in regard to which lying is possible, and in the case of which knowledge is shared with others by testimony.

This last remark points up one of the two regards in which it is indispensable to develop Strawson's approach if we are to obtain a credible and stable general account, namely by coordinating it with a general account of knowledge by testimony. The second regard is this: we need also to integrate this approach with a proper treatment of memory and knowledge of identity over time within the account given. Let us look at these key matters, of testimony and memory, before attending to the obscurities of such phrases as 'on the basis of' and 'logically adequate behaviour-criteria', and to the different ways in which the introspectionism and behaviourism which Strawson is at pains to avoid, may rear their heads again.

---

[11]Wittgenstein's Philosophical Investigations in *Knowledge and Certainty.*
[12]*Problems of Mind,* Part III.

(b) The sharing of states of knowledge and belief: the character of testimony

To reach a proper understanding of why, after a personal predicate (P-predicate) has been applied by a speaker to himself, it must be that the predicate has the same sense when the hearer applies it to the speaker, it is vital to grasp the character of human communication in statement-making as an extending to others of the speaker's states of knowledge and belief. In this context, we need to consider what it is to believe upon the word or testimony of another.

It is crucial that there is a distinction between, on the one hand, believing something on someone's word in a case in which either what they say is true or they are lying because it is within their certain knowledge and, on the other hand, merely taking someone's word as evidence that something is so. That is, there is the case of believing upon testimony, exemplified when one says "I know that P because Jones told me so" in a case when one knows that Jones must know whether or not P and must be lying if P is false: I do not have in mind the general case of believing what the expert says, since we can reckon on experts disagreeing and being often wrong, nor the case of what a man says he saw in obscure light or other bad conditions, but the common cases in which the question would not arise of the speaker being wrong (e.g., about its being wet outside when he has just come in, or about his intentions, or about Mary Jane not having come round last night) except in special circumstances, including that of neurotic self-deception in the speaker. But contrasting with this is the case when (e.g.) a juryman treats what one witness says as one bit of evidence amongst others to be weighed against what other witnesses say and what some of the circumstances suggest.[13]

The first of these cases is one in which the speaker takes Jones to have knowledge as to whether or not P, and takes his telling one that P as putting one in the position of also having knowledge, and its existence is part of the basis for saying that predicate "intended to X", "was in pain", "saw Brown at the party", "chatted to Smith"

---

[13]The contrast between using a person's word as evidence and taking it as authority is well-made by Josef Pieper, *Belief and Faith*, and is the lynch-pin of accounts of belief upon faith upon God's word in traditional Catholic and Evangelical accounts of Christian faith. Faith upon God's word was made the basis of non-immediate knowledge in Descartes.

have the same sense whether said by Jones using the pronoun "I" or said by the person who believes on Jones' word and reports "Jones intended to X", "Jones was in pain", "Jones saw Brown at the party", or "Jones chatted to Smith". That is, there is no way in which these predicates, ascribed by me to Jones, merely have the sense that Jones' behaviour, including what he said, was of a certain kind, viz., the kind of behaviour I would evince if I would ascribe these predicates to myself. For it is exactly the same thing (property or attribute) that I attribute to Jones as he attributed to himself or indeed as I, using his words, might attribute to myself.

We have here the underlying reason for our insistence that the predicates in question have the same meaning as applied by a person to others as they do when applied by a person to him or herself. The presumption (obviously often questionable) underlying human communication is one of trust so that in what each person says to another person he or she extends to that other person the same situation of knowledge or belief, with the same degree respectively of certainty or sureness, that he or she has him or herself.[14]

The existence of a presumption of this sort does not constitute an unspoken qualification of the sort "On the presumption that the communications I have received are honest, . . . ", accompanying every statement into whose acceptance the testimony of others has played a part. The supposition that it does is like the suppositions that "Probably, . . ." or "It seems that . . ." are implicit operators within every statement and is to be objected to on three grounds: the first, that an operator that enters into all statements is one which makes no difference and whose meaning is inaccessible; the second, that no presentation of what is known (i.e., no system of first order statements) can be founded upon an account of its credentials or how it is known (i.e., some system of second order statements); and the third, that the acquisition and the functioning of language depend upon some element of credence between established language-user and learner, speaker and hearer. It should be noted that mentioning this third

---

[14]The epistemological importance of knowledge and belief on human testimony, and, more extensively, on human authority, was set aside by Descartes and by Hume. But its importance was seen by Thomas Reid, and the most developed recent studies have been those of C. A. J. Coady. That in belief upon testimony, a person's word is 'how one knows', rather than merely a reason for belief, is of key importance to its place in the structure of human knowing, cf. David Braine, 'The Nature of Knowledge'.

ground does not make the presence of such credence into a criterion of whether the language-game concerned is properly established or valid, as if this were something which had to be tested for beforehand, but only marks that such credence will be found to be present constituting an indication of the already clear fact of the valid use of the language-game.

(c) The treatment of memory and identity over time

The second regard in which Strawson's account demands development, if it is to stand at all, is in the treatment of memory and one's knowledge of one's own identity over time. For it is evident that it is as common or more common for the first person statements which a speaker makes about himself, not on the basis of behavioural criteria (but fully warranted nonetheless) to be in the past, not the present, tense. Thus, we not only say "I am in pain", "I think that...", "I intend to...", "I see...", "I am engaged in building a tool-box", and suchlike, but also "I was in pain", "I thought that...", "I intended to...", "I saw...", "I was engaged in building a tool-box", and so forth. All these are cases of statements of whose truth others may judge on the basis of the use of behavioural criteria but whose truth I may know without using any such criteria. And what is involved in the truth of the second group of statements includes the identity of me, the speaker today, with the person who, at or within the appropriate past time to be understood from the statement, was in pain, thought..., intended to..., saw..., was building a tool-box, and so forth. And, although there are criteria for judging of the personal identity of me, as the present speaker, with a person who did indeed do these things at or within the time concerned, I myself do not (except in odd cases, such as when I retrospectively consider a case in which I have suffered amnesia) use these criteria.[15]

Berkeley in his earlier thought, revealed in his *Philosophical Commentaries*, conceived of the self in Hume's way as but a 'congeries of perceptions', but later realized the absurdity of supposing the existence of a perception, in the sense of a perceiving rather than of an object perceived, without the existence of a perceiver. In his *Principles* he conceives the self as the substance which is the subject of the relations

---

[15]We owe this clear way of describing the situation to Sydney Shoemaker in *Self-Knowledge and Self-Identity*.

of mind to ideas, such as perceiving, imagining, and willing, and regards neither the self nor these relations as objects of any kind of perception (the objects of perception being ideas, conceived of in the way Hume conceived impressions)—in this way, conceiving the self as an Aristotelian substance, the subject of perceptions and operations.[16] He thereby restored a logic in which operations were neither subjects nor objects but things designated by the complete propositions wherein relations of subject to object are asserted, the logic which Hume was to neglect. In all this he anticipated Kant who reckoned that there could be no experience without an experiencer, so that any experience or perception of an object required a knowledge of the experiencer and of the experiencing in the act of having perceptual knowledge of the object, but neither the experiencer nor the experiencing being objects of experiential knowledge.

This knowledge of ourselves, which is not a knowledge had by using behavioural criteria, should not be supposed to be limited to the knowledge that some person (perhaps ourselves or perhaps not) was at one time in one state of consciousness, some person (perhaps the same or perhaps not) was at some later time in another, some person (again perhaps the same and perhaps not) was at some yet later time in yet another, and so forth—all these times being past, together with our knowledge that we are at present in such and such states, as if we had no knowledge of ourselves as continuing through states. For each kind of 'state' is of a sort to be expressed in the form of a proposition: we have instanced such propositions as "I was in pain", "I am in pain", "I was engaged in building a tool-box", "I am engaged in building a tool-box", "I saw . . .", "I see . . .", "I intended to . . .", "I intend to . . .", "I thought . . .", "I think . . .". But the idea of 'state' is here used informally (we must distinguish what philosophers call 'states', following the ordinary

---

[16]That this is the fundamental logic of Berkeley's later position is made plain in *The Principles of Human Knowledge*, Part I, paras. 2, 7, 27, 86, and 89, which make plain that the self is not only that which acts but also that which perceives, and something 'entirely distinct' from ideas (Berkeley, para. 2). Berkeley carefully distinguishes subject, relation (perceiving or operating), and ideas as objects of relations, and these passages have a clarity quite overlooked in 'The Self in Berkeley's Philosophy' by A.C. Lloyd whose argument depends entirely on the earlier Notebooks (*Philosophical Commentaries*)—confusing the self with activity and confusing ideas with the consciousness of them (Lloyd, p. 192) in a way which the references I gave above show to be utterly foreign to the Berkeley of the *Principles*.

usage of the word, including dispositions, to contrast them respectively with achievements or acts; accomplishments, performances, tasks, or processes; and activities).

Each such propositionally expressible 'state' has some accidental and some non-accidental relations with others. Thus, I may be aware of seeing something while building my tool-box or at the same time as hearing something. Or I may be aware of running away out of fear of a bull which I saw moving towards me, and though I may not have had any intervening thought that a bull was dangerous I will certainly have been involved from the moment of sight in a conviction of its being dangerous, and of this as inspiring my running away, which I will certainly be aware of as being intentional, besides knowing its intention. Into this saga may enter many elements, the hedge over which I wondered whether I could jump, the gate which I climbed and fell off, the relief I experienced while resting in the wet mud the other side, and the excitement I felt while recounting the whole incident to my hosts at the farm and which remained with me as I lay in bed that night. Observation enters into this history, and with some of the observing, knowledge of the observing. I have some perceptual knowledge of my body, but I do not check that it is the same body which runs, which climbs, which gets muddy, which jabbers out its story, and which lies in bed. Thus, knowledge of my own identity is not just knowledge of discrete 'states' or sets of 'states' all at definite moments of time, but of continuance through 'states' of many logically different temporal types.

Once it is realized that we do not have to use criteria of identity in making past tensed statements of the kinds I have instanced any more than in making the present tensed ones, the sameness of the way in which these two kinds of statement—the one drawing upon memory and the other not—fit into the structure of Strawson's account becomes evident, along with their parallel status for the purposes of communication with others and of knowledge upon testimony.

Against this background, we do not need to introduce what C.O. Evans called a 'self-approach' in order to explain a 'native knowledge of the self' which does not depend on a use of criteria for sortal or 'referential' identification (i.e., upon criteria for deciding of what kind I myself am, and for distinguishing which thing of that kind I am).[17]

---

[17] *The Subject of Consciousness*, pp. 22–28.

He supposes that, if, in using the word "I" of myself in saying "I am depressed", I implied a classification of this 'I' which I am aware of as being depressed as a body or as a 'person' conceived of as a bodily being, I would have thereby presupposed a use of criteria for deciding that I was an entity of this sort. And, appreciating that we do not make any such use of criteria, he concludes that there must be some awareness of the self as conscious involved in experiencing which does not demand a use of criteria for being bodily, i.e., does not demand that use of criteria which he takes it would be necessary for me to make before ascribing 'states' of consciousness to myself in conversation with others.[18] But none of this construction is necessary once it is realized that it is presupposed even in conversation with others that we will not normally have had to use criteria to be in a proper position to make statements of the kinds concerned of ourselves in conversation. The idea he expresses that the persons-approach seeks to offer an answer to the question 'What are they?' asked of the 'selves', which it is the aim of the self-approach to identify experientially,[19] embodies precisely the idea of a self which one identifies in one's own case prior to and independently of the capacity to identify others, which it was the aim of Wittgenstein and Strawson to exorcise.

2. Our Knowledge of Others from Their Behaviour

The idea that we can ascribe mind-involving predicates to others simply on the basis of observing their behaviour seemed particularly obvious to Ryle and is deeply set in Wittgenstein as well as implicit

---

[18]The self or 'unprojected consciousness' is, in his view, that which experiences are *to*, not that which they are experiences *of* (i.e., not the subject of which they are predicated, the possessor to which they belong), *op. cit.*, pp. 25–26. The "to" connotes the passivity or role as receiver of the subject in experience.

[19]*Op. cit.*, p. 26. Of course, his design was to show that even this 'awareness of oneself', which he had invented as something distinct from knowledge of oneself *qua* person, was something which had bodily criteria and belonged to one as a bodily being, in his design of showing that even this self-knowledge was propositional and that it involved the body non-contingently in such a way as to be incompatible both with a Pure Ego theory and a bundle theory of the self (pp. 26–36). What is of value in Evans' discussion is the way he explains the presence of physiological elements in what he calls the 'unprojected consciousness' presupposed in attention, drawing on the ideas of TH. Ribot: this is important for the explanation of the quasi-behavioural criteria of continuity in 'stationary' conscious activity, e.g., watching, and for one's account of the interplay between self-knowledge not by observation and awareness of one's own body in such cases (*op. cit.*, pp. 70–73, 80–128).

in the system of thinking to be found in Merleau-Ponty's *Structure of Behaviour*. It was codified by Strawson in his insistence that there are 'logically adequate behaviour-criteria' for the ascription of 'P-predicates' to others.[20]

The idea seems, indeed, so natural that in many cases it is very odd to speak of 'criteria' at all—as if when I saw a person walking or when I heard what they said to me I merely had 'evidence' from which I might, on reflection, judge that they intended to walk or meant this or that. It is for this reason that Strawson draws attention to the case of intentional action in order to explain how it should seem natural to have a way of thinking and talking, a structure of discourse, within which the concept of 'person' and this class of P-predicates, other-ascribable on the basis of observation of behaviour and self-ascribable without dependence on such observation, have an, as it were, 'given' or uneliminable role.

In thus thinking of physical intentional action as something self-ascribed without reliance on the observation of behaviour at the same time as being other-ascribed on the basis of such observation, Strawson seems to be implicitly taking the same view of action as is to be found most developed in Anscombe's *Intention*.[21] It is the view already explained in Chapter IV whereby we have a knowledge of our own intentional actions in the respects in which we intend them simply in virtue of their being actions we do intentionally: we do not

---

[20]For Ayer's criticism of this presentation by Strawson, see *Concept of a Person and Other Essays*, in the title essay and especially pp. 96–102, 104–112.

[21]The idea that knowledge of the intentional character of the actions of others, and even what the particular intentions with which they were done, can be known (and not indirectly) from behaviour, has been commonplace (though often disputed) since the time of Ryle's writing in *The Concept of Mind*. Ryle supposes intention to be related to action rather adverbially than causally in the sense that being done intentionally is rather a matter of the manner of an action than its cause, a matter of its not being a defective case of human action in the way various things done 'not voluntarily' are, and an intention is rather a disposition in accord with which an action is done than an inner state or occurrence. But what is noteworthy in Anscombe and Strawson is the combination of such views as these (perhaps less crudely presented than in Ryle) about the ascription of intentional action and particular intentions to others with a much clearer grasp of the different basis of the self-ascription of these things. This insight is also present in Hampshire's *Thought and Action*, but more evident in his discussion of the intentional movements associated with perception (in varying vantage point, etc.) than in his discussion of intentional action, which is more occupied with our own knowledge of intention than with our knowledge of our own actions.

discover our picking up a bag of potatoes in a supermarket when this is done intentionally and precisely what we intended in our action, whereas the person watching our shopping without knowledge of our intentions will know of our action by observation.[22]

In thus thinking of physical intentional action as *a paradigm case of what it seems 'natural' to take in this way,* 'natural' to take as something self-ascribed without reliance on the observation of behaviour and other-ascribed on the basis of such observation, Strawson is taking a certain view of perception as well as of action. It is the view of perception involved by our approach in Chapter II.

Thus, any following through of Austin's understanding of the variety of 'objects' of perception, so that it is not only material objects that we see but also, along with shadows and other non-bodily things, the shapes of cats and men being shaved, will carry with it that we see *animals and people as such* and hear *speech in its meaning as such* so that perceived behaviour is not merely material. And this way of thinking of behaviour underlies Ryle: the statements about behaviour in terms of which 'mental' dispositions are specified and explained are not statements about the movements of conglomerations of atoms but about behaviour understood and described as intentional; the norm of what we think of and see as 'human behaviour' is to be 'voluntary', the point of such a description being understood by realizing the deviations whose absence it implies,[23] and the same would apply with 'free' and 'intentional'. The same conception of the perception of behaviour imbues Wittgenstein and is echoed in his remark 'My attitude towards him is an attitude towards a soul. I am not of the *opinion* that he has a soul.'[24] This way of conceiving our experience and perception of other people is most obvious in Merleau-Ponty, while the framework for seeing its *explanatory* importance in psychology is provided by Charles Taylor in his book *The Explanation of Behaviour.*

---

[22]Cf. Anscombe, *Intention.*

[23]These ways of thinking, or these insights, separately inspired in Ryle and in Austin, are presupposed rather than explicit in the writings that come to us. They are not codified into a systematized doctrine, with the result that Ryle has been misread as if he were a logical behaviourist, reducing the mental to the 'purely' physical, and Austin read as if what he said on perception had no implications for the 'other minds' problem.

[24]*Phil. Inv.,* II, iv.

(a) The quasi-autonomous or truly mental character of mental states ascribed on the basis of behaviour

However, the naturalness of this way of thinking of perception and in general of our experience of other people, its indispensability phenomenologically for describing what we perceive as we perceive it and describing our experience of other people as we experience it, must not prevent us from insisting upon some absolutely vital clarifications.

It must be kept absolutely unmistakable that what we ascribe to others on the basis of observing their behaviour is the very same thing as we ascribe to ourselves in the present or by memory or to others on the basis of their testimony. It is not merely a property of behaviour, but something just as mental as that which we ascribe to ourselves (e.g., when we say that we are in pain or depressed, or that we saw or heard such and such, or that we intend, believe or want so and so, or that we intentionally did this or that).

Thus, our capacity for self-ascription is not just an incidental property of these mind-involving predicates but essential to their meaning. And it is this above all of which the 'causal theory of knowledge' fails to take account. It represents us, not in a situation of knowledge in regard to our own mental states, but only in a situation of belief, belief happily caused in such a way that beliefs thus acquired tend to be true. In this way knowledge, authority, or the tendency to authority in respect of one's own mental states is implied to be entirely extrinsic to the character of these mental states, a logical accident arising from a standard causal context. But this means that those who accept the causal theory of knowledge cannot regard self-ascription as of itself ascription from a *prima facie* standpoint of knowledge, simply in virtue of the meaning of the terms for the mental states concerned, inseparably from the identity of these mental states for what they are—as fear, as anger, as pain, or as belief, intention or want. Rather they must regard this capacity for authoritative self-ascription as something only accidental to the meaning of the terms concerned, and therefore (despite themselves) have nothing to fall back upon except an account which defines mental states as behavioural dispositions.

It is the quasi-autonomy of mental states, whereby they cannot be defined simply behaviouristically but have to be understood in a way which allows for authoritative self-ascription, that has led empiricists from Mill to Ayer[25] to think that the so-called 'mental states' or 'states' of consciousness of other human beings, as supposedly distinct existences, must be problematic for us to know—inaccessible or else dependent for being known on an inductive argument by analogy from one's own case, rather than known directly from observation of behaviour.[26] Therefore, we must first achieve the epistemological clarifications needed to deal with the difficulties of Ayer and his company and second, ward off the incipient tendency for behaviourism to creep back, explaining the mental as if it consisted in tendencies or capacities in behaviour—a tendency which grossly distorts much recent philosophy of language.

(b) How we know mental states from behaviour: the presumption of normality and the stratification of criteria

The common conception of 'criteria of application of a concept' is that, for the application of some predicate F, a set of necessary and sufficient conditions can be laid down for the application of F. This amounts to giving some kind of 'definition' to the predicate, it being perhaps left open whether all definitions are such that their applications are tautologies or analytic propositions, or whether, like Husserl's accounts of particular essences, they might be (since the relations concerned belong to a special subject-matter, and are therefore in no way formal, trifling, or verbal) synthetic a priori.

---

[25]Ayer, *Philosophical Essays*, pp. 199–214, cf. Malcolm, *Problems of Mind*, pp. 16–23.

[26]Ayer has doubts as to whether any observations of behaviour can suffice to make certain some particular ascription of a 'conscious state', rather than merely 'inductively probable'. The difficulty in establishing the presence of a mental state on the basis of any finite set of observations of behaviour is raised in a quite different way by Kripke, in connection with how we gain from observation of a finite number of instances of the following of some particular rule (without knowledge apart from these observations of what the rule is), the understanding involved in being able to follow the rule correctly, or in knowing what rule it is intended by teacher or speaker that the hearer or learner should understand to be being followed. But here again part of the problem arises from the assumption that the hearer or learner approaches the problem without being in a position to make any presumptions including presumptions as to the type of disposition being exercised (a skill, *hexis* or 'many-track' disposition, rather than a mechanical behavioural regularity, mere habit or 'single-track' disposition, to put the thing in Rylean terms), and as to the normality of the particular disposition being exercised. I reserve fuller discussion to my collaterally planned work *The Expressiveness of Words: the key to the nature of language.*

However, a little attention to particular cases suggests a quite different model. 'Criterion' is an epistemological notion, and, if we consider our modes of knowledge (i.e., our modes of verification and falsification) of statements about other people, it is plain that we proceed in a certain order.

In brief, we presume a case to be 'normal' or to conform to some 'paradigm'[27] until some reason arises for doubting such presumption. Let us consider some examples of this.

We presume people not to be lying or pretending unless reason for doubt presents itself. We presume many common species of human action to be 'free', 'voluntary', and 'intentional' until this presumption is weakened. The point of such concepts as 'free' and 'voluntary' is seen when we envisage the spread of different cases in which an action fails to be free or voluntary, and when we say an action is 'free' or 'voluntary' we mark it as not failing of the paradigm in any of the open-ended list of ways in which such failure may arise. There is a parallel with the way Austin treats of being a 'real duck': we presume, if people in an unspecialized context speak of ducks, that they intend to refer not to toy, decoy, . . . , and to say that a 'real' duck was intended is to say that one is not occupied with any of these, in different ways, deviant cases.

The point we are concerned with is not a logical one, of the meaning of words like "real", but the epistemological one whereby a certain presumption is appropriate until it is, as it were, defeated. The same structure arises when we consider claims to knowledge: we often have adequate grounds for attributing knowledge, but however adequate the grounds, the claim may be defeated by new discovery, e.g., that the proposition said to be known is false or that the experiments on which the knowledge was pretendedly based were counterfeit or

---

[27] I have used the notion of norm or paradigm case. This notion is valuable even though there is nothing sacrosanct about it. We are familiar with the argument that there is no one paradigm type of case of being a game and with the suggestion that there is a spread of characteristics typical of games, but few or none that all games share. What is defective about most treatments of 'games' is that their internal features rather than their context is considered: what they have in common is that they are played: the difficulty should be considered to be, not what internal features are common to all games, but how we should characterize the type of play concerned. And it is at this point that the notion of paradigm may come back into its own. But it may often or generally be better to think of a range of paradigms analogous to one another.

that in some other way it was a pure accident that the supposed knower got it right.

In other words, most of the concepts we use have a meaning such that they may be properly applied, and knowledge claimed, when certain conditions are fulfilled, but also such that such applications and claims to knowledge are not infallible but defeasible: in each case, there is a spread of ways in which, despite the fulfillment of the conditions mentioned, the concept may fail to apply, and in connection with each of these ways we have further means of test as to whether or not they are arising in the case we are considering. In this way, a hierarchy of sets of conditions may arise: suppose a predicate F paradigmatically applies in circumstances C, and suppose that there are a number of ways in which F may fail to apply in the circumstances C, then for each of these ways there will be a type of explanation, account, or classification, E1, E2, E3, etc., indicating why the deviations arose or of what type the deviations were, and there will be paradigm ways in which E1, etc., arise; but then, in each of these cases, a similar situation may arise that the example we are considering does not exactly fit or is a case of some new peculiar type with its own characterization, but a characterization not as a peculiar variation on F but as a peculiar variation on (say) E1. That is, it is not just that there are paradigm cases of perception, or of intentional action, but that there are paradigm cases of illusion or of hallucination, or of the involuntary or the unintentional, or of that which is done by mistake or of that which is done by accident. And at each level we presume the norm or paradigm until reason shows itself to seek a more complex account. Our characterizations and divisions between types of deviation from a norm may change as we get a better understanding of the explanations of particular cases of deviation.

Therefore, we need to replace the notion of 'logically adequate behaviour-criteria' by the notion of a 'logically stratified set of groups of criteria' where the stratification is of such a kind that the meaning of the predicate under consideration together with the previously applied groups of criteria, the underlying strata, determine or structure the context of the later groups of criteria. Thus, in many cases the first group of criteria (that is, the first group of determinants of judgement) will be what the other person says, treated as testimony. But the meaning of the predicate will be such as to determine, not only that testimony normally gives knowledge, but also that certain behaviour (the second stratum) would verify such testimony and would normally be adequate to show that the predicate applies. But, beyond this, the meaning of the predicate will also set the structure whereby certain kinds of further evidence break the presumption that even this second stratum of criteria is decisive and determine the range of further criteria which should be looked for.

The question will be raised as to what defines 'normality' at each stage. Here what it is vital to resist is a definition of the 'normal' in terms of the criteria set by either a Humean regularity theory or a physicalist theory of causality. What is normal is made clear as the patterns of explanation in each area and at each stage become clear, and at the first stages of dealing with human beings and animals these patterns are holistic and teleological, as will become unmistakeable in Chapters VII and VIII: the privilege of memory-claims and testimony and of the character of normal patterns of relation of mental state and behaviour is inset, and it is only when we come to disorders in human and animal perception and behaviour that features which do not fit with these holistic and teleological patterns become relevant and rather to be understood statistically and physically.

(c) Incipient behaviourism: the mistake of identifying mental states with behavioural capacities or practical abilities

We must now see how easily the position we have outlined can be given a behaviourist twist.

We have already noted the neglect on the part of Ryle sufficiently to disambiguate his use of the word "behaviour", and earlier, his mistaken attempt to over-assimilate the modes of self-knowledge to the modes of knowledge of others. We also saw how Strawson not only avoids these mistakes but also the mistakes of Wittgenstein and the earlier Malcolm in denying that "I am in pain" is a statement or can express knowledge. What we have now to see is how even Malcolm's later explanations have a reductionist tendency of a behaviourist kind. It is especially important to refute Malcolm's suggestions because of their vicious effects when revived in the philosophy of language by Dummett and his followers, effects whose crucial importance will appear in Chapter X.

Malcolm in *Problems of Mind* interprets Wittgenstein's remarks about different mental attributions—understanding, intention, pain, and so forth—as arguing for the position that understanding the meaning of a word is present if and only if certain practical abilities are present. In this way he erects into a reductionist doctrine what had been represented only as a therapy: 'Always get rid of the private object in this way: assume that it constantly changes, but that you do not notice the change because your memory constantly deceives you'.[28] This is a therapy which fits with Wittgenstein's idea that 'a wheel that can be turned although nothing else moves with it, is not part of the mechanism.'[29] Malcolm postulates the possibility of a man, Robinson, who shows all the practical abilities required for ascription of pain to others but who has never experienced pain himself, and so, in respect of himself, denies that he has ever been in pain—and indeed has never exhibited behaviour such as would make it appropriate for others to ascribe pain to him. Such a man, in Malcolm's view, knows the meaning of the word "pain" and knows what pain is, and, in Malcolm's view, this man has fulfilled the requirements stated by Wittgenstein in the form 'You learned the *concept* 'pain' when you learned language.'[30]

But understanding the concept of pain turns upon gaining the capacities for self-ascription and for other-ascription in one act, or one unitary process of learning, so that the two capacities are inseparable and interdependent, or, we might better say, one and the same capacity—two only in specification. For the capacity for self-ascription not on the basis of behaviour is the capacity to apply understandingly to oneself a predicate which we understand as also ascribable on the basis of behaviour. Likewise the capacity for other-ascription on the basis of behaviour is the capacity to apply understandingly to others a predicate which we understand as also ascribable to oneself not on the basis of behaviour. Therefore, Wittgenstein's remarks do not have the tendency to reduce the understanding of a word to a set of capacities since the capacities are precisely capacities to use the word concerned understandingly and the understanding is unitary—not that there could not be a different usage, but then that different usage would embody a different language-game and a different understanding.

Therefore, in considering Malcolm's imagined case of the man Robinson, we must insist that the case of self-ascription is not just

---

[28]Wittgenstein, *Philosophical Investigations*, II, xi, p. 207.
[29]*Phil. Inv.*, Part I, Sec. 271.
[30]*Phil. Inv.*, Part I, Sec. 384.

another case, equal in footing or relevance to any of the many other person cases, but is, as it were, one of the twin foci of the ellipse, each equally integral to the language-game and unitary understanding concerned. A concept of pain in the case of which there was no necessary possibility of self-ascription without the use of behavioural criteria, a concept wholly explicable in terms of behaviour, would be a different concept from the one we have, just as a concept of pain defined in terms of stimulation of certain nerve cells would be a different concept. One could rightly compare the case of depression: a concept of depression defined entirely in terms of behaviour and not applicable by a person to him or herself without using behavioural criteria, would not be the concept we use when we say "I am depressed".

Further, we can add that if a person has never had any experience of pain, there will be no adequate warrant for the saying that he or she would use the word correctly in regard to him or herself, as I will now show.

Malcolm's Robinson might exhibit *some* 'pain-behaviour' but deny being in pain and show no distress or aversion and there is no scent of his exercising some special self-control—he writhes when some instrument of pain is used but says 'How pleasant! Go on', but there is no systematic evidence that he is a masochist—and we can find no reason, except the peculiarity of the case, to suppose that he is pretending when he denies pain. In such a case, our knowledge of human nature tends to make us presume self-control or masochism and presume that he is pretending, knowing how such instruments normally act on the nervous system and the common context of such writhing. But since we can also hypothesize that the writhing is just a physical reflex roused by our action upon the nervous system, just as we can rouse reflexes in the insensitive parts of paralysed people, there would be no adequate warrant for ascribing pain to him and for adopting, without any other substantiation, hypotheses of pretence, self-control, or masochism. In this way, there would be no way in which we could reassure ourselves that 'everything was in order in Robinson's use of the word "pain" ', and no way in which we could be assured that 'he knew the meaning of the word "pain" ' or 'knew what pain was' and that therefore he knew what other people were ascribing to themselves when he construed them as self-ascribing pain.

The capacity for self-ascription without observation is integral to Strawson's account. But unless cases arise in which Robinson both would ascribe pain to himself and has an overall behaviour pattern appropriate to being in pain, and not paradoxical in the way of the case just described, we have no warrant for saying that, in typical cases, Robinson would have ascribed pain to himself if he had suffered pain. (Of course, in ordinary life people can have pain in particular cases without noticing it, e.g., because their attention is altogether concentrated on something else. But such cases do not suggest that they do not know the meaning of the word "pain".)

In brief, then, Wittgenstein's argument and position do not involve breaking all connection between knowing what pain is and having known pain. Rather, he breaks the idea that the meaning of the word "pain" is gained through some exercise of 'inner sense' so that its connection with various kinds of pain-behaviour is logically (i.e., from the point of view of the meaning of the word) accidental. (And, we may remark, any imaginatively deeper literary or psychological penetration of 'what pain is' or 'what it is to know pain' will develop its portrayals, not by ever more developed 'descriptions' of something 'introspected', but rather by delineating the depth of its interference with the activities of life and their enjoyment, and its link with associated emotions.)

What I have argued in regard to pain applies *a fortiori* to the case of moods, such as that of depression, which is the instance which Strawson takes in order to explain by example how he understands his key class of P-predicates.[31]

3. Avoiding the Conception of Inner Sense

The finely balanced perspective whereby with mentalistic concepts we have one unitary meaning to which the possibility of each kind of verification is indispensable can be overthrown in two ways. One is by the revival of behaviourism we have just examined. The other is by restoring introspection and therewith the possibility of an introspectionist account of the meaning of the terms concerned. To see how easily introspectionism can return, we must grasp how Strawson's phrase 'on the basis of' is ambiguous and can still, despite his intention, be construed in a way compatible with a belief in inner

---

[31]Strawson, *Individuals*, pp. 108–109.

sense or introspection as the source of one's knowledge in one's own case. To avoid this mistake, I draw on the discussions of Austin, Wittgenstein and Malcolm.

Thus, if one said that one ascribed the predicate in question to oneself on the basis of introspecting an experience, either one would be back with the problems of apparent dual meaning (one meaning appreciated through introspection and another signifying a certain behaviour pattern), or else one would need to have knowledge of a synthetic a priori proposition connecting some basic meaning appreciated through introspection with various behaviour patterns, so that we would not observe pain or fear in others but only infer them, knowing of them only indirectly from behaviour. But it is clear that the idea that knowledge from behaviour is indirect is a key part of what Strawson is repudiating. And, as we shall re-emphasise below, precisely the insight to be gleaned from such authors as Ryle, Wittgenstein, and Merleau-Ponty is that we so observe others as to observe pain, fear, anger, and intention—not observing them in isolation, but in observing groaning with pain, cringing with fear, voice heightened with anger, and acts done intentionally. Therefore, if we suppose these thinkers to be right, it must be wrong to say that we know of these things only indirectly from behaviour.[32]

Therefore, we need to find some other interpretation of 'on the basis of', if we are to be able to interpret Strawson in a way which accords with his own or these other thinkers' intent.

In order to see the possibility of some other interpretation, we need to draw upon the distinction made by Austin between what puts one in a position to know (stated in answer to 'How do you know?') and what serves as a reason for belief, i.e., as evidence (stated in answer to 'Why do you believe?'). Strawson's 'on the basis of' is to be construed as 'on the basis of, as a ground of knowledge', rather than as 'on the basis of, as a reason for belief'.[33] This making of the

---

[32]The statement of the connection between pain and behaviour will, of course, still be a non-analytic a priori proposition, non-analytic in the technical sense that it does not arise from the formal logic and set theory which apply isomorphically to all subject-matters, abstract or concrete, but draws upon the properties of some special subject-matter. But the capacity to use the word "pain" understandingly both in self-ascription and in other-ascription does not draw upon (is not mediated through) this proposition, but is rather the source of our knowledge of it.

[33]Austin, 'Other Minds', *Philosophical Papers*.

distinction between what puts me in a position of knowledge and what counts as a reason for believing constitutes a practically indispensable background for an accurate grasp of what is essential in the rejection of private objects and any 'private language' by Wittgenstein and followers such as Malcolm.

The most obvious case of my being in a position to know a state of my mind, but not by any kind of inner observation, is that of my knowledge of my own beliefs and intentions. As Wittgenstein says:

> That he believes such-and-such, *we* gather from observation of his person, but *he* does not make the statement "I believe..." on grounds of observation of himself. And *that* is why "I believe P" may be equivalent to the assertion of "P".[34]

That is, there is no extra introspected private state witnessed to when a person says "I believe P" over and above what is already displayed when he asserts "P".

However, the main discussion of inner sense or introspection has centred on the case of pain. To this I now turn.

If by inner sense or 'introspection' I were able to attend to, and identify as of a certain kind, some inner object, e.g., a pain or other sensation, somewhat as by the sense of sight I am able to attend to a lion when there is a lion before me, and identify it as of a certain kind, viz., a lion, then I would be able to use the presence or absence of a pain within the 'field' of my inner sense as a criterion of whether or not I was in pain: I would check whether or not I was in pain by ascertaining whether or not I felt pain. That is, if I were asked "Are you in pain?" I could address myself to the task of answering it by, as it were, taking an 'inner look', somewhat as, if I were asked "Is there a bus before you?" I could address myself to the task of answering it by looking (I might keep my eyes closed and then look in order to answer it). It was the work of Wittgenstein to show that this way of thinking of pain, as a distinct introspectible sensation, known as distinct from other kinds of perception and precisely a sensation of the sort we call a pain by the exercise of introspection or inner sense, was entirely wrong-headed—but, if this needed confirmation, it is to be seen in the connections between pain and various emotions made clear in Chapter IV.

---

[34] *Remarks on the Philosophy of Psychology*, Vol. I, para. 504.

In this way, it is not that some *cogitatio* or *pensée*, 'perception of the mind', or experience (being in pain is clearly an experience) is the reason for believing that I am in pain, but that being in pain is what puts me in the position of knowing without any appeal to criteria or evidence that I am in pain.[35]

It is not that I think, or if asked would assent to the proposition that, I am in pain 'without warrant' or 'without reason', but that the answer "I am in pain" serves as an answer, not by indicating a check or verification procedure which I have carried out, together with its result, nor by offering supporting evidence or any reason which would allow an inference that I was in pain, but by indicating in which kind of way I was in a position of knowledge. There is no distinction between the statement "I am in pain" of which I am being asked why I believe it or how I know it and the answer "I am in pain" which tells how I know it.

In the case of seeing a bus, there is a distinction between there being a bus there, and my seeing of it. There can be no knowledge of my seeing of it which does not include a knowledge of me as seeing it, whereas there can be knowledge of whether there is a bus there in front of me which is not a knowledge of my seeing the bus. In the case of pain there is no parallel distinction between there being a pain there and my having it or my being in pain. And there is no knowledge of there being a pain there which is not a knowledge of me having a pain or being in pain.

The presence of a bus before me, the good conditions for seeing, the good state of my optic system, and my use of my eyes to see, are what put me in a position of knowledge that there is a bus before

---

[35]In this, I part company with Shoemaker's position in *Self-Knowledge and Self-Identity*, pp. 220–225, from the points where he says that 'In general, the question "How do you know that P?" and the expression "I know that P because..." have application only if there is more than one way in which we could know that P', and a moment later reveals his reason for thinking this in the remark that 'An explanation of how one knows something, moreover, is always an attempt to justify one's knowledge claim'. This second remark reveals that, contrary to Austin, he has conformed his notion of 'reasons for knowledge' to the common idea of 'reasons for belief'. How this is a mistake is made clear in David Braine's 'The Nature of Knowledge', Sec. 4.2, pp. 51–53 (reading "as" instead of "is" in tenth line from the bottom of p. 52).

I do not mean that being in pain is 'not a reason for believing' in the sense merely that it is 'not *just* a reason for believing, but a reason for knowing' but in the sense that it is not 'a reason for believing' at all, in the primary or ordinary meaning of "reason for believing".

me, and, if asked, in regard to "There is a bus before me", how I know it, I can answer "I see it" or "I can see it". However, it may be argued that the case parallel to that of pain would be that of my being asked, in regard to "I see a bus before me", how I know it or why I believe it, and answering "I do see a bus before me". But in the case of seeing a bus, whichever question is asked, further inquiry can be made. The person's position for judging whether or not there was a bus and they saw it may not have been good, and in that case query can be raised about the subsidiary conditions of their having been in a position to know and then within some context of real query why they yet believed that there had been a bus and that they saw it (the case of lying can arise, but I leave this aside for simplicity).

No such room for further query is present in the case of pain. But this is not because pain is an inner object inaccessible to others and about which my judgements are therefore incorrigible, nor because pain is like a stark bright light set in a dark background which can never fail to be seen by an unsleeping lidless eye, not discovered but obtruding itself, and as it continues still always possessed of the initiative so as to make the idea of checking out of place, but rather because it is not an object at all. Its quality and location are matters which we may register internally to the experience itself, inseparable from relevant awareness of bodily position and aptitudes to feel about with our hands and move in ways relevantly affected by the pain. Verification of the location may be assisted by exploratory movements of our hands and experimental movements of parts of our body; but neither the experience nor such process of verification is analogous to an inner feeling about (like an inner searching by touch) or inner looking about. The pain is never an object over against me, and it is never, in the kind of sensation it is, distinguished independently of my other emotions, of my movements with their awkwardness or ease, of other appreciation of damage, and of the behaviour which exhibits these emotions, this awkwardness, and damage; and it has the particular location in the field of intertwined emotions and movements, involuntary, quasi-voluntary, and intentional, which we described earlier.

Since the meaning of the word "pain" and in each particular case, its quality and location, together with its relations to fatigue, attention to other things, and long term temporal contour, are so inseparable from this web of other things, there is no place for an account of the meaning of the word or the meaning of terms descriptive of its quality, which severs ascription to oneself—not by immediately using criteria or observation but simply because it is one's own pain—from knowledge of behaviour, sensations, and damage. And what is thus true in the case of pain is true with appropriate variations *a fortiori* in the cases of anger, fear, pleasure, desire, intention, and belief, which I discussed in Chapter IV. In the last cases, linguistic behaviour and testimony assume an additional, quite new, role as we shall see later, not just expressing an emotion or disposition, but expressing the content of a wish, intention, or belief.

VI. The Primacy of the Agent
over the Event in Causation

We have seen in earlier chapters how, at the level of description and how we experience things, perception and intentional action are each alike focused upon or have as their hub a subject, the subject of experience, the agent. And we made it clear that this focus, equally for perception and for action, is the human being or animal as such, not a pure mind nor a mere body—the key facts and statements involved being irreducibly psychophysical in character.

However, the question is: is this agent, this subject of experience, also the focus at the level of explanation and causation, and therefore at the level of reality?[1]

Here, when we come to examine modern views, we find that the focal role for the agent is repudiated. Instead it is alleged that all agent-causality is to be explained away in terms of event-causality. And this suggestion is the natural effect of a dualistic account of human or animal action. Once the outward act has been separated in conception from the context of the unitary intentional human act, the question arises as to its causes, and these causes are thought of as in the brain or the soul. Dualists and materialists agree in the picture of states and events as causes, inner causing outer in intentional action and outer causing inner in perception, inner and outer logically independent of each other. For the dualist, the inner states and events are states and events in the soul which cause or are caused by states and events in the

---

[1] I make it clear that the levels of causation and explanation and of experience and description are inseparable and that considerations of causation and explanation place us at the level of reality in Chapter VIII, Section 4 below (cf. pp. 105–120, *The Reality of Time and the Existence of God*, for a more general treatment of the logic of this connection)—the level of reality when we are dealing with the things of nature is not some underlying unknowable, but something made accessible through the consideration of causes which experience makes possible.

brain, and for the materialist, the inner states and events are simply states and goings on in the brain, describable in two different ways, psychological and physical.

In this way, the dualistic ways of thinking of action which we were attacking in Chapter IV dovetail with the modern dogma that it is events, not agents, which are the true causes, and that all so-called agent-causality has to be explained in terms of so-called event-causality. And in this way also the mythology of 'experiences' and 'tryings' or 'volitions' has come to be supported upon a mythology of events and states, each imagined to be a 'logically distinct existence', logically independent of all others, these events and states alone being causes in a primary sense.

The effect of this on the consideration of human action is all too familiar.

From within the framework of a view which regards agent-causality as primary and not reducible to event-causality, it is not difficult to explain how a human action can be both responsible and free. It is only required that one's action should not have been caused by some thing or someone other than oneself, e.g., by misinforming one or subjecting one to force, and that one's action should have been intentional and not by mistake or accidental. It does not make a man's action in choosing to become a monk or choosing to go to the cinema unfree or 'not from himself' or unexplained just because (let us suppose) there is no explanation beyond the fact of his choice for his not going back on his ideas of possible monastic vocation or of going out.

However, if it is required that agent-causality be reducible to event-causality, the situation is quite otherwise. Within this different framework, the only sense in which a person's actions, intentions, emotions, or character can be causally 'from' the person is by their being determined by his or her previous beliefs and experiences, intentions, emotions and character. There seems to be no way of escaping the dilemma, 'either determined or by chance', and no way of combining the denial of determinism with responsibility. (Whether or not it be deemed 'from' the person for some legal or other practical purpose is beside the point.) But, if one's actions, intentions, emotions, and character are only 'from' oneself in the case that they are determined by one's previous states, then one seems to have become just as much the plaything of circumstance (one's genes or whatever) as if they were due to chance.

In this way, within the framework of explanation by events in the context of states of affairs, the actions and tryings of human beings can now seem to have the character of mere happenings, things which crop up within human life, arrive upon the human scene without the human being being in any way properly their author. Yet surely, it is felt, actions do not merely happen to the agent but are somehow 'from' him or her? There is no way within the framework of event-causality for catering for this 'feeling' that the action is 'from' the person or animal. However, rather than fumble about trying to resolve an irresolvable problem,[2] we need to attack the whole theory of event-causality head on.

At the level of description and experience, it is the human beings and animals which present themselves as the things which are acting causally within human and animal intentional or directed action. The theory of event-causality is revisionist, not analysing but displacing the idea of agent-causality, whether causality by inanimate agents or causality by human beings and animals, and the revision it proposes depends upon a mythology of events as objects, of which Davidson is the most influential recent exponent.[3] Our first task is to explode this mythology, showing its exact parallelism with an older Platonic mythology of properties, kinds, or 'forms' as objects, and revealing the mistakes in the theory of explanation which have encouraged belief in them.

---

[2]One proposed solution is that acts of will or tryings have a peculiar quality of 'voluntariness', supposedly privately introspectible, which somehow exempts them from a supposed general presumption that 'happenings' just arrive upon people and the world unheralded and without anyone being responsible (O'Shaughnessy, *The Will*, Vol. 2, pp. 259–261). But it is difficult to see how an introspectible quality could remove such a presumption (whose existence seems doubtful anyway), let alone how it could go proxy for the causal relation of being 'from the agent' which is being denied.

The introspectible quality of 'voluntariness' seems to be doing duty for the 'being caused by an agent' in Chisholm's recent discussions. But at least the latter achieves the restoration of some real authorship by the human being of his actions, even if this is achieved only indirectly (in Chisholm the only direct causation by an agent is of his 'undertakings', and the rest is still left to event-causes-event causality, the inner undertaking causing the outward action).

[3]I concentrate on Davidson because his attempt at accuracy serves beautifully to expose the implausibilities of his ideas of events and causation.

1. The Mythology of Events and States as Objects

Our starting point should not be one of attack, but of simple inquiry: what are events and states?

One's natural first attempt at explaining what events and states are is to say that they are things of kinds differentiated by their different relation to time. Roughly, an event happens at a time and is something about which we ask when or at what moment it occurred: it cannot occur, one and the same event (as opposed to one and the same kind of event), at different times—e.g., Alfred hit Bridget. A state goes on holding over a period of time, never just for a moment, but one and the same state at any time within the period—e.g., Alfred trusted Bridget. Alongside them, also in different relations to time, we also speak of activities and of processes or progresses towards an end. An activity goes on over a period in such a way as to have parts, no part of the activity being present at different times—e.g., Alfred was thinking. And a process or progress towards an end is a series of activities or continuing activity directed towards a completion which it takes a period of time to reach—e.g., Alfred was building a house, and later had built the house.

At this stage, the first and most obvious observation is that the distinction between states, events, activities, and processes has to be explained by reference to the distinction between kinds of statement. They are differentiated by being reported in statements of four different kinds, kinds differentiated by modes of tensing (what linguists call 'aspect') and logical behaviour in relation to time.

However, what is much more important is the seemingly obvious point suggested by this.

It is this: the primary way of referring to events is not by means of noun expressions such as "Alfred's striking of Bridget with his fist in the sitting room at 2 p.m.", but by means of propositional expressions such as "Alfred struck Bridget with his fist in the sitting room at 2 p.m.". That is, for instance, it is perfectly appropriate to ask the cause of the event which might be referred to by these expressions by asking 'Why did Alfred strike Bridget?' It would not have been particularly more appropriate to ask 'What was the cause of Alfred's striking of Bridget?' Rather such noun expressions are merely nominalizations of the more basic propositional expressions—nominalizations occurring in certain grammatical contexts according to certain lexical rules. (Whether we refer to an event by a propositional clause or by a nominalization, if our purpose is simply to identify the event, we tend to be economical in our specifications, going only so far as to refer to it in an, in context, determinate, natural way—so it is often unnecessary in context to bring in the 'with his fist' or the 'in the sitting room' or even the 'at 2 pm'.)

This insight, that the primary way of referring to events is by sentences or sub-sentences, not by noun expressions, must not be obscured by the absence of a simple correspondence between true statements and events.

Whether a statement reports an event is commonly not clear from the statement by itself. It may be a fact that Alfred struck Bridget on Tuesday, but if he struck her many times, no one event occurring at one time is referred to when this fact is stated. In general, if several events of the same kind occur within a period, they will be distinguishable in statements distinguishing subjects, times, places, and features such as means: Alfred may have struck Bridget with his fist in the sitting room at 2 p.m. and with a saucepan in the kitchen at 6 p.m., and in another case an avalanche of snow may have struck the north of the village at the same time as another struck the south.

No statement about mundane objects is completely determinate in respect of what might make it true. If I say "Alfred hit Bridget on Tuesday", this leaves open the exact time, the place, whether it was with his fist or with a saucepan, the exact route of his fist through the air, etc.

However, if in the ordinary course of life on a certain occasion Alfred hits Bridget and does it just once, and, knowing this, I ask, after the event, what was the cause of Alfred's hitting Bridget (or, as we say, why did Alfred hit Bridget), what happened is perfectly determinate as to subjects, time, place, and all other incidental features, and I ask it in a way which presupposes that the event did occur. Therefore, when, after the event, I ask in respect of this episode why Alfred hit Bridget, I ask the cause of a determinate event lying in the past, referring to it in a way which is in context unambiguous—Alfred did hit Bridget, he did not hit her twice, etc., and I am referring to it in a way which is, in the context of what actually happened, unambiguous. And it is evident that there is no difference between asking directly why this event occurred and asking why an event of this sort occurred—no difference between why that which occurred occurred and why what occurred occurred.

From this, what emerges is that, when used to make true statements, propositional expressions such as "Alfred struck Bridget with his fist in the sitting room at 2 p.m." state facts which are always, in some respect, general. But equally it is evident that the same expressions, used in appropriate circumstances, also serve to refer to events and constitute the primary way of doing this. Thus the remedy for the difficulty we have located does not lie in resorting to the misconceived theory of events as objects, but simply in distinguishing the ways and circumstances in which propositional expressions are used.[4]

The reason why this needs to be insisted upon can be seen from the rather peculiar view with which it contrasts.

This peculiar view is the one which supposes that when we ask 'Why did Alfred strike Bridget?' we are asking the explanation of a fact, whereas when we ask 'What was the cause of Alfred's striking of Bridget?' we are asking something quite different, namely, the cause of an object (an object of the sort called an event), viz., the cause of the object identified as 'Alfred's striking of Bridget' or as 'the blow Alfred struck upon Bridget'.

The idea of distinguishing explanations of facts from causes of events is bolstered by failing to make a distinction between two types of question: (1) simple questions, "Why...?", like why Alfred hit Bridget in which the only contrast is between Alfred's hitting Bridget and Alfred's not hitting Bridget so that the question is "Why P rather than not-P?"; (2) topicalized questions, "Why...?", like why Alfred hit Bridget on Tuesday rather than on some previous day, or why he hit her at the time he did rather than at a different time on that Tuesday, or why he hit her only once and not several times on Tuesday, or why he hit her with a saucepan rather than with his fist. In every case one is asking for the explanation of a fact stated in terms presupposing that the event did take place, but in these latter cases one's questions are topicalized or concentrated on one aspect of the affair so that one is asking why one thing occurred rather than this or that other thing where the two things are alternatives (contraries like being red and

---

[4]In this way, in these last paragraphs we have circumvented the confusions generated by Davidson's realization that sentences do not as such identify events (*Essays on Actions and Events*, pp. 129–137, 167–171, cf. 114).

being blue), not simple opposites (contradictories like being red and being not red).[5]

What we are here encountering is the doctrine that events are objects. For my car to collide with a wall is for it to be the case that there exists an event x, where x is a collision, such that x is by my car, x is with a wall, and x took place at some time. Or, to take a case recently discussed, for Sebastian to stroll through the streets of Bologna at 2 a.m. is for it to be the case that there is an event x such that Sebastian strolled x, x took place in the streets of Bologna, and x was going on at 2 a.m.[6] One finds that this event is supposed to be of the sort called a stroll and that what one does with strolls is stroll them, and in parallel discussions it appears that what one does with blows is strike them.

One is confronted here with what one might call the phenomenon of being mesmerized by the abstract noun. And this is the main point we must concentrate upon.[7]

If Alfred strikes Bridget, then—on the account being presented —we have not two objects, Alfred and Bridget, being spoken of, but three, Alfred, Bridget, and a blow, these being related so that Alfred struck this blow upon Bridget. What immediately sticks out is the analogy between this type of analysis and the much older analysis of the predication of properties whereby, if for instance Socrates is wise, we have not one object, Socrates, being spoken of, but two objects, Socrates and wisdom, these being related so that Socrates has or exemplifies wisdom.

What we have here are two mythologies.

---

[5]Davidson, *op. cit.*, p. 171, fails to distinguish these types of question.

[6]Davidson, *op. cit.*, pp. 166–167.

[7]There are of course many subsidiary objections to be made against these suggestions. For instance, strictly speaking, if an event were an entity or object, one should not speak of the cause of the object, Alfred's striking of Bridget, but of the cause of the existence or occurrence of this object. And, more obviously, one should be worried about the tensing of the expressions "there is an event x, . . .", "took place", and so forth: "there is now an event which took place . . ." is contradictory, since "took place" implies "in the past", and it cannot be that the same event 'is a collision' and 'took place (in the past)'. One might try to rectify the damage by saying 'there is, was, or will be an event x, such that x is, was, or will be a collision, . . ., and took, takes, or will take place at some time'. And one might further be worried that what was going on at 2 a.m. was not a stroll (which would be a progress with a beginning and an end) but a strolling, and not an event but an activity: no event of moving is accomplished in an instant of time, although an activity may be going on at that time.

The mythology of events means that whenever a statement mentioning n objects (one object, Sebastian, or two objects, Alfred and Bridget) reports an event, its meaning is to be analysed in terms of a relation between n + 1 objects, viz., the original n objects and one extra object, the event. And the notable feature of the case is that the extra object (Sebastian's stroll or Alfred's blow upon Bridget) seems to be denoted by a noun-expression exactly corresponding to the whole statement ("Sebastian strolled" or "Alfred struck Bridget").

The other mythology is that of properties and relations, first seen in the Platonic mythology of 'forms'. This is the mythology whereby, whenever a statement mentioning n objects (e.g., one object, Socrates, said to be wise, or two objects, Socrates and Plato, the first said to be older than the second) attributes a property or relation, its meaning is to be analysed in terms of a relation between n + 1 objects, viz., the original n objects plus one extra object, the property or relation originally attributed. And in this case the notable feature is that the extra object seems to be denoted by a noun-expression exactly corresponding to the predicate in the original statement ("is wise", "is older than").

I say that we have here two mythologies because in each case certain new subjects of discourse, such as events and properties, are being counted as 'objects' in such a way as to be put in a single pool with all other 'objects' as if 'objects' constituted a single category. What is wrong with this, I will now attempt to make plain.

Let us discover what we can learn from considering the older mythology of properties and relations—or in modern guise, the mythology of concepts, features, and classes.

In the earliest Platonic mythology, being wise consisted in sharing in an entity called 'wisdom' or imitating an entity called 'the wise itself' (the paradigm of all wisdom). Developing this line of thought, being wise, being red, being round, being an 's', and being human come to be regarded as being explained by treating them as cases of having wisdom, having the colour red, having the shape round, being an instance of the letter-type 's', and belonging to the species human being. In this way, the vision suggests itself of concrete things in such relations as having, exemplifying, instantiating, exhibiting, or being a member of to entities such as virtues, colours, shapes, and species, or more generally properties, concepts, features, and classes—or (one might say, speaking yet more generally) in some relation to some kind or other of 'universal'.

In this way, all of a sudden the world comes to seem populated not only with concrete objects but also with these abstract objects—objects in special relations to concrete objects, relations such as containing as members or being shared in, had, possessed, or exemplified by. Wherever there is a one-place predicate such as " . . . is wise" or " . . . is red", there is now also a two-place predicate such as " . . . has ——" so that "Socrates is wise" is equivalent to and has to be understood in terms of "Socrates has wisdom"—since, it is argued, if we could not first identify the feature called 'wisdom', surely we could not understand the original "Socrates is wise".

It is evident that, unless they can be first explained by reference to the sense of statements such as "Socrates is wise", there is no accounting for the nature or identity of these supposed abstract objects and no explanation of what is meant by the 'having', 'exemplifying', or 'sharing' concerned. Of course, if we recognize that Socrates is wise, we thereby know that he has what we call wisdom and we could say that he has the feature or property, wisdom; but we cannot use whether or not he has wisdom in order to decide whether or not he is wise, as if our task was to search about for some entity called 'wisdom' and determine whether it was in the appropriate relation of 'being had by' to Socrates; rather, if we did not already know what it is to be wise so as (e.g.) to be able to decide whether or not a person is wise (perhaps using what he said and how he behaved as a criterion), we would not know what wisdom is.[8]

The idea of the equal status of substances and properties is often bolstered by the argument that, just as properties cannot exist without substances (or so it is said), so substances cannot exist without properties, and therefore dependence is mutual.[9] But this rests on a quite mistaken idea of how substances are prior to properties or how properties depend on substances.

---

[8] It is also clear both that this general form of explanation of n-place predicates in terms of (n + 1)-place predicates produces an infinite regress, and that, in any case, at every stage there is no way of explaining the sense of the (n + 1)-place predicate except in terms of the n-place predicate, just as there was no way of explaining what it is for Socrates to have wisdom except in terms of what it is for him to be wise.

[9] The idea that the priority of substances over properties or the dependence of properties on substances would have to be explained in terms of substances being able to exist without properties has often been taken to imply a symmetry of status between the categories of substance and property. Davidson offers an exactly parallel argument for a symmetry of status between the categories of substance and event

Of course, substances cannot exist without properties but this leaves the essential point unaffected: for there remains a semantic priority of expressions like ". . . is wise" over expressions like "wisdom" and this gives a semantic priority to substances over objects such as wisdom which are in a subordinate category. The moment the semantic priority of ". . . is wise" over "wisdom" and thereby of substances over their properties is compromised,[10] the referring expressions "Socrates" and "wisdom" being treated alike as primitives, the result is that substances and properties are treated as standing beside each other in a common pool of objects. And this is the mistake, to treat 'objects' as a genus in which all objects of reference are gathered together. To introduce a theory of properties or features as objects as if it were explanatory is to make the mistake of treating subjects of discourse (persons and material objects, shapes, colours, and other properties or features, places and times, and so forth) as if they were all given together as semantic primitives in some single pool, all of them 'objects' in some single way or sense. Instead, we should recognize that 'being' or 'object' is not a genus, and that the things we speak of belong to different categories, and that the nature and criteria of identity for subordinate categories, indeed the point if any of treating them as having proper criteria of identity, require to be explained in terms of statements about things of more fundamental categories.

We can now see what is wrong with the mythology of events.

Just as Socrates' being wise has been represented as a relation between Socrates and an entity called 'wisdom', so the colliding between Smith's car and the wall has come to be seen as a complex relation between two ordinary objects and a further entity, an event called the collision between Smith's car and the wall. When we meet such

---

(*op. cit.*, pp. 174–175). But this is no argument against the kind of semantic priority of one kind of referring expression over another which I explain in the text.

[10]It is this which is compromised by Ramsey's key supposition that there are things called propositions such that "Socrates is wise" and "Socrates has wisdom" represent two analyses of equal status of the same proposition. I simply repudiate the existence of any such super-linguistic entities as these Ramseyan propositions, insisting that such logical form as is linguistically marked is essential to the identity of a proposition. In this way, I attack Ramsey's idea of a symmetry between substance and property on grounds of logical theory, grounds more fundamental than those adduced by Strawson in *Individuals* from epistemology and considerations of modes of identification, cf. Braine, *The Reality of Time and the Existence of God*, pp. 112–117.

theories, we should bring to bear the same sort of incredulity which we are inclined to bring to bear when we are told that, in the case that Socrates is wise or is white, this is a matter of a relation between Socrates and another object, the virtue wisdom or the colour white.

The trouble with such accounts is that they get things the wrong way round: they explain the sense of " . . . is wise" in terms of the 'having' of 'wisdom' instead of vice versa. Accordingly, what is required in this case is that the one-place predications of " . . . is wise" be treated as semantically prior to the two-place predications of " . . . has ———". Of course, the category of substances cannot exist without the category of properties, just as much as vice versa, but the question is not of whether Socrates cannot exist without properties (such as wisdom, folly, or immaturity) but of whether the primary way of referring to such properties is predicative (e.g., in the form " . . . is wise") or by a singular term such as "wisdom". And what we must insist is that in the primary mode of speech, only substances are mentioned by singular terms, and properties only predicatively—so that the other mode of speech in which singular terms such as "wisdom" appear is semantically secondary.

And the same medicine which dispatches properties, classes, and relations, putting them in their rightful secondary place, serves also to deal with events.

Of course, the category of mundane substances cannot exist without the category of events—Smith's car cannot exist without there being happenings or events involving it. But this is not to the point.[11] The question is as to the relative semantic priority of expressions like "Smith's car collided with the wall" and expressions like "the collision between Smith's car and the wall". The grand mistake involved in the mythology we are attacking is the mistake of explaining what it is for Smith's car to collide with the wall by saying that it consists in the existence of this object, the collision which Smith's car and the wall engage in. Likewise, the sense of "Sebastian strolled" in "Sebastian strolled" has been explained in terms of the existence of an event called a stroll which Sebastian strolls: in this way, the intransitive use of the verb "stroll" is explained in terms of a supposed transitive use, "strolled" being explained in terms of "strolled a stroll" or, as we more idiomatically say, "took a stroll".

---

[11]Cf. n. 9 above, with text.

The parallelism can be appreciated when we realize that, contrary to what this view suggests, we only know what a collision is from understanding statements in which one thing is said to collide with another, and only know what a stroll is from understanding statements in which (e.g.) somebody is said to stroll round the park. Further, we only know the relation between Smith's car, the collision and the wall, or of Sebastian to his stroll, through understanding the kinds of statements in which the nouns "collision" and "stroll" do not occur. It is just as in the earlier case when we registered that we only know what wisdom is, or what it is to have wisdom, from understanding the predicate "... is wise". And the theories which bring in events as objects as primary are vicious in just the same way as the theories which bring in properties or features as objects as primary. If these things are brought in as primary, then they are being brought in, as it were, in an indeterminate way or in a way which makes no categorial discriminations between them, in a common pool, cheek by jowl, events and properties with people and billiard balls, each enjoying different kinds of relation with the others.

What is involved needs to be seen in its essential crudity. By a similar logic, we could think of 'states' as objects, so that, for instance, a change of mind would become the substitution of one object, the intention to do X, by another object called "the intention to do Y" within a place called the mind—in a way formally analogous to the way one might substitute a lump of lead for a lump of iron within a certain place. And this 'substitution' of one object for another, this change of mind, will be in this heady way of thinking a new object, again of the type called an 'event' differently placed in time from 'states', and which will relate the two states of mind concerned cross-temporally.

It seems obvious that there is no one thing which is what it is to be an object. Furthermore persons, states, and events or processes are all of different categories—what is involved non-formally for each to be an object being quite different. The concept of object is a purely formal one, correlative to the formal structures of predicate logic with identity, the structures whose applicability it marks. Numbers and colours are objects, just as are events and just as are persons and billiard balls, but there is nothing, no non-formal property, which they have in common—nothing which warrants considering them together in some common pool. Object is a formal concept, not a genus containing substances, properties, and events together as all alike metaphysical and semantic primitives.

Of course, it will be said that nothing more is meant by saying that events are objects than that they can be generalized about, distinguished, and counted—to be referred by a singular term. And this is indeed all that would be meant if the term "object" were being used just as a term belonging to formal logic. But this is not the situation. The view we are attacking involves treating events as objects in a much stronger sense. It is not just that they are being regarded as capable of being referred to by noun expressions used as singular terms, but that this is being represented as the primary way of referring to them. They are being regarded as having a semantic parity with substances as if they lay together in a common pool antecedent to speech, and as if singular terms referring to events were just as primitive and just as indispensable as singular terms referring to substances. Indeed our philosophers tend to go further: they want to enthrone events in place of substances or agents as alone causes in what they consider the primary sense (and, since they suppose experiences to be one kind of event, they tend also to think that the primary objects of knowledge as well as the primary causes are events rather than substances).

Note on the relation of adjectives and adverbs: counting and describing actions

This distinction between the use of the word "object" purely in a logician's sense and its use to mark some sort of semantic priority is vital if we are to keep our bearings when we count and ascribe properties to specific kinds of events, e.g., describing some actions as clumsy, or counting kisses. Being logical subjects of properties and being distinguishable so as to be countable does not, in the least, imply semantic priority or objecthood in any metaphysical sense.

The idea that such things as actions and events have some semantic priority has been bolstered by transformational theories whereby sentences containing adverbial expressions are derived by grammatical transformation from sentences containing adjectival expressions. In this way, the adjective is made to appear semantically and grammatically prior to the adverb, and this is supposed to explain certain morphological facts—such as that in English and French it is normal for adverbials to be formed from adjectives, "clumsily", "slowly", and "easily" from "clumsy", "slow", and "easy", and even "twice" or "two times" from "two", although there is more parity between adverbs and adjectives in many other languages. E.g., in Latin *facile* is morphologically no more or less derivative than *facilis*.

However, rather than supposing "John carried the tray clumsily" to have the semantic analysis "There was an event (process) x such that x was a carrying of a tray, John performed x, and x was clumsy",[12] we can adopt a more nuanced theory. We will hold that the predicative expression " . . . carry the tray" has semantic, grammatical, and in typical cases morphological priority over the nominal "the carrying of a tray" (calling it a nominal because it is eligible to be head of a subject phrase). We will say that semantically the adverbial use of the morpheme "clumsy" is prior to the adjectival uses, so that clumsy persons are ones who act clumsily, and clumsy actions are ones which are done clumsily, and this is the right order of explanation. We will not regard any of the different morphological forms of the morpheme "clumsy" as grammatically primary as if the others arose by grammatical transformations from it. Rather we will regard the morpheme as something neutral as to morphological form and as drawn up in to different morphological forms according to grammatical function,[13] i.e., according to whether it modifies a predicate (i.e., is adverbial) or qualifies a nominal (i.e., is adjectival), in this way adopting the non-transformational perspective of contemporary grammatical theory.

Likewise, when John kisses Barbara and then kisses her again, we say he has kissed her twice or two times,[14] while since Peter was an apostle and Paul was another apostle we say Peter and Paul were two apostles. What we have in both cases is the summary of a conjunction in a quantified statement in which the quantity-indicator applies to the predicate indicating that the predicate applies twice, in one case to one subject at different times and in the other case to different subjects. We do not have to analyse "John kissed Barbara" as "John gave Barbara a kiss" in order to understand "John kissed Barbara twice" any more than in order to understand "John kissed Barbara clumsily". Here again, with "two" and "twice", just as with "clumsy" and "clumsily", we have a morpheme which is drawn up into different word-forms in different grammatical contexts, so that we have the same morphological process in

---

[12]This is the type of analysis to which Davidson would commit us: in general, adverbs and adverbial phrases including those indicating time and place are to be analysed in terms of predicates of events, *op. cit.*, pp. 105, 166–167.

[13]It will be noted that I am taking grammatical categories such as nominal, adverbial, and adjectival to be definable in terms of the relevant grammatical functions— an approach which is more compatible with Lexical Functional Grammar than with its rivals.

[14]I advert to this case because it is suggested by Davidson's argument (*op. cit.*, pp. 167 f.), and if we did not consider it our argument would be indecisive leaving an obviously open flank.

both cases despite the gulf between the semantic settings within which this process comes into play. None of the different morphological forms of such morphemes has grammatical priority although in this or that language this or that form may have morphological priority. In such contexts, we find different transformational relationships within the morphology of different languages, without elevating them to a role in a universal grammar.

The semantic analysis which suggests that we understand the verb "kiss" from understanding the verb "give" and the noun "kiss" is about as mad as an analysis which suggests that we understand the verb "state" from understanding the verb "make" and the noun "statement", or the verb "sleep" from the verb "have" and the noun "sleep". On the contrary, the semantic process proceeds in the opposite direction so that, when verbs like "kiss", "state", "sleep" and "stroll" are transmuted into a suitable formal verb like "give", "make", "have" or "take",[15] together with a noun. Accordingly, the behaviour of adverbs such as "clumsily" and "twice" does nothing to suggest that the primary way of referring to events or actions is by means of nouns rather than predicative expressions.

In this way, we can see how the fact that we describe and count actions has no tendency to imply that they are 'parts of the basic furniture of the world', basic objects in any semantic or metaphysical sense.

---

2. The Deceptiveness of Logic: The Limited Logicians' Sense in Which Events Count as Objects

(a) The significance of objecthood in logic

In order to see the radical nature of the differences of category concerned, we need to see in each case how it comes about that the things concerned—properties, classes, events, and actions—come to be regarded as objects. For this will give us the necessary clue as to the limited sense in which they can be counted as objects.

The proposed mythologies are defended on the grounds that we generalize or quantify over properties, classes, and the like, and even

---

[15]Each of these verbs has its own associations determining nuances of implication or suggestion affecting its suitability in a particular context. The constraints on which of such verbs is selected are comparable with the constraints which determine which preposition is selected in such cases as those in which we can say "assault on" instead of just "assault of".

distinguish them from each other and count them; and likewise that we generalize or quantify over, distinguish and count events, states of affairs, and processes. In each case, they are, we are told, therefore 'entities' or 'objects' and, it is insisted, not only that there is 'no entity without identity' but also that there is 'no identity without entity' (as if this told us something extra, as if being an entity or an object in the logicians' sense was being some one sort of thing).[16]

However, what we have to insist is that the sense of statements about the existence or entity-hood of logical subjects of some kind which we distinguish from each other and count, and in regard to which we generalize, is to be gauged from the sense of the statements which assert identity or distinction. Frege made it clear that this gave semantic priority to statements about lines and their relations (e.g., their being parallel to each other) over statements about directions—which have been regarded as classes of lines parallel to each other. And likewise he gave an analysis which made statements not referring to numbers as objects semantically prior to statements referring to numbers as objects. Of course, these analyses did not suggest any doubt as to directions and numbers being objects in the sense of being perfectly good logical subjects in regard to which there are statements of distinction and identity and over which there is quantification. But these analyses equally made clear a direction of explanation whereby statements which do not refer to directions or numbers as objects are semantically prior to statements which do.

The question which therefore remains concerns the sense of statements of distinction and identity in the different case of events, states, and processes—things which would seem to correspond rather to whole propositions than, as was the case of properties, classes, and numbers, to first or second level predicates. Here we will tend to concentrate on the case of events.

(b) The significance of identity statements about events

The principal reason for regarding events as objects arises from the consideration of causation. In ordinary speech, we speak both of agents (billiard balls, animals, and people) and of events and states of affairs as causes. *Prima facie*, we speak of an event or state of affairs P as

---

[16]Davidson, *op. cit.*, p. 164.

the cause of an event or state of affairs Q when we understand that Q is the case or came to be the case because P was or came to be the case, the "because" formulation being semantically more fundamental.[17] It seems that we regard a novel event or state of affairs Q as arising out of a background of previous states of affairs, standing conditions, and events out of which we pick one or two as the cause or causes of the novelty concerned. We select the cause or causes why Q, or decide what to adjudge to be that because of which Q, according to what our business in the case (so that we will specify the poor camber of the road as the cause of the accident if we are a road designer, the tiredness or drunkenness of the driver if we are a policeman, or the ice on the road if we are responsible for salting and sanding the roads) or according to what we judge abnormal or salient in the case (which may be the resolve of some agent).[18] In brief, we judge the causes and effects of P from a certain standpoint of interest which determines what is of importance or relevance.

Now it can be that from a certain standpoint of interest the causes of Q are also the causes of R, and that from this same standpoint what Q causes or explains (its effects) are the same as what R causes or explains. The interests which determine the counting of kisses do not require further clarification: once time, place, manner and person are clear, nothing else will make a difference to the patterns of explanation of interest in social life.

But the case of lightning is more instructive. From the standpoint of the physicist the causes of a discharge of electrons from earth to sky are the same as the causes of a stroke of lightning, and likewise the physical effects (e.g., the light and sound and their directions and the damage done) are the same. In such a case, we say the lightning *is* the discharge of electrons and vice versa.[19] Such a statement does not imply that everything true of or explained by the lightning is true of or explained by a certain discharge of electrons: the one is as such an

---

[17]In this view I share the view often stated by Geach, e.g., in *God and the Soul*, pp. 69 f., 81 f.

[18]In this, I consolidate the explanations given by Collingwood, 'On the so-called idea of causation', and Hart and Honoré, *Causation in the Law*.

[19]In these remarks, I introduce the notion of a 'non-strict' identity, relating it to considerations of explanatoriness and in this way reminscent of Nagel's idea of non-strict identity in "Physicalism", section III, an idea which will be again important to us in Chapter VIII, Section 3, below.

astonishing and frightening visual phenomenon and the other as such invisible, but these differences are of no concern to the physicist and so the statement of identity can stand. And, to take a quite different case, for the purposes of the ordinary conduct of human life, as distinct from the standpoint of the physiologist, it will normally be quite clear when a stabbing is a killing and when it is not, and our account will leave the uncertainties in the same place as they are found in the law courts.[20]

When we say that the lightning was a certain discharge of electrons and vice versa, we call this the "is" of identity because we have the "is" of identity whenever we have an unquantified convertible use of the copula. There is no magic in the "is" of identity—it is not a special relation but only a certain use of the copula and its use does not transmute a mere complement into an object in any metaphysical sense. If I say "To be a human being is to be a rational animal", or more precisely "To be a human being is to be a mammal of the species *homo sapiens*", I have not brought 'essences' into the fundamental ontology of the universe.

When we ask why something happened we are inquiring about the pertinent cause or causes (reason or reasons) which made a difference to whether it happened or not, which will be situations or goings on in the world or facts of some sort. We are not seeking a subject of active power or operative cause. The camber or iciness of the road, the tiredness or drunkenness of the driver, or his or her failure to notice the parked car were not possessed of any active power and are mere facts—situational aspects—adduced in the explanation or unfolding of the causes of what occurred.

What we ought to say is that a 'why something happened or came to be the case' is not an object but something aspectual, propositional in its specification, like 'that there was a vast deficit of electrons (positive charge) in the clouds' or 'there being a vast deficit of electrons in the clouds'. A cause in the sense with which we are here concerned is nothing else than a 'why something happened or came to be the case'. And to treat such things as objects in any metaphysical sense is as much a superstition as to suppose that when I have told you three things, that you are honourable, that you are expert, and that

---

[20]This approach sets the difficulties of Martin, Davidson and Kim (Davidson, *op. cit.*, pp. 133–134, 170–171) in a much more realistic setting.

you do not know everything, I have told you three objects: neither truths and untruths, nor facts or possible facts, nor events and states, are objects.

True, explanation requires, not just statements or propositions, but realities in the world or 'actualities'—realities such as events, states or situations, processes or goings on—just as what is called factual truth requires not just statements or propositions, but realities in the world. However, these realities in the world are not objects capable of being referred to and treated as having a identity except in a way geared to a possible role in explanation. And these realities precisely have to be things referred to primarily by propositional expressions rather than noun ones if they are to have the role in explanation and in making true which they do have. Realism—the view that truth and explanation are not just psychological, subjective, or conventional—does not require that all realities in the world should be basic objects or objects in a metaphysical sense, i.e., that they should be entities denoted *primarily* by noun-expressions (singular terms) rather than by propositional ones. Rather, any doctrine of truth, but especially realism, requires precisely the opposite: unless some realities were primarily referred to by propositions and only secondarily and derivatively by noun-expressions, there would be no truth and no explanation.[21]

(c) Summary of the logical situation

We are now in a position to clarify the general position. It is a question of getting underneath the technicalities involved in contemporary discussion.

Using the word "relation" in an informal sense, we can distinguish two relations. Firstly we have the relation of a causal agent to that of which he/she/it is the cause. And then secondly we have the relation expressed by "Q, because (*historically* or *causally*) P"—we might say, speaking informally, the relation whereby (P) *historically*

---

[21] It is that a situation obtains, rather than a situation as an 'object', which might have the property of obtaining or the property of not obtaining, which makes a proposition true, and strictly it is that an event occurred ('its occurring') which explains or causes the effect, not the event referred to as an object about which we might ask whether it occurred or not. (Grammatically, the use of the gerund 'its occurring' in English is analogous to the use of the infinitive in Latin to express *oratio obliqua*, and so is only a noun-expression in an ambivalent sense.)

or *causally* explains or is the cause of (Q), where (P) and (Q) are the events, states, or facts referred to by "P" and "Q".

But, this second relation is not a relation properly speaking in the technical logicians' sense. That is, "Q, because (*historically* or *causally*) P" does not satisfy the logicians' requirements of extensionality: i.e., "P" and "Q" do not appear as designations of independently specifiable entities with a range of alternative descriptions, such that for any such descriptions, P′ and Q′, "Q′ historically because P′ " would be just as true as the original "Q historically because P".

For this reason, our modern philosophers want to insinuate the idea that, quite distinct from the relation expressed by "Q, because (*historically* or *causally*) P", there is a third relation "(P) was the cause of (Q)", a relation meeting the strictest requirements of the logicians between (P) and (Q) as objects. (P) and (Q), the supposed cause and effect, are understood to be distinct entities with a range of alternative descriptions, freely intersubstitutable without affecting the truth of the relation asserted.

Now, what we have found is that the idea that there is any such third relation, distinct from that expressed by "Q, because (*historically* or *causally*) P", is a mere fancy of the philosophers. What we find instead is that there can be intersubstitutability of other expressions for "P" and "Q", *but only within the limits set by certain purposes of explanation*, not the free intersubstitutability which would be associated with an extensional relation between independently existing objects.

(d) Rescuing the theory of explanation from the idea of events as objects

The source of this fancy of philosophers, that events are objects, lies in a certain way of presenting Humean theories of explanation.

It has become conventional to think of 'ordinary causality' as being between events. And according to the view dominant since Hume, there is nothing more to this 'ordinary causality' than these events and states of affairs, each logically independent of the others, occurring in patterns in conformity to regular laws. This, we are told, is what is meant by 'causation' in the primary sense. In this view, the explanatory power of a statement that one event has caused another lies in the existence of an implication that these events and states of affairs are related by such regular laws, and this, we are told, is the only kind of 'causation' of which we have any clear understanding.

Yet even this view that the explanation of a particular occurrence consists in making plain how it exemplifies some generalization, and that the explanation of conformity to a generalization lies in conformity to a wider generalization, does not require one to treat events and states as objects. Someone might say that the match lit up because it had been struck because matches always (or usually) light up when struck, and that matches light up when struck because red phosphorus and potassium chlorate (which are the chemicals on the head of the match) always ignite when heated by friction. At no point in explanations of this type (of which these are oversimplified examples) has there been any need to refer to events, such as striking, lighting up, or igniting, as if they were objects.

However, the philosophers will represent these explanations as conforming to the following pattern: an event a of type A caused an event b of type B, because an event of type A always causes an event of type B, and this is because events of type A are all of type C, and events of type B are all of type D, and an event of type C always causes an event of type D. In this way, the philosophers by adopting a certain logical idiom create the illusion that Humean views require one to regard events and states as entities, each with its own identity and a range of alternative specifications. This indeed fits well with the requirement of the mind-brain identity theory whereby the same events in the brain, capable of purely physical specification, must also be identifiable in psychological terms. But it is entirely unnecessary to the Humean view.

Of course, the event a, which was the cause of b, can also be referred to as 'the cause of b', just as the point P which Smith just stated can be referred to as 'the point which Smith just stated'. But it does not in the least follow that events, any more than facts, 'points', or propositions, are objects in their own right, capable of being referred to in a non-explanation relative way, in the way which the mind-brain identity theory requires. We have already seen how events and states, goings on and situations, can have an explanation-geared identity which requires the primary way of referring to them to be propositional. But this is the only kind of identity they have.

In fact, the gulf set up by Davidson between causation as a relation between objects and explanation as a relation between facts or statements has a very peculiar effect. He tells us 'it is not *events* that are necessary or sufficient as causes, but events as *described* in one way or another'.[22]

We had already realized that the doctrine that mental 'events' (states or goings-on) were realized in or identical with 'events' in the brain required that the concept of 'event' should be topic-neutral so that the same event might be described indifferently in physical and psychological terms (which in turn requires that 'events' should have no criterion of identity associated with them generically).

But Davidson's account makes it clear that the situation is much more peculiar. The postulated entities called 'events' have to be conceived of as each individually having no nature relevant to explanation. The descriptions of them which are relevant to explanation have to be conceived of as accidental to their nature. They have to be entities, we know not what, which have descriptions accidental to their nature which come into explanations. This divorce between causation and explanation involves many other absurdities[23] but this is the primary one: the erection of 'events' as things in themselves to which all properties of significance in explanation are accidental. As against this, I insist that an event is nothing in itself apart from its

---

[22]*Op. cit.*, p. 172. This remark of Davidson's is one of many symptoms of the way in which an oversimple semantics (in this case derived from Tarski) can distort the understanding of metaphysics, and here, in particular, the understanding of causation.

[23]One is baffled by the prospect that an event as described physically may explain (presumably 'physically explain') other events (presumably '*as described* physically'), and that an event described in mind-involving terms may explain (shall we say '*historically* explain'?) other events (presumably *as described* in whatever way we normally do in ordinary historical explanations, e.g., not only 'the decision to blow up the bridge' but also 'the collapse of the bridge' so that the events historically explained include ones describable in purely physical terms), but that the events concerned which are going to be called causes of sundry other events should be things with a nature and existence in themselves to which the capacity to explain either physical or mental consequences is accidental.

It is not easy to count the puzzles. Physical causes operating physically are normally described in terms which makes the dispositional properties relevant to explanation consequences of their constitution. The idea of describing either constitution or dispositions in some way independent of causation, or describing physical causation without one's description having any explanatory significance, seem flights of madness. What we might have thought of as psychophysically described causes play an evident role in the historical explanation of many physical events, but what is proposed is a set of events in the mind happening to be also events in the brain to whose nature any physical effect is accidental; but the whole concept of a cause whose operation has no explanatory significance in itself, but only as described in a certain way, is puzzling.

relevance to possible explanations, that there is no divorce between events (as objects exercising causal powers) and facts (as things stated in statements) playing roles in explanations, but only certain criteria of identity which allow certain specifications of fact to count for certain purposes as descriptions of the same event.

3. The Role of Agency within Explanation

The way is now clear for an unobstructed view of the role of agency in the description of causation.

We have to distinguish three things: causal action by agents, the sorts of 'causal' relation between events and states of affairs which are specified in 'explanations' of what occurs, and knowledge of laws such as allows us to predict what will occur.

There is, of course, no suggestion that there are agents without action or relation, or without nature or disposition, and therefore no suggestion that there are agents without there being events and states playing a role in explanation. Indeed, an agent cannot cause an effect without its being by an action that he, she or it caused the effect, so that, if ever it is true that "x brought it about that P", it will also be true that "P because x brought it about that P", and, if it is true when something, (P), occurs according to and because of the action of x in A'ing, then it will be true that "P because x A'd". And this is itself an explanation, albeit a diminutive one.

But we have to ask what makes an explanation into a 'causal' explanation—for, after all, many explanations (e.g., in mathematics, geometry, and optics) are not causal at all. And the answer is that in all such cases, the explanation in which it is set forth that one event in the context of various other events and states of affairs has caused another event will make it plain that exercises of active power by agents (or the cessation of some such exercises) were crucial to what occurred. In other words, the meaning of "causally explain" or "cause" used in respect of events and states of affairs needs to be explained by reference to the meaning of causal verbs attributing causative activity to agents. Of course, we have to accept that in modern English the most common use of the word "cause" is in regard to events and states of affairs, not agents. This is because, derivatively from its original uses of causal agents, and thence its application to their causative actions, the word "cause" has come to follow the use of the words "why" and "because", somewhat as the word "condition" has come to follow the use of the word "if". But it remains that what is determinative of whether or not an explanation is to be called a 'causal explanation' is whether or not the explanation functions by bringing the event to be explained within the framework of the action and interaction of different kinds of causal agent within the same world.

And this is how causal or historical explanation works, by showing how the event being explained is the outcome of the action and interaction of the different natures at work in the world. Viewing causal relations in this way, it is natural to envisage different modes of causal action, and there is no temptation to be captivated by the physical case exemplified by the billiard ball. Rather, different agents act in different actions according to different dispositions, some involving teleology and some not, depending on the mode of agency concerned. Moreover, in this approach, the main accent has been removed from the idea that causal connection is between events or states each of which is a 'logically distinct existence', and instead put upon causal agents with different types of disposition entering into explanation in different ways. For this reason, there ceases to be any general and systematic obstacle to there being a priori connections between various physical and psychological states, and between various psychological states and each other (using the term "states" to encompass events and processes as well as states in the proper sense). In this way it ceases to be mysterious that such a priori connected states are sometimes explanatory of each other[24]—physical and sensory situations explanatory of experiences—beliefs explanatory of fears—beliefs and emotions explanatory of intentions— beliefs, emotions, and intentions explanatory of actions.

This perspective gives us a new freedom. No longer having to put on to 'causation' the whole load of 'giving an explanation', and no longer having to regard all knowledge of causation as knowledge of such a kind as would allow the inference of the effect from the cause or the cause from the effect, we no longer have to

---

[24]We shall see in the next chapter how unnecessary it is to try to ground a priori explanatory connections in a posteriori ones, and see the mistakenness of the reasons given for requiring this.

distort and stretch our view of causal action in order to fulfil such grandiose tasks.[25]

We can now envisage the knowledge of supposedly 'invariable' laws[26] as a distinct or separate matter from the knowledge of causes, and see only some, but not all, knowledge of causes as derived from knowledge of such 'invariable' laws. Laws will now turn out to be of several different forms, some involving teleology and some not, different kinds involving different degrees of approximation or of idealization, some (e.g., 'accidents cause injuries' or 'floods destroy bridges') as merely stating liabilities, and others as purporting to state invariable connections—all with different types of relation to the task of inferring effects from causes, or vice versa.

We can also grant that there are some laws which are not, as stated, causal laws at all, although they clearly provide a basis for predictions. For instance, there are conservation laws, such as those of mass, inertia, and energy,[27] or again the gas laws, laws of thermo-dynamics and Fermat's Least Time principle. We may note that some of these laws can be equally well regarded as teleological or non-teleological. Some of these laws which can be regarded either way are ones which can be reduced to other laws, but the idea that light in vacuo takes the path of least separation can be construed teleologically without there being the possibility of such reduction. Thus, of laws possibly involving teleology, some are causal and some are not.

The protagonists of events, insisting that 'agent-causality' must be reduced to or explained in terms of 'event-causality', ask the peculiar question as to what is the relation between an agent and his or her action—schematically the relation between Smith who brought it about (or made it to be the case) that p and his or her bringing it about (or making it to be the case).

---

[25]This is an especially important release because the Humean position transmutes causal relations from being (first order) physical or historical relations between events and states in a spatio-temporal framework into being (second order) relations between propositions whereby one proposition may be inferred from another, making any account of causes into a theory of the knowledge of invariable laws.

[26]I say "supposedly 'invariable' laws" because most such laws are understood either to draw upon idealizations in its statement or to refer to a system in some respect closed, e.g., not subject to interferences of quite unwonted types.

[27]Unlike Newton's Laws of Motion, the conservation laws do not employ the concept of force or action, and if they are explanatory they are so in a different way.

The correct answer to this question seems to be that the agent is the logical subject of the action and that the action is predicated of the agent. If one says that the action is 'from' the agent, or that the agent is 'cause' or (more idiomatically) 'author' of his action, one means to mark a difference between the predication of actions and other types of predication, the difference which might be marked by linguists by saying that the predications are causative. Causativity is internal to the sense of the verb phrase in such predications as aspect and tense are internal to it.

In asking this question, the protagonists of events seem to have already started on the path of thinking of the agent and the action as both objects, distinct objects between which there is a relation. However, their next move is to suppose that the believer in 'agent-causality' will believe that this relation is the relation of causing; they then ask the relation between the causing of the action and the action itself.

It is then argued that, if there is such a thing as agent-causality, then there will be a problem as to the relation of the agent (the person, the dog, the river, or the billiard ball) to his/her/its action.[28] Evidently enough, the agent's causing of the action (in whatever sense an agent, as distinct from an event or state of affairs, does cause what is done) cannot always be another action distinct from and prior to the action. Otherwise there would be an infinite regress, internal to any action by an agent, of the action whereby he/she/it caused that action, the action whereby he/she/it caused that causing of the action, the action whereby he/she/it caused that causing of the causing of the action, and so forth. Therefore, there must, in every case, be some causing of an action which is the action itself—the agent's causing the action is nothing different from the agent's acting, his/her/its doing the action. And this accords with commonsense: my being the cause of my kicking the football is nothing other than the action's being 'from me', nothing other than its being me that kicked the football, provided only that this was my action in the full sense, and (e.g.) we are not speaking of an involuntary action of some kind.[29]

---

[28]Davidson, *op. cit.*, pp. 52–53.

[29]One has, of course, to recognize that the questioner is foisting a thoroughly artificial use of the word "cause" upon the exponent of commonsense. As we have already remarked, kicking something, burning it, wetting it, and carrying it are all examples of causing something to happen. Causing is rather the genus of these actions than the relation we stand in to them. Causing an action, for the purposes

But the suggestion that my causing an action is nothing other than the action itself is met with the objection that the remark that I caused the action has no explanatory power, because it does not imply a connection between one event and another in a context of circumstances in which the later event, independently specifiable, follows according to law from the earlier event.[30]

However, this objection is quite unsubstantiated since no respectable proof has been offered of the doctrine that explanations, or explanations in some primary sense, must take this form. The remark that John Brown caused the action, or more simply that John Brown did it, suggests a background of patterns of motivation, intention, and belief or knowledge without at all suggesting that the action was dictated to happen by previous events and states of affairs by law. And those who put forward this objection have offered no refutation of the rival perspective which we have put forward, namely that causal explanations derive their explanatory power from our natural or acquired appreciation of the active and passive powers[31] of the different natures operative in the universe, making intelligible their common patterns of action and interaction. It is not, we say, that there are no laws, or that prediction is never possible, or that cases do not arise in which wrong prediction shows wrong explanation, but that it is quite wrong-headed to make the requirement that any account of an event has to have the implication that the event occurred in conformity to law before it counts as an explanation of the event concerned.

We are now in a position in the next chapter to accept variety in the dispositions which enter into historical or causal explanation, accepting teleological and mind-involving patterns of explanation in their own right, and not making them parasitic on mechanical or physical explanations. And, having dethroned events, we will then, in Chapter VIII, be able to see human and animal life as focalized upon the human beings and animals concerned, not only at the level of experience and description, but also at the level of explanation and reality.

---

of considering Davidson's argument, ought to be considered to be causing a causing, and should be considered analogous to dreaming a dream: 'a dream' does not specify a content dreamt, and similarly an action is not an object caused.

[30]Davidson, *ibid*.

[31]Their powers or propensities to act on other things or be acted upon.

VII. No Presumption in Favour of Mechanism: The Possible Autonomy of Teleological Explanation

In Chapters II to V we established the main logical and epistemological features of the mind-involving statements which we make about people and the higher animals and do not make about inanimate bodies, and we made clear that such statements are basic, uneliminable from our *description* of the life and behaviour of such animals and people. In Chapter VI we opened out the possibility that such statements would have a key role, not only at the level of description, but also at the level of *explanation*, in particular 'historical' or 'causal' explanation. Mary's hearing John say that he would meet her at a stated time and place several months later is part of the historical explanation of Mary's being at that place at the stated time, waiting for John. And, in an analogous way, the dog's seeing his master put the meat in the cupboard the evening before is part of the historical explanation of the dog's excitement when his master went to the cupboard the next day.

Generalizing, we may reasonably say that every true statement about persons of the kinds we have been concerned with, ascriptions of personal, or what Strawson called P-predicates, has an actual or possible role in what we may call 'historical' explanation. And likewise every mind-involving (or, as one might say, 'consciousness'-involving) statement about animals.

By "historical explanation", I mean the accounting for later events and states of affairs by narrating some of the key previous doings and happenings, together with longer term conditions, which explain why they occurred or came to obtain. Of course, many explanations are not of this kind, e.g., explanations of why the gas laws hold in terms of a kinetic theory of gases or explanations of surface tension phenomena by the tendency of faster molecules to escape the surface of a liquid so as to leave the remaining molecules nearer the surface slower, on average, than in the rest of the liquid—or explanations in mathematics, e.g., of why triangles with two sides and one angle equal need not be congruent.

Whenever the statements about human beings or animals are of sorts which we would not make about material bodies, we are liable to find certain recurring features in the explanations in which they are involved. Thus, we typically find that they involve teleology or the explanation of the doing or happening of something by reference to some end aimed at by an agent, that they involve holism or the explanation of the behaviour of parts by reference to facts about the wholes of which they are parts, that they depend upon the continuing identity through time of the subject or subjects of personal or consciousness-implying predicates concerned, and that they are 'basic' in the sense that explanation in terms of them cannot be 'explained' or 'reduced' to explanation in quite different terms. It is these themes which I shall develop in this chapter and Chapter VIII.

By "explanation in different terms", I have in mind, for instance, the way in which historical explanations drawing upon facts about the changes in the volume and temperature to explain changes in pressure can be 'explained' or reduced to explanations in which average molecular kinetic energy is mentioned instead of temperature. Or again, there are many simple systems in which there is a tendency for small variations in some parameter in either direction to be rectified so that the system returns towards some 'normal' median state, e.g., ships whose centres of gravity are below their metacentres, thermostatic devices, and electrical systems making use of negative feedback. In all these cases a teleological explanation in the form "It returns to such-and-such a normal state because it has a tendency to return to this state" can be replaced by an explanation of a non-teleological kind of how it is that small variations in the parameter concerned bring into play some force or process operative in the same direction until the median state is reached.

(Of course, ships, thermostats, and various electrical devices have been built precisely in order to achieve this kind of stability, so that, while a non-teleological account is more basic in regard to the behaviour of the system, a teleological account may be more appropriate if the enquiry is into the motives of the builder. E.g., 'Why do ships tend to return to the vertical after listing?' may not be directed towards discovering 'Why do things built the way ships are built behave this way?' to which the answer is 'because their centres of gravity are below their metacentres', but towards discovering 'Why, when we build things to serve as ships, do we build them so as to behave this way?' to which the answer is 'so that they won't tend to capsize'. If we then ask 'How are we to build them so that they will behave this way and not tend to capsize?', the answer is 'by building them with their centres of gravity below their metacentres', so that we might ask 'Why, when we build things to serve as ships, do we build them with their centres of gravity below their metacentres?' to which the reply might be 'so that they will behave in the way mentioned, and this so that they will not tend to capsize'.)

1. The Nature of Teleological Explanation

(a) **The structure of teleological explanations
   and their possible empirical backing;
   two notions of dispositions and natures**

The form of a teleological explanation does not involve that some end is an efficient cause, but that some system is such that the fact that some development is conducive to a certain end is a reason for that development's taking place. There is, we might say, a tendency or disposition in the system towards the end specified. In deliberation the reason for wanting or choosing something lies in the end which presents itself as desirable or to be aimed at, but in historical explanation the end is not a cause or element in the historical explanation of what happens or is done; it is rather the tendency to the end (of whatever type the tendency is) which is an element in such explanation. Such tendencies or dispositions towards an end are not future to the developments which they explain in the way in which the end is future to these developments, but previous and present to them.

There can be cases in which the tendency or disposition concerned arises out of the structure of the make-up of the system concerned and the properties of the parts or elements of which the system is made up and which are related according to this structure. In such a case, the tendency or disposition concerned is explained by the 'inner constitution' of the system concerned. We have just given instances of this with our examples of the stability of ships, thermostatic devices, and the like. In such cases, the tendency or disposition can be considered as a property of an apparatus or structure describable in two ways, the one according to the effect of which it is the cause, and the other according to the way it is related to the constitution of the apparatus.[1] But in all such cases, the teleological style of explanation is not basic and its availability can be considered a by-product or consequence of the underlying make-up of the system concerned, a by-product highly relevant to human planners who can see a use for such systems.

However, there is no general a priori ground for assuming that all such tendencies or dispositions are rooted in this way in the make-up of the system concerned, the way it is structured of parts, what we might call its material make-up or constitution—thinking of the matter of the thing, not as that out of which it is made (i.e., as something formerly existing), but as the parts or stuff which, continuing to exist, are structured together within it. For it is perfectly conceivable that what the different developments which we observe in the behaviour of things of a certain kind in certain situations have in common is not, so far as we yet can tell, a common materially explained rooting but simply that they are all conducive to a certain outcome or upshot. That is, our observations of a spread of situations of a particular kind may sometimes suggest that what the goings on observed within the framework of this kind of situation have in common is that they are results of a certain type of cause, but may also sometimes suggest that what these goings on have in common is that they tend to a certain type of effect or outcome.[2]

Thus, there is no epistemological reason to suppose that a tendency or disposition towards an end has to be conceived of as a state of some apparatus or mechanism, whether material or immaterial. And especially there is no epistemological reason why a state of mind or mental disposition should be conceived of as the state of some mental apparatus, whether brain or mind, within the person. Wittgenstein's opposition to this way of thinking whereby understanding, meaning,

---

[1]Wittgenstein seems to have regarded the expressions "state of mind" and "disposition" as limited to being understood in this way. To speak of the knowledge of the ABC as a state of mind, he thinks, is to be thinking of 'a state of a mental apparatus (perhaps of the brain) by means of which we explain the *manifestations* of that knowledge', and 'there ought to be two different criteria for such a state: a knowledge of the construction of the apparatus, quite apart from what it does', and 'Such a state is called a disposition.' (*Philosophical Investigations*, I, 149).

[2]In this account, I have, albeit with some alterations, made use of the account offered by Charles Taylor in *The Explanation of Behaviour*, Chapter I.

intending, and so forth are conceived of as states of some mental apparatus is one of the reasons which made him refuse to call them 'states' or 'dispositions'.[3] But, since the words "state" and "disposition" do not normally connote the state or disposition of an apparatus, I shall feel free to use them in order to explain the teleological perspective without this connotation.

In this, I mean to restore Aristotle's conception of state or (in modern parlance) 'disposition' (*hexis, dynamis*) which was quite open and not at all tied to the idea of being the resultant of the state of an apparatus. It was a notion particularly important for Ryle. Ryle distinguished between 'single-track' and 'many-track' dispositions, but his explanations disguise its importance. All dispositions involve the truth of various hypotheticals whereby, if certain preconditions are fulfilled, then a certain type of behaviour or upshot will follow. But the question is as to whether the class of hypotheticals is a closed one and the types of precondition specified in them are defined in a way which does not require to be understood by back-reference to the character of the disposition concerned, or whether our understanding of the disposition is determinative of an open class of hypotheticals, in such a way that we cannot list beforehand the types of possible case in regard to which the disposition may have consequences. In the example of the skilled mountaineer, there is no specification beforehand of the types of situation which his degree of skill may enable him to deal with. As we shall remark later, such 'many-track' or open dispositions are of peculiar importance in the understanding of our use of language. We have to escape the prison set by the modern use of the word "disposition" to mean conformity to a confined set of behaviour patterns, and recover the more open Aristotelian use whereby the paradigm cases of dispositions were the moral and intellectual virtues and varieties of expertise both theoretical and technical or practical.

The widespread way of thinking to which Wittgenstein objected, and for which there is no epistemological reason, is well represented by David Armstrong's account in *A Materialist Theory of Mind*. The introspectively known state of mind called belief is, he supposes, empirically discovered to be identical to a certain neurologically definable state of the brain. The neurological state causes the appropriate behaviour in a way to be understood empirically and mechanistically.

---

[3] *Philosophical Investigations*, Part I, para. 149.

It is at this stage that the account becomes convoluted. We are told that, because of the brain's supposed self-scanning capacity, we know of this state of belief introspectively, i.e., without using criteria, albeit knowing it not as a neurological state of this or that physical kind but in mentalistic terms as a 'belief'—but yet thereby, by the very meaning of the word "belief", knowing it as an aptitude or disposition to behave in certain ways, albeit (the theory of contingent connection between the mental and the physical requires) only in loose logical connection with this behaviour.

In this way, what seemed to be a priori causal relation between the belief as introspectively known and the behaviour is understood to coincide with the supposed empirical causal relation between the neurological state and the same behaviour. We appear to have a double explanation of behaviour, the one a priori in terms of the non-accidental implications of belief as ordinarily understood, and the other in terms of the empirical connections of a neurological state imagined to be identical with (or the realization of) the state of belief with the same behaviour. Recent philosophers have jiggled with ways of making these accounts seem compatible, ways whose bankruptcy will appear in Chapter VIII, but what we are here concerned with is their background: the presumption that a tendency or disposition, even one conceived mentalistically and teleologically, has to be understood as the state of some mechanism whose operation will lead mechanically to the end which the tendency is a tendency towards.

Before I consider the deeper reasons why philosophers have so often tended to think that teleologically understood tendencies or states must have a non-teleological basis, I will explain some important further features of teleological ways of thinking.

(b) Teleology in the description of ends, and in the description of the conditions of the attainment of ends

If we accept the propriety of teleological patterns of explanation, then we will be liable to say, in certain cases, that it has come to be found that a thing is of the nature to, or has a disposition to, follow courses which tend to a certain end. At this stage, it is important to note that the types of description of the end which are available to us are as wide as our way of experiencing things may suggest to us. Therefore, if there are ways of describing things which do not correspond to any straightforwardly physical or mechanistically defined property, these also will be available to us as descriptions of ends which bring together a spread of possibly very disparate things as means to that end. Thus, if a person wants to find a satisfying career, there will be a very wide range of things which may count as means to this end. Or again, if we want to find a proof that one cannot trisect an angle by a construction using a ruler and compasses only, we may try a wide variety of gambits. Or again, the question might be of the means of travelling from one place to another by a scenic route.

Next, it has to be noted that the non-physical character of the definition of the end may infect the range of descriptions which are acceptable of means to the end. Thus, if we view how animals perceive things as something relevant to the explanation of their behaviour, we will expect the modes of description of the objects of perception to be of kinds relevant to the directing of behaviour towards the ends characteristic of the species or more general kind of animal concerned. In this way concepts associated with danger and with various differentiated kinds of source of danger, with food and differences in the type, direction, and means of acquisition of food, and so forth, will come into the description of objects of perception as perceived by the animal—and very obviously these will be descriptions which, far from being in mechanistic terms, will involve the categories of the continuous, the living, the animal, and even the human.[4]

Or, to take an example of relevance to our later discussions, if our aim is to get at the truth by means of deductive argument from some given information, the means will be by using valid forms of argument: but typically for any one form of argument there will be many different idioms in which it may be realized. For instance, if our concern involved a use of an argument of the logical form "Any A is B; Any B is C; Therefore, Any A is C", we might not be bothered as to whether the information given to us used the linguistic forms associated with "any" or whether it instead used those associated with "every", "each", "all", or "whatever".

Learning to see things in a greater variety of different ways opens more possibility of discovering what is relevant to the attainment of a goal. And what we learn can be relevant to more than one goal. If we

---

[4]In writing this, I have in view the fuller discussions of Charles Taylor in *The Explanation of Behaviour*, Part 2, and the ideas of Merleau-Ponty in *The Structure of Behaviour*.

think of paths followed by rats in order to get to a certain goal-place, they may be very disparate. When selection is made between different things, there is great variety in the types of difference which can turn out to affect behaviour. Seeing things as so and so can take many forms, somewhat as recognizing things as being of the same logical form can be realized in different ways. To know what aspects of things are relevant to behaviour with a certain goal we need to look amongst other than purely physical descriptions.

(c) The shape of causal explanation: dispositions and natures are not causes but marks of distinction between different modes of causal agency

We have noted that teleological patterns of explanation do not involve regarding an end or goal which lies in the future as the efficient cause of something in the past. What we must now grasp is that neither do they involve treating natures and dispositions (understood in the Aristotelian sense as *hexeis*), 'purposes', or 'intelligences' as new entities acting as efficient causes.

In Charles Taylor's account it is not a matter of introducing new theoretical entities whose existence is unverifiable (unless it is supposed that they are known by introspection), but explaining the phenomena to be explained in terms of laws of a different form from mechanical laws. But, if we are not dealing with laws whose subject (if any) is the whole universe, but with laws whose subjects are (for instance) entities belonging to particular natural kinds, human beings, horses, dogs, mammals, vertebrates, and the like, then what we need to insist upon is more particular: namely, that the dispositions or nature of this or that particular substance or subject of one of these kinds under consideration are not new types of cause or entity in their own right, but mark the presence of a different mode of causality. The subjects of this causality are still bodily, but their modes of action are to be understood according to a different pattern.

What we have to do is to rescue causal agency, which is a kind of criterion of being real, from the prison of mechanism and accord it its full generality, so that the prototypical examples of causal agents will be, not billiard balls, but persons and animals exercising a mode of causality which is intentional or directed. We may then envisage the various causal agents or 'substances' as exercising modes of causality fuller or less full, the case of the billiard ball being a genuine case of causality but the most deficient, and envisage these agents as acting together in the same world. We may remark that these agents, living and non-living, are paradigms of the concrete, that which does not have to be spoken of in abstract modes of speech.[5]

Within this world, each agent, substance, or whole acts according to the mode of causality belonging to it. Into this arena we do not have to admit, we do not need to admit, vital forces and energies, nor even dispositions, whether non-teleological or teleological, as if they had any active power or reality in their own right.[6] Rather, as we have seen, speech about them is circumlocutory for speech about substances. In dealing with animals and human beings, instead of admitting vital forces[7] and energies as entities, we recognize different modes of causality, modes whereby agents act according to different types of disposition.[8]

2. Misplaced Methodological Reasons for Rejecting Teleological Elements in Explanation

We have seen how it is just as possible for a teleological explanation of a phenomenon to be well-grounded as for a mechanistic or non-teleological one to be so. And we have seen that such explanation in no way depends on treating either future ends or present tendencies to these ends as efficient causes in their own right. But there remain other roots of prejudice against teleological explanation which do not depend on such misconstructions. I think we can usefully disentangle three of these: firstly, the idea that, unless there is a mechanical explanation underlying the teleological one, the teleological one will

---

[5]The analysis in this paragraph is set forth more fully in my *The Reality of Time and the Existence of God*, pp. 76–81, 105–120, cf. 287–293.

[6]The main problem for this perspective is set up, not within biology or psychology, but within physics, by the need to give an ontological status to forces, fields, and forms of energy, in a way not readily reducible to the existence of substances, although co-ordinate with and dependent on it—cf. my *The Reality of Time and the Existence of God*, pp. 51–56, cf. 150–156.

[7]Aristotelian forms or souls, if understood as efficient causes, perhaps described as 'entelechies' (transliterating Aristotle) as by Driesch, would fall under this head.

[8]We have in fact already shown the needlessness of admitting vital forces or energies, or indeed any other kind of force of disposition, as entities when in Chapter VI we showed the grossness of the mistake of regarding events and states as entities in their own right.

turn out to have no more content than the explanation of sleeping in terms of a 'dormitive power'; secondly, the idea that teleological and mechanistic explanations are like oil and water, and do not mix; and thirdly, the idea that the only scientific method is always to look for a mechanical explanation and never to rest satisfied with a teleological one. It is probably the third of these roots of prejudice which has had most influence, but let us for clarity deal with the others first.

The first line of objection is based on the idea that if, for instance, we explain sleeping in terms of the power to sleep, and have no conception of what is involved in having the power to sleep which is in any way distinct from our conception of what it is to sleep, we are doing no better than explaining a thing in terms of itself. To say that sugar dissolves because it is soluble seems to add nothing to our knowledge. On the basis of such examples it is suggested that cause and effect, *explanans* and *explanandum*, must always be logically independent so that relations between them are a posteriori.

It will be recalled that the kind of view of explanation which I refuted in Chapter VI combined two elements, one the requirement that the explanation reveal the particular cause-effect relation as an instance of the satisfaction of covering laws, and the other the requirement that cause and effect should be logically distinct existences and so be specifiable in logically independent terms. Accordingly, some protagonists of 'ordinary causality' insist that every explanation must carry the implication that there are properties of cause and effect which make each cause-effect relation fall under some causal law.[9] But others see the hallmark of 'action-explanation' as being precisely a supposed presence of explanation without the implication of subsumability under general laws. But continuing to envisage subsumption under general laws as the paradigm case of what counts as explanation, these latter still require an account of what 'action-explanation' has in common with this imagined paradigm in order to make it count as explanation.[10] And all the parties concerned agree that at least

---

[9]This is Davidson's view, *Essays on Actions and Events*, Essay 1.

[10]Peacocke says that the question 'is not what is distinctive of action explanation but why or whatever is distinctive of it is sufficient to make it *explanation*' (*Holistic Explanation*, p. 168). He requires that there be some independently specifiable property

the minimum of what these kinds of explanation have in common must include that they should involve the causation of one event by independently describable other events and states of affairs according to connections known a posteriori.[11]

In this way, the requirement that cause and effect be logically distinct existences is made to appear sacrosanct. Now, as we have observed, we commonly find thoughts of danger seeming to explain feelings of fear, and these to explain aversion from the object feared—beliefs and desires to explain actions—one group of beliefs to explain another—and in general various psychological phenomena seeming naturally to explain others or to explain bodily movements. And, as a result of this requirement of logical distinctness or a posteriori connection between causes and effects, it is suggested to us that when we accept these ordinary explanations as explanatory, we are presuming that each psychological phenomenon has some independent existence (perhaps a realization in the brain) so as to be describable in its intrinsic nature in some way which gives it only a posteriori or empirically learnt connection with the things which it is supposed to cause or of which it is supposed to be the effect.

But all this seems a mere extravaganza—the result of an arm-chair philosophical doctrine run wild. As Chapter V made unmistakably clear, it is an essential characteristic of the central kinds of mind-involving predicate that when they are applied to human beings they should have a double mode of verification, one as we apply them to ourselves without resort to behavioural checks and to other people simply on their word, and the other on the basis of behaviour. As a result, it cannot be said that the defining character of any mental predicate is given in just one way, e.g., that fear is defined by aversion behaviour in the context of believed danger as if fear was not also something felt and testified to in its own right. The ideas we have of different mental phenomena are neither so given as to make the phenomena reducible to each other as if they did not constitute distinct existences, experienced or attended to or affecting us each

---

which both explanation by causal laws and explanation of human action share (*ibid.*), a property conforming to the requirements of explanation in general.

[11]This requirement on all explanations is laid down by Peacocke at the first stage of his discussion (*op. cit.*, pp. 144–153) so that whatever the different kinds of explanation have in common must include at least this.

in their own way or ways, nor so given as to be logically independent of various other related phenomena.

The second worry, that if we allow teleological explanation into a field at all it will exclude all mechanistic explanation because they are like oil and water and do not mix, is quite unsupported and can be dismissed quite briefly—though we shall recur to it in later chapters.[12] The common idea that what is treated teleologically must be treated non-mechanistically in all its aspects embodies a simple mistake. When we have a whole with parts which are not fully describable in their nature or principles of behaviour except with reference to the whole, we also find that the whole is not fully describable in its nature or principles of behaviour without reference to the parts. And from this it follows that the parts have some descriptions that do not depend upon their being parts of this whole, descriptions in virtue of which the behaviour of the parts and even the whole may be explicable in some aspects. Accordingly, physical and even 'mechanistic' explanation will certainly have a role in dealing with living bodily things, even though some 'abstraction' is involved wherein other aspects and a total view of these things are 'abstracted from', ignored, or not attended to. This leaves a plenteous and ample role to the physical and the 'mechanical', and therefore as I shall remark later also to computer studies in the study of the sub-processes of human behaviour.

However, the most common objection to the introduction of teleology at any point is that it *ipso facto* blocks off further enquiry. This methodological objection arises from already giving privilege to one particular methodology. In this methodology, the process of discovery is seen as proceeding in well-regulated order, at each stage the problem set being cut and dried.

This way of thinking is neatly represented by Dennett. He wants every problem posed to the living or human being to be broken down successively into different stages, at each stage leaving on the one hand something 'mechanically' settlable and on the other hand

---

[12]It is evident that linguistic activity has to incorporate phonetic processes, and likewise human and animal activity typically involve the human body as a body with organs, i.e., involve a physiological structuring whose activation is internal to the activity in question (cf. Chapter IX below).

some new question (independent of whatever had been mechanically settled) in regard to which alternative answers can be posed to each of which a yes or a no answer would be appropriate.[13] Then the question arises as to whether these yes-or-no answers are determined by some 'unexplained intelligence' (or 'undischarged homunculus'), or whether mechanically by the physically defined inner or outer environment of the system, or whether in a mechanically (as well as from the point of view of intelligence) random way. Within such a plan of inquiry, for psychology to leave anything to be explained by 'unexplained intelligence' appears no better than ascribing it to God's design, and so psychology appears unscientific if it abandons the mechanist ideal.

But to conceive the matter in this way is to beg many questions. For instance, suppose the question under consideration was the explanation of the use of a certain word or concept. It seems quite unlikely that more understanding will be gained by the mechanical approach just described, than by some more holistic and teleological view. I consider the linguistic case because it is convenient for *demonstrating* the inappositeness of the mechanistic methodology.

Let us consider this case. Many concepts might be supposed to apply to an indefinitely large spread of types of use in virtue of one and the same 'understanding' (e.g., the concepts of truth or of method of verification or proof), and before Dennett's approach could get going it might seem that his machine would have to decide mechanically which of this non-recursively defined set of distinguishable types of use of the concept was concerned. But this would be impossible, and so it might be supposed that the machine be required to check only for some finite number[14] of such distinguishable types, leaving the possible residue to be dealt with 'in the wash' later. Only after this first stage had been got over in one way or another, could the machine try to proceed mechanically according to some one of these types of use. But then it would need to deal with further questions when it was discovered that some type of use had not been so distinguished as to leave no questions to be resolved in a different way—as well as to deal with the effects of the 'residue' left at the first stage. The machine could be imagined to be such as to deal with some of these later arising questions, but then there would be a new residue, to be

---

13 *Brainstorms*, pp. 84–86.
14 Or 'constructive ordinal' number.

partly dealt with in yet another way, and then another residue, and then another and so on *ad infinitum*.

The types of problem which arise will, of course, differ according to the concept concerned: i.e., according to whether we are trying to give a mechanistic account of the understanding of concepts like truth or proof or whether we are trying to give an account of the understanding of concepts like (say) play, or game, or love, or pain over the full range with which these concepts arise linguistically. In the second group of cases there may be fewer problems at the first stage, and more at later stages.

But it might well seem that it was the same 'understanding' or teleologically understood *hexis* or state which was exercised both in drawing up the initial list of types of case with their definitions or modes of distinction, and with dealing with the various different species of question later—and the initial list, even if short, was drawn up, one might have presumed, according to the same 'understanding' but not (at least if the understanding concerned was of truth or of proof) in any mechanical way. Therefore, the approach which brought in the 'understanding' of the concept concerned, together with any teleological bearing which that concept might have, might well seem not only simpler but also more viable than that which Dennett has in view.

I may be reproached for having loaded the dice against the mechanist by considering a case of linguistic behaviour—the mechanist always says that one should begin by considering the simplest kinds of behaviour first and might expect to get to language last. To this I would reply that at every stage it is a question of finding appropriate structures of explanation, and by limiting oneself to the simplest cases one confines ones vision of the possibility of different kinds of structure. Moreover, the idea that a more holistic and teleological account, even stated quite informally, may cover a greater range of cases with greater predictive power than any mechanical account seems right not only in the case of language but also, for instance, in explaining the categorization which takes place in perceptual discrimination and learning amongst animals.[15]

Accordingly, a preference for the non-mechanistic approach in such cases may be well-considered and not in the least obscurantist. The 'intelligence' or 'understanding' spoken of is not, of course, a

---

[15]Cf. Charles Taylor, *The Explanation of Behaviour*, Chapters VI and VII.

distinct introspected mental state with merely accidental or inductively learnt connections with behaviour, especially linguistic behaviour, but something the very concept of which involves behavioural criteria in the way sketched in Chapter V. Nor is it a merely theoretical entity inferred from behaviour, or an 'intervening variable' between people's observations of the linguistic behaviour of others and their own linguistic behaviour, since this would imply that they could have no non-inferential knowledge of their own possession of understanding.

Studies of animal behaviour and its simulation, when considering 'understanding' or 'insight', tend to concentrate upon problem-solving behaviour. I consider the case of linguistic understanding because it is less 'bitty' than the 'insight' involved in problem-solving, and more definitory of the human species. I have no doubt that learning amongst other higher animals, and the phenomena associated with perception and intentional action amongst such animals, show parallel problems. But in a way the case of 'understanding' or 'intelligence' presents a reasonable test case because it is the elected concern of those who adhere to an 'Artificial Intelligence' approach on methodological grounds—perhaps, like Dennett, considering it a top-down or 'forwards' approach to the same promised conclusions to which psychological behaviourism offered a bottom-up or 'backwards' approach.[16]

Therefore, what we should conclude is that the impression given by such an argument as Dennett's is a product of a certain pattern of analysis, a pattern which a wide span of examples suggest is inappropriate. But, in the absence of a clearly difficult and testing type of example such as the linguistic understanding of various concepts, the plausibility of such a defective pattern of analysis may seem compulsive. However, once the pattern has been seen to be non-necessary, in no way inescapable, this compulsiveness is removed, and the conspiracy between a mechanistic view of semantics (or more precisely, of the way a lexicon is to be put to use), as well as of perception and of motivation, and a mechanistic view of the human being is revealed.

Once it is clear what a plenteous and ample role a teleological framework leaves to the physical and the 'mechanical', the plenteous role to which I referred before, and once the spell of the mechanistic pattern of analysis just described has been broken, the anti-teleological

---

[16] *Brainstorms*, pp. 80–81.

methodology loses what little attraction it had. It creates a schizophrenia in thought, divorcing the theoretical from the human world, for the sake only of substituting a promise for a reality—substituting the will of the wisp of promised a posteriori mechanical explanations for the rich human understanding of language and behaviour which we already have—not that these allow of no amplification but that this should be within the framework set by them.

3. Exorcising Mechanism: Its Deceptive Roots in the Theory of Meaning

However, the compulsion often felt towards mechanical models does not spring only from misunderstandings of what is involved in teleological explanation, nor even from the two methodological motivations which I have just described. Rather, the underlying and fundamental source of this compulsion arises from certain false presumptions of a quasi-logical kind, presumptions as to the supposed conditions of the possibility of words having meaning. That is, what ultimately drives materialists to adopt their view is not epistemology or methodology, but a certain sense of awkwardness in speaking of states when such speech has, as it were, no material or quasi-material content.

It is not easy to diagnose the inspiration of what one might call a 'gut-feeling' amongst philosophers. What we are here concerned with is the sense that any tendency, disposition, or state even if initially understood teleologically must be ultimately describable as the state of some system, apparatus, set-up, or mechanism, whether material or mental. Thus dispositions or states (understanding these terms in an Aristotelian way), such as belief, intention, desire, understanding, and so forth, must be states of an inner apparatus, whether within the body or within the soul,

This presumption seems to rest upon the feeling that the paradigm case of being 'real' is provided by the example of bodies with some solidity, an example which involves some distribution of stuff of one or several types, or of parts, over space, and some causal properties, instanced by that resistance to penetration which we call solidity. And, in this way of thinking, it is important that because of the spatial distributedness and solidity involved with such structures, they are typically picturable—we picture things as we see them, they need to be distributed in space in order to be seen as solid and in perspective, and this is typically how they are seen.

The 'real' is then supposed to need to bear some analogy or likeness to such physical structures, structures composed of parts or of spreads of different kinds of stuff, in order for there to be any content to statements presupposing or implying their 'reality'. That is, it is felt that, unless predications or ascriptions of states or dispositions involve something about some such 'substantial' set-up—analogous to that which is spatially structured and distributed and which has causal properties arising from the character of what it is composed of (although not necessarily spatial and not exercising causal action physically)—the predication or ascription must be empty and a mere hanging of words on to a subject without there being any corresponding reality. Merely to have a logical subject of which predications are made, i.e., of which things are said ascribing things to it, the world being empty of any 'substantial' structure (in some way analogous to the physical structures we have indicated) in or around the logical subject, so that the predications cannot denote any state, disposition, or change in this structure, is to mouth empty words—or so it is felt.

It is not exactly that it is being felt that, in Locke's terms, we are using words without ideas, but that we are using words and ideas which imply that there must be 'things' which they denote in a setting in which it is being denied that there are any such 'things'.

Something like this, then, is the reason why ascriptions of states of consciousness, and indeed all statements having a role in teleological explanation even if not about people or animals, are felt to be empty if the states ascribed are not to be regarded as analogous to physical states understood according to a mechanical model.

If it is once granted that ascriptions of 'mental states' must denote the state (or disposition of parts and relations of parts) of some physical or non-physical set-up or apparatus, it will immediately be taken that, when they are historically explanatory of some physical movement, this is because the state which they denote (*qua* state of a set-up or apparatus) is mechanically causative of what they explain—'mechanically causative' in the sense of being analogous to mechanical causes in their mode of action, external to and determinative of their effect. In this way, we see at once the generation of the structure we observed in Armstrong, an inner state of an apparatus (according to him, the brain) externally causing a bodily movement, and this account strangely superimposed upon the given pattern of a state of consciousness being of its very nature, or a priori such as to be explanatory of the behaviour which included this bodily movement.

We must grasp the peculiarity of this general position.

Firstly, we have in our hands a class of statements, the sort which we can ascribe to others on the basis of behavioural criteria but which we ascribe to ourselves without any need to utilize such criteria, of which it is not in doubt that they have sense and content. What we lack is an agreed systematic account of how it is that they have content, just as we lack such an account for most or all other types of contentful statement. But, thanks to the integration of the physical and the mental in the psychosomatic structures concerned in the ways explained at the end of Chapter IX, we *are* able to give some constructive sense to statements such as "I see a man walking towards us with his dog", "I have a griping pain in my stomach", "I was furious with him, and still am", and "I am making a Christmas cake". All of these announce dispositions or the inception of dispositions which play a part in the historical explanation of pieces of human behaviour. And all of them involve both straightforwardly physical and consciousness-involving aspects, the two inextricable from each other in our account of what same thing it is that we ascribe to ourselves without using the criteria we use in regard to other people. (It will be noted that there is no plausibility in taking these statements—which, not as decomposed into imagined mental and physical components but as they are, are stated in the form relevant to historical explanation—as referring solely to an inner mental or brain state.)

But in regard to these statements, which we already know to have content, it is being alleged that it is a condition of their having content that certain analogies with the physical states, described and thought of in physical terms, of physical structures should hold. The analogies concerned are in regard to what allows a physical structure distributed through space to be mechanically causative and in regard to what allows it to be picturable. But at this stage of the argument no justification has yet been offered for these requirements beyond a 'gut-feeling', and to regard them as required for the statements concerned to have content is curious for the following reason: that, even if these requirements were satisfied, it would seem to do nothing to explain or illuminate that sense or content which they do have. For instance, it belongs to what we understand by 'an understanding of a proof of Pythagoras' theorem' that the person who has it should in principle be able to explain to another person how to prove this theorem. This seems to us thoroughly intelligible, and is not made more so by bringing in a theory of structured states of brain or soul and showing how these might be mechanically productive of the same sound-effects from the person's mouth.

This example brings us to the second peculiarity.

There is something which we already know, namely that a state of consciousness of the sort which people ascribe to others on the basis of observing their behaviour and to themselves not on this basis is by the very concept we have of it explanatory of certain behaviour-patterns.[17] But it is proposed to explain this by saying that this state of consciousness, known in a quite different way and described in terms of quite different concepts, viz., as a state of an apparatus (perhaps a part of the soul or perhaps the brain), mechanically causes the physical aspect of such behaviour-patterns. In this, a connection between the state of consciousness and behaviour which was already thoroughly intelligible to us is re-explained in a way quite foreign to the original explanation. Why the state of an apparatus described as such should be identified with the state of consciousness concerned described in personalistic terms is said to be: because each is known to be the cause of the same behaviour. But, besides that the idea that some state of an apparatus (e.g., the brain) is such cause is quite unsubstantiated, the state of the apparatus would be a cause in a quite different way from that in which the state of consciousness is a cause.

We traced the inspiration of this way of thinking to the require-ment that 'real' states have to be analogous to those apprehended by sight and touch, 'substantial' in virtue of an analogy with the solid, or causally resistant or active, things apprehended by touch, and picturable in virtue of the analogy with things apprehended by sight.

For a person's having a belief, or having an understanding of something, to be explanatory of something else, e.g., his answering a question in a certain way, or his being able to explain something, involves its not being 'a nothing', but hardly seems to involve its

---

[17]It is 'explanatory' in the way a capacity (e.g., the ability to swim) is explanatory of its exercise, a moral virtue of acts done according to the virtue, or knowledge explanatory of remembering or of telling someone else, i.e., in the logical way a *hexis* in Aristotle is explanatory of its acts, and not in the way the make-up of something is explanatory of its behaviour.

being analogous to 'substantiality'-involving states of material bodies of the sorts recognized by the sense of touch, such as solidity or resistance to penetration—states which involve distributedness in space. If anything analogous to these states is involved, it would seem to be only indirectly, through a general requirement that persons be bodily or that such states find bodily (e.g., verbal) expression. Therefore, if a causal or explanatory role is a criterion of 'reality', there is no need for such 'mental' states to have a quasi-physical character in order to be candidates for having such a role and thereby being 'real'.

There indeed has to be something about the person which makes it true that he or she has a belief, or has understanding, and so forth, but this does not have to be represented as picturable, because it is not by the provision of models to be pictured that propositions get their content, let alone only by such provision. We picture substances, and we picture situations in which substances interrelate, and the content of this image of 'picturing' depends upon the substances and situations being distributed in space and upon their being conceived of as spatially 'out from' and 'over against' the picturer. (In this way, states of consciousness and persons as they figure in them as subjects are *ipso facto* debarred from being pictured because of the self-ascribing aspect of the meaning of the predicates ascribed.) But it is not by such picturing that content-possessing propositions get their meaning or content: a proposition is not, even in the most generalized sense, a picture. As we shall see later, in Chapter XI, neither a statement nor a fact is an 'object' such that one might be compared with the other and realized to be a picture of the other.

What we have been dealing with has been a theory of meaning which demands that some degree of isomorphism with the physical structures which arise at the level of human acquaintance be a condition of meaningfulness or possession of content in factual statements. It is a theory of meaning of the kind from which Augustine had escaped when he came to see Plato as showing that the real need not be material, but might be intellectual, so that God did not need to be conceived of as an everywhere present stuff distributed like the ether, part by part, through all space. It is a theory of meaning whose life has returned to it with the decay of such a Plato-inspired conviction. But we do not have to resort to consideration of the intellectual as such but can see what is wrong with this theory of meaning. Rather it suffices to take a more human-level approach and envisage the constructive sense possessed by personal predicates of sorts which human beings share with the higher animals. What we have to envisage is the way ascriptions of perception, sensation, emotion and intention have meaning independently of this form of material rooting in the way explained in Chapter V and further in Chapter IX, Section 5.[18]

---

[18]It can be argued quite separately that the meaningfulness of the statements of modern physics at the microscopic level cannot depend upon the applicability of models arising at the level of human acquaintance.

VIII. The First Refutation of Mechanism: Psychophysical Unity at the Level of Explanation and Reality

In Chapter VII we refuted the presumption of mechanism. There is no general reason for supposing a priori that whenever something is explained in a way which involves teleology there must always be an underlying mechanical substructure which would allow it to be explained mechanically. On the contrary, particularly when the involvement of teleology stems from the involvement of mental or mind-involving concepts, the natural presumption is rather the other way. That is, the natural presumption is that the ordinary teleological mind-involving explanations on which the conduct of ordinary life relies are adequate in their own right—or, as we might say, autonomous, in no way presupposing the possibility of a more basic mechanical explanation of the same phenomena. In this chapter, Sections 3 and 4, we shall establish the stronger conclusion that mind-involving explanations positively exclude any more basic mechanical or physical explanation of the phenomena concerned—and that this is true not just at the level of the 'phenomenon', the level of experience and of description tailored to experience, but at the level of fundamental explanation and reality. It is not the involvement of teleology alone, but the involvement of mind-involving concepts which enables us to demonstrate that these explanations are basic, and thus to demonstrate that physicalism is false.

But first, in Sections 1 and 2, we must enlarge our conception of what we are committed to when we accept mind-involving explanations as autonomous and even basic. For, firstly, any system of causal or historical explanation carries with it certain presumptions about identity. In particular, the mind-involving explanations concerned turn upon giving a special place to animals and human beings as the possessors of a continuous identity through time, and involve regarding them with their natures as basic entities—for the entities

249

which are basic from the point of view of considerations of explanation and causation are basic absolutely. And, secondly, the same mind-involving features which compel us to view animals and human beings as having a basic status ontologically also compel us to view them holistically, as essential unities to be viewed as psychophysical wholes. These wholes fit into the general perspective outlined by David Bohm of the diversity of things that may exist in the universe, diverse in the levels at which they arise and in the kinds of law associated with them as fundamental particles are diverse from atoms, ions and molecules, and these from living organisms and from masses of stellar or planetary scale, but having it in common that at each level things have some degree of autonomy and stability in their modes of being.[1] But what our argument will have achieved is the giving of a particular significance to the autonomy of those middle level entities we call animals and human beings.

As we shall see in Section 2, this holistic viewpoint prevents the conception that mind-involving explanations are autonomous or basic from having the effect of excluding further enquiry. It is not just that there can be deeper enquiries into motives and structures of understanding such as novelists, psychoanalysts, or linguists may suggest, i.e., deeper enquiries still keeping at the level of considering the animal or human being as a whole. But rather, precisely because human beings and animals are psychophysical wholes, they have physical parts, structures, and functions of which a physical account is required, an account which considers lower units, the organ, the cell, sub-cellular masses, as having some relative autonomy and stability.

However, it remains that in these physical treatments we are abstracting certain aspects of human and animal life, considering certain elements of the human being in their behaviour in abstraction[2] from the life and behaviour of human beings or animals as wholes which can only be understood holistically, teleologically—understood as organic psychophysical unities. The psychophysical life of these wholes is itself set within a wider environmental context, so as to again have aspects which can only be understood in relation to a yet larger whole than themselves. Yet they have a peculiar status because, in their case, the autonomy and stability of their identity is associated with their nodal

---

[1] *Causality and Chance in Modern Physics*, pp. 139 f., cf. 144–146, 149 f.
[2] Cf. *ibid.*, p. 146 (cf. 150, 154–156).

place in a framework of psychophysical law, and this of its nature brings in something absolute, a centre or focus of consciousness or self-consciousness. And it is the task of this chapter to make this peculiar status plain.

(At this stage I must enter a caveat: in this chapter, and indeed in this book I concentrate on certain kinds of 'substance' as subjects of active power and holding a privileged place in explanatory schemes, because human beings and other animals are just such sorts of substance; but I do not wish to exclude there being other kinds of subject of active power, not substances, yet still important in physical science, such as fields;[3] but it is just that these are not the subject of this book.)

1. The Significance of the Role of Identity Statements in Explanation

(a) The limits to the role of convention in deciding questions of identity are set by considerations of explanation

It has been for a long time a commonplace to insist that a judgement of identity, e.g., "a is identical to b", presupposes a concept under which a and b fall and which sets criteria of identity, so that a fully explicit statement would take the form "a is the same A as b". It has been held in addition that, until such a concept is supplied, the statement "a is identical to b" is ambiguous.[4] Thus, for two subjects of discourse to be the same 'man' is not for Locke for them to be the same 'material substance' or the same 'person'. Spatio-temporal continuity in a bodily being undergoing constant changes in matter but enjoying the same form of life defines the same animal or human being, but not what it is to be a body with the same matter, and not for Locke what it is to be the same person.

I may at a certain time be able to identify a certain thing, e.g., my bicycle, without being able to answer all questions of identity in

---

[3]Cf. R. Harré and E.H. Madden in *Causal Powers*.

[4]David Wiggins disputes this (*Sameness and Substance*, p. 47, cf. especially pp. 27–44, 90–99, 206–210), but his later argument does not absolutely depend upon disputing it in general, but only upon disputing it in a certain key class of cases, viz., the case of the identity of substances where the general concept concerned is that of a natural kind. These are precisely the cases where I take relevance to explanation to limit or eliminate any relativity of identity. Cf. my discussion of plants and flatworms below.

regard to it. I need some general concept, e.g., that of 'a bicycle', in order to identify it at all, or to count the number of distinguishable bicycles present in a certain place. But I do not need to be able to deal with all questions, e.g., as to whether it counts as the same bicycle if I repair whatever at any particular time counts as my bicycle so constantly that after a time no part is still materially the same as the corresponding part of the original bicycle—and, if no tandems have come into my purview, I may well not know whether to count a tandem as a bicycle or not. However, it is perfectly possible to stipulate (perhaps for legal purposes, to decide questions of disputed ownership) that, however much the parts have changed, the spatio-temporal continuity of something subserving the function of a bicycle is sufficient to be deemed to establish sameness of bicycle.

There are many plausible cases where there could be two concepts A and B, such that a thing, a, counted as the same A as a thing, b, but as a different B, and other concepts leaving the matter indeterminate. In such cases, we could speak of the correct answer to the question whether a was identical to b as a matter of convention or choice, inasmuch as the answer depended upon what choice we made amongst several possible concepts in order to determine the answer—or what choice society or the law made.

However, there is an important limit to the extent to which choice or convention can be conceived to enter in, namely the limit which is set if we wish identity statements to be relevant in certain ways to explanation.

Consider, for instance, the explanatory role of statements of identity about dogs and about persons. If on one day your dog sees you put meat into a cupboard in an enclosed dish emitting no scent and the next day you leave the cupboard door open and the dog sees the door open and remembers you putting the meat in and goes to the cupboard, dislodges the lid and gets and eats the meat, then the explanatory value of the account just given depends upon the truth of numerous identity statements. For the explanation given to work, it is vital that it was the same dog as between one day and the next, the same dog that is the subject of seeing, remembering and of certain sorts of activity in relation to knocking lids off and to poking about on shelves. Likewise, if a person says that they know something because they remember seeing it happen, their present knowledge and memory has to have the same subject as the seeing earlier: that is, the person who has the knowledge by memory has to be identical with the person who earlier had the sight of the happening concerned, if what the person says is to be accepted—and it is not just that we would not call it knowledge by memory, and would not count it as remembering, if these identity statements were not true, but that the acceptance of the "because", i.e., the acceptance of the person's having earlier on seen the happening concerned as an explanation of their knowledge depends upon the truth of these identity statements.

It does indeed seem that it is considerations about explanation which motivate the view one is apt to take of what judgements of identity one would make in certain of the strange hypothetical cases which have been proposed. If a person whom we met today said that he was Julius Caesar, seemed to be honest, and told the truth in regard to many matters of history belonging to the lifetime of the historically known Julius Caesar as if he knew them by first-hand memory, including some unexpected matters outside the ken of present-day historians and archaeologists, numerous of which were put to the test of further archaeological study, then we would want an explanation of how it was that he got so many matters right. The attraction of accepting his claim that 'it was because he remembered seeing, hearing, or doing these things' would be that it seemed to provide an explanation of the conjectured phenomena.

Accepting such an explanation, if the imagined case arose, might push us towards an acceptance of a dualistic conception of the soul and of possible reincarnation. But, if two such persons were being conjectured to be 'in play' at the same time, this explanation would seem to deal with only one, leaving the apparent knowledge of the other to be explained in some other way, e.g., in terms of extra-sensory perception; but, if in this way some other type of explanation was brought in, and if as with extra-sensory perception it would account for two cases as readily as for one, such other explanation (not involving Cartesian souls and reincarnation) would seem preferable.

However, it is perfectly open to us to say that imaginability or a certain novelists' describability are quite insufficient to establish real possibility, or even to establish the absence of conceptual incoherence of less obvious kinds (we are well aware of the possibility of a novelistic portrayal of the aftermath of time-travel, and should be quite unwilling to accept this as proof of the coherence of supposing it, let alone its real possibility). We might allege the dependence of memory upon brain-function, and even the conceptual necessity of its dependence upon some bodily continuity; or we might be game for the hypothesis of Cartesian souls, but insist that more than one case at the same time was impossible, perhaps even incoherent to suppose. As to extra-sensory perception, we might suspect it of already implying dualism, or be unwilling to consider it on other grounds. However, whatever view we came to, it would be quite wrong to say "It is a matter of convention which explanation or type of explanation we accept, and therefore derivatively just a matter of convention whether we should accept, in such an imagined case, that it was because he remembered that he knew and got it all right". Except in the case of merely *ad hominem* explanations (like explaining surface tension phenomena to children in terms of liquids having skins), explanation cannot be arbitrary in this way.

Such thought-experiments confirm the explanatory role of iden-tity statements, and it is clear that it is related considerations which influence philosophers' sympathies in the nowadays more popular thought-experiments which conjecture cases of brain-transplants. And here again it is open to a person who adopts the perspective argued for in this book simply to deny the possibility of such transplant. They involve, for instance, that one person might emerge from an operation with the body of one former person and the mind of another, but this would involve that the 'outer' and 'inner' were so distinguishable and contingently related as to make this possible—a view quite excluded by the holistic perspective established earlier in this book.

Even Hume can see the importance of identity in connection with explanation, although this does not transparently appear when he is discussing identity in Part IV of Book I of his *Treatise*, nor when he is discussing the nature of necessary connection as an element in causation. But earlier, in Part II, he tells us that there is only one kind of reasoning, namely causal reasoning, which is operative in regard to the three kinds of contingent relation: relations of space and time and relations of identity as well as of what he calls relations of causation, after his classification of "philosophical relations" (i.e., propositions) into his seven different kinds. Suppose I put a book on my bedside table at night and I waken the next morning and find a book exactly similar there and not recognizably different, I assume it to be the same book. Otherwise I have to invent hypotheses as to who removed the one copy and who came in and substituted without my knowledge of either event another volume similar to the first.

Sometimes, therefore, identity—even material identity in the case of inanimate objects—plays a role in explanation of goings-on in the world and this involves identity through time. This link with explanation involves, on any non-Humean view of explanation, a concept non-conventional and non-arbitrarily determining identity, whether it be concept associated with material stuff, e.g., of which the book is made, or whether it be the concept of person or whether it be the concept of dog.

Let us generalize what we have indicated: for there to be identity in this non-arbitrary way of a thing (or 'temporal substance') over a time, depends upon the thing having a certain nature, where by "nature" I mean some character, relevant to its classification, which is determinative of its forms of behaviour and the ways in which it can be acted upon. It has to have a nature, not in order that as a matter of epistemology one should be able to make judgements about it, but because its having a nature is part of what is involved in being a thing or temporal substance about which judgements are to be made. The 'natures' concerned are those which are determinative of 'behaviour' in the broadest possible sense, including patterns of nutrition, growth, regeneration of injured parts, and decay, general physiological and morphological features, and so forth, as well as 'behaviour' in a more ordinary sense.[5] A nature thus thought of has been thought of as an 'internal law', 'source of non-accidental change and rest', that in a thing in virtue of which it by nature maintains a certain shape and form, has in itself the cause of its continuity, and so is a unity in a stronger sense than that which is held together by glue, nails, or rope.[6] The things which have such a nature, and a unity of this kind important to explanation, are what we may call 'natural wholes', with a 'natural' or 'essential' rather than a merely 'accidental' unity: to the question of the relationship of parts to the whole within such unities, I turn in discussing 'holism' below.

---

[5] In this way, after a very sketchy discussion, and despite a less complete rejection of the relativity of identity (relativity to the concept in respect of which identity is to be assessed), I converge towards the conclusions reached in the closely argued treatment of identity of David Wiggins in *Sameness and Substance*. He concludes that the fundamental kind of identity is that of Aristotle's primary substances, for which sameness of individual identity is inseparable from continued membership of the same natural kind (in his Chapter 3).

[6] I here bring together the ideas drawn from Aristotle and Leibniz which Wiggins quotes with favour in expounding his own view in Chapter 3 of *Sameness and Substance*.

Even in the case of plants and some of the lower animals, some room for an element of convention or arbitrariness can enter into the consideration of identity. Thus, it is not clear at what point in processes of asexual reproduction amongst plants, e.g., by the formation of suckers, or the modes of reproduction of strawberries or of potato-plants by the formation of runners, we should describe a new plant as having arisen. Likewise, it is not clear how we should describe the case of flatworms when their heads are surgically divided and two heads form. But once what I shall later call focalized subjecthood arises, and in particular the subjecthood associated with perceptual consciousness, there is no more room for convention or arbitrariness at all.[7] In this way, non-arbitrariness in the ascription of identity through time is peculiarly associated with persons, whether rational animals such as human beings or immaterial spirits, if there be such, and in general with all higher animals who share perceptual conscious-ness, i.e., all of what we may call psychosomatic beings. These two concepts—"person" and "psychosomatic being"—identify the hubs of explanation because of their character as range-concepts, concepts marking out the range within which the terms key to the relevant explanatory schemes (in the case we considered of the dog, terms such as "see", "imagine", "remember", "desire", "goes", "dislodges", "gets" and "eats").[8]

(b) Note on the concept of substance

Since I have spoken of 'substances' as subjects of the key kind of identity statement, and will often use the term in my later argument, it is important to clarify its meaning.

The way in which I use the word "substance" in this book is roughly that of meaning 'logical subject of concrete predicates' where amongst 'concrete predicates' I include predicates ascribing action or movement. These are the 'first substances' of Aristotle's *Categories*, and the things which Strawson ranks as 'basic particulars'.

---

[7] For Wiggins, the human person is a substance the form of whose life, belonging to man as a natural kind, is marked by the features Locke associated with personhood (*Sameness and Substance*, Chapter 6, pp. 148, 176–179, 187). There is no room left for arbitrariness after the unitariness of the organism whose nature is to grow to full expression of this form of life (cf. *Sameness and Substance*, pp. 220–221).

[8] Cf. Chapter IV, nn. 3 and 4 together with associated text.

In this, I set aside many other uses of the word. Thus, the most common use of the word "substance" is to mean 'stuff' or 'kind of stuff', and as such it corresponds better with Aristotle's notion of matter than with his concept of substance. Likewise, in much modern philosophy, by the "permanence of substance" has been meant rather the permanence of matter than the permanence of Aristotelian substances. Since the Greek word *ousia* used by Aristotle and translated *substantia* in Latin and thence 'substance' in other languages has the original meaning 'being', as a noun formed from the verb 'to be', it is unsurprising that it should have a great variety of usage. Aristotle himself notes a large variety of types of application of the word *ousia*. As used to pick out the subjects of concrete predicates, it covers all natural bodies or bodily things, including even celestial bodies and the universe[9]; but it can also pick out natural kinds of such substance (species such as man and dog, and their genera), and also kinds of stuff; because of these usages, it can also be used to mean matter or that which underlies change, but thence even matter as that which persists through substantial change, as when a dog dies, or logs become ashes, or water becomes steam.[10] But quite apart from these uses, the word *ousia* can mean essence or the object of definition, or form understood as that which combined with matter makes up a substance in the first mentioned sense.[11] (When Aquinas wishes to disambiguate *substantia*, according to whether it means the subject of concrete predicates or whether it means essence, he uses *subsistentia* for the first and *essentia* for the second.)[12]

In the *Categories*, elaborate explanations are given to make sure that first substances exclude not only predicates of any kind, but also things which can be spoken of as 'in' substances but not as parts, such, it seems, as surfaces and particularized qualities or actions such as Socrates' being healthy or Socrates' action on a particular occasion. At this stage of his thought, the parts of first substances also counted as first substances. When, at a later time, Aristotle came to characterize

---

[9]*Metaphysics*, Zeta, 1028b 8–14, 1040a 28ff.

[10]For Aristotle, this last is a change in substance, not just an alteration or change in quality, *De Gen. et Cor.*, I.4, cf. II.6.

[11]Whereas it is the individual subjects of concrete predicates which are 'first substances' in the *Categories*, in the *Metaphysics* we can find essences or forms being referred to under this title.

[12]E.g., *S. Th.* Ia, Q. 29, Art. 2, cf. Q. 75, Arts. 2, 3 & 6.

natural bodily things as composed of matter and form, more privilege was given to the natural wholes which have parts, the parts being substances only derivatively or counting only as matter in relation to the whole in the way explained in my next section.

It is this use of the word "substance" to refer to natural wholes which are subjects of concrete predicates to which I keep in this book.

There is a narrow sense of the word "logic" in which it includes only principles which bestraddle all subject-matters, even independently of whether they are abstract or concrete, and includes therefore, propositional and predicate logic, together with arithmetical principles such as "Two things of a sort and another two things of the sort are four things of the sort". Such a logic has no concern with time and no concern with what depends on the continuity of space and movement; it has no concern with the distinctions between predicates ascribing sensory quality, shape, size, place, action, or passion; it has no interest in distinguishing states, acts or acheivements, performances or processes, and activities according to their temporal aspect. Such a merely formal logic is in utter contrast with a properly 'general' logic which takes account of all these distinctions and has been counted as 'metaphysics'.

The notion of substance belongs then to such a 'general logic' or 'metaphysics'. We could call it the notion of 'basic particular' so long as this notion was developed in terms of concepts of logical structure drawn from the philosophy of language, not from epistemology. It was developed by Aristotle as a concept of such a 'general' logical theory, rather than of physics. In his thought, it antedated his theories of change and of form and matter in physics, and no notion of being made of matter or stuff, or of being solid or spatial, is involved internally to the concept—although certainly hardness, and various types of spatial property (shape, size, position, and posture) are amongst concrete predicates. Developing the concept further today, we can see it as co-extensive with the concept of causal agent.

Since this notion does not belong to physics and is not 'second-order' or epistemological, it is natural to say that it belongs to metaphysics—but it is less misleading to call it a transgeneric term than to call it metaphysical, because, at the stage at which it is introduced, all that needs to be grasped is that it is of greater generality than the various genera introduced by physics and that it is not part of the concept to be limited to the physical. In this it follows the pattern set by the concept of causal agent—that is, it is introduced before and independently of any development of metaphysics as an integrated account of the world, e.g., before and independently of any development in the direction of cosmological or theistic theories.

2. Wholes and Parts: The Aristotelian Conception of a Natural Whole or Non-Accidental Unity

(a) The interdependence of wholes and parts:
the Aristotelian conception of natural
whole or non-accidental unity introduced

The idea that the method of understanding things is always by picking out their parts and considering the inter-relation of their parts—explaining away the behaviour of the whole in terms of the behaviour of the parts—represents the arrival in the seventeenth century of materialism in its first *prima facie* successful form. Even in physics, on examination, it turns out this appearance is deceptive. It is violated in so far as matter—waves, fields, or anything else— are treated as having some sort of continuity in a continuous space. It is violated as a consequence of quantum theory. It is violated by cosmological theories and theories of gravitation which involve treating the universe as a whole in some way. The depth of the significance of such violations was grasped by Whitehead in his conception whereby events, far from being entities whose existence and nature are non-relational, are 'prehensions into a unity' at nodes within a system of relations,[13] and is vividly illustrated by David Bohm's consideration of how what is contained in, is to be explained within, a cubic metre of so-called 'empty' space is, through the presence of radiation from the most distant parts of the universe, a microcosm of the whole, not intelligible or explicable apart from relation to the rest.[14] We not only find that the exploration into ever more minute structures helps explain more macroscopic features, but again and again that the consideration of wider contexts introduces new understanding of the minute, especially so as to make intelligible and even predictable what might have appeared to be deviant phenomena at the lower level, and to present the macroscopic as explaining and even determining the microscopic, so that the relationship between

---

[13] *Science and the Modern World.*
[14] David Bohm, 'Quantum Theory as an Indication of a New Order in Physics'.

laws relating to the macroscopic and laws relating to the minute is reciprocal.[15]

The existence of these violations of a general mechanism even within purely physical theory merely marks the incoherence of any overall or complete rejection of holism. All substances, not only 'purely physical' ones, exist only within a field which is in its character and totality holistic. But to respect the phenomena of continuity, to note the holistic features of quantum theory and much cosmology, and to insist upon the place of relations, not just within the behaviour, but also within the nature of whatever substances there are, does not involve one in treating either the continuous as such or the universe as a substance. What the incoherence of a total rejection of holism adverts us to is the fact that the mechanistic approach can only proceed at all as a special growth within a field which is in its character and totality holistic. It is in fact that special growth which arises by treating as substances physical bodies or particles at some particular level, whether it be the level of billiard balls, nuts and bolts, the level of molecules and ions, or some deeper level.

However, we are not immediately concerned with these general violations of mechanism not involving the phenomena of life and consciousness, except to mark the holistic character of the general context within which life and consciousness arise has ultimately to be conceived. Rather, our concern is with the living substances we have referred to as 'natural wholes'—causal agents with a persistent identity through time inseparable from their place in certain types of explanation.

For we have seen that it is characteristic of the kinds of statement, those involving consciousness, that their meaning gives them a role in teleological explanation—they bring teleological explanation into play by their very meaning. Further, the kind of teleological explanation which they bring into play involves their subjects, human beings and higher animals, as wholes. Furthermore, it is in respect of 'substances' of these kinds that our earlier chapters have shown the need of a holistic approach, in particular one which does not divide the human being into an 'inner part' (the mind, soul, or brain) and other parts thought of as 'outer'.

---

[15]David Bohm, Causality and Chance in Modern Physics, pp. 132–134, 138–139, 143–146.

It is to a holism relevant to such living substances as human beings and the higher animals, which are the nodes of mind-involving explanations and which must not be divided or atomized into 'inner' and 'outer' parts, that Aristotle's approach provides a key.

We shall find that the perception of a reciprocity between the macroscopic and the minute of which we spoke above is an echo of the insistence on reciprocity between wholes and parts which is the hallmark of Aristotle's conception of nature, and it is this which provides the key to the understanding of human beings and animals.

Aristotle's conception of natural unities or wholes presupposes the notion of nature as the principle of a thing's behaviour, taking the word "behaviour" in the widest sense, so that it is the principle which governs the manner and direction of growth and regeneration, patterns of nutrition and of decay, as well as modes of action and passion. Against this background the parts of a natural whole will have natures which can only be understood and specified according to their place and function in the whole with its behaviour, i.e., natures which can only be specified in terms of the nature of the whole.

For instance, in order to obtain a rounded or global view of the nature and principles of behaviour, not only of fingers in general, but of this or that particular finger, one has to understand the finger as being a part of a living human being. There is no complete knowledge afforded by the physiologist or any amalgam of computer theorists and of other mathematical and physical scientists—no full explanation of the behaviour of a finger without resort to the concept of the finger as being used by a living human being. Accordingly, a man's finger cut off is a finger in name only[16] because what it is (its 'nature') is no longer the same. In this conception what a finger is is only properly to be understood in terms of its being part of a hand understood in relation to an arm of a biped of a certain kind, viz., a human being, the finger functioning in the way characteristic of a human being while alive. It is not, of course, that there is no connection between the use of the word 'finger' in regard to a severed finger, removed in battle, and its use as a functioning finger of a living man. The connection of the two uses of the word is in some way obvious. There is a similarity of shape and internal physiological structure as

---

[16]Aristotle, *Metaphysics*, 1035b 23–25.

well as a relation of origin since it was once not severed. But, as Aristotle would have had it, it is the same in matter, but not the same substance because not the same in nature—that is, not the same in regard to that which is relevant to identity because of the way in which it is relevant to explanation (or more precisely, while the same in respect of the explanation of certain abstracted aspects of behaviour, not the same overall, and not the same when considered in what makes it a unity.)

The view of the status and nature, and along with these of the identity, of the parts of natural wholes is a corollary of the view we took of the relevance of considerations about the appropriateness of certain modes of explanation to the treatment of the identity of the wholes.

We need to understand that what is meant by 'not being an accidental unity' does not have to do with the mode of origin of things, e.g., that they were brought together 'by Nature' rather than by the design of an artificer or by chance. The contrast is rather between things whose parts are capable of separate existence without being denatured, such as parts of heaps or parts of chairs, and things whose parts have natures which make them incapable of existence apart from the wholes of which they are parts without changing their natures and criteria of identity. The Aristotelian expression "accidental" (*kata symbebēkos*) as used of chairs and heaps does not have to do with origin, but is the opposite of "of itself" (*kath'auto*, commonly translated 'essential').

Such then is the character of the notion of natural whole or 'non-accidental unity'.

Against this background, we can recognize a key corollary of the role of substances—as natural wholes in the sense just explained—within the explanation of phenomena. This is the corollary that no such substance can contain another. As Aristotle argues, no such[17] substance be composed of other substances present in it in complete

---

[17] I add the word "such" because Aristotle is not speaking of primary substances in the sense which would include not only parts of substances but also the universe (*Metaphysics*, Zeta, 2), but only the familiar perishable natural wholes which he thinks of as composed of matter and form, not those which he thinks are eternal or unique (1040a 28–29).

actuality.[18] For, in the relevant conception of substance, a substance is of a nature which includes everything determinative of its principles of behaviour. In the case of human beings and other animals, the laws and principles of physics and allied sciences do not, in his conception, include all the principles determinative of their behaviour, but, on the contrary, leave unexplained much which has an explanation if a more global view is taken. In Aristotle's conception we must view human beings and other animals globally in a way which allows an uneliminable role for teleology and consciousness. This allows the explanation and even the prediction of much that is not even in principle predictable or explicable in terms of sciences utilizing only physical concepts.

It should be no surprise that Aristotle should insist that no substance can contain as a part another substance in complete actuality, since it generalizes his rejection of the atomism of his day. And therefore equally it should be no surprise to us that the seventeenth century believers in the self-containedness of material explanation should have found the Aristotelian conception of natural wholes and non-accidental unities unacceptable. It was so 'evident' to them that material substances were, in Aristotle's terminology, substances in complete actuality that they could no longer understand the concept of 'non-accidental' unity and the holism from which it sprang. They purported to reject the so-called 'substantial forms', but the real object of their attack was this holism which contradicted their conception of the self-sufficiency of material explanation within the sphere of the material—a holism which can be stated in the way we have done above without bringing in any conception of form as correlative to matter or any conception of 'substantial forms'.

(b) The aspectual character of scientific laws

We must now insist upon the opposite side of the same coin.

It is not just that the nature of the parts requires explanation in terms of place and function in the whole with its behaviour, but also, conversely, that it belongs to the nature of the whole to have such

---

[18] *Metaphysics*, Zeta, 13, at 1039a 2–14, where Aristotle indicates that this statement arises from his critique of Democritus's atomism, with its connection with one of Zeno's paradoxes—although in the context he is using this principle to mark what is impossible in any conceptual atomism of Platonic forms.

parts. Statements about the parts are not like statements about aspects of a thing or consequences of its nature, but have some standing in right of the whole's having them as parts, not aspects or consequences. The whole concerned must be understood as a whole which has parts which by abstracting in a certain way, ignoring certain aspects of their functioning, can be described independently. Thus, to take some instances, one can describe the anatomy of a finger and consider at one level the neurology and at another level the mechanics of its operation, but also one can speak of the different kinds of cell which it contains and generalize about types of cell indifferently to their relation to fingers or even to human beings, as well as treating of chemistry and physics as they relate to types of substance in certain physical conditions indifferently to whether they are parts of the constitution of animate beings or not. The fact that bodily parts and substructures and their functioning can in identifiable respects be considered as it were in their own right is key to the possibility of their having a functional role within various key mental activities—a possibility whose importance will be brought out in Chapter IX. And it is this fact which secures the limited autonomy of the various biological and physical sciences which we have described.

That is, on the one hand, it is an essential part of the kind of holism which we are considering that such subjects as physics should be considered to be dealing, not with the whole nature of things, but only with certain aspects of this nature, so that it is in this sense dealing only with certain 'abstracted' aspects of things, not their whole reality. But, on the other hand, it is also essential that such abstraction be possible—that is, it is essential that parts should have aspects which allow their description and identification in other terms than as parts of this or that accidental or non-accidental whole.[19] In other words,

---

[19]I present the point here without reference to Aristotle, and implicitly with a greater range of examples of types of 'abstraction' than he considers. I use the word "abstraction" to cover a wider range of cases of 'ignoring other aspects' than is, for instance, covered by his phrase 'separation from matter'.

Some 'forms', Aristotle tells us, are not tied to particular kinds of matter, e.g., the circle; but other forms, e.g., the form of 'human being', are thus tied, viz., to the kind of matter we call flesh and bones, so that although he says such matter does not belong to the form, we cannot abstract from the type of matter ('perform the separation') when we define the nature of the human being—this seems to be the doctrine of *Metaphysics*, Zeta, 1036a 26–b 7 and many other places. All natural substances have particular kinds of matter in their definitions, and the forms which are

the validity of the physiological and the physical approach to relevant problems—the validity of the explanations they offer of what goes on in human and other living bodies in the aspects they deal with—is not compromised by regarding their status as involving an 'abstraction' or partial consideration. We are free to adopt Ryle's perspective whereby laws can exist and be obeyed but no more need to be conceived to determine what transpires in a global way than would the laws of cricket if obeyed. We do not have to consider a set of laws as all-determining, as reducing, at every juncture, all possible outcomes to one: the laws we meet with in physics, physiology, and so forth do not deal with every kind of juncture however defined, and we have no need to conceive them even as limiting, at every physically defined juncture, all physical outcomes to one. In practice, we describe situations in certain limited physical respects, not completely even as regards the physical; and laws limit outcomes, excluding some but not all—they limit outcomes to one only in the respect they are concerned with.

(c) The status of human beings and other animals as substances

It may be asked why we should give special status to animals with consciousness, human beings amongst them, and not simply, as if to follow out the logic of the Aristotelian way of viewing things further than he did, to regard the universe as the only natural substance existing 'in complete actuality'. For, after all, do not animals and human beings only exist or live with their characteristic kind of life in integration with and dependence on the general system of Nature?

To this we must reply that what is required for a thing to be a 'substance existing in complete actuality' is not complete independence from the rest of nature but only its being a subject of action in its own right. By a subject of action in its own right I mean something

---

not tied to a kind of matter are not forms of substances, but of shapes as with 'the circle' and so forth, so that a kind of matter will come in again in specifying (e.g.) the natural thing which has the shape.

In mathematics, we 'abstract' from matter, while in physics we 'abstract' from (e.g.) what makes the difference between non-living and living things. In physiology, we might be considered to be considering what belongs to flesh, bone, or tissue of different types, without any necessary reference to the type of living thing concerned, or we can consider the tissues of just one type of organism without the other aspects of its functioning. And so forth.

with a rounded nature of which the action is a realization, possessing 'a rounded nature' in the sense in which subordinate parts do not have rounded natures because interdependence and interrelation with other parts is internal to the actions proper to each of them.

The universe is not a substance or subject of actions and passions but the context of substances. It is not a contemporaneous whole with the kind of contemporaneity in existence between its parts necessary to acting together in a co-ordinated way. Nor is it the subject of passion or being acted upon as a whole or as such. The propositions we make about it are laws concerning the behaviour of what makes it up, and questions of the cause or causes of its origin and continuance along with accounts of its history are questions and accounts concerning what makes up the universe. The things in the universe are members of a system in such a way that their natures cannot be understood apart from the underlying patterns and laws of that system and cohesion with other things within the universe in accord with these patterns and laws, but not in such a way as to make the universe as such an agent, let alone something acted upon.

By contrast, the ordinary loci of identity are things with some degree of autonomous and stable existence within the universe, subjects of action and passion. And amongst these the position of animal subjects of consciousness is singular. The autonomy and stability of existence in one continuing identity of these organisms within the physical world is inseparable from their autonomy and stability of existence in one continuing identity as subjects of consciousness. Now, as we have seen, such identity as subjects of consciousness has a special role in explanation, a role which this chapter will show to be fundamental or uneliminable. This identity has a special character inasmuch as while there can be material division of one body into two bodies, there can be no material division of one centre of consciousness into two centres of consciousness. In these ways, this kind of identity has a certain absolute status.

I have described a certain kind of holism. Such holism has nothing obviously false about it and it is only metaphysical prejudice, not scientific proof, that has lead to its being set aside. One may further remark that dualism is in one way only a variant upon mechanism in that it suggests that in addition to the material parts of the human being there is an extra part, namely, some immaterial part called the mind, soul or spirit. But dualism still leaves one with the picture of human beings as aggregates of parts inter-related in various ways, so that their nature and behaviour can, in certain ways, be explained away in terms of the nature and behaviour of these parts and their inter-relations. We shall comment on this later in the light of a comparison with the way in which a broom may be conceived of as a broom-handle screwed into a brush.

3. The Incoherence of the Theory That Determinism and Freewill are Compatible

(a) The form and strengths of the 'common-sense' position

On the face of it, it appears that the types of explanation with which we have been concerned, those involving the mental (and thereby an uneliminable teleology arising, with all animals with perceptual consciousness) carry with them certain concepts for judging questions of identity and a certain ontology—an ontology presenting certain natural wholes or substances as explanatorily basic. They are presented as being basic in the sense that these explanations, carrying with them this ontology, is not liable to displacement by advances in understanding of the multiple processes involved.

We are well aware of the difficulties in 'reducing' chemistry and biochemistry to physics. We are not in doubt that whatever is determined in chemistry or biochemistry is determined physically—but we cannot carry out the calculations. In the meantime we proceed quite well using concepts and principles which are not strictly those of physical theory. We do not expect—though perhaps we sometimes may not exclude—the explanations which we offer using these higher, chemical and biochemical, concepts and principles to be displaced, in the sense of being shown to be untenable, by any later success in doing the calculations and thus performing the 'reduction'.

The situation is sometimes imagined to be the same in regard of the relation of our ordinary consciousness-involving explanations of the behaviour of human beings and other higher animals to explanations in terms of physiology, biochemistry, and physics. However, this does not seem to be the case. We are not confident that whatever is determined or predictable according to our ordinary consciousness-involving ways of understanding human or animal behaviour is, even in principle, determined physically. On the contrary, it appears to

us that, if something predictable or explicable in terms of these ordinary ways of understanding human or animal behaviour turned
out to be predictable and explicable in terms of these other sciences, we would have to reject the particular psychologistic explanation offered previously.

Whereas we have no tendency to suppose that to regard the
reduction of biochemistry and chemistry to physics as impracticable
involves regarding the entities treated in biochemistry (molecules,
ions, radicals, or whatever) as other than physical, or inanimate bodies
as other than 'merely' physical bodies—by contrast, we do have a
tendency to suppose that people, animals, and, perhaps, even plants
are not just 'not *merely* physical bodies', but not properly spoken of
as 'bodies' at all. After all, does it not seem that 'there is something
absurd—so unnatural that the upshot is simply falsity—in the proposition that people's bodies play chess, talk sense, know arithmetic, or
even run or jump or sit down'?[20]

There is a seemingly 'common-sense' approach according to
which this apparent datum presents no problem. This is represented
in one form in Ryle, in another in Woodger, and gives plausibility to
the relevant argument of Wiggins.

For Ryle, mechanism was a bogy, an unreal object of fear. In
order supposedly to show this he merely adverted to the possibility
of there being several different types of law, none all-determining,
applicable to the same phenomena; and with them, several types of
explanation, none deterministic, of different facets of the same event.
There was, for him, no reason to anticipate a set of deterministic
physical laws, at every juncture limiting possible outcomes to one,
and he did not take time to consider the view that things were thus
determined. He therefore did nothing to refute the view that all the
physical movements of parts of our body which are involved in what
we think of as an action are physically determined. Since he spoke
nearly always in the material mode of speech, he never doubted human
freedom or feared lest some proof of mechanism should undermine it:
mechanism was for him no more serious a view than dualism, indeed a
view whose mistakes were yet more elementary. One could undertake
a study of the physical aspects of human action and constitution

---

[20]Wiggins, *op. cit.*, pp. 163–164, and related thoughts are to be found in Ryle,
e.g., *The Concept of Mind* (Hutchinson), p. 189.

without carrying with one any such dead weight as a methodological determinism.[21]

There can be the idea that the concept of person is not a 'material' concept in the sense of one which is 'definable or properly describable in terms of the concepts of the sciences of matter', so that it is 'both primitive relative to the concepts that pull their weight in the sciences of matter and primitive relative to the concept human body'.[22] And one can understand this concept as a transgeneric one, applying to any kind of animal to whose form of life as a species it belonged to be 'a thinking intelligent being, that has reason and reflection, and can consider itself as itself, the same thinking thing, in different times and places'.[23] And one could think of some such concept as "animal" or "psychosomatic being" as in a parallel way transgeneric, applying to any natural kind of animal to whose form of life as a species perception and intentional action belonged (in a weak sense of "intentional").

Utilizing such ideas, one might see the teleology-involving modes of explanation we have instanced as having application primarily in virtue of the applicability of these concepts. As we remarked earlier,[24] such concepts have precisely the character of concepts marking the range of significance of certain families of predicate. These predicates define these range-concepts and are just those predicates involving consciousness which play interlocking roles in just such explanations. And clearly this perspective is quite independent of any

---

[21]Woodger argues to a similar conclusion along a different line: 'If you want to reduce biology to physics and chemistry, you must construct bi-conditionals which are in effect definitions of biological functors with the help of those belonging only to physics and chemistry; you must then add these to the postulates of physics and chemistry and work out their consequences. Then and only then will it be time to go into your laboratories to discover whether these consequences are upheld there. From the fact that people do *not* do this, I venture the guess that they confuse reducibility of biology to physics and chemistry, with applicability of physics and chemistry to biological objects.' He associates this reducibility with 'the metaphysical doctrine, that living organisms are "nothing but" physical systems'. J. H. Woodger, *Biology and Language*, pp. 338—in Wiggins, *op. cit.*, p. 148.

[22]Wiggins, *op. cit.*, p. 164.

[23]Nothing in the argument of this section turns on whether the term "person" is taken in the more restricted sense of 'personal bodily being' defined by Wiggins, *op. cit.*, p. 171–173 (cf. n. 7 above), usual amongst Anglo-Saxon philosophers, or in the wider way described in Chapter V, allowing its application to God and the angels.

[24]See Chapter V, n. 4.

belief that where such explanations involved dispositions or states teleologically defined, these dispositions or states were identical with physical states of an organism or of some such part as the brain—as if teleological explanation as such had to be rooted in mechanical. In this way, one has not at all committed oneself to any form of physicalism or mechanism, but remains within the ambit of 'common-sense'.

(b) The counter-claims made by physicalism

But such 'common-sense' seems to many simply uncritical, and indeed almost ostrich-like. Hampshire, taking seriously the possibility of a determinism or sufficiently determining explanation as in principle within reach of an 'objective' knowledge, saw it as in possible tension with the subject's subjective knowledge of his own freedom in his action inseparable from the knowledge he has of his own actions because he did them intentionally.[25] In this way, the spectre of determinism and even physical determinism, which oppressed Kant, is seen undispelled in Hampshire as well as, implicitly, in Merleau-Ponty—whose position leaves the physical sciences as much limited to the phenomenon rather than the unqualifiedly real as any sciences of the living or the human, and therefore in no special authority, but nonetheless provides no refutation of the hypothesis of a set of physical laws all-predicting in relation to movements involved in action.

This 'common-sense' is indeed ostrich-like in relation to common convictions and programmes of research to be met with today. The inspiration underlying a great deal of Artificial Intelligence research has been the belief that the processes determining the relation between sensation and behaviour are ultimately physical, and that AI is the most powerful theoretical tool for describing the possible structures of mechanical processes.[26] And the belief, that not only memory, but all thinking-processes, must have a neurological correlate, and that all dispositions or states of mind are 'realized in the brain', is so deeply rooted that, as it was remarked to me even in the early 1960s, 'one would be ashamed to be heard thinking anything else'. And such opinions do not depend upon a generalized physical determinism, but only on the supposition that, when something physical is

---

[25]Cf. *Thought and Action.*

[26]The way of thinking concerned is represented in Daniel Dennett, *Brainstorms*, e.g., Ch. 5, pp. 80–86.

determined in some physical respect somehow (e.g., so as to be capable of prediction and explanation in consciousness-involving terms), it is determined physically in that respect.

The way of thinking concerned appears amongst many thinkers little occupied with the problems of 'reducing the mental and biological to the physical'.

Thus, to take an eloquent instance, Wiggins treating identity as if in a way inspired by Aristotle and Leibniz takes it as a praiseworthy feature of Leibniz's thought that he reckoned the laws or natures within substances or 'nomological foundation of activity' as always 'supervenient upon the fundamental laws of nature'.[27] And he goes on to represent biological organisms including human beings as if they were nodes of a temporary stability within the total field of phenomena, existing by being 'exploitations' of 'basic laws of nature', so that 'lawlike norms of starting to exist, existing, and ceasing to exist by reference to which questions of the identity and persistence of individual specimens falling under a definition can be arbitrated' are 'supervenient on basic laws of nature'. This 'kind of account of living substances' is, he tells us, amplified for us a posteriori by biologists, seeing these living substances as 'systems open to their surroundings but not in equilibrium with them and so constituted as to be able, by dint of a delicate self regulating balance of serially linked enzymatic degradative and synthesizing chemical reactions to renew themselves at the expense of those surroundings—the renewal taking place under a law-determined variety of conditions and always in a species-determined pattern of growth and development towards, and/or persistence in, one particular form'.[28]

In these remarks, he makes it intelligible to us how he can hold that the kind of concept for identity which we ordinarily employ 'is rarely or never a scientifically basic concept'[29]—a concept for identity

---

[27] Op. cit., p. 85, referring to the passages in Leibniz quoted on pp. 76 and 84, although in fact in these passages Leibniz speaks only of the 'law' within a substance determining the continuous succession of its states as also determining its accord with 'the laws of nature which govern the whole world' (p. 76) and the activities or qualities of a substance as being derived from their natures as intelligible modifications of them (p. 84), in no way implying that these laws or natures within substances were not fundamental, but merely consequential upon more general laws.

[28] Op. cit., p. 86.

[29] Op. cit., p. 144.

used in some, for us, basic explanatory science.[30] Indeed, although he expects our more ordinary explanatory schemes and concepts to be co-tenable with the 'scientific' ones, and, more than this, insists that they must be so since the ladder upon climbing up which science depends cannot be pushed away,[31] nonetheless he expects the concept of continuant (covering persons, animals, plants, bodies, and all other ordinary substances, as well as rivers, springs, mountains, volcanoes, and so forth) to be absent from fundamental science even though the concepts of event, process, and stuff remain.[32] It is against this background that he tells us that 'A person is material in the sense of being essentially constituted by matter', and that the continuity principle for persons 'defines a material entity in the "matter-constituted" sense of "material"', while going on to speak of the body of a person or animal as 'that which realizes or constitutes it while it is alive'.[33]

The problem is that Wiggins does not explain, except by example or suggestion, what it is to be constituted of or by something. But this suggestion that a person 'is constituted of matter' and is 'a material entity in the "matter-constituted" sense' seems to go together with the suggestion that the 'laws' inherent in the identity-determining natures of human beings, animals, and other living things are not amongst the 'fundamental' or 'basic laws of nature', and the concepts concerned 'not scientifically basic'. Neither suggestion seems to have any justification offered for it beyond a certain rhetoric or association of ideas. In fact, by 'is constituted by matter', Wiggins appears to mean 'consists of the same material parts as'.[34] It is difficult to see

---

[30]In all this he improves on Thomas Nagel's account of what physicalism requires in regard to non-strict identity in the case of substances. Nagel in 'Physicalism', sections III and IV, makes such non-strict identity depend on the conjoint holding of causal and conditional statements (cf. our discussion of the identity of such things as lightning in Chapter VI), but physicalism requires an asymmetry whereby it is the physical kinds of causal statement which are fundamental and this Wiggins' view provides.

[31]*Op. cit.*, pp. 194–196.

[32]*Op. cit.*, pp. 196–197.

[33]*Op. cit.*, p. 164, so that, although persons and animals are not bodies, 'we may define the body' of a person or animal as 'that which realizes or constitutes it while it is alive and will be left over when, succumbing to entropy, it dies'.

[34]On *op. cit.*, p. 43, Wiggins opines that there is a use of "is" to mean "is constituted of". For further illumination we look to pp. 30–33 where we are told that "is the same collection as" can mean "is constituted from the same collection as", and the case mentioned of a jug whose china parts find themselves regathered as a coffee pot seems to suggest what I call 'consisting of the same parts'. I find his

how this can be construed except as a sophisticated return, not just to physicalism, but to mechanism. But in any case the supposition that the only basic or fundamental laws or concepts are those of physical science would still seem to express a physicalist position.

We shall see later that the fundamental lines of Wiggins' approach, making considerations about what are the proper modes of explanation of different phenomena determinative of the concepts appropriate to use in order to determine questions of identity, and thereby determinative of what things we consider exist to be subjects of identity, provide us with an avenue of escape from physicalism.

In the meantime, however, the chief difficulties of physicalism, unsurprisingly, remain in Wiggins' actual view. Not only has no reason been given for supposing that the most general laws of nature, simply because they are the most general, are the only fundamental or basic ones, but also it has not been shown that this view is compatible with the acceptance of our ordinary consciousness-involving statements about human beings and animals with the explanatory role that they have.

(c) The incoherence of compatibilism demonstrated

The problem is that consciousness-involving explanations of the activities and beliefs of human beings and the behaviour of animals do not apply in a different world from physical explanations of the movements of bodies. If the physical movements and changes logically involved in human actions and speech are already fixed by physical law, the freedom of action and the possibility that action and opinion be guided or determined by reasons precisely in virtue of their being recognized as reasons are removed. The position whereby freedom, and determination or guidance, by reasons *qua* reasons, are solely in respect of inner intentions and thoughts, and in respect of the purposes or reservations with which things are said or done (or, as some would say, in respect of the descriptions under which they are said or done),

---

position puzzling since to consist of the same material parts as something else seems to involve the survival of some, perhaps minute, material parts (such as molecules, ions, or atoms, or else such as some more fundamental 'particles'), and thereby to leave the conception of continuant unviolated. (His remarks on pp. 196–197 do not dethrone continuants from their place in modern physics but relate to an imagined four-dimensional language.)

and not in respect to the physical movements involved in speech and action, depends upon a dualistic analysis and an introspectionist understanding of self-knowledge which we have already excluded in earlier chapters. But this position also denies to human beings the freedom and capacity in action and in communication which they want, or, to put the point more strongly, undermines the point of forming plans and intentions and making communications in the first place, since in all these cases the intention is directed primarily towards the external act.

Discussions of the issues here are apt to concentrate upon the case of freedom of choice in action. There is a popular view that there is no incompatibility between saying that a certain physical bodily movement was physically necessitated, or such in the background circumstances that it could not not happen, and saying that the agent could have not done the action involving it (in which case the physical bodily movement would not have occurred).

What seems to be proposed here is that in the assertion of physical necessitation we have a properly modal statement in which the modal operator, "at time t, it is physically impossible that", applies to a properly complete propositional clause apt to identify a determinate fact (and therefore including indication of a time later than that marked in the modal operator).[35] By contrast, it is imagined that in the assertion that the agent could have not done it we have an ascription of an ability, ascriptions of ability being understood to be in respect of sorts of action, the ability-verb not being applied to a proposition at all. Thus, if it is said "Jones can swim", we may agree, even though Jones is in hospital with a broken arm, because we take it that a general ability is being indicated which has not been destroyed but merely had its exercise suspended by the circumstances. And this is much more obviously the right thing to say if Jones is in a desert or in prison. And in the common compatibilist view espoused by Hobbes and now again popular, whereby free-will is supposed to be compatible with actions being determined beforehand, statements like "Jones could have done otherwise", "It was possible for Jones to act otherwise than he did", and "Jones can go swimming today at

---

[35]Or propositional function with a variable ranging over times bound by a prenex quantifier.

Linksfield pool, but it is quite possible for him not to go", are likewise ascriptions of abilities.

Against this, we must insist that, if we say that "Jones can go swimming today at Linksfield pool" we no longer seem to be expressing a general ability in regard to a sort of action, but a possibility which is now in regard to a 'possible fact' (as some philosophers speak), i.e., in regard to what is stated fully propositionally: that is, we now have what we did not have before, a properly modal proposition, in which a modal operator is applied without qualification to a proposition.

Or, to explain the matter in a different way, it is plausible that the assertion of a possibility is equivalent to the denial of a conditional statement, i.e., that "Possible that (P and Not-Q)" is equivalent to "Not the case that (If P, then Q)". In this way, in effect, "He could have not gone swimming" (i.e., meaning "It was possible for him not to go swimming") it is equivalent to "It is not the case that (If Jones was in a going-swimming-situation, automatically it would result that he went swimming)". Now, the compatibilist supposes that ordinary assertions of the possibility or freedom of A not to X are equivalent to saying "It is not the case that (If P1, P2, P3, ...and Pn, then automatically it will result that A X's)", where {P1, P2, P3, ...and Pn} constitutes an incomplete description of the situation in which A will choose and act. The compatibilist holds that what is required for freedom is not that an action not be determined by previous events and states of affairs, but only that it not be determined in a way incompatible with the action's being due to choice.[36]

By contrast, the libertarian or defender of free-will will insist that even if the specification {P1, P2, P3, ...and Pn} constituted a complete description of the situation previous to A's choice and action, the conditional would still be false because the real possibility which is important for the understanding of free-will is the possibility which is left open even when the whole situation[37] prior to choice and action

---

[36]In this he follows the path suggested by Hobbes and opened out afresh by such writers as G.E. Moore, H.A. Hart and P.H. Nowell-Smith, and now followed by a herd of others. In his "Freedom and Determinism", pp. 150–152, 155, Kenny substitutes the combination of an ability and opportunity (the absence of two types of preventing factors) for a possibility not subject to any conditions.

[37]Libertarians are not, of course, committed to the view that the whole situation has a complete description in propositions: that is, they are not committed to the view that human language has the capacity to give the desired 'complete descriptions' of

is set up. [And, of course, libertarians are not willing to see the choice as determined and then to regard the action as free simply because it is (proximately) 'only' determined by choice. And, if they understand matters in the way we explained in Chapter III, they will realize that bringing in a division between choice and action is a red herring, since the primary expression of will is in intentional action itself and not in anything separable from the action such as a previous choice which might be gone back upon.]

Thus, the assertion of the freedom of an action involves the assertion of a real possibility in regard to 'a possible fact', a possibility not subject to any conditions, and so (contrary to what the compatibilists say) is in full and direct contradiction with the assertion of physical necessitation.[38] To say this is, in fact, just to give a particular example of the general significance of the truth that explanations in consciousness-involving terms of human actions are also explanations of the bodily movements they involve, and so come to bear upon the same world, and in possible contradiction to, proposed physical explanations of the same bodily movements.

The worry about determinism is a real worry because it is not the case that freedom is at the level of noumena or 'things as they are in themselves' and determinism at the level of phenomena 'things as they appear to us' in the way followers of Kant might suppose; nor is it the case that there are two 'phenomenal' or 'empirical' worlds. To bring the matter down to earth, it is not that we have two kinds of world of explanation dealing each with different things, as if the ordinary man or woman—who explains and predicts the bodily

---

the situations out of which action proceeds or indeed any local or global situation in the universe.

[38]In this I take the view represented in J.L. Austin, 'Ifs and Cans', *Philosophical Papers*, G.E.M. Anscombe, 'Causality and Determination', *Collected Philosophical Papers II*, and David Wiggins, 'Towards a Reasonable Libertarianism'. That this is the issue is shown up in Kenny's remark (*op. cit.*, p. 155) "It [Wiggins' argument] assumes that the modality involved in talking of a physical impossibility is the same as that involved in talking of human ability and opportunity"—here we see Kenny willing to allow the two worlds of explanation, two worlds or types of historical possibility and necessity, at last come to the surface. (The matter is confused by the previous argument: the supposition of historical inevitability at t' or of physical contingency at t' of other states of affairs or events only makes sense in regard to states of affairs and events at later times, cf. Braine, "Varieties of Necessity", pp. 159–163, so that the sense of the propositions numbered (1), (2), (3), (6) and (7) on p. 154 of Kenny's discussion is quite obscure; it is also evident that in at least one place t' is a misprint for t.)

movements of human beings in a way which utilizes mind-involving concepts like desire, judgement and choice—is occupied with the explanation of a quite different set of things from those which the promised neuroscience promises to explain in physical terms (assisted, doubtless, by cybernetics). On the contrary, both the ordinary human being and the supposed future neuroscientist are or will be occupied with the historical anteceedents and the explanation of one and the same event, e.g., the movement of a certain football as a result of the impact of a certain footballer's foot. The two kinds of explanation presented to us do not bear upon different worlds or different events, but on one and the same world, a world in which bodily beings of varied principles of action interact, and even upon one and the same event within that world. Explanation in mind-involving psychophysical terms is not an *ad hominem* device without explanatory force or predictive value in respect of physical events but a key element in the integral complex which explains physical events and which in ordinary life commonly (indeed often) even makes them predictable. It is not just that we do not have two worlds, a world of minds and a world of bodies, but also that we do not two worlds of explanation, two segregated areas for exercises of causation or action. Rather, we have just one world within which a variety of different kinds of bodily being, with different principles of action, act upon and are acted upon by one another.

But it is a mistake to consider the case of free action in isolation, because it is merely a particular case of a general difficulty, a case which compels attention because of the directness of the contradiction involved.

There is the same incompatibility whenever something is ordinarily represented as due to reasons *qua* reasons, whether they be reasons for action or reasons for assent, and so represented as explicable in this way, but now presented to us as determined and explicable in purely physical terms. And there is the same incompatibility when we have rival explanations in an analogous fashion in the case of lesser animals than man.

The general difficulty can be conveniently presented by considering the way it arises in the case of the mind-brain identity theory.

If the identity between brain-state B and mind-state M is contingent, and if an action A is explained in terms of M, then *ex hypothesi* (since the connection of M and B is said to be contingent) one can raise the question whether A would have occurred if M had occurred but A had not occurred.[39] If the answer is 'yes', then B is not the cause of A; and if the answer is 'no', then M is not the real explanation of A.[40] Either way the appearance which the mind-brain identity theory gives of having salvaged ordinary explanations of action turns out to be pure deception.

An exactly parallel argument arises whenever it is proposed that the validity of some teleology-involving explanation of some action, intention, choice, belief, or other mind-involving fact about a person in terms of other such facts is rooted in the existence of mechanisms causally linking corresponding physical facts. In every such case one can raise the question as to whether the facts interrelated in the teleology-involving explanation would have still fallen out the same way if the supposedly corresponding physical facts had been different. In other words, the mechanist account is quickly uncovered for the sham that it is by a short consideration of relevant counterfactual conditional statements raising the question whether any difference would have been made if the extra physical facts brought in by the mechanist

---

[39]One was tempted to say 'if M had occurred and not been identical with B', and then would have fallen foul of the oddities which Wiggins notices in *Sameness and Substance*, p. 95, in supposing that something might have been a different entity from the entity it actually is. The trouble in fact lies in treating 'facts' as objects about which identity propositions are appropriate, and assimilating statements like 'Mind-state M is identical to brain-state B' to statements like 'The Morning Star is identical to the Evening Star'. In fact, such states are propositional entities, liable to be related, not in the ordinary way by the relation of identity, but by such relations as '. . . if and only if ——', or '. . . explains and is explained by all the same facts as ——', and it is in fact the latter of these relations which the mind-brain identity theorists should really try out (although for reasons I explain in the text, even then they will fail). After all, lightning is a phenomenon to sight whereas a discharge of electrons is not, so that it is just not true that the two are identical if Leibniz's law is to be obeyed—but it may very well be true that everything within physics which we want to explain about lightning can be explained by thinking of it as a discharge of electrons.

[40]It has been objected that this argument only works if one holds that "B causes A only if it is logically impossible for A to occur if B does not", which is equivalent to saying that the argument only works if one holds that "B is not the cause of A if it is logically possible for A to occur and yet B not occur" [since it is natural to read the 'if' in 'if B does not' truth functionally]. But this objection is mistaken.

I only say that B is not the cause of A if "A would have occurred if M had occurred but B had not occurred" is true (I could have said 'whether or not B had occurred' or 'even if B had not occurred' instead of the weaker 'but B had not occurred', and the same point would still be being made). This seems a very natural line of argument.

had not obtained. If it would make a difference, then the teleology and consciousness involving explanation would be shown to be mistaken; and, if it wouldn't make a difference, then the mechanistic explanation is shown to be wrong and the relevant theory of mechanisms is shown to be a wheel upon which nothing turns.

Any view which tries to represent explanations which involve consciousness and teleology as having their validity rooted in the existence of some mechanism securing the required effects has the same problems (or worse) as the mind-brain identity theory. This theory[41] involves a peculiar correspondence. On the one hand, we have the *a priori* and *non-accidental* connection between mental states understood in mentalistic terms and behaviour implied by Strawson's account—the mental state is understood in such a way that it is an a priori truth and that it is of a sort to be explanatory of certain behaviour (typically intentional behaviour, and therefore including bodily movements thereby explained mentalistically), if that behaviour occurs. On the other hand, we have (supposedly) an *empirically known* connection between a state of the brain and movements of the human body—this latter connection is supposed empirically known with the help of scientific theory, and is therefore according to official doctrine *contingent* or *accidental*). It will be remembered that in such theories the mental state is then, by means of some reasoning (involving considerations of economy of hypothesis as well as more ordinary science), supposed to be empirically known to be identical

---

Considering the objection requires us to consider the following propositions:
(1) "A would have occurred if M had occurred but B had not occurred" is true.
(2) It is logically possible for A to have occurred and yet B not to have occurred.
(3) B is not the cause of A.

I argue that (1) implies (3): it is presupposed that conditions are normal, and the setting is one in which it is taken to be true that A occurred because M, the conditions being normal. This inference does not seem doubtful even though how subjunctive conditionals are to be analysed is obscure. My argument doesn't draw on (2) at all.

The objector thinks that this implication would only hold if (2) implied (3). But (2) plainly does not imply (3). However, this is no worry for me since (2) has very little relation to (1): true, (1) implies (2), but (2) is much too weak to justify (3), and it seems wild for the objector to suppose that one needs "(2) implies (3)" as a justification for supposing "(1) implies (3)".

[41]D.M. Armstrong, *A Materialist Theory of the Mind*, presents a fairly sophisticated example of this—sophisticated at least in his attempts to circumvent the problems surrounding introspection and to do justice to the relation of belief to behaviour.

to it (and therefore 'contingently' identical)—this makes them mind-brain identity theories.

This 'rooting' of a form of explanation involving a priori connections in a form of explanation not involving these is, of course, in accord with the requirements of the atomism inspired by Hume described in Chapter VI in its demand that the connection between cause and effect be contingent. The baselessness of this requirement we have already shown.[42] However, this 'rooting' proves too much! In thus representing what we understand to be a priori and non-accidental as merely contingent, it goes against the logic of our ordinary discourse so as to imply that what we say in this ordinary discourse cannot be true. In this way it knocks away the ladder (of ordinary consciousness-involving statements) on which it ultimately depends. And this criticism will apply whether we are dealing with some mechanism in the brain, or some mechanism in a mind or soul conceived as if structured of immaterial stuff—any such theory represents a non-accidental connection understood a priori as being in fact a contingent connection to be known empirically or to be postulated and subject to empirical falsification. In this way, all such theories are self-undermining.

(d) The source of the beguiling plausibility of determinism and compatibilism

Philosophers are dragged into compatibilist positions as into a vortex as a result of one crucial initial mistake. They begin from the received orthodoxy that substance-causation has to be explained in terms of state and event causation, so that in the sphere of causality what is fundamental is the causal relations between previous states of affairs and events and later states of affairs and events in a context of overarching law, and not any supposed real causal action on the part of substances, whether inanimate things or living beings. From this vantage-point it appears that there is no alternative: either a particular action (or a particular choice) was determined by previous beliefs and thoughts, determinations, preferences, desires and emotions, character, knowledge and experience, in which case it might seem to be in some sense from the person or an expression of his or her will; or else

---

[42] *The Reality of Time and the Existence of God*, pp. 280–284, cf. Chapter VI above.

it was not so determined, but all these things left it open how he or she would choose and act, so that how he or she chose and acted was a matter of chance, indeed one might as well say pure chance, and so not the responsibility of the agent at all except perhaps in a legal sense.

In this approach, there is thus only one paradigm accepted for the consideration of causality, the paradigm whereby states and events identified by tensed or time-determinate propositions occur in conformity to law and in which the only alternative is for law to leave the outcome undetermined. In this way, there is no alternative to being by chance except to be determined. It does not matter that everybody knows that in the common view of physicists, determinism is false, and that very slight sub-atomic events, slight chances in human affairs (illnesses or successful assassinations), localized explosions may trigger or bring about enormous effects in physics, history or the weather, and that the same might be true in the functioning of the brain, so that, if chance enters in, its effects, though perhaps unsystematic, may be enormous. It suffices that, if at any level of description there is conformity to law, then to that extent the reign of chance is reduced, so that, even though chance may enter into the sub-structure of individual biography, nonetheless so far as real responsibility (the action really expressing the character, preference and desire of the agent) exists, the action must still be determined according to law, law at that level of description—chance and the absence of responsibility being the only alternative.

In order to escape from this vortex the remedy is simple.

We need to accept what we have already proved in Chapter VI, namely that it is state and event causation which needs to be explained in terms of the workings of the natures at work in the world, of which prime examples are provided by the exercises of active power by substances or bodily things; and it is not at all substance-causation which needs to be explained in terms of state and event causation. Rather, the various kinds of substance-causation are primitive, and the propositional constructs called 'states of affairs' and 'events' with their relations exercise no causal action at all.

Against this background, we have to recognize that the main opposite of being by chance is not being determined according to law but being intended or according to plan. The alternatives in the case of an action are not (a) being caused in the determinists' sense and (b) being by chance, but (a) being the intentional action of a being capable of intentional action, (b) being the outcome of the workings of other natures at work in the world (lower animals, plants and non-living things), and only in the third place (c) being by chance. When I do something freely, and in a case when this was not predictable, I am the author of my action, the agent or cause, and in order to refute the charge that the action was 'by chance' or 'by accident' it suffices to show that it was intentional—there is no need to go beyond this and exhibit it as determined according to law.

In a parallel way, to refute the charge that my giving of trust to another person's word or my making of a certain judgement in a particular case was 'by chance', it suffices to exhibit me as the author and to exhibit the trust as voluntary and the judgement as the free rational working of my mind. That is, to generalize, what is required for me to be the author of my action, judgement or trust is that it proceed from me freely, voluntarily and according to my own use of reason, and not because this has been caused or contrived by others (e.g., contriving that I am deceived) or results from some disposition not belonging to my reason or will; and it is to be presumed that they proceed freely, voluntarily and according to my own use of reason whenever it is intelligible that I should choose, judge or give my trust in this way. Considerations of reliable predictability are beside the point.

We are mesmerized by the philosophers' misuse of the notion of chance. That which is by chance or accident comes under one or more of the following headings: it results from coincidence and is not according to plan; or it results from the intrusion of some alien cause or from something atypical or not according to the normal working out of the natural process concerned; or it is the random by-product of random processes. In this way being by chance is not incompatible with being determined—many coincidences known to astronomers have been long predictable and, in an idealized consideration, the 'random processes' involved in the behaviour of the molecules of a volume of gas were conceived classically to be completely determined—although in modern physics 'pure' chance seems to have again entered in.

To sum up: my own authorship of my actions, judgements and givings of trust—their being determined by me according to my reason and will—is only brought into prejudice when some alien cause (duress, the use of drugs upon me, kleptomania, the contriving of some deception whether in the individual case or by some all enclosing propaganda, or suchlike) is the determinant, or when it is simply unintelligible that these things should be being determined according to my reason or will because they are not of sorts of which it is intelligible that they should even seem to be good, reasonable or right, so that it must be that alien cause or chance has entered in. But, if the physical aspect of my action, or the expression of my judgement or giving of trust were determined according to physical laws, this would remove it from being determined by my exercise of reason and will; and for my action, judgement or giving of trust to be in any other way determined other than by the exercise of my reason and will would likewise remove it from my authorship; for we have seen that there is no place for two equally basic levels of explanation here, and so if these things are thus removed from my authorship they can only be the issue of alien cause or chance.

4. No Need to Contrast Appearance and Reality When Considerations of Explanation Give Us Access to Reality

The picture of the natural sciences as presenting a framework of homogeneous laws governing all physical events, and of teleological and holistic perspectives as involving the intrusion of new and abstract entities, souls, vital forces and energies, and suchlike, into the realm of the physical, and so as introducing a kind of pseudo-science, has provoked many philosophers to demote the status of all science to the level of the 'merely descriptive', or of the 'phenomenon'.

Thus Merleau-Ponty tells us in *The Structure of Behaviour* that 'In reality, the two arguments [mechanism and vitalism] consider the organism as a real product of an external nature, when in fact it is a unity of signification, a phenomenon in the Kantian sense. It is given in perception with the original characteristics which we have described [he takes it to be given to perception with the teleology-involving 'significations' which he has indicated]. Scientific knowledge finds physico-chemical relations in it and little by little invests it with them. A counter-force which would intervene to break these correlations is inconceivable. But nothing forces us to think that the cycle of physico-chemical actions can completely enclose the phenomenon of the organism, that explanation can rejoin the givens of the description or that the phenomenal body can be converted into a physical system and integrated into the physical order. The totality [the organism] is not an *appearance*; it is a *phenomenon*.' And he quotes with agreement[43] the saying of Goldstein that what we are looking for in the idea of life 'is not the terminal stone of a building, but the building itself in which the partial phenomena, at first insignificant, appear as belonging to a unitary, ordered and relatively constant formation of specific structure . . .; we are not looking for a real foundation (*Seinsgrund*) which constitutes being, but for an idea, a reason in knowledge (*Erkenntnisgrund*) in virtue of which all the particular facts become intelligible.'[44]

To back up this picture, Merleau-Ponty portrays causality as having lost its 'mythical meaning of productive causality' with the result that 'laws can no longer be conceived as that which engenders the existence of the facts', so that with full appearance of even-handedness he can go on to say that '"Signification" is to the final cause what the relation of function to variable is to the "producing cause"'.[45]

In this way, Merleau-Ponty's predicament in the face of the empire of physical science and the helplessness of vitalism was to resort to a view of physical causality whose home is in positivism, and to insist upon the equal validity of two different perspectives in the subject in regard to the object, without allowing any bringing together of these perspectives in any general account of the object.

We have cited Merleau-Ponty because he is in what he says representative, not only of phenomenologists, but also of others, both positivists and supposed 'ordinary-language' philosophers, with an inbuilt anti-metaphysical bent.

But in order to escape the spectre of a physico-chemical realism which excludes any teleological ideas from having more than an *ad hominem* value, and gives the physical sciences a quite different status from any accounts drawing on teleological concepts, we do not have to embrace the Kantian distinction between the phenomenon and the noumenon, or between how we speak of things and how things are. For this purpose, all that is required are such things as the refusal to eliminate the category of causal agent in favour of the categories of event and state, the refusal to explain the notion of causal action in terms of the notion of law, the refusal to treat laws as all of one

---

[43] *The Structure of Behaviour*, p.153

[44] K. Goldstein, *Der Aufbau des Organismus*, Nijhoff, p. 242 (*The Organism*, p. 401).

[45] *The Structure of Behaviour*, p. 160.

kind as if either all or none were non-teleological in form, and the refusal to treat laws at any level as an all-determining system. We have to to avoid a false picture of physics as substituting a framework of laws of an all-determining kind for our ordinary discourse about the actions and interactions at different times of bodily things in various spatial relations. Rather this ordinary discourse is presupposed by any framework of physical laws; and the framework of physical laws, not all-determining, undergirds it, giving us fresh insight into how and why things are and behave as they do. (The Kantian distinction itself, of course, was presented as having roots of quite a different kind from these difficulties about the relation of physical science to the rest of our ways of thinking, epistemological roots of a kind which are not the concern of this book, roots of a kind which present a false ideal of 'things as they are in themselves', meaning by this, things without external relations and which are objects of the intellect alone.)

The causal agents with which we are acquainted, and about which physical science still tells us, are not mythical but real. They include, not only billiard balls and planets, but also human beings, other animals, and plants. The laws which the sciences propose to us are not homogeneous, and these causal agents do not exercise only one mode of causality (not even only one mode of physical causality) but several. Teleological and holistic ways of thinking arise without any dependence on the introduction of abstract terms such as soul or vital force or energy, or even disposition, all such abstract modes of speech being circumlocutory for talk about substances, that is, causal agents exercising different modes of causality.

We can admit the exercise of causal agency as a criterion of reality or of some kind of substancehood, without stultifying further inquiry. We have already seen how the admission of human beings and animals as psychosomatic beings exercising the teleology-involving kinds of causal agency which consciousness carries with it in no way excludes, but rather requires, the possibility of treating of their bodily parts under descriptions other than as parts, i.e., other than as subjects of mechanical study and law. And there is no way in which the admission of causal agency of one kind at one level excludes the admission of causal agency at more macro or more micro levels, typically different modes of causal agency. What is excluded is regarding any single system of laws as giving a global account of the nature and behaviour of the objects we encounter, rather than an account of certain aspects of this nature and behaviour.

We saw that the problem posing itself to Merleau-Ponty in *The Structure of Behaviour* was the problem as to how to reconcile the perspectives of the orders of the living and of the human with the perspectives of physical science. And we saw that in order to resolve this problem he demoted all these perspectives to the status of having to do with 'the phenomenon', glossing this from Goldstein in terms of having to do with a ground of knowledge and intelligibility rather than a ground in reality. What we have shown is there is no reason, in this problem at least, to resort to any such distinction. If we are giving an account of what there is, and have in mind what there is at the level of the concrete, or as we might say at the level of basic particulars (not being anxious to list numbers, colours, shapes, places, events, states, and so forth over and above concrete things or substances), we will list every kind of causal agent, whatever its mode of causality, human beings and other higher animals conforming to paradigms involving consciousness and teleology as well as inanimate things.

5. The Theory of Explanation as Disproving Physicalism

We know that human beings and other animals which we regard as having perceptual consciousness are possessed of bodily parts and are logical subjects of bodily predicates. But we do not speak of them as bodies. The question was posed to us in Wiggins' terminology as to whether we should nonetheless regard them as 'material', as 'constituted by matter', and as 'material entities'. The question needs to be given a determinate meaning before it can be answered. Wiggins' motivation for judging that we should answer these questions in the affirmative seems to be that he thinks that they are aggregations of material parts whose identity is to be judged according to a principle of bodily continuity, the body concerned exhibiting a certain pattern of behaviour and change characteristic of the species—the continued existence of such entities being an exploitation or resultant of the application of the fundamental laws of physical science.

Accordingly, it looks as if the reasonable way to give determinate meaning to the question whether persons and at least the higher animals are 'material entities' or 'constituted by their matter' will be to say that they are such and are so constituted if everything about them that is determined is determined according only to laws of physical science. Conversely, they should not be so described if, on the contrary, the fundamental laws of the universe which determine their behaviour and change include uneliminably laws concerning respectively human beings and animals with perceptual consciousness and treating them as unities of a psychophysical kind. And a demonstration that they should not be so described will be especially decisive if it can be shown that the fundamental laws determining even just the physical behaviour of human beings and other higher animals require this treatment.

That this is the appropriate way of approaching the question is confirmed by considering a range of other examples. We need to distinguish two quite different kinds of motive for saying that something is not 'just a material object'.

We may well feel inclined to say, not just that a human being or animal is not 'just' these material parts in these relations but an entity of a different kind, and likewise that water is not 'just' hydrogen atoms and oxygen atoms in certain proportions and bonded together in a certain way but something of a different kind, and that a broom is not 'just' a broom handle screwed into or otherwise attached to an appropriate brush but a whole and a thing of a different kind. That is to say, we are heavily reluctant to accept any of these formulations involving this dismissive "just" because we recognize that it ignores the Gestalt which is involved in the way that the thing concerned enters into our experience and life—in the same way as happens when someone says that lightning is 'just' a discharge of electrons between the earth and the clouds, whereas it is clear that lightning is a startling phenomenon and electrons are not phenomena at all. We sense that a broom is not just a brush and a handle, because that's not how we think of it or operate with it—that's not the whole meaning in our lives. Likewise with water—it's not just hydrogen atoms and oxygen atoms bonded in some way, because that is not how it enters our lives.

But what we are concerned with is a different and much stronger motive for saying that this or that is not 'just a material object'.

For we would be willing to say that a broom consists of an appropriate brush and handle suitably attached to each other, and that water consists of hydrogen and oxygen combined in the required way, while it still sticks in our gullet to say that human beings and animals 'consist' in their material parts in appropriate relations in an appropriate environment (temperature, pressure, air, and ground with gravity so that walking is possible). Accordingly, it seems that what one has to do is to distinguish between what we ascribe to things in virtue simply of our way of thinking of them, using them, etc.—i.e., what we state of them in concepts which belong to the descriptions of the states of people relating to them in ways involving intentionality—and things which come into the explanation of the behaviour of the things in question (and of their nature as a principle of this behaviour).

In suggesting this as the appropriate basis for deciding whether to say that human beings and the higher animals are 'material entities' and 'constituted by matter', I am in fact following the path suggested by the fundamental lines of Wiggins' own approach. For I am making considerations about the proper modes of explanation of different phenomena determinative of what sorts of thing we should judge to exist at the basic level. These will be sorts of thing for which we will have criteria of identity determined in accord with these modes of explanation.

Once we see the question posed in this way, the answer to it is plain from our previous discussion. In that discussion we saw it as inseparable from acceptance of the use of consciousness-involving predicates that the statements in which they are ascribed should have a role in a type of explanation which involved teleology uneliminably, the substitution of explanation in terms of mechanisms being excluded. In conclusion, we have no choice but to accept the concepts of 'person' and of 'psychophysical being' as explanatory concepts that will not go away; we must accept teleological laws relating to such wholes (human beings and higher animals) as amongst the 'fundamental laws' of the universe; and we must see the refusal to speak of human beings and higher animals as 'bodies', as if it were bodies which saw, remembered, imagined, desired, or knew things, not merely as a deep-rooted quirk of idiom, but as a recognition of a fundamental fact about the ontology of the universe.

David Bohm gave some more precise idea of the way in which some degree of autonomy and stability in existence arises at each of many levels within physics, and why it may be expected to so arise.[46] In this he gave an account adapted to physics and to beings and organisms in their physical aspect which accords with the much more informal and unpolished ideas of Teilhard de Chardin,[47] ideas which intended to bestraddle the physical, the biological and the sphere of reflective mind. Our concern in this chapter has been less general, and

---

[46]See n. 1 above.
[47]In *The Phenomenon of Man*.

to pick out just one level of autonomy and stability in existence, and to show in regard to this level (whatever may be said of the other levels) that, because of its essential involvement or consciousness, it has in certain respects an absolute status.

Conclusion

We have recognized that there is a large range of types of statement of a sort in regard to ourselves known without using behavioural or observational criteria, and in regard to others known either by testimony or by using behavioural criteria, which (though our judgements in these cases are not infallible) are not as a whole class open to coherent doubt. What these statements have in common is conveniently summarized in labelling them as 'mind-involving'.

We have seen that these mind-involving statements are, by their very meaning, uneliminable from explanation and explanatorily basic. And we have seen that this implies that the subjects of these statements, the human beings and animals concerned, are basic entities—not just as bodily beings, but in their irreducibly psychophysical natures, the physical and the psychological inextricable from each other in the descriptions and explanations we have to give. In this way, it is a datum at once of self-knowledge and of knowledge of the world that within the basic inventory of the furniture of the universe there stand, uneliminably, beings which are irreducibly psychophysical—human beings and other higher animals amongst them.

IX. The Community of Human Beings with Other Animals: Five Aspects

1. The Radical Rejection of Physicalism Implied by Our Treatment of Animal and Human Behaviour

The materialist has supposed that in human beings and other animals we have a 'material entity' or 'body' with properties of special kinds. The dualist supposes that in them we have a 'material entity' or 'body' with an immaterial spirit called a soul interacting with it. Both agree on a map which allows of at most two basic kinds of entity or substance, the one purely material and the other purely immaterial.

The consequence of what we have shown in Chapter VIII is that this map is false. The stark reality is that nature is full of things which are, from the point of view of materialist and dualist alike, hybrids—things the fundamental laws governing whose behaviour include uneliminably principles referring to life and consciousness.

We might have thought that within the realm of the physical there arise systems of ever increasing complexity and close-knitness, so that, from the point of view of physical science, it was and is inevitable that when physical systems of such complexity as (for instance) viruses arise, the modes of description and explanation appropriate to living things should come into application without the need to conjecture any new principle as being at work. And there might seem to us to be a similar inevitability at each stage in the unfolding development as new types of life emerge: bacteria; one-celled plants and animals; higher plants, fungi, and sponges; more complex animals which we do not have to think of as possessing perceptual consciousness and so as being psychophysical beings; and then higher animals which we do think of in this way; and finally human beings and any other animals belonging to the category of persons. And, in accord with this perspective, we would see the generation of each new individual plant or animal as likewise involving no new principle as being at work, but equally inevitable within the given setting.

But what we have demonstrated is the untenability of this position and perspective. In particular, we have shown that when human persons and other psychophysical beings arise within nature, we have the arrival of beings (natural wholes or substances) whose principles or manner of functioning involve treating these beings in consciousness-involving ways, and so of which the ensemble of the physical sciences can never give an explanatory account. That is, these natural wholes are such that many things are explicable and some even predictable according to the types of consciousness-involving account which we ordinarily give, but not predictable or determined according to physical law, besides not being explained in the same aspects.

It is not at all a question of introducing a fresh argument for a *deus ex machina*—or even of introducing a soul *ex machina*. It is merely a question of recognizing the full significance of the statements that, in animals and human beings, we have a new kind of nature—a new kind of thing or substance which is not to be ranked as 'a body' or 'a material entity'.

One is tempted to express the point in the following way. If one had thought of higher animals and human beings as combinations of two substances, a material body and a 'soul', then—despite the fact that it had been the characteristic feature of evolution that radically new types of life should arise, and the most usual thing in the world for living things at every level to reproduce their kind—it would seem to us astounding or extraordinary that psychsomatic beings should arise at all, and each new production of a further individual would seem no less astounding and extraordinary. It would seem astounding and extraordinary in this way, that it was beyond the powers of the merely physical to explain.[1] But now one should say that it is no less astounding or extraordinary in this way that there should arrive such radically new types of substance or natural whole upon the scene as these essentially unitary *psychophysical beings*, animals with perceptual consciousness and human beings—astounding metaphysically, although no surprise empirically.

---

[1] It would, of course, also be astounding and extraordinary in other ways, e.g., that it involved all the difficulties which are associated with dualism and that it involved something novel in a quite different way—not the arrival of a new kind of bodily thing, but the arrival of a new kind of thing which was not bodily, and this in a novel relation to bodies. But we are not occupied with these extra marvels, since they are the fictions of dualism.

Inasmuch as our argument turned upon the irreducibility of mind-involving explanations to other forms of explanation, one might anticipate a parallel argument in respect of lesser animals and plants which we also commonly regard teleologically. But, since the demonstration of such irreducibility in these cases requires appeal to types of consideration different from those which have been the concern of this book, I do not here develop this point. (It is also important that the irreducibility of the biological to the physical in these areas has a looser connection with individuation or one which requires to be differently stated: one conscious animal subject cannot bifurcate into two in the manner of plants, amoebas, and flatworms.)

One could find another way of expressing the same point. The continuance in existence of Nature in its order requires, not only the arrival of each type of life when the physical is in an appropriate state, but also the arrival, at appropriate times, according to the regular order of nature in animal and human reproduction, of new individuals possessed of a nature whose operations transcend the power of the physical. But what the regular order of nature thus requires transcends, we have seen, the power of the physical—indeed cannot be defined as a whole in terms of physical concepts.[2] Accordingly, it is not only that it could be argued that the continuance in existence of temporal substances in their nature, powers, and order requires a transcendent cause such as God—but also more particularly that it could be argued that, since this continuance requires the coming to be of things outside the power of the physical to cause or explain, the power of God is required in the coming to be as well as in the continuance in existence of such living things as these human persons and animals with perceptual consciousness.[3]

---

[2] It can only be specified in physical terms in some of its projections, as bodily movement is a projection of an action and body of a person, as it were, onto one geometrical plane—a capturing, as it were, in one plane of existence.

[3] No 'God of the gaps' would be here involved, as if the role of a 'God' in explanation was to plug gaps in our understanding of why things come to be or happen as and when they do, since the involvement of God in coming to be would be here but a facet of His upholding all things in their natures and order. And the reason for accepting that God is thus involved in the continuance of things would be that having a cause is a condition of this continuance, not that supposing such a cause satisfies some desire for understanding. Cf. *The Reality of Time and the Existence of God*, pp. 220–223, 253–254.

The relevance of these remarks is to dramatize the sense in which persons and psychomatic beings transcend the physical order. They so transcend it that their existence is as much—or as little—ground for argument to the existence of God as cause as would be the existence of souls, dualistically conceived.

In being able to dramatize the matter in this way one is trading upon the fruits of materialism in its pruning back of the belief in teleologically conceived forces within the world.

For us today there remain the standing nodes of teleological explanation which our immediate knowledge of ourselves and the world throws up to us: persons, animals, plants, and possibly bacteria and even viruses. But, in so far as teleology is thought of in non-physical terms, it is tied to the subjects of some kind of life, these basic particulars which I have just instanced, and conceivably other personal beings spoken of in ways formally analogous to those in which we speak of human beings. We know the aptness of the physical in several stages of organization to be the vehicle of each successive level of life, and we may dispute (as we do in this book) whether or not the personal, the psychophysical, or lower levels of what is called life, transcend the merely physical. And we can duly recognize the wonder of the physical universe and its order, and at each level the wonder of order as it is found together with this aptness to be the vehicle of such new types of life. But we no longer go beyond this in our fancy to imagine 'seminal forces' within the physical universe at each successive level of organization, at each level pregnant with and causative of the next stage and its unfolding as extra occasions of wonder. Rightly or wrongly, contemporary thought has no place for 'seminal forces', 'emergent tendencies', and suchlike when these are imagined without a subject but only, as it were, in anticipation of a subject.

We have the teleological elements in physics mentioned earlier (such as that light *in vacuo* takes the path of least separation), but we understand these so far as we do without seeking any analogies with the phenomena of life. Beyond this, we have come to seek no ways of thinking teleologically which are not nodally centred on subjects such as persons, animals, plants, bacteria, and perhaps viruses—or sometimes their individual parts, e.g., cells.

It is against this background of the de-animization and demystification of the universe at large—rendering it bare of spirit—that the demonstration that certain of these living things are uneliminable nodes of non-physical explanation stands out in its stark significance. Our demonstration of this turns only upon the irreducibility of explanations involving consciousness and its associated psychophysical structures, and so on the character of human beings and the other higher animals.

We are not here introducing a philosophical mythology of 'transcendental subjects' as if such subject only entered into our explanations in order to mark a limit of explanation, and as if for the rest explanation in terms of states of affairs and events could proceed without reference to them.[4] Rather, as we have seen in Chapter VIII, reference to these persons and higher animals as subjects is integral to any viable or valid empirical explanation of what occurs in the world. These subjects do not have a merely 'formal' or 'transcendental' role without any function within 'empirical' explanation. On the contrary, they do not exist apart from the natures and characteristic spreads of active and passive powers, specification of which indeed involves teleology and mind-involving concepts; and as such they are involved in the functioning and intelligibility of any explanation in term of events and states of affairs whatsoever in this area. And explanations involving them are as well known to be empirically verified as any other explanations we meet with in the field of nature.[5]

It may well be that some other more general demonstration of the irreducibility of the biological to the physical is possible, based on more general features of biological life. It no more follows from the openness of the physical to the realization of the biological patterns of pre-conscious life within the physical sphere that pre-conscious biological explanation and causation is reducible to physical, than this follows in the case of the patterns of conscious life. (It would fit well with the general view of this book to regard some of the

---

[4]That is, neither the teleological nor the psychological involve any transcendental subject or any seeking out of a metaphysical subject as a limit of the world or of explanation (contrary to what is suggested in Wittgenstein's *Tractatus*, 5.641).

[5]The difference between these explanations and those of physical science is not in respect of whether or not they are empirically based and supported, but in the character of the 'theory' brought within them, in the one case a theory whose character is seen, for instance, in the elaborate semantic structures for talking about human beings and other animals which grammar exhibits, and in the other a highly mathematizable theory of the type we meet in Newton or Clerk-Maxwell.

earlier stages of de-animization and demystification as misguided and
to allow teleology and holistic approaches an uneliminable role in dealing with the life of plants, lower animals, and some animal colonies.
Such approaches would have relevance also to aspects of the life of
human beings and the higher animals, aspects which can be considered
in abstraction from the psychophysical as such. This arises in two
quite different ways, one in seeing teleology within the functioning
of parts and subsystems within the animal or human being, e.g., in
the functioning of individual cells, and the other in envisaging the
whole animal or human being holistically, but in ways abstracted
from consciousness.)[6]

However, it is for other studies to consider the possibility of any
such more general demonstration based on aspects of life which do
not involve or depend on consciousness. Our concern here is only
with a demonstration based on the character of consciousness and the
psychophysical.

Aquinas argues that 'It is impossible for the action of a material
force to give rise to the production of a force which is wholly spiritual
and immaterial—for nothing acts beyond its kind (species).'[7] He is
arguing that the production of a form which is subsistent because it
has an operation which is not through any bodily organ is outside
the power of things whose operations are all through bodily organs.
We have been identifying a different application of the same type of
argument, an application in which it is argued instead that the production of substances, some of whose operations are not mechanically

---

[6]This latter may be of relevance in giving a general account of reproduction
and regeneration, but also more particularly in considering, for instance, the theories
underlying acupuncture, which may connect up with general modes of functioning of
the autonomic nervous sytem together with ill-understood aspects of general resilience
and of the experience of pain.

[7]*De Potentia*, Q. 3, Art. 9, the second argument in the body of his reply. He
goes on 'in fact, the agent must be more perfect (*praestantius*) than the patient', in
this way arguing that the human soul must be created by God.

That persons and living things transcend the possibilities of physical explanation
is important to arguments to the existence of a personal and living God. Any argument
from the livingness and personhood of some of the beings which God upholds in
existence to the livingness and personhood of God is liable to depend upon the premise
that the kind of life and personhood which is argued from transcends the nature and
powers of the material or physical. We met this pattern of argument in *The Reality of
Time and the Existence of God*, pp. 278–280, 284–287.

conceivable,[8] is outside the power of things purely physical. Our purpose has been only to secure that the proposition that persons and other psychophysical beings are not 'bodies', not 'material entities', is properly understood.

Our point, then, is that for such living beings to have natures, to be substances, and not to be material things, even though still possessed of bodily parts and subjects of bodily predicates, is not at all for them just to be material things about which certain types of discourse involving non-physical concepts, conformed to our modes of experience, can go on so as to 'keep our intellects happy'. Rather it is for such living beings to be nodes of explanation and prediction in regard to things not explained or predictable, nor even 'determined in principle', in physical terms, so that these types of discourse are doing some real explanatory work. In brief, it is for such living beings to be causal agents *qua* persons or *qua* psychophysical beings, exercising a mode of causality different from that exercised by 'material bodies', marking their difference in nature and thereby a difference in what we should say exists. For a human being or higher animal to exist is not for certain aggregations of different kinds of material stuff to exist in certain relations to each other, every component of such aggregations exercising its characteristic physical powers, and the whole to continue in a certain state of stability amidst change as a result of all these exercises of powers in the context of these relations. Instead it is for there to be a whole or unity present whose functioning and behaviour is not in general thus explicable but rather requires explanation in a holistic, teleological, and psychophysical way—so that, when this functioning and behaviour is determined, it may be determined not physically, but for reasons only exhibited in this quite different kind of explanation. Its character is, therefore, not to consist in just these aggregations of matter in these relations exercising these powers, but to be a natural whole of the psychophysical kind we have made clear.

In this way, the admission that persons and other psychophysical beings in general are not bodies or material entities marks a real enlargement of our ontology beyond the material, in a way which is not at all dependent upon any recognition or postulation of souls.

---

[8]As we have seen, they are only conceivable in terms of dispositions and developments in these substances conceived in a way which involves teleology.

2. The Psychophysical Structures Shared by Human Beings with Other Animals

(a) The character of our knowledge of other animals

The starkness with which the irreducibility of human beings to the merely physical stands out has been shown by consideration of features belonging to their nature as psychophysical beings. That this has been the basis of all our arguments up till now means that our demonstration of the incoherence equally of dualism and of mind-brain identity materialism along with any mechanistic view of the human being has depended only upon features of human beings which they are liable to share with other animals.

It is mad to envisage the psychophysical nature of human beings, which precisely reveals them as essentially animals, and then to fall back on thinking of the animals as mere automata. It is strange: *first*, to *reject* the idea that we need an argument by analogy in order to know that other people have minds and to know mind-involving facts about them (as if we directly apprehended a certain correlation or connection between what is in our minds and our behaviour and, thence, from perception of parallel spreads of behaviour in others, argued by analogy to their minds); and *then*, to *insist* that we do need this type of argument in the case of other animals.

It is manifest to us that it is people who are speaking to us, eating at table with us using knives and forks, walking together, embracing, etc., and what it is in these respects that they are doing, and it is manifest to us that it is a dog that we see running after a stick that we have thrown, trying to get food off a bone or to break the bone, cringing in anticipation of a blow, etc. The perceptual judgements we make in regard to people are corrigible, and likewise those about animals. We tend to think of animals in ways analogous to those in which we think of people to the maximum extent that the phenomena allow. But, if reason arises to judge that such a way of thinking is inappropriate in regard to some particular piece of behaviour on the part of some higher animal, or in regard to some whole branch of behaviour in the case, for example, of a bee, perhaps because we find it to be automated in certain respects in such a way as to destroy the analogy between it and the human behaviour of which we speak in parallel terms, then we alter our judgements. But always the way of speaking which holds the fort until displaced is that which accords with our way of perceiving, and this way of perceiving persists unless we are trained out of it.

The encounters between individual human beings and individuals of other species begin in childhood. In some types of case (e.g., dogs and, in suitable conditions, many other mammals), they are elaborate enough to give structurally strong reinforcement to initial attributions of sight, hearing, smell, memory, desire, fear, anticipation, and (in a weak sense of "intentional") intentional action. By contrast, in other types of case (e.g., flies and bees, and *a fortiori*, paramecia), they give only structurally weak reinforcement to such attributions. E.g., we might in some cases after reflection be willing to say only that the animal was influenced by differences in distributions of light, influenced by differences in the chemical effects of vapours or gases, influenced by differences in the chemical effects of liquids, rather than that it saw, tasted or smelt, and say this because there is an automation in the way action follows stimulus uncharacteristic in the mammals we get acquainted with.

Again, in the case of all species, some of the behaviour of individuals is only intelligible with respect to function in the group. However, whereas in the case of mammal groups (wolf packs, prides of lions, and different groupings of elephants) this is compatible with much behaviour being individually learnt and learning having an effect on the working out of these roles, by contrast it might seem that, for instance, in the case of insects this is not so. We still have an individuation associated with unitary organization and bodily continuity in something whose behaviour shows teleological aspects, but the distinction between being a member of a colony and being a cell in a community of cells constituting an individual, although it can still be made, e.g., by considering the reproductive unit, lacks the distinctive significance of the individuation associated with individually learnt behaviour. This makes it unsurprising that in the lower animals individuation should be less absolute (as we indicated by our example of the surgical division of flatworms) and this is another part of the background in which we may become hesitant in our attribution of perceptual consciousness.

At a more elemental level, we experience and think of all living things in terms of growth, regeneration and disease, and reproductive development, all presenting themselves in terms which involve teleology, although not in brief experience of them but in more extended relation with them. I mention this in order to indicate the fuller variety amongst living beings, not to develop the point in its own right.

In all these inquiries, we must hold firm to a certain principle: if we are not to break the structured unity of the order of nature, then at each stage, when something radically new arises in the unfolding of living nature, we must show its homogeneity with what has gone before.

Thus, to take the instance with which we are primarily concerned, if we recognize in human beings the presence of psychophysical unities, then we must recognize some of the higher animals as psychophysical unities as well. If we express this in terms of a conception of soul, it must be a conception of soul applicable to these other higher animals as well as to human beings. (We shall explain two such conceptions of soul in Chapter XIII.)

And the same principle will hold also at each earlier stage. If we form some concept of 'animal life' applicable to some much larger class of animals than those higher animals with which we credit these psychophysical structures of which we have been speaking, but not applicable to all living things, the same principle will again apply. If we recognize the higher or 'psychophysical' animals as possessing 'animal life' in this more general sense, then we must find structures of description common to the life of our 'higher' animals and the life of the other animals grouped with them as possessing this 'animal life'.[9] Then if we also recognize all such animals as having something in common with living things in general, sponges, fungi, and bacteria being included as well as the more obvious kinds of plant, then we must find yet other more primitive structures of description common to all living things. And at the last stages, if perchance there is some community between living things and viruses, there will be other

---

[9] These will involve structures described by O'Shaughnessy in terms of desire, awareness or sensation, and *sub-intentional striving* (*The Will*, Vol. 2, pp. 95–100, cf. 224f.) but in regard to which the terms "desire", "aware" and "feel" are too psychological because implying consciousness. Exhibiting directed behaviour in independent movement and ingestion of food in response to touch, light, vibration, and alien chemicals in the medium of movement seem to mark animal life, but it is not easy to achieve a watertight philosophical differentiation of animal and plant.

structures of description before we reach what would count for present purposes as the basal level of the structures of description common to all 'middle level' bodily things—intermediate between celestial bodies and fundamental particles.

It is only against this background that we can properly pursue our inquiry further as to what structures of 'psychological subjecthood' and individuation are common to human beings and the highest other animals.

Nothing we have said so far has depended upon any talk of 'souls'—I shall discuss in Chapter XIII what ways of speaking about souls are legitimate. But it is the peculiar vice of talk about 'souls' in post-Cartesian times that it has reinforced a theory which divorces human beings from the other animals, representing the animals as mere bodies and mechanical automata and the human being as a soul in ill-understood relation to just such an animal body. The Hebrew conception of soul had no such implications in regard to the animals. It enshrined a non-dualistic conception of the soul in the human case, but this general conception was not philosophically articulated.

Likewise, it was the strength of the Aristotelian framework for thinking about human souls that the structure for his conception of the soul in human beings was set by his way of thinking about the soul in animals and other living things. And this, amongst philosophers, is almost the peculiarity of the Aristotelian and Thomistic tradition. Almost, one may say, but not quite, inasmuch as Aristotelian ideas reappear in the thought of vitalists and emergentists, with the unfortunate dependence on the introduction of abstract entities (vital forces, energies, 'entelechies', and the like). Again, more importantly, I say 'almost but not quite' because of the avenues opened by Merleau-Ponty and Charles Taylor and because of the structure opened out in different aspects by Ryle and Wittgenstein. It is one of the weaknesses of the treatments of human personhood in Anglo-Saxon philosophy over the last fifty years that, although it has made plain the psychophysical nature of human beings, its exposition (with such honourable exceptions as I have indicated) has so turned upon its account of language in its full human-found structure as to open no bridge to understanding the community of human beings with other animals—and indeed also no bridge to the understanding of the community of human beings with each other.

(b) The character of psychophysical structures in animals other than human beings

I have spoken of there being two structures involving consciousness, a simpler structure which human beings share with other higher animals which I have associated with 'psychophysical beings' in general or whatever has 'perceptual consciousness', and a more global structure exemplified in human beings involving all the features of personhood. There are the problems, firstly, of identifying when these structures become first present in the evolutionary series, and, secondly, of how we should speak of their emergence in the development of the individual.

The line between animals which have the life of persons and other animals may seem clear because of its direct association with language in the way I will describe more closely in Part II of this book (in Chapter X)—that is, as I shall explain, with language not as just any communication system but as a communication system in which communications are through their parts (e.g., words) expressive of what is communicated. But the structure which I have presumed human beings to share with the higher animals, associated with 'perceptual consciousness', may seem more puzzling.

How are we to draw a line between the 'higher' animals to which we should ascribe perception, emotion, and intentional action, and 'lower' animals to which we should not? At what stage in evolutionary series does 'consciousness' come in? What is this structure involving consciousness even amongst animals lower than the human, and how are we to describe it and how identify its presence? (Our task is to identify the structures to be associated with consciousness, not to describe the more general structures associated with animal life in general as distinct from merely plant life, nor to describe the structures common to all living things: these are other tasks beyond the scope of this book.)[10]

The way in which the chief different elements of this structure, perception, knowledge, memory, imagination, emotion, and 'intentional' action are interrelated can be exhibited by consideration of an adequate range of examples. In, for instance, a dog's being a perceptive and reactive being, all these elements are involved interdependently.

---

[10]Cf. n. 7 above.

Firstly, as we argued earlier, a key element internal to perception is the coming to be of certain behavioural aptitudes, aptitudes exhibited in 'intentional' behaviour. And, conversely, it is equally vital to recognize that intentional action is only possible in the context of prior perception and sensation, i.e., in a context which allows it to be perceptually directed.

But also, secondly, to consider behaviour as 'intentional' in that diminished sense in which the word "intentional" applies to animals lower than human beings depends upon the possibility of envisaging a background of desires, in a context of some possibility of at least imaging goals or of whatever would give some genuine content to the idea that the animal 'knew' what it was going for, an appreciation of a goal such as might give 'direction' or 'intention' to behaviour.[11] If there is no kind of knowledge or appreciation of a goal whatsoever, an activity in a living being may be teleologically directed but cannot properly be described as 'intentional' or 'voluntary' even in a diminished sense.

There is no way, in the absence of linguistic behaviour or of the sorts of pieces of thinking it expresses, of separating perception and memory, memory and imagination, or action out of emotion such as fear or desire from all three. In the case of a dog going to hide behind a sofa when threatened by its master with a stick, we have to conceive of some memory of hurt or harm from past attack by a stick thus brandished by a man or by his master, contemporaneous with present perception of such brandishing, and some anticipation of similar hurt or harm as a background to fear, and these together with some anticipation of escape by being behind the sofa as a background to the desire to get behind the sofa. There is a certain continuity between the initial perception of its master in threatening posture and the presentation of the object of fear in memory image as the dog faces and moves away from its master, and between the image of behind the sofa as a place of refuge and (if the dog succeeds in getting behind the sofa and finds it momentarily a place of refuge) the perception of being behind the sofa as a place of refuge.

---

[11]Because there must be some role for imagination or imaging in connection with the behaviour associated with desire or fear, we see no difficulty in attributing dreams to dogs when they exhibit some of the behavioural signs of, for instance, fear during sleep, even though they tell no tales of dreams.

The symbiosis of sight and intentional action, along with touch and kinaesthetic sensation, which we discussed in Chapter II, presents an instance of a realization of one key part of this structure. It exhibits the way in which we have to regard 'exploratory' activity of an 'intentional' kind, integrated with knowledge from touch and some kinaesthetic sensation associated with these 'intentional' bodily movements, as internal to what we call perception. Such exploratory behaviour involves the coordinated use of different senses, appreciation (for instance) of the differences and interconnections between sight and touch, hearing and sight, and so forth, and in this way appreciation of the so-called 'common sensibles' (the properties appreciated by more than one sense) as common, an appreciation shown in behaviour.[12]

It is important not to over-intellectualize the definition of key features of human and animal life. It is for this reason that in Chapter I I defined intentional action as 'action springing from emotion and directed towards an end', close to Aristotle's notion of the 'voluntary'.[13] Such intentional action involves the non-observational knowledge of what one is doing and of what the action is directed towards, and these types of knowledge are revealed in animals in the co-ordination in their behaviour and in disorientation if some end to be expected is not attained. What distinguishes human action is its background of deliberation and its being typical for knowledge of the end to require linguistic concepts: hence it is the norm for human intention and desire to be known by the intender answering questions as to what he or she intended and why, not just from behaviour.

Likewise, in explaining the intentionality of human emotion and perception, we must not over-intellectualize and say that whenever we aim at or desire, are angry at or fear, see or hear something, we only do

---

[12] The appreciation of these things will belong to what Aristotle and Aquinas call the common sense.

[13] The word in Aristotle customarily translated as 'voluntary' has no etymological connection with 'will' (*boulé*) and is treated by him as clearly applying to the higher animals less than human beings, while the word closest in meaning to 'intention' in the sense restricted to human beings is normally translated 'choice' (*prohairesis*, meaning something like 'deliberate preference'). Aquinas explains this wider notion of voluntariness as attributed to irrational animals 'inasmuch as they are moved to an end through some kind of knowledge' (*Summa Theologica* Ia IIae, Q. 6, Art. 2, Reply to obj. 1).

so under some description as if all the attitudes and states concerned presupposed language. Rather all that is required is that these ways of being mentally directed towards something should involve some teleologically directed patterning or re-patterning of behaviour, such as we readily ascribe to animals.

It is important to realize that the phenomena associated with 'consciousness' by anthropologists and students of animal behaviour do not require explanation in terms of states to which the animal could testify, although this is their most obvious feature in the human case. The complexities of behavioural patterns can show the presence or absence of conscious states even in what may seem intricate cases. Thus the sophisticated awareness that it is the blemish on one's own fore-head which one is seeing in a mirror is a realization of a consciousness correlative with a pattern of exploratory behaviour and learning within the context of this common sense rather than something requiring to be understood in terms of some higher, linguistically realizable, form of expression. Or to consider a more specialized example, there are instances in the human case of behavioural responses to visual stimuli in which the relevant part of the neocortex has been damaged and there is no awareness of having seen the things to which response is made, even despite this, as a result of effects passing from the optic nerve to brain centres affecting behaviour without being mediated by the neocortex, and it is speculated that amongst animals lower than the human there might be analogous phenomena.[14] Such parallel phenomena amongst animals could be behaviourally exhibited by the animal's betraying ignorance of the sensory mode involved, e.g., where sight is concerned by allowing its eyes to be covered or looking away and in this way indicating the absence of consciousness of seeing despite the occurrence of some behaviour appropriate to sight. What we are concerned with here is the general phenomenon of what is commonly called 'unconscious cognition'.[15]

I have spoken of how action out of emotion presupposes per-ception, memory, and imagination. But conversely there can be no perception, memory, or imagination without an orientation towards discriminatory activity—and, in the absence of the activities which

---

[14]See the discussions in R.E. Passingham, *The Human Primate*, pp. 240–241.
[15]See n. 24 below.

linguistic behaviour might express, the orientation must be towards or away from or against objects precisely as objects of desire, fear, and aggression.[16] In the case of animals lower than the human, perception, memory, and imagination—each of them—require a connection with intentional action via desire or other emotion[17] in that perception, memory, and imagination are always of an object as having a 'meaning' in the sense of some relevance to emotion and action from emotion.[18] Possibly the most developed account of these relations within empirical psychology, at least so far as relatively simple motivations are concerned, lies in Gibson's theory of 'affordances' which are what is responded to or estimated as to 'what the environment offers the animal, what it provides or furnishes, either for good or for ill'.[19] In the human case, this is not required because of a structure of activities

---

[16]I mean by aggression the emotion expressed when a dog attacks a trespasser on his territory or snarls when one takes a bone away from him. It is not precisely anger which seems to presuppose thoughts in a stronger sense than we attribute to dogs; nor is it annoyance because this is either too intellectual in its implications or too weak to express the ferocity expressed or held back in these cases; resentment is again too intellectual to describe the latter case.

When I speak of something as 'expressing' an emotion or sensation, I mean something expressive of the emotion or sensation as groaning and grimacing are expressive of pain, hitting at the object of anger expressive of anger, whimpering expressive of misery, cringing expressive of fear. None of these things neccessarily involve deliberation or self-consciousness and all of them are attributable to animals lower than the human. What is required is that they be recognizable by members of the same species (again without this recognition involving any self-consciousness or any formulated, reflective or non-behaviourally realized expression of consciousness), recognizable in such a way as to produce appropriate responses of sympathy, counter-aggression, reinforced attack and suchlike. We need to be wary of over-restricting the use of these analogous or polymorphous expressions.

[17]Desire is always involved in action from any emotion, but it is not a genus of which other emotions are species. Consider the case of fear earlier in the text.

[18]This is what Merleau-Ponty describes as 'functional value' (*The Structure of Behaviour*, pp. 116–120) and 'sens' (*The Phenomenology of Perception*), cf. Charles Taylor, *The Explanation of Behaviour*, pp. 63–71. The same conception seems to be embodied in Aquinas, when he considers amongst the powers inseparably connected with perception proper what he calls the estimative power which amongst the animals makes judgements discriminatory of what is relevant to good and evil. In this way, in Aquinas there are thus four powers inseparably connected with perception proper, common sense (cf. n. 9), memory and imagination (which we discussed in the text), and now this estimative power (*S. Th.* Ia, Q. 78, Art. 4).

[19]J.J. Gibson, *The Ecological Approach to Visual Perception*, p. 127 and throughout chapter and book, *passim*.

such as those expressed in language which have a less direct connection with the motivation of behaviour.[20]

However, there is no sense in attributing such 'meanings' to objects, or to attributing knowledge or perception or any of the elements in the structure I have mentioned if relevant learning and adaptive behaviour is not shown.[21]

We can exhibit this by considering a very simple instance. We are told by biologists of complex pieces of animal behaviour such as that exemplified by certain wasps which, having built a burrow in which to lay eggs alongside paralysed crickets which will serve as food for the wasp grubs which hatch from the eggs, inspect the burrow prior to putting a paralysed cricket into it and laying the eggs. The cricket is paralysed and put just outside the burrow before the inspection proceeds, and, if during the inspection the cricket is moved a short distance away, after the inspection it will be replaced and inspection repeated, and up to forty repetitions of this cycle have been observed.[22] This shows that the apparent inspection does not produce 'knowledge' but only (if the burrow is satisfactory) triggers the next move in the behaviour. But it further shows that it is out of place to speak of 'memory' or even of 'perception' in those primary senses of these words in which knowledge is implied. (It will be noted that there remains in such insect behaviour a certain apparent teleology, but this is standardized to the species.)

---

[20]There is still a distinction between perceptual judgements and others, so that perceptual discriminations still have to have some relevance to behaviour: the judgements that a face is cruel or that a painting is well-composed, erotic, or fierce are perceptual, but not the judgement that the stars are more distant than the planets. The distinction made by Merleau-Ponty between functional value and symbolic form which involves, in both cases, discrimination relevant to action, but in the latter case involves having a range of discriminations at the same time open endedly available to prompt different actions, is reminiscent of the distinction made by Aquinas between the way in which this discriminatory or estimative power is realized amongst the animals lower than human beings and the way it is realized amongst human beings. In the latter case he calls it the 'cogitative power' or 'particular reason' because it makes particular (rather than universal) judgements using general concepts, but still of things discriminated by the senses relevant to some kind of behaviour.

[21]The importance of learning is dwelt upon by Jonathan Bennett in *Rationality*, but wrongly associated by him with rationality rather than with the lower level of conscious structure which we are occupied in delineating.

[22]D. Wooldridge, *The Machinery of the Brain*, p. 82.

A ramified consideration of examples would fill out one's picture of the structure involved. This would include giving an account of the nuances of relation between the different senses, allowing, for instance, of cases of blindness and even unsightedness amongst animals possessed of consciousness. But, while retaining Aristotle's idea of the prime necessity of touch, it would still insist on a more complex account of the 'sense' of touch distinguishing being influenced by tactual contact and the sense of touch proper. Touch as a mode of perception would involve the structures described above, involving memory, imagination, and discriminations relevant to emotion liable to be initiatory of intentional movement, as well as the structures of exploratory behaviour and learning. The difficulty for us is to conceive a functioning of imagination (which is connected with having a conception of the world in the sense of what grounds 'knowing one's way about') involving touch alone.[23] A fuller account would also have to embrace the phenomena of play and sexuality,[24] and bring in pleasure and enjoyment, as well as pain, distress, and the mourning of loss.

In these ways, we must envisage animal consciousness as present only when there is a working together of many different aspects in an integrated way. From among these aspects, let any of the key ones be absent, and we must say that consciousness is absent in the case concerned.[25] It is typical for these aspects to have each a different

---

[23]A study of the case of Helen Keller and other work with the deaf and blind (e.g., at Zagorsk) is clearly appropriate here.

[24]Sexuality in human beings is of special logical interest, not only because the emotions which its definition involves are essentially psychophysical, but also because their objects are only intelligible by reference to the emotions themselves, sexual attractiveness being only intelligible by reference to sexual desire as colour is only intelligible in reference to sight (by contrast, harm and risk of harm are intelligible without reference to fear). That is, we do not and cannot first define the sexual properties in virtue of which the person is found sexually attractive and then define the emotions from these properties, but have to begin by defining the emotions in their psychobiological contours. (I owe this observation to Karol Wojtyla's *Love and Responsibility*, p. 48 f.; by "urge" is meant roughly 'orientation', p. 46.)

[25]In recognizing the involvment of many different ('modularized' or 'parallel') sub-systems with different physical aspects, and the way in which what counts as consciousness is only present when there is an adequate synergism between them, I am in accord with D. Alan Allport in 'What Concept of Consciousness?'. I have also carefully given place to unconscious 'cognition'; indeed I regard it as integral to the ordinary functioning of higher animals and not to be associated only with the

physical sub-system subserving it, so that defects in a particular sub-system can have the effect of removing a piece of 'cognition' or reason for 'behaviour' from consciousness; yet these defects will typically not have altogether removed the teleology characteristic of life or indeed of animal life (at a pre-conscious level) from the phenomena concerned. However, we must not allow the fact of the existence beside each other of many sub-systems each with a physical aspect within the life of the higher animals lead us to deny the fact of consciousness when it arises. For, in the life of animals of many species, it is normal for consciousness to arise in the context of an adequate degree of synergism between physical sub-systems upon which its realizations may depend. And for this consciousness to be present is not for some isolated 'cognitions' to be 'conscious' but for the whole life of the animal, perception, sensation, memory, emotion and action, to be integrated within the framework of the particular kind of mind-involving explanation which we identified in Chapter VIII. The attractiveness of thinking of sub-systems working in parallel with one another must not blind us to the whole of which they are parts: they must not be regarded as autonomous mechanisms.[26]

---

behaviour of higher animals defective in some 'sub-system' or with the behaviour of the lower animals.

However, it is vital not to require perfection, but only adequacy, in synergism between the supposed sub-systems. Consciousness is not a theoretical ideal in the life of animals, rarely or never realized in practice. Rather, it identifies the overall framework for the understanding of the main body of their biographies.

[26]For the life of the animal to continue in a way which is not made deviant or defective by the non-conscious elements which enter into it, these elements must have the appropriate integration with the overall framework referred to. If different activities continue contemporaneously, each requiring its own level of attention (which may in some cases amount to little more than the capacity to notice interference with it) and each perhaps pre-occupying different sub-systems, it remains that there must be something about their mode of connection with this overall framework which makes them count as activities of the animal or human being concerned. Therefore, the system of control cannot be unqualifiedly heterarchical (contrary to some of the drift of D. Alan Allport's 'Patterns and actions' and 'Attention and performance': note, e.g., pp. 31–39, 142–148). Cf. the discussion of 'parallel distributed processing' (PDP) in Section 3 of Chapter XII below.

Further, it cannot and must not be simply assumed, even in the cases where it is undisputed that a sub-system has a physical aspect, that the sub-system concerned constitutes a 'mechanism'. Neurological systems cannot be simply assumed to function like computers: if it is conceivable that cells have irreducibly teleological aspects, this is not inconceivable in the case of neurological sub-systems. The introduction of

I do not propose to go, in this book, beyond these general indications of the pre-human pre-linguistic pre-rational level of consciousness and the way examples serve to bring out the way its elements interlock. The type of analytical approach represented in Merleau-Ponty and Charles Taylor will serve to establish more precisely the criteria which will identify which animals have this kind of consciousness and which rest at the lower level of what Merleau-Ponty calls, more generally, the vital.

What I have been trying to do is to mark out some of the features of that kind of consciousness which we ought to attribute to the higher non-human animals as well as to human beings, features which in these animals are closely integrated in ways some of which I have indicated but not set in the context of reflection or language-use. It is vital to the recognition of the existence of an animal level of consciousness, a level homogeneous with human consciousness in its relations with behaviour and in the way it enters into explanations of this behaviour, but of a pre-reflective and pre-linguistic kind, not to falsify the picture by a surreptitious re-introduction of self-consciousness. For instance, Nagel's idea that if a bat is conscious, then there must be something which it is like to be a bat is quite wrong if it implies that a bat must be aware of what life is like for it,[27] i.e., must be self-conscious in this respect. Of course, the form of bat life is different of that of human life and so what it is like to be a bat (which is something psychophysical) is different from what it is like to be a human being, but this is shown in different patterns of behaviour in relation to different behaviourally-differentiated modes of perception, in brief in a different form of life, and does not imply any self-consciousness or 'awareness of what it is like to be a bat'.

To contrast the human case, let us consider in the first instance perception: as it occurs in human beings, who are language-using and self-conscious, any perception exhibits both aspects revealed in non-linguistic behaviour and behavioural aptitudes and aspects which are not just behavioural but judgemental, that is, revealed only in

---

teleology does not mean the end of disciplined study or experiment—we need to end the worship of the idea of 'mechanisms'. The idea of 'finitary' reasoning has a much wider application in mathematics than the idea of 'mechanical derivability'; the imposition of the forms of mechanist explanation in physics seems outdated; and so attachment to them in psychology seems merely obscurantist.

[27] Nagel, 'What is it like to be a bat?'.

linguistic behaviour and aptitudes. That is, the discrimination implicit in any perception (any perception must be determinate in some degree in that there is something which the object of perception is not perceived as being) is exhibited not only in behavioural setting and aptitudes but also in propositional judgements, the two inseparable.[28] A second key instance is provided by emotion which, again, even in the animals lower than the human, is geared to the discrimination of such features as the pleasurable, the good to eat, the dangerous, the harmful and the painful, but which does not involve reflectiveness or self-awareness, nor any non-behavioural (here I mean linguistic or language-dependent) exhibition of the identification of the aspect of the object of the emotion which provoked that emotion, whereas in the human case there is always awareness of this or at least a capacity to become aware of it.

It is an integral part of the form of animal life that the animal develops and that its potentialities unfold in stages—in the case of mammals stages both inside and outside the womb. It is only in stages that the forms of description appropriate to conscious life become applicable. Thus, to take a simple instance, I have spoken of the dog as afraid when his master threatens him with a stick and of this as presupposing a learning from previous experience of hurt or harm from attack with a stick. Underlying such processes of learning are primitive instinctual patterns of reaction common to the species and developed in response to earliest nurture. It is characteristic of animals to develop by an unfolding of potentialities. However it remains that it is only the adaptivity of the dog or other animal which warrants the coming into play of such descriptions as I have offered.

The problem of how we should describe the development of the individual, both at the stage of learning late in the womb and outside it, and at earlier stages, is quite different from the earlier problem of laying down criteria to determine when consciousness or the structures which mark psychophysical life arise within the evolutionary series. It is, in one way, more intractable, inasmuch as in many cases acts of consciousness seem to be such as to presuppose other previous

---

[28]For instance, the perception's behavioural setting and the aptitudes arising from it are key elements in the identification of the objects of the perception about which judgement is made.

conscious acts and yet the series cannot go back without limit, but in another way, more straightforward. It is more straightforward because of the clear connection between identity of a subject and the continuance of a being whose identity is inseparable from a certain nature, independently of whether all the potentialities which belong to that nature have yet been realized or still remain realized.

To put the matter in other terms, we have here explanations of kinds which will only work if the continued identity of the individual concerned *qua* member of the animal species concerned can be presumed. In particular, as soon as an individual is established in the womb *qua* member of the human species, the identity of this individual will be key to the validity of explanations of developments and phenomena in its life, albeit that at an early stage the explanations coming into play will not involve consciousness and at a later stage will involve consciousness. Accordingly, it is a mistake to build phylogeny into one's description of the generation and development of the individual, and separate the emergence of the subject of consciousness from the earlier emergence of the biological individual. The subject of consciousness begins in a state where it does not exercise consciousness and over the course of time its potentialities unfold.

Consider the human case: as soon as individuality is established—according to some at the first stage of the existence of the zygote (or in the case of identical twins at the two-cell stage), and according to others at some later stage not later than the fourteenth day (the time at which we plainly have begun to have a 'body with organs' in presence)[29]—we have an identifiable individual in whose nature it is

---

[29]Since in the case of identical twins, they seem at each time to be at the same stage of development, their time of coming to be as individuals would seem to be the same. Individuality cannot be considered established if twinning has yet to occur, and requires not just a determinate genetic code but also its physical realization. And it would seem reasonable to say that the individual exists as soon as there is some embodiment to serve as locus or focus of individuality, e.g., by the importance of its co-ordinating influence on other cells and future development. It would seem that such locus is established at least as soon as distinct inner cell masses are established, and there is no need to wait for the incipient body with organs. How soon there is such locus or focus can only be gauged from an understanding of the processes involved (what Wiggins calls the relevant 'nomological and factual findings', *Sameness and Substance*, p.221); at the present stage of research it would seem to be anyway no later than the eighth day, normally evident between days three and five, and arguably established in an asymmetry of role between cells after the first cell division in the monozygotic case.

to develop into a more mature being with the structures of human consciousness fully actualized. We do not have first, the emergence of an individual with a nature extending just to the realization of the structures of the vital, then the emergence of an individual with a nature extending just to the realization of the structures of pre-personal consciousness, and then the emergence of an individual with a nature extending to the realization of properly personal consciousness. (This last emergence would occur sometime after birth, all in the midst of relationships, first with the mother beginning within the womb and then with others outside it, relationships both preceding and following it.) Rather, we have from the start, whenever that may be, i.e., as soon as we have a biological individual at all, an individual whose nature extends to the realization of all these stages.

True, there may be nothing for some weeks or months in the womb which requires description and explanation involving perceptual consciousness, and perhaps nothing for some little time after birth which requires description and explanation in terms involving personhood. But there is no individual with a merely living nature which transmutes into an individual with a psychophysical nature but not the nature of a person which transmutes into an individual with the nature of a person. Rather, there is one individual with a human nature which is such as to unfold in stages as soon as there is any individual at all.

3. The Focalized Subjecthood Involved by Perception and Judgement

Subjects of perception, emotion, imagination, and intentional action (which are also in some cases subjects of linguistic understanding and judgement) have special kinds of criteria of identity. It is not just that they had the kind of persistence through time of such bodily things as plants, amoebas, and flatworms, a bodily continuity compatible with processes of regeneration and reproduction, which at certain stages leave it arbitrary whether we view there as being one or two individuals present. Nor are the patterns of teleological explanation such as to leave the explanation of the behaviour of bodily individuals to group directed ends, or as to leave the behaviour automated so far as the individual is concerned and only end-directed when considered from the point of view of the good of the species, as with much of the behaviour of insects. Rather the unitariness and persistence in identity involved in the particular kind of teleological explanation concerned is a unitariness and persistence in identity of the individual precisely *qua* subject of potential or actual consciousness.

We must now inquire into the character and root of this unitariness.

We may be described as inquiring into the character of the unity of the 'self', 'I', or Ego, but in fact our inquiry is wider than this since the higher animals lower than the human do not present themselves as an 'I' or 'me' with self-reflection, but only (we may conveniently say) as a 'he or she'. What is clear to us as a preliminary is that the unity after which we are seeking is not some unity of organization in the brain or in the brain and body taken together such as cognitive scientists drawing on neurology and computer science might hope to discover, because—whatever it is—it is already well known to us in understanding the terms "person", "human being", and "animal" (so far as this last is conceived as implying the psychophysical structures we have described). Nor is it the unity attributed to a Cartesian "I" as a spiritual substance, since that, we have shown, is not anything we know in knowing what human beings are, but something which, in relation to human beings and *a fortiori* to animals, is purely fictitious.

The structure, whereby the subject is, as it were, focalized in an 'I', a 'he or she', undivided and indivisible is part of the ontological structure of the human being. It is clear from our earlier discussion that computers are debarred from being models of animal operation by having no activities requiring teleological or holistic account involving what we called a 'psychophysical being' or animal as subject. For the account we gave of perception and action applying also in the cases of higher animals excludes a mechanical or deterministic system in the sense of the words "mechanical" or "deterministic" as used in computer theory, and it is a key feature of this account that it involves a structure only describable in terms of a subject directed towards 'objects'. And this structure is not simulable by a computer because they do not require description as subjects. Metaphorical descriptions of computers as if they were subjects of knowledge and decision will always be equivalent to non-metaphorical ones not involving such descriptions. Thus the primary reason for the human being's not being a computer or simulable by a computer is that he is a psychophysical being—it is only within this framework that we go on to discover further reasons, e.g., ones relating to language and understanding, debarring human beings from this.

Always we adopt the method of recognizing what belongs to the human being simply as an animal before going on to consider what differences arise from what is peculiar to language and linguistic understanding, i.e., the things distinctive of human beings which are the concern of Part Two of this book.

What the consideration of sight and of judgement both bring into view is the presence of some kind of polarity, of the 'I', the 'he or she' (the "he" and "she", not as connoting sexedness, but as marking that the subject is a subject in a 'psychological' sense) as a pole or logical focus. (By a "subject in a 'psychological' sense", I mean a subject of perception and intentional agency—also of judgement and understanding, if these are present.)

The temptation is to think that the psychological subject or 'I', the 'he or she', is some inner part of the whole substance or being, whether animal or human being, an inner self, centre of consciousness, mind, or soul, which is a pole or focus out from which the other parts and features of the animal or human being, as it were, radiate, or to which they are attached (and modern thinkers will then propose to identify this inner self or mind with the brain). Understood in this way, the human being or animal as logical subject, that to which we ascribe properties of many different kinds, bodily properties and psychological ones, would have a focus or centre which would be a part or point within the whole—it would not be that this bodily being, this logical subject, was as a whole or as a unity a focus for anything, but that some part or point within it was a focus of some kind.

But there is no need to think of the focalized subjecthood of humans beings and other animals like this.

Rather the 'I', the 'he or she', which judges and understands and the 'I', the 'he or she', which perceives and exercises intentional agency is the same as the 'I', the 'he or she', the animal, the human being, which has bodily parts and which physically moves. No other entity or being, no special element or inner part, is being spoken of when we speak of the 'I', or of the 'he or she', which perceives and judges, than is spoken of when we speak of the 'I', or the 'he or she', which acts and travels from place to place. Nor is this subject some 'transcendental Ego' distinct both from a supposed empirical self and a biological bodily thing, as if the locus of the unity of apperception of which Kant speaks was outside, and unqualifiedly over against the world.

The problem at this stage is therefore to explain the special character of 'being focalized' which arises with human beings and the other higher animals, but not with rocks, roads, planets, and so forth, and seemingly not with plants.

The bodily thing which is a human being or is an animal is not only integrated, its parts into a whole, in the manner of a plant or tree alongside other simpler organisms, but is a unity in a more peculiar and intimate way. And it is this more peculiar and intimate way of being one or unitary which we need to explain.

A block of wood is divisible into parts each of which is also a block of wood. Very evidently with plants, and it seems perhaps also even with flatworms, even though enjoying each plant and each flatworm a kind of bodily continuity tied to the exercise of a form of life, we also find a divisibility by various forms of asexual reproduction or by surgery into things of the same kind, and in some cases in such a way as to seem to make it arbitrary whether we say that the original individual survives or not.

By contrast, there is no question of dividing an 'I', or a 'he or she', into parts. The 'I', or 'he or she', presents itself as undivided and indivisible. And the root of this undividedness and indivisibility lies not in some greater degree of integratedness of bodily parts (or at least not of integratedness in any physical respect) but, at least in so far as integratedness in the case of parts is concerned at all, in the possession of a different kind of integratedness, namely integratedness into the life of a conscious subject. But when we think of the 'I', or the 'he or she', as undivided and indivisible, we are *somehow* denying that, as such, it has parts at all rather than thinking of some special kind of integratedness of its parts. And this unitariness and indivisibility— what I am calling 'focalizedness'—is because of what is involved in conscious subjecthood as such, rather than this focalized subjecthood being because of some kind of integratedness of parts making for unitariness and indivisibility as a bodily thing.

I say 'somehow' denying that as such the 'I', or the 'he or she', has parts at all despite the plain fact that (e.g.) my legs and arms are certainly parts of me. Yet the 'I', or 'he or she', is not *made up* of parts, and as we have remarked there is no question of dividing an 'I', or a 'he or she', into parts.

We might say that persons and psychophysical beings in general are focuses. It is not just that they are logical subjects on which we can hang reports or descriptions, but that they are, as it were, point-focuses—focuses which are as such (i.e., in virtue of their natures) undivided and indivisible, not distributed equally, part by part, over a space. What we are trying to give an account of is precisely this focalized subjecthood, this kind of unitariness or indivisbility.

There is a paradox here. The human being and other higher animals have bodily parts and in this way appear as composite things. But by their nature they are persons or psychophysical beings possessed of consciousness and so, by nature, things of kinds to be unitary and indivisible in the way which is puzzling us. The modes of explanation on which our accounts of their behaviour turn involve kinds of predicate which apply to them only as unitary subjects, and these kinds of predicate do not apply in the same sense to their parts. The parts of coloured surfaces and heavy bodies themselves have colour and weight, but the parts of people and animals do not see, desire, intend, imagine, remember, or any of the like—indeed, when I grasp something with my hand, it is not even true that my hand grasps it in the same sense that I do, since it is not implied that the hand has intentions.

In this way, it is as if the composite bodily being (and the human being is a bodily being) presents itself as something which is in a key respect incomposite. Moreover it presents itself as something thus incomposite *by its nature*, the nature associated with the criteria of identity and modes of explanation appropriate to the thing concerned. I say this because something belongs to an entity *by its nature* when it belongs to it according to that which determines the modes of explanation appropriate for accounting for its behaviour and determines how we judge of questions of identity in regard to it. And being a person, or being an animal with perceptual consciousness, are the central and most generic parts of the nature of people or animals with perceptual consciousness.

We have here a kind of inversion, as if within nature amidst ever-increasing complexity certain new kinds of structure and new kinds of simplicity or unity are born. The first of these new kinds of structure is that associated with psychophysical beings in general and perceptual consciousness. The second is that which integrates the features associated with animals with perceptual consciousness or psychophysical beings in general with those associated with speech and language,[30] understanding, reasoning, and reflection. Neither are they any longer structures specified as it were from the bottom upwards, but rather from the top downwards.[31] My concern has only been with those structures associated with consciousness which are determinative of identity and individuation and which are associated with consciousness. (I have not brought into consideration those underlying teleological structures which underly growth, regeneration, and reproduction, or whatever is involved in species-determined behaviour of sorts which individuals cannot adapt through learning.)

In order to understand this 'focalization', we need to take account of the ways in which men and animals relate to their environment (the word "environment" being understood in the most general sense). They relate to their environment not only physically, by being spatially distributed and placed within it and subject to physical interaction with it, ways which give no unqualified privilege to one part or aspect over another, but also as perceiving, intentional agents and as subjects of judgement and understanding. In these latter ways of being related the human being or animal can no longer be conceived as a mere aggregate of parts, nor even as a whole of parts with some teleological directions exhibited in growth, regeneration, and spread or reproduction. Rather they have to be conceived as subjects with relations of being mentally directed towards other things, and in the case of subjects of judgement and understanding relations of intellectual (whether 'speculative' or 'practical' or 'volitional') directedness: relations which either bring into prominence only the parts which they internally involve (like eyes in seeing, and legs in walking) but within a context which still involves reference to the whole, the animal as unitary subject, or which bring into prominence no parts at all but only the human being, undivided, as subject.

The 'focalization' involved is therefore not a matter of a part of the animal or human being (e.g., the mind or brain) being a focus in respect of the whole animal or human being, but of the animal or human being as a unity being a focus or centre in its relations with

---

[30]To take this second structure in full generality, one would have to understand 'speech and language' as applying to any communication system of the kind we have called 'linguistic', whatever its 'linguistic substance', e.g., whether sounds, marks on paper, or whatever.

[31]This is explained by Aquinas in a striking way in his *Comm. De An.*, 773–774.

the world. A psychological subject is *qua* psychological subject in key relations with the world, not just as a distributed body all of whose parts have relations and interactions with the world, but precisely as a unitary subject in the way indicated.

The focalization is not upon a part of the animal or human being, but simply upon the 'I', the 'he or she', as such. The animal or human being is a 'focalized subject', not in having a head, brain, soul, or mind as a focal centre within it, but in having its relations with the world (or those which differentiate its nature) focalized upon it as an *anima*, a psychological subject, as such undivided and indivisible.

In order to carry the matter further it may be helpful to raise a general question which arises also in the consideration of novels and paintings.

In a novel it may happen that the reader through explicit or implicit indications gains some sense of the physical appearance of a character, but it is plain that what is primarily projected and appears, as if highlighted, is the persona of the person concerned, or in different types of novel the stream of consciousness or again the retrospective outlook or attitude of the person centred upon. Actions come in with their obvious involvement of the body, but they are present only in their relation to the actor, the spectator, or the interaction involved with the emotions and actions of others. In drama it is persons and actions in relation to them which stand out. Some parallel remarks may be made in the case of some kinds of painting, notably icons.

If we ask what is thrust forward for attention when we encounter another human being, we might be inclined to say that it was not the person's body as a whole but rather his or her face—not that this is or needs to be literally thrust forward but that it is this that thrusts itself upon our attention leaving the rest of the body as context or background. But, upon further reflection, we might say that even this is not exact, because it was not so much the face as the expression on the face which drew attention to itself, and then not so much the expression on the face as what it expressed or rather the person as expressing himself thus. In this way, it is the person *qua* person which thrusts itself on our attention—likewise with the dog who presents himself as a living, conscious, and reactive being.

One could say that the 'he or she', the psychological subject, has an existence in the world which is 'headed' or 'pointed', not in the sense of being focalized in or through a head in the biological sense, but in the sense that it is under an aspect whereby it is 'focalized' or unitary and indivisible in the way indicated,[32] not under the aspect of being a bodily thing distributed over a space.

We have here also an inversion of a second kind, that in our perception of human beings and animals, although what is presented to the senses is presented as distributed over a field and what we encounter is a mass of different pieces of behaviour, the multiplicity is pushed into the background so that what presents itself is presented in a Gestalt so that what we are primarily aware of is the person or animal with this multiplicity involved only incidentally or consequentially with it. And it is not only in our perception, but also in our understanding, that this inversion is seen: because the inversion appears not only in our account of the phenomena as they present themselves, but also in the explanation of these phenomena, so that in this explanation it is upon the concepts of person and of psychophysical being that the working of the whole explanation turns. It is not just that being a person or an animal with perceptual consciousness is a mask or guise[33] in which the phenomena present themselves to us, or that they are categories which our understanding imposes and which shape our experience, but that they are the basic features of the natures of these kinds of object experienced, persons or animals, determining the criteria of identity and modes of explanation appropriate to them.

Somebody might have thought that our envisaging the animals and human beings in our thinking and perceiving as animals and human beings was a matter, not of what they are, but of how we think of them, or of how we experience them. He might have thought of it as a matter of intentionality—that we think of or aim at things according to certain concepts or under certain types of description. But then he would go against the fact that being a person or psychophysical being was the determinative part of their natures, the fundamental feature of what they are and how they behave, not just of how they

---

[32]One could think, to take a weak analogy, of the case of a pencil: this has a 'head', a point which gives it its function and role, a point whereby it relates to the world in a function which requires it to be in key respects undivided and indivisible.

[33]One original meaning of *prosopon* or *persona* in classical times was that of a mask worn by actors in plays. In respect of this, we must say that the character or *persona* which is projected, if deception does not enter in, is not a mask but a revelation of the nature of the character portrayed.

present themselves. Thus, we have to grasp that our envisaging the animals and human beings whom we perceive or think about has to be through these concepts, and not (for instance) through the concept of 'ordered *ensemble* of bodily parts', in order to be true to the nature of the things perceived and thought of.

Again somebody might say that it is as a person that a person projects him or herself upon the world. He would then be in danger of thinking that seeing or grasping a person as being a person was a matter of capturing a certain projection from the entity called a person in a certain plane, the plane within which talking about persons was intelligible or primary. But then he would be thinking of a thing's being a person as relative to a certain frame of description, whereas it is fundamental to its nature.

4. The Human Standpoint in Perceiving and Judging as a Standpoint from Inside the World: Avoiding the Cartesian Mistake

In raising the question as to what must be the nature or structure of a person or animal in order to be the subject of such consciousness-involving attributes, we are prone to a constant temptation. This is the temptation which we have been constantly fighting against to think of the human being or animal as composed of two parts, a conscious self set over against the world in perception and in judgement, and a body or the rest of the human being or animal. The modern context of this temptation has been set by a certain epistemological perspective.

The question is of whether and how the human being or higher animal is transcendent in relation to the world. Aquinas draws from Aristotle the idea that 'the mind needs to be unmixed with matter in order to command or to know', inspired by Anaxagoras, but the question is as to how this idea should be construed or developed. In Descartes and in the empiricist tradition following him, the mind, self, or consciousness is thought of as standing above or over against the world in order to desire and choose or to experience and judge, the relation between mind and world being wholly contingent.

(a) The way the perceiver is both over against and in the world: some contrasts with understanding

Some of the motivation of the thought that 'the mind must be unmixed with matter, in order to command or know', can be seen in the natural thought that, literally or metaphorically, one has to 'get one's head above water' in order to see or to judge.

What is the point in this context of 'getting one's head above the water'?

It seems, firstly, to have to do with the capacity in the case of the sense of sight to look about and vary one's vantage point. We have, in general, the picture of the see-er as proud of what he sees (i.e., as it were, stood over against it), and at the same time as a vigorous exploring agent initiating different relationships to what he sees. The capacity for independent movement in respect of the objects of perception is as important as his being over against or out from these objects as an element in our understanding of the freedom or independence of matter required for the perceiver to be proud of, distinct from, what he perceives, whether the perceiver is a human being or a dog.

The idea of the need to 'get one's head above the water' also explains how the sense of sight has come to be described as 'the least immersed' in its medium and its objects—the least immersed in matter and the 'most spiritual' of the senses. For it is seemingly the least dependent on its medium for the knowledge it gains: that is, whereas in touch and taste the organ is the medium and operates by physical contact with its objects, and with sound the organ suffers physical vibration from the vibrating air, in sight the medium is rather a construction of theory ('the ether') than a physical reality for the organ to be physically integrated with.[34] In the case of the sense of sight it is as if there was, in the ideal case, an unobscured direct presentation of the object as it is to the see-er, unmediated by vibrations in the air or other medium, and not arising from a directness of physical contact between the organ and the object of sense. What is required of the medium is, rather, that it should not get in the way by its obscurity or partial opacity and that from some source light should be thrown on the object (if the object is not itself luminous).

---

[34]In Aquinas' thought, the medium in the case of sight is not affected or altered (i.e., changed in respect of elemental qualities, hotness or dryness, coldness or wetness, that is, those qualities which were supposed to be relevant to one substance's altering another by contact) and so does not receive any form from the medium or from the object via the medium naturally (cf. n. 36 below). It is thus that sight is the 'most spiritual' of the senses.

This is the background out of which it arises that most of the metaphors which we need to rely upon to describe understanding and 'intellectual' knowledge derive from sight. Whether we think of the objects of the intellect as the particular things of certain natures or think of its objects as being these natures themselves, in the act directed towards these objects the intellect stands proud of the world containing these objects somewhat as we imagine the operation of the sense of sight to be distant from and proud of the objects of sight and their background. When Lucas discusses the difference which will remain between the human mind and a machine of whatever power, the latter limited to proving things within some system (however extended), he speaks of what the mind 'standing outside the system' can do.[35] Here we have at work the same primaeval thought, that the mind (like the seeing eye) must have freedom from being immersed in matter or controlled by a mechanical system, must be able to stand outside the system in order, knowing it (or seeing it), to make judgement.

There are, however, some obvious contrasts even on the surface, as well as the deeper structural ones we shall discuss later.

Although, in the case of sight, light stands as a means enabling things to be seen rather than (except in the case of the luminous) as an object of sight, it remains in the case of sight that light belongs to the world of the objects. By contrast in the case of the intellect, what is metaphorically called light does not belong to the world of the objects at all but is nothing different from the power to think or know, i.e., the intellect, itself. Again, whereas in the case of the sense of sight obscurity belongs to the world of the objects, in the case of the intellect obscurity is not a property of the some medium or of the objects but a matter of a failure (for one of several reasons) of the intellect to acheive its desired act.

This brings out one of the ways in which sight is not so immaterial as it might seem. The nature of the dependence on 'light'[36] and the 'lack of obscurity of the medium', as well as the role of the sense-organ bring this out. In regard to the latter, thinking of the sense of sight

---

[35] *Philosophy*, 1961, p. 117.

[36] We think of light as a physical phenomenon physically causative of certain physical effects in the sense-organ. This way of thinking is not logically forced upon us. Yet light for Aquinas is still a particularized property of the medium, even though not strictly 'physical' but 'intentional'.

with its organ as distant and proud of its objects goes together with thinking of the operation of the sense of sight as dependent on the formation of a particularized imprint or impression, e.g., a *species* or structuring of light in the pupil of the eye, as in the theory of Aristotle and Aquinas, or a retinal image or alteration deeper in the brain, as in more modern theories—which is in some way isomorphic with the object of sight and which plays a role in shaping how things are seen.

But the most important way in which sight and the see-er are still in the world which is seen lies in the intimate symbiosis of sight and intentional action. We have already just mentioned looking about and changing one's vantage point. The sense of sight must never be divorced from intentional action exemplified in exploratory movement involving also the sense of touch and some 'feedback' in respect of bodily movements in kinaesthetic sensation. All this involves the see-er in being in amongst, and not just over against and out from, the objects in the world. The judge-er is also in the world, and does not only in some metaphorical sense stand above or over against it. But the ways both of being in the world and of being over against it are different in the two cases.

(b) **The way the judger is in the world as a background for considering how he or she 'stands above' the world: false models suggested by the consideration of seeing**

We seem to have plain in our minds the model of the perceiver as over against, out from, confronting and confronted by the objects he or she perceives, the same perceiver who also is an exploring agent, freely moving—more accurately we might say, self-moving, self-guiding, him or herself initiator of his or her exploratory movement—amongst and in respect to the objects he or she perceives, in a watchful monitoring relation to them, a cognitive but still real relation. The perceiver is physically, and (to consider the case of sight) by the structure of the act of perception as a matter of logic geometrically and so physically, out from and over against the objects of perception.

We are tempted to transfer this model of being over against and out from the objects of knowledge to the consideration of the relation of the judging subject of knowledge to what is known. In this way, as well as in others, we are led to a picture of a triad: the judging subject, language or whatever else structures his or her thought, and reality—the reality which he or she is supposedly over against.

In this way of thinking, the judging subject is either helpless or else a cognitive God—one who masterfully frames 'conceptual schemes' with which he or she 'orders' or 'conceptualizes' the 'material' of his or her perceptual experience. This judging subject stands above, or as judge in respect of, both the supposed alternative conceptual schemes and 'reality' itself. This subject's language at a particular moment enshrines a conceptual scheme and describes, not reality as it is in itself, but a picture or representation of reality. 'Reality' as the judging subject is in a relation to it may be real materially but, cognitively, although judge of, out from, and over against reality, this subject has no real relation to reality. The world is bracketed from the subject in Husserl's sense: that is, the thinker has to bracket the world in order to analyse his or her own consciousness and thence to consider the status and nature of things. This bracketing is the supposed price of role of subjects as judges, masters of their thought, chooser between conceptual schemes, or recognizer of the limits of whatever conceptual scheme is given to them, whether by the conditions of their form of sensibility or form of understanding, or by their nature, or by their culture.

We have here a way of thinking which envisages the situation of the philosopher as that of being confronted by the need to consider the relationships amongst the members of a triad: the judging subject, language, and the world. This way of thinking gives philosophical primacy as a matter of method to a certain kind of epistemology, whether (following certain preconceptions) it be called 'critique of reason' as by Kant, 'philosophy of language' as by Dummett, or 'metaphysics' as by Wright. Any such way of thinking involves some form of 'transcendental idealism' with some kind of 'transcendental ego' (or transcendental subject of judgement). The commonest symptom of its presence is some kind of conventionalism, although this is not found in Kant or Dummett.

We shall see later how any such picture of a triad, of subject, language, and reality, is excluded by the philosophy of language itself, properly conceived.[37] Language and reality are not objects in relations, so as to be available to be compared with one another.[38] Unless this triad is insinuated as a preconception at the very start, there is no

---

[37]Chapter XI, Section 1, below.
[38]Chapter XI, Section 1(b), below.

way in which the philosophy of language can lead one (let alone force one) into it, and no way in which transcendental idealism can get a footing.

The subject of perception and agency is in the world, in physical relations internal to perceiving and to the relevant kinds of acting, and the ways in which this 'being in the world' of the subject which stands out from or is over against its objects and is self-moving in respect of them, has already been described. But the subject of judgement is in the world also, and the subject's way of being in the world requires explanation: the point which we are here making is that the model of being over against the world, derived from the physics and geometry of visual perception, invites a quite false picture of how the judgement is over against or above the world, which excludes any right understanding of how the judging subject is in the world.

How is the judging subject in the world?

Most obviously, one's perception and one's intentional knowledge of one's own actions (that is, one's knowledge of them *qua* intending them, so that nothing to do with technical notions of intentionality is involved here) involve internally one's being in real relation, what we described as real cognitive relation, with the world.

But it is not enough to say this.

We must say further that this perceptual and intentional knowledge is of a piece with one's knowledge by reflection. That is, one does not, by reflecting on one's modes of knowledge, get into a 'world' (an inner world) or frame of thinking in which one prescinds from all perceptual and intentional knowledge. There is no meta-language or system of propositions which has sense independently of some first order language, so-called 'object-language', and which stands in judgement in mastery over it.

It might be objected that, conversely, there is no language in the proper sense, no expressive system of symbols and capacity for using it expressively and, therefore, with understanding, which does not contain its own meta-language. The 'first order' terms which we use would not have the meaning they do, their sense in use, indeed would not have linguistic meaning at all, except in a context in which they could also be used within a 'second order' framework. This will be part of the significance of our argument in Chapter X, Section 3. However, it remains that, within the structured whole which is human discourse, within which there can thus be no first order terms without openness to second order contexts, the first order has a priority, a priority without which critical thought would be impossible.[39]

Thus the reflective subject who raises second order or critical questions does not in his or her act of thus thinking prescind from his or her nature or from the world of which he or she is part, to be part of which belongs to his or her nature. Even when the physical *qua* physical is not attended to, it is not bracketed.

How is the judging subject to stand above the limitations of material conditions so as to obtain objectivity of judgement? Not then, from what we have said, by standing outside or over against the world, but by having open concepts which permit the unlimited extension of modes of enquiry and, even more crucially, of modes of response to enquiry. This is a key point at which there is an interdependence between the arguments of the present work as presented in Chapter X below[40] and a more extended treatment of the problems of knowledge.[41]

It is in these ways that we must systematically veto any attempt grounded in epistemology to remove human beings from their place amongst the animals and divorce each human being and consciousness from the world.

5. The Intimacy of the Unity between Body and Mind in Human Being and Animal

(a) The question of the nature of mind-body unity

Our early chapters showed how perception and intentional action are focalized upon a subject, and how this subject is essentially

---

[39]This perspective is clearly presented in *The Reality of Time and the Existence of God*, Chapter VII, Section 1.

[40]Section 4 in conjunction with Section 2.

[41]It is my hope to treat this in a later work, *The Structure of Knowledge: Two Kinds of Critical Philosophy*. The key point of test for the account I offer is aired in *The Reality of Time and the Existence of God*, pp. 245–246; but it depends essentially on the understanding that every language, in the full sense applicable to human languages, must include its own meta-language, for the reasons presented in Chapter X, Section 3 onwards, cf. XII, 2(d).

psychophysical. In Section 3 of this chapter we explored the peculiar character of the unitariness of this psychophysical subject, what we called its focalizedness, so that it can only be thought of as a personal or psychological unity, not an aggregate of parts. And in Section 4 we further highlighted the wrongness of conceiving the perceiver or judger as a psychological entity, a mind, set over against the world which is known, rather than a psychophysical entity set within it.

To consummate our grasp of the intimacy of the unity between mind and body both in human beings and in other animals, there are two further things we need to appreciate: the strategic role of concepts of perception and sensation, and the relevance of the organic structure of the body to the psychophysical unity of mind and body.

What we are doing is exploring further aspects of the concepts of 'irreducibly psychophysical subject' in general and of 'irreducibly psychophysical subject with a human level of consciousness' in particular.

I do not begin by using the word "person" because, as we pointed out in Chapter V, it has to be realized that there are two meanings of the word "person" in vogue. The one most common among Anglo-Saxon philosophers, and represented in Strawson, limited the word to referring to all those beings of a bodily nature which are personal, such as human beings but presumably any other animal beings which also turn out to be personal.[42] This notion of person, as a personal animal being, we saw to be a specialization of the more general meaning of the expressions "person" and "being personal" which marked the range of appropriate joint application of such predicates as "know", "understand", and "judge", "desire", "prefer", "rejoice in", "intend", and "choose", and literally or metaphorically "speak" and "hear", all predicates which have been applied to God and to angels,[43] the meaning of the word "person" which will be important in Chapter XV.

Now, our concern is with 'persons' in the first and more restricted and least controversial sense, and we want to make it clear that, according to our general perspective, human beings are not persons peculiar in being psychophysical, but psychophysical beings peculiar in being personal, and it is viewing things this way round which is important at this stage of our argument. And in explaining the

---

[42]Cf. Chapter V, Section 1 (a), above.
[43]Cf. Chapter V, n. 4, above.

intimacy of mind and body both in psychophysical beings in general and 'persons' in particular, I shall be able to rehearse and set in a new perspective a lot of the earlier argument of the book.

Approaching the matter informally, we can see it as the most obvious mark of 'persons' in the restricted sense, i.e., irreducibly psychophysical beings with a human level of consciousness, that they are subjects of three strikingly different types of predicate. Firstly they are subjects of intellectual sorts of attribute like understanding and thought—reckoned by Descartes to be attributable not only to the human being as such, but also to the mind by itself. Secondly they are subjects of bodily properties like shape, size and weight—which seem attributable not only to the human being as such but also to the human body considered in abstraction from whether it is alive or dead, as well as to inanimate bodies. Thirdly they are subjects of things such as perception and intentional action which seem to bestraddle the mental and the physical.

Now the question is raised as to why we should attribute all these to the same subject rather than attributing the first group to the mind and the second group to the body, while viewing the third group as analysable into things which belong to the mind (experiences and intentions), things which belong to the body (alterations and movements), and co-ordinative relations between them.

In response to this question, some philosophers have proposed so-called transcendental arguments, supposed to show that thought and experience must be attributable to the same subject as the bodily properties because, otherwise, they will not be attributable to any subject at all.[44] Other philosophers have argued that there must be

---

[44]Thus, in *Individuals*, Chapter 3, Strawson excludes such analyses on the basis of a *reductio ad absurdum* argument, to the effect (i) that the 'no-ownership' account of experiences suggested by some remarks of Lichtenburg and of the middle Wittgenstein, and involved in any 'bundle' theory of the self such as might derive from Hume, can give no account of what makes the experiences non-contingently the experiences of the same person, and (ii) that the Cartesian dualist account gives no adequate explanation of why the experiences concerned should have a subject at all. One might think that although he had indeed produced a *reductio ad absurdum* argument in regard to the no-ownership account of experiences, the basic reason for the wrongness of that account is not the one which he gives (despite its validity) but that the notion of an experiencer is internal to the notion of an experiencing (and we have no notion of an experience distinct from the notions of an experiencing or

something wrong in supposing two subjects, a mind and a body, on the more obvious ground that no account could be given of the supposed causal or co-ordinative relations between the mental and the physical. Both these kinds of argument are essentially negative, arguing to the mental and physical's having the same subject only by reducing alternative views to absurdity. These arguments are, thus, entirely non-constructive, giving no positive insight into the unity of the supposed single subject—the thing they call a 'person'. They purport to show that thought, experience and intention belong to the same subject as bodily property, alteration, and movement, and that this attributing them to the same subject cannot be a mere legal fiction, but only by arguments which, in imaginary situations, would prove that a block of wood shaped like an animal which moved and seemed to talk was a person. They give us no insight into what it is which makes it a reality, not a legal fiction, that a bodily being with bodily parts and properties is also the subject of thought and experience.

We may contrast these negative approaches with that of Aquinas. He argues in effect: firstly, the perceiver is none other than the thinker (that which thinks is the same as that which perceives); secondly, the perceiver is a bodily being in the world (that which perceives is not a mere soul, but that which moves); therefore, the thinker is a bodily being in the world (that which thinks is the animal which moves and perceives).

The first proposition does not seem problematic.

It is unmistakable that perception has to be attributed to the same subject as intellection.[45] As Merleau-Ponty tells us: 'I say that my eyes see; that my hand touches, that my foot is aching, but these naive expressions do not put into words my true experience.

---

of its object), as both Berkeley and Kant recognized. But, since the notion of an experiencer is thus internal to the notion of an experiencing, the dualist is obviously right in insisting that experiences must have a subject. Therefore, the primary objection to Cartesian dualism which Strawson actually puts is not actually valid; however, this does not affect the force of the rest of his argument, in effect raising problems such as those raised by Locke as to why the same subject should be conceived as continuing so as to have different experiences at different times and as to how these experiences at different times are marked as experiences of the same subject.

[45]This is not to say that Aquinas does not use *reductio ad absurdum* arguments to rule out what would seem today perfectly mad views associated with Averroes and his followers whereby thought was to be attributed to some single intellect which moved the animal which was at the same time subject of perception and motion.

Already they provide me with an interpretation of that experience which detaches it from its original subject. . . . I distribute through my body perceptions which really belong to my soul, . . . If I consider them from the inside, I find one single, unlocalized knowledge, one single indivisible soul, and there is no such difference between thinking and perceiving as there is between seeing and hearing.'[46] In this way of thinking, Descartes and Merleau-Ponty, Plato and Aquinas, are one.[47]

But it is at this point that the divide occurs. For it is here that the question arises: what is this 'perception'? Is it a *cogitatio* of a mental substance, mysteriously united with a body, an 'experience' in the sense spoken of by the empiricists, Grice and Strawson?[48] Or is it an experience (at once an undergoing and an activity) of a bodily being as such?

(b) The key position of the question of the character of perception, emotion and sensation

To this question of the nature of perception, for Aquinas the answer seemed obvious: it was for him straightforward, or not a matter of dispute, that sight was the operation of a human being using a bodily organ (involving an *immutatio* in the pupil of the eye). From this involvement of the bodily organ it followed straightaway that perception was predicated of the human being, precisely as a bodily being, that is the subject of bodily predicates and possessed of bodily parts.[49]

---

[46] *The Phenomenology of Perception*, 212–213.

[47] The point seemed especially clear to Aquinas since he regarded the natural mode of use of the understanding as involving the use of imagination to provide its objects, refusing to consider human thinking in a purely formal way or in the abstract as if one might equally well be dealing with the way angels think.

[48] This way of conceiving experiences is to be found not only in 'Perception and its objects' (1969), but also in the seemingly much more alien context of *Individuals* (1959) where we strangely find depression and intentional action, but not perceptual experience, treated as the most natural examples of the logically psychophysical, and no argument making the physical or behavioral internal to perception.

[49] It should be noted that for Aquinas it was not just the act of perceiving as a whole which was irreducibly psychophysical; rather even the alteration in the sense-organ (*immutatio*, the imprint or impression on the sense-organ, in that sense of the word "impression" as the change in the sense-organ, not something purely psychological or purely mental, which it kept until Hume changed the usage) was something psychophysical which had to be described intentionally, i.e., in a way

The same view of perception as in its internal character involving the body, and therefore by implication as essentially predicated of a bodily being is the one which we argued in Chapter II, not chiefly on the basis of the involvement of a physical *immutatio*, but on the basis of the integration of perception and behaviour, the integration indicated by Merleau-Ponty and Hampshire. And in this way perception is one of the things which holds for us a key median position. Let us call it 'a psychosomatic attribute'. It is vital that there should be psychosomatic attributes which provide a bridge between the more intellectual attributes of the human being and the purely physical ones.

First, and most obviously, these attributes allow proof that there is, indeed, one subject for both mental and physical attributes. Thought has the same subject as the psychosomatic attributes, and these psychosomatic attributes have the same subject (the animal which is also a bodily thing) as bodily movement. This structure of argument, present in aboriginal form in Aquinas, works equally with any property or attribution of which it is conceded both that it belongs to the same subject as intellection and that it belongs to a subject of bodily predicates, possessed of bodily parts. Whether it be anger, pain or other forms of distress, various forms of desire or pleasure, and whatever the reason for making these two concessions—because of the physiognomy of their expression, because of the actions which reveal them, because of their realization through a bodily organ, or because of the experienced bodily excitement or sensations involved— it will remain that, once this pair of concessions is made, an argument of this structure will follow.

But it is not just that such psychosomatic attributes allow one to prove that there is one subject, the person or psychophysical being, for both mental and physical attributes but, secondly, that they begin to give content to these ideas of psychophysical being or 'person' and its unity. They exhibit how the conscious and the physical are united in a seamless web. In each case what they reveal is not primarily an inner mechanism corresponding to each such feature to the extent to which it involves the body, but primarily the integration and involvement of the body in a network of interrelated psychophysical attributes.

---

involving reference to the kind of mental directedness which it made possible, not in any merely physical way (George von Riet, *Problemes d'Epistemologie*).

If such attributes exhibiting this integration were absent, there would be no content in the assertion that intellection and bodily properties belong to the same subject. There would be no content, not primarily because the sameness of subject could not be proved, but because to assert it would explain nothing—it would be something upon which nothing turned, whereas, in fact, such unity is crucial both to the intelligibility of our ordinary descriptions of human life and to the explanation of what takes place in it.

We can dramatize the difficulty with which we are now concerned by considering the case of intentional action.

For a spirit or person to be a bodily thing, or equally, conversely, for a bodily thing to be a person, the body must not be, as it were, a mere appendage or adjunct to the person. There is no sense in saying of a homogenous lump of matter that it was the body of a person—even if a body was moved as chairs and such like are supposedly moved by spirits or poltergeists, the body concerned would not be, any more than the chairs, a subject of intelligence or intention. If writing began to appear in the sky regularly, we might infer that it was due to the will of an intelligent being, but would not be warranted in saying that the intelligent being was in the place where the expression of intelligence was located, i.e., up in the sky, any more than we assume the author of a book is where some copy of the book is—let alone warranted in saying that the intelligent being was to be identified with some physical reality present in the place concerned. The prime difficulty is as to what adequate reason has been given in such supposed cases either for attributing some bodily movement to the supposed spirit, or for attributing the thinking and willing of the spirit to some material body.

Any intentional agent as such—prescinding from the question whether he or she be God or angel, or whether he or she be a human or other bodily being, and from the question whether pure spirits are even possible—has a knowledge of his or her own action which is not by observation. This is part of the formal structure of intentional agency, and (leaving aside questions as to the real possibility of divine or angelic action) would cover the case of God's action in creating and conserving things in being and the supposed movement of bodies by devils and poltergeists, as well as human action.

We can readily bring perception within this context: if we could have thought of perception as something purely mental or intellectual, then we might have thought of the whole of the human being's conscious or mental life as possibly played out within some inner sphere so that the thing which was alive or lived a life was essentially a soul which stood in external relation to the body, external as a pilot is external to his ship, or a person is external to the clothes he wears.

What is it then, which forces us to say in the case of human action that the same thing causes movement as moves, rather than it being a soul or intellect which causes movement and, distinct from it, a body which moves? What is it about the very concept of perception which forces us to say that it is the same thing which has perceptual experience as moves?[50] How is it that the attribution of thought, the causation of movement and experience to the same thing as we attribute the movement itself and bodily alteration not merely chimerical—like attributing thought to a piece of sky in which a message appeared written or consciousness to a block of wood?

To these questions, as we have seen, it is no use returning non-constructive arguments alleging that, unless we accept sameness of subject, we will come to the absurd or impossible in accounting for personal and animal identity or for causation between the mental and the physical. For such arguments give no insight into the character of the unity of a person or psychophysical being, no insight into how it is that the attribution of both mental and physical properties might have the same subject. We may be able to argue transcendentally that the concept of psychophysical being—or of 'person' if we ignore other animals—is primitive, and not built up from separate concepts of mind and of body.[51] But this, by itself, does nothing to give any content to the concepts of psychophysical being or 'person', and nothing to explain what makes it non-chimerical to ascribe mental attributes

---

[50]It will be noted that I regard perception as an essentially psychosomatic concept, necessarily the attribution of mental and physical properties to the same subject, whereas I regard intentional action as essentially psychophysical in the human and animal case but only because of its integration with perception and sensation, not because the concept formally excludes two subjects.

[51]For instance, Strawson argues that it is a condition of our being able to ascribe mind-involving states ('experiences') to ourselves that we should also be able to ascribe them to others (*Individuals*, p. 99), and that it is, therefore, a condition of being able to ascribe such states to ourselves that the concept of a psychophysical being (as something which is subject of both mind-involving and purely physical properties) should be prior to that of an individual consciousness or mind (*op. cit.*, 102–108).

to something bodily.[52] This is what makes the hybrid character of
mind-involving predicates, whereby they involve logical connections
between the mental and behaviour, so crucial to the possibility of a
constructive content-giving approach to the concepts of psychophysical being and 'person'.

The question is of what makes it seem evident to us that the
'I', or the 'he or she', to which thought, agency or causation of
movement, and experience are ascribed is itself a bodily being. We
know ourselves not as external beings influential on movement and
affected by alterations in the body, but as being ourselves bodily
beings—the perceiver, the subject of emotion and sensation, the agent
being precisely the bodily being, animal or human, which moves and
is physically affected. And we understand and experience other human
beings and animals in the same way, not as if they might be machines
or purely physical systems in external relation to a dynamo (whether
a pure spirit or a brain), but as unitary bodily beings, at once bodily
and enjoying the life of a human being or animal.

And the answer seems to be that it is above all two things
which make it thus evident: firstly, the integration of perception with
behaviour, especially prominent in quite different ways in sight and
touch; and secondly, the integration of touch (as a kind of perception
involving contact) with behaviour, bodily sensation and the emotions
associated with these.

We have seen that the formal structure of intentional action does
not by itself formally exclude the case of a spirit or brain moving a body
while remaining distinct from it. It is the integration of intentional
action with perception, so that it is the same subject who sees where
the table is who also avoids walking into it or who touches it, which
primarily shows that the focus or centre of action is not a pure spirit
or mere brain, but the bodily being, animal or human, which moves

---

[52]Strawson has it in mind that it is a condition of these mind-involving states
being ascribable in the same sense to ourselves and to others that there should be
logical connections between these states and behaviour, allowing a double mode of
verification, and this is the next part of his argument (*op. cit.*, 105–108). However,
although this brings the hybrid character of mind-involving predicates, whereby they
involve logical connections between the mental and behaviour, to the fore in his
presentation, it does not make this hybrid character or double mode of verification
itself part of the initial transcendental argument. Rather this initial argument speaks of
'experiences' in a Cartesian way, prescinding entirely from their hybrid character.

about and explores. In a parallel way, it might be thought that the formal structure of visual perception did not exclude the case of clairvoyance, or seeing as it were without eyes from a vantage-point independent of the body. And again it is the integration between visual perception and behaviour, so that our visual perception is that of a being who looks around, walks or otherwise moves, and even explores, which primarily excludes thinking of the focus or centre of this perception as a pure spirit or something realized in the brain and shows it to be again the bodily being, animal or human, with its perception dependent on localized sense-organs.

But the bodily character of the being who touches, tastes, or smells, or who acts bodily or experiences anger, fear, or sensual desire or pleasure, is made clear also by the integration of these things with bodily sensations and awareness of varied kinds: the perception is not experienced separably from the bodily awareness or sensation, and kinaesthetic sensations and sensations associated with the emotions are experienced as integrated with the particular bodily action or emotion concerned.

It is wrong to give any particular privilege to bodily sensation. It is part of key structures of human and animal life, but not a peculiarly privileged part. For again the relation within the structures concerned is not one-sided—as if (for instance) it were only the sensation which plainly involved the body in its own right, and the perception, action or emotion only consequentially because they involved sensation. Rather sensations are only known as the sensations they are, in the bodily character and location which they have, through their being experienced as in essential connection with touch as in the case of pressure or heat, with movement as in the case of kinaesthetic sensation, or with various emotions evinced in various kinds of behaviour in the case of pain, or in other connections in other cases. A Cartesian might say that sensation does not require a body any more than a pain felt in a phantom limb requires an actual limb; but the integration of the different kinds of sensation with the other structural elements of psychophysical life is essential to their identity, and they could only be experienced even by a disembodied spirit *as if* it were embodied, just as the pain we know to be phantom is felt *as if* in (e.g.) the knee.

Each of the features we have instanced is essentially psychosomatic and will carry the weight of an argument of the structure we set forth above. But, in each case, the character of the feature concerned as essentially psychosomatic can only be established unmistakably by showing how, in animal and human life, it is locked into wider structures involving both perception and what I have called 'intentional' behaviour. And it is these wider structures, linking perception with intentional action, and linking perception, bodily action and emotion with sensation, which give content to the concepts of psychophysical being and 'person', and help explain what makes it non-chimerical to ascribe mental attributes to something bodily.

(c) The human body as a 'body with organs': the importance of a material underpinning of animal function

However, we have not yet gone the whole way necessary in order to show all that is wrong with Locke's flight of fancy that a material body might be the subject of thought, or our earlier mentioned fancies that a piece of sky in which messages appeared or a block of wood might be the subject of consciousness. More is required for a bodily being, that is a being which is subject of bodily properties and possessed of bodily parts, to be also the subject of mind-involving attributes. It is not just that the bodily thing has to behave in the right way—we can picture a lump of metal suitably painted and with suitable variations of shape grimacing, groaning, seeming to speak as if it had heard, and otherwise behaving as if it were a human being. But if the bodily thing is to be a human being, the matter of its body must play a functional role. The human body is as Aristotle said, 'a body with organs'.

We have already implicitly begun to fill out this picture. For what we have said implies that the body of a psychophysical being, human or animal, must be a body with all the organs needed for the being concerned to go in for the kinds of action, perception and expression of emotion characteristic of its species.

However, we need to go further than this, because there seems something misleading in the suggestion that it would make no difference to our certainty of our understanding that was a human being if his head was full of sawdust.[53] The inspiration of such a suggestion

---

[53]Kenny makes the milder suggestion that this would make no difference to our thinking that he had a mind (*Metaphysics of Mind*, p. 30), and it is true that behaviour could show mind even though the non-involvement of the brain would imply a difference in biological class. Malcolm's discussion in *Problems of Mind*, pp.

would seem to be the idea that, if everything about a being's behaviour were appropriate, then we could be certain from this that it was a human being. But, besides that, if its head turned out to be full of sawdust, we would be certain to classify it as of a quite different biological species so that the idea would seem simply mistaken, there seems to be something more deeply wrong: it seems to be implicit in this idea that for a bodily being to be the subject of mental attributes, all that matters is that it should behave the right way, whereas it also seems vital that its parts and organs should have a function in enabling it to behave in the right way.

It need not be a part of our ordinary pre-scientific concept of a human being that it is the brain rather than the heart or the liver which has this or that function in respect of enabling us to imagine or remember things or feel emotion, but it would seem to be part of this concept that something bodily (if not one thing then another) must have a positive role in respect of various such functions.[54] And a priori reasoning on Aristotelian lines would suggest that there must be some bodily functional structures to support all these functions, as well as the functions of sight, skin-sensation, etc., besides the more obvious structures of bone and muscle supporting the mechanics of movement. One would expect empirical studies to converge with such a priori or theoretical reasoning in establishing the kinds of dependence that different mental functions have on bodily ones[55] and to fill out the picture of how, in each case, this dependence works.

We said earlier that for it to be non-chimerical to suppose something bodily to be the subject of mental attributes it is required that there be the psychosomatic structures in human and animal life interrelating different attributes which we described. But now we have gone further and established that it is required that bodily function be internal to various key mental functions.

73–77, shows the same point of view. But it remains that bodily organization must be functionally relevant to human and animal behaviour as involving mind in some respect for the assertion of the unity of mind and body to be non-empty.

[54]In general our ordinary ways of thinking would not lead us to expect parts of the body with no functional structure at all.

[55]The idea of theoretical and empirical considerations converging is alien to atomistic empiricism but is a familiar feature of traditional geometry and the development of theoretical physics, and is to be expected within a framework of holistic and teleological explanation.

We saw in Chapter VIII that the sciences which proceed by considering bodily parts, individually and in their functioning together—for instance, the sciences of cell-physiology, of muscle, bone and joint function, of endocrinology, of neurology and the physiology of perception[56]—must retain a certain autonomy simply because any holistic view requires that bodily parts and substructures and functioning can, in identifiable respects, be considered in their own right. This was a corollary of the Aristotelian perspective whereby there is an interdependence of wholes and parts.

But now the conception of the internality of bodily function to various key mental functions will give new importance to the integration of these sciences which as it were work upwards from the parts with the over-arching psychophysical system of description and explanation which considers human beings and other higher animals in mind-involving terms.[57] We saw this earlier in a notable case in the involvement of different physical sub-systems of a neurological kind in various of the key mental functions integrated together in lives to which consciousness is integral.[58]

In these remarks I indicate the consequences of recognizing that the internality of bodily function to key mental functions is a part of what is involved in giving real content to the statement that human beings, like other animals, are bodily beings. The subject which thinks, lives and experiences is also the subject of bodily properties and possessed of bodily parts. But all this is within the earlier established framework whereby to be an animal with consciousness is to be

---

[56]For instance, the physiology of visual perception sheds important light on how the physiological registration of continuous movement is distinctively separate from the registration of distinct positions at different times relevant to the knowledge that something has moved. The experience of continuous movement exhibits the human being or animal as a psychophysical unity, but in this way we discover a physiological substratum to this experiencing of movement as continuous, rather than as merely a succession of distinct states.

[57]These sciences will, of course, also have to be integrated with other systems of description and explanation which consider human beings or other animals holistically, i.e., subordinate levels which abstract from the conscious or psychophysical—e.g., the level to which theories of acupuncture give access, albeit obscure—or if, independently of this, there are holistic aspects of life-structure which animals with consciousness have in common with the lower animals.

[58]But see n. 24 above.

ipso facto a being whose nature and behaviour transcends the physical in its description and explanation.

Conclusion of Part One

We have now accomplished a double purpose.

Firstly, we have demonstrated the falsity of materialism, and done this not by resorting to dualism, but simply by drawing out the consequences of what it is to be an animal with consciousness, drawing not upon something peculiar to human beings, but something they share with the higher animals. We shall see later, in Part Two of this book, that there are other arguments, ones drawing on things peculiar to human beings which have the same consequence that materialism is false. But it is vital that the falsity of materialism should not be regarded solely as a consequence of something peculiar to human beings, as if we could happily relegate the other animals to the level of biological *mechanisms*, and take satisfaction in supposing that human beings alone transcend the physical or mechanical. Rather those things which human beings share with the animals, viz., perception, sensation, emotion and intentional action, suffice to reveal—firstly at the level of description and secondly at the level of explanation—that neither human beings nor the higher animals can be regarded as mechanisms (not even a kind of mechanism labelled 'biological').

Further, we demonstrated this by showing the impossibility of conceiving human beings or higher animals as organizing minds or brains set within machines as if these realities—perception, sensation, emotion and intentional action—could be compartmentalized into distinct, causally related inner and outer aspects: inner aspects to do with mind or brain and outer aspects to do with behaviour, the sense-organs and the perceived world. Rather, these realities compel us to treat both human beings and the higher animals as wholes. It is not that thought, experience and intention have a mind, soul or brain as their subject or locus and that behaviour is to be attributed simply to the 'outer man', but that all are together to be attributed to the human being or animal as such.

Secondly, we have established the footing from which the rest of our thinking about human beings should proceed. We do not begin by considering human beings as persons in the generalized sense who just happen to be embodied, with their bodies parts of the natural universe. Rather we begin by considering human beings as bodily beings, parts and members of the natural universe, in community with the rest of that universe. This is their nature, what is required for their coming to be, for their maturing, and for the natural operation of all their faculties. For, as we shall see in Part Two, even what is peculiar to the human being, linguistic understanding and thinking, is something of its nature to have an expression, language, which is peculiarly psychophysical in character. And other seemingly distinctively human activities are equally unmistakable in their psychophysical character, notably the appreciation of art and music and the artistic production they involve.

And this is the background of any rounded consideration of human good. For it is part of this good to enjoy the natural universe in all its aspects, wondering at physical and biological nature, enjoying the whole range of bodily activity appropriate to human beings, and doing this in a context of respect for and community with the rest of nature. All these things are liable to take on a variety of distinctively human forms. And in general every body-involving experience or activity is liable to be affected by its being set firstly in the context set by self-consciousness, reflection and language and secondly, by the context of human relationship. But it remains that these contexts do not do away with the role of the material and biological in human life, nor with the community between human beings and the rest of the natural universe.

We can give these points edge by making clear their importance for any theology. For if the starting-point for our thinking about the human being is that human beings are parts and members of the natural universe, and if God has made the human being capable of responding to him, then this means that he has made a part of this universe capable of responding to him. It is mad to suggest that God is interested only in souls and pure spirits and sees no value in the physical universe except as a training ground, since the part of the universe which he has made capable of responding to him is also a part which sees value in and marvels at, participates in and is in community with, the universe of which it is a member—and yet, more than this, is a part the natural functioning of whose higher faculties involves the physical. No, rather, if indeed human beings along with the rest of the universe are the work of a divine creator, then this God in his design must have seen intrinsic value in the physical universe and set upon making some part of it capable of responding to it on behalf of the whole.

Therefore, if we are to see the human situation in a theological perspective, then precisely we must see the role of the human being (and any other reflective animal being which may exist in the universe) as being to respond to God as representative of the whole natural universe, in a context of community with and care for this universe. The body then is not some prison to be shackled off leaving some pure immaterial spirit free, and the physical and the physical universe some extraneous extra outside the scope of God's ultimate plan. Rather the whole point of creating human beings must include there being some permanent point in the physical and in the kind of expression and community the physical makes possible and involves.

Therefore, even if, as I shall argue in Part Two of this book, the human being is able to continue to exist, not only without legs or eyes, but in more global deprivation, the deprivation we call death, it remains that this death is a real privation, a real parting, a real sundering. The point of human existence from a theological perspective cannot be attained just by the disembodied human being enjoying the vision of God, but can only be realized in a completion which involves the restoration of the body—what is called a resurrection.

But now we must move forward to consider what is peculiar to the human being, and this is above all language and the understanding and thinking expressed by language—language not just as a communication system such as we may find amongst the other animals, but something whose structures are explored by linguists and whose intrinsic flexibility is exploited in every typical human communication, and whose structures involve not just consciousness but self-reflection.

And we shall discover in language, itself so clearly reflective of the psychophysical nature of the human being, the way in which human beings peculiarly transcend the physical. It is not only that their nature and behaviour like that of other higher animals requires explanation in non-physical terms, but that the understanding and thinking expressed by language are not themselves the operations of any bodily organ. This means that in their deliberations human beings are not limited or controlled by physical structures so as to be enclosed or predetermined in their thought. But more than this, it means that their existence is not limited or terminated by the body.

These are the concerns of Part Two of this book.

PART TWO

The Human Being as Spirit: Human Transcendence Revealed in Language

Introduction

In Part One, we saw firstly how the human being has to be treated as a single whole in *describing* human mental life. The mental, in perception, imagination, emotion, and intentional action, is not something which goes on in the brain and is not something which goes on in a distinct, non-material part of the human being or animal called the mind. Rather, the mental, in all these things, has to be attributed primarily to the human being as such as a psychophysical unity. The mental is inextricably linked, logically and not just causally, with the patterns of bodily behaviour in which it is reflected, and it is this inextricability which first gave us the conception of the human being as a unitary psychophysical whole rather than as an organized aggregate of parts, whether a physical aggregate of the brain with the other parts of the body or an aggregate of an immaterial soul with the physical parts of the body.

Then secondly we saw how the human being has to be conceived of in this way, not only for the purposes of *description*, but also for the purposes of *explanation*, even the explanation of human physical behaviour. If we consider the physical in the human being in purely physical or physiological terms, we are considering human behaviour only in certain aspects, abstracting these from a more rounded consideration. And if we abstract in this way we leave many things to seem uncaused and undetermined which can be seen as caused and determined in a more rounded psychophysical consideration. The fact that physical explanation is not self-sufficient even within its own sphere needs constantly to be kept firmly in view. It shows itself in the explanation of the forms of behaviour which the human being shares with other animals as well as in the explanation of human linguistic behaviour and the mutual understanding of speech between speaker and hearer on which we shall dwell much more below. It is not just that the mind in the living human being is not to be conceived of as something separate, but that the body itself is not to be conceived of as something either separate or self-contained. The body, when considered merely physically, is just as much an abstraction, got by ignoring other aspects of the reality with which one is dealing, as the mind. What we have in the human being is something in itself irreducibly psychophysical, neither body nor mind self-contained in nature, but simply the human being as such needing to be considered as a unitary subject or single whole.

From this it followed that human beings are not 'material enti-ties' or 'bodies' in the sense of 'things the fundamental laws governing whose behaviour are physical'—and this is simply because some of these laws are not physical but irreducibly psychophysical. Rather, while they are indeed bodily beings—things with bodily properties and parts—they also have mental or mind-involving properties and have to be understood not as 'bodies' but as essentially psychophysical entities, *sui generis* in nature.

And we showed all these things by considering the nature of such things as perception and intentional action. From this it followed that the same things will be true of all those animals which share with human beings such things as perception, imagination, memory, emotion and intentional action—intentional in the sense we described in Chapter IX. That is, all these animals have to be conceived in this same holistic way as essentially psychophysical unities. They are like human beings in being bodily things in the sense of having bodily properties and parts, but also like human beings in having other irreducibly psychophysical properties key to their nature and to the understanding and causation of their behaviour. Therefore, these animals are no more 'material beings' or 'bodies' than human beings are: it is just not true that all the fundamental laws governing their behaviour are physical.

In this way our account placed human beings firmly amongst the animals. Indeed, if we get away from the false idea of animals as biological machines, and recover the conception of an animal as an organic whole with a certain kind of life requiring its nature and behaviour to be understood holistically, we could regard the statement "The human being is an animal" as precisely capturing our central contention.

In all this, we restored the holistic Aristotelian perspective which was mostly abandoned in the seventeenth century. It had been aban-doned in favour of the idea that the material is self-contained in its nature and that its behaviour is to be explained in terms of this purely physical nature except in so far as external entities, Gods, minds or others, interfere with it. And this idea, we had shown, is grossly misguided: the material and physical is not thus self-contained. Materialism as an account of biological nature has to be rejected, not in the name of dualism, but in the name of holism.

It is against this background that, in this Part Two of the present book, I explore the significance of language as what differentiates human beings from other animals.

My primary purpose in Part Two of the book is to make clear schematically how the transcendence of the body implied by language is compatible with the holistic perspective. My argument turns on a certain theory of language. But in this book I present this theory only in bare summary—to do otherwise would be to turn aside into elaborate discussions of semantic theory and grammar belonging to another book, not to a book on the nature of the human being. For within the philosophy of human nature, the main need is to grasp how it is that we can recognize the human being's transcendence of the body without any return to dualism. It belongs to quite another book to develop the details of the required account of language.[1]

For our present purpose, what matters is that human life exhibits kinds of understanding and a kind of thinking which cannot be explained in behaviouristic terms and cannot be regarded as the state or

---

[1] I develop the required theory in my *The Expressiveness of Words: the key to the nature of language* (forthcoming).

Let me mention some of the elements of this theory which I draw upon in my argument in Chapters X to XII. For instance, we have to show how it is the norm for some context-indicated elements to be integral to 'sense' as the concern of semantics, redefining the boundary between 'semantics' and 'pragmatics', and relegating pragmatics (conversational implicatures, perlocutions and the like) to an entirely secondary and derivative place. This is key to the proper understanding of the *langue/parole* distinction central to Chapter X. Again, like Wittgenstein, I regard force as a component or aspect of sense and reject the current orthodoxy that the two are separable. This contributes to the argument of Chapter XI. Thirdly, I indicate how syntax is to be regarded as the projection at a formal level of constraints introduced by semantic structures. This is relevant to my view in Chapter XII that there does not need to be a neurological basis for grammatical functioning.

But merely to specify these points, the relation of semantics to pragmatics, the relation of 'sense' to 'force', the relation of grammar to semantics, is to make plain that establishing them against objection will take us into quite different areas of controversy and technical argument than those on which the present book is centred.

operation of any bodily organ or material system—in particular not as a state or operation of the brain.

In all this, I do not begin in the abstract with the notions of understanding in general or of thinking in general, but with that particular kind of psychophysical activity which defines the difference between the human being and other animals, namely language. I am concerned here with language in the full sense—not language in the loose sense in which we may attribute it also to the higher apes—language as that which includes within itself the whole range of structures with which linguists are typically concerned. I argue that the whole working of language involves understanding at two levels, an understanding of *langue* in virtue of which words or elements of speech have some meaning in their own right and an understanding of *parole* or speech, which is the exercise of the underlying understanding of *langue*. These kinds of understanding are exercised both in speaking and in thinking in the medium of words. And it is these kinds of understanding and this kind of thinking which I argue cannot be the states or operations of any bodily organ or material system.

This opens out a second avenue for the refutation of mechanism.

But it also raises a further question. Even granted that these kinds of understanding and thinking are not bodily states or operations, does it follow that human existence transcends the body?

And this question puts us in face of a puzzle.

While the holistic account of human nature offered in Part One was plainly incompatible with materialism, quite excluding the reduction of the human or the animal to the physical or mechanical, it might at the same time seem to exclude any after-life for the human being or any idea of human existence transcending the existence of the body. It might seem that we had made the bodily essentially involve mind but had done this only at the expense of making mind or soul essentially dependent on body. If, like Aristotle and Aquinas, we express the holism we have spoken of in terms of a doctrine of soul, does it not seem that this non-dualistically conceived soul will be just as dependent on the body as the body on the soul—for, in Aristotle's terminology, are not form and matter correlative?

The case is not an open-and-shut one. How these questions were dealt with within the Aristotelian framework in earlier times can be understood if we grasp that the most indispensable feature of that framework was not the dependence of soul on body, but rather the fact insisted upon in Chapter VIII, that the material is not self-contained in nature, that its behaviour is to be explained holistically in psychophysical, not just physical terms. In Aristotelian terms this means that a body cannot exist without its form and so in the animal case means that the animal body cannot exist without the soul. Hence, it comes about that an Aristotelian will explain the essential unity of soul and body primarily in terms, not of the dependence of soul or form upon body, but of the dependence of body upon soul. The dependence of body on soul, independently of other reasons, by itself suffices to make soul and body constitute one substance, not two. And in this way the Aristotelian idea of soul as form leaves room for saying that, in some case, the soul might continue to exist after the living body, but not vice versa.

But one can accept the Aristotelian holism of Part One without committing oneself to the language of matter and form or the idea of the soul as form of the body.

Therefore the question arises, firstly, of the viability of any non-dualistic account of soul and, secondly, of the coherence of supposing in the Aristotelian and Thomistic way that in the human case this non-dualist soul can exist separately after the perishing of the body. It is essential to a non-dualistic conception of soul that perception, memory, imagination, understanding, thought, and all other such concrete attributes are predicated primarily of the human being or animal as such, and that, if they are predicated of a human or animal soul, what is meant has to be understood by reference to what is meant when these things are predicated of the human being or animal. And it is vital always to hold to the principle that whatever we express by speaking about the soul is to be explained and understood in terms of what we can say about the human being or animal as such.

And it is in accord with this that I show how non-dualistic ways of speaking of the soul are to be understood as embedded within an overall holistic viewpoint. When it came to considering how it is that human existence transcends the body, Aquinas was able to give coherence to Aristotle's idea that, although in other animals soul could not exist separately after the body had perished, in the human case *nous* or mind could do so. He suggested that, although the human soul has to originate with the body and needs the body for its natural mode of functioning, nonetheless it has an existence in its own right because it has an operation in its own right, namely, understanding. Now it is this last, the connection between a thing's having an operation in its

350 THE HUMAN BEING AS SPIRIT

own right and its existing in its own right, which gives us the clue to how we should express human transcendence of the body. For us, the primary way of expressing this transcendence should not be in terms of the soul existing in its own right and not by right of the body, but in terms of the human being existing in its own right and not by right of the body because it, the human being, has states and operations which are not bodily. And it is because we can speak of the human being as existing in its own right that we can speak derivatively of the human soul in this way, and not the other way round. This is how it is that even here ways of speaking about the soul are embedded and underpinned by ways of speaking about the human being as such.

This then is the argument which we shall explore in the next six chapters, an argument that human existence transcends the body, but an argument of an entirely non-Cartesian kind—an argument not from consciousness (because, as we have argued, perception, imagination, and emotion, besides being shared with other animals, do not involve such transcendence), but from language and linguistic understanding and thinking—in this way, as we shall see, taking its starting point from the specifically animal form of intellectuality. In this argument we have no truck with dualist conceptions of mind or soul and leave the human being still standing foursquare with the animals—with an animal nature and an animal form of life, sharing perception, imagination and the like with them. The being whose existence we show to transcend the body remains a true member of the physical universe, in his or her thought and concern not determined by matter but able to reflect upon the world and its situation and be in a special way representative of it and its value. And it is as such a member and representative of the physical world that, if the whole world has God as its author and sustainer, he or she stands before God.

X. Language and the Understanding of Language

1. Language as What Differentiates Human Beings from Other Animals

We have seen how the human being is an animal, and seen what human beings have in common with the higher animals—perception, imagination, emotion, and perceptually directed action from emotion. What we have now to identify is the key peculiarity which differentiates the human being from the other animals, and this, I shall say, is language—language in that primary sense of the word whose structures, each inseparable from the others, I will be sketching in this chapter.[1]

In specifying the fundamental peculiarity of the human being amongst the animals, one is not trying to name some property (say, intellectuality) independent of being an animal as, for instance, concavity is independent of being a nose, but to name that particular form of intellectuality which fits human beings as animals in the way that (say) snubness is the form of concavity which fits being a nose. We do not have any way of imagining forms of intellectuality appropriate to angels or to God, even though in regard to them we may adopt structures of speech appropriate to persons and beings with understanding. But the only form of intellectuality of which we have any grasp, which is not merely structural, or of whose realizations we have any imagination, is coordinate with rationality or the use of reason—in the way that, to take two very different cases, the understanding of a theory and the understanding of a person are coordinate with the understanding of an ordered exposition of the theory or with explanations of the person's motivations. And we have no concept of rationality which is not the concept of something linguistically expressible.

---

[1]The sense in which the 'languages' learnt by chimpanzees under human instruction are indeed 'language', but only in a secondary sense, will be clarified later at the end of Section 3 of this chapter.

351

In speech, which we here identify as the characteristic realization of the kind of intellectuality which differentiates the human being from the other animals, we have what is obviously still an animal or bodily activity because it involves the mouth, the tongue, and in brief the voice. And whatever the 'substance' used in language, whether sounds, marks on paper, the dots of braille, the signs of deaf-and-dumb, or other, the activity of producing linguistic signs is a bodily one showing all the features of the psychophysical which we have dwelt upon. (What we have to see here is that what makes speech bodily and animal in mode is that the characteristic expression of intellectuality is bodily, not that the understanding expressed in it is some inner bodily state: that would be quite another matter.) And, although there can be communication with properly linguistic structure in media other than sounds, it belongs to the nature of the human species that the spoken word is the mode of linguistic communication primarily characteristic of it.

Indeed, in the inseparability of sentence and sense, we come upon the most extreme example of the unity of mind and body in an action, here not just the unity of intention and act in intentional action but the unity of understanding and speech in 'understandingly speaking'. And in 'understandingly hearing' we have the most unmistakable and rich example of the unity of the act of 'perceiving as' wherein what is perceived and how it is perceived (that is, not the means of perception but as what it is perceived) cannot be extricated from one another. At the same time, in speaker-hearer knowledge of both sentence and sense, we have the paradigm example of the sharedness of first-person and other-person knowledge and community in the meaning of what they say.

(a) The peculiarity of human language

Some will say that language is essentially a communication system and that communication systems are common amongst the highest non-human animals. But I say that it is a mistake to take communication systems as a genus of which human language is a species within a scientific classification. Squids and fishes are both sea-animals and have structures geared to submarine life, but they are not thereby of one biological genus or phylum. In like manner, non-linguistic signals and language-dependent expressions of sense both have structures geared to inducing beliefs in others, bringing about actions on the part of others, etc., but this does not mean that being signals or being geared to such effects (even if convention is involved) is what is most fundamental in their nature. It is not, I shall say, signalling which is the genus to which speaking belongs, perhaps with the presence of certain kinds of convention as its differentia, but something quite different—what I shall call 'expressiveness'—which is the essence of language.

We have to ask what it is about human linguistic capacity which gives it at once its extraordinarily integrated structure and at the same time the open-endedness which is characteristic of it. To this question I reply that the answer lies in the right understanding of the relation of words to sentences, and it is this feature whereby words do not merely identify the meanings of sentences but *express* these meanings which I call the expressiveness of language and which I regard as the clue to all the other features of language. The products of speakers and writers are not mere tools to achieve certain ends, but are expressions of a sense, so that as well as speaker and hearer there is this third thing, an object of understanding, situated in between—the expression with its life or sense.

Words can only have this expressive capacity (with the result that 'sentences' express something, since, after all, 'sentences' as speech-units are nothing but words in a certain order, intonation or mode of combination, and context) because of the double way in which they have meaning. On the one hand, as dictionary-items (lexemes or items of *langue*) they are nodes of a skill—what we may call knowledge of their *langue*-meaning—a skill realizable in an informally understood open-ended range of logically distinguishable types of use of the word concerned, i.e., in a spread of ways of speaking which cannot be captured in any effectively applicable rule. Yet it follows from this that, on the other hand, as words in use (sentence-factors, to be understood as they occur in speech or *parole*) they possess in each use something which we may call speech-meaning, a different speech-meaning for each of the logically distinguishable types of use just referred to. It is because the words we use in speech are not just counters or cyphers but possess *langue*-meaning, i.e., because they are nodes of understanding in their own right, that when we use them in speech they are able to express something with the result that the speech itself expresses something.

It is this leeway between word-meaning in *langue* and word-significance in *parole*, in use in the full speech context which gives language the open-endedness, flexibility and fecundity associated with it, as well as being the root of its unformalizability.

The much vaunted capacity to make infinite use of finite resources which is characteristic of human intellectuality does not result from the indefinitely large number of times we can repeat certain operations in logic or in grammar—operations such as conjunction, negation and conditionalization, addition, multiplication, and exponentiation. In thought we can reach to a comprehension of only a small number of iterations in speech. The capacity to extend this comprehension by surveying pieces of writing and in an indirect sense by deeming computers to do it vicariously shows very little of importance about the nature of human intellectual capacity—after all, it is not by iterating an operation 10^{20} times that we estimate some galaxy to contain 10^{20} stars, and we do not need to complete any very long process in order to prove the results we want in mathematics in the calculus or analysis (of course, there is no question of completing any infinite process). Rather, what matters is our capacity to initiate and respond to new types of enquiry and to handle new situations in thought. This is where the unlimitedness or potential infinity of what the human being can do with finite resources arises, and it is a result of the open-endedness and flexibility of words, the result of the leeway between word and sentence and of the many-track character of the kind of disposition or skill which is called 'knowing the meaning of a word'.

Rather, therefore, this much vaunted capacity to make infinite use of finite resources results from this fecundity associated with the use of words, the fecundity whereby in the context of language the *langue*-understanding of a particular word opens the door to an indefinite number of logically distinguishable types of use of the word as a sentence-factor, an unlistable spread of different *parole*-meanings arising out of one initial node in *langue*-meaning.

This, then, is the distinctive locus of unformalizability of what some think of as the non-mechanical and non-rulebound in human thought. In this way, it is the understanding exhibited in language—and not the ingenious leaps in thought whereby a stick becomes a tool, or two sticks are discovered to dovetail and made to form a longer tool—which provides the differentia of the human species amongst the animals. I thus avoid the conception which makes understanding in general, or the understanding which is important for differentiating the human being, consist in insightful leaps from one thought to another thought or from an experience or set of experiences to a thought or from a thought to a decision as to how to act upon it. Such insight is common amongst the highest non-human animals and is hardly peculiar to human beings in a way that language is. Rather the kind of understanding which differentiates human beings from beast and angel alike is the kind of understanding exemplified every time a sentence in speech or writing is understood—every time the appreciation of the *langue* of words is exercised in an appreciation of their *parole* in speech.

In this book, I present only a sketch of the account of language which needs to be given, leaving the required fuller discussion of the view I propose to another place. In this book, I shall offer only such broad strokes of the brush as are conducive to convey the general picture—to make it intelligible, not here to prove it.

(b) Why we pick on language as the differentiating feature of human beings: answers to objections

It may be asked why I pick on language as the key peculiarity of human beings, rather than thinking in general, or the general capacity for reasoning and deliberation, or the capacity to make intuitive leaps of thought, or some form of understanding or contemplation conceived of as the goal of the intellect.

In giving a glimpse of the fecundity and open-endedness in thought which language in its *langue/parole* structure opens out, I have already given some indication as to why language should be given such privilege. But this becomes even more plain if we take a global view of what is required in a specific characterisation of the human.

As already remarked, we have no concept of rationality except in terms of what is linguistically expressible and that what we are looking for is, not something (be it intellectuality or rationality) abstracted from its human mode of realization, but something defined according to its specifically human way of being realized. And, in general, in judging of human capacities one should define them according to their humanly most complete realizations. Accordingly, since the humanly most complete realization of the capacity for reason and deliberation is in speech, it is in terms of a relation to speech or possible speech that we should define rationality. That is, as intention is to be defined and understood according to its role in intentional action, and it is intentional action which is the complete realization of the capacity called the will, so it is (for human beings) understandingly speaking and understandingly hearing which are the most complete realizations of the capacity called the reason. We betray the conception of the human being as an animal in favour of a dualism of mind or brain and body when we abstract intention or choice from action, and likewise we betray the conception of the human being as an animal in favour of this dualism if we abstract thought from its expression. And as human beings we have no means of disciplining our thoughts and judgements except through disciplining how they are expressed, no access to or handle upon them which does not involve their actual or possible expressions.

The clue that in considering the character of a human capacity we must consider it as orientated towards its complete realization enables to see two further apparent problems in their proper light: firstly the problem of how it is that the typical expressions of linguistic capacity are not isolated statements of judgement or pieces of inference, but extended pieces of linguistic interchange, discourse, poetry, drama, and so forth; and secondly the problem of how one should speak of human development. Let us consider each in turn.

(1) Propositions and series of propositions in which the later derived logically from the earlier do not occur in isolation or have their proper meaning and significance except in some context of linguistic interchange, carrying with it the presumption of something of human interest, truth, understanding, sympathy or some other good. And such human contexts and concerns may set a place, not only for statements intended to express truth or for conversations of different kinds, and, in more formal settings, for interrogations in law courts and series of propositions intended as demonstrations, but also for much more extended pieces of linguistic performance. We should envisage here such works as the *Iliad*, the tragedies of Aeschylus and Sophocles, Shakespeare's *King Lear*, and Goethe's *Faust*; the *Phaedrus* and *Phaedo* of Plato; the Psalms and the Book of Job; the Song of Songs, Augustine's *Confessions*, Dante's *Divine Comedy*, and the poems of St. John of the Cross taken together with his commentaries. We should also include Thucydides' *Peloponnesian War*, the *Elements*

of Euclid and the *Principia* of Newton, *Das Kapital, Pride and Prejudice, The Brothers Karamazov,* and *Ulysses.*[2] It is important to note that the capacity for extended linguistic work does not arise only or primarily with the written word, but is present in the unwritten oral linguistic production: there were extended poems, speeches and rituals before they were written down.

These, then, are amongst the works, the realizations, or products —in Aristotle's word, the *erga*—of language. They have a unity, at once a unity of thought and a linguistic unity, whereby the meaning of words and sayings in the earlier parts of a work is unfolded in the whole—and indeed not even so completely unfolded as to be incapable of further unfolding by the author or by later interpreters, so long as it can be clear that the unfolding is a true unfolding, faithful to the intent and direction of what went before, and not alien in respect of it. And this is not peculiar to works of literature and theoretical study, but common to all speech and writing in the conversations and interchanges of life and love, of anger, fear, and hope, of friendship and of worship.

(2) Next we come to the problem of how we should speak of human development.

Certainly, children, who have just been born, and for some time following, cannot speak, but have to learn how to vocalize, how to reciprocate linguistically by imitation, how to play using language talking to themselves as well as with others, and thus, in stages, how to communicate linguistically. But likewise we should say that their capacity to think advances in stages, and not independently of their advance in the capacity to communicate linguistically in some linguistic substance (not necessarily words as the example of the blind, deaf, and dumb Helen Keller shows). Human beings are animals and thereby beings whose basic capacities can only achieve their realization in stages. One must not think of the learning to speak and to understand what is said as a development in which a fully developed mind finds expression, rather than as a development in which the mind itself develops. Thought can, as it were, develop a little ahead of speech,

---

[2]These remarks are not compromised by the fact that many of the large scale works one will bring into consideration here are, to some extent, compilations, cf. n. 6 below.

but it can only advance that little way ahead in virtue of symbiosis with some already achieved unfolding of linguistic capacity. This is for two reasons, one because of what I shall later call the allusiveness of thought and the other because of the way one stage in language learning may be incipient of the next. Language has, I shall argue in Section 3, a unitary structure so that all human learning of language takes place within the context of this structure as an unfolding of a unitary basic capacity for language. Because of this, utterances made at an earlier stage of learning a particular language may have a meaning which is only differentiated linguistically at a later stage (I mean merely at a somewhat later stage, not the final stage of the adult mastery of the language). Now all thought takes place within the context of such unfolding of linguistic capacity and may, therefore, have a content only expressible at a later stage.

It will be recalled that I asked why we should pick on language as the key peculiarity of human beings, rather than thinking in general, or the general capacity for reasoning and deliberation, or the capacity to make intuitive leaps of thought, or some form of understanding or contemplation conceived of as the goal of the intellect. My answer to three key objections will make clear how all these issues are to be dealt with.

(i) Objection that thinking can be in images, not words

Firstly, it is argued that thinking need not be in words because it can be in images.

To this I reply that there is no pure thinking in images. Rather what is called thinking in images involves not the imagination alone, but this in the context of some thinking in the medium of words. An image or model is useless without whatever enshrines the under-standing of how to handle it. It is not that the images always came voluntarily or that it is as if they were there before the mind first and one then decided what to do with them and how to handle them. Clearly, thinking in images is not like this. Accordingly, one would do better to say that an image or model is functionless without whatever enshrines the handling of it. In the case of subhuman animals its 'meaning' is determined by its context of behavioural disposition. But, if the handling of images is an activity distinct from what be-longs to behaviour and behavioural disposition, still always there has to be some activity determining the context or role of the image. E.g., if the image is of one's husband and is to have some role in thinking, it is not enough that the image float about in the mind, but rather it is necessary also that it be thought of in some way, for instance as the image of one's husband: and what is involved here is of the sort which is linguistically expressible or coordinated with linguistic understanding.

I do not wish to denigrate the role of the imagination. On the contrary, if we consider language not just as a system of signals, but as having expressive content, it absolutely depends on imagination. Without the imagination, language would present only a formal structure without content. Even concepts as general as cause, act and substance depend for their possession of content, the content which debars them from applying to abstract subject-matters such as numbers, upon the possibility of presenting examples in the imagination. Imagination here (as relevant for instance to the concept of "cause") is, of course, not to be conceived in terms merely of the having of images, as it were in the presentation of a series of snapshots, but rather as analogous to a living through or living through again of various interactions and histories—the way of living or re-living them which we call 'living or re-living in the imagination' (cf. Chapter XI, 3).

However, it is vital not to misconceive the role of examples. The key thing to understand is our freedom in the use of them. Indeed, when we speak of the imagination we usually have this freedom in mind much more than any involvement of images, and in particular the capacity to use language in an intelligible way going beyond already given paradigms. This is most obvious in literature, but is vital to general enquiry in every field. We are not tied in our use of words to the learning situation, whether, as in the case of less general words, this type of situation is of a kind to define their literal meaning, or whether, as in the case of the more general words, the literal meaning has no proper definition. If we speak of the imagination in terms of the notion of 'images', we find the image of the sweet transferring itself from tastes to persons, the image of the loud transferring itself from sounds to colours, and so forth, so that in such cases what is called imagination has to do with the freedom to use images to give content or body to our thought even though what we might call the pictorial or sensory content has been departed from. And this freedom is primarily a function of intellect, showing itself in how we use language, not a function of simple imagination.

Moreover we should note further that the range of this freedom is exactly the one marked by language with its open-endedness, not limited in its workings to the range which keeping to formalizable rules would require. That is, this freedom is a function precisely of the kind of intellect exhibited in language and not of any supposed merely ratiocinative intellect conceived of as limited to the range allowed by some set of formalizable rules.

(ii) Objection that there are many unverbalizable forms of intellectual experience and activity

Secondly, it may be argued that in considering the kind of intellectuality which differentiates human beings from other animals one should not consider intellectual activity in general, but some form of understanding or contemplation conceived of as their goal. And this, it may be held, is some kind of experience which is not verbalizable in the ultimate (it may be suggested), the vision of God, but also (more obvious to us) such things as the contemplation and enjoyment of the wonders of land, sea and sky, by day or by night, the different enjoyment of the wonders presented by the theoretical scientist or by the mathematician, and the enjoyment of works of architecture, art, and, most notably, music.

However, in order that these things should enter into the life of a rational animal, they have to enter as objects to be preferred for some reason or because of something which the heart or mind apprehends as a reason, and not merely in the way that sensory pleasures enter into the lives of the higher animals in general without there needing to be anything apprehended as a reason. That is, they have to enter into the structure of the life of a rational animal in a way appropriate to them, and this involves their presenting themselves to deliberation in an appropriate way. In the second place, although in each case the good which is wondered at (what makes it good) is not expressed or not fully expressed by discourse, in every case discourse—not bare individual statements, but extended pieces of discourse such as we spoke of above, taken in context—can express something of why the object of wonder is such and do this in such a way as to be distinctive in each case of the case concerned.

Thus, in these two ways, the kinds of experience concerned do not enter into human life in an arbitrary manner, as intrusions in no integration with or no hierarchical relation to other facets of that life—in the way that a dualist might imagine some strange new introspectible sensation, of different quality to all others and for no assignable reason enrapturing the soul in a distinctive way. Rather, in these ways, we have marked out how these kinds of experience or contemplation—even in the case of the vision of God which surpasses any possibility of imagination, expression or comprehension—enter into and fulfil human life in a structured and determinate way. Furthermore, because our explanation has required that these kinds of experience or contemplation should enter human life in a determinate relation to possible deliberative and linguistic activity, it does not matter for our argument whether they are strictly 'purely intellectual' or whether they involve the senses or, if they involve the senses, how they do so.[3] It does not matter because whatever the character of the experience or contemplation, there will still be this same requirement.

Therefore, it is not these kinds of contemplation and experience as such, but rather the structures of deliberation and linguistic capacity which set their place in human life which mark the form of intellectuality distinctive of human beings as opposed to 'pure spirits' such as God and the angels are believed to be. And it is this form of intellectuality, shaped to an animal form of life as snubness is to a nose, rather than intellectuality as such which we have to take note of in order to understand the human place amongst the animals.

Our treatment of these in varied ways passive forms of contemplation and experience provides the key to our approach to a spread of forms of non-linguistic activity which still seem intellectual. I have in mind particularly musical composition whether it take place in the mind or on paper or in improvisation in the act of performance, although there are a multiplicity of other examples with other arts, crafts and skills. Again our argument does not require us to draw a precise line between 'purely' intellectual and other activity, e.g., to assess the extent to which an activity involves sensory and behavioural capacities, as in 'hearing' the relation of sounds while writing a musical composition.

We must, of course, distinguish between two ways in which musical composition or production, and in different ways other forms

---

[3]It seems obvious that there is an integration between sense and intellect in the appreciation of nature, music, art and architecture, even that which enters into religious worship, but an integration which takes different modes in different cases.

of artistic production and practical activity, are intellectual activities. In one way, they are intellectual activities (and this extends to dancing, rock climbing and tennis playing) inasmuch as there is rational or deliberate planning or judgement exhibited in the activity concerned, e.g., in the musical case both in global planning and in the detailed ordering of the notes, the adjustment of the tempo, etc., etc. However, although such planning or judgement is typically expressed only in the action and does not need to be expressed in thinking in the medium of words beforehand, nonetheless it is of a sort to be linguistically expressible, and is not what we are concerned with. Rather, what matters to us is a second way in which such activities may in some cases (let us keep music in view as representative) be properly described as intellectual, namely that they express, deliver or communicate something—typically not something expressible or intended to be expressible in words, something which may be spoken of in terms of such things as excitement, struggle, fury, anxiety, expectancy, foreboding, sadness, joy, serenity, wonder, or a sense of worship. The music may even communicate a sense of the object or kind of object of the emotion concerned; but it does not do this in a linguistic way as if it made a statement about the object, unless in a metaphorical sense of the expression "making a statement". It may seem to prescribe an attitude, but again this is not the 'issuing of an imperative' except in a metaphorical sense.

It is not for this book to give an account of music or the other arts, in their composition, production or performance, or of how they are intellectual and emotional in the way we are concerned with. Rather what matters for our present argument is that, in order for them to have their proper place in a life which is properly human and not purely angelic nor purely animal or instinctual, they still need to be integrated, equally in production as in experience, in a determinate relation to possible deliberative and linguistic activity.

At this point, we should add in a subsidiary comment arising from the alleged possibility of distinctively human cognitive capacity independently of linguistic capacity.

Now we have just seen how, for a cognitive capacity to be of a distinctively human kind, it must be in some integration with fully human patterns of action, and (we might add) human social relationship, both of which require integration with the exercise of linguistic capacity. However, it is a mistake to envisage what we call 'natural language', by which we mean something tied to the mode ('modality' or 'substance') of sound or voice, as the only form of such exercise.

Rather, we should picture an underlying general linguistic capacity, open to being realized in many different ways according to the upbringing or culture in which it matures and the variable modes (voice, writing, gesture, etc.) in which this realization (in different degrees) takes place. Such a realization we call a *langue*—effectively a different *langue*[4] according to particular stages of maturing and disabilities, as well as more obviously according to different linguistic cultures. And any such *langue* will show itself in *parole* or linguistic communication, in the understanding of *parole* or linguistic communication, and in thinking in a linguistically formed way. Therefore, when one is confronted with the lack of development of *langue* in a particular dimension or mode—perhaps because of disability or the shape of a particular culture—or from loss (due to injury) of the capacity to use pre-existing language abilities in a particular dimension or mode, one is not to infer that the underlying linguistic capacity has found no development in any dimension. In particular, there is no general inference from the presence of cognitive capacity without 'natural language' (with its dependence on all the sub-systems involved in the use of the spoken word) to its being independent of human beings' underlying linguistic capacity to be unfolded in some dimension or other.[5]

Accordingly, the possibility of some distinctively human development of cognitive capacity without natural language implies nothing contrary to our general perspective. It may be independent of a corresponding rounded development of natural language, but it is not

---

[4]Or perhaps, at stages which are incomplete because of immaturity or disability, what we should call a 'quasi-*langue*', since we may well think of a *langue* as a sociological reality correlative with a community of adults.

[5]I develop these perspectives further in Chapter XII, Section 3, and mention them here in order to supply a corrective to such apparent suggestions as those of D.A. Allport in 'Language and Cognition' and 'Components of the Mental Lexicon' (p. 399 f.). In particular, the way in which a *langue* or quasi-*langue* as realized in a particular individual may involve a differentiation of word-meaning for the same 'word' in different 'modalities' (speech, writing, etc.) should be considered a standard possibility, and therefore constitutes no particular difficulty if realized in peculiar forms in people subject to this or that handicap (*pace* E. Funnell and D. A. Allport, 'Non-linguistic cognition and word meanings').

independent of some unfolding of human beings' underlying general linguistic or semantic capacity.

(iii) Objection that it is the giving of reasons in deliberation which is the key differentiating feature of man

Thirdly, it may be argued that it is precisely the giving of reasons in theoretical and practical deliberation which is the distinguishing feature of human beings and that of this the expression of these things in language is a mere symptom.

In arguing in this way, the objector makes the capacity for seeing what follows, if certain assumptions are made, for discovering valid inferences and judging whether suggested inferences are valid, into the centre of attention in thinking about what differentiates the human being from the other animals. In this the objector has considered only the capacity for valid argument or for the selection of technically appropriate means and paid no regard to the truth of the premises taken or the value of the ends, and no regard to the question whether the suggested conclusions or means are not so objectionable as to bring the acceptance of these premises or the pursuit of these ends into question. The objector has thus entirely neglected any global consideration of what is required for getting at truth or the attainment of understanding and any global consideration of what is required for getting at or respecting the good. But to do this is to leave out consideration of the point of valid inferences in theoretical and practical reasoning in human life—for the point of requiring one's inferences to be truth-preserving arises from the value of truth and is quite lost if the starting-points of the inferences are not true. The objector has substituted valid inference for right understanding and right judgement, action and pleasure, and substituted cleverness for theoretical and practical wisdom, as the ends and virtues of human intellect.

If we are to understand how the human being is addressed towards truth, understanding, and preference for the good, we have to realize that it involves many different ways (for different types of proposition) of being true, many different ways of being recognized or shown to be true, and many different ways in which a thing can be appropriate to be preferred. There are no formal rules which allow these different ways of being true, known to be true, or good to be brought under one definition or to be made commensurable with one another. In using expressions like "is true", "is provable (capable of being shown to be true)", or "is good", we are using notions which cannot be formalized or applied according to mechanical rule. It does not follow that they cannot be used or that they cannot be used objectively. There is nothing non-objective in our transitions from Aristotelian to Newtonian and then to relativistic mechanics, or from proofs proceeding only from Peano's axioms in arithmetic to proofs which draw on Gödelian arguments or model theory. And concern for truth and understanding forces one into foundational enquiries, precisely involving non-formalizable exercises of judgement using the concepts instanced. The shape and character of such enquiries is exhibited most vividly in Aristotle's works,[6] in his *Physics*, in his *De Anima*, in his *Ethics*, and in his *Analytics and Topics*, but is likewise well exemplified in Frege's *Foundations of Arithmetic*, and the papers of Einstein and Gödel first establishing special relativity and the incompleteness theorems respectively—to extend the list of foundational theoretical works listed earlier, Newton's *Principia* and the like, as examples of extended works of language.

The capacity to understand linguistically expressed concepts, "true", "show to be true", "good" amongst them, is not separable from the capacity to use them rightly in judgements. The linguistic capacity which enables us both to understand and to use such concepts rightly is not separable from the 'intellectual' capacity it exhibits. But likewise the intellectual capacity concerned is precisely a capacity which has to do with linguistically expressible judgements—whether expressed in the medium of sounds, the gestures of deaf-and-dumb or some other medium. It is not the capacity realized in a contemplation or vision which does not have the articulation of language and is therefore not conceptualized in such a way as to contain concepts such

---

[6]We can consider the *Physics* not as a single work, but as a number of discrete, albeit inter-related, enquiries in Books I to IV, a distinct polished treatise in Books V–VI, and separate, albeit related, discussions in VII and the later VIII. Parallel, though more complex, comments need to be made about the *Ethics* and the *Organon*. In the latter case, the *Prior Analytics* stands out as a polished work to be compared with *Physics* V-VI, while the last chapter of *De Sophisticis Elenchis* (Topics IX) represents a fitting postscript to the *Topics* and *Analytics* taken together.

But the character of these works as compilations, to some extent typical of extended works (literary, historical, religious or scientific) where there is nearly always a greater or less amount of sewing and joining coupled with judgements as to the appositeness of such sewing and joining, in no way compromises my remarks in the text.

as we express in sentence-factors, speech-elements like " . . . is true" which are essentiallly incomplete, i.e., which require to be articulated together with other speech-elements.

Therefore, the kind of intellectual capacity which is exercised in reasoning and deliberation—if this is considered broadly, not just in terms of capacity to derive formulae from various other formulae, but as the capacity exercised in foundational and non-rulebound as well as in straightforward deductive argument—is not distinct from linguistic capacity. What we have is one capacity considered under two different aspects. And, in every case, it is the capacities or skills embodied in knowledge of *langue* relating to a concept which alone anchor the spread of judgements made using that concept within a properly human life in its animal and social dimensions and provide us with a necessary means of disciplining our use of the concept.

One may further remark that making *langue* central to the understanding of the special character of human intellect enables one to avoid setting up the false chasm imagined by Jung and others between two kinds of thinking, the one 'rational' and directed by the concious ego out of its own resources, and the other a kind of thinking which is described as 'intuitive', 'associative' or 'lateral'.[7] This is because the capacities denoted by the word *langue* are precisely the ones which give human thought its special flexibility and open-endedness—give it the means of finding ways of expressing oneself in response to new experiences, enquiries or mysteries which are not restricted to what mechanically applicable or formal rule might allow. It also allows one to see how foundational enquiries (called 'dialectical' by Aristotle in his *Topics*) and 'heuristics' as the study of methods of discovery can be brought together with deduction and 'demonstration' as all the work of a single intellectual capacity.

Of course, the associations which make shifts in human thought intelligible are of a highly variable nature. They may arise from history, biography, or the suggestions reflected in etymology, and need not arise from similarities given content by the imagination, even in an unconscious way such as might be explained in Jungian terms: indeed it is because of the existence of such connections in thought,

---

[7]The contrast between intuitive or associative and rational thinking is particularly emphasised by Jung, e.g., in 'Two Kinds of Thinking' in *Symbols of Transformation*, while the term 'lateral thinking' is derived from de Bono.

connections not to be explained in terms of similarity at any level, that the notions of image and model have had to be supplemented by the notion of symbol. Now we have to remember that mutations in modes of behaviour amongst animals, and likewise leaps in thought, do not as such require to be explained in terms of the exercise of either intellect or imagination. (They have to be integrated into human or animal life in some way, but this need not be in terms of them being products of the operation of intellect or imagination). And it is at this stage that the introduction of the idea of an intellectual capacity identified by its connection with knowledge of *langue* allows a useful sifting out of what arises from the synergism of intellect and imagination in connection with what is alive in *langue* from shifts in thought of a more accidental kind including those suggested by chance likenesses in word-form or dead facts of etymology.

2. Words as Expressing, Not Identifying, Meanings

We must now develop our account of language in the respects important to our later argument. This involves first opening out our basic ideas of the expressiveness and the articulated or word/sentence[8] structure of language, i.e., unfolding the philosophical, not just linguistic, importance of the linguists' distinction between *langue* and *parole*. This will prepare the way for the grasp of the other key features of language required for an appreciation of the deep mistakes in any form of mechanism or behaviourism in treating the phenomena of speech, and provide the groundwork for a proper theory of linguistic understanding.

I present this account of language only in summary form, in order to make what I say about understanding and thinking intelligible, because the concern of this book is not with detailed argument in the philosophy of language, semantics and the theory of grammar but with a general account of human nature and human psychology.

I have said that the essence of language lies in what I have called expressiveness. By this I do not mean its capacity to express

---

[8]One could say the threefold structure of word-as-lexeme/word-as-sentence-factor/sentence, meaning 'speech-unit' by "sentence".

emotion, mood, or attitude, distress or pain, but the capacity of words to express meaning—so that they do not merely identify but express the meanings of the sentences they make up. Two things are involved here: firstly, the distinction between just any system for deliberately signalling messages and a linguistic system[9] and, secondly, the role of what I shall call the articulatedness of speech in enabling it to express a sense. It is a question of making a conscious use of the term "express" as the underlying primitive idea in our account of language, instead of merely the unreflective, unself-conscious, uncritical, albeit certainly natural use found in writers of quite opposite approaches.[10] One can have a very extended system of signals, e.g., where numbers indicate messages listed in a phrase book, in which it is clear that the expressions used in signalling do not express the content of the messages.

A sentence, utterance, or saying, is precisely words uttered in a certain order in a certain manner in a certain context. For a sentence to express what is meant is for its words issued in this order, manner and context to express what is meant and conversely for these words in this order, manner and context to express what is meant is for the sentence to express what is meant.

The result of the feature that a sentence expresses, and does not just identify a meaning, is that, as well as the speaker and hearer, there is this third thing, the *expression* of meaning with its life, sense, or direction, in between. The uttering of this thing in between constitutes a complete human act, an act containing within itself two cognates, first the sentence or complete speech-unit as the expression of meaning and second the meaning of such a sentence or speech-unit,

---

[9]We can say that a sentence expresses a belief, a judgement, a wish, or a command, as well as that it expresses a meaning. And this might seem to make sentences similar to non-linguistic signals. For sometimes we may say that a non-linguistic signal expresses our belief, although this is not a natural way of speaking if the belief is a complicated one. But the difference becomes evident if we reflect that we can never say that the non-linguistic signal expresses the content of the belief, judgement, wish, or command. If I indicate my wish or issue my command that the door be closed by pointing at the door, I precisely do not express or make linguistically explicit (in any linguistic substance, sounds, marks on paper, or whatever) what my command is. The content of a belief is expressed by a sentence (in this case a statement) whose sense or meaning is what is communicated in expressing the belief.

[10]As different as Blackburn, *Spreading the Word*, pp. 35f, 140, and Sperber and Wilson, *Relevance*, pp. 55, 73.

twin coordinate and inseparable objects of linguistic understanding, the understanding of *parole*. It is because the uttering of such an expression of sense is a complete human act that there is a distinction between what is done in saying something and what is achieved by saying it—between, as Austin put it, 'illocution' and 'perlocution'.[11] Hence the sense or meaning of the speech-unit is what is expressed in the sentence or speech-unit, not what is achieved, or what is to be expected according to convention to be achieved, by means of expressing it.

It follows from what we have said that a sentence cannot be un-structured or unarticulated, but must always be articulated of different parts with different roles blended together and none of them having sense on its own.[12]

The idea that a simple unstructured utterance might express a sense by stipulation[13] is simply confused. Stipulation can no more make a sound into a sentence or an expression of sense than listing commands in a phrase book could make "303" express the sense 'I have lost my passport'—the utterance of "303" is aimed to achieve, as a result of the existence of a convention, a certain effect, be it the imparting of a belief or the securing of appropriate action, but

---

[11]J.L. Austin, *How to do things with words*, pp. 101 ff.

[12]I give this fuller discussion in *The Expressiveness of Words: the key to the nature of language* (forthcoming). Common examples of one word utterances such as "Fire" meaning in one case 'There is a fire' so that the one word is a noun and in another case 'Fire the gun(s)' so that the one word is the second person imperative of the verb "to fire", are deceptive, lexical articulation still being present. "Ow!" and "alas" have an etymology and can be translated and can be seen to be words from the way they enter into fuller linguistic contexts, "Ow! it hurts", "Alas, all is lost", revealing a diminutive grammar, readily extensible to encompass, for example, "Alas that he has gone". In the absence of the possibility of any such coordinated occurrence within a fuller linguistic context, these sounds might be pieces of pain or distress behaviour but not expressions of linguistic meaning, elements of *langue* and of *parole* requiring the appropriate kinds of understanding. As to Wittgenstein's so-called 'language'-game including such utterances as "Slab!" and "Beam!", if this subsisted independently of any connection with the ordinary language which gives the words "slab" and "beam" a certain meaning and grammar, it would not be a 'language'-game at all but only a signalling system whose components were uttered to secure a certain effect, not to express a certain meaning.

[13]One meets this suggestion in Gareth Evans, p. 102, *Varieties of Reference*. He envisages that such unstructured sentences might arise by stipulation, but this would leave them in no different situation from mere signals which, as we have indicated, are not, as such, expressive or sentences at all.

has no meaning besides its designed effect as a signal. There is no reason to attribute an expressive function to the signals over and above or underlying their perlocutionary function. In short, the notion of something unstructured being the expression of a sense has an absurdity about it analogous to the absurdity of the supposition that a number might have a soul or be alive.

I say that the words of the sentence or speech-unit do not merely identify its meaning but express it. It is therefore not to the point that the words used in a sentence together with other clues—context, intonation, and so forth—permit the calculation or identification (by whatever process) of a meaning. This is not their primary role, which is rather—as if they were alive—to express the meaning of a live utterance. As incomplete factors within a sentence they carry a sense and direction determined by the sense and direction of the sentence. But we deliver and hear the sentence in this sense and direction in delivering and hearing the words as having this sense and direction.

The whole, the utterance whether spoken or written, is such as to have parts and to have no existence apart from the parts, and a meaning not determined by but expressed by these parts. The parts as the sentence-factors[14] have no existence apart from the sentence which, in their nexus together, they constitute, somewhat as the spoken syllable with consonants has no existence apart from its consonants while its consonants and vowels have no existence apart from it. (I use the terms "sentence" and "sentence-factor" to refer to parts of speech, whether spoken or written, not parts of *langue* or language.)

This is the speech-meaning of subordinate expressions within sentences, words amongst them—their *parole*-meaning, associated with them as sentence-factors (typically functorial expressions like " . . . saw ——") taken 'in the live'[15] or as they occur in speech. The speech-meaning of an expression is its meaning taken in a logically distinguishable use, each such use constituting a distinct mode in the exercise of a skill. The words or other smaller or larger lexical

---

[14]I take this term from Ryle, 'Categories', *Collected Papers* II. This idea is more general than the notion of functor, accessibly explained in Adjukiewicz, 'Syntactic connexion'. I develop both notions in my work *The Expressiveness of Words: the key to the nature of language* (forthcoming).

[15]Jespersen, p. 116, *The Philosophy of Grammar*, tells us that 'A junction [of expressions] is like a picture, a nexus like a process or drama'.

components in a sentence all have a *langue*-meaning, a meaning as a dictionary item, so that it is the node of a skill, antecedent to use. This *langue*-meaning or skill is exercised in each of the many different logically distinguishable uses of the expression or types of exercise of the skill concerned. And, as we have remarked, this structure of a single disposition or skill, the appreciation of a *langue*-meaning, opening out into a multiplicity of speech-meanings, is the basis of the open-endedness and flexibility of language.

Correlative with this understanding of the role of words in sentences as expressing the meanings of the sentences, or whole speech-units, is a certain view of sentences or complete speech-units. We do not first compose a sentence or select it from a store of 'possible sentences' and then put it to use, or at least we do not do this in the archetypal or typical case (the case where reflection is not on the mode of expression but on the matter in hand). Rather, the sentence, its sense, and the senses of the words as functors or as in use are all constituted in the act of utterance, as the sound of a trill or musical sequence is constituted in the act of performance, or, to take a more ancient parallel,[16] as the sounds of consonants and vowels are constituted in the act of pronouncing a syllable, and vice versa.

We do not speak of 'expressing' in these cases because there is nothing which stands to the notes and the trill, or to the phonemes and the syllable, as sense or meaning stands to the words and the sentence. The sentence or speech-unit and its sense or meaning are twin co-cognates of speech and hearing and linguistic understanding. And we say that the words express a sense, the sense of the sentence, words and sentence having sense in the same act. If we wanted a vivid analogy, we might say that a sentence or complete speech-unit stands to its sense or meaning as the body stands to its life or soul; and we might say that, as the parts of the body have life and movement as functioning parts of the human being in the same act as the whole body has human life and movement, so the parts of the sentence have life or sense and direction in the same act as the whole has life, sense, and direction.

Here we have a crucial difference between sentences and words or lexemes. The home of the notion of sentence is only at the level of

---

[16]Ryle, 'Letters and Syllables in Plato', *Collected Papers I*.

speech or *parole*, and of function.[17] The conception of sentence-form is entirely secondary and derivative, as the form of those things which conventionally subserve this function. By contrast, it is essential to lesser units such as words, whether as lexemes or as word-forms, that they should have a home both in *langue* and in *parole*.

This fact about words can be seen by reflecting upon the way in which the language-user, even the child, knows both speech-words (so that the word-forms "cow" and "cows", "do", "does", "did", and "done" count as different words) and language-words (so that these are different forms of the same 'word' or lexeme),[18] whereas he or she does not, in the same way, know both speech-sentences and language-sentences—there is no knowledge of language-sentences embodied in *langue*.[19] There are two things to be noticed here. Firstly, and most importantly, the whole theory of *langue* and *parole* involves that words as lexemes have a double aspect as being at once nodes of *langue*-meaning and speech-unit-factors ('sentence-factors') and

---

[17]Larger speech-units can be built up incorporating smaller ones. To take a simple example, a question constitutes a speech-unit, but so also does the the interchange consisting in the question supplemented by the answer "No!". At the other extreme, Newton's *Principia* or Thucydides' *History* also constitute larger speech-units incorporating smaller ones. What is important in such building is that the function of the incorporated statements is not altered by their incorporation into the larger whole. The cathedral may be extended but, e.g., the sanctuary is not changed into the porch. Within this framework, we may define a sentence as the smallest speech-unit whose function is preserved in the building up of any larger speech-units which may incorporate it. (It is not for this book to deal with the problems of how sentences occur within the context of extended works with an oblique way of communicating what they communicate, e.g., in *King Lear* or *The Brothers Karamazov*; nor with the simpler problem of how they occur in quotations.)

One may contrast what occurs when something which, if it occurred on its own would be a statement, occurs instead as a conditional clause or as an alternative in a disjunction or with the words "Suppose" or "Perhaps" prefixed, or when the context or intonation makes it plain that what has the appearance of a question is a rhetorical and not a real question. These would not be function-preserving incorporations and the clauses do not count as sentences in the sense we are concerned with.

[18]The child knows these things, even though he or she does not know the meanings of such terms as "noun", "plural", or "tense", and has never tried to disambiguate the word "word", let alone tried to distinguish word-radical (morphological stem), word-root (etymological derivation), and lexeme (as what is common to "obey" and "obeys", but not to "disobey").

[19]Unless in the case of petrified idioms or memories of decontextualized examples in grammar books. By contrast, even the remembering of aphorisms, famous quotes, songs, and the like is an exercise of *langue* rather than part of it.

involves that the notions of word as lexeme and of sentence or speech-unit are interdependent, neither eliminable in favour of the other. We cannot define away the notion of lexeme in terms of that of sentence, nor vice versa. This means that it is fundamental to such lesser units as words[20] and lexemes to have a place in linguistic theory both as elements of *langue* and as factors in *parole*. Secondly, it is essential to speech-words to be defined both in respect of form as distinct word-forms which is a matter belonging to *langue* and in respect of function so that the end of a word marks a point from which speech might unfold in different ways.

When I speak of a logically distinguishable use of an expression I mean a use such as might invite a different paraphrase (this is typical in attempts at clarification in ordinary life) or require a different definition or specification of truth-conditions for its application, or such as might be marked out by a certain primary mode of verification or hierarchy of modes of verification or by some other feature of logical, epistemological or attitudinal significance.[21] It is vital to recognize that, when we are distinguishing uses or meanings at the level of speech or *parole*, we are concerned with use, meaning or sense at the level at which philosophers and logicians are concerned with it, the level at which assessments of truth and accuracy, of proof and disproof, of interest and direction of concern, come into play.[22]

---

[20]Also lexical components which are not words, including significant morphological features within words and petrified idiomatic phrases. The fact that lexical components which are not words also have this double aspect of being both elements of *langue* and factors in *parole* is especially important in considering agglutinative languages, but is also important for the consideration of the one word utterances instanced in n. 12 above.

[21]In a more extended account I would develop the idea that the differences between "and" and "but", "dog" and "cur", "negro" and "nigger", proposing that any differences which would invite a different translation into another language will count as differences in sense. This means that, if two expressions are not 'intensionally isomorphic' (Carnap, *Meaning and Necessity*, pp. 56–64), they will not count as having the same sense. And we shall say that "P" and "It is true that P" have different senses because the later takes 'P' (or 'that P') as something believed, stated or judged which attains the goal of truth, whereas the former does not have any such sense (cf. Dummett, *Frege: Philosophy of Language*, pp. 228–229).

[22]The only reservation to be made is that the features which belong to meaning or sense, 'speech-meaning', at the level with which we are concerned have to be internal to the speech-act (what is done in saying what is said), rather than merely with what is achieved or comes about by means of saying what is said. These latter, at least when

It was Ryle[23] who was most explicit in focusing attention on the distinction between *langue* and *parole*, drawn from linguists such as Saussure and Gardiner, specifically in order to reveal its particular logical and philosophical point. It is units of speech rather than of language which are true or false, obeyed or disobeyed, and it is components of speech ('sentence-factors' to use Ryle's apposite phrase) rather than units of *langue* which have their meaning 'defined in the context of a proposition', an idea strategic for Frege, Russell, and Wittgenstein—and it is always meaning in the context of a proposition or other speech-unit which the philosopher is concerned with.

And there is something further to be grasped, namely, that the 'speech-meaning' of a sentence-factor, " . . . f ——", (unlike its *langue*-meaning) is affected by whatever things arising out of its *langue*-meaning may alter the truth-conditions, modes of verification, etc. of the statements in which it occurs; and obviously it will therefore be normal for the 'speech-meaning' of an expression to be affected by the context of the utterance of statements containing it. It is the fundamental mistake of most recent semantic theory to conceive a sentence as primarily a unit of *langue* with a settled meaning determined by the *langue*-meanings of its grammatical components and their mode of combination, a settled meaning determined at the level of *langue* and without respect to context of utterance, to which implications accrue externally from the context of utterance. In this way, context of utterance is wrongly conceived to make no difference to the meaning of the sentence-factors within it, taken at the level of *parole* or performance, so that (in this view) there is no *parole*-meaning of subordinate parts of sentences distinct from *langue*-meaning—despite the commonsense fact that we often give different paraphrases of the same subordinate expression used in different contexts of utterance.[24]

---

aimed at, are what Austin called perlocutions (*How to do things with Words*, pp. 101–103). Some cases of what Grice calls 'implicatures' would also count as external to the speech-act (but cf. n. 21 above): they are external to the speech-act in its sense and force when they do not make any difference to truth-conditions, to methods of verification, to attitudes marked by nuances of *langue*, etc.

[23]In 'Use, Usage, and Meaning', *Collected Papers II*.

[24]When I speak of *langue*-meanings and *parole*-meanings I do not mean abstract objects of any kind, but what I shall call at the beginning of the next chapter 'cognates'—they are cognates of different kinds of knowledge or understanding, in the way, for instance, to know the meaning of a word as a dictionary item is different from knowing the sense of a particular statement. The understanding of a word which

To help make clear what types of difference of use in terms we are concerned with, let us consider some particular examples.

Let us begin by considering the most general terms or concepts (since each term or expression is the object of *langue*-understanding, it does not matter whether we discuss terms or discuss concepts as the meanings of terms). We cannot lay down a set of criteria for being true, or for being provable, or for being good applicable in all cases, nor for being an individual, existing, or being a set, nor for being an example of thinking, or of some kind of knowing. All these concepts are in Ryle's terms 'polymorphous', or in an older vocabulary 'analogous', so that the uses they have in different contexts are logically distinguishable in how they might be informatively defined so as to be applicable according to rule or formalized. It is a familiar fact that it can be useful to offer definitions of particular terms, e.g., "true", "provable", or "good" applicable within limited fields ('good' parties, screwdrivers, farmers, or friends being defined separately) or over limited ranges within a field. E.g., we can define what is provable in natural arithmetic according to Peano's axioms but this leaves what is provable by Gödelian arguments to be covered separately. There is no single criterion of being a proof which covers all cases; and, in general, we can only give many separate sets of criteria for what counts as a proof in the empirical sciences (and not just set of criteria for each science but many sets, one for each different way of establishing results).

In the case of each concept or term it is not that we have a list of uses which could be enumerated, each of which uses could just as well be represented by a different word or symbol in a formalized language; rather there is a real unity in the concept concerned such as invites the use of one word or expression and the different uses of the concept cannot be enumerated because the spread of uses is open-ended in a way which defies enumeration. It is not that the number of uses of these and most other concepts is simply too large, but that it is indefinite, having a kind of potential infinity corresponding to the spread of possible situations or types of case in which the concept might find a publicly intelligible use, whether literal or metaphorical.

The predicament that we cannot satisfactorily formalize or define (even contextually by a set of axioms) the most general terms—

---

we bring to the context of communication is not identical to the realization of this understanding in the understanding of a particular piece of *parole* or speech.

"true", "provable", "good", "individual", "exists", "set" were instanced above—is well-known but often ignored as if it were of no significance for concepts in general but merely a consequence of these particular concepts being apparently purely formal ones. However, these concepts in their lack of delimited criteria of application are typical of concepts which are by no means purely formal—not only "think" and "know" as already instanced, but also (to take a convenient example) "see".

According to the primary logical use of the verb "see", "a saw b" implies the existence of a and b, the use of the eyes, the presence of light and so forth. But, as we observed in Chapter II, different contexts of statement and variations in the logical type of "y" give "x saw y" quite different and various logical powers. And, inasmuch as there is no pre-set limit to the types of quasi-visual situation with which the human or other animal may be presented and to our capacity to deal with them using visual idioms and yet still maintain public intelligibility, these are not to be dealt with by using a disjunctive definition of " . . . saw ———". It is equally plain that it would be quite wrong to require different words to be used in the logically differentiable cases— if different words were used we would find that we were without means of expressing the experiential similarities between the cases. It will be noted that I have been speaking so far only of non-metaphorical uses of "see", but the same arguments apply if we consider the various metaphorical uses of "see" in connection with 'intellectual' seeing— except that we might try to express the similarities between this wider range of cases by using some other more general polymorphous word such as "know" (with which, of course, parallel problems will arise).

The conception of disposition or state (*hexis, dynamis*) which we developed in Chapter VII, Section 1, is crucial here: it allows us to say that the achievements of understandingly speaking and understandingly hearing are realizations of open or many-track *dispositions*, proximately the disposition called the understanding of *parole*. This understanding of *parole* is in each particular case a realization of the interlocking dispositions which constitute the understanding of *langue*, while these latter are realizations of an underlying capacity for language (the capacity for speech as an exercise of *langue*).

The speaker speaks, the hearer hears, and in both there is an inception of an understanding of *parole*. The speech and hearing cease but the understanding of what is spoken is a state or disposition whose inception is in the speaking and hearing,[25] but which does not cease with them. Where the learning of *langue* is concerned, the inception of the understanding of an element of *langue* is born in some fresh understanding of some piece of *parole*, but, once born, this understanding of *langue* is exercised, not just in the way instanced in the learning case, but also flexibly in a multiplicity of other types of case. I deal with the chief objections to this conception of the flexibility of language in Sections 4 and 5.

3. The Integrated Structure of Language

We have seen one aspect of the structuredness of language, namely the aspect whereby sentences are articulated of words, words express the content of sentences, and words are able to do this because of the relationship of *langue* and *parole*—a relationship whereby words as nodes of meaning have an open-ended flexible use in speech. We must now see a different aspect of this structuredness, inseparable from the first, namely, the way in which the whole of language, the interlocking capacities we call the understanding of the different elements of *langue*, constitutes an integrated whole.

If a bodily thing (e.g., some foreigner or some electronic machine) issues the sounds represented in "That is red", the question arises whether it has made an utterance with the meaning which an utterance in context by an English-speaker of the sentence "That is red" would have. Most obviously this has the character of a proposition about which one might ask whether it is true or false, accurate or over-simple in regard to the object spoken of, and suchlike, rather than the character of a command or a question. To this we will recur later.

The next most obvious observation arises from the subject-copula-adjective structure of this sentence in English. Let us note the three groups of aspects which arise from this: first, the aspects involved in being able to distinguish types of subject of such sentences according to the spread of other types of predication to which they are susceptible (e.g., an animal or person, a body, a surface, a shadow, the Sun, or the sky), second, the aspects involved in the type of verbal

---

[25] The coming to be of a state such as understanding is not a process with stages unlike the speaking and the hearing, any more than seeing is a process with stages: what is being built has not yet been built but what is seen has been seen.

structure here exemplified, and third, the aspects associated with the particular predication made.

The first is the most straightforward. It is a sign that the sound "That is red" has not been produced as an utterance with the meaning which "That is red" would ordinarily have if the producer of the sound (some imagined humanoid machine) could not use the predicate " . . . is red" in a discriminating way of the same range of different types of object.

More notable is the second point. In order to be understanding the word "red" in the meaning it has in its normal context, one has to be able to understand the subject of this predicate within such a sentence as susceptible of other predications, and, since "is" is a tensed verb, other types of predication, including ones's differing in respect of time (past, present, or future) and aspect (states or episodes of different types reflected in the use, e.g., of continuous, perfective, or aorist 'tenses' according to the mode of 'placing' in time concerned).

In any use of the present tense, there are presupposed the capacities to speak of the past, and also to speak of the future or the possible.

We need to understand the depth of the mistake enshrined in Dummett's remark: 'We learn the use of the past tense by learning to recognise certain situations as justifying the assertion of certain statements expressed by means of that tense.'[26] He speaks here as if there could be a capacity to use the present tense in its proper meaning in the absence of any capacities to speak of the past or the possible future, and as if the capacity to speak differentially about the past was a separable skill—as if, for instance, statements about the past were constructions out of statements about the present which we represented to ourselves as inferences from pieces of evidence in the present to past (now absent) states of affairs. But this picture of our appreciation of the past in its pastness as being something quite external to our appreciation of the present cannot be right, as one can see if one considers the implications of the following features of human life. In knowing my hitting someone I know that I have hit him, in knowing that I see a certain thing I know that I have seen it, in knowing that I am moving across a space I know that I have been moving across it, so that always I know the present as a

[26]Dummett, *Truth and Other Enigmas*, p. 363.

completion or a continuance of some past: it is the juncture to which a certain past has come together. But it is also a juncture out of which I and other agents act, and action involves an orientation towards a future, not yet existent or established, a future to be determined by action: in carrying something I bring it about that something is moved, in burning something I bring it about that something burns, in eating something I bring it about that something is eaten, in wetting something I make it wet, in every case so that some change occurs, a change brought about by the action, and liable to persist, be extended, or reversed as time continues.

Thus we do not have a merely external or observer's knowledge of the meanings of past and future tenses, or of the kinds of modality ('real' contingency) and of practical desire and hope associated with the latter, let alone a merely inferential knowledge of these things. We do not know changes of state solely by observing different states at different times, but proto-typically in knowing the acting which is the causing of the change and the changing which is its effect. And we know the present as the time of present doing, whether on the part of ourselves, other persons or animate agents, or inanimate things, and whether act, process towards a completion, or other activity. And time and aspect (to use the linguists' terms for tense) have to be understood as internal to the propositional or utterance structure concerned.

In the third place, in order to understand the sentence "That is red", one also has to be able to make an adequate range of contrasts— to be able to distinguish the white, the pink, the red, and the black; the yellow, the orange, and the red; the red, the green, and the blue; the red and the brown; and so forth. And one has also to understand these as discriminations in respect of colour, not of brightness, and not pertinent to senses other than sight.

This last brings us to a capital point, that—if one is understanding the formula "That is red" in the way English-users understand it—one has to understand the discrimination which it expresses as a discrimination made by sight in respect of objects of sight as opposed, for instance, to a discrimination made by hearing in respect of objects of hearing: i.e., one has to be able to understand the verb "see" in its contrasts with "hear", "feel (by touch)", "smell", and "taste". And one has not understood what it is to use sight as a means of discrimination if one has not therein understood it as a means of knowledge, affording knowledge by memory after the experience has passed. Further, one has to understand that knowledge by such means as sight and the other senses is to be distinguished from, for instance, knowledge at the testimony of others, knowledge by inference, and knowledge of one's own beliefs, intentions, and emotions. None of these is knowledge by sense.

But, if one knows something by sight, one is aware not only of what one knows by sight but also that one knows it and that it is by sight that one knows it. In this one has a certain self-knowledge, perpetuated by memory.

But with the concept of knowledge come the concepts of truth, of assent, and of the ground on which something is held to be true. There is also the conception of mistake or error, and of reasons for judging that mistake has occurred, and the anticipation of there being some explanation of the mistake. This is all involved in the application of the concept of knowledge to language-using animals in the sense in which we are understanding "language". This is part of how the capacity of human beings for self-reflection includes or is inseparable from a capacity to reflect upon, partly identify, and criticize their procedures for getting or extending knowledge and the particular applications of the procedures.

In this we come full circle, back to the first point we made, namely, that what is uttered must have in this case the structure and nature of a proposition, i.e., a linguistic entity (normally an utterance or piece of writing) of the sort which is by its *parole*-meaning either true or at least put forward as if something true. But we must carry this point further and insist that, in order to have the nature of a proposition, it must be cognized as having this nature—as being of a sort to which it belongs that it should be true or put forward as if something true. Indeed, we can go further, since in the case under consideration the proposition is logically of a subject-predicate type and (if understood) understood as such, and insist that it is cognized as being of the form, "a is red", wherein it is presupposed[27] that either it ("a is red") or its negation ("a is not red"), one of the two, must be true—the existence of the subject being presupposed—i.e., one has

---

[27]Presupposed, but perhaps presupposed mistakenly, as when the subject does not exist although mistakenly thought to do so (a situation which can even arise when the subject-expression is "That", as when I point in a determinate direction at what I take to be some object close to my finger, but in fact the appearance of there being such an object close to my finger is the result of a cunning optical deception).

to understand "That" as being a singular term or referring expression for the purposes of the logician.

Accordingly, with every singular proposition is carried the presumption of the applicability of one or more specific forms of the Law of the Excluded Middle. I mean by a 'specific form' of this Law a form restricted to one proper type[28] of subject, e.g., principles such as that every proposition is either true or not true (the principle of bivalence which is simply a particular application of the Law of the Excluded Middle) or that every visual object is either unqualifiedly of a given colour or not unqualifiedly of that colour—and which specific form of the Law is applicable is determined by the type which the subject of the singular proposition belongs to, which must be determinate if we have a genuine subject-expression.[29] Such presumptions of the applicability of the Law of the Excluded Middle are carried by every categorical[30] affirmation whatsoever, the Laws of the Excluded Middle and Non-contradiction being given at the same time by the very meaning of the word "not", and the capacity for using this word being inseparable from the capacity for affirmation. *A fortiori*, if the question of decidability can arise, the capacity to use the word "not" is present whether or not it is in use.[31] At the same time there is given the second-order or reflective and critical capacity to consider the ways in which indefiniteness can arise whereby such presumptions may fail.

It is incoherent to suppose that a bodily being which issues the sounds contained in the sentence "That is red" is engaged in human discourse and uttering a sentence with the meaning which "That is red" would have for an English-speaker, and thus involved

---

[28]A type is a general kind which is the range of significant application of a predicate. Given a predicate F, we will have a range R which will be the type such that every R is either F or not F.

[29]Cf. Wittgenstein's insistence that a naming ceremony, e.g., "That is Tommy-Noddy", would not be effective unless it was clear what sort of object was intended to be named, e.g., in the case of a use of "That" with pointing, what sort of object it was intended to point at.

[30]I note that conditionals, "Any"-sentences, disjunctions, and statements of the type "A certain man hit me", amongst others do not have negations with any sense determined in natural language, although the law of bivalence applies to them.

[31]Dummett asks us to consider 'a fragment of natural language lacking the sentential operators, but containing sentences not effectively decidable by observation' (*Truth and Other Enigmas*, p. 316), but my argument indicates that there can be no such fragment.

in propositional discourse, without the at least implicit (i.e., whether or not the appropriate vocabulary has been learned) possession of the concepts such as knowing by sense, knowing, truth, assent, mistake, and so forth, in some form, as well as the concepts of bodily being or substance and of the subject of knowledge and perception.

That is to say, not that the person who utters "That is red" with the meaning which it has for an English-speaker must possess all the vocabulary required for full self-reflective and critical discussions, but that it is part of the linguistic capacity involved in what he or she does that he or she has at least the capacity to appropriate the requisite vocabulary. Children may not use the words "time", "thing", "truth", "assent", and suchlike, or may not use them in the way of adults, but they have the capacity to appropriate the full range of modes of speech we have indicated.

In this way, the more specific linguistic capacities (say those associated with particular shades of colour, or the specialized taxonomy of animals, or, to take a different type of case, various highly theoretical branches of study) all presuppose more general capacities which are inseparable from one another and together constitute a single unitary linguistic capacity.[32] Thus, linguistic capacity is unitary in its essentials, and these essentials reach deeply into the structure of human life, including the interrelation of perception, action, and emotion and the integration of these with the procedures of deliberation both 'theoretical' and practical. And the recursiveness or self-reflexivity of linguistic operation is only one facet of this structure, albeit a facet on which one branch of our argument in Chapter XII will turn.

In all this we have, in the meantime, presented a sobering challenge to any would-be simulator of human linguistic capacity by a computer model: human linguistic capacity has to be simulated in all the structural features which I have set forth in order to have

---

[32]This is a holism well argued for in Blackburn, *op. cit.*, pp. 35–36. The full working of this requires discussion in another place. In short, human beings' underlying semantic capacity is realized in stages, firstly as they appropriate adult grammatical means of expression, and secondly as their thought advances into new fields or a new way of grasping an old field is attained. In regard to the second, what we observe should be represented as the arrival of a new understanding, not itself a linguistic matter, which allows pre-existing linguistic capacity richer realization, rather than an addition to pre-existing linguistic capacity, presupposing it but external to it.

been, *qua* language, simulated at all—with only this reserve, that the computer need not be supposed to have the same sensory modes as the human being (although it must be able to distinguish sensation and perception). However, as we shall see in our next section, this is the lesser of the two challenges with which the computer simulator is presented.

We have sketched the integrated structure, incorporating for a start self-other distinction and tense, putting this in the context of self-reflection in regard to the procedures of judgement, but above all marked by the open spread relation between *langue*-meaning and *parole*-meaning, which belongs to 'language' in the primary sense—the sense of concern to linguists—and the sense differentiative of man. Even the most sophisticated utterances and differential responses to utterances on the part of chimpanzees—'Elizabeth give apple Amy' in 'words' and 'Please Roger tickle Lana' in gestures have been instanced[33]—fail to exhibit this global structure. Hence, such utterances of chimpanzees are not to be construed as if pregnant with the meaning that they would have if expressions exhibiting the rest of the global structure were to follow naturally in the learning sequence in the way they do in the case of human children. And, in the absence of the linguistic capacity co-ordinate with this global structure, it may be unsurprising that each new development is learnt with such difficulty.

Linguistic capacity is something unitary and therefore comes, the whole or not at all, all in one step. If there is some structuring of hardware correlative with or indispensable to the realization of this linguistic capacity it is to be expected that the key move in its development will be some single move within the whole structure so that, until this move is made, the whole will be impotent. [It is striking to note that, whereas evolutionary theories of continuous adaptation at an earlier date led one to anticipate a process of continuous change from sub-human animal to man, modern materialistic theory would suggest exactly the opposite. When the hardware structure of a machine, a television set or computer, is all set up so as to show one logical structure of behaviour, it will be by some one further mutation in hardware structure (or one combination of such mutations, none of them any use by itself) that the logical structure of behaviour will be

---

[33]Passingham, pp. 216, 221, *The Human Primate*, gives these examples, and his pp. 201–222 give a convenient review of and references to recent work.

transformed. And so even a materialist should expect the human type of linguistic capacity to arrive, in all its integrated together aspects, in one single move, even if the unfolding of the exercise of this capacity takes many generations.]

We have to realize, however, that this underlying capacity for language, which when possessed at all is possessed as a total integrated whole, is a capacity whose realization in explicit forms of *langue* exhibited in speech unfolds over many generations in developing stages. Modern European languages are, in certain respects, more developed than those of some so-called primitive peoples (e.g., the only number-words of some 'primitive' languages are one, two, three, four, five, and many, by contrast with modern European languages. Also, modalities and differences in the force of an utterance from being indicated by intonation and context may come to be marked by distinct idioms, "I order you to . . .", "I ask you to . . .", "I suggest that you . . .", etc.). But children of peoples of more primitive language, if brought into a European context, can develop the whole gamut of European idiom.

In respect of 'language' amongst higher animals and children, whether in speech or in other media such as gestures, we should adopt the same approach as with perceptual consciousness as described in Chapter IX: we should presume the presence of integral linguistic capacity until its absence is evidenced. Experience suggests that, in the case of human beings, this linguistic capacity belongs to the species but that even the chimpanzee lacks, not just the capacities for vocalization dependent on the shape of the mouth and suchlike, but the underlying linguistic capacity for command of a language-system proper—lacks the features which at the same time have to do with words expressing and not just identifying a meaning and with the propositional structure co-ordinate with self-reflection (as well as lacking the capacities whereby mothers or elders teach or assist in the learning of language).

4. No Calculation of Meanings

There is a seemingly very common-sense view of the procedures of language learning and language use which, as we have already said, shows to be radically misguided. It is indeed this so common-sense view which chiefly inspires the view that human linguistic procedures not only are but must be computer simulable. And it is only the demonstration that this view is untenable, and the exhibition of why it cannot be right, which can satisfy the mind that these procedures not only are not, but cannot be computer simulable.

According to this plausible account, calculation, whether conscious or unconscious, comes in in two ways, and communication depends upon the 'effectiveness' of the procedures of calculation concerned.

How is calculation supposed to come into linguistic procedures?

Firstly, it is supposed that we have experience of language-use, predominantly the language-use of others, and from this we calculate the elements of *langue*, identifying the *langue*-meaning of each lexeme or each morphological item and of each grammatical mode of construction, while learning whatever elements in intonation and context carry semantic significance. Meaning, it is said, must be exhaustively manifested in use. On one view, perhaps not very plausible, the human being begins with a mental apparatus unfurnished with any information or any pre-programming and, thus bare, programmes itself in a way adapted and in a way set by incoming data and builds up an understanding of language on the basis of these. On another view the human being begins with a system for receiving incoming linguistic data, only according to a certain pre-programmed structure. But however the picture is set up, human beings are (on the views here concerned) able to identify the meaning of the elements of *langue* by calculation in the context of an appreciation of their structured use together in speech-acts.

Secondly, human beings, after having accomplished this task of calculating the *langue*-meanings of significant components or aspects of speech, are supposed to be able to calculate back again from these *langue*-meanings to the meanings of complete sentences or speech-units. In this they manifest their understanding, for there is nothing to understanding meaning beyond capacities to use in appropriate ways: understanding is a set of capacities to use.

Against the view here represented, involving two sets of calculation (whether conscious or unconscious) as the very condition of the possibility of human communication, we have two objections to set.

In the first place, these ways of thinking have no regard for the distinction we have made between the *langue*-meaning and the *parole*-meaning of words, and if they were correct would make the *parole*-meaning of words (the meaning they express) redundant, leaving sentences only identificatory of meaning, not expressive of it—the expressive function would be redundant.

For we need to say the following.

On the one hand, what is appreciated in hearing understandingly (even and especially in the learning situation) is a *parole*-meaning and only therein and therewith a *langue*-meaning, and to take the opposite view enshrines the false view of perception whereby at a first stage we apprehend some relatively unformed data and at a second stage we interpret them. And, on the other hand, granted a knowledge of the *langue*-meaning of an item *of langue*, what is spoken understandingly or with meaning with a view to being heard understandingly is spoken directly in its *parole*-meaning, and what is involved no more involves calculation from *langue*-meaning than walking involves calculation from muscle properties and relations. (To this it might be objected that there is no incompatibility between unconscious processes having to do with muscle properties, etc.—described in some technical sense as 'information processing' or 'calculation'— and the conscious procedure of walking intentionally. But to make such a comparison is to misrepresent the matter: whereas no particular knowledge of muscles is internal to walking, whatever *langue*-meaning is involved in speaking understandingly is utilized knowingly internally to speaking.)

Underlying this first objection to the view which postulates two kinds of calculation is the realization that the approach we are criticizing involves a deep misconception of the logical character of *langue*-meanings and *parole*-meanings as if they were objects to be identified rather than things to be expressed. This is a misconception whose nature will become clear in Chapter XI. For the processes of calculation envisaged all involve treating, in the one case, the *langue*-meaning of each particular element of *langue* as the value of a function of the *parole*-meanings of the experienced utterances of others, and, in the other case, the *parole*-meaning of a sentence as the value of a function of the *langue*-meanings of its elements and its context of utterance, in both cases involving regarding *parole*-meanings and *langue*-meanings as objects to be identified.

But it is not by identifying entities which we might call the *parole*-meanings of sentences that we get by calculation to identify other entities which we might call the *langue*-meanings of elements of *langue*, and it is not by identifying *langue*-meanings and performing another calculation that we identify the *parole*-meanings of the utterances others utter or we propose to utter. The trouble is not that such calculation would have to be unconscious, but that the whole process of learning language and the whole process of using it has been misdescribed. In learning and using language, our starting point is not the identifying or picking out particular meanings—identifying in each case which, out of a general class of objects called meanings, we are dealing with—but in each case the understanding of the meaning of some expression, somewhat as in dreaming a dream we do not identify a dream and then dream it, but simply dream it without processes of identification coming in. It is not that there is any particular similarity between speaking and dreaming, but that, as we shall indicate in our next chapter, there is a similarity in the logical character of noun-expressions 'denoting' dreams and noun-expressions 'denoting' sentences and meanings—for in the way explained in our next chapter both are examples of denoting 'cognates' not 'objects.'

In the second place, the processes of calculation postulated are not only mythical but impossible.

What we have to realize is that something quite new is introduced with the idea of calculation. It is, of course, perfectly possible to have a philosophical notion of effectiveness whereby, for a method of coming to conclusions to be 'effective', all that is required is that it suffices to establish public certainty. This is quite compatible with supposing it to draw on perception, understanding, and the capacity for nuanced judgement in a non-mechanical way. That is, the view that experience of other people's speech (supposedly their sentences), coupled, perhaps, with attempts to imitate it in different respects and even to join in with it, can make knowledge of *langue* (centred on word-meanings) publicly accessible does not of itself compel one to view knowledge of *langue* as the result of calculation. Likewise, the view that knowledge of *langue* (centred on word-meanings) together with an appreciation of the context of speech can make an understanding of speech (i.e., of 'sentence'-meanings) publicly accessible does not itself compel one to view understanding of speech as the result of calculation.

However, once it is supposed that knowledge of *langue* is derived from experience of speech *by calculation or inference*, and that understanding of the speech-meaning of sentences is derived from knowledge of *langue* together with knowledge of context *by calculation or inference*, the situation is transformed. In place of the general epistemological notion of effectiveness mentioned above (in terms of which going to look or getting someone to go and look might count as an effective method for coming to conclusions in a publicly accessible way, there being a great spread of procedures 'effective' in this general way), we are asked to limit our consideration to a notion of effectiveness applicable to procedures of calculation or inference. And if the person assessing the effectiveness of a procedure of calculation or inference is not allowed to reassess the acceptability of the particular premises or general axioms from which inference proceeds or of the rules of calculation or inference relied upon, then the notion of an effective operation becomes that of one which could be performed mechanically.[34]

Such possession of an effective procedure for performing the two kinds of calculation envisaged depends upon being able to bring all the relevant data for such calculations into a single enumeration, in the one case an enumeration of all the (possible) speech-sentences of a language together with laws relating them to their semantically significant features, and in the other case an enumeration of all the elements of *langue* and other semantically relevant features of utterances together with all the laws relating them to speech-sentence meanings. Of course, when we have an effective procedure for achieving a certain kind of task, we do not have to use it since there are commonly short ways of achieving the task in particular cases, much shorter than relying upon a general procedure designed to work in all cases. Nonetheless, if communication is to be guaranteed over a certain range and if the achievement of communication is to depend on the possibility of calculations in the two directions mentioned, then enumerations of

---

[34]I.e., by a Turing machine. I here imply acceptance of Church's thesis in the form given to it by Turing, whereby in mathematics what is effectively calculable is Turing machine computable, the form in which Gödel found it intuitively acceptable (see p. 110, Solomon Feferman, 'Kurt Gödel: Conviction and Caution'). I will give a fuller discussion of the notions of the effective and the mechanical in my *The Expressiveness of Words: the key to the nature of language* (forthcoming).

If proofs are formalized, and premises and methods of proof are enumerable, the question of whether we can decide a question, producing a proof or formal derivation either for the answer "Yes" or for the answer "No", is equivalent to the question whether some corresponding function is computable (cf. S.C. Kleene, *Mathematical Logic*, pp. 227–229). It is against this background that I have not troubled to separate (a) computing numbers from numbers from (b) deriving propositions from propositions.

everything relevant over this range will have to be possible. However, the idea that such enumerations are possible seems a fantasy—not only in view of the diversity of semantic clues arising in a potential infinity of types of situation and literary usage, and not only in view of the kind of potential infinity in the speech-sentences individuated by their distinctive senses which we may utter or write according to the situation and human inventiveness, but also because of the character of the types of law referred to above.

There is no single set of criteria for the literal application of any of the following predicates or functors: "...exists", "...is a set", "...is true", "...is a definition", "...can be shown to be true", "...is a mechanically effective method of determining ——", "...is good of its kind", "...knows ——", "...sees ——", "...plays ———", to take only a few salient examples.[35] In the case of the first six of these the point can be mathematically demonstrated. The other three are but the beginning of a long list of structurally key general concepts whose generality is not such as to bestraddle all subject-matters abstract or concrete, but of which the same point, of the lack of a single set (even disjunctive) of criteria for literal application is true,[36] but not open to the same mathematically formal proof.

When we come to the last of the examples just listed, we are moving into the field of predicates or functors which are sufficiently specific in the type of subject-matter to which they have application so as to have non-literal as well as literal applications. *A fortiori*, we have no single set of criteria for the whole range of such sometimes non-literally used expressions (always, of course, limiting our considerations to types of use in which communication of the same meaning from speaker to hearer is achieved relying only upon what is public about the language and its use). But in all cases it is important to note that disjunctive definition is no use because the only available type of disjunction has to be between a finite number of actual types of use whereas what is required would have to be between an indefinite number of possible types of use, types of use arising not according to law but according to the exigencies of novel situations and turns of questioning.

---

[35]Ryle instances 'thinking' as another such (what he calls) 'polymorphous' concept in 'Thinking and Language', *Collected Papers II*.

[36]Cf. the discussion of transgeneric and polymorphous concepts in *The Reality of Time and the Existence of God*, pp. 72 ff.

Each type of use, logically distinguishable according to distinctive criteria, constitutes what I call a distinct *parole*-meaning or meaning-in-use. But the capacity for the whole range of *parole*-meanings embraced in each case is grounded in the understanding of a particular element or item of *langue* within its structured situation within more general linguistic capacity.

The understanding of *langue* which grounds, in the case of each expression or lexeme as an item of *langue*, the understanding of an indefinitely varied range of word-functors realizing that expression cannot be encapsulated in a mechanically applicable rule. This is a consequence of the unformalizability of natural language: this unformalizability was demonstrated by Tarski drawing on the properties of the expression " . . . is true", but other demonstrations are possible on the basis of consideration of any of the first five predicates or functors listed above. Any mechanically applicable rule either fails to cover the whole range of the use of a word or else generates contradictions and misuses, so that it is only an understanding of a sort which cannot be encapsulated in such a rule which does or could do the job.

The general understanding of *langue* which goes with the integrated structure sketched in the previous section provides the public means, not only of distinguishing the literal and the non-literal and the implications (so far as they are determinate) of each logically distinguishable use of an expression, but also of unpicking paradoxes as they arise—in each case discerning how they arise. This latter task, of unpicking paradoxes and discerning how they arise, is a public one, accomplished not instantaneously but through extended reflection and debate. Likewise, the former, interpretative, task of distinguishing meanings and implications is only in part achieved in the act of speech and can be a matter again for extended reflection and debate.

From all this it follows immediately that there can be no calculation of the *parole*-meanings of sentences (utterances) from the *langue*-meaning of elements of *langue*. This is not because inflection and order of words, intonation, and context of utterance leave the *parole*-meaning of these elements private or indeterminate. On the contrary, the *parole*-meanings of the expressions concerned are grasped in the act of grasping the *parole*-meaning of the total sentence or utterance, and this *parole*-meaning is public. But for calculation of a *parole*-meaning to be possible it would have to proceed by taking amongst its bases some semantic fact about each of the lexical items given (this 'semantic fact' might, of course, be very complex in its specification).

However, the ways in which the unformalizability of natural language can be established show that there cannot be adequate codification of the relevant 'semantic facts' in the case of the most general concepts, those the use of which is presupposed in any utterance whatsoever; accordingly, the supposed calculations of the *parole*-meanings of sentences (that is, for our purposes, complete speech-units) are not only fictitious but impossible.

5. Linguistic Understanding Is Not a Mystery: The Systematic Mistakes Shared by Dummett and by Cognitive Scientists

It will be complained that I am here introducing a mysterious inner entity or reality called understanding, in order to explain in a mystifying way a puzzling spread of linguistic phenomena (both in the learning and in the use of language), and that this is no more use than the fond explanation of the event of going to sleep in terms of a dormitive power.

However, the proper reply to this complaint is that the forms of understanding spoken of, understanding of *langue* and understanding of speech, are not mysterious or unknown in their nature or in their criteria of ascription, but well familiar to us both in our self-knowledge and in our knowledge of others. That is, for instance, we have no systematic difficulty in deciding whether or not another person knows the meaning of a particular word in a language, and no systematic difficulty in deciding whether or not he has understood a particular statement or question. Nor do we have any systematic reason for being uncertain in regard to our own knowledge of the meaning of this or that particular word, or as to whether or not we have understood something said to us.

Underlying the original complaint is the same syndrome we have already met with in regard to so-called 'mental states' in general, whether cognitive, like perceptual experience, or conative, like the emotions and intention. They are allegedly only to be allowed into 'science' or regarded as explaining anything, in so far as either they can be identified with some neural or brain state or with some operationally defined disposition towards certain physical behaviour patterns (or with both at once as when, as with the concept of gene, the physico-chemical and the functional come together). The incoherence

of this general approach, and its baselessness, has already been sufficiently exposed in Chapters V and VII. All we have to do is realize
that common treatments of linguistic understanding are just further
examples of the same syndrome.[37]

The desire of Dummett is to represent behavioural capacities
as criterial for states of linguistic understanding. Believers in mind-
brain identity and typical cognitive scientists represent these states of
understanding as inner states (states of the brain) generative of just
these behavioural aptitudes or tendencies (these inner states sometimes
being called 'functional states'). But the definition of these behavioural
dispositions, interrelating a variety of kinds of linguistic behaviour with
each other and interrelating linguistic and non-linguistic behaviour,
must either bring in the very states of understanding whose nature
it is being attempted to explain or else be infinite—since the relevant
behavioural dispositions in respect of each element of *langue* have to
be in regard to an indefinite and non-enumerable spread of possible
types of situation and turns of questioning. Accordingly, the positions
represented in Dummett's arguments and in those of typical cognitive
scientists together with the concepts of behaviour they enshrine cannot
be right, as the argument of the previous section shows.

It is easy to see how the questionings about linguistic understanding come to have an exactly parallel structure to doubts in regard
to other so-called 'mental states'. Thus it is presumed that the presence
of such understanding has to be exhibited and evidenced in 'manifest
behaviour', but this is required to be described in terms which do not
refer to language-related states.[38] Yet, this allows sentences so-called to
figure only as the products of acts producing sounds or marks, and not
as structured of elements of *langue*, elements which carry at one and
the same time *langue*-meaning and *parole*-meaning, the two not being
identical. As a result, the concept of 'manifest behaviour' in Dummett

---

[37]For instance, we should regard Quine in his questions about the determinacy
of translation as simply raising problems about linguistic understanding parallel to
the problems Ayer raised about all mental states. There are, of course, false ideals
of definiteness of sense which public language has never had to live up to, but the
failure to conform to these false ideals does nothing to suggest that there is some
intended object of understanding to which the hearer of speech has no access—as if
all speaker-hearer communication was systematically frustrated.

[38]Towards such an approach, misguided though it be, Grice might be envisaged
as having made a key contribution ('Utterer's Meaning, Sentence-meaning, and Word-
meaning'), opening up the possibility of reducing 'semantics' to 'pragmatics' or, one
might say, the reduction of what belongs with illocution to perlocution.

may not be exactly the same as the concept of physically defined behaviour, but, because of what is excluded from its description, it is sufficiently close to it to raise the same problems: the same problems in Dummett as in the very different thought of Quine, and these the same as in behaviourist and operationalist approaches in psychology, and these the same as in the myths of Artificial Intelligence. The failure to give an adequately nuanced account of the relation between understanding of *langue* and understanding of *parole*, resulting in a reductive definition of the former in terms of the latter is common to all these approaches. However, without such a nuanced account we are driven back to a physicalistic description of linguistic 'behaviour'. In this way, the problems of describing and explaining linguistic behaviour come to fall back into the general problems of describing any human behaviour and become merely particular cases of the problems dealt with in Chapter V in our criticism of Malcolm.

The relevance of the *langue/parole* distinction needs to be made absolutely clear.

The key point to seize upon in reviewing Dummett's approach and those rival to his, approaches whereby attempt is made to define understanding in terms of behavioural or 'practical' abilities, is that the definition is always in terms of the handling of utterances or sentences. This is true whether attention is concentrated on truth-conditions as by Davidson, or on verification-conditions as in Dummett, or on what counts as an appropriate response as when imperatives are the centre of attention.

This starting point has the defect of making there to be only one fundamental concept (the sentence) and one fundamental level (speech or *parole*, of which written communication can be taken as a special form) in language—instead of allowing two such concepts (lexeme and sentence) interdependent but neither reducible to the other and two such levels (*langue* and *parole*). But it also has the other associated defect of treating a 'language' as a set of sentences or speech-units—a set of what we may call 'speech-sentences',[39] i.e., of 'utterances' in that sense in which we may make the same

---

[39]It is crucial to the consideration of what is involved in this debate that the word "sentence" is being used, not to mean 'sentence' in the grammarian's sense, but "possible statement", i.e., something which (usually in a way which depends on its context) has whatever definiteness of truth-conditions, appropriate modes of justification and appropriate response ordinary life would expect of statements—or else

utterance, characterised by the same logical import or use, on different occasions.[40]

And Dummett, Wright,[41] and others have the concept that one
can consider a 'fragment of a language' and consider the practical abilities involved in expressing meaningful use of this fragment and then
go on to ask about the practical abilities essential to some extension of
this fragment of language. And, just as a language is supposed to be a
'set of sentences', so a 'fragment of a language' is to be a 'set of sentences'. Thus Dummett tells us: 'If we consider a fragment of natural
language lacking the sentential operators, but containing sentences not
effectively decidable by observation, it would be impossible for that
fragment to display features, embodied or embodying our recognition
of the undecidable sentences as determinately true or false.'[42] In this
we may observe the supposition that one could *first* have a fragment
of a language lacking sentential operators, presumably allowing the
rejection of some of the sentences of this fragment as 'not true' (since
this possibility is presupposed if the question of decidability as to truth
or otherwise is in play) and *then* consider whether or not to add the
principle of bivalence, thereby rendering indirectly provable things of
which no direct proof is available.[43, 44]

"possible question", "possible command", etc. One could say that what was meant
was what Lyons calls a 'text-sentence' (*Semantics*, I, p. 29).

[40] I speak of an 'utterance' (utterance-type) distinguished by its logical import
or use where Strawson speaks of the 'use of an utterance' in "On Referring" (pp. 6–8).

[41] *Realism, Meaning and Truth*, Blackwell, Oxford, 1987.

[42] *Truth and Other Enigmas*, p. 316.

[43] In this, he not only ignores the fact, adverted to in Section 4, that the principle
of bivalence is only a consequence of the Law of the Excluded Middle (the false
proposition either being simply one which is not true, or else, with a more restricted
application of the law of bivalence, being one whose negation is true) so that it is
about the Excluded Middle (and not bivalence) that questions ought to be raised,
but also he seems to envisage the possibility of fragments of 'language' which do not
include negation amongst their structural or structuring features.

[44] Dummett sees that language has to be fragmentable in some way in order
for it to be sufficiently revisable for us not to be landed with accepting falsehoods
as linguistically necessary truths, or with 'creatively' 'proving' nonsense. But this
recognition is sufficiently realized if we root out illegitimately creative inferences, as
from being a dog to being a cur to being contemptible, by an exercise of a variety
of elements of *langue* conjointly against the background of an understanding of the
integrated structure delineated in the previous section. What is required is freedom or
reflectiveness in the handling of distinguishable elements of *langue*, not distinguishable
fragments of language in the sense of totalities of possible speech-sentences.

We can now see that the type of argument deployed by Dummett and Wright in favour of what I have described as a variant of behaviourism turns upon this misconception that what is given in *langue* is sentences—either the complete corpus of the 'sentences' (speech-sentences) of a language, or else fragments of a language each fragment likewise conceived of as a set of such 'sentences' (speech-sentences). In order to see the illegitimacy of this conception we need to grasp that there is no set of rules governing the interpretation of speech-sentences utilizing a given element of *langue* which, as it were, gives the meaning of the class of all the speech-sentences utilizing that element of *langue* beforehand as if this was an already definite infinite totality. Rather, the knowledge of *langue* is given a skilled and situation-geared use by the users of a language, a use wherein they deploy their understanding of the elements of *langue* in understandingly speaking and hearing parts or stretches of *parole*, and these do not constitute a completed totality, but an open set, i.e., a set which comprises possible as well as actual pieces of utterance of no definite number of kinds: knowledge of the *langue*-meaning of a word is a potential towards an indefinitely wide spread of meanings-in-use or *parole*-meanings.

Knowledge of an element of *langue*, e.g., knowledge of the meaning of a word, is gleaned from an experience of some instances of *parole*, but does not consist in the acquisition of rules pertaining to an imaginary totality of all the possible speech-sentences in which the word concerned might appear. There is no such totality.

In short, Dummett and his like conceive linguistic capacity as a capacity or disposition in respect of utterances instead of a capacity in respect of the realization of *langue* in utterances, regarding *langue* as a dispensable or eliminable element in its definition. In this way, they misconceive what kinds of state or disposition we are meeting with whether in the understanding of *parole* or in the understanding of *langue* which it presupposes.[45] A language is an enumerable and,

---

[45]Wittgenstein objects to conceiving understanding a word as if it were just one kind of thing in the sense of one kind of behaviour-pattern or one kind of inner state, to thinking of it as an 'occurrent mental state' in such a way that the whole use of the word was laid out before the mind of the user, or to thinking of it as the inner state of an apparatus (*Philosophical Investigations*, I, 36, 66–77, 143–155, 193, etc.). Again Kripke shows the incoherence of the view that such understanding is a 'disposition' in the restricted modern sense of an operationally defined state. But all these objections

indeed at any one time, a finite set of elements of *langue*, but it is not any kind of set of utterances.

The objections which we have raised against the approaches of Dummett and Wright are sufficient to exclude also various other older or more popular approaches.

Thus, firstly, the idea of separating off some large fragment of a natural language, treating this separated fragment as a set of sentences which can be spoken of as an 'object-language', and regarding it as formalizable and, in general, 'well-behaved', and then of separating off successively larger fragments, referred to as meta-languages, meta-meta-languages, and so forth, each set of sentences and each formalizable and well-behaved, but never treating natural language as a whole with unrestricted self-reflexivity built into the meaning of any one of its parts has been commonplace since Tarski. Ramsey gave his blessing to this approach, which has thenceforward been respectable within almost every school, but it remains useless as a framework for considering natural language or thought.

Secondly, it has been a point of method amongst cognitive scientists to separate out areas where a certain approach, always one involving the effective determination of some class of response for a subject in an appropriately trained state by some class of stimuli with allowance made for some scatter or statistically anticipated error (not due to error in observation, but due to deviation of the subject from the model). Accordingly, since, quite rightly, complete utterances and judgements in regard to them are regarded as the primary data, the result is that only limited ranges of utterances are considered, so that the approach is compatible with conceiving of fragments of language as sets of sentences.

The correct approach for the empirical scientist in this field as in others is to find an adequate model for an adequate spread of phenomena. As in physics, so in linguistics, a large part of the work is theoretical: in Section 3 we saw some elements of the shape of any appropriate theory in this area, a shape incorporating a certain reflexivity, tense-structure, and so forth. And this shows that the whole

---

are beside the point if we utilize the concepts of state and disposition (*hexis, diathesis, dynamis*) in the way they occur in Aristotelian thought (cf. Chapter VII, Section 1 above)—the way of thinking which underlies their prominence in Ryle.

idea of separating off fragments of the language which do not include these structural parts is mistaken.

The conception of expecting some exceptions, 'a rough fit' between scientific model and empirical data, is one which the cognitive scientists share with the philosopher Davidson.[46] But in accepting this conception, they fly in the face of the evident fact that the exceptions are not due to roughness but perfectly determined according to the understanding we have. Both the cognitive scientists and Davidson have regarded the object of their science of language as *parole*, and it is at this level that formalizability fails and, at the same time, understanding gives knowledge outreaching mechanical rules.

---

[46]'Radical Interpretation' reveals at the end the extent of his retreat from the forward positions put forward in 'Truth and Meaning'.

XI. The 'Objects' of the Mind in Speaking and Thinking

If intellectuality arises within animal life, then it takes the form of language: this is the form of intellectuality specific to animals. What then are we to say, if anything, as to the structure of linguistic understanding and of thinking in the medium of words? We have to consider these questions of the structure of linguistic understanding and of thinking in the medium of words as a preliminary to any discussion of the nature of that which understands and thinks. We write against a background within which the tendency is for theories of understanding either to take a behaviouristic form or else to give prominence to the notion of modelling (of which 'picturing' is an example).

Our own view is easy to state. The words we speak are meaningful and not empty, not because when we think or speak there are models, representations, words as symbols, or images of any kind as objects within the mind towards which the mind is directed, but because they say something—in simple cases, some expressing the sense of a statement, some the sense of a question, some the sense of a request or command, and some the sense of a wish. Now the way we think about speaking is the guide to the way we think about thinking in the medium of words, and linguistic understanding is the stuff, grist, and underlay of any kind of human theoretical understanding. But saying something is not an example of presenting a picture,[1] any more than it is an example of naming; and it is not the presenting of a 'symbol' either. Accordingly, it is mistaken to analyse understanding or thinking in terms of modelling—or, for that matter, in terms of 'symbolizing'

---

[1] This key objection to favoured approaches amongst computer theorists is developed in Section 2 below: in brief, to produce a model B of A is not to say that A is like B, let alone to say that A is like B in this or that respect; and no multiplication of acts of modelling, or of modelling of modelling, will achieve the transmutation of the production of a model into the saying of something.

(in any of the common meanings given to this ill-defined term). Let us now give edge to our own way of thinking by considering the alternatives proposed.

For our approach has to hold its own against a multiplicity of rival accounts all of which involve that in speaking meaningfully and in thinking, the mind must contain or be directed towards or 'handle' objects of some kind, whether 'representations', 'ideas', or 'images'. Thus, for many, thought has been conceived of as inner speech involving words passing through the mind as images. Again, thinking and judging involve general concepts, and these have been supposed to be objects of the mind of a kind called 'ideas' gained by a process called 'abstraction', and for Locke the great evil was to use words without such ideas. Yet again, that language represents the world or that it enables the mind to represent the world, has become for many a commonplace. And, even amongst those who escape all these positions, it has sometimes seemed that, in order for the mind to know or think about external objects, it must at least have images of them presented to it as internal objects.

As against all these positions, we should hold to the position that in thinking the mind must not contain within itself intermediate objects of awareness or be directed towards anything apart from the object to be known itself, a position perhaps traceable in Aristotle's remark that it is necessary that the understanding 'be unmixed, as Anaxagoras says, in order that it may be in control, that is that it may know. For anything foreign which appeared in the mind incidentally would hinder or block this mastery or knowledge. . . .'[2] What we have to do in this chapter is to show that speaking and thinking involve no such intermediate objects to the mind, neither images of external objects, nor representations of states of affairs, nor abstracted ideas, nor words as images. In Chapter X we remarked on the importance of the involvement of the imagination in the workings of the intellect, but in explaining the way this works in Sections 2 and 3 below we will see that it is not by means of intermediate objects to the mind of any kind.

We have seen the special kind of indivisibility associated with human beings and some other higher animals as 'focalized subjects', because they are psychosomatic beings. What we are now occupied

---

[2] Aristotle, *De Anima*, 429a 18–22.

with is the peculiar kind of simplicity which belongs to human beings as the subjects of linguistic understanding and of the kind of thinking which is expressed linguistically. This involves a certain indivisibility, not only in the subject of understanding and thought *qua* subject of understanding and thought, but also in the 'operations' of understanding and thinking so that these must not be thought of as composed of sub-processes. Understanding and thinking, and their subject as involved in them, neither *are* nor *present themselves as* complexes.

In earlier times, we might have been said to be inquiring into the 'simplicity' of intellectual substances. In a more modern idiom, following the thought of Ryle and Wittgenstein, we might be said to be exploring the reasons for saying that the mind neither is nor has an 'apparatus' structured of parts or elements in relation to one another—whether the brain composed of physical parts or some soul-substance composed of non-physical parts.

In the present chapter we shall see how it is that understanding and thinking *present themselves as* 'simple': the logic of our concepts of understanding and thinking allows for no 'objects of the mind' internal to the mind, no 'mental contents' making these 'operations' into complexes involving parts and relations between these parts internal to the mind. I leave it to the next chapter to inquire whether understanding and thinking could yet be, 'as they are in themselves', complexes of sub-states and sub-processes of some material kind, in the way it is fashionable to suppose—despite the fact that they 'present themselves' or 'appear to us' as simples or indivisible unities. We are not concerned in this chapter with whether such a supposition could be explanatory of anything, or whether it is empty or incoherent. Rather, in this chapter, our concern is with the preliminary and less extravagant task of examining the 'phenomenology' of thinking—what arises directly from the 'logic' of the concept.

1. Language and Thought Do Not Represent the World: Sentences, Senses, and Facts Are Not 'Objects' to Be in Relation with One Another

Words as sentence-factors are expressive, and thereby sentences are expressive—expressive of the meaning or sense of the sentences or more extended pieces of discourse of which they are part. We shall see that neither language, nor thought, nor the world consists of

objects—sentences, meanings, or facts—such as might be in relations
to one another. And it is not in virtue of such relations that sentences
have sense or meaning. Neither a sentence nor a sense is a picture
or representation. Sentences or complete speech-units have meaning,
not by representing facts or the world, but by expressing whatever
they express. They may express the statement that something is so,
the question whether something is so or why or how it is that is so,
the command that something be done, or the wish that something be
so (or in other cases something requiring more complex description).

I shall say that sentences, senses or meanings, and facts are none
of them 'objects', in this following in an honourable philosophical
tradition of those who, from Plato onwards, have insisted that saying
is not naming or designating. It is not by identifying meanings but
by expressing them that words and sentences have meaning. Neither
sentences nor meanings are, we should say, 'objects' so as to be
subjects of identity statements. Nor is a fact an object in such a way
that sentences or senses might correspond with it or represent it.

Our first task is to demystify this assertion that none of these
things are objects.

(a) Preliminary critique of representational theories of meaning and thinking

Let us consider first the idea that in speaking and thinking the
mind is occupied in some way with representations.

The myth that language or thought is representative of reality as if statements and thoughts represented facts is ever recurrent
amongst philosophers. Statements in particular have been held to have
a 'descriptive content' or 'sense' which made them representative of
reality, while other kinds of utterance have been imagined to have a
meaning dependent on these—so that, for instance, if "P" were the
statement that P, then the imperative would be "Make it to be that P"
and would have been obeyed or as the jargon goes, would have had
its satisfaction-conditions satisfied if the statement "P" had its truth-
conditions fulfilled, so that the descriptive content or 'sense' of imperatives would be limited to their supposed propositional component.

This myth can be shown up for its implausibility by the consideration of very simple examples.

We can form representations or mental pictures of what is seen,
and even of a person or animal looking at it, but not of a person's act

of seeing it. Of course, we know what it is to see something, and we are tempted to say that this is because we know and can imagine what it would be for us ourselves to see something, but this knowing or imagining what it would be for us to see something includes knowing what it would be to reach out to touch it, to move in amongst the things seen, or to re-orientate ourselves in regard to what is seen, and is not at all a matter of picturing ourselves seeing it: likewise, to imagine others seeing something is not at all just to picture the others in certain bodily and spatial relations to it. Along the same line, we can now go further and say that, indeed, we know what it is for someone to wish or to order something to be done, but this is not by picturing wishing or the relation between people involved in ordering. Knowing what it is to wish or to order something to be done is derivative upon knowing the meaning of optative and imperative moods and forms of expression or of knowing the force of speech-acts involving these which, at least according to the doctrine we are criticizing, is not part of the 'descriptive content' or 'sense' of these speech-acts.

In a more sophisticated way, we should be aware of the position set forth in Wittgenstein's *Tractatus* as the most distilled and formal presentation of what is involved in a representational or 'picture' theory. *In his presentation, all that propositions are required to have in common with reality in order to be able to represent it is logical form (i.e., this is all that pictorial form comes to in the case of a proposition). Accordingly, everything which tells against that picture theory tells against any representational theory whatsoever.* And in the hindsight of over seventy years reflection or discussion (Wittgenstein's own and that of others later), we should be aware of all its untenability of this type of theory—aware of the impossibilities generated by logical atomism even for the simple problem of colour incompatibilities—aware of the structured spread of true or false assertions to which the theory cannot apply, the spread indeed of which the *Tractatus* itself offered an initial map picking out quantified propositions, ascriptions of number, logical laws, modal statements, laws of nature and assertions of causal connection, psychological and evaluative assertions as outside the theory's reach—aware of the folly of supposing that every sense-expressing act, even the Neapolitan gesture of contempt,[3] has a 'logical form'.

---

[3]N. Malcolm, *Ludwig Wittgenstein: A Memoir*, p. 69.

However, such representational theories remain always with us. Thus, in a strange echo of the *Tractatus*, Dummett tells us that 'A sentence is a representation of some facet of reality', speaks of attempting to 'explain the way in which we contrive to represent reality by means of language', and identifies 'the content of a sentence' with 'its representative power',[4] while Wright speaks of 'the realist's idea that depictive powers may outstrip our cognitive capacity'.[5] And it is in accordance with this preconception, whereby language represents the world, that it has been said that it is 'the theory of meaning' which 'lies at the foundation of the whole of philosophy',[6] or that 'the attempt to understand the relation between thought and the world' should be described as 'constitutive of metaphysics'.[7]

It may be helpful to make some rather looser informal remarks at this point. Having a mental model is not judging, whether as an act of thought or an act of speech. If there were a model or picture involved in giving content to a judgement, the most natural way to suppose this to occur would be to suppose that the judgement was the judgement that the world was like the model in some respect, or that the two in some way corresponded or fitted. The judgement would then include modes of reference to the world and to the model, but would not include the world or the model (any more than a statement would). The sense of a sentence is not something which depicts the world and hangs about in the mind while it is being considered as to whether it is true or false—or whether it 'corresponds' to the facts it is meant to depict or whether it does not so correspond. (Entertaining a proposition is a common phrase for this supposed having a sense in the mind with a view to considering whether it is true or false, but there is no such hanging about the mind in an indeterminate way prior to a 'mental action', whether of thought or of speech, whether of questioning or of judgement.) On the contrary, it is judgements and statements which are true or false, not some other entities called senses with a supposed depictive relation to the world—or with a 'descriptive content', a content not as to what the world is like in some respect

---

[4] Dummett, *Truth and Other Enigmas*, p. 309.

[5] *Realism, Meaning and Truth*, p. 3. He here presumes that the cognitive job of statements is to depict, and that the question is of whether we can always determine whether reality is as they depict it as being.

[6] *Truth and Other Enigmas*, p. 309.

[7] *Realism, Meaning and Truth*, p. 1.

(this would make it a statement or judgement that the world was like so-and-so) but a content which fits or 'corresponds to' the described possible state of affairs.

However, we must avoid allowing our rejection of such depictive or correspondence theories from leading us to make such perfectly mad statements as that 'there is no connection between language and reality',[8] imagined by Hacker to be a consequence for Wittgenstein after 1929 of the 'autonomy' of grammar whereby grammar is a matter of notation and a notation is not true to the facts.[9] Still, to be speaking of language and reality (constellations of sentences or senses and facts) as if they were constellations of objects, and yet to do this in the act of denying any connection between them, is to have the worst of both worlds. If one thinks like this, of course one cannot help but become prey to transcendental idealism and to conventionalism—but what one ought to have done is to realize that what is wrong is to think of language and reality, sentences or their senses and facts, as objects or constellations at all.

Rather, the connection between language and reality must be thought of in a quite different way, not in terms of a correspondence between linguistic entities (e.g., sentences) and non-linguistic entities (e.g., facts or states of affairs), but in terms of a coincidence of major grammatical categories and major metaphysical ones. Thus the philosophy of language should take cognizance of such distinctions as those in relation to time between continuants (subjects persisting through time) and states, episodes, acts, and activities (the things respectively distinguished by their posture in time), and between these and time itself; or in relation to space the distinctions between first substance, shape, size, and place; or in relation to causal agency the distinctions between (i) first substance, (ii) the nature of such a substance or thing as what determines its modes of action and passion, (iii) actions and passions, and (iv) the terminal and intermediate states from which or to which these substances, according to these natures, are carried by these actions and passions, i.e., by which the stages and end-points

---

[8] *Insight and Illusion*, p. 185. This is far stronger claim than the claim that there is 'no isomorphism between language and reality' (pp. 186–188) which merely embodies a rejection of a picture or representational theory of the meaning of statements.

[9] *Insight and Illusion*, p. 207.

of changes are marked, and (v) time as that with reference to which change is measured or ordered; and all these distinctions belong to physics or some first order study wider than physics as well as to the science of language. In this way, not only does speech tell, but its structure shows, something of reality—but not by there being an isomorphism between language and reality as if these were two objects which might be compared as to structure. It is rather in this way that 'the harmony between thought and reality is to be found in the grammar of language'.[10]

Accordingly, our critique of representational theories of the meaningfulness of speech and of thinking must be more radical. We must, first of all, reject the very idea of statements, senses, and facts as objects between which there are relations—there are no such objects in or before the mind because these things are not objects at all, and to suppose that they are is to make a grammatical mistake. Secondly, we must kill the notion of sense, whether devised to fit these representational theories or devised for quite different grounds, and so remove one of the terms of the supposed relations.

(b) Sentences, senses, and facts as 'cognates', not objects

I come now to the task of demystifying this assertion that none of these things are objects. The way to this is by showing the natural way in which it arises simply as a point belonging to logic and to grammar. Then, afterwards we need to make vivid the significance of this point.

It is evident that the verb "to be" takes many different kinds of complement, some of them what we describe as adjectival and others which, because of their other grammatical features and relations, we regard as noun-like. We have already distinguished between the logical and grammatical status of expressions for possible logical subjects of discourse and so-called intentional objects, respecting the difference

---

[10]Wittgenstein, *Philosophical Grammar*, p. 162. For Hacker, on the contrary, it is the conventionalism of the later Wittgenstein which reveals the sense in which grammar is autonomous and shows how the meaning of this remark is to be understood (*Insight and Illusion*, pp. 193–194). However, the main example Hacker gives (pp. 185 ff.) is only the relatively superficial feature of colour classification, and he does not notice deeper structural distinctions such as those embodied, for example, in Aristotle's eight principal categories.

in significance between "There was something he ran into (it might have been a lamp-post)" and "There was something he imagined (it might have been a cow)". What we are now occupied with is a third class of case: "There was something which he knew but did not tell me", "There were several points he made", "There was something he said", "There was something he meant", "There was something which he said that very clearly meant", and so forth. What I wish to say is that, whereas in the first two classes of case it is appropriate to use the word "object" and to speak of relations or directedness towards 'objects', in the third class of case this is not appropriate.

At this stage a short piece of technical clarification will be helpful: the reader will find afterwards that it exactly fits his ordinary intuitions.

I shall present the matter in the following way. The expression "the sentence "The grass is green"" refers to the same sentence as the expression "The grass is green", but cannot be used as a sentence. By contrast, the expression "The grass is green" can be used as a sentence, and, just because it can be used in this way as a sentence, the same expression can also be used to refer to a sentence, viz., to itself. Thus, the expression "The grass is green" according to one mode of linguistic use is used as a sentence but according to another is used to refer to a sentence, whereas the expression "The sentence "The grass is green"" has only the one mode of use, namely to refer to a sentence and does not have another mode of use whereby it may be used as a sentence. Likewise, the expression "the predicate " . . . is a horse"" refers to the same predicate as the expression " . . . is a horse", but only the latter can be used according to two modes of linguistic use, the one as a predicate, and the other to refer to a predicate. Again, the expression "the name "Smith"" refers to the same name as the expression "Smith", but only the latter can be used according to two modes of linguistic use, the one as a name, and the other to refer to a name. It will be noted that in every case the primary use of the sentence, predicate, or name, is as a sentence, predicate or name, and the secondary use is as a way of referring to itself, but that out of this secondary use other derivative modes of reference arise, viz., the ones mentioned first in our above examples.

Against this background, I shall say that an expression is an expression denoting an object when that to which it refers has other noun-expressions referring to it, and all the expressions referring to it have always the same mode of linguistic use and are, therefore, intersubstitutable without change of mode of linguistic use: these expressions I call object-designations. There are other cases in which there are two expressions referring to a thing, but in which it is not the case that these expressions have always the same mode of linguistic use and which are not, therefore, intersubstitutable without change of mode of linguistic use: these expressions I call cognate-designations. I call them cognate-designations because the primary designations concerned, viz., the sentences, the predicates, and the names, become designations at all only because of the way in which in various linguistic combinations they become cognate to verbs such as "know", "tell", "say", "ask", "order", "mean", "understand", "think", "wonder", "believe", and so forth. According to which verbs they are cognate to, they are described as (e.g.) designating facts, designating sentences (complete speech-units), designating words, designating senses or meanings of sentences, or again sometimes designating the *langue*-meanings and sometimes designating the *parole*-meanings of words.

So much then for the technical meaning of saying that none of the expressions "The grass is green", "that grass is green", "grass's being green" designate an object, whether the object be a sentence or proposition, a thought or a sense, a fact or a state of affairs. And so much, likewise, for the technical meaning of saying that words and other subsentential expressions, whether mentioned or used, do not designate any such objects as words and expressions, or meanings, whether in *langue* or in *parole*, or properties, classes abstractly conceived,[11] or 'features'[12]—although, of course, when used rather than mentioned, certain of them (viz., names in the proper sense, e.g., "Smith", "Saturn", "red") may designate objects properly so called such as people, planets, and colours.

But by saying that such expressions, when they designate without designating objects, do something else—namely designate cognates— I mean to say something positive in regard to them, not merely negative. For I bring them into analogy with other cognates: we do deeds, dream dreams, see sights, feel feelings, etc. And the cognate

---

[11]I count a class as something abstractly conceived if there is such a thing as an empty class and if there is a distinction between an object and the class containing it and nothing else. Collections as ordinarily conceived are not abstract in this way: I may keep equally one shoe, a pair of shoes, or a collection of shoes under my bed.

[12]These are a recent surrogate for properties, favoured by modern theorists who think of statements and thoughts as involving the recognition of a general feature as being exemplified in a particular thing or situation.

need not have the same morphological stem or etymological root as the verb concerned, nor need the verbal expression be single-worded: thus, we perform actions, feel pains, pleasures, desires, and sorrows, have worries, pains, and hallucinations, play games and pieces of music, enjoy games and other pleasures, and so forth. But we need to put beside these a second set of examples: we make statements, give orders, have beliefs and thoughts, present arguments, perform plays as well as pieces of music, and along with these things we utter sentences, hear and understand them, understand words and understand their meanings, learn or get to know facts sometimes by being told them, and so forth. And this second set of examples should be analysed and understood, logically and ontologically, in a parallel way to the first.

Let us speak of these matters more informally, utilizing what comparisons and metaphors come to hand.

In every case, we could, if we wanted, think of the cognate as having a sort of existence (after all, they do figure as complements to the verb "to be", as in the already instanced types of context such as "There was something he said"). But this will tempt us to invent a new kind of 'being' or *Sein* in a Meinongian fashion, and to introduce distinctions between supposed kinds of 'being' (*esse* or *Sein*) possessed supposedly by different categories of 'being' (*ens* or entity) as if they were prior to distinctions between the modes of speech appropriate to the various grammatical subjects and objects involved, treating the supposed entities as given first, so that then one will have to inquire into their metaphysical relations. In this way, one will have added to one's mythology of kinds of *Sein* a mythology of kinds of entity. Instead of all this, one should treat the distinction between modes of speech (or of thought in the medium of words) as primary, so that there is nothing beyond some formal structure in speech in common to the different things which are said to 'be'—hence Berkeley was almost right in saying in such a case (a substance and its 'ideas') that the 'things' have nothing in common except the name 'being',[13] but not quite, because there is this shared formal or grammatical structure.

Senses or meanings, therefore, and sentences as complete speech-units or the completed expressions of sense, have only what we might

---

[13] *Principles of Human Knowledge*, sect. 89.

describe as a dynamic existence, akin to a drama as the linguist Jespersen put it, set within the context of the performance called a speech-act. In this their 'relation' is analogous to the 'relation' of a person's life or soul to his body, each made what it is in the dynamic act of the person's being or living: and as the person's life or soul is not a second thing externally related to his body as a first thing, requiring to be related by some third thing (some system of correlation, isomorphism and causation), so the sense or meaning of a sentence is not a second thing externally related to the sentence as a first thing, requiring to be related according to some system. Rather, as the soul is what makes the body what it is, so the sense of a sentence is what makes the sentence what it is, makes it the sentence it is. And as soul and body may be thought of as constituted in the dynamism of the person's existing, so sense and sentence are constituted together in the dynamism of the speech-act as its twin cognates—as a deed is constituted in the doing, a game in the playing, and a dream in the dreaming.

In sum, then, there are no objects with any standing in their own right, senses or meanings, such as could have relations of isomorphism or otherwise with sentences or facts; and sentences and facts themselves are not objects, let alone ones with relations of isomorphism (the early Wittgenstein) or lack of isomorphism (Hacker) between them.

(c) Force internal to sense and to thought: no thought without attitude

Fitting in with representational theories, although often with independent reasons, philosophers have developed a technical theory of 'senses'.

In order to make clear what is involved we must distinguish between, on the one hand, what we may call complete senses, associated with sentences as complete speech-units, the cognates of complete speech acts, and, on the other hand, the senses of sentence-factors.

Philosophers have developed a mythology according to which, as well as statements and judgements, there are also the senses or contents of statements which are entertained by the mind without any determinate attitude or posture internal to them, such senses or propositional contents being called 'thoughts' by Frege. These thoughts or senses are not supposed to be themselves judgements, beliefs, or anything expressible as a statement: the force associated with judging, asserting, or stating is imagined to be external to them. And it is these forceless senses or thoughts which are alleged to be the primary subjects of truth and falsity and to have a depictive or representational relation to the world in virtue of which they are capable of being true or false.[14]

But this is all a cloud of the philosophers' own making.

The primary subjects of truth and falsity[15] are statements, judgements, beliefs, and thoughts. When we consider the logic of truth-functions such as "... and——", and say that "P or Q" is true if and only if at least one of the component propositions ("P" and "Q") is true, what we should have said more accurately is that it is true if and only if one of the component propositional clauses ("P" and "Q") would have been true if it had occurred on its own, i.e., contextually as a statement or judgement. If we state as an instance of a logical law 'If "P" is true and "If P, then Q" is true, then "Q" would be true as well', we have envisaged "P", "If P, then Q", and "Q" not as statements or judgements actually made but as statements or judgements which could be made: there is a problem about possible acts of stating and judging which falls into its place within the general problem of the status of possible facts, a problem to which I will attend below. But it remains clear that the cognates even of possible acts of stating and judging are statements and judgements—not some entities (labelled 'senses' or 'thoughts') to which force or direction is external.

We may rightly speak of models, images or representations as having a role in connection with thinking. But propositions, statements and senses are not such models, pictures or representations: rather they incorporate force or attitude. They not only explain or make plain the possible use or function of a model (or picture or representation),[16] but because they incorporate force or attitude give

---

[14]In Wittgenstein's precise formulation: 'A proposition *shows* its sense. A proposition *shows* how things stand *if* it is true. And it *says that* they do so stand.' (*Tractatus*, 4.022)

[15]Primary subjects of truth and falsity, that is, where what is concerned is the intellect operating in the manner of a deliberating animal and answering to how things are, rather than a matter of how things are answering to the prior intention of an artist.

[16]It is only within a context shown by an utterance or thought that models can have any role at all, and this is not by being parts of the utterance or thought (we do not say or think the model); rather, they are the things shown or alluded to in thought, illustrative of the way things are being said to be, cf. Section 3.3 below.

the model this direction, point or function. Models, etc., are, as such, dead and without direction.

The idea that something called a proposition, say "P", occurs unasserted as a component in the negations, conditionals, and disjunctions "Not P", "If P, then Q", and "P or Q", was the root of Frege's view that such entities as these 'propositions' had sense such as sufficed to make them the subjects of attributions of truth and falsity without having force, e.g., as statements asserted or judgements assented to. But today we meet an approach which makes the main function of 'force' something quite different, namely to distinguish between statements (also called assertions), commands, and wishes—entities which Frege had held to have different sense, and not only different force.

In respect of commands and wishes we should hold to the general form of our position on statements: it is the statements, commands, and wishes which are the primary subjects to which sense should be ascribed, force being a component or aspect of sense, and there is no abstractable 'sense' belonging to the whole but not including force. Wishes like judgements and questions[17] can occur either as thoughts or in outwardly expressed form, and when they so occur mentally rather than in outwardly expressed form, they occur again with 'force' or direction—with posture, force, direction or attitude internal to them. It is the inner wish as well as the outer wish which can be fulfilled, the inner question as well as the outer one which can be answered, and what is fulfilled or answered is the wish or the question, just as what is true or false is the judgement: what is fulfilled, answered, or true or false is not a supposed sense abstracted from force, something to be spoken of as a 'descriptive content',[18] but the wish, question, or judgement itself.

The conception that there is an object towards which the mind is in certain mental acts mentally directed, in particular an object of understanding, distinguished in Frege's terms as a 'sense' or a 'thought', and by others as the 'propositional content' of a sentence,

---

[17]I have not brought these in earlier because Frege's position in regard to questions changed, first regarding the difference between assertions and questions as analogous to the differences between assertions, commands, and wishes, and so a difference of sense, but later regarding the first difference as a difference in force. But this historical detail is not germane to my present discussion.

[18]Dummett, *Frege: Philosophy of Language*, p. 308.

is therefore baseless—a creature of the philosophical logician's own making, born of a mistaken line of thinking. There simply do not exist any such objects as these supposed 'senses' available to stand in a relation of 'representation' to some facet of reality.

2. Abstraction and Judgement: The Capacity to Use General Concepts Cannot Be Explained in Terms of Abstract Ideas as Objects to the Mind

The question arises as to how the use of any general concept (the concept F, for example) is possible. By a 'general concept' I mean a concept of the kind which typically figures in the three interrelated sorts of proposition called singular, universal, and particular: that is, propositions of the forms "The object a is F", "Every A is F", "Some A is F"; or, expressing these forms using quantifiers and taking quantification over the domain of the A's of which a is a member, "Fa", "(x)(Fx)", "(∃x)(Fx)".

Historically, we meet with two most popular accounts of how such use of general concepts is possible, one bringing in a theory of acquaintance with objects called universals (Platonic theories), and the other depending upon the theory of a capacity to compare sensible ideas and to judge likeness (the classical 'empiricist' theories). These theories have been subject to an enormous volume of criticism, both within the circles of 'ordinary language philosophy' and outside it, including criticisms found within the writings of the empiricists themselves. But, for the most direct and clear treatment of the whole matter, we can do no better than to draw fairly directly on the analysis presented by Aquinas, in this way avoiding the frequent indecisiveness and inconsequentiality of later discussions. [Into Aquinas' account there enters some mention of entities called *phantasmata* (the Greek word for 'images' being used here), and we shall consider what we should say about these and about Berkeley's representative ideas not in this but in the following section.]

All such systems of human judgements, singular, universal, and particular, with the human capacities to make and understand them which they presuppose, imply associated judgements of similarity and dissimilarity, and these in respects both more general and more determinate, and also such judgements in relation to imagined and supposed cases. The question is as to what makes the global ensemble of such judgements possible.

It cannot be by means of some kind of 'acquaintance' with objects called 'universals' conceived of in a Platonic way for three reasons, well-known from discussions of the so-called Third Man argument.

(i) It is not clear how a relation not yet explained to an extra kind of object of knowledge would assist in or relate to ordinary knowledge. What we need to know is the significance of the predicate (e.g.) " . . . is a man (human being)" as applied to Plato, Socrates, and other human beings, not to how some knowledge of a further entity called Man or 'being a man' in some obscure relation to ordinary human beings. (ii) The nature of these 'universals' has not been explained, and it does not seem that there is any good reason for supposing that any such 'objects' exist. Acquaintance with them, whether directly or through reminiscence, would not help in getting to know ordinary objects. (iii) No account can be offered of the relation between these supposed 'universals' as objects and ordinary objects. The relation between ordinary objects and the 'universals' has been variously described as one of participation, imitation, exemplification, having, instantiating or belonging. But what are these relations? We might think of (e.g.) explaining "participates in whiteness" or "imitates the white itself" in terms of "is white", or explaining "has humanity" or "belongs to the species man" in terms of "is a man", but giving such explanations is excluded by the theory of 'universals' which involves that we get understanding the other way round, and only understand these ordinary predications from first understanding the supposed relations to universals.

In short, the proper object of the human intellect, i.e., of the human being *qua* operating intellectually, is not a universal as such but the universal or nature as it exists in individuals.[19] I.e., when we learn that 'man is an animal' or that 'animality is a part of humanity', what we have learnt is not some truth about abstract objects called

---

[19]This is the reason why the intellect, in order actually to know a sensible nature, e.g., the nature 'human being', has to know it as presented in particular instances, through perception or imagination (as Aristotle and Aquinas say, in the *phantasmata* or images). For the role of the imagination and relevant references, see Section 3 below. In Aquinas' theory, it is not the object of insightful knowledge which is universal in its nature, and free from individuating conditions, but the means of knowledge, i.e., these principles (called *species*) of the things known as they exist in the knower.

the species man or the property humanity but that human beings are by nature animals.

Presented with empiricist theories whereby the basis of the judgements, "a is F", "Every A is F", and "Some A is F", is the capacity to compare external objects with each other or to compare external objects with ideas, the question still remains as to what makes such comparative judgements between external objects (e.g., that they are alike in colour and in particular in being red) or between an external object and an 'idea' or sample in the mind (e.g., the idea of 'red') possible. This cannot be explained in terms of isomorphism or the possession of samples. Given an idea, schema or sample, as an object to the mind—whether a schema of being red not tied to any shade, brightness, shape or size, or whether a representative sample to be used in a certain way—it remains that the object has to be judged like in form or isomorphic with or similar to the idea, whether schema or representative sample, and judged 'like in respect of colour' and, more explicitly and determinately, 'like in the respect that both are red'. The empiricists may think they have got over two of Plato's problems: their 'ideas', unlike Plato's Forms, do not have to be remembered from an earlier period of existence or are not innate but 'derived' from experience; and they are known, we are told, by imagination. But these do not help them explain how the use of general terms or concepts is possible, how judgements of similarity and dissimilarity are possible.[20] No additional objects of the mind, whether external to it like Plato's Forms or internal to it like the empiricists' ideas, can serve any function in making such judgements possible.[21]

---

[20]The uselessness of multiplying samples without introducing things which are not samples, but principles for considering the sample, is made plain in Wittgenstein (*Philosophical Investigations*, I, 74) as well as Aquinas (cf. the discussion in 'Intellect and Imagination in Aquinas', Anthony Kenny, pp. 285–288).

[21]There is an ambiguity in the empiricists as to whether ideas (e.g., as faint images of impressions, or as particular 'perceptions of the mind') are particular existences so that the idea of red which I have at one time is numerically distinct from the idea of red which I have at another time, or whether we can have the same idea at different times—in which case ideas seem to be types (or universals of some kind) rather than tokens. If they are types or universals we have all the problems indicated in the text with Plato's theory of Forms, and if they are particulars then adding some additional internal or mental particulars to the initial spread of external particulars does not help the problem about how we can generalize about (or make judgements of similarity and dissimilarity in regard to) particulars at all.

Therefore, the answer to the question as to what makes any such human judgements possible does not lie in proposing some further objects to the mind's attention (whether ideas as universals as in Plato or whether ideas as analogous to images as in the empiricists). Rather it lies in merely insisting that there must be within the causal or historical explanation of such human operations a disposition, principle or root of some kind which is shaping or formative of the intellectual operations concerned, 'intentional' of the objects in that it is the 'that whereby the mind is directed towards them' (corresponding not to the objects of the rifle's aim but to what is involved in the rifle's being aimed at such objects). The requirement that there be such a principle is structural—a structural requirement of any explanation of the operations concerned but not something which gives any non-formal content to the explanation. (This principle of intending or pointing, or 'property in virtue of which, or whereby' objects are intended, is not itself the object of the acts concerned but only their principle, and is known only through reflection upon the acts concerned, a reflection belonging to sciences of natural things, in this case the science of psychology, and to metaphysics.)[22] That it is some principle or disposition which we must look for, directing mental acts, rather than some extra object of the mind over and above ordinary external objects, is confirmed by the way in which in more sophisticated empiricist accounts the role of the use of images and habits in the use of images begins to overshadow the role of the images themselves.[23]

---

[22]S. Th. Ia, Q.85, Art. 2, Comm. De An. 718, Q. D. De An., p. 27.

[23]Hume introduces an elaborate system of habits whereby, in effect, if what is involved is the image of (e.g.) a horse, then that it is being used as the image of a horse and not that of a bay horse is shown by our realization of the equal serviceability of images of other kinds of horse and that is not being used as the image of a quadruped, of a footed animal, of a land animal, or of an animal is shown by our realization of the non-serviceability of other images such as of a cow, an ostrich, a snake or a fish—a great number of further judgements of similarity and dissimilarity being here involved. In all this, we seem to have a theory of customs or habits in the use of images brought in to explain our habits in the use of words and to explain how they have content, and what everything turns upon is not the ideas as images on which the empiricists laid so much store but whatever is involved in these habits in the use of words. In this way, dispositions as to use whether of images or words seem to have assumed a larger importance in Hume's account than images themselves as supposed available objects to the mind. And, one may remark, within Berkeley's account of the meaningful use of words in regard to the objects of the mind, the mode of use of representative

The conception that, for our capacity to use general terms meaningfully, what is vital is not an extra object of the mind but a new set, or disposition, or principle of operation of the mind was thought of by Aquinas as parallel to the way in which, in our act of seeing things, the alteration in our sense-faculty is not an extra object of the mind (a representation or sense-datum) but only a something in virtue of which we see.

Aquinas called such a principle of intellectual operation an intelligible *species* by analogy with the sensible *species* which he thought were involved in vision. Neither of these kinds of *species* was in Aquinas' understanding an image (*imago* or *phantasma*) since neither was an object of the imagination or of acts of perception, and neither was a principle of operation or object to any act of the intellect (except as an object of second-order theoretical study of the conditions of perception and intellection). In his account the sensible *species* had the double aspect described earlier in both being likenesses of the objects of vision and being the principles whereby the animal was directed appropriately towards the objects in the act of seeing, i.e., the principles in virtue of which the animal saw the objects. We do not wish to retain the particular theory of vision (whereby they were 'imprints' of the objects captured in the pupil of the eye, present somewhat as light is present *en route* in a window):[24] it was because of this theory that, in the case of vision, these principles were regarded as 'likenesses' of some kind and in virtue of this called '*species*'. But we do wish to retain the conception of there being principles, both in the case of intellection and in the case of vision, in virtue of which the person's mind is directed towards the objects so as actually to be able to know them (comparable, as we remarked, rather to a rifle's being aimed rightly than to its objects).[25]

---

ideas overshadows the role of the idea taken as representative. Therefore, even in the empiricists' own accounts, the key to a theory of meaning must be of the existence of some principle or disposition underlying the use of words or of images and words in connection with each other, not the existence of images or ideas in addition to external objects as objects to the mind.

[24]Cf. Chapter III, n. 45 and text.

[25]In my way of understanding the word *species* in Aquinas, I was assisted by two primary things: firstly, Lonergan's insistence in his book *Verbum* on the distinctions, very clear in Aquinas, between (a) *species* as the principle through or according to which a cognitive act is achieved, (b) *species* as the natural kind or nature which is the object understood or judged about, and (c) the *species expressa, verbum,* or definition

Although we do not use the word *species* because it is now for us a misnomer, we do want to retain the concept of 'principle of cognitive operation' for which Aquinas used this word. We also want to retain, both in the case of intellection and in the case of vision, the feature whereby these principles in virtue of which the person's mind is directed towards the objects so as actually to be able to know them is, in some way, determined by these objects—the concepts or 'intelligible *species*' determined by experience through 'abstraction' and the 'sensible *species*' formed in the act of perception.[26]

The question now is as to what more can be said a priori as to the nature and genesis of these 'principles' in the case of understanding and thinking.

---

formed as a result of the act of understanding; secondly, the account of intentionality as it figures in Aquinas' theory of perception in Chapter II, *Problemes d'Epistemologie*, George von Riet. This structure is key to understanding Karl Rahner's account of 'Uncreated Grace' in *Theological Investigations*, vol.I: Jesus, as the Word or *species expressa* of the Father, is the *species impressa* or *intelligibilis* which is principle to the human act of seeing God. In addition, Professor G.E.M. Anscombe alerted me to the fact that Aquinas speaks always of the pupil and, unlike Descartes, never of the retina of the eye: the pupil must be transparent and without colour (like a perfect window) as a background for the idea that a colour materially in the pupil would alter the colour seen, thus explaining why the non-materiality of the alteration to the pupil, indeed its material colourlessness, would be vital, and how the comparison with vision suggested that 'intelligible species' of objects must 'be' their objects only intentionally, never formally.

Because the *species* concerned are in no way objects of the mind in the cognitive acts of which they are principles, the translation of the word *species* by the word "image", found in the English Dominican translations of the *Summa Theologica* of the early 1900's (2nd ed., Burns and Oates, 1941), and perpetuated in their more recent translation (Blackfriars, 1961–70), is particularly to be abominated. The comments in Appendix 1 to Vol. 12 of the latter do no justice to the rich evidence to be derived from the *Comm. De An.* and *Q. D. De An.* as to the steadiness with which 'intelligible *species*' means *species impressa*, not *species expressa*, in the relevant contexts. The madness which overcomes translators of Aquinas whereby either sensible or intelligible *species* become rendered as 'images' (Aquinas has quite other words for 'image', viz., *phantasma*, *imago*) is difficult to understand, especially in the context of his war with representative theories of perception and intellection.

[26]Each kind of *species* is formed in a way shaped by the previous life-history of the person concerned according to principles ('dispositions' or *potentiae*) intrinsic to human nature, i.e., while relevantly different features of experience differentiate different *species*, these features of experience are not in their causal or qualatative aspects adequate by themselves to determine these *species* in either form or content— the human being is not operated upon mechanically, but the exercise of its own nature is involved (including, in the case of concepts or 'intellective *species*', the so-called 'active intellect').

Let us keep in view the function of these 'principles of cognitive operation'—what they are 'principles' of.

These principles are to make possible two things: (i) the specifically human mode of exercise of the sensory powers, whereby we perceive things as such and such, i.e., as falling under certain universal concepts, understood as universals (i.e., as applicable to many things)—that is we grasp the *phantasma* or the sensible object as exemplifying a certain nature or universal;[27] (ii) more generally, all the acts of defining and of stating, embracing all types of assertion which involve general concepts, whether definitional or propositional, affirmative or negative, singular, existential, or universal.[28]

If the human being comes into existence a *tabula rasa*, he or she cannot gain these principles innately or by reminiscence but only by something which, for lack of any other agreed name, we may call abstraction. The activity of the intellect (this will be an aspect of the intellect wherein it is active)[29] in abstracting these principles involves the coming into existence in the mind of these principles

---

[27]This is the point of Aquinas' remark about "the universal reason which, so to speak, overflows into the cogitative and memorative powers" (*S. Th.* Ia, Q.78, Art. 5), and the contrast he makes between the estimative power in animals and the corresponding power (called 'cogitative power' and 'particular reason', because it involves the particularized application of universal concepts) in human beings (*S. Th.* Ia, Q.78, Art. 4, in corp.; cf. Ia, Q.83, Art. 1, on how reason enters into judgements even about particular acts, and how human freedom depends on this.)

[28]These will be acts signified by the voice using words, signifying the *ratio* or definition of something, and, in the case of assertions in general (*enunciationes*), signifying or expressing composition or division, cf. *S. Th.* Ia, Q. 85, Arts. 2 and 3. (These latter will include judgements of the sensory powers, as in (a), as well as universal judgements).

[29]Aquinas' account of the active or agent intellect and of the receptive or 'possible' intellect is a highly sophisticated account of the formal conditions of the human being's being a *tabula rasa*, with only a loose connection to the obscure remarks of Aristotle which purported to be its inspiration but which received very natural and quite opposite interpretations from other commentators. Because human beings begin each as a *tabula rasa*, they have to have a capacity for being active in 'abstracting' these 'principles' or 'ways of conceiving things' (so-called intelligible *species*), and intellectual capacity in this aspect is what is referred to as the active or agent intellect. But subsidiarily, in order to retain these principles from a learning situation into a non-learning situation of their use, the human being's intellectual capacity must have a non-active aspect, the so called receptive or 'possible' intellect: the human being does not in each new act of thinking or speaking start from scratch, look again in his imagination at all the varied range of previous cases, re-form a 'way

in such a way that they exist in the mind without being tied to any of the individuating conditions associated with the occasions of their acquisition.[30]

In regard to this activity of 'abstraction', I have three points to make.

In the first place, abstraction has to be explained in terms of judgement. The act of abstraction as the act of acquiring the principles (means) whereby objects can be known cannot be understood or defined except in terms of the activity of exercising (using) these principles in judgement (or activities of reflecting or contemplatively understanding presupposing judgement). The separateness of the principles from the individuating and material conditions of the circumstances of their acquisition is tailor-made to their function of making it possible to 'consider the nature of the kind concerned without considering the individuating principles represented in the sensible examples or images'[31] or to 'consider one thing without considering another, but without judging them to be separate; considering them separately but not as separate'.[32] I.e., it is tailor-made to the exercise of these principles in judgements about the objects known: the objects of *intelligere* (understanding or thinking about) being, not strictly speaking the images or *phantasmata*, but the nature of a kind as individuated in material things, whether presented through perception or through imagination. To take examples from a later style of presentation of the position concerned, what is required is the establishment within the human being of precisely that possession-of-principles-able-to-be-exercised-independently-of-the-identity-of-the-learning-situation which will allow of an application of the concept "round" to round yellow objects although hitherto only (say) round red, white and blue objects have been met with, so that the person can judge a thing to be round without implying anything as to its colour.

In the second place, 'abstraction' and 'judegment' are acts of the human being *qua* animal. In the 'act' of abstraction, the consideration of sensible particulars plays an essential role in that this consideration

---

of conceiving' things, prior to re-using this 'way of conceiving' in a new instance, but retains 'ways of conceiving things' from earlier experience.

[30] *Q. D. De An.*, Rowan's translation, pp. 24–25, cf. pp. 8, 21 (Obj. 20), 22, 27 (Ad. 5, 6), 182–183; *Comm. De An.* 692–693; *S. Th.* Ia, Q.85, 1.

[31] *S. Th.* Ia, Q.85, Art. 1.

[32] *Ibid.*, cf. *Q. D. De An.*, Rowan's translation, p. 43 (ad 8).

is not just the occasion of the formation of a general concept or of the acquisition of the 'principle' in virtue of which it is possible to use the general concept concerned in judgement, but indicative of the character of the principle which is acquired. For, although the upshot of the 'act' of abstraction is an existence of this 'principle' free of material or particularizing conditions, equally it has the character precisely of being a principle intending objects which are particularized. Hence, although (or so we shall argue in Chapter XII) neither the abstraction nor the exercise in judgement of such principles is a material process, nonetheless both abstraction and judgement involve that the mind typically takes material things as objects, whether as presented through perception or through imagination—for as we made clear earlier it is concerned not with natures or universals as objects in their own right, but with particulars (typically material things) as realizing natures or having general terms predicated of them. So in no way are human beings other than animals and this is seen strikingly even in their being talking animals.

In the third place, because it is essential both to abstraction and judgement that the principles referred to be received in the human being in a way to which the presence of a material isomorphism between any physical structure in an organ and the objects of knowledge would be functionless or counterfunctional, neither abstraction nor judgement can be acts of a bodily organ, even the brain. This is the consideration which we shall develop in the next chapter.

There is, then, no reason to fancy the existence of abstract general ideas, whether as Platonic forms or concepts or as images, as objects to the mind as involved in human judgement or its possibility. We must now turn to consider the character of the supposed role of the *phantasmata* in the above account.

3. The Misconception That Images Are Objects and the Way the Imagination Enters into Thinking and Understanding

I have taken Aquinas' account of abstraction and judgement as having greater clarity in certain respects than those to be found in later discussions. In it we found that, on the one hand, in the abstraction establishing the possibility of the use of a general concept in judgements, a principle of operation had to be established in the mind (that is, in the person) which was in no way tied to particularized conditions such as those of the learning situation. Nonetheless, on the other hand, in the act of judging itself there had to be a presentation of material objects, whether through perception or through imagination, and so, in the typical case, there has to be what Aquinas refers to as a *conversio ad phantasmata*, a turning to *phantasmata* or images. The fundamental reason for this requirement is that in human knowledge of 'natures' such as 'human being', 'horse', 'dog', 'red', 'blue', and 'round', they are known not as abstract objects but only as predicated, i.e., as exemplified in particular instances. This is a corollary of the linguistic and sentential or articulated character of human knowledge.[33] This involvement with particular instances presented 'in the *phantasmata*' is constantly insisted upon by Aquinas,[34] but the idea of the need of a *conversio ad phantasmata* is in Aquinas relatively unformed, and so we need to give it some determination, taking advantage of some of the later insights of Berkeley and Hume.

1. One should say that, when it is said that the subject cannot think without *phantasmata*, it is not that mental images are objects of the mind in thinking, but that the objects of the mind are the things imagined, the things which the images are of. It is not, for instance, that we imagine images of cows, but that we imagine cows: as our account in Chapter III indicated, in thinking and imagining, the mind is not occupied with or directed towards (e.g.) images of cows as 'intentional objects', but cows.

There is a constantly recurring confusion whereby it is supposed that, in the imagining of cows, there are some extra objects—not cows—but images of cows before the mind's eye.[35] This is like

---

[33]This is what Aquinas refers to when he speaks of it as being knowledge by 'composition or division' ('division' is intended to indicate the case of negative statements, denying something of something).

[34]*S. Th.* Ia, Q. 84, Art. 7, *Q. D. De An.*, Art. 15 resp. (Rowan's translation, pp. 194–201, especially 198–199), cf. Kenny, 'Intellect and Imagination in Aquinas', pp. 288–290.

[35]We can, of course, imagine a picture of a cow, imagining such a picture as some artist might have painted on a wall or put on canvas and enclosed in a frame. Likewise, we can imagine a picture of a diagram done on paper, imagining the paper as well. But imagining cows is not like imagining pictures, and forming a mental image of a cow is not forming in one's mind an entity which is a picture of a cow. We are confused by the case of diagrams because, often when we are doing geometry in the

supposing that, when people have hallucinations of pink rats, there are before their mind's eye, not only pink rats, but also some extra objects called hallucinations. What one has to realize is that nouns like "image" (referring to 'mental images') and "hallucination" are, like the noun "dream", cognate to some verbal formation or set of verbal formations: we have or dream dreams, we have or see hallucinations, we have or form mental images or they arise before the mind—saying that we-imagine images has something of the oddity of saying that we dream dreams, see sights, and state statements, and is a secondary way of speaking.

G.E. Moore noted how in speaking of 'the idea of X' the description of X is internal to the description of the idea:[36] it is, for instance, irrelevant for the purpose of specifying the idea whether or not X, or an X, was the cause of the idea. And such remarks apply whether ideas are features of imagining or of thinking.

But the question is of the correct diagnosis of the cause of this fact of logical grammar! The proper explanation is this, that as a particular sight is a sight of what is seen, a particular view a view of what is viewed, a particular hallucination an hallucination of that which the hallucination is of, a particular dream a dream of what it is a dream of, so a mental image is an image of what it is of. That is, whenever we have some class of 'entities' which come in as cognates to certain verbal formations, e.g., sights, views, hallucinations, dreams, and images, the cognates concerned are always 'of' what we might describe as the proper objects of whatever verb determines the character of the cognates concerned.

2. We now have to see how the imagination is involved in the kind of understanding and thinking expressible linguistically with which we are concerned.

In order to employ the general term "cow", whether in saying that this particular animal before us is a cow, recognizing that it is part of the nature of cows that cows are quadrupeds, or in saying that this cow is black, that some cows are black, or that all cows are black,

---

mind's eye, what we picture is not a circular material object like a metal ring, but a diagram of a circle. Our attention is on the circle in the diagram, or on the diagram, not on the mental image of a diagram.

[36] *Some Main Problems of Philosophy*, pp. 65–66.

using the term "cow" as the name of a nature or natural kind, one has to understand the term thus used. In order to do this, one has to understand it as applying to particulars, understand this nature or this property of being a cow not as an abstract object but as realized in particular animals. The propositions concerned are not relational propositions, relating particular perceptual objects to some abstract object or relating two abstract objects, but predications, involving the understanding of "cow" as a predicate term. Such natures or properties cannot be known properly or as they are except as they are known as realized in particular things: we do not know a part of cowhood as it is when we know that four-leggedness is part of it, but know a part of the nature of cows as it is when we know that cows are four-legged. Therefore, in order to understand the objects most appropriate to its mode of understanding (the natures of bodily things), the human being has to turn to particulars (whether presented through perception or through imagination) in order to contemplate (look at, attend to) these general natures as realized in particular things.

It is not a matter only of the requirements of understanding bodily things (which are things which have natures of a kind to be realized in many spatio-temporally distinct instances), but of the requirements set by a linguistic, predicational, mode of understanding orientated towards dealing with such things.

3. The perception of a cow as a cow may not in itself involve the understanding of the general concept "cow" if, by this, one means the kind of understanding expressed in the linguistic utterances we have noted. In the higher animals lower than human beings it may be exhibited sufficiently in forms of non-linguistic 'intentional' behaviour, 'intentional' in the weaker sense I indicated in Chapter IX. In contrast, the understanding or 'possession' of the general concept "cow" with which we are now concerned is one exhibited or expressed only in ways coordinate with capacity for the linguistic realizations mentioned. In other words, this possession of the concept "cow" is not sufficiently exhibited by appropriate behavioural responses to perceptions, memories, and imaginations of cows, but requires a wide range of judgemental discriminations whose natural expression includes those linguistic ones which we have picked out as central.

This might lead us to distance thinking from imagining in such a way as to separate them.

However, it is integral to the exercise of human linguistic capacity that it integrate with, or have integrated within it, the 'sensory' discriminatory powers or propensities which I have mentioned. This integration has two aspects, the one bearing upon the character of perception and imagination, and the other upon the character of understanding and thinking.

In the life of higher animals, physical processes[37] in the sense-organs and the brain are integrated within the activities of perception and imagination and given a new character and unity thereby. In an analogous way, in human life the activities of perception and imagination are integrated within the total life of a linguistically intellectual being, and therein given the character and kind of unity distinctive of the human modes of perception and imagination.[38] The role of physical process within perception and imagination is not the same as the role of perception and imagination within understanding and thinking, as we shall have reason to insist later, but in both cases there is in animal or human life the subsumption of the 'lower', 'more material', or less multi-levelledly organized process or activity within the 'higher'.

But conversely the 'lower' level process or activity sets the shape of the 'higher' level activity inasmuch as the latter has to take such a form as to allow the subsumption of the former within it. Not only does appropriate discriminatory linguistically expressible judgement dovetail with appropriate non-linguistic discriminatory propensity, but such integration is internal to the sense of the linguistic expressions of judgement.[39]

Accordingly, 'as anyone can experience in himself, if he attempts to understand something, he will form some images to himself which serve by way of examples, in which he can as it were inspect what he attempts ('studies') to understand. This is the reason, indeed, why, when we want to make someone understand something, we propose

---

[37]It is not required for our argument here to make distinctions in regard to the 'physical' processes in the sense-organs of the kind which Aquinas would insist upon between strictly 'material' processes and natural processes in a more general sense which, in this case, he would require to be described in intentional terms, cf. *Comm. De An.*, 776.

[38]*De Anima*, 431a 18–20, together with the notable comments of Aquinas, *Comm. De An.*, 773–774, cf. 766–769.

[39]*De Anima*, 431a 14–18, together with Aquinas, *Comm. De An.*, 770–772.

examples to him, from which he can form images to himself in order to understand the thing concerned.'[40] Thus, in order to understand how triangles with two sides and one angle equal, not the included angle, can fail to be congruent, a person might be shown a diagram with two lines crossing at a given angle at a point A and a circle drawn round a point B on one line crossing the other in two points C and D, and have it observed to him that the triangles ABC and ABD have two sides and one angle (not the included angle) equal but are not congruent, and that the same will arise in any like situation. He will then be able to perform the same experiment in the imagination and see for himself that the same upshot will arise, and be able to do this at any time.

In such a case, the diagram or the imagined diagram serves a representative function in the way envisaged by Berkeley. It is not that there is an idea of the lines, points, and circle considered which is of a configuration involving no particular angle or relative lengths (AB and the radius of the circle) or size within the visual field, but that some one diagram or image represents all other relevantly like ones—no attention being paid or inference made from features other than those mentioned. The diagram or image is representative of others by its use, wherein only certain features are pointed out or attended to, not by similarity in other respects.[41]

4. Let us advance one further point before moving on to the next phase of our argument.

At this stage we must make a new application of Aristotle's remark that it is necessary for the mind 'to be unmixed, as Anaxagoras says, in order to be in control, that is to know',[42] different from the one we previously made. The kind of imagining which is relevant to linguistic understanding and thinking involves a freedom to explore and move about in some way analogous to that in which the kind of sensation which is relevant to perception involves a freedom to explore

---

[40] S. Th. Ia, Q. 84, Art. 7, resp.

[41] Because of this non-requirement of any unqualified similarity, we might almost as well be guided in thinking of what it is for an image to be representative by thinking of the weak sense in which one person may be a representative or spokesperson for others—except that literal similarity in some respects, the relevant kinds, is required for the image to serve its function and also for it to be an image rather than a symbol.

[42] De Anima, 429a 18–19.

and move about. We must be able to imagine different things at will, to know the difference between imagining a cow and imagining a horse, a dog, a fly, or an elephant, or between imagining any of these and imagining a mountain, a hillside, a tree, the sun, a blue sky, a chalet set in snow, or other objects visualized as static. It is this freedom to move about in the imagination—a freedom which it has been suggested differentiates human imagination from that of the other animals—presumably obvious to earlier thinkers, to which Hume draws our attention.

It is the fact that this freedom is possessed by human imagination and not by human perception which makes imagination, not perception, key to the explanation of how the mind is presented with its objects. This is the reason why it has to be said that in human life the exercise of the understanding in speaking, hearing understandingly, or thinking involves a *conversio ad phantasmata*, and not just a *conversio ad sensibilia*.

To sum up the present stage of our argument in a simple-minded way, let us say the following.

Cows are sensible particulars. Human beings get knowledge of what cows are either through perception conjointly with testimony or through testimony trading upon knowledge of other types of sensible particular, so that they can, in some degree, imagine what it is for something to be a cow, knowing the difference between this and what it is for it to be (e.g.) a horse or a dog. But this capacity to imagine cows and what it is for something to be a cow in such a way as to differentiate being a cow from being (e.g.) a horse or a dog is not a mere by-product of the process of getting to know what cows are, but internal to the present knowledge of what cows are.

5. The question arises as to the role of the imagination in the capacity to use the more general concepts, but consideration of this requires some further observation on the nature of what we call 'imagining'.

The word "imagining" has two kinds of connotation, the one narrower and tied to picturing or visual imagination, and the other wider, not just in admitting images associated with the other senses, but in signifying a kind of re-living of the experiences which need not be limited to acts of the external senses—what we call a re-living in the imagination. (Non-circular definition is impossible here, and only contextual definition or explanation is possible.) Thus, in the first way we cannot imagine the seeing of something, although we can picture a person looking at something, as we can also picture his walking along, hitting someone, or knocking something over: in these examples we 're-live' the experience of one who *perceives* such a looking, walking, hitting, or knocking over, but is not himself doing the looking, walking, hitting, or knocking over concerned. In the second way, we can imagine seeing, walking, hitting someone, or knocking something over (whether intentionally or unintentionally) as things which we ourselves do, re-living in imagination the doing of these things, as it were, from the first-personal standpoint.[43] It will be realized from these examples that in the human case the first 'way' of imagining is a particular case of the second.[44]

Against this background we can now speak of human imagination with the proper generality.

Human imagination is not only exercised when such concepts as horse, red, round, seeing, and walking are exercised, concepts which have contraries imaginable in the same style, cow, green, square, hearing, and running, but also when more general concepts are used. It belongs to a different book, an extended treatment of epistemology, to make the accurate distinctions here required. Let it suffice for the present to make the following further remarks. First, the imagination is exercised in exploring its limits: thus, for instance, we can form no model of a process whereby something at a later time might cause something at an earlier time. Second, we can imagine a bodily object being in a place (that is, in a context set by other objects spatially related to it) and we can imagine the place being empty of any such object which would mean that there did not exist any such object in that place: this capacity for imagination set up the context for our being able to assert or deny existence. (When we assert the existence of an angel or God, we are able to assert these things in virtue of something analogous which makes the ordinary cases, e.g., of the existence of stones, animals and human beings, share something with the non-ordinary cases concerned, but in a context in which we can

---

[43]In the case of unintentionally knocking something over, this will involve re-living the having of certain kinds of perception in the context of the absence of certain intentions.

[44]It will also be realized from our earlier discussion in Chapter IX that, with all its behavioural connections, imagination has the character of a re-living in the case of all animals with imagination, and not only in the case of human beings.

also make plain what further things are implied in the ordinary cases which are not implied in the non-ordinary ones.)

6. We must now explore the question of the relation of the various things we call 'imagining' to the various things we count as 'thinking'. We can use the word "thinking" both in regard to linguistically expressible acts and more widely. In the latter way, imagining can be an example of thinking, and 'thinking of' can fail to be linguistically expressible.

As a preliminary we need to identify the kind of 'thinking' which I speak of as something linguistically expressible—whether as exemplified in long pieces of deliberation, inquiry, or argument, but which is also exemplified in the having of particular thoughts.

We are not here speaking of thinking in the sense of 'being of the opinion that' which is a kind of state of belief or disposition to opine. Nor are we concerned with what is reported after something sudden has happened like a car accident when we say things like 'I thought he was going on across in front of me', said truthfully by a driver of a pedestrian because of whom he had just done an emergency stop, when perhaps 'everything happened in no time' and he was explaining his behaviour. This is not a clear case of the 'having of a thought' or of the activity of thinking as something discrete from behaviour. (Perhaps it is characteristic of non-dispositional 'thought' amongst animals lower than man to be in this way not discrete from behaviour.)

The thinking we are concerned with is exemplified in many different types of thought. Not all thoughts are specifiable in declarative clauses preceded by "think that". On many of the occasions when we say something of the form "I thought...", the thoughts are questions, wishes, or decisions, and their specification can include expletives. Pieces of thinking may call for specification as short as a simple sentence or as long as an extended piece of prose. Activities of wondering, inquiring, deliberating, are all examples of the activity of thinking.

We think such things as: 'Heavens! The post has gone'; 'This pain has got worse, and with that foot all swollen, I'd better phone the doctor'; 'Is he going to stay here the whole afternoon? I've got to get that work done. If I don't get that report done today, when will I get it done?'; 'He must go. If he doesn't, the whole office will be at loggerheads with each other'; 'We ought to get home' or 'I wish

I could get away' (or as one would have naturally said in specifying a thought in earlier times, 'Would that I could get away', 'Oh that I might get away!'). Or, most extendedly, we might think:

'If I draw a line on paper, which is going to be one side of a triangle, and then draw a line at a fixed angle backwards from the right hand end above it and towards the left across the paper, and am going to have a line upwards from the left hand end, a line of fixed length whose direction is determined by the requirement that its end is to be where a circle round the left hand end (the one whose radius is this fixed length) hits the other line drawn backwards as it comes from the right above the original one, and obviously if the fixed length is long enough it will hit the other line at two points—so being given two sides and one angle [the lengths and angle being fixed], can't be enough to make triangles congruent'.

The nature of the intimate relation between the thinking and its specification or expression will require attention later as part of our main argument. What I have been doing in my remarks above is to indicate the range of acts and activities I have in mind as 'thinking' in the sense in which I am concerned with it, separating them from states of belief or knowledge and from such 'thought' as is only very doubtfully discrete from behaviour.

7. It is instructive to consider the place of imagining in thinking by setting it within the context of the ways in which the 'intentionality' of thinking arises—features of thinking which make it disanalogous to speaking.

The extension of the ideas of the phenomenologists using the vocabulary of 'intentionality' to the treatment of thought and imagination appears strikingly in Ryle. He rejects any incipient tendency to treat the expression of thought or the thinker as in the position of having a 'thought' as its 'intentional object',[45] for the reasons which we have already seen. Instead he sees thinking as, in effect, 'intentional' (to use a vocabulary which is not his) in relation to objects in that it is a thinking of objects as falling under certain descriptions, and indeed as

---

[45] Ryle, 'Are there Propositions?', *Collected Papers* II (where he is even suspicious of Meinong's 'objectives', deliberately distinguished by Meinong from 'objects', p. 35 n.).

falling under certain descriptions understood in context to presuppose an, on reflection, open-ended number of other descriptions:[46]

> A rowing enthusiast says that he had been thinking about the Oxford University crew; and if asked bluntly, would deny that he had at that moment been thinking about the Cambridge crew. Yet it might transpire that his thought about the Oxford crew was, or included, the thought that, though it was progressing, it was not progressing fast enough. 'Not fast enough for what?' we ask. 'Not fast enough to beat Cambridge next Saturday.' So he had been thinking about the Cambridge crew, only thinking about it in a sort of threshold way. Or I ask a tired visitor from London what he had been thinking about. He says, 'Just about the extraordinary peacefulness of your garden.' If asked, 'Than what do you find it so much more peaceful?' he replies, 'Oh, London, of course.' So in a way he was thinking not only of my garden but of London, though he would not, without special prompting, have said for himself that he had London in mind at all. Or my visitor says, 'How lovely your roses are,' and then sighs. Why does he sigh? May he not, in a marginal way, be thinking of his dead wife who had been particularly fond of roses?—though he himself would have said, if asked, that he was only thinking about my roses. He does not say to me or himself, 'Roses—her favourite flower.' But roses are, for him, her favourite flower. The thought of them is an incipient thought of her.

Ryle goes on to press the point that all these relations of the first identified thought to those other thoughts which gave part of its point or sense are internal to the first thought, rather than previous items in a stream of consciousness, items of which one might be reminded as one might be reminded of the last but one telephone call which one made where the telephone calls in question were unconnected, and had only an external temporal relation. The kind of intentionality

---

[46]'A Puzzling Element in the Notion of Thinking', *Collected Papers* II 30, p.400–404. He also extends parallel ideas to the imagination (disparaging 'images', which we may suppose still need some discussion, whether they are images in dreams, or images in waking life): 'imagining' and 'modelling' are not as close to supposing or pretending as Ryle seemed to think, but remain more like 'thinking of in a certain way' than like forming mental pictures (*The Concept of Mind*, Chapter VIII).

we are encountering here is what, in the next section, I speak of as the 'allusiveness' of thought: meaning by this, not the directedness of thought towards 'objects' (so-called 'intentional objects'), which would be nothing new, only a banal commonplace; but I mean the way in which it is typical for intentional directedness towards some subsidiary or presupposed object to be internal to the intentional directedness of the thought towards some more immediate, evident, or central object of attention.

We should now consider to what extent imaginations are internal to the episodes of thinking concerned. In every case, we can express the background thoughts and express them in their connection with the first identified thought linguistically: the thoughts and their connections are all of a character to be linguistically expressible. But in the typical case also it is natural to envisage the imagination as involved: it would be strange to suppose that the rowing enthusiast did not know what a rowing eight in their boat and what a river looked like, or that the visitor from London had no images of the noise in London, and no images of his wife and expressions of her love of roses.

Such imaginings are not internal to the thoughts as words are internal to the linguistic expressions of the thoughts. Nor are they internal to the thoughts logically, as one thought can be internal to another as its logical presupposition or part of its connotation. Yet they are not external to the thoughts as if it would still be human thinking of the kind we know in this world if the thoughts occurred otherwise than in the context of such imaginings.

And we can say further that these imaginings do indeed play the role envisaged for them by Aquinas of presenting the mind with its objects, of making it true that the thoughts were indeed directed towards rowing crews and boat races, noise or its absence, the beauty of roses and the fondness of a deceased wife for them.

In one sense, the only objects of reference in propositions are the objects referred to by singular terms in singular propositions (subject-predicate propositions in the strict sense), but in a looser sense we refer to kinds of animal, kinds of stuff, colours, shapes, activities, and so forth when the terms 'mentioning' them do not occur as singular terms, as when we say that some cows are black, some chemical substances are hard, or that Jones plays golf. Because the objects of reference in this wider sense are multiple in kind, entering into discourse in the structured way set by it, the objects of human imagining can be likewise multiple in kind.

It would be mad to suppose that perception and imagination entered into the learning and use of language only in respect of the names of first substances, and not also into the use of other expressions. But we do not learn the names of kinds of animal, colours, or kinds of activity by becoming acquainted with abstract objects (e.g., red as denoted by the subject term in some propositions); and in our primary use of them we do not use them as singular terms. Rather we learn to use kind-terms, colour-words, and the multifarious kinds of verb-expression for activity predicatively. The gross mistake is to suppose that by a process labelled 'abstraction' we form ideas, whether abstract objects or paradigm samples, which are objects to the mind, acquaintance with which is involved in our every use of the general term concerned. However, to move from the repudiation of this mistake to the supposition that in speaking understandingly and in thinking the intellect functions independently of the use of the imagination is just to make some opposite mistake. Every capacity to use words understandingly involves a capacity to use the imagination with appropriate freedom in conjunction with the family of uses of the word under consideration.

8. I indicated earlier that the way in which physical processes are subsumed within the activities of perception and imagination might be very different from the way in which these latter are subsumed within the activity of thinking.

The physical processes of perception, in the eye, the optic nerve, and the brain, are internal to the act of perception as the physical processes of speaking and making sounds are internal to understandingly speaking and as a multiplicity of processes in the nervous system and the muscles are internal to intentionally walking.

Aquinas supposed that, in some fashion parallel to that exemplified in perception, some physical processes in the brain were internal to the act of imagining (these processes being describable in terms of there being in the brain some particularized pattern isomorphic with what is imagined, as in visual perception there is in the changes in the retina some particularized pattern in the relevant respect isomorphic with what is seen). One may suppose that Aquinas conceived imagining oversimply, by analogy with visual perception: in visual perception the mind was directed towards an object as particularized (e.g., this actual cow) by means of a form, species, or imprint on the sense-organ (a 'physical' change, albeit of an intentional kind), as a forming of images as objects to the mind through imprints, forms, or species; since, in imagination as in perception, the mind is directed towards an object as particularized, this imagined cow instead of this actual cow, Aquinas supposed that the principle or form (what he would have called a '*species*') whereby it would be directed towards this object would be as particularized as the imprint on the sense organ is particularized, and therefore equally requiring a material organ.[47] As we have indicated, a more complex account, both of animal and of human imagining, whereby imagining involves a kind of re-living in the imagination of something with behavioural connections, is required. But, if in the animal case one anticipates some complex physical structure as internal to imagining, so in a corresponding way one may anticipate that there will be some structure (structured in some respects in a parallel way) internal to human imagining.[48]

However, the role of the imagination in thinking is not to provide non-external objects of reference of a special kind called images, nor to provide symbols which might be mental or verbal means of reference to objects external or internal, but to make reference possible. Accordingly, activities of imagining are not internal to activities of linguistically expressible thinking either as mental objects or as mental words have been supposed to be. Indeed, as we shall see in the next section, linguistically expressible thinking is not a process in any proper sense and so not a process such that imagining might be internal to it as a part (as if it might be related as sub-processes described in hardware terms are related to more global processes, open to more global description, within a computer). Rather imagining is internal to the human thinking we know, not as a material part, but logically as providing objects of reference to it.

---

[47]This is the a priori reason why Aquinas supposes that imagination must have a material organ, the reason neglected by Kenny (pp. 290–291, 'Intellect and Imagination in Aquinas'). And it is this which explains the contrast in Aquinas whereby the imagination must have and the intellect cannot have a material organ, the contrast which puzzles Kenny—the fact that the *species* or forms whereby the mind is directed towards the objects of intellect (typically, the natures of kinds of material thing) precisely must not be thus particularized is exactly what, in Aquinas' view, debars the intellect from having a material organ, one of the arguments I discuss in Chapter XII.

[48]This point is presented in terms of considerations other than those which influenced Aquinas in Chapter XII, Section 1 (a) below.

4. The Nature of Thinking Compared with Speaking: Words Are Not Images in Thinking

At this stage, the question arises as to what is to be said about the nature of the kind of thinking, spoken of in the previous section, whose nature is to be linguistically expressible.

It is tempting to envisage this kind of thinking as a 'saying to oneself', but barring the way to such a way of understanding the nature of this kind of thinking there stand three obstacles. First, words do not figure as images in the activity of thinking to oneself in the medium of words. Secondly, the thought has a kind of unity which the sentence lacks. Thirdly, the thought has a kind of intentionality which the sentence lacks.

We have recognized the peculiarity or differentiating feature of human animality as being, not thought, not rationality, not the capacity to make insightful advances from one thought to another, but language. It belongs to this understanding also to recognize the prototypically human way of thinking as a thinking in the medium of words,[49] and therefore in close analogy with speaking, as if it were a kind of inner speech, or as Geach has it, 'a saying in one's heart'.[50]

---

[49]It is appropriate to associate this with the naturalness of speaking of 'thinking aloud', of envisaging thinking as going on in a world where one's moving about is amongst words, and with the observation that we tend to speak of communicating through the medium of words, of music, of painting, adverting to the 'substance' of *langue* rather than to the completed units of communication: thus, we speak of words rather than statements or gestures as the medium of communication (that is if by a gesture is meant something conveying a complete message, rather than an element within a communication in deaf-and-dumb language).

[50]Geach takes this from the Psalm which tells us 'The fool has said in his heart that there is no God' and he also instances 'They said in their heart let us destroy them together', *Mental Acts*, p. 80. It is commonly but wrongly said that utterances like "Let us destroy them together" and "Let us go" are first person plural imperatives, as if they were imperatives in the same sense as "[You] destroy them" and "[You] go", but in truth they do not express an order, advice, or request, but the taking of a resolve on the presumption of an accord of mind. If those set on evil are a community, they can know their accord before its expression, so that after the chairman has said "What more needs to be said?" they all get up together to set to the work, knowing that it has been resolved upon, the taking of the resolve being in the moment of accord with the thought of the chairman that nothing more needed to be said. It is thus that they can say in their heart let us destroy them together. The nearest parallel idiom in the singular seems to be "I will go".

Against this background, it is of key importance to observe the disanalogies between thinking (in the sense identified in the previous section) and speaking.

(a) Words do not figure as images in thinking

When a person draws a geometrical figure in the imagination, we also speak of his seeing and considering what is thus drawn. If the cases were properly parallel, we should expect that if a person's thinking something to him or herself were analogous to this, speaking in the imagination as the analogue of drawing in the imagination, then there should be also something analogous to hearing (in the imagination) in order to consider what is thus spoken. It is vital to understand why this is not so, and how the analogy breaks down.

In brief, in thinking in the medium of words, words do not figure as images or imagined, whether auditory images of vocal sounds or visual images of words on paper.

In order to understand this, let us, as a preliminary, contrast the cases of drawing a picture on paper and drawing a picture in the imagination. In both cases we have a partly intentional activity, but in the former case there is not only a knowledge, as it were, in advance of what is done and what is drawn because the drawing is intentional, but also a knowledge by a means independent of this by sensory observation of the drawing process and of what is drawn. In the case of drawing a picture in the imagination there is no such independently based double knowledge—the one a priori or beforehand in virtue of authorship and the other a posteriori or after the event by observation.

Yet, despite this, we can somehow speak in the case, for example, of visual imaging of seeing or of considering what is imaged, and we need to see the sense of speaking in this way and how it arises. We shall then be able to see that there is no parallel sense in speaking of the words which pass through the mind in thinking as if they figured as images or imaged.

It might seem that there are different kinds or aspects of imagining, active and passive. Let us consider the more active cases, e.g., trying to remember or the free picturing of things in the mind first.

I imagine a Swiss mountain and a chalet on the hillside and a huge window and seeing what is inside, a long table with one, no two, vases on it—and as I imagine I see. As I draw each part of the picture, or each part is drawn before me, I know what is drawn. There is no independent observational knowledge, so how can we speak of 'seeing' at all?

In order to get to understand this, let us consider the case of drawing diagrams in the mind: I draw a line and another at an angle to it crossing it (so that they look like a large multiplication sign squashed from above) and I take a point on the left side on the lower line and draw a circle round it, which must be either too small to touch the other line, or will just touch it at a tangent, or cut it in two points on the left hand side of the join of the lines or, if it is bigger, cut it in two points one either side of the join: all this I see as I picture in my mind successively larger circles; at each stage I am led in my train of thought to picture a larger circle in order to see how it will be, and as soon as I do this I see what must be the case. Hence, in this way there is discovery, and I speak of seeing, but there is no gap between drawing the picture in my mind and seeing the upshot—it is not like an experiment in which I set up the apparatus and set things going, and then have to wait and watch to see what happens, what happens not being determined in my mind as soon as I have set things going. Thus, the act of picturing sets, constitutes, or fixes, what is seen—there is knowledge by intention of one facet or aspect and knowledge by observation of another inseparable facet or aspect.

Against this background, upon reflection, we realize that the same structure is present even in the case of the imagining of a chalet on a mountainside. We draw certain things in our imagination and these carry with them necessary concomitants, e.g., related to perspective and distribution or related to the directions in which there are further questions to be raised, possibilities to be considered, types of further feature which might be drawn in, and to the limits set by the already given structure to what features might thus be added—although these concomitants were not considered in the initial drawing of the picture in the imagination.

Obviously, in deliberate remembering—as when someone who lives in Aberdeen deliberately envisages following the road as it runs southward along the coast from Stonehaven—we discover things, as it were, they come back to us: in the example given, by imagining ourselves following the route, recalling in our mind's eye progressively which way the road curves, Dunnotar Castle on the left and the other places one can see from the road, where and where the trees are. . . . So it is as if the images are before us as objects of observation. But there is still never any double knowledge—quasi-intentional knowl-edge (as if it were us as authors drawing the images) and observational knowledge of the images drawn. And if the images do not come voluntarily (in the course of ordinary undeliberate remembering, or in dreams, flashbacks, . . .) still there is no double knowledge—as if the imagining or having of the image and the seeing what is in the image are separable—but nonetheless certainly there is discovery.

We now come to the contrasting situation of words in thinking.

If we have images, models, or representations in thinking, that would be one thing—but words don't come in in this way at all. To think of words as like auditory images would bring us in under the aspect of hearers not speakers. We don't come in as if hearers or readers of our own words in thinking—so the parallel of images is out of place. There is nothing in thinking in certain words corresponding to attending to these words in imagination or to discovery by means of such attention. It is not that we do not know, if we have thought in words, in what words we have thought, but we do not have this knowledge by remembering auditory or visual images of the words concerned which we had while thinking.

We can, indeed, try words out for sonority by forming images of them—but we have to imagine producing a whole utterance, in its context of speech, to try them out for meaning. There is no dis-covery of meaning relations by considering auditory or visual images of words, but only by reflecting on utterances—whereas there can be discovery of geometrical relations by considering imagined diagrams, simply as objects of visual imagination and without any imagining of the drawing of the diagrams.

In thinking about thinking we must take seriously the analogy between thinking and speaking, but must be careful in the way we apply it. In speaking we may choose our words, hesitating as we realize that the word we were about to use was inapposite, but this hesitation does not appear in the straight report of what we said. Contrastingly, if we try to produce the verbatim expression of thought as it proceeds 'in the mind' (as we say), all these hesitations show up in the words of this verbatim expression of thought. I can, while speaking, reflect on the ill-advisedness of a word I was about to use and choose a different one instead. But, if I am expressing verbatim the chain of thought I had while thinking through a certain matter in the medium of words, changing my mind about the best word to use as I go, the old word and the new one and perhaps 'no' and 'a better way of putting it would be' and perhaps a few reasons will all come explicitly in the expression of the thought as it was had.

Let us develop the point involved here.

We could have a certain paradigm of speaking, according to which speaking other than spontaneously, speaking in such a way as while speaking to make a reflective choice of words, was an elaboration rather than the fundamental case. It counts as an elaboration because the relevant kind of reflection is never total in regard to what was said but only partial within an already largely predetermined structure. In rock-climbing we may choose our hand-holds and our foot-holds without attending to the way we hold our fingers or what training has built in as skill in our way of disposing our feet. If in projecting a bodily movement we tried to attend to it in its every facet and aspect, we would never move at all. In a parallel way, in speaking we can only reflect and be self-critical in respect of some facets of our vocabulary and sentence construction, not in respect of all. In the kind of uncontrived speaking which I am envisaging as paradigm or prototypical, we would use words but not attending to them and be entirely unreflective in respect to the words used. Within this paradigm kind of speaking, the direction of the mind is towards the content of what is to be said, towards the matter in hand, not towards the words and constructions used in expressing what we want to say.

Actual speech, of course, typically deviates from this paradigm, but what we need to recognize is that thinking perfectly accords with it. Within the verbatim expression of thought *everything* is brought to the surface. We might, for instance, have a thought whose appropriate expression was like this (the passages in square brackets are put in to make intelligible to the reader why the thought ran on in the way that it did):

> 'These drums—this clarinet—this is rather a splendid effect—when is this?—after 1820!—what shall I say to the folks? [I used to joke with the people I live with that the music they put on for me must be pre-1820]—is it 20th century?—is there an orchestra? or is this just two instruments experimenting in rather a 20th century sort of way?—how old is he? [the clarinetist]—his hands are a bit creased—rough-skinned—too much washing-up—or has he a farm?—no! not so old—classical musician's sort of face—it's rather sombre [the music not the face]—leading up to death—will I be able to listen to the end? [I only turned on the

TV after finishing work five minutes before I expected the person helping me to get to bed (I am a paraplegic)]—damn it—must be mid-19th century [after a conclusion of the clarinet/drums piece, the words 'Fourth Movement—The March to the Scaffold' had shown up on the screen]—wish I knew the dates of those people—yes! here's the orchestra—great [not because it was great to have an orchestra, but in regard to the music as it went on with more varied effects]...'

This is thinking in the medium of words, and human life is full of it, but within it the words in no way figure as auditory or visual images as if there was some process of listening or watching which went on all the while so that it was by remembering the previous auditory or visual images that we were enabled to proceed with the thought—producing in some cases improved formulations of what we were aiming or feeling towards.

One is author of one's thought as one is of one's speech or of one's walking. We have here a knowledge of what is being done which is not by observation or memory but in virtue of the fact that what is being done is being done intentionally.

It is instructive to compare the case of thinking with that of outward action. I do not, as I reach for a can of Oxtail Soup in a supermarket rack, know of the first stages of the movement of my arm only retrospectively by observation, even if late in the movement I decide to pick up the adjacent can of Mulligatawny Soup by preference. I do not, as I draw or paint and alter the direction of my stroke in midstream, know how the stroke began only by observation. Likewise, I know the words I utter inwardly as I know the words I utter outwardly in virtue of the thinking or speaking being intentional, part of the same action. Again, if I change the direction of my thought, just as when I change the direction of my speech, I have an intentional knowledge of this—just as in general when I change my mind I have an intentional knowledge of my earlier and my later intention internally to knowing the change of mind.

However, whereas in the case of outward utterance I can have perceptual knowledge after the event (important for knowing when and how an utterance has been faulty), by contrast, in the case of inward utterance or thinking there is no such double knowledge, but only intentional knowledge. And, as we have seen, there is no function even for speaking of images.

It should now be clear what we should say about the puzzle as to whether we should speak of thinking as an 'expressing of our thoughts to ourselves'.

Judgements, decisions, and wishes, unlike commands, advice, and requests,[51] can be mental acts or thoughts as well as, in other cases, public actions. We commonly express our judgements, decisions, and wishes—as it is said, our inner thoughts—to others. The question arises whether we 'express' our judgements, decisions and wishes to ourselves. And one's first inclination is to say that I do not in thinking 'I am a fool' express my judgement to myself but make a judgement, I do not in thinking 'I must go' express my decision to myself but reach my decision, or (one should as well say) decide, and I do not in thinking 'I want to get out' express my wish to myself but wish. In this, one is responding to a sound instinct, namely that, as in saying outwardly "I promise . . .", I do not report a promise but make one, so, in thinking "I want to get out", what is going on is not my telling myself or posing to myself of a wish but a wishing, so that any supposed 'expressing to myself' is incidental to the wishing.

One has to distinguish the cases, firstly, of thinking something and, secondly, of rehearsing the words of such a thought to oneself in such wise as one might be able to reflect upon them, consider their eloquence or sonority as possible words to utter. In both cases one can speak of 'expressing something to oneself', but only in the second case are images (auditory or visual) involved. In the second way, one might express even commands to others to do things to oneself beforehand to see if they sounded or read offensively or were clearly formulated.

(b) The unity of the thought

Having words as a medium for thinking is not like having words as a medium for talking or writing, or instrumental sounds as a medium for playing a piece of music.

When I have the thought 'Heavens! The post has gone', as soon as the word "Heavens" has entered my consciousness it is clear that I already know what my surprise is at. I do not think 'Heavens!—oh, that means I am surprised at something—what is it?—ah, the post—

---

[51] I can give an order to others "[You] let me go" or "[You] release him", but although I can rehearse these words to myself I do not think '[you] let me go' or '[you] release him', cf. n. 50.

so that what I am surprised in regard to—but what is it about the post that has caught me by surprise—ah!—that it has gone', as if I knew nothing of my thought until a series of words had passed one by one through my mind, or as if my thinking of my thought consisted in a serial process of one word following another until the thought was through.

In this way a thought is not composed of words—even of 'words passing through the mind—as a sentence is composed of words, of syllables, or even of phonemes, or as a musical performance is composed of instrumental sounds. This truth about thoughts reinforces the point made above about words not figuring as images within the act of thinking in words. But it is not only that they do not figure as images, but that they do not figure as anything occurrent of any kind whatsoever—as if each occurrent word in the mind, whatever kind of entity it be, passed through the mind as an element or component part of the stream of consciousness to be followed by another until the thought is complete.

In this way, we meet the conception of the thought as a unity of a special kind, composite in its expression, but not composite in our thinking of it, this act being indivisible. Some acts are indivisible in some respects but not others: thus, hitting someone is indivisible under the aspect of being the object of an intention but divisible in respect of the bodily movements which it logically involves. And saying something may be indivisible *qua* intentional act and in respect of the thought expressed, but cannot be indivisible in respect of its words, morphological components, syllables, and phonemes. But the act of thinking is not divisible in any analogous way, that is, it is not divisible in itself but only in its expression. (We shall refer to the difficulties in this conception of the indivisibility of the act of thinking with its associated indivisibility in respect of time—difficulties which arise with any extended pieces of thinking—later below.)

This must make us resistant to any suggestion that thoughts are structured, as if they had parts inter-relating (even holistically) with one another. Evans tells us 'it is simply not a possibility for the thought that a is F to be unstructured—that is, not to be the exercise of distinct abilities'[52]—evidently one ability in respect of identifying a, and another ability in respect of picking out the 'feature' F—but

---

[52]Gareth Evans, *Varieties of Reference*, p. 102, cf. 104.

we must not allow this misleading use of the word "structure" with its connotation in other contexts of composition or the possession of parts.[53] It is a grave mistake to think of thought *qua* mental state or act as structured or articulated.

It is a mistake to explain the structuredness and articulatedness in the linguistic expressions of meaning as arising from some relation to a corresponding prior structuredness or articulatedness in 'thought': certainly, the structuredness or articulatedness in the expression of a thought arises from its capturing an element or aspect of the way in which the thought is woven into the structure of human life in its relation to reality. Human life cannot be logically atomized and the thinking of or the having of a thought cannot be logically severed from the change in the structure of behaviour inseparable from it, the change in dispositions both to linguistic and non-linguistic behaviour, the changes which determine what the thought is, i.e., express what is thought about what. But this element or aspect of the way in which thought is woven into life is expressed (and in that sense identified) only in its linguistic expressions, and it is these that are structured and articulated in themselves. It is in the nature of a human thought as such to be expressible, but it is not the thought as such but the spread of its linguistic expressions which have structure internal to them.

Where others have misleadingly spoken of the structuredness of thought, we should, instead, speak of its teleology and intentionality. Let us deal with its teleology first—in this way dealing with a difficulty which should have been obvious.

The point about the unity of the thought which we have high-lighted above has been made by Geach[54] in order to show that think-ing a thought cannot be a process because it does not have stages so as to take time, but must be conceived of as instantaneous.[55] There is, of course, a technical notion of 'instant' which derives from a

---

[53]We must also forbid this Platonic conception of 'features' as things to be picked out. This would involve one in a regress of abilities, firstly to identify a, then to pick out F, and then to attribute F to a.

[54]*God and the Soul*, p. 36.

[55]This does not, by itself, show that thinking does not involve internally various bodily processes so as not to be itself a bodily operation in the sense that seeing something is a bodily operation. This can be seen from the fact that seeing something moving (as distinct from first seeing it at one place and then seeing it at another, or seeing that it has moved) must be instantaneous in the same sense.

consideration of continuous motion: granted that something passes without stopping through a continuous series of places, there must be conceived of as existing 'instants' corresponding to each 'point' it passes through, instants like points being dividing points in a continuum, themselves occupying zero time. The sense in which an act of thinking, and anything which is instantaneous in the same way, is instantaneous is more primitive: what is implied is only that it occurs at a 'moment', moments being defined as the *times at which* indivisible acts happen (that is, acts which are, in some respect, indivisible), by contrast with periods as the *times over which* things happen. What happens in human life as an indivisible act at a time (moment) will happen after some physically defined instants and before others, but may not have determinate before-or-after relations with all the instants in between.

We must now consider how we should speak of more extended pieces of thinking. We have identified the unity of a thought whereby every part of its expression has a sense pregnant in context with the whole, as in the case of 'Heavens! the post has gone'. But now we have the problem of hesitations in thought whereby we cast about for a word while in mid-sentence, or do not know at the beginning of a sentence how it is going to go on, especially with long sentences. This is dramatized for us in the case of thinking aloud.

We must say here that the earlier part of the expression of the thought carries a meaning-towards-the-whole within which the rest unfolds. We can contrast the case which arises in conversation, but not in thought, of beginning saying the wrong thing and then artificially constructing a polite completion: in such a case, the sense of the beginning of the utterance was not incipient with the sense of the whole. In thinking, we do not except in imagination construct polite completions so as to produce monsters, analogous to the trunks and heads of men being joined to the trunks and legs of bulls as with a centaur, satisfying certain aesthetic or grammatical conditions but not possessed of a single sense (any more than an interrupted gesture of greeting towards a person we thought we knew but realized in mid-stream that we did not know possesses a unified intention): rather in thinking we come to an inconsequential halt, and start again not from the end of our half-thought, but from some earlier stage in its unfolding.

There is a teleology in the expression of thought, even in the case of more extended pieces of thinking, of the earlier words being directed towards the whole. As in speaking, the initial phonemes limit what can follow, the initial morphemes limit what can follow, the initial words limit what can follow, so the initial parts of a thought, identified by how they would be expressed, limit how a piece of thinking can unfold. But in thinking there is an additional constraint present, namely that—if it was genuinely thinking with some direction[56] rather than merely airing, or playing with words in the mind—there is the constraint of an initial pre-conception, aim, sense of what one is about, or direction governing whatever unfolds.

We think of having a thought as an act or an event—happening at a time—but we also think of thinking as an activity going on over a time. The thinking which goes on over a time is not composed of discontinuous acts of thought as a line might (mistakenly) be thought of as composed of dots. The thinking which goes on over a time is not a constant like heedfulness or watching, nor even like seeing something moving as we watch it through different parts of its path, but is indeed an unfolding activity whose unfolding is exhibited in the expression which would be appropriate to it, just as the act of thinking which seems instantaneous is exhibited in the expression which would be appropriate to it. And the parts of this unfolding over one three minute period as they would be exhibited in the expression appropriate to them will be different from the parts of that unfolding over the next three minute period as they would be exhibited in the expression appropriate to them.

At key stages the further parts of the unfolding are, in more than one respect, free, free in respect (say) of examples one may develop one's thought through, free in respect of the line of argument (perhaps suddenly altering in its bent in midstream, e.g., from the more theoretical to the more empirical) which opens out in what may be a path of discovery or exploration. But they are at no stage totally free, but rather at each stage governed (in a way in which speech is not governed) by an already established direction and context for thought—as a tree has its growth determined by the placing of its roots and by the mode of growth characteristic of its species, even though the way the growth unfolds may be influenced by the weathers

---

[56]This direction or sense involves inseparably the force, posture, or attitude with which the thought is coming and the type of content which it is to have. There is no separation here, above all none in the inception of a thought, between what contemporary philosophers have mistakenly separated as 'force' and 'sense' or 'content'.

which shine and blow. In the case of thinking, unlike that of speech, this already established direction and context which determines or limits the thought or the course of the thought is something set, not merely externally by the facts of *langue* and the conventions of communication, but internally by the 'intention' of the author of the thought.

The unity of the simple thought, the instance which we considered first, of thinking 'Heavens! The post has gone', is clear. What we have now explained is the teleology of the more extended thought whereby the whole of it is embraced or comes within the context and direction set by its *arche* or beginning in the mind—so that whatever comes later comes as part of the same tree, an element in the unfolding of the same course of thinking, so that in this way the unity of the thought remains, a unity stronger than that of the unity of the expression of thought. Within what is presented as the expression of thought there is always liable to be that which is adventitious, and there may even be a revolution in the direction or sense so that the supposed unity of the expression is no longer a true unity of meaning or thought, but a unity only in some sociological sense.

(c) The 'allusiveness' or intentionality of thought

What I call the intentionality of thought arises from its directedness to objects in relations to each other where these relations are expressible in statements, and, since a thought of x is always a thought of x as Y, always expressible in an open-ended list of statements as to what the thought of x is a thought of, viz., not only as of Y but also as of Z and, by connection with Z, of W.[57] This is what we met earlier in Section 3 in our citation from Ryle. As I explained in that context what I mean by the intentionality of thought is not the directedness of thought towards 'objects' (so-called 'intentional objects'): this, I remarked, would be nothing new, only a banal commonplace. What I mean is the way in which it is typical for intentional directedness towards some subsidiary or presupposed object to be internal to the intentional directedness of the thought towards some more immediate, evident, or central object of attention.

---

[57]The naturalness of introducing the word "intentional" here is evident from its parallels with the structures of description "seeing a as F", "shooting (intentionally) a as F", introduced in our earlier discussions in Chapter III.

This conception of the intentionality of thought is of key importance.

For it has to be realized that, because of the integrated structure of language spoken of in Chapter X, Section 3, within any thought is contained internally, not only a directedness towards its more obvious objects, but a directedness towards whatever further objects the integratedness of language makes it presuppose. Thus, a thought about a particular colour, or of something's being of that colour, will carry with it an intentionality towards a spread of different colours (the colours with which the given colour is naturally contrasted) and towards the sense of sight and the spread of different kinds of distinction made by sight together with the spread of senses with which the sense of sight is contrasted. But it will also carry with it an intentionality towards those more general kinds of distinction and concept towards which most or every thought is at the deeper levels directed, distinctions between perception and memory, knowledge and action, past, present, and future, and so forth.

In this way, internal to every thinking of a thought, and therewith also to the understanding of any piece of speech, is the thinking or understanding of all the relevant connections of this thought or piece of speech with the more general features of existence in the world, exhibited in the structures I have mentioned.

XII. The Second Refutation of Mechanism: Linguistic Understanding and Thinking Have No Bodily Organ

In this chapter, we shall discover that linguistic understanding and thinking in the medium of words have no bodily organ through which they operate, and no neural correlate. That is, they have no physical states or processes internal to them in the way in which we may suppose perception, imagination, and emotion to have physical processes internal to them. This we shall show in this chapter, exploring its consequences analytically in later chapters, showing that to be of a nature to have language is to transcend the body.

First let us review the overall context of these discussions.

We have rejected earlier any attempt to erect the mind or soul into an inner part of the human being on the basis of the Cartesian picture of human experience and judgement. We saw how deeply mistaken it was to conceive the perceiver or the thinking subject who understands and judges as an inner part of the human being, set over against, outside, and over against the world of bodily things. This way of thinking sprang from false pictures of the operation of sight and mistaken analogies between the operations of understanding and judging and those of perception. The ultimate root of the Cartesian error could be seen to be the separation of perception and judgement from action, exploratory behaviour, and behavioural aptitude—as if perception, other experience, and judgement could be logically or conceptually extricated from action and the arena of action so as to be thought of as things essentially 'inner'. We also saw how the rejection of the Cartesian perspective, and the conception of the mind and the mental as something inner, carried with it the rejection of the modern fashion of identifying the mind with the brain.

We registered that explanations utilizing mentalistic or psychosomatic concepts such as those of perception, imagination, and emotion could not be reduced to mechanical explanations, and had a predictive power in various systematic respects outstripping the mechanical. This entailed that human beings and higher animals sharing at least some key psychosomatic structures with human beings were not 'ontologically', or from any point of view of 'ultimate explanation', describable as 'material entities'.[1]

But these explanations involving the mental or the psychosomatic in the cases we considered did not exclude the mechanical or physical from a role within the overall teleological and psychosomatic structure. On the contrary, these explanations absolutely required that the mechanical or physical should have some role in this overall structure, requiring it as something integral to the psychosomatic as such— and in very obvious ways perception, action, sensation, and emotion exemplified this.

However, what we shall establish in this chapter goes far beyond any of this. For we shall show that the properly intellectual in human beings, characterized by its relation to linguistic expression, has no such physical or neural element internal to it despite dependence on integration with other states and activities involving such internal physical elements. And this creates an entirely new problematic.

The Cartesian and materialist picture of the mind and the mental as inner, perhaps identical with the brain and with what is 'realized' in the brain, has been ruled out in Part One of the book. In this chapter we shall establish that in linguistic understanding and thought human operation does indeed transcend the body—does not have a bodily process or state internal to it—leaving it to the following three chapters to find appropriate non-Cartesian ways of giving an accurate account of what this transcendence implies.

1. Summary Statement of Four Main Lines of Proof

The understanding of *langue* and the understanding of *parole*, together with the kind of thinking we have been concerned with (what we described as thinking in the medium of words), require the body for their expression—whether in speech or writing or in some other way. However, whereas speaking and hearing, writing and reading, are all bodily activities, it is not in the same way obvious that these

---

[1]See Chapter VIII.

kinds of understanding and this kind of thinking are bodily states or activities.

We have seen that operations of the person or animal such as perceiving, imagining, emotion, and intentional action are not themselves physical and cannot be conceived mechanistically because of the way in which they enter into explanation: the teleological explanations which turn upon them cannot be reduced to mechanical explanations. But we have also noted how, in each of these cases, some physical process, in the sense-organ, brain, and/or other parts of the body, is internal to the operation (state or activity) concerned.

What we have now to see is that the reverse is true in the case of the understanding of *langue*, the understanding of *parole*, and the kind of thinking we have been speaking of. Certainly they have physical preconditions, but not only can they not be conceived mechanistically, as if they were physical states or activities, but also they cannot have any physical process internal to them as physical processes are internal to perception, imagining, emotion, and intentional action.

I will speak of the kinds of understanding and thinking here concerned, along with perception, imagination, emotion, and action, all as 'operations', since we need some word and "thing" seems a poor one. I leave comment on this word "operation", along with "activity" and the like, till later.

There are four reasons why these kinds of understanding and this kind of thinking cannot have any physical state or process internal to them—or indeed any state or process in any other supposed inner apparatus, para-mechanical soul-substance, or whatever. These are reasons why these kinds of understanding and this kind of thinking cannot have any neural correlate at all, since any such correlate could be conceived of as internal to the operation concerned.

Let us state these four reasons summarily, and then in our next section comment on each in turn in more detail.

(a) The kind of thinking which is characteristic of human beings is in the medium of words, and the ways in which this thinking differs from speaking do not make a difference to those analogies between them in virtue of which their main physical correlate, in the case of thinking as much as in the case of speaking, is their expression, not some going on in an internal mental apparatus. It would be less mistaken to say that the voice was the organ of thinking than to say that the mind or brain was this organ. But in fact, thinking has no organ because inner speech has a purely 'intentional' existence involving no inner voice or inner hearing, no image-involving process at all, as internal to it.[2]

It is the person or human being who understands, speaks and hears, and thinks, and these are not operations of some inner part of him or her but of the person him or herself. Moreover, it is as misguided to attribute the meanings of the linguistic expressions of thought or feeling, this statement, this wish, this dialogue, this poetry or prose, to brains or souls rather than to persons as it is to attribute the thought and feelings themselves to brains or souls rather than to persons. The content of these expressions does not subsist apart from the force or attitude,[3] as if it were an imprint or structure in the brain or in an inner apparatus of soul, but only exists as it issues from the person.

(b) The use of general concepts requires a principle or 'formative cause' of operation[4] which does not function in virtue of any material isomorphism. That is, they do not function in virtue of any sameness of structure between the determinate capacity in regard to these concepts exercised in using them and the objects, natures, actualities, or facts known. Further, any such sameness of structure would be irrelevant to their operation.[5] But it is only by means of such sameness of structure that any material state or process could be relevant to, so as conceivably to be internal to, the possession or exercise of these determinate capacities.

Perception and imagination have a role in supplying objects to the understanding of *langue*, the understanding of *parole*, indeed in supplying objects to speech and to thought, but this role does not make them internal to the operations of being directed towards these objects, but only indispensable to the natural operation of understanding, speech, and thought—which fairly evidently cannot function without objects.[6] They are indispensable to the natural operation of understanding, speech, and thought because the world within which we live—within which, as it were, our soul functions, to use the way of speaking of the next chapter—is not a Cartesian or empiricist

---

[2]This was shown in Chapter XI, Section 4 (a).

[3]This was shown in Chapter XI, Section 1 (c).

[4]"Principle" or "formative cause" in the sense we indicated in Chapter XI, Section 2.

[5]These things were shown in Chapter XI, Section 2.

[6]This was shown in Chapter XI, Section 3.

inner world of perceptions or ideas as mental objects but an outer or public world.

(c) The understanding of *parole* in hearing and speaking involves a capacity, on the basis of the understanding of *langue*, to use words in an indefinite number of logically distinguishable types of use (or as we expressed it earlier, polymorphously as distinct functors or sentence-factors).[7] These kinds of understanding cannot be supposed to function in a way which requires a material correlate, because any supposed correlate would lack the flexibility, or extensibility in type of relation to different types of case, which is required.

(d) The structure of linguistic capacity involves a judging subject and within it structures of self-reflection and of reflection on procedures of coming to judgements. This structure is unitary in such a way that, without these and other essential substructures, there would be no capacity for language or linguistic understanding or for thought in the medium of words.[8] But there could not be any mechanically operating system which exemplified these structures—and therefore no material system, since the phenomena of geometrical continuity are irrelevant to the representation of thought. And the procedures of critical reflection could not be tied to having any particular kind of physical process internal to them, because, if they were so tied, they would lack the generality or open-endedness of structure whereby they are applicable to structurally varying types of case. The extent of this structural variation, the indefiniteness of the number of structurally differentiable types of case which may have to be embraced within the same concept (e.g., 'shows it to be true that . . .', 'is a definition', 'is a method for showing to be true/for mechanically deciding . . ./for defining'), is most evident when self-reflective or critical procedures are taken into account because of the indefiniteness of the number of points at which critical enquiry may be pursued and the indefiniteness of the number of levels to which it may be carried, all within a single language-system—in natural languages, critical capacity bringing with it its own resources for avoiding paradox and diagnosing apparent paradox, in the way we summarised.[9]

---

[7]This was shown in Chapter X, Sections 2 and 4.
[8]This was shown in Chapter X, Section 3.
[9]Chapter X, Section 4.

If by the organ through which a capacity is exercised is meant some part of the organism such that the operation of the organ is internal to or vehicle of the operation of the capacity, then there can be isomorphism between parts, sub-states, or sub-processes and the whole or its states or processes, but nothing corresponding to a critical judgement by the whole upon the operation of the whole. By what we called the 'allusiveness' of thought (its 'intentionality' in one sense of that word), every utterance or thought is pregnant with the whole inter-connectedness and structure of language.[10]

I put the objection that thinking in the medium of words cannot be a material process or comprise material processes as internal to it in the first place, not because by itself it will seem to the would-be materialist decisive, but because once fully grasped it enables the other objections to be seen in their proper light.

The possession or use of a concept is not the bringing of an internal object (an 'idea' or representation) into relation with the object to which it is applied, but the saying—the expressing—of something. The use of a concept in thought is like its use in speech—polymorphous, each meaning in *langue* being realized in multiple kinds of way in *parole*, each node of thought-capacity being realized in multiple kinds of way in actual thinking. The use of any concept is only within the context of something expressible as a complete speech-act, and therefore involves an author (that is, a subject) giving the speech-unit concerned the force it has, whether the force of a statement, of a wish, or something else quite simple, or something more complex. That is, the use of any concept involves in any case a subject with self-reflection and involved in evaluation and so forth, with all the structures which these will bring with them.

In all this the key point is that what belongs to the thinking's being expressible in a certain way must not be thought of as an inner process within some complex of parts, whether this apparatus or complex of parts be the brain or the soul, but as what issues from a person who is, *qua* subject of thinking, indivisible and not composed of parts. We have to return to our primary insight, that it would be less mistaken to say that the voice was the organ of thinking than to say that the mind or brain was this organ. Thinking has no organ

---

[10]This was shown in Chapter XI, Section 4 (c).

because inner speech has a purely 'intentional' existence involving no inner voice or inner hearing internal to it.[11]

It has been held that, although thinking and understanding 'as they present themselves to us' might be simple or materially uncomplex, they may yet, 'as they are in themselves', be some materially complex processes or states. The materialist will expect that such a supposition will prove explanatory. This expectation is ruled out as hopeless by our third argument drawing upon what we established in Chapter X as to the impossibility of calculating speech-meanings from *langue*-meanings, despite the fact that the understanding of *langue* is something publically accessible and shared between speaker and hearer which explains the intelligibility of speaker to hearer. At this stage, the suggestion of the occurrence of material processes precisely correlated with the procedures of understanding and thinking becomes not only impossible—there can be no such precise correlation—but also redundant, serving no purpose in explanation. In the same act as becoming redundant, the supposition becomes empty and contentless: we no longer know what meaning to attach to the suggestion that this brain-state or process which happens to be about the place is identical to this state of understanding or activity of thinking. The suggestion is reminiscent of the absurdity considered by Frege that the square root of 16 might happen to be Julius Caesar—the two 'objects' or 'states' seem to have no relevant connection, nothing relevant to do with each other.

That is, once we have got to this point—of seeing that the materialist suggestion is non-explanatory, redundant, and empty—we can grasp how it is that the suggestion was misconceived in the first place. The types of structure which can be envisaged by the materialist (and any structures comprising inter-related elements or parts, even non-physical, analogous to these) are, as it were, entirely 'out of joint' with the structures of thinking and understanding as they present themselves to us. The explorations into the roots of intelligibility which the linguist may offer are not thus foreign, bringing to light as they do connections in meaning and parallels in structure of which we might not have been conscious but which, when pointed out, seem of a piece with our general way of understanding and thinking.

---

[11]See Chapter XI, Section 4 (a).

The way we conceive seeing is such that there is nothing out of place in the explanations provided by optics and neurology of the way the nervous receptors are acted upon and the way the 'information' is organized, but only, as it were, an already open role for them. The way we conceive speaking and hearing leave a likewise open place for explanations of the mechanisms of speech and the use of the vocal chords and of hearing and its phonological aspects. But there is no such parallel between the structures of *langue* and *parole* and the types of structure envisaged by the materialist. The former are in a certain sense on the surface: I mean by this that the road to understanding them more deeply lies in what we may think of as the human or holistic sciences, not in delving into the realm of material explanation.

It is vital to avoid any mistake here. There is no room for *any* kind of 'mechanisms' by which the intellect might work, whether soul-mechanisms or brain-mechanisms. Yet, if we do not understand the point rightly, we shall no sooner escape materialism than fall back into dualism—exchanging a material apparatus of mind for a mysterious immaterial apparatus, and in either case doing away with what the mediaevals called the 'simplicity' of understanding and thinking, falsely reasoning from the 'material' complexity of their expressions to their being materially complex themselves.

The supposition that there might be a close correspondence between the dynamic neurological structures of brain operation and the internal structures of some digital computer, a correspondence which explains understanding and thinking, represents a survival of what Ryle speaks of as the Cartesian para-mechanical view of the mind's workings. If we follow Ryle's arguments, it was a retrograde step for us, having escaped the error of explaining linguistic understanding in terms of the working of mechanisms in the soul, to substitute the error of explaining it in terms of neurological structures and mechanisms: the mistake was a mistake in 'logical grammar', that of thinking of understanding as to be explained in terms of, or realized in, the laws and structures of subordinate internal parts or 'mechanisms' at all.[12]

---

[12] *The Concept of Mind*, Chapter X, cf. 'Mowgli in Babel', pp. 99–103.

It does not matter for the argument whether the 'mechanisms' are in the soul or in the brain, and it does not matter whether they are 'biological' or 'neurological' as in Searle, *Minds, Brains and Science*, Chapter I, or whether they are of the computer theoretical sort espoused by the 'cognitivist', scorned in Searle's Chapter III.

Blackburn provides a good commentary on the issues in *Spreading the Word*, pp. 26–37, where Ryle's approach is the second view represented (p. 30, led up to

But this perspective cannot be reached securely except by the wisdom of retrospect. If we begin with it, introducing it uncritically, it can only appear obscurantist—dismissive in advance of what may seem potentially rich seams of inquiry. It is only after appreciating the four deeper reasons for the 'out of jointness' to which I refer that it can be seen that the putting away of material explanation in this field is not obscurantist but records a liberation of thought—like the putting away of phlogiston theory.

Let us therefore review these four key reasons for regarding the idea that understanding or thinking has a material embodiment distinct from its outward expression in language as misguided.

2. Subsidiary Comment on These Four Lines of Argument

(a) Key to the first proof: thinking in the medium of words is material in its expression, not in its operation

Thinking, *par excellence*, is supposed by modern fashion or orthodoxy to be a brain-process. But according to our first line of argument, at least that kind of thinking which is in the medium of words cannot be such—whatever the situation with other kinds of so-called thinking. Let us now make some side-observations upon the argument we offered.

It is said that in the course of dreaming, with the eyes closed, there is a great deal of rapid eye movement and it is supposed that this is co-ordinated with the objects dreamt of and that it is the result of sundry processes in the brain. It is further supposed that such serial processes, in the brain or in the sense-organs, are internal to the activities of imagining as well as of perceiving. It is evident that in dreaming there is also some incipient behavioural propensity internal to it, as is sometimes evidenced by the shuddering, cringing, and even (in the act of waking) more violent movements which reveal the behavioural aspects of the emotions and experiences concerned. Aquinas' reasons for presuming imagination to be analogous to perception may not be ours,[13] but the correctness of thinking that imagination is of a

---

by the argument of pp. 28–30). The idea of an innate grammar nowadays takes the form of supposing it to be realized in neurological mechanisms, and this is open to the same objections (cf. Blackburn, pp. 32–37).

[13]Chapter XI, Section 3.8.

piece with perception in having behavioural 'sets' internal to it, and may therefore be expected to have structures in the brain related to behavioural anticipation internal to it in a parallel way to that in which they are internal to perception is clear: the directedness is indeed, as Aquinas recognized, towards the particular, and this directedness towards the particular, whether as revealed in rapid eye movement or in incipient action, involves physical structures as internal to it.

It might now be suggested that in some analogous way sub-threshold variations in muscle tension in the speech organ and, more importantly, various underlying neurological processes are internal to what we have called thinking in the medium of words.

I make no judgement as to whether any such neurological and muscular changes proleptic of speech go on during thinking, since my argument in no way depends on whether they do or whether they do not. What is important to note is that, if they do go on, they are of a sort to be germane to the outward expression of thought and linguistic understanding, rather than of a sort to be internal to whatever mental 'operation'—state, act, process, or activity—these outward expressive activities might be supposed to be expressive of.

We made it clear that thinking does not involve a directing of the mind towards images or towards words as objects imaged (words did not figure within thinking in this role), so that there is no reason on the basis of analogies with imagining for attributing a serial character to thinking. In discussing the unity of the 'act' of thinking or 'having' a thought, we made clear the non-serial character of thinking as distinct from the serial character of the expressing of a thought—with our example of thinking 'Heavens! The post has gone'. Accordingly, thinking in the medium of words cannot be conceived of as including as serial parts of it physical sub-processes (electro-chemical or otherwise) corresponding to the verbal or morphological components of its expression—as if it were a directed and organized passage through an integrated series of sub-processes in even the way talking and playing a musical phrase can be conceived like this.

It might, of course, be proposed that thinking was a brain-process which had material sub-processes as parts, but not ones cor-responding to words or anything else of which the person having the thoughts concerned might be conscious. This brain-process would be one of which the liability to be expressed in certain ways was a mere by-product but which, in itself in its internal reality, had no parts serially occurring in any way analogous to that in which the parts which make up a piece of speech occur serially. But then what we might say about the brain-process would be so out of relation with how our thoughts or thinkings presented themselves in our experience or knowledge as their authors that it would be obscure what was explained by supposing the brain-process to be internal to the thinking, let alone identical with it. And we would seem to have represented the thinking (now supposed to be in itself a brain-process) as if it were only in an external causal relation to its expression, whereas what the phenomenology or logic of 'thinking' suggests is that how it would be expressed is internal to what the thinking which had occurred was. This is the 'out of jointness' between material explanation and the 'phenomena' to which we referred earlier.

It might be complained that we are falling into a trap spoken of by Wittgenstein in these terms:

> 'And we do here what we do in a host of similar cases: because we cannot specify any *one* bodily action which we call pointing to the shape (as opposed, for example, to the colour), we say that a *spiritual* [mental, intellectual] activity corresponds to these words.
> 'Where our language suggests a body and there is none: there we should like to say, is a *spirit*.'[14]

That is, it might be complained in a Rylean spirit (in the context of quite different examples, e.g., tennis-playing) that because there is not just one bodily action which exhibits a certain stretch of thinking activity, we are concluding that there must be some theoretical activity antecedent to action to which 'thinking' refers. Or it might be complained that we are inventing as something extra and behind the physical act of pointing an intellectual act of 'intending' the shape of a thing, whereas the fact that the outward act is an act of pointing at the shape is not a matter of its being preceded by a prior intellectual act of intending a shape but of a context of behavioural pre-occupation plain to the onlooker and hearer envisaged in the act. And, worse, it might be complained that we are introducing not only an inner operation of thinking, but also an entity, a spirit, to perform this operation.

But our case is quite different. We have an 'operation' on our hands, the operation of 'thinking in the medium of words', which

---

[14] *Philosophical Investigations*, I, 36.

is not adverbial or aspectual to some bodily activity which can be considered in itself as a rounded psychophysical whole (the intentional activity of tennis-playing, pointing to a shape, or speaking some word), but an activity in its own right. And this 'operation' or 'activity' is not one whose mode of exhibition is obscure, scattered, or in its primary character ('pointing') ambiguous, but one whose mode of exhibition in its primary character (linguistic) is clear: consisting in the expressing of the thought. But the thinking which can be thus expressed is not, when not expressed, some inner whisper heard only by the thinker. The mistake is not in saying that the thinker is a spirit (that would merely be at this stage obscure, since nothing has told us what a spirit might be), but in supposing this spirit to be some inner thing analogous to a body capable within its own non-physical soul-stuff and inner soul-world of an inner non-physical speaking and hearing.

We must not jump out of one mistake—mind-brain identity materialism—into other mistakes, whether behaviourism, or Platonism as exemplified in Descartes and the empiricists. We must, at this stage, simply record what we have shown, namely that thinking in the medium of words is not a bodily operation, leaving it to Chapters XIV and XV to inquire what may follow from this.

(b) Key to the second proof: the 'principles' of intellectual operation in speaking and thinking can have no material embodiment or realization

The basis for my second line of argument was set by the shape of our rejection of Platonic and empiricist theories of abstraction, following the lines suggested to us by Aquinas.

We can argue that the principles or 'formative causes' in virtue of which we understand and are able to apply general concepts cannot be materially isomorphic with the objects or natures which they make it possible to understand or attribute on three principal grounds. It is the first of these grounds that we are pursuing here, namely the consideration that any such material isomorphism would be irrelevant even in the case of quite specific concepts. We pursue the other two principal grounds under (c) and (d) later. The second ground, pursued under (c), rests on the consideration that to require any such isomorphism, an isomorphism not in some informal sense but in some univocal or formally definable sense, would involve a restriction of the intellect's own freedom of operation, a freedom of operation exhibited in the full range of enquiries associated with the most general concepts. The third ground, pursued under (d), draws upon the idea that any requirement of material isomorphism would interfere with the intellect's own capacity for self-reflection, which exemplifies the exercise of a key part of this general freedom.

The notion of material isomorphism here concerned is the only concept of isomorphism currently in fashion, parts corresponding with parts, the parts being elements or continua, the isomorphism being only in respect of such structures as allow elements and continua to be related according to them.[15]

In the line of argument which we are immediately concerned with, we draw upon only the first of these principal grounds for objecting to the suggestion of any isomorphism in this sense. The point here is that the possession and use of general concepts would be in no way assisted by the existence in the brain or in any physical or non-physical part of the human being of any structures isomorphic even in the most formal way to the objects known, e.g., the general natures of this or that type of thing, such as human being, dog, cow, star, angel, etc. This is because what is required is not another sample of something like the object known but a capacity or principle of operation making it possible for the human being to grasp the essence of the likeness between the different instantiations of the concept concerned, e.g., the essence of the likeness between different human beings. And the existence in the human being, e.g., in the brain of some physical structure, electro-chemical or other, which was even in only the most dilute sense isomorphic to all the various individual human beings, would be no more helpful than the existence in the imagination of an image of a human being, or for that matter, the perception of an individual human being (yielding an image on the retina, which is not itself an object of perception or of imagination). Indeed, such things would be no more helpful than there lying about in some part of the human anatomy of an effigy of a human being or *homunculus*. Rather, what is required is whatever is needed for the

---

[15]The idea of an intentional isomorphism towards something such as may be enjoyed by a thing in virtue of its having some property ('being informed' in the appropriate way) whereby it is cognitively directed towards another, called an isomorphism (a sharing of the form or *species*) arises from the theory of visual perception described in Chapter III, n. 45. It is absent from modern thinking, so that Searle lacks excuse in using the word "represent" (Chapter III, n. 46).

human being to be able to stand back from all the individual human beings which are objects of knowledge and judge them to be human beings, with a knowing of the kind that involves the understanding of that in which their likeness consists, in virtue of which they are all human beings.

If any correspondence between some physical structure in the material, either the whole body or some particular organ within it (e.g., the brain), and the objects of knowledge is to be causative in a formative way of the exercise of human understanding in judgement, i.e., of 'intellectual' knowledge of these objects, this can only be by this correspondence's being an 'isomorphism' (the concept of 'isomorphism' is such an open one). The notion of 'material isomorphism' can be in respect of structures as 'logical' or 'systems descriptive' as any computer theorist or systems analyst might care to think up so long as it is essential to it that it be a structure exemplifiable in principle by a mechanical system, i.e., a system whose behaviour is, in principle, explicable considering it in terms of physical relations of physically related parts, whether elements or continua.

Any relevant correspondence must be an isomorphism and any isomorphism of the kind considered ('material') would be irrelevant. If irrelevant it would have to be a consequential accident, i.e., so that as the intellect went so the material variations followed the intellect around although serving no function in the intellect's operation, like a kind of material by-product. There is no point in supposing this. In order to be a principle of operation in the relevant sense, it would have to be *qua* form causative, but this has been excluded.

It will be noted that the possession of general concepts with which we are concerned is that kind of understanding which is exercised in the linguistic act of making a statement, the kind of understanding in which the words express the meaning of the statement, rather than merely identifying this meaning. But, by concentrating on the most specific concepts, we have taken the case which should present least problems to the hypothesis of a material isomorphism between the concept, 'idea', or principle of understanding concerned and the thing or nature understood—least problematic because of the possibility that in such cases the concept is univocal so that there is only one logically distinguishable *parole*-meaning associated with the *langue*-meaning of the term concerned.

(c) **Key to the third proof: the understanding of *langue*
and the understanding of *parole* can have no material
or neural correlate or element internal to it**

In my third line of argument, what I am doing is using the
impossibility of calculating sentence meanings from lexeme-meanings
to show the ubiquitous presence of understanding in any use of words
in sentences as something which cannot be regarded as physically
realized in any biological apparatus (or in any 'material' apparatus
of a para-mechanical or supposed non-physical kind analogous to it).

It is not just that lack of calculability shows a lack of mechanical
simulability but that there is something positive which we do or
achieve (understanding in speaking and in hearing) which is not a
mechanical process or state, and has nothing mechanical involved in it
in the way in which seeing involves processes in the retina and nervous
system.

Understanding is not a functional state which is definable behaviouristically as if it were a set of behavioural capacities. It appears
to be something which underlies or is behind behaviour, realized in[16]
although not exhaustively expressed in it since it is of its nature a
many-track (not a single track) disposition, but for reasons already
evident cannot be a mere state of the brain explanatory of behaviour.
The comprehending or explaining of behaviour here involved is not
in mechanical terms any more than any other teleology-involving
explanation bringing in consciousness. We have already seen that no
reduction of consciousness and teleology involving explanations to the
mechanical or physical is possible, but now, *a fortiori*, we have to see
that, in the case of linguistic understanding, the physical cannot be
internal even in the way we find in the case of perception and of the
imagination which takes place in dreaming.

The fact that understanding explains something, without there
being a deterministic mechanical process involved, is shown by the
impossibility of calculating rather than 'seeing' meaning, in a context in which is evident that ordinary 'mentalistic' explanations are
still doing some successful work. This is evident from the fact that

---

[16]In the Aristotelian sense that potentialities or dispositions are realized in, and
understood by reference to, the spread of actualities in which they are fulfilled—not
in the sense that they have their reality in certain brain processes or states.

these explanations make it intelligible that the hearer should reliably understand the speaker in a mass of communications which cannot be encompassed in any mechanical rule. This implies that there is an activity of the person or intellect which is, in no way, mechanically simulable, and which cannot be regarded as a physical process.

Let us fill this out.

One can perform a thought-experiment. One can imagine a computer being put to many uses, each according to a different programme, each corresponding to a different speech-sense of a certain word. One might imagine a multiplicity of different users, one for each speech-sense, or just one user turning the hardware to all the different uses. Somebody might then suggest that such a computer was an analogue of the brain.

Let us treat the environments of the words, though necessarily this will be contrary to fact, as a constant for all these different speech-senses, constant in the sense of not themselves requiring differential programming.

Two principal problems arise. Firstly, the presentation suggests a definite number of speech-senses for each word corresponding to an enumerable set of uses/programmes. But, if our exposition in Chapter X was right, there will be no enumerable set of speech-senses corresponding to a given *langue*-meaning for a word, and no function in any extended list of specifications of types of example of speech-sense as if speech-sense could be calculated from such a list, but rather an open set of possible uses arising within the open set of possible situations, of no definite number and not enumerable. There is nothing in the computer corresponding to such a non-enumerable set, but only a capacity to be used in a non-enumerable variety of ways; a football has the capacity to be projected in a variety of ways corresponding to the real numbers, because the directions of projecting it are distinguishable according to a physical, in this case geometrical, concept. However, the ways of using a computer do not correspond in number either to the natural or the real numbers, because they are not thus distinguishable but distinguished according to the plans of computer users, these plans not being enumerable because characteristically only in the realm of the possible rather than yet actually adopted requiring to be adapted to a non-enumerable range of possible situations, projects and systems of co-operation in projects. Accordingly, this 'capacity for an indefinite range of use' is not an internal feature of the computer, or even of the computer taken together with any set of already given programmes, but a property of the computer users.

Secondly, there is nothing in the computer corresponding to the unity and interconnection between the multiple speech-senses arising from the *langue*-meaning of a given word. This unity and interconnection lies in the understanding of the computer user. This understanding is in no way represented or embodied in the computer even taken together with its already given programmes.[17] Yet it is this understanding of *langue* which is common property of speaker and hearer, and quite adequate to explain the capacity of speaker reliably to communicate with hearer, expressing a determinate *parole*-sense to him.

We can view this whole matter more broadly.

It is not open to human beings to lay down beforehand the limits either of their possible enquiries or their capacities for new types of response to them. Two features of this openness need particular note, both of which are required for a proper understanding of what is involved in speech and writing.

One of these two features has already been much publicized, namely, that there is the capacity for new inquiries to be initiated at a second order or meta-level, and the possibility that these meta-level inquiries generate new conclusions and results even at the first order level, a feature incidentally not only of natural arithmetic and reflection about its methods but also about, for instance, estimations of distance in astronomy and methods of assessing these, to take an instance at random of what has become recognized, through the influence of Einstein and Heisenberg, as one of the fundamental features of physics. Whenever one paradigm of explanation or analysis is supplanted by another, as when physicists turned from Aristotelian to Newtonian and then to relativistic models, or quantum mechanical

---

[17]It is not embodied in the 'capacity for the range of use exercised in this spread of uses corresponding to speech-senses' because this is an accidental reflection of the global 'capacity for an indefinite range of use'. This global 'capacity' marks a global indetermination of the computer corresponding to its merely physical character carrying no meaning in itself in regard to any concept whatsoever, let alone any meaning related to some particular item of *langue*. The computer is free for multiple use, but all uses are given by the computer user, and the various spreads of uses associated with particular items of *langue* are not represented in it or in its already given programmes.

approaches were accepted with some idea of complementarity between wave and particle models, second-order reflection is involved. Yet the result is nonetheless a real increase of publicly received and objective knowledge at the first-order level, including verified predictions. And we must always be open, in mathematics as elsewhere, to the possibility that conjectures may receive a mixture of a priori and a posteriori confirmation.[18] For we must let there be no mistake about the matter: the second-order reflections with which we are concerned, whether they be in mathematics or in physics or some other empirical science, are fruitful of results which are not effete or out of the way but within substantial first-order areas of concern of the sciences concerned. The Gödelian reasonings about natural arithmetic give proof of natural seeming combinatorial results already suggested by model-theoretic conjectures and not hitherto suspected of any second-order link-up.[19] As Kreisel amply shows in mathematics, so also, in general, finitary reasoning goes far beyond the mechanical. Thus, while Gödelian and other finitary arguments in mathematics are deductive, despite not being formally based, the types of reasoning in empirical science which justify alterations of paradigm in method of explanation, alterations observationally tested and confirmed, are not thus deductive, but nonetheless coercive. Second-order reasoning is much involved, and it is on the capacity for this that our fourth line of argument will turn.

But underlying this more publicized feature of the openness of human capacity for inquiry and response to inquiry is another more general one, and it is this more general feature with which we are concerned in our present, third, line of argument. For it is an underlying feature of all human inquiry that in our inquiries—

---

[18]It is very instructive to see the way in which Gödel thought of the presence or absence of fruitfulness in producing results at a less general or more testable level as a sign of the truth or untruth of such conjectures as the Continuum Hypothesis ('What is Cantor's Continuum Problem?', 1964). He had a real anticipation that a priori insight would coincide with genuinely a posteriori 'confirmation' in the form of new results. One may compare Gödel's attitude with that of Einstein in which quite a priori considerations conspired together with the empirical Michelson-Morley observations to suggest the Special Theory of Relativity (cf. Polanyi, *Personal Knowledge*, pp. 9–15).

[19]The finite Ramsey theorem (cf. *Foundations of Mathematics and Other Essays*, Paper III, F.P. Ramsey, cf. *Ramsey Theory*, Ronald L. Graham, Bruce L. Rothschild, Joel H. Spencer) for natural arithmetic is provable from Peano's Axioms, but the natural-seeming infinite Ramsey theorem is not thus provable. However, Paris and Harrington have proved that this stronger theorem follows from Gödel's Incompleteness theorems ('A Mathematical Incompleteness in Peano Arithmetic', 1977).

quite generally whether they appeal to second-order considerations or not—we use concepts which are in Rylean terms 'polymorphous', not susceptible of being captured by or having their meaning encapsulated in any single set of criteria or any single definition, nor of having their unity explained by the mere listing of their agreed uses in a disjunctive definition. It is well known that second-order predicates like "is true", "is a definition", and "can be shown to be true (is provable)" cannot have their meanings captured by any single set of criteria or definition. However, this is equally the case with the most general first-order concepts: existence, causation, life, knowledge, goodness, desire, enjoyment, thought and the like. And it is the openness of such concepts as these which has the effect that there are no definite limits upon the opening out of new inquiries and the dealing with these inquiries, a freedom reflected even within quite ordinary areas of empirical knowledge.

Standing back from these lines of argument, (b) from the nature of judgement and (c) from the character of the most general concepts involved in our judgements and inquiries, we can summarize the situation as follows. It is part of human nature, firstly, that a human being's knowledge has linguistic expression (in Aquinas's terms, that it be a knowledge of truth by composition and division) and, secondly, that it involves some engagement with reasons or argumentation (that is, in Aquinas's terms, that it is discursive), no intuition existing in isolation from the context of the possibility of review and consideration by some kind of argument or other, demonstrative or dialectical (to use the Aristotle's terminology in the *Topics*). That is: firstly, all human use of the intellect (including that use which underlies freedom of choice) involves the capacity for judgement; and, secondly, the use of general concepts, including those most general concepts whose applicability in a literal or proper sense cannot be limited according to any one definition or set of criteria. And from each of these it follows that the capacity with which we are concerned is one whose exercises are not operations of any material system.

Always, it should be remembered that the possession of general concepts with which we are concerned is that kind of understanding which is exercised in speech, the kind of understanding in which the words *express* the meaning of the statement or other speech-unit, rather than merely *identifying* this meaning. That is, we are never concerned with the understanding of *langue* as if it were something with standing in its own right, but only with the understanding of *langue* as something to be realized in the understanding of *parole* or speech.

And in all this, in speaking of openness and flexibility, we must reiterate that we are not speaking of indeterminacy of meaning or indeterminism as to how speech is to be understood. The openness of a unit of *langue* to polymorphous use, the flexibility which allows us to use words meaningfully outside the type of context within which they were learnt, the flexibility of which metaphor is only one example, involve that *langue*-meaning does not by itself determine *parole*-meaning—but this is not why they are important for our present argument. Rather, the key point is that this openness and flexibility still allows communication and so still allows the public determination of *parole*-meaning which this requires. Further, it not only allows the opening out of new questions but also allows these to be answered in a publicly agreed and objective manner. The understanding of *langue* which is exercised in speech makes speech intelligible and explains how it comes to have as determinate a meaning as it has, and in these circumstances determines what is understood, but explains and determines it in a non-mechanical way; and this non-mechanical determination of meaning can carry with it a non-mechanical determination of judgement. To repeat the point again, things can be determined without being determined by a mechanism.

(d) Key to the fourth proof: the structures of self-reflectivity internal to language, and implicit in every utterance, cannot be exercised through a material organ

What we have here is a perfectly general question about the conditions and implications of the self-reflective and critical capacities of human beings. We already noted the importance of these second-order procedures, not only in (and not principally in) natural arithmetic, but also much more widely in physics, astronomy, and elsewhere under (c) above.

But we must now take account of the strategic situation of the structure involved here, as a structure imported with the very act of judging itself.

We have already recognized that having an image, a model, or a representation of any kind is not the same as making a judgement. No isomorphism between any structure within an apparatus within a person, whether this apparatus be the brain or some supposed non-physical part of human make-up, and some object to be known or understood would constitute a judgement. It is not just that a model needs a context to serve as a model, and that a way of conceiving things cannot be a model although it might include an appreciation of how to use or interpret models, but that models and ways of conceiving things need to be put to use in one of the particular ways characteristic of different kinds of speech-act before we have any example of the exercise of linguistic understanding or of thinking at all.

But once we introduce the act of judging, we do not have on our hands only some brain or soul about which (if it had parts like an apparatus) it might be imagined that something within it was isomorphic in structure with the object being judged about; but we also have on our hands the person who makes the judgement and his or her act of judging. Accordingly, if we persist with this way of thinking which we have already seen to be wrong-headed, the way of thinking whereby knowledge and judgement involve an isomorphism between some inner part of the knower or judger and the thing known or judged about, then we will be landed with the need for some modelling in the brain or soul, not only of the object known or judged about, but also of the act of knowing or judging about it. But, if we are to model the act of judging itself, then we will have to model the whole structure which judgement involves, at least in its behavioural expression. But, since a formalized language cannot include its own metalanguage and it is integral to the structure of natural language to do this, and since it is this which most reflects the structure of the self-reflecting critical judger in the act of judgement, there is no way in which a material system functioning mechanically can exhibit isomorphism with human beings in respect of the relevant structure.

A computer can be programmed to check some of its procedures, but it cannot be programmed to check or review all of its procedures. Probably, there can be no general method for deciding whether or not something is a method of deciding a type of question (no algorithm for deciding whether or not something is an algorithm) and, in particular, no general programme for deciding upon the consistency of formalized systems. But more particularly and to the point, a programme for deciding questions within a formalized system cannot include a programme for deciding the consistency of that system as a whole. By contrast, as we have explained, any natural language of its nature includes its own metalanguage, thereby allowing questions to be raised about its own statements and procedures. There can be nothing in a computer as a mechanically operating device which corresponds to this generalized capacity.

It is important that for the purposes of this chapter nothing hangs on whether or not a 'computer' is an artefact. If human beings managed to construct out of material parts a structure which did not function overall in a mathematically mechanical way, it would not count as a computer for the purposes of our discussion.[20]

The consideration of this perfectly general question about what is involved in human capacities for self-reflection has achieved a certain notoriety through being narrowed to a consideration of the significance of Gödel's first Incompleteness Theorem for natural arithmetic. The effect of this theorem is that any formalizable system for proof in natural arithmetic, if consistent (yielding no contradictions), will be incomplete in that there will be propositions of natural arithmetic capable of being shown to be true but not according to this system. Since a digital computer operated according to a definite given set of programmes can only simulate proof in natural arithmetic so far as it is restricted to some given formalized system, no such combination of a computer with a definite given set of programmes can simulate a certain particular ability of human beings: viz., the ability in respect of any given formalized system for proof in natural arithmetic, to show to be true some proposition of natural arithmetic not provable within that formalized system. In this way the capacities of any human being in one particular systematic respect in principle outreach the capacities of any digital computer/programme combine. The significance of this is that the human being therefore cannot be conceived of as analogous to any mechanically operating system whatsoever since the mathematical or structural description of what could count as a digital computer and programme is so general as to cover any properly physical system or organization of discrete physical relations of physical parts.

It is of course true that each time we find a new Gödel formula, provable by informal argument but not derived within the already given formalization of arithmetic, we can add it as a new axiom. And

---

[20]If it can happen over thousands of millions of years, as it were in the factory of Nature, that there develop organisms whose material parts are complexes of organic chemicals but which do not function in a mechanical way, it cannot be excluded a priori that in human factories there should develop bodily systems whose material parts are of a different kind (including pieces of metal, silicon chips and the like)—or, if this is impossible in principle, it will be because the genetic coding required for regeneration and the like cannot be realized in materials such as these (e.g., because they physically do not allow of adequate complexity) or for some other physical reason.

we may suppose, for any constructive ordinal number, the possibility of having a system which included as axioms all the Gödel formulae which could be imagined to have been successively added in the appropriate order up to that number. We have no system for naming (i.e., giving what are called Church-Kleene descriptions of) higher constructive ordinals, but if intuition (or non-formal finitary reasoning) correctly suggests the name of any high constructive ordinal, then we could have a formalization of arithmetic including all the Gödel formulae corresponding to ordinals up to that number.[21] And there could be a computer with powers to derive anything derivable in that system. But we could never complete the process, since there is no highest constructive ordinal, and there could be no computer with powers to derive anything derivable in any system expanded up to any constructive ordinal. And in the meantime, besides that a non-mechanically guided act of intuiting the name of a high constructive ordinal would intervene in the identification of any system, the human being, granted such intuition and identification, could yet again step beyond the system identified to form another Gödel formula outside it.

There is a familiar riposte to arguments of this sort, namely that human beings are no better than computers in the respects argued about in that they are no better than computers in making the judgements about the consistency of formal systems.

The first easy reply which suggests itself is that computers do not make judgements at all, but that it is computer-users who make judgements, sometimes in the light of the behaviour of computers. But this reply will not satisfy the person who imagines a computer which has become self-reliant and self-sufficient, as it were using itself, simulating or extending human capacity in such a way as to be able to be spoken of as making judgements itself. Nor will it deal with the more modest idea of computer-users who, as it were, depute all their decisions to be made according to the indications offered to them by some particular computer.

Therefore, this fundamentally right reply that computers do not make judgements at all needs to be supplemented. The human being has the capacity to judge that, understood in their standard application, i.e., as applying to the natural numbers, Peano's axioms are true,

---

[21]A.M. Turing, 'Systems of Logic Based on Ordinals'.

and to judge this in virtue of insight into the subject-matter—and
likewise to judge the validity of the standard rules of inference used
in deriving conclusions from them within natural arithmetic—and to
judge these things because he or she sees why they must be true and
why such conclusions must follow. From this truth and validity the
consistency of natural arithmetic follows and, therefore, the consistency of formalized arithmetic (even though this is compatible with
non-standard interpretations) from which incompleteness follows. But
the computer has no such reason for judging formal arithmetic to
be consistent, indeed no reason for judging anything. Rather, how
a computer 'decides' things is simply determined by the way it has
been programmed.

The idea that human beings are no better off than computers
in respect of being able to decide questions of the truth of axioms
and of validity and consistency fits with the fashion amongst cognitive
scientists and philosophers of a materialist persuasion for espousing
the causal theory of knowledge in epistemology—often gilded with a
veneer of conventionalism. We might think that certain things could
be seen to be true, not in a foundationalist spirit as if nothing of any
kind could be said in favour of accepting that they were true and
that we have the kind of understanding which would enable us to see
them to be so, but in the sense that such acceptance did not wait
for its warrantedness upon such things being said, but was already
provided by this understanding spoken of. But the point of view we
are considering denies that we have any such warrant or any such
understanding in the cases concerned—or indeed in any case at all.

Let us look at this view in all its absurdity. The suggestion is
that what we experience as a knowledge or understanding sufficient
to enable us 'intuitively' to decide questions of truth, validity and
consistency in the cases in question is nothing objective, but a matter
of how 'Nature' has programmed us. When we question what we
are thus caused to think we know, we can back it up with all the
resources offered by a conventionalist epistemology, the agreement of
the human and scientific community and the reinforcement provided
by considerations such as simplicity, elegance and apparent consilience
with other things accepted. But it remains that there is no rational
compulsion to accept what these considerations suggest, and in this
way acceptance of the results of the envisaged 'programming' by
Nature is as optional, or as free from reason rather than cause or
choice, as the programming of a computer. According to this view,

we have no insight which shows us that two plus two must equal four, or that for any natural numbers, a and b, a + b = b + a, or in general that the principles of the type of system of natural arithmetic Gödel considered are true or valid, or that to deny any of these things would make nonsense—just because insight is not allowed in at all.[22] Indeed, even the considerations suggested by conventionalist epistemology have no *rational* force upon us. All ends up in an acceptance which is caused or else 'chosen' in a decision upon which understanding or reason has no influence.

Such is the view which the idea that human beings are no better off than computers (*qua* mechanically operating systems) in deciding questions of consistency pushes us back to. It is the causal theory of knowledge met with in Chapters I and V revealed in its most implausible aspect.

What follows from all this? It clearly follows that the human being cannot be a mechanical system and that, in operations involving self-reflection, including these kinds of reasoning to conclusions in natural arithmetic, the human being does not operate as if it even might be a mechanical system. But does it also follow that mechanical processes are not internal to the procedures of understanding and judging involved, as they are internal to the procedures of seeing, suffering emotion, and so forth?

We have already seen that the kind of understanding of a concept in *langue* which is realized polymorphously in *parole*, in speech and thought, can have no material realization internal to it. And it is these concepts of 'being true', 'showing to be true', and so forth with which we are concerned in considering the judgement as the self-reflective and critical act of the subject who judges. These second-order or 'meta-level' concepts provide the most indisputable cases of the understanding of a concept in *langue* which cannot be simulated by the operations of, and is not represented by any structure in, a machine.

---

[22]One might ordinarily think that when insight was questioned the questioning could be dealt with by bringing in supportive argument, itself involving insight or understanding of some kind, and if this supportive argument was questioned further supportive argument could be brought in, and so on. However, wherever the process stopped there would remain some reliance on understanding and insight in regard to something. But this is what is disallowed in the position we are considering, and so argument can never be allowed a starting-point.

This might be thought to be the principal role of arguments drawing upon the peculiarities of relying upon the Gödel procedure to prove a proposition to be true. And the idea that the rules for 'showing a thing to be true' cannot be formally axiomatized even for the sphere of natural arithmetic might seem trivial in the light of the seeming obviousness of the impossibility of capturing in one rule or formalized system all methods of 'showing to be true'. The disparateness and informality of the kinds of reasoning utilized in history and law, in archaeology and palaeontology, in cosmology, in physics, in physiology, in political and moral affairs, in aesthetics and literary study, should be evident—and these are all areas within which numerous quite different kinds of judgement arise.

But are we confronted in this self-reflectivity of the subject in the act of judgement with some additional argument that there can be no material realization internal to the understanding and judging we are concerned with?

Aquinas says that no material faculty can reflect upon itself. Let us reformulate this: there can be isomorphism between part of the material faculty[23] and the whole but nothing corresponding to a judgement by the whole in regard to the whole—no reproduction in the material organism of the structure whereby the organism in critical judgement reflects upon itself or critically (reflectively) judges. This is the argument to which we gave succinct statement originally.

Note: The acceptability of speaking about thinking and understanding as 'operations' or 'states'

At this stage, we must briefly comment on these words "operation", "activity", "state", and the like, words with which we may be accused of having been too free.

We made it clear earlier that it is perfectly proper to call these kinds of understanding 'states' and this kind of thinking an 'activity'. Understanding of *langue* is a *hexis* or state in an Aristotelian sense, as virtues and vices, the possession of various branches of knowledge and kinds of skill are also *hexeis* or states; and the understanding of speech, whether by speaker or hearer, is another *hexis*, a realization of the understanding of *langue*; both are *hexeis* or states by reason

---

[23] By "material faculty" is meant here, not the mere fact of the possession of a capacity whose exercise involves a material organ, but the organ itself considered as that through which the capacity is exercised.

of their posture in time, contrasting with those of acts, processes, or activities—of which speaking and thinking are examples.[24]

Further distinctions in respect of posture in time are required between processes as things which proceed in stages and are not completed until the earlier stages are got through (like building a house), acts as things which do not have stages but, if present at all, are complete in themselves (like noticing something or winning a race), and activities in a restricted sense as things which unlike acts go on over a time but still are not described as proceeding in stages (like watching something). It is sometimes useful to use the words "act" and "activity" informally, so as not to have to bother as to whether speaking or hitting someone is an act or a process, or whether thinking is an act or an activity. All these are occurrent or episodic or 'in' time, rather than states holding over a time.

It is useful to have another concept in play which will cover positive states, acts, processes, and activities alike, so long as they are attributed to a subject and are realizations of some capacity of that subject: let us call them 'operations' for lack of a more convenient term.

Amongst operations, all the ones with which we are presently concerned will be realizations of an underlying capacity for language, thinking of language as something realizable in many different kinds of linguistic substance—vocal sounds and marks on paper being the most obvious to us.

The reluctance to allow the use of such global terms as "state", "activity", and "operation" is often a veil for a certain kind of transcendental idealism. In this way of thinking, we are permitted to describe how we speak, our existing 'language-games' but are not permitted to generalize beyond them. 'Things as they appear to us' in this philosophy are 'things as we speak of them', and we are not permitted to advance to any kind of generalization lest we introduce false models. But this is the path to obscurantism, not to understanding.

---

[24]Cf. Chapter VI, Section 1.

As to Aristotelian meaning of the words "state" and "disposition", see Chapter VII, Section 1 (cf. Chapter X, end of Section 2); we dealt with the objections of Wittgenstein and Kripke to calling understanding a state or disposition rather cursorily in Chapter X, n. 46, referring to the fuller treatment in my book on language.

As to the use of the word "activity", there is no implication in calling something an activity, act, or process that it is something of one kind with a single definition or paradigm, rather than a spread of kinds of thing enjoying some family-resemblance and entering into discourse in partly analogous ways—as games enjoy a family-resemblance and are one grammatical kind of cognate to the verb "to play".

Rather, when we have used examples to show something, e.g., to show some distinctions in temporal posture or in structures of explanation, we should allow ourselves to co-opt terms expressive of what we have shown, accepting that we will need to fend off misleading connotations.

3. Notes on the Roles of Neurological Subsystems and Computer Simulation in Cognitive Science

In sum, we are arguing that there can be no neural correlate or other inner physical embodiment of the understanding expressed in linguistic activities. This understanding has a public expression, physical in its way, but the understanding which underlies it, of which it is the expression and *ergon*, has no physical character. And that inner speech which is called thinking has no organ, no inner voice waiting to be inwardly heard. In brief, there are no mechanisms of any kind, non-physical or physical, digital or analog, internal to linguistic understanding and to thinking in the medium of words.[25]

The principal impulse in recent times towards supposing that there is an underlying neurological mechanism within linguistic capacity has been the idea instilled by Chomsky that there is some universal grammar possessed innately by all human beings combined with the presumption that it can only be possessed innately by being neurologically embedded. We should note that here we have, once again, the substitution of physical neurological mechanisms for the spiritual para-mechanical mechanisms attributed to Descartes and other dualists, where we should instead substitute quite different paradigms of explanation.[26] For, as I will suggest elsewhere and as is suggested by the approaches of contemporary theories of language learning in psychology, the structures of grammar may constitute a projection at a particular formal level of constraints set by semantics. Therefore, if what I have called linguistic understanding is not to be understood in terms of neurologically embodied structures but, in Aristotelian terms,

---

[25]Of course, nobody has seriously suggested that analog processes should play any part in semantic or syntactic procedures, as distinct from perceptual ones, but it remains that the statement which requires to be made is quite general: applying not only to digital mechanisms but mechanisms of any kind including whatever combination of the digital and the analog.

[26]Cf. n. 10 above.

in terms of form rather than matter, then neither is grammar to be understood in terms of neurologically embodied structures.

At this stage some more detailed comment may be desired.

Of course, it is certain that the normal exercise of linguistic capacity, viz., in speech and writing and, with them, in hearing and reading, involves neurological structures. There will be, therefore, processing structures related to each 'substance' in which linguistic communication is realized, structures in perception and structures in utterance, and these typically become adapted to the recognition or production of intermediary units (phonemes as meaning-relevant units within a particular language, and word-forms within a language) and of rule-determined configurations of such units, so that, as it were, the matter (the physically based structures) is appropriate to the form (use within the context of the full free play of linguistic understanding) as Aristotle conceived flesh and bones (unlike substance not organically organised) to be the matter appropriate to soul as form. This brings into the theory of language function the notion popular amongst psychologists of 'modular sub-systems'.[27] (It is commonly supposed that grammatical capacity depends on such a physically-based sub-system: however, I believe that further study will show that underlying grammatical structures are ultimately dictated by semantic ones, and this will make the idea of a modular neurological sub-system for grammatical functioning unnecessary and objectionable in the explanation of normal speech.)

Outside the context of the full free play of linguistic understanding, these physically based structures may retain functionality in limited respects somewhat as the sub-systems within a corpse—or in a less extreme case in parts of a living body affected by injury—retain some of their previous modes of behaviour. It will, therefore, be a question to be examined separately in each case how far this or that species of defective behaviour is to be understood in terms of the overall structures of full linguistic understanding merely interfered with or held back by some defect of subsidiary perceptual or other capacity or in terms of the structures of some physically-based sub-system originally shaped to be subsidiary to the play of those overall structures.

Our underlying picture should then remain that of an underlying capacity for language, realized in different cultures in different ways

---

[27]Cf. D.A. Allport, 'Distributed Memory, Modular Subsystems and Dysphasia'.

(and perhaps differently within a culture in different modes of expression, and certainly differently if deprivation means the absence of some key normal modes) and so in different *langues* or structures of understanding at the level of *langue*[28]—each such structure or *langue* being realized in *parole*, the understanding of *parole*, and what I have called thinking in the medium of words. My argument has shown that none of these can be coherently conceived as physically based or realized, even though they play a key part in determining or limiting the possible or useful shape of numerous physically-based sub-systems.

In recent theory attempting to suggest how cognitive processes might be capable of being simulated by a computer, or even how the human being or brain might constitute a computer, much has been made of the possibility of 'parallel distributed processing'—the functioning of modular neurological sub-systems being supposed to be analogous to parallel distributed processing between computers.[29] And, combined with this, we may also meet with the idea of 'heterarchical control' so that, within a set of mechanical systems working in parallel and mechanically organised to cooperate together as a unity, the locus of decision may vary between one system and another. But we must not get confused by this. No such set of systems working together can have a power greater than a single possible Turing machine, albeit they may achieve their results using much less hardware with a much greater efficiency and speed. And, although in a certain sense the locus of a decision may lie in one of the subordinate systems in one case and in another in another case, there has to be some organization which makes the 'local decision' count as a decision of the whole.

---

[28]Because a particular culture or a particular upbringing shaped to a certain deprivation may give different word-meanings to the written, spoken or gestured form of the same 'word', such a structure or *langue* will include any differential notes between such word-meanings of the same 'word'. D.A. Allport, in 'Language and Cognition' and 'Components of the Mental Lexicon', argues against a single modality-independent (what linguists following Saussure would call 'substance-independent') lexicon. My position would deny that any mental lexicon is part of the underlying universal linguistic capacity, but that as the learning of a *langue* advances a lexicon forms, that at each stage the entries in the lexicon formed are modality-modulated according to the stage of learning and capacities (and disabilities) of each person, and that, in general, to each *langue* there is a different lexicon—and conversely each different lexicon marks a different *langue* or in the cases of partial learning and systematic disability 'quasi-*langue*' (I call it a quasi-*langue* because it is not a *langue* in the fully fledged sociological sense).

[29]Cf. D.A. Allport, *op. cit.*, and discussion and references in Chapter IX, n. 23.

Therefore, if there had been no obstacle in principle to the simulation of human linguistic behaviour by a Turing machine, then theories about parallel distributed processing would certainly have been likely to help make it intelligible how the hardware in the brain might be adequate to the task. However, we have shown that it is impossible in principle for linguistic behaviour (and therefore the two kinds of linguistic understanding we have spoken of) to be simulated by a Turing machine—therefore it follows that they cannot be simulated by any system of parallel distributed processing however cunningly conceived whatsoever.

The conclusions that the human being's underlying linguistic capacity, and with it the two kinds of linguistic understanding we have distinguished, have no physical or neurological sub-system internal to them, and that they cannot be regarded as the working of mechanisms, and so cannot in any way be simulated by a computer, are likely to seem scandalous. We cannot remove the scandal, but we may be able to mitigate it by making clear the positive role which does arise for the consideration of computer models within cognitive science. This arises in three quite different ways.

In the first place, there are mechanically simulable aspects of our global behaviour, e.g., in working out problems in propositional logic or in arithmetical computation by 'mechanical' methods, to take two of a vast number of examples. The methods are 'mechanical', not in the sense, for instance, that it is determined at what time we will make the next move in our derivation of a result (e.g., how many cigarettes we will smoke while taking time off), but in the sense that they are determined according to an 'effective' (in the sense of computable) rule.

But these zones of application for 'mechanical procedures' exist precisely as 'protected areas' whose existence and boundaries we discover by means of exercises of the understanding which are not thus formalized or formalizable. And this must be so. For, as we have seen, in general our exercises of linguistic understanding are in general unformalized and unformalizable because the way in which, on the basis of *langue, parole* is understood is not by calculation and therefore not a candidate for being mechanically simulable in the way reasoning may often be.

I have said that the number of types of such example is vast. The scope for 'mechanical procedures' within logic and set theory is well studied, and their scope within grammatical studies is becoming better known. We may also anticipate that much defective linguistic behaviour is free from certain of the semantic controls provided by the understanding, and therefore likely to conform to simpler patterns than the totality of linguistic behaviour. We can, therefore, surmise that some types of such behaviour may be more open to computer simulation.

These types of 'simulation' can be called 'modelling' in order to mark that it is only structures of behaviour which are 'modelled', i.e., between which there is an isomorphism, without there being any suggestion of an isomorphism in the thing which 'behaves'. It is a 'logical' similarity between the structures of the computer software and cognitive processes which is here being regarded as instructive, not any similarity in any supposed hardware.

In the second place, and of a quite different character, we have the simulation of some material processes relevant to knowledge acquisition, e.g., some of the processes affecting what is perceived, such as the need for the retina to receive a certain number of 'bits' of 'information' in order for a threshold to be reached, e.g., in registering a change of brightness. I say that the importance of this is or is likely to be of a quite different character because part of the interest of the relevant research lies in the possibility that the parallelism in the behaviour of the simulating machine and the behaviour simulated arises from some isomorphism in the 'hardware' involved in the two cases.[30]

(Thus I do grant that, at least if one follows modern theories, there will be a large role for (e.g.) 'mechanisms of visual perception'. It might be imagined that this way of thinking involved that there be, in the end, some brain-state which was what was brought about by these mechanisms, and from this concluded that this innermost brain-state must either cause the 'experience of seeing xyz' or else be itself identical with the 'experience of seeing xyz'. In that case, in this way of thinking, I would have backhandedly reintroduced the 'experiences' which I had been at pains to expurgate in Chapters II and III. However, this is a false representation of the situation. These so-called 'mechanisms' have to be conceived teleologically. The constraints upon evolution, combined with the capacity of the physical to subserve holistic fuction, make it possible for the operation of the

---

[30]It will be noted that analog elements in computer construction may have place here, whereas they would have no place in the simulation of the first type, let alone in any imagined 'calculation of meanings'.

whole living organism to be so adapted or developed that its physical systems are geared to response according to complex patterns (e.g., of the kind envisaged by Gibson in the 1960s) which are geared to behaviour of the kind appropriate to and exhibitory of the level of life and consciousness reached, stability at each level only being reached when the integratedness appropriate to that level is attained. As a result, what is affected by these mechanisms is not an inner brain-state, logically independent of the states of the more external parts of the sense-organ and of the world and in principle capable of being caused otherwise than by the reality reckoned to have been seen, but a cognitive relation involving internally both facts about the sense-organ and about the world seen—a cognitive relation, or relational state, not analysable into internal and external elements in causal relation.)

In the third place, computers can be programmed for use in the solution of statistical problems. And there can arise some province for statistical variation wherever we have two variables which vary in a way between which there is no systematic relation.

The consideration of the behaviour of large numbers of human beings, and the consideration of cases where defects of human pro-ceeding arise, introduce the possibility of a complex interplay of all three of the aforementioned roles for study assisted by the considera-tion of computer simulation. For instance, error may be significantly related to material factors but also significantly limited by higher level (e.g.) grammatical and semantic structures (in these examples I have in mind study of the incidence of some kinds of grammatical mistake and study of the speech of schizophrenics). Of course, if the higher level structure relevantly escapes formalizability, it will also escape computer simulation, but errors or deviations in respect of it will not escape statistical study. But this is not the place for any more extended discussion of a complex field, only an indication of its existence.

[A question arises when we have systems whose global behaviour (whether or not they involve freedom) is determined according to deliberation or intelligible reasons or motives so that certainly the physical is affected as well as involved. But in many cases these reasons or motives seem in no direct relation to many physical properties of the minute parts of the organisms concerned. Accordingly, whether or not we can also describe physical variables as without systematic relation in these cases is more obscure. We cannot say absolutely 'Yes, there is no systematic relation', but in many studies we can ignore any connection.]

XIII. Animal and Human Souls: Two Non-Dualistic Conceptions

Once having realized that linguistic understanding and thinking are operations which do not have a bodily organ, as made clear in our last chapter, the question arises as to whether this implies that either the human soul (if there is a non-dualistic way of conceiving of souls) or the human person has some existence which transcends the body. In this chapter, I address the question of how we can speak about souls.

We must see how the idioms of speaking about 'souls' can be used, and primordially always were used, to express the holistic and non-dualistic understanding of the human being which we struggled to articulate in Part One of this book—what we might call the 'unistic' conception of the human being as a psychosomatic unity.

In Aristotelian Greek, *empsychon* or 'ensouled' is one of the commonest words for 'being alive' or 'animate'. It is normal for words meaning breath, e.g., *anima* and *spiritus* in Latin and *pneuma* in Greek, to come to mean "soul" or "spirit", and this seems to be because issuing breath is a key embodiment or symbol of being alive. It has been said that in Hebrew thought man is 'an animated body', not 'an incarnate soul'.[1] The Hebrew *nephesh* used for "soul" has roots associating it with the windpipe or throat and thereby, not only with breath, but also with a range of emotions, greed, desire, and suchlike, and so in more than one way with life itself.[2] It is, within these contexts, as much a mistake to think of the soul as a particular part or component of the human being as it would be to consider the word "heart", when used metaphorically, or (a different case)

---

[1] Cf. H.W. Robinson, 'Hebrew Psychology', and also his *The Christian Doctrine of Man*.

[2] I owe knowledge of this striking history to the doctoral work of Keith Whitefield drawing on Aubrey Johnson's *The Vitality of the Individual in the Thought of Ancient Israel*.

480

to consider the word "life", as designating some particular part or component of the human being.

In giving philosophical development to holistic ways of speaking about the soul there have been two tendencies: the one to speak about the soul in more concrete and phenomenological terms; and the other to speak about it in more abstract terms related to explanation. Both conceptions are represented in Aristotle, but the second may be regarded as specially Aristotelian as he was the first to articulate it. In the first two sections of this chapter I examine each in turn. We shall find that the idioms associated with each present themselves as in both cases optional but also appropriate. However, these two ways of speaking, the one concrete and the other abstract, seem incompatible:[3] how, as Aquinas asks, is it possible for the human soul to be both a form and a concrete individual thing?—this is the problem which I address in Section 3.

1. The Phenomenological Conception of Soul

I shall begin by sketching what I shall call the phenomenological conception of soul. This is represented in the primordial agreement as to which workings or 'operations'[4] of the human being or animal are to be ranked as workings or operations of soul: seeing and hearing, being pleased and being distressed, wanting, hoping, being afraid, being angry, believing and intending, remembering, imagining and thinking, and suchlike.[5] There is an equally plain primordial agreement about what operations of the human being or animal are not on the list even though they involve intention or mind, e.g., touching and feeling by touch, speaking and writing, and intentional action in general. Additionally the sorts of predicates which we apply to inanimate bodies as well as to human beings and animals obviously do not apply to the

---

[3]The same problem of apparent category-mistake arises for some explanations of how we can speak of pure spirits such as God, e.g., for I.M. Crombie's explanation of this in 'The Possibility of Theological Statements', pp. 57–62.

[4]The word "operation" is a convenient cipher drawn from such philosophers as Aquinas and Berkeley to refer to the mixed bunch of attributions concerned. I gave what limited definition is possible in Chapter XII.

[5]Roughly speaking, these workings or operations being attributed to the soul are what Aristotle referred to as 'affections' (*pathē*) of the soul and Descartes and the empiricists less neutrally as *pensées*, perceptions of the mind, or experiences.

soul. In short, the soul does not eat or walk, and does not weigh ten stone.

In the ways of speaking involved the soul is a subject of many concrete predicates, consciousness-involving predicates of human beings and animals. I call them concrete predicates because we predicate them of concrete things or substances.

I call these ways of speaking primordial because there seems to be such perfect or almost perfect agreement as to which things are 'operations of soul' and which are not. We are dealing with the ways of speaking which misled Plato and Descartes, but which are not in themselves at all tied to dualism—represented in Aristotle throughout his *De Anima*,[6] relied upon by Aquinas in his demonstration of human unity, and still drawn upon in the sayings of Merleau-Ponty and Wittgenstein.

We must fight to discover the guiding principles which underly this primordial agreement. We shall find that these principles and this agreement in no way involve the Cartesian mistake which we made clear in Chapter IX, the mistake of supposing that the human being's standpoint in perceiving and judging is a standpoint, not in, but over against the world.

The first principle underlying this primordial agreement seems to be a negative one, roughly speaking, that the body in a certain sense in no way 'obtrudes' within the operations counted as 'operations of soul', what I will sometimes call 'psychic operations'. This we must now explore.

(a) The sense in which the body 'does not obtrude' in operations of soul

In order to understand the relevant idea of 'not obtruding', it is convenient to begin with the case of seeing.

Seeing something involves internally to it subordinate states and goings on, some having to do with the objects seen, the light con-

---

[6]Aristotle's ambivalence towards these ways of speaking is evident in Book I of his *De Anima*, but, despite his account of soul in Book II seeming to have excluded treating the soul as the subject of such operations as imagining, we find him quite unhesitatingly treating the soul as subject of both thinking and imagining in *De Anima* III. 7. He is also somewhat ambivalent as to whether or in what sense the soul is the subject of movement.

ditions, and background, and some states and goings on in the eyes, optic nerve, and brain cortex. But awareness of these subordinate states and goings on in the eyes (and, *a fortiori*, of those in the rest of the optic system) is not present to consciousness even in the way that some awareness of the subordinate movements of the legs is present in the case of an unreflective walking across a room with a purpose. The comparison is difficult because the kind of subordinate state or process involved is so discrepant in these cases. But the same contrast between seeing as an operation in which the body 'does not obtrude' and operations of which this is not true is made vivid in the contrast between sight and touch: we are not aware of alterations in the eyes and activities of the eyes themselves in the act of seeing in any way parallel to that in which we are aware of these in the organ of touch in the act of sensing heat or pressure.

In a certain way, we are not aware of the eyes at all within the act of seeing.

One commonly speaks of using the eyes in seeing, and we are aware that we use our eyes when we open or close our eyelids or put our hands in front of our eyes, especially while watching these activities in a mirror. But there seems to be a good sense in which awareness of our using our eyes is not internal to the act of seeing or to our awareness that we are seeing something. Our using our eyes is the seeing, and vice versa (it is not an activity subordinate to or a means to seeing), but it is not as 'using our eyes' that seeing presents itself to us. In order to direct our look, we do not intentionally move our eyes in contrast to the case when in order to get across the road we intentionally walk and intentionally move our legs. In directing our look we may move our whole body or our head, not just our eyes, and we are little aware of how much, in directing our look, is accomplished by each of these. As a result, in some respects, it might be less misleading to say that we see with our bodies, than to say that we see with our eyes. Intention can enter into the movement of head and body in this context, but not into moving the eyes which happens incidentally in directing our look.[7] Again, when we walk along, the direction of our look varies often in a random way, in the course of which we notice things, and in general our knowledge of the direction

---

[7]It would be more accurate to say that we move our eyes by directing our look than we direct our look by moving our eyes.

of our look is derived rather from our appreciation of the spread of what we see than from knowledge of our head and body movements. But whichever way we know of our head and body movements when these are relevant to directing our look, this does not make these movements internal to the act or operation of seeing, and *a fortiori* such relevance does not make knowledge of eye movements part of this act or operation.

But our lack of awareness of the eyes within the act of seeing can be envisaged under a different aspect. If we think of seeing through the eye as analogous to seeing through a window, then the eye, or pupil of the eye, must be thought of as an ideal window, a window which contains no murkiness, has no colour, and gives no reflections in such a way as to make itself an object of sight or awareness in the act of seeing or as to alter what is seen.[8] If there is obscurity in vision or what is seen is blurred, the obscurity or blur belongs to the object of vision, not to the eye or parts of the eye which may have caused it. If there are floating bodies (*muscae volitantes*) within the liquid in the eye, they are not seen as floating bodies in a liquid in the eye but as specks in the field of vision—even though we may know that such floating bodies are the cause of our seeing what we see.

These things explain why it is thought that the sense-organ and its activity within the operation of seeing are not parts of the experience of seeing.

Now, it might be suggested that in all the operations we are concerned with the person or soul is exposed directly, in a way not experienced as mediated by the body, to its objects and to the operations whereby it is directed towards these objects. However, this definition will not quite do. Firstly, it is not clear that all 'operations of soul' are accurately described as 'directed towards objects'—e.g., there are puzzles about some kinds of anxiety. Secondly, it is clear that we regard intentions and many 'mental' acts which are intentional as 'operations of soul' in the sense we are trying to define; but in whatever sense intentions towards certain intentional bodily actions have to do with objects, these actions themselves have to do with the same objects; the relevant kind of 'direct exposure' to intentions and to intentional 'mental' acts seems to be that of authorship and not

---

[8]This is the key to Aquinas' theory of vision referred to in Chapter III, in Section 2 and in the 'Note on the vocabulary of intentionality'.

experiential. We seem to have the same author's kind of knowledge 'in a way not experienced as mediated by the body' of our intentional bodily actions—and we clearly would not count these bodily operations as 'operations of soul'.

We could make the mistake of saying this: seeing and being angry do not involve the body in the description of the experience as it is experienced—and so the subject of these operations is not presented in the descriptions "sees" and "is angry" under the aspect of being bodily. However, how we experience one thing can be taken in a larger or in a more restricted context. In the primary way of speaking and the prototypical case, we should rather say that we experience seeing as in some context of appreciation of the position or situation from which the perception is made, so that this is presupposed in the experience itself, and as of some object or spread with which the perception reinforces or creates some behavioural relation—as when, in the example we have given before, seeing where the table is enables us to touch it or to avoid walking into it, or seeing a star we know where to direct our binoculars.

Therefore, we must rather say this: that the operations we are concerned with are ones which are conscious, the awareness of which is not the awareness of a movement of or development in the body, which involve no subordinate conscious bodily acts or states internal to them, and which do not have any part of the body or bodily action as an intermediate object of awareness within the act. This, then, is what I mean by 'the body's not obtruding'. It will be realized that the word "obtrude" is somewhat misleading, since what is excluded is even a passive availability to consciousness at certain points within the 'acts' concerned.

Thus, in the case we have concentrated on, within seeing we have no consciousness, whether intentional or experiential, of goings on in the sense-organ and neither the image in the retina nor anything in the pupil of the eye nor any action in respect of the eyes is an intervening or presupposed object towards which the mind is directed in being directed towards its principal object.

Likewise, in a quite different type of case, the case of anger, an emotion which takes different forms, some proximate to immediate action and some to longer standing plans or frustration, it is in the typical case (even just because it involves excitement) attended by bodily agitation, and Aristotle's judgement that this was internal to 'being angry' seems correct. But consciousness of any such agitation is not part of being angry but rather a distraction from it, and such agitation is not an object of the mind within the act—not something one is angry at, nor (as part of anger) something one is aware of. I take the case of anger because, the problematic cases of sensory pleasures and bodily pains apart, it seems the most body-involving of the emotions. The feelings one has in the pit of one's stomach when one anticipates something with fear may draw one's attention to one's being afraid but, although in the particular case the feelings may be part of the experience of being afraid, consciousness of them is not (although it may add to anxiety), and they are not involved as objects of fear or of awareness in the fearing of something.

By contrast, the bodily pains or sensory pleasures are not operations of the kind which we are concerned with. It cannot be said that in the case of a pain in the foot that the body does not obtrude in the experience concerned in the sense we have explained. As we saw in Chapter III, the difference between perceptions and sensations was precisely this, that the former but not the latter are to be analysed in terms of mental directedness towards an object—the word "pain" no more indicates a content or object of feeling than the word "dream" indicates the content or object of dreaming. Rather, sensations represent forms of non-observational consciousness of the body, and the idea of a pain in the foot as an operation of soul is a bizarre Cartesian aberration (connected with the Cartesian mistake of making infallible knowledge an implication or a criterion of being a mental operation)—an aberration of a piece with the complete privatization of the affairs of the soul in Cartesian and empiricist tradition described in (c) below, a privatization totally alien to the primordial conception of soul as I am presenting it.[9]

(b) From 'operations of soul' to 'soul'

Against this background, logically, we can present the situation as follows. Certain predications of a human being, certain facts in human life, are being described in two ways: one the standard way simply involving reference to the human being as such, indifferent

---

[9]This is confirmed when one examines the contortions Aquinas gets into in Q. D. De Anima when trying to explain how disembodied souls could experience the pain of fire in Hell. Instead one should say that at least until resurrection terms such as fire and all other terms referring to bodily sensations and activities ('weeping and gnashing of teeth') are used metaphorically to describe non-bodily distress.

to the differences between different types of predication and how it involves the body, e.g., as to whether their meaning involves the non-obtrusion of the body mentioned or whether they do not; and the other a way speaking of the soul or self as the subject in those cases where the body does not obtrude.

Now, there is no understanding of the 'phenomenological' use of the word "soul" with which we are concerned except in terms of the non-obtrusion of the body spoken of. But arising out of the non-obtrusion of the body in the operations concerned, there is a second albeit subsidiary thing which gives point to our speaking of these operations not just as operations of the human being or animal but of soul.

Of course, we know perfectly well that the human being and the animal are proper subjects of all these operations. Yet, to take a particular instance, when we think of the human being as seeing through his eyes, we think of that which sees as in the relevant respect (we might say, 'aspectually') behind the eyes. This which is behind the eyes we call, in the phenomenological sense with which we are concerned, the 'soul'. The 'I', the 'he or she' which is aspectually behind the eyes is evidently not in the eyes; but then one would not expect the 'I' to be in any particular part of the body rather than being the whole bodily being itself; however, the point of saying that the 'I', the 'he or she', is as soul not to be identified with the whole bodily being itself or with the human being or animal as such is that the latter cannot be described as behind the eyes.

Likewise, aspectually what hears hears as if it were in the region of the head, but not as if it were *in* the ears. The ears and what is going on in them do not obtrude at all in the relevant meaning of the word except in the case of some imperfection or disturbance of sense. The ears come into our experience of hearing in that, for instance, we may ask someone to speak into our better ear or turn our head to hear better, but not in the sense that we feel anything in our ears (except in the cases mentioned).

The sense in which we see from 'behind' the eyes, or hear in the region of the head, is not an ordinary spatial one—as if it were from a certain particular identifiable location or as if what sees or hears were a physical object. Rather it seems to be a behavioural one determined by how we direct or use our head with a certain sense of geometry.

The 'I', the 'he or she', which sees and hears is in the primary mode of speech certainly not identical to the head or anything 'behind the eyes' or 'in the region of the head' because it is what touches with its hands and acts in other ways—it is, taken in the primary way, the human being or animal as such. However, what sight and hearing make plain is that phenomenologically and aspectually these operations can be spoken of, not only as operations of the human being or animal, but also as operations of something (some grammatical subject) which, as we have seen, is not identical with the human being or animal because it does not (e.g.) eat, walk or weigh ten stone, but is none the less in this non-spatial sense experientially as it were 'behind the eyes'.

It is natural to call this subject thus spoken and thought of 'the soul'. And it is natural, although unnecessary, to speak of it metaphorically as 'inner', not meaning by this 'in the head', but to mark a contrast with 'the outer'—meaning by "the outer" what goes on in the sense-organs and outward behaviour.

This subject or 'soul' which sees and hears is naked before the objects of vision and hearing, exposed unprotected to them, nothing obtruding between that which sees and the bull or the tiger which is seen. And, in an extension of the same line of thought, this subject is also naked to the images which may form before it, as the bull or tiger I see in my dreams or imagine to myself with my eyes closed passes into the bull or tiger I remember the other side of the imagined field and this passes into the bull or tiger I imagine as running at me as I shake or quiver in anticipation.[10] And, in response to these perceptions or images, the same subject is shaken by fear and moved in different ways by other emotions.

The 'I', the 'he or she', thus spoken and thought of as 'soul' is not unknown to us: we recognize its presence in the dog who shakes, whimpers, or barks and hides under the table in a thunderstorm, or who shakes and quivers while asleep in some dream—that we can speak of recognizing it in the case of the dog is a symptom of our knowing the same syndrome, the same physiognomy of experience, in ourselves.

We have no knowledge of the soul apart from operations of the soul, and no knowledge of operations of the soul except as operations

---

[10]When the anticipation is of bodily sensations or of touch (as when after falling one is about to hit the ground), we wake up in the moment the anticipation would be fulfilled. (I speak of first-person dreaming, as when one dreams of falling, not as when one dreams as if seeing oneself falling, dreaming as it were in the third person.) Thus the 'soul' still experiences no bodily sensations or sensations of touch.

which are also operations of the human being or animal—indeed which exist as operations of soul only in being operations of the human being or animal. Accordingly, we do not have any direct experience of the soul or of what it is as if it were an object which we could view and study in the mind's eye by introspection.

We ought to consider the logic of talk about 'soul' before any delving into metaphysics.

Logically, the relation of the concept of 'soul' to the concepts of 'human being' and 'animal' bears some analogy with the relation between the concepts of 'surface' and 'body'. Souls are subjects of seeing, hearing, anger and fear, belief and intention, and the like but not of eating, walking and weight somewhat as surfaces are subjects of colour, shape, touch, reflect, without being the subject of any predicates involving solidity, or three-dimensionality. The relevant attributes are attributed to the soul in the very act of attributing them to human beings or animals, and vice versa, somewhat as one attributes colours to surfaces in the act of attributing them to bodies, and vice versa. And one would not attribute weight or bodily movement to souls any more than one would attribute weight or volume to surfaces.

We say that bodies *have* surfaces and in the way of speaking we are examining it is commonly thought natural to say that persons *have* souls. But so long as we have not erected surfaces or souls into separate parts within an aggregate of parts supposedly making up the body or the person we should not have a problem as to how the same things can be predicated of persons and of souls any more than we have a problem as to how the same things can be predicated of surfaces and of bodies. The attributive 'has' does not imply two distinct objects but arises from the use of the genitive to express what we might call 'logical' or 'formal' relations. That is, the expression "the soul of. . ." is to be compared with such varied expressions as "the surface of. . .", "the wisdom of. . ." or "the nature of. . .". In each case a description of the ways of speaking wherein talk of the two kinds of thing spoken of as if one was 'of' the other arises makes clear contextually what 'relation' is being spoken of—what kind of 'attribution' is concerned.

This logical parallel should not of course be allowed to hide the gulf in other respects between the two cases. One does not attribute agency or activity to surfaces but rather to bodies, so that there is no temptation to attribute to surfaces the kind of reality we attribute to bodies. By contrast, activity or operation is characteristic of souls, so much so that it might seem that the soul was the heart of that

which existed, lived, and acted in the case of human beings and
higher animals. Therefore, these logical remarks, while not inviting
a 'metaphysics' of soul, do not exclude it.

One last logical remark: the concepts of 'soul', 'person' and 'psychophysical being', 'surface' and 'body' are all of them range-concepts,
each marking out the range of sensible application or significance of a
certain group of predicates. And this helps to explain a second way in
which the conception of soul is not at all that of a substance. Just as
'person' is not a proper genus or species, a proper answer to a question
of the type "What is it?" but covers quite discrepant types of being
(human beings, angels, and God), so likewise soul is not a proper
genus or species specifying a kind of thing, an answer to a "What
is it?" question.[11] Suppose we may rightly speak of souls, it remains
that the souls of different kinds of living thing, human beings, higher
animals, lower animals, plants are not at all one kind of thing. But,
more than this, whereas 'person' is, at least, a term applied to beings
in a complete nature, the opposite is true in the case of souls: the
very meaning of the predicates we have mentioned makes it clear that
the soul cannot function in any or most of its operations without the
body. Seeing and hearing and such emotions as being angry logically
involve bodily processes internally to their operation.

The soul, as introduced in the way of speaking we are concerned
with, is introduced not as a substance, but, we might say inasmuch
as it is subject of concrete predicates, as an 'as-if-substance'—a quasi-
substance. The soul spoken of in the way we are now concerned with
cannot be a substance properly speaking because it does not have a
complete nature. I do not mean by this that souls in general considered
in themselves apart from the body (I don't mean existing without the
body, but considered in their own right) are like horses which have

---

[11]Human being, horse, primate, mammal, fungus, bacterium, and the like are
genera or species of nature—not only determinative of identity of a sort for being
relevant to explanation in the way explained in Chapter VIII, but also principles of all
the behaviour (at every level) of the things of that nature. "Person" in the wider sense
does not signify any common nature in this sense—a nature such as God, angels, and
human beings might share so that 'person' would overlap 'animal' and 'mammal' in
the case of human beings. "Person" in the narrower sense would still cover any kind
of intellectual animal. In either sense, "person" is a range-concept (marking the range
of significance of certain predicates) and as such has no content such as might allow
it to 'unfold' or 'express' a contentful answer to a question "What is it?".

lost a leg or are blind but which are still horses. The possession of four legs, like being sighted, is a part of the nature of horses but not indispensable to being a horse. Rather the soul fails to be a complete nature or a substance in a complete nature in a more radical sense, namely that the operations we have mentioned all involve the body as part of that substance which operates for their natural mode of functioning. It is in this way that indeed as Aquinas puts it 'My soul is not I'.[12]

Thus, in the way of speaking we are considering, it is said that the soul sees through the eyes: but the eyes are part of the human being or animal which sees and without them there would be no seeing. The eyes are not like a telescope which the soul takes to itself to use, nor like a window external to the soul towards which it turns to look in order to see. Such dimensions of living as sight, hearing, and, I argue,[13] imagining and fear with them are ones which would be absent if their subjects were not bodily, and in this way the substance to be subject of such operations cannot be the soul but must be 'a complete nature' in respect of having whatever bodily parts are required for the operation concerned to take place at all as parts of it. And, as I have argued,[14] the intellect operating in a way appropriate to human nature involves synergism with the imagination.

We could speak of the soul so far as all its operations involved bodily process internally as having an existence which consisted in being dynamically related to the body, dynamically in the sense that (e.g.), in the operation of seeing, the soul as spoken of as seeing is in the operation itself related to the eyes, i.e., dynamically related to a part of the body, since the human being or animal has to use his eyes in order to see. Yet even to speak in this way is to speak of the soul as if in this phenomenological way of speaking it was *given* as an entity, albeit an entity with perhaps no existence except in certain relations—but it is not as a term for an entity that the term "soul" and the ways of speaking concerned were *introduced* (even if it *may* yet be discovered at a second stage of thought that there is a sense in which the soul, in the human case, although not initially thought of in this way, does have existence in its own right).

---

[12]Geach draws the following from Aquinas' commentary on I Corinthians 15: 'my soul is not I; and if only souls are saved, I am not saved, nor is any man' (*God and the Soul*, p. 22).

[13]In Chapter XI and Chapter XII, Section 3.

[14]In Chapter XI.

The sense in which the soul is not given as an entity in this way of speaking can be seen by considering the type of identity which had relevance to explanation we recognized in Chapter VIII. This was the sort of identity involved when we say of a dog "He saw me put the meat in the cupboard yesterday, remembered it, and that is why, being hungry, he was scratching at the cupboard when we came in today"—the explanation obviously depends on its being the same dog. This was the identity of substances and in the human and animal case belongs primarily to the human being or animal who is liable to touch, make noises, and go in for other intentional behaviour, and only secondarily and derivatively if at all to souls.

(c) The non-Cartesian character of this conception of soul

Two things are immediately striking about the way of speaking of souls which I have delineated, the first that it is as natural in regard to the higher animals as to human beings, and the second that it is in no way Cartesian: it is primarily real objects, not just imaginary ones, which I see and hear and which my soul is naked to and prey to emotions about; sensory perception involves the sense-organs internally, and I would argue that imagination and anger likewise involve bodily processes internally; and it is part of the character of emotions, as well as of perception, to show themselves in relevant behaviour and bodily states. This structure is particularly plain in the case of the higher animals, and it involves nothing of the inner room theory of the soul whereby the soul or 'self' is locked up, not with bulls and tigers from which escape might, perhaps vainly, be sought, but with its impressions or images (whether attributed to sense, to memory, or to imagination).

Phenomenologically, seeing and hearing, imagining, being afraid or angry, and so forth, are just as good candidates for being operations of soul as understanding and thinking. And it follows from this that one will naturally speak of operations of soul in the case of all those animals to which one attributes perception, memory, imagination, and emotion.

We enunciated earlier a key principle of homogeneity whereby whenever something radically new arises in the unfolding of nature it must be in a key way homogeneous with what has gone before. This meant that if human beings are psychosomatic unities so must the highest animals be, but now—to our present purpose—it means also that if we express this in terms of a conception of soul, it must be a conception of soul applicable to at least some other higher animals as well as to human beings. This principle is satisfied by the phenomenological conception of soul we have delineated.

How was this phenomenological conception of soul distorted by Descartes?

He supposed (wrongly) that the mental or conscious element in all these workings or operations of mind or soul was conceivable without contradiction, even in the absence of their normal bodily accompaniments, and supposed (again wrongly) that it followed from this that they had a real possibility of existing without these accompaniments—on the ground that God could bring about anything which we could conceive without seeing a contradiction in our conception. In this way he got to conceive these workings or operations of mind or soul as having an existence as operations of a mental substance independent of states and goings on in the material world. That is, he ontologized the phenomenological conception of soul, making the mind or soul simply in virtue of being conscious and having operations of the kind we have picked out into a substance in its own right.

How did he come to think of all these workings or operations of mind or soul as independent of their normal bodily accompaniments? He pictured the experiential element in perception as thus independent, i.e., as not necessarily directed towards any real objects or essentially integrated with behavioural relations to a real natural environment.[15] As a result, the emotions came to be conceived by him as essentially related to mental objects provided by this perceptual experience; at the same time it became conceivable to him that bodily sensations such as pain should be compatible not just with not being caused where they are felt to be (which is commonplace) but even compatible with the total non-existence of the body and that touch might be deceived not just as to the quality but even as to the existence of its object, then, experience as well as intellect being thus internalized or conceived as compatible with the non-existence of external or physical objects, it seemed obvious that acts

---

[15]For Descartes sensory percepts remained distinct from concepts, even though detached from real objects. For Leibniz they became confused concepts, and such intellectualization of perception suggests another way of being separate from matter.

of will might be directed towards ends in an imaginary world. Thus, whereas in the primordial phenomenological conception the objects of the natural world presented in perception, our own body known non-observationally in sensation, and our outward intentional actions known pre-observationally in virtue of being according to intention, are as immediate to us as our 'operations of soul', in the Cartesian conception it is quite different. Each person's world has become privatized. The person has been conceived of as enclosed with immediate relation only to mental entities whose form and content is logically independent of how the world is.

The soul, then, taken in the primordial non-Cartesian sense, is not something of special importance to epistemology, as if it was the sum of what we had immediate knowledge of. Freed of the Cartesian distortions, the concept of the soul has importance in the human case in morals, but in a quite different way.

We do not have authoritative knowledge of our own motivations, and the overall set or direction of our motivations and behaviour may be quite different from what we superficially and perhaps self-deceptively think it is—and it is just as likely to be a wise counsellor as private reflection that brings this to light (that is, it is not that the things of the soul are typically out of reach of our knowledge, but that the reflection which brings us knowledge of them does not have to be private). Obviously, how our motivations and behaviour appear from an outward view of limited segments of our behaviour, and to a person with no knowledge of many things set in our past or present which are relevant to our judgements and motivations, are likely to be very imperfect. Therefore, indeed there is much in regard to which, because of what memory and awareness we do have in ready access to our mind, we know better than those ignorant of our past, ignorant of changes of attitude or conversions of mind or priority well-known to us. But there is none of this which is, in principle, epistemologically private, although much that we may not wish to parade to the world.

These remarks accord with what appears in the Gospels. There what is 'inner' or 'comes from the heart' is not peculiarly private, and by this is meant what matters for whether or not man loses his soul (this losing of the soul is a matter of moral and spiritual betrayal, not a matter of the ordinarily thought of temporal loss, the loss of faculties).[16] Thus it is said 'Do you not see that whatever goes into a man from outside cannot defile him, since it enters, not his heart but his stomach, and so passes on? . . . It is what comes out of a man which defiles him. For, from within, out of the heart of man, come evil thoughts, fornication, theft, murder, adultery, coveting, wickedness, deceit, licentiousness, envy, slander, pride, foolishness. All these evil things come from within, and it is these which defile a man' (Mark 7: 18–23). This repudiation of epistemological privacy entirely accords with Jewish tradition, and is to be found with equal force in Indian and Chinese religious tradition as well as most primal religion. The idea of the epistemologically private and of the subjective (as that which is thus private to me, even in the exercise of my conscience, as if nobody could call me to account except for betrayal of what is thus private) as the pivot of moral concern is a peculiar excrescence of post-Reformation thought, whether expressed by preacher or atheist, empiricist or existentialist.

(d) Conclusion

The explanations we have given allow the 'soul' a certain standing in the phenomenological description of human and animal life. We would better say 'incarnate *soul*' than speak of 'incarnate *consciousness*'. The more concrete term "soul" is more appropriate to a 'quasi-substance', that is to what is still a subject of concrete predications, than the more abstract term "consciousness". What we have done is to escape a Cartesian and also any other kind of substantialist account of 'soul'.

We know what a person is, and what a psychosomatic being is, in knowing these operations and this kind of 'non-obtrusiveness'. And we can make sense of the motivation for speaking of the soul as the subject of these kinds of operation in understanding their special character—even if we do not speak in this way, of 'souls'. 'Souls' are not parts of mythology, but elements in a dramatic idiom of speech which we can understand whether or not we adopt it. In this idiom many higher animals, and not only human beings, have souls.

---

[16]It is what Gabriel Marcel has in view when he speaks of a 'threat to the soul' in *Being and Having*.

According to this way of thinking and speaking about souls, either we know of souls and their operations immediately in the very act of knowing these operations to be attributable to a person or a higher animal—or we do not know of souls and their operations at all. Souls as subjects of operations are either in this sense known directly or non-theoretically, or not at all. They are not theoretical entities, to be known through metaphysical reflection upon the act of understanding or upon types of explanation, nor even through self-reflective epistemology. Rather, knowledge of the existence of souls, if it exists at all, is anterior to such critical reflection.

Within the context of modern man's Cartesian pre-conception of soul, there is no room for speech about 'souls'—it is squeezed out between the millstones of dualism and materialism. And this engenders a certain cultural destitution, whereby, for instance, even the most appropriate sayings read like unintelligible archaisms—e.g., Wittgenstein's remarks that 'The human body is the best picture of the human soul' and 'My attitude towards him is an attitude towards a soul. I am not of the *opinion* that he has a soul'.

Yet the rival way of speaking and thinking which I have sketched, understood at the phenomenological and experiential level which I have expounded, remains ever accessible because of the unchanging structures which I have distinguished. And in this way, assisted by the survival of literatures within which this primordial way of speaking is still present, there is still possible a cultural renewal which will make the human and animal world not dead and inanimate in human conception but 'full of soul', enrichening a new humanism[17] which views man not as a mind in a machine but in full openness and community with the physical and biological world within which he lives.

2. The Aristotelian Conception of Soul
as the Form of the Living Bodily Thing

We come now to a very different development of the idea of 'soul'.

---

[17]The struggles for such a new humanism are evident in the tensions between the more technological and the more 'emotional' motivations for ecological programmes for human advance or in the tensions between more Aristotelian and humanistic and more 'materialistic' interpretations of Marxism.

The realization that psychosomatic beings, human beings and some other higher animals, do not 'consist of' their material parts in their dynamic relations is instantly likely to be construed as meaning that they consist of these plus something else, a soul. But in Aristotle and the tradition initiated by him this is not construed in a dualistic sense, as if human beings and animals were composed of elements, some material and one immaterial, but in quite a different way.

In order to understand how Aristotle understood what it was for the soul to be a 'form' and not an 'element', his own exposition at the end of *Metaphysics*, Zeta 17 is exactly to the point.

He considers the case of the syllable 'ba', compounded of elements 'b' and 'a', and notes that the syllable is not identical with its elements[18] any more than flesh is fire and earth (or whatever its elements are, e.g., the hot and the cold), since, when these are separated, the syllable and the flesh exist no longer even though the elements still exist, so that there is more to the syllable and the flesh than just their elements. 'The syllable, then, is something, not only its elements (the vowel and the consonant) but these and something other'; but this something cannot be another element in the make-up of the thing (let alone be itself composed of elements) else the argument will proceed again, i.e., we will be able to say that the whole is not just the elements (now three or more) but these together with something else, and so on, *ad infinitum*. Accordingly, he says, 'this other' which is required 'is something, not an element', and 'it is the cause which makes *this* flesh and *that* a syllable—and similarly in all other cases. And this is the *ousia* (essence) of each thing (for this is the primary cause of its *einai* or being).' Now, of course, what makes some things what they are may be some accidental relation between their parts brought about by an artificer or arising by chance. But, 'while many things are not substances, the *ousia* (essence) of those that are substances are formed in accordance with a nature of its own and by a process of nature would seem to be this kind of *physis* (nature), viz., what is not an element but a principle. An *element*, on the other hand, is that into which a thing is divided and which is present in it as matter; e.g., 'a' and 'b' are the elements of the syllable.'

This kind of *physis* which he is chasing, the correlate of matter which, in the rest of Book Zeta and elsewhere he calls 'form', precisely

---

[18]The Greek for elements is *stoicheia*, or literally 'letters'.

cannot be an element or have elements, cannot be a part jointly with the other parts and cannot be made up of parts as elements. The form, or soul as form, must not be an extra part (made of extra stuff, even immaterial stuff) so as metaphysically to give extra 'body' to the thing.

And such is Aristotle's conception of the soul of a living thing: that it is the 'form' which makes these bodily parts into this living thing of this determinate species with this characteristic behaviour. The 'form' is the principle of unity and operation of the thing of which it is the form, the kind of unity being shown by the kinds of operation. Such general notions as 'form' and 'principle' cannot be defined, but can only be made clear by the consideration of an adequate spread of examples, examples such as those we review in Section 3 (c) below.

This Aristotelian conception of the soul as the form of a living bodily thing—and as this even in the case of animals lower than human beings in the case of which, except on a Platonic or Cartesian view of animal perception, no suggestion arises that it be subsistent or a 'particular thing'[19]—of itself constitutes a scandal to materialism. For it means that the physics—including here the chemistry, physiology, and even neurology—of living bodies is only an abstraction, the separating out for attention, of just one aspect of a reality which is not merely physical in the modern sense.

This conception, as we discovered in Chapters VII and VIII, does not primarily involve that the soul is dependent for existence on the body (although in the case of 'accidental forms', that is 'forms' of 'accidental' unities, e.g., geometrical arrangements of pieces of chalk, there is such dependence) but that the body has no existence apart from the soul. Whereas the materialists and dualists of the seventeenth century agreed in holding that the bodies of living things, including human beings, had a self-contained existence as complete substances in their own right (even though they might be in external relation or interaction with immaterial substances called minds or souls), the conception of Aristotle and Aquinas excluded this. 'A substance cannot consist of substances present in it in complete reality', Aristotle tells us in *Metaphysics*, Zeta 13,[20] and the parts of animals in no way exist in complete reality or as separate things except when the animal

---

[19]In Aristotle a *tode ti* and in Latin translations a *hoc aliquid*.
[20]1039a 3ff.

is dead or they are cut off (like fingers in a battle) and become parts in name only (Zeta, 11 and 16)—so that to consider them only in the aspects which they share with inanimate things is to consider not their natures as a whole but only some aspects of these natures.

It is because it is the dependence of matter on form which embodies the heart of the Aristotelian position, and the root of its rejection of atomism, that it is not necessarily contradictory to suppose that in some case (viz., the case of the rational soul) the form of a body should be subsistent, or exist in its own right, and therefore be capable of continuing to exist even after the body had perished. But this suggestion of Aquinas in regard to the human case is quite outside the original conception of form as the correlate of matter, although, as we shall see, not excluded by it.[21]

3. The Relation between the Aristotelian and the Phenomenological Conceptions

(a) Background of the question

The phenomenological way of speaking about souls is a pre-philosophical by-product of primary modes of speech about persons and animals, while the Aristotelian way of speaking of forms and therewith of souls as forms is a philosophical creation—an entirely optional way of expressing the presence and fundamental character of a spread of teleological and holistic modes of explanation in the case of those beings we count as 'living'.

---

[21]This conclusion seemed less strange to Aquinas than to us, not only because (as we stated earlier) within the Aristotelian approach the key dependence is not that of form on matter but of matter on form, but also because he already had within the purview of his philosophy the conception of God and of each angel as a subsistent form. In this he may have been deceived by confusing two different uses of the word "form" of quite different origins: on the one hand, we have the use of the word "form" to refer to 'natures' or 'predicates' concretely (the idioms "The horse is a quadruped" and "The circle is a figure" are representative here) from which there arises the notion of self-subsistent natures, within which there is no individuation correlated with matter but identity between the nature as subject of concrete predicates and the individual realizing this nature, as supposedly in the case of God and the different species of angels; and, on the other hand, we have this notion of "form" as a correlate of matter (originating with the idea of shapes, such as circularity, as forms of material things such as metal rings).

The question arises of the relation of these two quite differently founded modes of speech, and in particular of whether we can generally or ever identify soul in the one sense with soul in the other. The antecedents of our answer to this question are clear. Firstly, both Aristotle and Aquinas took the soul to be something already partly known even in advance of its being defined as 'form of the living body'—known as the 'cause' or principle of movement in living things but primarily as the subject of such operations as we have mentioned. For them, the soul was known as an already given reality, given in its phenomenological character, before some further account was sought and a philosophical theory of 'form' as the correlate of matter was offered—providing a notion of soul which belongs to the general theory of explanation. Secondly, there seems to be something altogether right in an account which brings together the phenomenological or descriptive and explanatory, abolishing the apparent gap between 'how things appear to us' and 'how things are in themselves'.

Since Aristotle paid no attention, even indirectly, to the problem as to how these two notions of soul could be brought together, his discussions are, in this respect, less instructive than the more analytical treatment of Aquinas. The latter considers with care only the human case, but this is the one which is of key importance to us for the reasons which will become clear in Chapter XIV.

In relation to the understanding of Aquinas, it is clear that both notions of soul are actively at work in his arguments. Explicit assertions that the soul is the form of the body recur with great frequency, so that what we need to make unmistakable is how he is also committed to the phenomenological conception of the human soul.

This latter commitment appears firstly in his general treatment of the relation of perception and imagination to thought or understanding (*intelligere*), and secondly, more importantly, in his account of how the problem of explaining human unity arises.

As to perception, Aquinas asks whether the human being who perceives is simply a soul using a body, the human being and the soul being identical, both being (in the way of thinking he is attacking) in essence something non-bodily.[22] In this debate, it is presumed that the soul which perceives is the same as the soul which thinks,

---

[22] *S. Th.* Ia, Q. 75, Art. 4, Resp. and footnote c, p. 19, Vol.11, Eyre and Spottiswoode edition, 1970.

and the question is as to whether perception like intellection is an operation in which the body does not share or whether perception is essentially an operation shared in by the body, so that its proximate subject is the animal or human being as such, the thing which also acts bodily and moves. Now, for Aquinas, the receiving by the sense-organ of an imprint from the object of sense was internal to the operation of perceiving. Therefore, perception being thus an operation essentially shared by the body, one could conclude that the soul was not situated in the human being as a pilot in a ship[23] and did not merely use the body but constituted one thing, one integrated nature, with the body. But in all this the phenomenological way of thinking whereby perception is attributed to the soul is not questioned—only it is insisted that it is an operation shared with the body.

As to imagination, the question arises whether that which perceives and imagines is indeed the same as that which understands and thinks. To this question, the answer was obvious to Descartes, but not to the mediaevals because of the existence of a peculiar theory due to Averroes. Aquinas shared with the followers of this theory the presumption that human understanding had to be of objects presented in phantasms or images, but, contrary to their peculiar view that the human animal did the imagining while a separate intellect did the understanding, he insisted that it had to be the same subject which did the imagining as did the understanding.[24]

---

[23]Descartes later returned to the same answer that the soul is not in the body as a pilot in a ship, but unlike Aquinas gave no analysis of perception which supported this.

[24]Aquinas' response to the theory in S. Th. Ia, Q. 76, Art. 1, is more instructive than the theory itself.

According to the theory which Aquinas' contemporaries drew from Averroes, the intellect was something separate from the human being who perceives and moves bodily so that, somehow, in virtue of the existence of phantasms or images in the animal (to be objects to this intellect), understanding took place in this separate intellect in virtue of which the human animal was moved to action. Thus, the intellect itself was something separate which causes the animal or body to move.

For Aquinas it was a datum that the act of understanding was the act of this or that particular human being, 'for each person experiences that it is he himself who understands', and he argues that the Averroistic theory can give no account of how this can be so. For there to be principles for understanding in a separate intellect abstracted from phantasms or images while the phantasms themselves are in Socrates would do nothing to explain how it was Socrates himself who understands by means of these principles. Whether there be one separate intellect for all human beings, or a separate intellect for each, no explanation has been given for the attribution of understanding to

But this merely highlights his acceptance of the Aristotelian view, embraced by us in Chapter XI, that in human beings the intellect addresses itself to objects which are presented through imagination. His whole theory of the normal working of the human intellect depends upon maintaining, whether one is speaking of the human being as such, or of the soul, that whatever in the human case is subject of understanding in its natural mode of operation is also subject of imagination and, if of imagination, then before and with this also subject of perception.

So much for the incidental indications of Aquinas' view. What is more important is the way in which the phenomenological conception of soul is vital to Aquinas' understanding of how the problem of human unity arises.

The first stage for Aquinas is to suppose that something called the soul which is not identical to the human being is the subject of the operations we have picked out as 'operations of soul in the phenomenological sense', understanding or thinking and sensory perception amongst them: the soul is that by which the human being is 'subject' of these operations as the part, aspect, or power exercised, but in such a way not just to underly them or be their principle but to be a logical subject of which they can be predicated. These operations are attributable to the human being and the soul at the same time, somewhat (one might say) as colours belong to bodies and to surfaces at the same time. But Aquinas presumes that he has a positive conception of the soul as the subject of these operations, somewhat as we might suppose that we have a positive conception of surfaces, even though souls and surfaces are not identical respectively to human beings and to bodies.

The second stage is this, to argue that in the case of the human animal, at least, one of this family of operations (viz., understanding or thinking) is not shared by the body, and that from this it follows that in the case of the human being this phenomenological soul must

---

the same being, the man Socrates, who perceives, has images, and moves intentionally. And to suppose that Socrates is moved by this separate intellect leaves this intellect as a mover externally related to Socrates as the thing moved, so that bringing in the relation of understanding to intentional movement does not help.

For Aquinas, the Averroistic theory merely represented dualism—whose absurdities he demonstrates in many places (*SCG*, II, 56–58, cf. 59–78, is representative)—albeit in a new form, more implausible than most.

be considered to subsist or exist in its own right. This is the argument which I consider with all its difficulties in Chapter XIV below.

It is then at the third stage, after it has been presumed that we have a positive or constructive or contentful conception of the soul as the subject of what we have called 'operations of soul', and supposedly proved in the human case that this soul subsists, that the question arises as to how it can be that the human being is a single thing—since it also comprises a body. To this Aquinas's response is that the human soul and the human body can be one only if the soul as subject of intellection is none other than the form of the body conceived of in an Aristotelian way—a response whose coherence I shall consider shortly below.

Thus, the problem of human unity arises for Aquinas only because he has first accepted the phenomenological conception of soul, and his resolution of this problem absolutely depends on his identification (at least in the human case) of the phenomenological soul, a subject of concrete predicates, with the soul as form.

We have to grasp that the conception of the soul as the form of the body has no tendency by itself to suggest that in the human case the soul will be subsistent. This conception is designed to encapsulate an holistic view of the whole human being so that it cannot be conceived of materially, i.e., as some aggregate of material parts in external relations to one another, nor as this with the soul as an extra part.

The key question will be of the sense in which the operation of intellection is not shared by the body. It will not be shared in this sense: that there is nothing in common, no common or shared form, between the human being and the body such as could ground a claim of isomorphism between the structure of intellection in the human being and some structure in the body. But, unless one already has it as a datum that there is something called the soul, conceived of as subject of this family of 'psychic' operations, which is logically distinct as a subject of concrete predicates from the human being as such, one could not state this in the form that there is no isomorphism, nothing in common, between the act of intellection in the soul and any structure in the body. One could not state it in this form because one would not yet know of the existence of any entity called the soul distinct from the human being as such, to have or to lack something in common with the body. One will have the whole human being as the subsistent subject of intellectual operations and will have no basis for saying that the form (the soul as form) is a subsistent subject of anything.

Thus, unless one already has the soul on one's hands as subject of psychic operations, it will achieve nothing in regard to the soul if one shows that intellection has no bodily organ. One will have the whole human being as such on one's hands as an 'intellectual substance', but nothing demonstrated in regard to anything called the soul.

(b) The objection that the identification of the phenomenological soul with the soul as form constitutes a category-mistake

The soul phenomenologically conceived is, as such, the subject of concrete predicates—and this can be said independently of whether or not in one particular case, the human, it has operations which are not operations shared by the body, and whether or not it could be argued from this that it has existence in its own right or 'subsists', as Aquinas argued.

Many authors simply assume that to identify this phenomenological soul with the soul as form is to commit some kind of category-mistake.[25] The soul conceived as form—the correlate of matter in the Aristotelian conception—seems to be the opposite, as such 'something abstract' incapable of being subject of concrete predicates, let alone subsistent or 'concrete'. This is typified by the way in which, for instance, it seems evident that so-called accidental forms like 'being arranged in a square' or 'being circular in shape' are abstract in the very obvious way that the expressions for them result from turning statements or predicates into nouns—for it seems evident that 'these four pieces of chalk being arranged in a square' is in some way an abstract entity by contrast with the pieces of chalk themselves which are in this relation.

The idea that a category-mistake had been committed in the supposition that the human soul is both the form of a body in the Aristotelian sense and a particular thing or something which subsists was one of which Aquinas was well aware. He has an objector saying that *forma est quo aliquid est, et sic ipsum esse formae ipsius formae*

---

[25]This assumption is well represented in Antony Flew's *An Introduction to Western Philosophy*.

secundum se, that is, the form is the principle by which some subject is something or other, e.g., this gold ring is a ring (in virtue of circularity) or this animal is alive (in virtue of its soul), and so existence is not something which the form itself has in its own right (as if circularity or a soul existed apart from subjects in which they were realized).[26]

The suspicion that a category-mistake is being made remains with us when we are confronted with Aquinas' presumption that the soul is 'the primary thing by which we operate in all the operations of life', regarding this as making it the primary thing, not only by which we understand and perceive or sense, but also by which we are nourished and move in place[27]—all the while that he is also willing to speak of the soul as itself understanding, perceiving, and having images. Thus the soul is supposed *both* to be that by which the animal or human being operates *and* that which in the same act itself operates. Yet it is not only not a phenomenological datum that the soul in the phenomenological sense is that by which we are nourished, but quite obscure whether the supposition even makes sense.

The suspicion remains with us when we consider Aquinas' subsequent argument. Thus, when Aquinas speaks of 'the primary thing by (or according to) which' this or that operation is attributed to a human being, there seems to be an ambiguity between respect or aspect and 'part', without there being any clear conception of 'part'.[28]

---

[26] *S. Th.* Ia, Q. 76, Art. 1, Obj. 5.

[27] *S. Th.* Ia, Q. 76, Art. 1, in his first paragraph of the reply.

[28] In the second paragraph of the reply in *S. Th.* Ia, Q. 76, Art. 1, we are presented with three alternatives from Aristotle: of acting *per accidens* as when it is said that a white thing builds, of acting according to the whole of what one is, or of acting according to a part. Aquinas argues that the human being who recognises that he both understands and senses cannot be a soul since sensation involves the body 'so that the body must be part of the human being': in this argument, it is presumed that the soul is something of which the body is not part, and therefore not the whole human being. It is also presumed, evidently because understanding is not a bodily act, unlike sensing, that since Socrates includes the body as a part it cannot be that Socrates understands according to the whole of himself: from this it is inferred that he must understand according to a part of himself, the intellect ("intellect" here refers to the '*principium* of intellectual operations' which the Article is proving to be the form of the body—i.e., what has intellectual capacity, not the capacity or faculty itself). However, a doctor's healing is taken as a case of something acting 'according to its whole self' because it is *qua* doctor that the doctor heals, so that X acts according to Y means 'X acts *qua* Y' or 'Y is the aspect or respect according to which X acts'. The expression "the primary thing according to which X is Y" could also refer to a faculty or, if Y was (e.g.) a colour, a surface.

One might be attracted to saying that the human being understands, not according to the whole of itself in the sense of 'according to all its parts', but simply *qua* human being, but not in respect of any bodily part or aspect; then, when asked in respect of what aspect understanding is to be attributed to the human being, one might say in respect of its intellect or soul, without implying that this was a 'part'. Accordingly, when the intellect or soul as that 'according to which' the human being understands is spoken of as a 'part' and as subsistent, one might again suspect a category-mistake had been committed, smuggled in under the veil of treacherous expressions like "the primary thing by (or according to) which".[29]

When a category-mistake has been committed it is only in special cases that a contradiction can be proved to result—special cases such as those which generate logical paradoxes such as Russell's, the derivation of a contradiction being possible because of the possibilities of self-reference which they open out. In the normal case, careful disambiguation of predicates will usually show that no formal contradiction is involved, e.g., in Frege's example of "Julius Caesar is a number",[30] or in "Green ideas sleep furiously". As Ryle perceived, the mistake involved in so-called 'category-mistakes' lies at a deeper level than that of contradiction. Contradiction arises between propositions which are already formed of appropriately combined terms, whereas a category-mistake is what arises when terms are inappropriately combined.

(c) Response to this objection

Therefore, we should not expect the approach which proceeds solely by showing that no contradiction is present to carry conviction in proving that no category-mistake is present.[31]

---

[29] The plain ablative and the use of the prepositions *secundum* and *per* in Aquinas' Latin correspond to the Greek *kata*.

[30] *Foundations of Arithmetic*, sec. 56. Of course, the "is" will need to be disambiguated so as to be divested of temporal significance, lest it be supposed that before Julius Caesar was conceived a certain number did not exist.

[31] Yet this might seem to be Aquinas' predominant approach: to prove by *reductio ad absurdum* argument that the human soul as subject of intellection must be identical with the form of the body, and then to show that no contradiction results. This approach is most clear in *SCG* II and *Q. D. De An.*, Art. 1.

Rather, our approach should be to insist that the conception of form as the correlate of matter is not the conception of something determinate in category, and to be prepared to consider each type of case separately.[32]

It is, in any case, plain that the model provided by considering 'accidental forms' does not fit all cases. The written syllable may be certain letters in certain relations, so that it is clear that only an accidental form (an arrangement or system of relations between independently existing objects) is involved. But in the case of the spoken syllable the phonemes have no existence apart from their dynamic unity in the whole, and in this way are in their own way abstractions from the concrete reality which is the whole. And parallel remarks may apply to atoms joined in valency bonds to constitute molecules, to sheets of metal in complex ways sharing their electrons, and to the parts of biological organisms. In many of these latter cases we still talk of the parts, the atomic nuclei, the electrons, the molecules or larger biological parts, and suchlike as distinct subjects, and thereby in a certain way as 'things', but how we should describe the status of whatever 'unifies' them into larger wholes is in many cases quite obscure.

Leaving aside the uninteresting case of purely accidental or external relations, there seem to be at least four other types of case to be considered.

In the first type of case, the right view seems clearly to be that there is nothing to be understood in regard to the category or general logical character of the 'form' as what unifies the 'elements'[33] in these cases, beyond what is already clear from the initial specification of the whole concerned in its context. Thus there is nothing mysterious, nothing requiring further explanation, about the 'category' of what unifies the phonemes into the syllable within the context of the general modes of human utterance and hearing, or about what unifies the 'elements' of the molecule or the metal sheet (granted the acceptance

---

[32]The conception of form as the correlate of matter is the conception of a certain kind of 'explanatory factor' or a 'that in virtue of which so-and-so'. We are familiar from the case of biological genes that we can formulate a theory of explanatory factors of a certain kind (viz., genes in Mendelian theory of inheritance) long in advance and independently of any notion that these may be identical to something material, such as in this case an element in a chromosome, *qua* exercising a certain function.

[33]Whether these be discrete like particles or whether they be conceived as continua.

of some theory of the role of electrons in the different kinds of bonding involved, or some other theory describable as 'physical'). When I say that the 'category' of the unifying 'form' is sufficiently clear, what I mean is that it is clear what general types of inquiry might be apposite to it and, for instance, that it could not be itself the subject of concrete predicates in the way that the 'elements' united and the resulting whole are such subjects.[34]

The second type of case is presented by pre-conscious living organisms, the ones to which we do not (or on reflection should not) ascribe such concrete predicates as perception, knowledge, memory, imagination, emotion, and action from emotion. If we call the unifying 'forms' of these living organisms into the functioning wholes they are, functioning according to the natures they have, 'souls', then it is not clear that these 'souls' will be subjects of any concrete predicates whatsoever. We may say that they are principles '*by which* the living thing operates in all the operations of life', but they will not themselves operate at all. The notion of 'form' or 'soul' here is serving a certain role in marking the appropriateness of a certain kind of holistic treatment of the living things concerned, a holistic treatment required by teleological accounts of nutrition, growth, regeneration, reproduction, and suchlike—holistic in depending on treating the thing concerned as a non-accidental unity in some of its 'operations'. It also marks how we are pre-reflectively drawn to describe plants and other such organisms—how we 'experience' them, the terms in which we describe our day to day perceptions of shape and growth (presupposing identity) and appreciations of 'need' (e.g., of water). But it carries no connection with the phenomenology of perception, imagination, memory, and emotion, since our experience does not call for the ascription of these things to these lower organisms.

In the third type of case, that of those higher animals to whom we do rightly ascribe perception, imagination, memory, and emotion, but not linguistic understanding or things tied to it, the situation is more problematic. In the case of these highest animals, I have suggested that we can speak, at a descriptive or phenomenological level of their souls as perceiving, imagining, and undergoing emotion.

---

[34] If a 'valency bond' is an example of a 'unifying form', then, although some perhaps ill-individuated electrons being shared in certain ways may play a strategic role in the unifying of the whole, the bond is not itself an electron.

But we still do not speak here in a way which allows the attribution of these operations to these supposed souls without there being bodily processes internal to the operations, and so still do not speak in any way which makes the soul into a 'thing' or something 'subsistent'. Accordingly, there is a question as to whether the soul spoken of in this way at a phenomenological level can or should be identified with the Aristotelian 'form' as that which unifies and gives nature to the organisms as organisms exercising this kind of life, associated as it is with kinds of explanation for their behaviour which involve the kinds of psychosomatic structure and unity which we have described. The concept of soul here concerned belongs to phenomenology, whereas the concept of form belongs to the theory of explanation and to ontology so far as it is determined by considerations of explanation.

In regard to this question we should say the following. On the one hand, there is no meaning to the statement that the soul as phenomenological subject of these operations of higher animals lower than human beings is identical to the Aristotelian 'form' of these kinds of organism—no meaning because neither these souls in the phenomenological sense nor these forms are 'things', and the ways in which talk of them enters discourse is quite different. There is nothing which the soul as phenomenological subject in the case of these higher animals does in its own right, and there is no reason for thinking of the Aristotelian 'forms' of these higher types of organism in any different way so far as category is concerned from the forms of lower organisms—even though they are specifically different in the way we have mentioned, viz., that the focalized subjecthood or unity they determine is inseparable from the applicability of a special kind of holistic and teleological explanation, viz., the mentalistic. However, on the other hand, it is in virtue of precisely the same structures in human life that *both* talk of animals' souls in this phenomenological idiom *and* talk of this kind of Aristotelian form tied to the applicability of this kind of explanation are appropriate. This fully explains the deceptive naturalness of a general identification of animals' souls with Aristotelian forms.

We now come to the case of the human soul.

If Aquinas is right that the human soul in the phenomenological sense has some existence in its own right or subsists, human beings will represent a fourth type of case. In this case we have been given a reason to suppose that the soul of the human being, phenomenologically conceived, is a subsistent thing. This enables it to be conceived to have a status which is not just phenomenological but ontological: it is a thing about which one can inquire its relation to the bodily parts of the human being and to the body as a whole. Once one has raised this question, it is clear that if the form of the human body, that is the principle determining its nature as exhibited in its life, behaviour, and unity, were anything else than this human soul then the body would constitute an independent thing with independent nature and existence alongside the soul, and one would have a fully fledged dualism on one's hands with all the impossibilities which that involves. Therefore, if the human soul as subject of understanding and will subsists, then it must itself be the form or principle of unity and operation of the living human body—so that the living human body as what it is has no existence independently of this soul—some aspects of its behaviour, e.g., physical and chemical, can be considered in abstraction from its complete nature, but its behaviour considered globally cannot.

At this point we can clear up the objection alleging the presence of a category confusion between abstract and concrete. Suppose we had had on our hands a constructive, contentful category-determinate concept of the form of the human body and also a constructive, contentful category-determinate concept of the soul as subject of understanding and will. Then it might have seemed that we had two competing *reductio ad absurdum* arguments, one from Aquinas that the two must be identical in the human case or else all the absurdities of dualism will result, and the other from his critics that to identify an abstract entity with a concrete one in the supposed way is an absurd category-mistake. We would then seem to be on difficult ground with two constructive contentful notions but no constructive model of how something might be both things at the same time.[35]

However, this is not our situation: there is no such difficulty because as we stated at the start the notion of "form" as the correlate

---

[35]It could be argued that this happens in physics. Not to have constructive notions is common in physics: we can have a constructive notion of things as particles, and of the same things as waves, without having a constructive notion of how they can be both at the same time. Again, it seems to be almost the norm in theology for us to have something belonging to two categories at the same time without us being able to form a constructive notion of how this is possible, although it may be obscure whether the categories concerned are ones of which we have constructive notions rather than merely formal ones.

of matter is not a determinate one—and, what is important here, it is not even determinate as to category. Therefore, we do not have to introduce any theories to explain why a category-violation might be licit in this case.

The concept of form as the correlate of matter is a formal one, not contentful, and not even category-determinate, and that the category of the particular 'form' may be determined in any of the generically different ways indicated above. "Form" may either refer to accidental relations, or to non-subsistent principles of unity and operation of non-accidental wholes (syllables, molecules, and living things provide very different cases of this), or, if the human soul be subsistent, the subsistent principle of unity and operation in the human being. The question in regard to the human case is not as to whether a category-mistake has been committed in supposing the human soul to be subsistent. Rather, the question is firstly as to whether the phenomenologically rooted way of speaking of the soul as I described it is well-conceived and, secondly, as to whether the arguments for its subsistence in the human case are valid. If they are, since if the human soul is subsistent then it must necessarily also be principle of human life and unity, and so be a 'form'. If they are not, then we will say just the same about the relation of the phenomenological soul and the soul as form in the human case as we said in respect of the other animals.

We have seen how the nature of human beings as amongst the animals and their situation of real relation to the world is the fundamental given in our thought about them. And we have also now seen that there is no viable conception of soul which is not 'unistic' or anti-dualistic in character and which does not also have application to some other living things. We have represented talk of 'souls' as a by-product of other discourse though appropriate: what we have to say about this or that kind of soul is always derivative from and determined by—a mere reflection of—what we have to say about this or that kind of living bodily being. In the next two chapters we shall examine how this works out in the case of human souls and their 'being' or *esse*.

XIV. How Human Beings Transcend the Body: First Explanation — the Transcendence of the Human Soul

In Chapter XII we demonstrated that the human being has certain operations, namely linguistic understanding and thinking in the medium of words, which are not bodily operations. We might choose to express this by saying that these operations 'transcend' the body and that in these operations the human being 'transcends' the body, meaning by these things nothing more than has already been demonstrated.

However, it seems very natural to go further, and infer that the human being has some part which, as it were, stands above the body and is exercised in these operations: a mind, intellect, or soul. That is, when we have grasped that understanding and thinking are not bodily activities and do not involve bodily activities internally to them, unlike intentional action, speaking, and hearing, and unlike perception in general, imagination and emotion, we want to say that there must be some other deeper non-bodily part of the human being which is exercised in them. We are not satisfied with the explanation that these operations are operations of the whole human being as a whole. They are obviously not like tennis-playing, involving just about every bodily part of the person, and do not seem to involve his arms or legs—or, as we have seen, any part of his body at all. As states or activities they do not involve the body internally, but only for their expression. Moreover, we are convinced that there is much more of a person than is expressed in tennis-playing and other non-linguistic activities, indeed more even than is or, we suspect, could be expressed in language.

Alternatively, or additionally, it may seem natural to say that the human being in his or her existence transcends whatever kind of existence his or her body has. The notion of existence or *esse* may well seem more difficult even than the notion of soul, but it remains that, if it be granted that human beings have operations which in the sense I have indicated transcend the body, we are strongly drawn to supposing that human existence must transcend the body.

In this chapter and the next I explore whether any such consequences can be drawn from the fact that linguistic understanding and thinking are in no way bodily operations—exploring first of all what is to be said about the human soul, and then, secondly, what can be said about human existence or being. We shall find that what requires to be said about human existence or being stands independently of what we say about soul.

Our first task is to rule out certain false starting-points for talking about the human soul.

1. No A Priori Argument to the Existence of Souls as Subsistent

Now, according to the way of talking about the soul which I described in Chapter XIII, Section 1, the soul, if we can speak about it at all, is in a certain way well known. It has a status in phenomenological description which leaves its position in human life absolutely clear. If this mode of speech cannot be accepted in some such way as was there explained, at least at the phenomenological or descriptive level, there is no way the soul as subject of operations, even intellectual ones, can be brought in afterwards. That is, the soul cannot be introduced as a theoretical entity to whose existence we might reason.

In Chapter IX we excluded any adoption of Descartes' way of thinking whereby because, metaphorically, human beings stand over against and above the world in order to see, assess, and make judgement about it, and from this to be free in their choices, their explorings, their imaginings, and even (some have held) their emotions and attitudes in regard to it. On the contrary, not only the perceiver, but also the judger are set within the world—the focalized subject, the focus, who is the perceiver and judger, is nowhere else but here in the world.

In this way we have excluded what is to modern man, not only to Descartes but also to the empiricist and to the existentialist, the most obvious avenue to a conception of the human mind as a metaphorically inner part of the human being, a part which transcends the body.

However, what it is vital to insist further is that not only is this Cartesian avenue of approach closed but also there is no other line of a priori argument to the soul available.

In particular, there is no approach by pure metaphysical reasoning from what is involved in human understanding, knowledge, and freedom. Aristotle has been cited as thinking that the intellect must be unmixed with matter in order to command or to know: human beings must be like metaphysical centaurs with one part sticking up above matter—like a periscope above the water—with freedom to move and look about in their intellectual operations.

But this a priori metaphysical way of arguing depends entirely upon physical metaphors and models, and brings in with them a picture of the mind or soul as itself substantial, not just in the logician's sense of being the logical subject of concrete operations, but in the sense of having (metaphorically of course) volume, depth, and solidity. In addition, the mind is now likely to figure as a kind of internal apparatus, a complex or structure, which we put to use in understanding, thinking, and choosing; and in this way it has suddenly come to be presented, not as the subject who and which understands and thinks, but as some organ put to use by the subject. We now have on our hands an immaterial part of the person to be united with the ordinary bodily parts by some principle we know not what, and we have a puzzle on our hands as to how, out of this conglomerate of parts (a mind to be used in thinking along with the ordinary bodily parts), we are to have a personal subject who as a focalized unity or focus uses them all and makes them a unity. Moreover, this mind which is supposedly unmixed with matter and exercised in understanding and thinking, because it is thus unmixed, cannot also be exercised in perceiving, imagining, and emotion so far as these involve the body.

No 'intellectual substance' can be thought of according to such physical models, and accordingly no such line of reasoning as the above has any validity even in regard to human beings or animals.

There is no way in which the focalized subject of intellectual operations can have a part, immaterial or otherwise, which is the organ of these operations. For we cannot conceive it as having a part alongside other parts except according to a spatial model which carries with it that it has a complexity of sub-parts within itself. There is no logical room for a composition of immaterial parts to form the apparatus of an intellect any more than there is room for a composition of material parts. The arguments which exclude material parts exclude immaterial parts by the same structure of reasoning. It is not only that the human being does not have parts material or immaterial to be organs of intellectual operation, but also that there is no conglomerate with parts, nothing with stuff, or as it were (as we say in English) nothing solid or substantial (meaning by this 'analogous to material substance'), such as might be called soul or mind to be subject of these operations. No intellectual substances, neither God nor the angels, are in this way solid or substantial, possessed of interrelated parts—we literally cannot imagine them.

What we are here meeting again is what the mediaevals called the 'simplicity' of the intellect, of which we spoke in Chapter XII.

When we were considering the tendency of people to presume that teleological explanation must have its validity grounded in explanation in terms of underlying mechanisms, we found that the deep-rootedness of this presumption lay in a survival of a picture-theory of meaning.[1] It is this same picture-theory of meaning which encumbers us in thinking about linguistic understanding and thinking. The moment one thinks of the soul (during a person's lifetime) as a subsistent thing which does not include bodily parts, and, therefore, as a distinct part of a person or human being, and not identical to the person or human being—and thinks of this soul as the subject of understanding and thinking, one seems to have imagined a bit of the person which stands above the other bits (the bodily bits). And, because one has pictured it as a bit which is thus along with (although over above) the other bits, one has started to picture this bit as if it were itself material—even if its matter be non-physical.

What one should say is that what is wrong may not be talk about the soul as such, but rather this particular use of the imagination— this 'picturing'. One may conceivably be able to say (and to assent and think) that this soul is a bit of the human being while it is alive which is distinct from the bodily bits, but one cannot validly picture it as a bit alongside, behind, or over above the other bits, because no intellectual substance is imaginable or picturable.

But the kind of a priori metaphysical reasoning which we were considering depends on precisely such picturing. We might well think we had the picture of the human being as having hidden depths so that, as it were, the centre of gravity of the human being was not in the

---

[1]Chapter VII, Section 3, above.

body but in the unplumbed depths beneath the surface. However, this metaphor of a 'centre of gravity' together with the spatial metaphors (depths below, behind, or above the body) associated with it, brings in the same physical model of an extra stuff-containing part, a type of model whose inappropriateness we have already noted. And, indeed, should we not rather say, if we resort to physical metaphor, that the centre of gravity—the heart of the presence—of the human being is right here in the world, behind the eyes or set in the body where feelings of touch, muscle sensation, and pain are had?[2]

2. The Human Soul in the
Phenomenological Conception as Subsistent

(a) The existence of non-bodily operations of soul as the basis for argument to its subsistence

We have shown that there is no possibility of putting forward a conception whereby the human soul exists in its own right on the basis of a purely a priori approach, whether from epistemology or from pure metaphysics. In Chapter XIII we saw that there is no route into this conception on the basis of the Aristotelian notion of soul as form in the sense of the correlate of matter, or not on the basis of this taken by itself—i.e., from the general theory of explanation without reference to phenomenology. Rather, the only conceivable approach to such a concept was via the phenomenological conception of soul, following the path mapped out by Aquinas. I cite Aquinas *in extenso* because he has been the only major philosopher to press through a precise analysis of such a non-dualistic conception of a subsistent soul.

The higher animals lower than human beings see, hear, imagine, remember, and suffer emotion. They also then, like human beings, can be spoken or thought of as having souls which are subjects of these operations, and in this subjects of concrete predicates. But all these operations whether in the human or in other cases involve, we have argued, bodily processes internally to them.

---

[2]In this we would follow along the line of Merleau-Ponty's conception of incarnate consciousness.

But we have argued that this is not true of the kinds of linguistic understanding and thinking of which we have spoken. These are operations of the human being, and according to the phenomenological way of speaking described in Section 1 also operations predicable of the human soul—but operations which are not bodily operations. From this it seems natural to argue that the soul which operates in these operations (is the subject of these operations) must exist as something non-bodily in its own right. As Aquinas states this conclusion: 'the soul has a complete *esse* of its own',[3] and there is an '*esse* in which the soul itself subsists',[4] and 'the intellectual *principium* has being of itself and is something subsisting'.[5] It is in his view due to some deficiency in their mode of *esse* that the souls of lesser animals are incapable of an operation which is non-bodily, not vice versa.[6]

Moreover, it is not that the human soul subsists, or exists in its own right, only in the sense that it has a capacity to go on existing after the body has perished. Rather, it is *because* the human soul has an *esse* in which it itself subsists that (Aquinas says) 'the human soul continues in its *esse* when the body is destroyed, whereas the other souls do not'.[7] In the relevant sense, in the case of the human soul there is such a thing as its '*esse*' which is not the case with other souls.

Let us spell out the most extended statements of Aquinas' argument to this conclusion, picking out the key principle on which they turn later.

In his disputed questions *De Anima*, he tells us that 'the soul is a particular self-subsisting thing because it operates of itself: for its act of understanding is not performed through a bodily organ, as is proved in [Aristotle's] *De Anima*';[8] For 'in the case of the rational soul . . . it is quite impossible for it, in performing the operation peculiar to it, to have anything in common with a bodily organ, as though something corporeal might be an organ of understanding, just as the eye is the

---

[3] *Q. D. De An.*, 1, Reply to the First Objection.

[4] *S. Th.* Ia, Q. 76, Art. 1, ad 5.

[5] This is how he summarizes the conclusion of *S. Th.* Ia, Q. 75, Art. 2, in stating Objection 5 in Q. 76, Art. 1.

[6] Thus he says 'Although the soul's *esse* belongs in a certain measure to the body, the body does not succeed in sharing in the soul's *esse* to the full extent of its nobility and *virtus*; and it is from this that the soul has an operation in which the body does not share', *Q. D. De An.*, I, Reply to Obj. 18.

[7] *S. Th.* Ia, Q. 76, Art. 1 ad 5.

[8] *Q. D. De An.*, 1, in the 'Sed contra', referring to Aristotle's *De Anima* III, 4.

organ of sight . . . Thus the intellective soul, inasmuch as it performs its proper operation without sharing in any way with the body, must act of itself. And because a thing acts so far as it is actual, the intellective soul must have a complete *esse* in itself, depending in no way on the body. For forms whose *esse* depends on matter or on a subject do not operate of themselves. Heat, for instance, does not act, but something hot.'[9]

The same perspective appears in his earlier disputed questions *De Potentia*: 'The rational soul differs from other forms in that the latter have a being not wherein they subsist but whereby the things informed by them subsist, whereas the rational soul has being in such wise as to subsist therein: and this is made clear by their respective modes of action. For, since only that which exists can act, a thing is referred to operation or action as it is referred to being: so that, since the body must, of necessity, take part in the action of the forms, but not in the action of the rational soul, which is to understand and to will; it follows, of necessity, that being must be ascribed to the rational soul as subsisting, but not to other forms.'[10]

Now the key principle on which these arguments turn is that a thing can only act according to the way in which it exists. The disciples of Averroes argued that the intellect could not be the power of a bodily thing such as the human animal but must be something separate because 'no *virtus* or power could be more immaterial or simple than the thing (*essentia*) from which the *virtus* or power derived'. The idea that no operation of a bodily thing such as the human being could be immaterial, not involving bodily processes internally to it, still appears to modern man to be entirely common-sense. To it, Aquinas responds 'if the act of existing of the human soul, when joined to the body, belongs also to the body, then the act of understanding, which is the operation of the soul, will belong both to the soul and the body';[11] and he supposes that if the human soul was immersed in matter or wholly comprehended by it, i.e., as to mode of *esse*, this would prevent it from having some non-bodily activity.[12] That is, he agrees with the disciples of Averroes and concludes that the non-bodiliness of an operation of

---

[9] *Q. D. De An.*, 1, resp.
[10] *De Potentia*, Q. 3, Art. 9, Resp. under first argument.
[11] *Q. D. De An.*, 1, Obj. 18. He then tells us that this was shown to be impossible in Aristotle's *De Anima* [III, 4, at 492a 18].
[12] *S. Th.* Ia, Q. 76, Art. 1, ad 4.

the soul implies its existence in its own right. In the *Summa Theologica* he states 'nothing can act of (*per*) itself unless it subsists of (*per*) itself, for there is no operation except of actual being (*ens in actu*), so that something operates by the mode by which it exists'.[13]

It is in this way that Aquinas reaches his seemingly paradoxical conclusion: in its natural mode of operation the soul requires the imagination to supply the intellect with objects, so much so that the action of God is required to make possible a different mode of operation to the soul without the body;[14] nonetheless, because the intellectual act in regard to these objects is not itself bodily, the being or *esse* of the soul must transcend the body.

It is to this principle, that a thing can only act according to the way in which it exists, to which I will return in Chapter XV in attempting to open out a way of explaining the transcendence of the human being over the body in a way which does not turn upon the in origin phenomenological idiom of 'souls'.

(b) The idea of the human soul as the 'least amongst intellectual substances'

In Aquinas, the soul is conceived of as subsisting, i.e., as a *suppositum* or logical subject of the kind which is subject to concrete predicates, the subject of 'operations' such as thinking, understanding, knowing, and loving. The idea of subsisting is a philosophically technical one. In Aristotle's thought, first substances have a position contextually defined by their situation correlative to, or at the hub of, a system of categories or types of predicate or attribute. In Aquinas' thought, that which subsists is in the same way understood as the subject of predicates and attributes, not itself predicated of or in anything (unless as a part), but more particularly as correlative with operation

---

[13]*S. Th.* Ia, Q. 75, Art. 2, Resp.: he gives as an example that it is not the form heat which makes hot but rather the hot thing. But his argument shows that the primary deficiency of heat whereby it cannot act in its own right is not that it is a form and that it is the whole (the hot thing) composed of form and matter which acts, not the form, but that this form is not an *ens in actu*.

[14]Aquinas' most refined treatment of this, distinguishing modes of knowledge but never modes of being, amidst a magnificent *exposé* of the problematic of avoiding dualism, is in *Q. D. De An.*, Art. 15. Much earlier he had tried the foreign idea that the soul has different modes of being before and after death (*S. Th.* Ia, Q. 84, Art. 1, cf. Q. 76, Art. 1, ad 6).

or activity. In this way, what subsists is, above all, that which acts, and a thing which subsists (a substance or *subsistentia*)[15] thereby stands in contrast with what I have elsewhere called 'actualities' (activities, i.e., ways of being active rather than that which is active). In his conception the *subsistentia* is that which has *esse*, or which 'exercises' *esse* (to use a somewhat misleading and picturesque way of expressing that it is the subject of *esse*), whereas the *esse* is an actuality.

In the case of the soul, this particular thing, *hoc aliquid* (Aristotle's *tode ti*), or thing which subsists, is conceived by Aquinas to have come into existence at the same time as the body on the grounds (a) that it was not a complete nature but something whose proper nature, as a soul, requires union with the body of the animate being whose soul it is, and (b) that its individuality with its conditions of individuation depends on its origination in unity with the body. This entity, even spoken of as a substance, in this conception continues to exist all through a person's life along with the body, being 'left behind' to exist after the perishing of the body—the substantial unity of soul and body arising primarily not from a dependence of the soul for its existence on the body, but from a dependence of the body for its existence and nature upon the soul—albeit that the soul derives its individuation from its origin with the body as constituting one substance and has a nature defined by reference to the principles of operation of this substantial unity and so only properly exercised and expressed in union with the body.

The conception is that a thing must subsist or have concrete existence in order to be the subject of concrete predicates attributing operations or acts; if the operation is not a bodily operation, as we have proved in the case of linguistic understanding and of thinking in words, the existence is not essentially bodily; therefore the thing with this concrete existence (here, the human being or the human soul) has no cause for ceasing to exist just because the body ceases to exist. If traditional faith be true, then this thing remains in existence, available to be resurrected and restored to its full range of normal modes of operation including normal modes of intellectual operation, but also,

---

[15]Aquinas uses the term *subsistentia* in the course of discussion of the Christian doctrine of the Trinity in order to disambiguate the term *substantia* which he said sometimes meant *essentia* and sometimes meant first substance in Aristotle's sense. He used *subsistentia* to mean the latter, taking it to be equivalent to the Greek *hypostasis* (*S. Th.* Ia, Q. 29, Art. 2).

even before this resurrection, available to be given the exercise of other modes of intellectual operation not against its nature but also not natural to it—above all the mode whereby it may enjoy the vision of God which throughout its natural existence, even before death, has been its underlying natural desire recognized or unrecognized, making it unsatisfied in other things, but also secondarily modes which will allow it some knowledge of lesser things even in this supposed middle state between death and resurrection.

The term "substance" is for Aquinas preferentially used of that which subsists in a complete nature, but anything such as the soul which subsists in its own right so as to have operations of its own can also be spoken of as a substance.[16] It is true that, if Aquinas' view is right, then the human soul has a persistent identity with an explanatory role in relation to the nature and the continuance of the human being as a whole—the nature of this explanatory role becoming clear in Section 3. But one is constantly tempted to think that the human soul is a 'thing' in the sense of having a nature which is complete in the sense of supplying a criterion of identity sufficient to make plain its place in *all* the explanations in which its operations figure: in this way, human souls would, as it were, stand on their own feet in *all* the explanations in which they figure. We have seen that neither 'soul' nor 'human soul' is such a nature, and in this sense neither is any use as an answer to the question "What is it?"[17] 'Intellectual substance' is no better. For there is not one kind of 'understanding' common to all possible intellectual substances any more than there is one kind of 'living' common to all 'living' things, and the 'rational soul' does not, in Aquinas' view, exercise the way of understanding natural to it except in conjunction with imagination and perception and thereby with the body.

But, with this reservation only, Aquinas viewed the human soul as in its nature the least noble of intellectual substances, but an intellectual substance nonetheless.[18]

---

[16]It will be a substance in a stronger sense than bodily parts of substances with a complete nature, in that these do not exist in their own right with a fully determinate nature apart from the wholes of which they are parts.

[17]Cf. Chapter XIII, n. 11 above and text.

[18]This hierarchical conception is presented vividly in the *Summa Contra Gentes* and receives some of its fullest expressions in the *Q. D. De Anima*, perhaps Aquinas' last expression of thought in this field. It appears in the introduction to Q. 75 in the *Summa Theologica*, Ia.

The same perspective appears in his account of the difference between human generation and the generation of other living things. Thus, he says: '. . . being must be ascribed to the rational soul as subsisting, but not to other forms. For this reason the rational soul is the only form which can exist separate from the body, and hence also it is clear that the rational soul is brought into being not as other forms are, which properly speaking are not made but are said to be made in the making of this or that thing. That which is made is made properly speaking and *per se*. And that which is made is made either of matter or out of nothing. Now that which is made from matter must be made from matter subject to contrariety [i.e., the matter proceeds from being in one state to being in another] . . . For which reason, since a soul has no matter at all or at least none which is subject to contrariety, it cannot be made out of something. Hence it follows that it comes into being by creation as being made out of nothing. By contrast, to maintain that the soul is made by the generation of the body is to say that it is not subsistent and consequently that it ceases with the body.'[19]

(c) Recovery of the phenomenological sense of the 'doctrine' of soul: the soul as 'laid bare' to whatever language lays it bare

The human soul is thus something which, according to our phenomenological perspective, is laid bare to the objects which perception, imagination, and memory present to it, and shaken or moved by the emotions which these objects arouse. This same soul, now realized to be all the while subsistent, is also something which, according to the same perspective, is laid bare to whatever language exhibits it as laid bare.

Accordingly, within this conception whereby the soul which suffers the exigencies of human experience is subsistent and therefore capable of continued existence even after bodily death, the soul may in this life be wracked or caught up in emotions of desire and aversion, fear, anger, and hope, fascination and wonder not only in regard to the objects of this world, but also in regard to God. According

---

[19] *De Potentia*, Q. 3, Art. 9, Resp. in continuation of his first argument.

to this conception, it is the same soul which is in this life exposed to the loveliness and harshness of this world, the love and the anger of parents, the wonder and the fear of tigers, the calm and the roaring of the sea, which is also capable of being exposed naked in loving and fearful immediate knowledge or 'vision' to God.

What I have explained in this section in terms of 'soul' may perhaps be better explained in terms of the whole human being, or the human being as such, so that one may speak not just of the soul being laid bare or exposed naked to the objects mentioned and seized by the emotions concerned, but of the human being being thus laid bare and seized—the human being always in the relevant respects an indivisible or 'focalized' subject. In this way, in our argument in Chapter XV it will be not the soul but the human being as such which we present as exposed at once to whatever it may be exposed to, including whatever language or other modes of communication and expression may expose it to. And it is only inasmuch as we can speak of the human being as such in these ways that, in virtue of the double way in which 'psychic' operations present themselves for description, we can also speak of the soul in these ways.

In all this we must hold fast to the perspective whereby it is the same human being and the same soul which is exposed to other people, other animals, the trees, the land, the sky, sun and stars, the weather, and the sea—the whole natural world—which may also be exposed to God. And it is the same human being or soul which will be wracked or caught up in the emotions appropriate to these objects. In setting the roots for any thinking of human being or soul phenomenologically, we allow no divorce between the human animal who enjoys and endures this life and the spirit who, whether as bodily being or whether deprived of body, is revealed by language as being open to wider and more ultimate orientations.

3. The Explanation of Human Unity

Human unity, the unity whereby the human being is a focalized subject, the unity whereby it is the same subject which intentionally moves which also sensorily perceives but whereby also the same subject which sensorily perceives also imagines, understands, and thinks, is a datum of human experience.[20] There is no way in which the phenomenological soul portrayed in Chapter XIII, Section 1, whose imagining is inseparable from its capacity to perceive, and which perceives and moves as well as thinking and understanding, can fail to be a single integrated nature with the body. In the phenomenological conception of soul, the soul only exists (in that sense in which it does exist), at least when one is thinking of certain of its operations, in dynamic relation to the body since in these operations it does not function apart from the body, so that there is no way in which the bodily organs of sense and of action can be conceived of as extras additional to, or external to, the 'being' of the soul.

Aquinas holds that the *esse* which the soul has in its own right is communicated to the body so that the *esse* of the whole human being ('the whole composite') is none other than the *esse* of the soul.[21] Likewise, he says 'the soul has a complete act of existing of its own . . . the same act of existing is conferred on the body by the soul so that there is one act of existing for the whole composite'.[22] There is no *esse* which the body has in its own right whereby it could be said to subsist. The body has no *esse* independent, over and above, or alongside, the *esse* of the soul—no *esse* apart from the *esse* of the soul as that which makes the body live with the life and unity it has, makes the body be what it is (in Aristotelian terminology 'the form of the body'). And there is no *esse* of the whole human being distinct from the *esse* of the soul, inclusive of it as a part.

However, the moment that the soul seems to have its own *esse*, independently of the continuance of the body, we feel that a problem has arisen because we think according to physical analogies according to which the soul has become, in our imagination or picturing, something alongside the body, the body or bodily parts thereby being envisaged as of equal status as 'substances' alongside the 'soul'. That is, if Aquinas' line of argument is right, then in the human case this phenomenological soul is something which exists in its own right—in his way of speaking, something which has an existence or *esse* of its own, not dependent on the body. This seems paradoxical because in

---

[20]As Aquinas says: 'Each experiences that it is he himself who understands' making it clear in context that the 'each' covers each human being who perceives and moves, *S. Th.* Ia, Q. 76, Art. 1.

[21]*S. Th.* Ia, Q. 76, Art. 1, ad 5.

[22]*Q. D. De An.*, 1, Reply to the First Objection.

treating the rational soul as existing in its own right or 'subsistent' one seems to be treating it as a particular entity, and then bodily parts and even the whole body will appear additional to it (not that they are added, but that they are realities and distinct). Thus, one seems to be putting oneself in the position of thinking of the soul and the body as two distinct things whose mode of union one has to discuss.

Yet this way of thinking, guided by the inappropriate use of the imagination, is what we already excluded in Section 1 of this chapter. Liberation from this way of thinking can, however, only be achieved by doing justice to the associated questions which arise about explanation and dealing with them in the way suggested by Aristotle.

For the right answer to these questions seems to be that *it is the existence of the body and its parts, not that of the soul, which is dependent and incomplete in its nature by itself.* Let me explain what I mean by 'incomplete in its nature by itself'. In Chapter VIII we made clear that, for purposes of considering explanation and causation, the purposes relevant to judging substantial identity, the human being has to be considered a psychophysical whole: there is no rounded explanation of behaviour in its physical aspect, and not even attainment of the full degree of predictability possible in regard to it, by considering the physical in abstraction from its context in the life of the human being as a psychophysical whole. The body and its parts are, in a way, abstractions, their criteria of identity being defined by reference to the identity of the living human being as such. This already makes the existence of the body and its parts dependent or incomplete considered on their own: they have no existence as what they are, considered in all its aspects and not just in some abstracted aspects, apart from the human being as a whole. All this can and must be said even before anything is said or agreed about the soul.

However, in the Aristotelian explanation of the matter, this is expressed in terms of the dependence of the body on the soul, considered as the 'form' or principle of unity, identity and operation of the body—in the case of the animals lower than human beings clearly an interdependence.

Now, once the human soul, considered as the subject of understanding, perception, imagination, memory and emotion, i.e., considered phenomenologically, has been granted to have reality in its own right, and not merely phenomenological status, there is a compulsion to regard this soul as what gives the body the kind of life (nature understood in terms of and realized in behaviour) and thereby the

kind of unity which it has, giving unity, nature, and function to
the parts of the body. That is, there is a compulsion to identify the
human soul, understood phenomenologically, with the human soul as
understood in the way Aristotle understood the form of the human
body. Otherwise, we will inevitably be landed with a return to dualism
with the impossibilities which that involves.[23] For, if the human body
with its form (that which gave it unity, identity and operation) were
one substance and the phenomenological human soul is something
which exists in its own right, then we would have two substances in
a dualist way.

To dramatize the point, recalling what we said in the Introduction to this Part of this book: the effect of regarding the material as
self-contained for purposes of the consideration of causation, prediction of behaviour, and identity is to make belief in the subsistence of
the soul or in the after-life into the superstition called dualism. And
this is what happened in seventeenth century thought—and this is
why the return to an Aristotelian perspective, whether or not it be
stated in terms of a doctrine of the soul as form, is absolutely crucial.
And it is this Aristotelian or holistic perspective which we established
in Chapter VIII.

We can now return to our general exposition.

We have made it clear that, once granted that the human soul,
phenomenologically considered, already established as subsistent,
nonetheless has to be united with the body without there being some

---

[23]This is the background of the statement of the Council of Vienne (1311–12):
'we reject as erroneous and contrary to the truth of the Catholic faith any doctrine or
position which rashly asserts, or calls into doubt, that the substance of the rational or
intellectual soul is not truly and of itself the form of the human body. . . . We define
that from now on whoever shall presume to assert, defend, or obstinately hold that
rational intellectual soul is not in itself and essentially the form of the human body, is to
be censured as a heretic.' This was, it appears, directed against the peculiar Averroistic
doctrine that the intellect is a separate entity from the human animal who imagines,
perceives, and moves, cf. Chapter XIII, n. 24, above. It appears that what was here
defined and canonized was not the Aristotelian doctrine of form and matter as such,
but that the intellectual soul was constitutive of the nature, form of life, and unity
of the body—that is, there was no canonization of any particular model of how the
soul was thus constitutive (e.g., the model suggested by Aristotle's other examples,
e.g., those arising in physics), but primarily the exclusion of any doctrine which made
something intermediate (e.g., a vegetative or animal soul) rather than the intellectual
soul into principle of the nature, life and unity of the body.

other yet extra principle or form uniting the body and the soul as if they were just parts of equal status of some larger whole as dualists imagine, then the only explanation of this union open to us is that it is united to it as its form or principle of unity, identity and operation. But this conclusion recommends itself, not only on the basis of a *reductio ad absurdum* argument to the effect that the opposite supposition leads to the absurdities of dualism, but also positively inasmuch as it is these activities of understanding and thinking, perception, imagination, memory, and emotion which give direction to human life within the sort of life towards which human existence from the start is orientated.

It is evident that the structure of thinking here forced upon us in the case of human beings could be regarded as a particular case of the structure which Aristotle proposed for all living things whereby in each the soul as form was what gave nature and unity to the bodily parts. But we represented this way of thinking in the case of living things in general as an entirely optional way of expressing a certain teleological point of view. The situation in the case of human beings—if Aquinas' argument works—is quite different: there will be nothing optional about regarding the phenomenological soul as what gives nature and unity to the human body and its parts, and nothing optional about regarding the body as having its existence as a humanly functioning body which is entirely dependent upon the soul. We can utilize the much more general Aristotelian conception of 'formal cause' and apply it to the soul, but it is, in my view, entirely optional whether we apply to the soul the separate (and in the development of Aristotle's thought, later) idea of 'form' as the correlate of 'matter'.

In identifying the root of human unity, what makes the human being with his complexity of parts and aspects a focalized subject or indivisible unity, as being the phenomenological soul (the 'I', the 'he or she', under the aspect of being subject of the 'psychic' operations we have singled out), we have brought the explanatory back into accord with what we experience, the 'phenomenological'.

In this way we give the phenomenological in the human case an explanatory and ontological status and thus avoid the evil in dualistic and materialist explanations which has always included the inventing of a gap between how we 'experience ourselves' and 'the realities as they are in themselves'. Thus, for instance, although we experience ourselves as incarnate consciousnesses,[24] the dualists have represented us as being in reality a composite of a spiritual substance in some external and contingent relation to a body. Or, although we know what it is to understand and to think in a way which makes complexity of a material kind quite alien, we are told that in fact understanding and thinking are states or processes in some apparatus such as the brain. These positions—involving the gap referred to—have been shown to be incoherent.

Nonetheless, aware that in the case both of the higher animals in general and of the human being in particular the relation between soul and body is a dynamic one only intelligible in terms of their functioning together, we may well look for some different way of speaking of the whole matter whereby soul and body are constituted together in the 'act' of existing which in the animal and human case is the 'act' of living. It is an alternative way of speaking along these lines which we will be seeking in Chapter XV.

4. The Objection That This View Re-Erects a False Contrast between Human Beings and the Other Animals

According to our account it is really only in the human being that the phenomenological way of speaking about the soul develops an explanatory and ontological aspect. But, on this basis, it might be strongly objected that we have re-erected a gulf between our ways of speaking about human beings and our ways of speaking about the other higher animals. However, all we need here is a certain clarity.

What is common to human beings and the higher animals is the fact that certain kinds of psychosomatic concept in regard to them as wholes are indispensable to the description and explanation of their behaviour and life, and that, in consequence of the character of some of these concepts, what I have called the phenomenological way of speaking of souls is viable and appropriate. This establishes community between human beings and their fellow animals, primarily at the level of perceptual, imagination-involving, and emotion influenced life, and secondarily at the more general teleological level of living things in

---

[24]This is to say 'incarnate souls' since "consciousnesses" means nothing new or different from "souls", whatever that means.

general. And these two kinds of community remain independently of whether or not in the human case this latter phenomenological discourse about 'souls' has some special ontic or explanatory function. What human beings and animals have in common is not that this phenomenologically given soul is an explanatory principle, let alone that it is subsistent, but these kinds of psychosomatic structure.

Aquinas forbids us to say that human souls are made in the making of their bodies, whereas he would allow us to say that, for instance, the souls of other animals are made in the making of the bodies of these animals, and this would appear to put human beings in stark contrast with other animals.

But perhaps he has here stated the matter too simply. It would seem that, on the one hand, one should say both that human souls are made in the making of complete human beings and that the souls of other living things are made in the making of the complete living things of which they are the souls, and, on the other hand, that one should deny, if the word "physical" is used in a modern sense, both that human souls are made in a physical process of making their physical bodies and that the souls of other living things are made in a physical process of making their physical bodies.

God's act of creating beings (in certain natures within an order of a certain nature) differs only logically from his act of upholding these beings (in these natures within the order of this nature), inasmuch as the second is a continuance of the first, so that what we have is the same species of act differently described according to what comes before it: the same power is involved in each. In his upholding of the order of the world it is required (if this order is indeed to continue) that in generation human beings should procreate human beings, horses should procreate horses, dogs should procreate dogs, and so forth, and in general that everything should proceed in accord with the general natures of things already in existence.

But it is no more true that the procreation of dogs by dogs or of horses by horses is a merely physical process than it is true that the procreation of human beings by human beings is a merely physical process. For, as Aquinas observes, even the operations of the vegetal soul require some principle surpassing the active and passive qualities of the elements (i.e., supposing those physical properties of things in the modern sense of "physical", which, he says, play an instrumental role in nutrition and growth), and the operations of the sentient soul transcend the merely physical in further ways:[25] generalizing, he says, that 'inasmuch as the active and passive qualities are dispositions of matter, they do not transcend matter',[26] in this implying that the dispositions of vegetal and sentient souls as well as of rational souls transcend matter, including of course the dispositions exercised in reproduction.

Therefore, it is not Aquinas' view that, apart from the aspect of the divine upholding of the physical elements in their nature, there is nothing involved in the reproduction of the sub-human animals and the plants beyond physical process, taking the word "physical" in a modern sense, whereas in the human case on top of the divine upholding of physical elements in their nature and physical process within this context, one has to postulate a creation of soul, soul to be inserted into the physical world. This description of what is involved in the continuance of nature is false to Aquinas, as well as defective in itself. The 'physical' in the modern sense of the word does not explain the biological or animal, let alone the human, and the creation of the human soul is not the insertion of an alien element into an otherwise self-contained and self-sufficient physical field. Rather the creating of the human soul as something existing in its own right is not a separate act, but something done incidentally, in keeping the normal course of things, within the very act of upholding the universe in all its aspects in its order and, according to this order, constituting a new human being in existence.

For, what we should say is that the difference between the human case and the case of other living things is this: that, in the human case, what comes to be is a human being, a human person, which is something which can continue to exist, albeit in a deprived state, even after the perishing of the body, because something has come to be (the human person or the human soul) which exists in its own right. Rather, in the sub-human cases, nothing comes to exist which can survive the perishing of the body, because nothing has come to be which exists in its own right even apart from the body.[27] If we speak of the soul as the principle of unity and operation of the living thing, then, inasmuch as in the human case the living thing can persist after

---

[25] *Q. D. De An.*, Q. 1, Resp.
[26] *Ibid.*
[27] *De Potentia*, Q. 3, Art. 9, Resp. in his second argument, is instructive.

death, we must say that the human soul also thus persists, and that this principle, the human soul, which came into being when the human being was procreated, was immortal and came into being with such a nature as to be thus persistent or immortal. By contrast, we will say that the souls of sub-human living things have no such persistence or immortality, and did not come into being with such a nature as to have any such persistence or immortality.

We shall therefore certainly say that, in relation to whatever lies within the powers of the physical as such, the coming to be of a new human being involves, not just an upholding of the physical, but a new creation—of something which is capable of persisting after the perishing of the body, because possessed of the capacity for operations which are not bodily (I mean such operations as those of linguistic understanding and thinking in words as exercised in this life)—whether we say that what is newly created is the human soul, or whether we say that it is the human being as such incorporating pre-existing matter.

The problem is not of what we should say in the human case, but of what we should say in the case of sub-human animals. Certainly, in relation to whatever lies within the powers of the physical as such, the coming to be of a new animal involves, not just an upholding of the physical, but what would appear to be a new creation—albeit not of anything capable of non-bodily operations or persistence after the perishing of the body. Whether we describe the coming to be of a new animal as involving a new creation depends on whether or not we conceive the bio-physical sphere as constituting a self-contained system, of animals and plants with their constitutions grounding their behaviour and relations, in a parallel way to that in which we conceive inanimate bodies as having constitutions grounding their behaviour and relations in such a way as to make the physical, to that extent, a self-contained system.

Therefore the problem here concerned is not about what we should say in the human case, but about our general view of the biological: the question is of the possibility of conceiving there to be some degree of self-containedness at the biological level analogous to the kind of self-containedness which is presumed at the physical level. One could dramatize the question by asking: is the cosmos a biosphere? But this is not a question which this book has to answer.

XV. How Human Beings Transcend the Body: Second Explanation—the Transcendence of the Human Being as Such

1. Introductory Remarks: Reasons for Seeking an Alternative Approach Which Explains the Human Transcendence without Reference to Soul

I wish now to explore the possibility of explaining human transcendence of the body in a way which turns only upon general concepts of existence, living, and situation, and which does not depend upon the particular phenomenological way of speaking about soul which we charted out in Chapter XIII.

Why should we seek out such an alternative approach? We showed that our phenomenological view of soul had nothing Cartesian in its inspiration and, indeed, was incompatible with Cartesianism or dualism in any form. It married with an Aristotelian holism which explained how the body had no status independent of the human being as a whole. We made it clear that we had not erected human souls into a separately definable entities as if they were a kind of thing in their own right, and that they could not be conceived of as 'parts' of human beings alongside other parts. An intellectual being could not be conceived as having its intellect as a part alongside other parts, as if it understood and thought by a part of itself, since (amongst other objections) this involved a distinction between the subject of understanding and thought and some apparatus by which it understood and thought, contrary to the requirement that intellectual substances be simple *qua* intellectual substances. All this was allowed for in our account of 'soul'.

However, it remains that the phenomenological idiom we canonized remains disputable in its credentials. It seems to be an idiom we can make some sense of, but not one which is forced upon us. The human soul thus spoken of only seems to have existence in dynamic relation to the human body, as in perception, imagination, and emotion, and even in the normal mode of exercise of the understanding which is in connection with the imagination, the use of models, and suchlike—or else only to have existence within the context of the existence and life of the human being as such within whatever context or situation this existence and life is set. Therefore, at least we should seek an account of this existence, life, and situation, in its own right even if only to underpin what has been said about soul.

The appropriateness of this approach should also be clear from thinking about the body. It is only the dynamism or *energeia* of the human being's existing or living which makes the body what it is—so that the body is not what it is statically as if what it is was a lump of matter which is how the imagination used in a certain way presents it. It is only by the person's existing or the animal's existing that the body exists, lives and is one. And, as we saw in Chapter VIII, we do not have to bring in the 'soul' to explain this—even though, granted that it be true that the body only exists by the person or animal's existing, this may license us to speak about soul in each of the two ways we have discussed.

2. Existence, Activity, and Actuality

The question is as to how we should think of existence.

There is an analytical question as to what general sorts of thing should be said to exist. This is the question as to what categories of thing we should attribute existence, and as to how we should explain the interconnection of the different uses of the word "exist" in regard to these different categories of thing. To this question I have elsewhere[1] returned the reply that there is one primary use[2] of

---

[1] *The Reality of Time and the Existence of God*, Chapter V, pp. 105–123, 126–129. In that book it was predominantly efficient causal activity which was taken to mark first substances (*subsistentiae, hypostases*), but, of course, any proper account of persons or intellectual substances would draw on the cases of the immanent activities of knowing and loving, and these will come indispensably into any account of the Trinity.

[2] Strictly speaking, in connection with each category of logical subject or 'entity', there are three distinguishable uses, one to mark the non-emptiness of a domain over which generalization is made, another to mark the instantiation of a property by at least one object within a domain, and a third to mark that a singular term has reference. These distinctions are made in *The Reality of Time and the Existence*

the word "exist" in regard to the subjects of acts, in a broad sense of
the word "act"[3]—the things which Aristotle called 'first substances'.
Arising out of this primary use there are also other uses in regard
to things we attribute to first substances and regard as contributing
to 'positive existence',[4] and there are also uses which arise by formal
analogy with this primary use so as to apply wherever the subject-
predicate structure of discourse has application—so that even so-called
'universals' have existence.[5]

Analysis thus gives primacy to the existence of substances.

But what is this 'existence' or what is it for a substance to exist?
To this question we can best give answer at least initially by ruling
out certain false pictures. (We have already elsewhere[6] dealt with the
objection that to exist is nothing more than to be a subject of predication. To say this is to transmute a first order statement presupposed by
other first order statements into a second order statement, to confuse
a thing's existing with the truth of a statement that it exists and to
disguise the contrast between what is non-formally involved in the
existence of substances and the formal or second order conditions of
the existence of anything, concrete or abstract.)

There is a tendency to think of existence, even the existence of
substances, as something static. Thus, we may think of things as just
being statically (one might say, stolidly) there, unmoving as rocks and
houses present themselves when objects to the imagination, available
to have existence stated of them—this existence, of course, adding

---

of God, Chapter IV, where the third—recording the existential presupposition shared
by a pair of contradictory singular subject-predicate statements—is shown to be most
fundamental.

[3]I mean here by "act" to cover all those predicates whose meaning requires
distinction according to posture in time, what grammarians call 'aspect', i.e., what
I have elsewhere called acts, processes, and activities, and which stand in contrast
with 'states'.

[4]The notion of positive existence is explained more precisely in *The Reality of
Time and the Existence of God*, pp. 108–112.

[5]This structure whereby there is a primary use of the word "exists" in regard
to substances, a spread of secondary uses ascribing 'positive existence' related to it by
paraphrase, and a setting whereby in regard to any logical subject the word can be
used by formal analogy with its use of substances, is described in *The Reality of Time
and the Existence of God*, pp. 126–129.

[6]*The Reality of Time and the Existence of God*, pp. 98–112, 126–129. We had
there to deal first with the misguided point of view which gave primacy to quantified
over singular existential statements.

nothing to them, but also not identical with any activity or going on in them. Or we may think of the subjects of which existence is asserted as possible things or concepts, having an unmoving being in a world of possible things or concepts, but of which existence is again asserted without being identical with any activity or going on.

To correct these ways of thinking is not easy. One's first inclination is to make the obvious remark that there is a certain incoherence if one treats a thing and its statically being there as if they were identical, so that there is no difference between a thing and something called 'its being', but then goes on to speak of existence as something we stated about the thing as if this existence (as the fact stated by an existential proposition) was something different from the thing said to exist. But this seems to be a difference only in one's mode of speaking.[7] Tritely, one can say that there is no separation between a thing and its existence in that there is no separation between a thing's existence and its existence. More pertinently, one can say that unless it is conceived in relation to activities a state is no different from a mere fact.

For one can advance further when one distinguishes existence as what is stated in a proposition from existence as an actuality in the world, and then further notices that the existing of a substance as an actuality in the world always consists in some activity.[8] Thus, for instance, we discover from science that the rock which appears to exist purely statically, as if its existence over a period might be merely the continuance of an existence which it might have instantaneously for a single instant only, in fact involves a massive pulsation of activity of an enormous number of protons, neutrons, and electrons in dynamic relation involving continuous change and movement—so that the

---

[7]Marking this difference in mode of speech is still vital. For it is only the existing not the thing which exists which is caused, really possible, or necessary. But real causation, possiblility, and necessity only arise with the concrete.

[8]Or is realized in this activity, and inseparable from this realization. An activity is always something inseparable from a subject, logically presupposing it (this does not mean that the subject is metaphysically prior to the activity, but only that the activity is understood as something logically predicated of the subject and not coming into our discourse otherwise)—I prescind here from the case of fields in physics which require further discussion. When I speak of "consisting in activity", I do not mean that the activities concerned can be understood (as it were as a heap of subjectless 'events' or 'goings-on') apart from the unity and connection which they have in virtue of being activities of the same subject, but only that the existence of the subject is not some other activity distinct from and underlying its activities (in the broad sense concerned) but has its realization in them.

idea of the instantaneous existence of substance within time is not only unimaginable and linguistically meaningless but also scientifically foolish. But in wide ranges of types of case one does not need science to tell one that existing, or (which is the same) continuing to exist, involve and indeed consist in some activity or going on: thus, for an animal, existing is living and bodily living consists in sundry activities characteristic of life and bodiliness.

When I say that in a certain case at a certain time existing or living consists in certain goings on or activities, or quite generally that existing and continuing to exist are the same, I do not mean that the statement asserting that a thing exists means the same as the statement that it continues to exist or the same as the statement that (e.g.) it is living, or that any of these statements mean the same as the statements describing the activities of particles, etc., or the activities of life pertinent at a particular time. All these statements have quite different meanings and functions in discourse. The question of what is meant by a statement is quite different from the question of what (if any) activity or 'actuality' it refers to, if true. Logically, the actuality called existence stands to various activities as trunk to a tree or a main current to variations of flow within it. Created actualities are not 'things', and not discrete from one another.

Analytical consideration, I have said, shows that substances are the primary subjects of existence and this in virtue of being subjects of predicates ascribing action or activity. What we are now saying is that this existing of substances is itself an 'activity', 'going on', or 'actuality'. This inseparability of substancehood and actuality, the notion of actuality bestraddling the notions of situation and activity, and situation and activity being inseparable, is something I have attempted to explain with greater precision elsewhere.[9] But what is in point at this stage of our argument is that the existence of substances is itself an actuality. It is in regard to substances rather than to other things that one has to insist that, as well as existence as what is asserted in a proposition (and might be asserted of abstract objects such as colours and numbers and of things whose existence consisted in the absence of something, such as holes and blindness), there is also existence as an actuality. This is what Aquinas occasionally called an 'act of being'— but some word like "activity" or "actuality" may be less misleading

---

[9] *The Reality of Time and the Existence of God*, pp. 138–161.

than the word "act" to render the Latin *actus* or the corresponding Greek *energeia*, since existing is not an action or act predicated of what exists but presupposed to any predication.[10]

3. The Existence of Human Beings, and Its Transcendence of Matter

It is against this background that we should consider the question of what is involved in the existence of human beings.

The existence of a rock, of a sheet of metal, or of a house, to take examples from our earlier discussions, will consist in activities which involve a mass of parts—atomic nuclei, electrons, and suchlike or, in the model example of a house, the bricks in relations involving various forces between them. However, the activities which constitute the living and existing of human beings and the higher animals of which we have been speaking include mind-involving operations, and thereby include operations of which the objects concerned are subjects. It is because of this that the activities concerned are integrated in such a way as to make the existing into the existing of what we have called an indivisible or 'focalized' subject, focalized and indivisible because subject of these mind-involving operations.

But now we have to recognize that, in the case of human beings, some of the operations concerned, in particular linguistic understanding and thinking in the medium of words, are not bodily operations. This we have demonstrated.

For we made it clear that the understanding of *langue* and the understanding of *parole* exercised in speech and hearing, and the sort of thinking which is 'in the medium of words', are 'operations' of the human being which have no inner neural realization: they have a bodily expression in speech, and are typically directed towards bodily objects (bodily things as real or intentional objects), but are not operations of any bodily organ.

---

[10]If one wanted to give theological expression to the above analysis, one might say the following. God does not give existence to a being as if there was a being and then he gave existence to it. God does not constitute beings in existence as if first there was a being in his mind and then a being in external existence. God does not constitute a thing's existing as if what he constituted was not the thing but an action of the thing, but what God constitutes is the thing existing, the thing and its existing inseparably in one act.

Therefore, some of the activities of the human being in which its existing or *esse* may wholly or partly consist are ones which do not involve the body, and because of the nodal character of these activities it follows that the human being has an *esse* which transcends the body.

We must not misunderstand this as if it implies that the human being in its essential nature was non-bodily. Under the aspect under which the human being transcends the body, viz., as the subject of understanding and thinking, it is undivided and indivisible in a way in which no body is and many lower living things are not; but, more than this, it has the kind of unity which any intellectual substance must have—that is, no division into internal parts in the aspect which is relevant to these operations which transcend the body. However, while the human being is alive, the subject of understanding and thinking is the human being itself which has bodily parts (even though these parts are not internal to these operations) and these bodily parts belong to the completeness of human nature. Nonetheless, while it is essential to human nature that the subject of linguistic understanding and thought be also the subject of perception and imagination, it remains that distinction of bodily parts and bodily function are not internal to the operations of understanding and thought as they are internal to the operations of perceiving and imagining.

The matter may be stated in the following way.

Since the operations of the human being are, in the case of some operations, not the operations of a bodily organ, the *esse* of the human bieng does not consist in the *esse* of the ensemble of its bodily organs. The activities in which its existence consists do not all have bodily activity internal to them, and so this existence transcends the body.

If the *esse* of the human being does not consist in this, there is no cause why it should cease at death.

The matter turns on this, that the existence of the subject is primarily correlative with activity as such, and the character of this existence is set by the character of the activities. If some of the activities, especially ones most nodal to life, transcend the body, then existence and life transcend the body. This way of presenting the matter embodies the kernel of the view of Aquinas as we saw it in Chapter XIV, shorn of its Aristotelianism and shorn of its dependence on speaking of souls.

By contrast, the nature of a subject is the principle, not just of some, but of all the activities of that subject—in the case of a human being, not just its understanding and thinking, but the whole spread of its animal and bodily activities including their physiological aspects. What we have in the human being is an animal with an *esse* which does not depend on the body. The nature of the human being is to be a 'rational animal', a psychosomatic being with linguistic understanding and thought.

We could say that the nature of the human being is to be a person conceived with and living animal life—but to say this is to speak less well and indeed misleadingly because it is not additional and external to an already constituted person to be conceived and to live animal life. Person (in the wider of the two senses we picked out) is not a genus of nature, happening to include God, angels, and human beings, specifying a 'what it is' of some individual which we have picked out and said something about: there is no such common nature. That is, whereas animal, plant, human being, horse, and the like are genera or species of nature, person is not another such overlapping the classsification 'animal' in the case of human beings.

However, the concept of person (in the wide sense), like the concept of first substance, is helpful to us in a different way: these terms apply to subjects of predication, not under the aspect of being of a certain nature, but precisely under the aspect of being subjects of 'acts'—whether causal actions, or acts of knowing and/or loving (taking these terms in a very open sense), or these latter as interrelated with forms of causal action. Wherever we have 'acts', we have a structure of substance as subject or *suppositum* and act or actuality, substance and actuality being correlative[11]—and 'personhood' simply marks the correlation with certain types of 'act', for to be a person is simply to be the subject of those kinds of act which are personal.

It is *qua* bodily being that the human being or other animal sees, because sight is the operation of a bodily organ. But it is not *qua* bodily being that the human being understands since understanding is not the operation of a bodily organ, but rather simply *qua* person. It does not follow that the essence or nature of the human being is

---

[11]This was the structure I groped towards in *The Reality of Time and the Existence of God*, Chapter V, especially articulated in pp. 112–123 and 138–161.

simply to be a person (in the unrestricted sense), rather than to be specifically a human being—and to the nature or essence of a human being bodiliness is an essential part, just as having four legs is an essential part of the nature of a horse, so that, though there can be horses who have lost a leg and these are still horses, this counts as a being deprived of something belonging to their nature. But it does follow that the *esse* of the human being, as precisely that which is presupposed to this kind of being's operations ("presuppose" is used here in its technical logicians meaning), does not involve bodiliness internally to it. [The concept of person as we are here using it is the concept of person in the less restricted sense explained in Chapter V, i.e., the sense in which it marks the whole range of application of predicates such as knowledge and love, and therefore covers angels and God if they exist as well as human beings. Taken in this way, it is (as we made clear in previous chapters)[12] not at all a proper genus or 'name of a nature', since angels, God, and human beings have natures calculated to quite different modes of understanding or knowledge.]

When one has died, one is not a nothing but one has no body: we could say that one is a soul, but this would not be a statement of what one is as if a soul were a sort of thing. We could say that one is oneself but that again is in a parallel way not a statement of what one is, as if one had not been oneself or not 'a self' when one had a body. Rather, a human being when he or she dies is a deprived person—and will continue to exist only in a deprived state without bodily parts and therefore also without the possibility of bodily expression of thought and without any bodily realization of togetherness or community unless or until there is a resurrection. When we speak of a person after his or her death as knowing and loving, we may also speak of his or her soul as knowing and loving, but it is logically important that this second way of speaking is just as much a secondary mode of speech as if, during his or her lifetime, we were to speak of his or her soul knowing and loving. After death it is still the person *qua* person which primarily knows and loves, not the soul or person supposedly *qua* soul, just as before death.

When a human being comes to be, we have the coming to be of a focalized subject of a nature to have operations which are not bodily, and thus the coming to be of a being whose *esse* transcends the body. This being persists through life and does not cease at death.

---

[12]In Chapter XIII, n. 11 and text, cf. Chapter XIV, Section 2 (c).

According to our earlier argument in Chapter IX the higher animals are also focalized subjects, standing in and relating to the world in key respects as indivisible. But, if one speaks of souls, then in the case of the souls of animals lower than the human, all the psychic operations—the ones in which the body does not 'obtrude'—predicated of these souls will contain bodily operations internally to them. These animal souls will be the subjects of concrete predications, but not without these predications involving the body sharing in the operations predicated. Therefore these souls cannot be spoken of as having any *esse* which transcends the body. Therefore, if we ask what there is of these animals as well as their bodily parts, there is nothing—in particular no soul—which has *esse* in its own right, or in brief nothing which has *esse* in the primary sense which we are concerned with.

It is against this background that I gave an explanation of soul which incorporated from the start that it is the subject of concrete predicates because it is (in the case of human beings and the highest animals, during life) nothing distinct from the human being or animal itself, considered in its role in operations in respect of which it figures as essentially indivisible. It is not a part of the human being enjoying separate existence from other parts (the bodily parts) and interacting with them. Rather the psychic operations of human beings by their very nature present themselves phenomenologically in two ways, the first as having the human being as such as their subject and the second in the way explained in Chapter XIII as having the soul as their subject, the two in the same act. Thought of in this way, in the case of human beings and the highest animals, the *esse* of the soul is nothing other than the *esse* of the whole being, and constitutive of the nature and unity of the body. In the human case, its *esse* transcends the body, and, if one can speak of what there is of the human being besides the bodily parts, this that there is besides the bodily parts (this soul) is subsistent, created in the coming to be of each human being and continuing after death.

But one does not *need* to speak in this way in order to show that the continuance of human existence does not depend upon the continuance of the body. In that the existence of a substance, in this case a human being, consists in activities or operations and, in the human case, these activities or operations transcend the body—human existing therewith also transcending the body.

Does what we have said about the human person's transcendence explain and underpin this earlier way of speaking about souls? It seems that it does. For it was said that the *esse* of the human soul was none other than the *esse* of the human being as such. What this later argument has established is this: that there comes to be in the coming to be of a human being a principle of activity which is a focalized subject, which has an *esse* which transcends the body, and which, therefore, does not cease at death. Now, if it is legitimate to talk of the phenomenological soul at all, then one will certainly say these things of the human soul and its *esse* will indeed be none other than that of the human being as such. But in speaking of its transcendence in *esse* one will say nothing which one has not said in speaking of the transcendence of the human person.

In the meantime, our general account of the nature of the human being remains one to which the capacity for bodily as well as non-bodily activity is integral. There is no question of a pre-existing soul coming in to relation by incarnation or re-incarnation with a separately originating body, but only the conceivability of a human being as a unitary psychophysical being coming into existence as a unity, then becoming deprived by death of faculties depending on the body, and then being resurrected, the body re-constituted. For the human being has no identity apart from its origin and history, a history in which it matures from being a *tabula rasa* without determinate intellectual and practical virtues and vices to the stage in their determination which it has reached at time at which its identity is being considered. Therefore, although we can make some sense of the notion of resurrection as a restoration of capacities to a being by nature bodily, we can make no sense of a notion of re-incarnation whereby one and the same dualisti-cally conceived soul might live and mature many times through many separate histories associated with different bodies. Indeed, rootedness in history is part of the global character of human situatedness, of which I will now speak.

4. The Human Situation and Human Nature as Co-ordinate, and Both as Revealed by Language: The Question Raised by Death

It has been held that there is no being for human beings which is not a 'being there'[13] in the sense of a being in a situation. But

---

[13]Such an idea might be suggested by the connotations of *Dasein* in Heidegger.

the question is how, for each kind of being, this situation should be conceived. And, most obviously in the human case, this situation must not be conceived in an atomistic and discontinuous way, as if, for instance, there would be a problem as to how one and the same human being could exist first in one situation on one day and then in another, after sleep, on a later day. Rather, the situation of the human being is always a global one, the situation set by being of such a nature as to continue through from one day to later times, the situation at the earlier times being partly set by the possibilities, desires, hopes, and unknowns of later times. Our account of this human nature which exists in and co-ordinately with this global situation must be co-ordinate with our account of this global situation, and vice versa.

The bringing of language into the heart of the description of the human case allows one to see how it is that human nature and the human situation are not just co-ordinate but internally related to one another. The nature specific to human beings includes the capacity for language, a capacity for speech or *parole* which is expressive because it is a realization of *langue*, i.e., a capacity which involves the whole integrated structure of concrete subject, tense, and self-reflection described in Chapter X. That is, each new human individual is geared to be laid open, not only to what he or she is laid open to as an animal, but this and more in virtue of his or her linguistic capacity. And one's situation as an individual human being is defined not just according to the types of relation to one's environment which one shares with other higher animals but more generally by the scope of what language lays one open to—so that one's perspectives are not limited to one's immediate opinions and interests, one's locality and tribe and its customs, but extend to questions of 'fact' or 'objective truth', the good and the right, one's larger environment and community with nature, the cosmos and to God.

With the question set by the fact of death, there is raised the anxiety as to whether, as a human being, one is locked into one locality in space and time in suchwise that wider perspectives, wider directings of wonder and concern, and even the attempt to be critical of the opinions and values of the tribe, are all without point or sense. They might then be only like sand castles, not real ones—perhaps hedonistic diversions, but with no realistic orientation whatsoever—what is realistic in that case being only what is in accord with the felt interests of the individual and the tribe, the value of criticism being limited to the more efficient securing of these interests. If, as a human being, one is in fact a merely material being, one's sense of understanding and one's judgement being in fact neurologically determined according to systems preferentially perpetuated by evolutionary laws of the survival of the fittest, or, to the extent that this is not the case, determined only by chance, then one may as well accept one's condition and forswear the paths of anxiety. Whether one does or not is of course of no great matter.

However, the fact that linguistic understanding and thought in the medium of words transcend physical processes in the way we have demonstrated gives the lie to such limitation of human vistas, wonder, and concern. There is no basis for regarding such limitation as realistic. The human being's situation after death may be one of deprivation and emptiness—for philosophy this is the land of the unknown. But it remains that one's real situation as a human being is not one of entrapment, metaphysically or in the determination of one's thought and will, within confines set by one's neurology, by the evolutionary emergence of his species, by one's individual character, or by one's tribe.

On the contrary, it is entirely realistic for the human being to accept the wider perspectives suggested by the seeking after the objectively true, reasonable, right, and good. And it is entirely appropriate for human beings to find object for wonder and for concern in the cosmos and in their wider environment, and to see in this occasion for wonder at the cause of this cosmos and of its continuance. As well as hope and desire for truth and respect for truth, good and respect for good, in themselves and amongst their fellows with whom they have a given community, it also belongs to their nature as revealed by language to have religious wonder, hope and desire—and for it to be possible for them to have the perspectives of this life set by this wonder, and even for them to have hope and desire for an immediate loving knowledge of God. And the fact that the human being is not by nature a being whose existing consists in activities to which the material is integral shows that this hope and desire is not chimerical. It is not a datum that death is a door whose closing closes all hopes and all life. Rather, from the standpoint of philosophy, the datum is that, because of the way human linguistic understanding and thought transcend the material, death is not a closure of life or hope, but only a closure of knowledge of and control over what is to come.

The works or products of language are not the only elements in human life which exhibit human transcendence. Human transcendence is also involved in the enjoyment of music, the perception of the wonders of nature in their wonder, the appreciation of works of architecture and painting. But it is language which is the differentiating feature of the human species of animal, and it is language which, in the way we have shown, offers dialectical or philosophical proof of human transcendence. It is also the works of language which not only allow this proof (a proof which is itself a work of language) but also exhibit most explicitly the range of experience to which human beings are open, the full scope of the proper objects of human fear and anger, hope, desire, and wonder, and in this way the full character of the human situation.

Bibliography

Standard works, e.g., Plato, Aristotle, Augustine, Descartes, Locke, Berkeley and Hume, are not listed where no particular edition is referred to.

Ajdukiewicz, K., 'Syntactic Connexion', in *Polish Logic*, 1920–1939, ed. Storrs McCall, OUP, Oxford, 1967.

Allport, D.A., 'What Concept of Consciousness', in *Consciousness in Contemporary Science*, ed. A.J. Marcel and E. Bisiach, OUP, Oxford, 1988.

———, 'Language and Cognition', in *Approaches to Language*, ed. R. Harris, Pergamon, Oxford, 1983.

———, 'Distributed Memory, Modular Subsystems and Dysphasia', ed. S. Newman and R. Epstein, Churchill Livingstone, Edinburgh, 1984.

———, 'Patterns and actions: cognitive mechanisms are content-specific', in *Cognitive Psychology: New Directions*, ed. G. Claxton, RKP, London, 1980.

———, 'Attention and performance', in *Cognitive Psychology: New Directions*, ed. G. Claxton, RKP, London, 1980.

———, 'Components of the mental lexicon', with E. Funnell, *Phil. Trans. R. Soc.*, London, 1981.

See Funnell, E., and D.A. Allport.

Anscombe, G.E.M., *Collected Philosophical Papers*, Blackwell, Oxford, 1981.

———, *Intention*, Blackwell, Oxford, 1958.

Anscombe, G.E.M., and Geach, P.T., *Three Philosophers*, Blackwell, Oxford, 1961.

Armstrong, D.M., *Perception and the Physical World*, RKP, London, 1961.

———, *A Materialist Theory of the Mind*, RKP, London, 1968.

Aquinas, see Thomas Aquinas

Austin, J.L., *Philosophical Papers*, OUP, Oxford, 1961.

———, *Sense and Sensibilia*, OUP, Oxford, 1962.

———, *How to do things with words*, OUP, Oxford, 1962.

Ayer, A.J., *Foundations of Empirical Knowledge*, Macmillan, London, 1964.

———, *Philosophical Essays*, Macmillan, London, 1954.

———, *The Problem of Knowledge*, Macmillan, London, 1956.

———, *Concept of a Person and other essays*, Macmillan, London, 1963.

———, *Metaphysics and Common-sense*, Macmillan, London, 1969.

Bennett, J., *Rationality*, RKP, London, 1964.

Blackburn, S., *Spreading the Word*, OUP, Oxford, 1984.

Bohm, D., *Causality and Chance in Modern Physics*, RKP, London, 1957.

————, 'Quantum Theory as an Indication of a New Order in Physics', *Proceedings of the Enrico Fermi International Summer School*, 1971, pp. 412–469.

Braine, D., 'The Nature of Knowledge', *Proc. Arist. Soc.*, 72, 1971/2.

————, 'Varieties of Necessity', *Proc. Arist. Soc.*, suppl. vol. 46, 1972.

————, *The Reality of Time and the Existence of God*, OUP, Oxford, 1988.

————, 'Human Animality: Its Relevance to the Shape of Ethics' and 'Human Life: Its Secular Sacrosanctness', in *Ethics, Technology, and Medicine*, ed. David Braine and Harry Lesser, Gower, Aldershot, 1988.

————, 'The human and the inhuman in medicine: review of issues concerning reproductive technology' (forthcoming).

————, *The Expressiveness of Words: The Key to the Nature of Language* (forthcoming).

Carnap, R., *Meaning and Necessity*, University of Chicago, London, 1947.

Chisholm, R.M., *Person and Object*, Allen and Unwin, London, 1976.

Coady, C.A.J., *Testimony*, OUP, Oxford (forthcoming).

Davidson, D., 'Truth and Meaning', *Synthese*, vol. 17, Dordrecht, 1967.

————, 'Radical Interpretation', *Dialectica*, 27, 1974.

————, *Essays on Actions and Events*, OUP, Oxford, 1980.

De Chardin, Teilhard, *The Phenomenon of Man*, Collins, London, 1959.

Dennett, D., *Brainstorms*, Harvester, Hassocks, Sussex, U.K., 1979.

Descartes, R., *Descartes' Philosophical Writings*, selected and ed. Norman Kemp Smith, Macmillan, London, 1952.

Dummett, M.A., *Frege: Philosophy of Language*, Duckworth, London, 1973.

————, *Truth and Other Enigmas*, Duckworth, London, 1978.

Evans, C.O., *The Subject of Conciousness*, Allen and Unwin, London, 1970.

Evans, G., *Varieties of Reference*, OUP, 1982.

Feferman, S., 'Kurt Gödel: Conviction and Caution', in *Gödel's Theorem in Focus*, ed. S.G. Shanker, Croom Helm, New York, 1988.

Flew, A., *An Introduction to Western Philosophy: Ideas and Arguments from Plato to Sartre*, Thames and Hudson, London, 1971.

Frege, G., *Foundations of Arithmetic*, Blackwell, Oxford, 1959.

Funnell, E., and Allport, D.A., 'Non-linguistic cognition and word meanings: Neuropsychological exploration of common mechanisms', in *Language Perception and Production: Relationships between Listening, Speaking, Reading and Writing*, ed. A. Allport, D.G. MacKay, W. Prinz and E. Scheerer, Academic Press, London, 1987.

Gardiner, A., *The Theory of Speech and Language*, OUP, Oxford, 1932.

Geach, P.T., *Mental Acts*, RKP, London, 1957.

————, *God and the Soul*, RKP, London, 1969.

See Anscombe and Geach.

Gettier, E.L., 'Is Justified True Belief Knowledge?' *Analysis*, vol. 23, 1963, Blackwell, Oxford.

Gibson, J.J., 'The Concept of Stimulus in Psychology', *American Psychologist*, vol. 15, 1960.

————, *The Senses Considered as Perceptual Systems*, Houghton Mifflin, Boston, 1966.

————, *The Ecological Approach to Visual Perception*, Houghton Mifflin, Boston, 1979.

Gödel, K., 'On Formally Undecidable Propositions of Principia Mathmatica and Related Systems' (1931), reprinted in *Gödel's Theorem in Focus*, ed. S.G. Shanker, Croom Helm, London, 1988.

————, 'What Is Cantor's Continuum Problem?' in *Philosophy of Mathematics: Selected Readings*, ed. P. Benacerraf and H. Putnam, Blackwell, Oxford, 1964.

Goldstein, K., *Der Aufbau des Organismus*, Nijhoff, The Hague, 1934 (*The Organism*, New York, 1938).

Graham, R.L., Rothschild, B.L., and Spencer, J.H., *Ramsey Theory*, John Wiley, New York, 1980.

Grice, H.P., 'The Causal Theory of Perception', *Proc. Arist. Soc.*, suppl. vol. 35, 1961.

————, 'Utterer's Meaning, Sentence-meaning, and Word-meaning', *Foundations of Language*, 4, 1968.

Hacker, P.M.S., *Insight and Illusion*, revised ed., OUP, Oxford, 1986.

Hamlyn, D., *Psychology of Perception*, RKP, London, 1957.

Hampshire, S., *Thought and Action*, 2nd edition, Chatto and Windus, London, 1982.

Harre, R. and Madden, E.H., *Causal Powers*, Blackwell, Oxford, 1975.

Harrington, L., see Paris, J., and Harrington, L.

Hart, H.L.A., 'The Ascription of Responsibility and Rights', reprinted in *Logic and Language* (First Series), ed. A.G.N. Flew, Blackwell, Oxford, 1951.

Heidegger, M., *Being and Time*, Blackwell, Oxford, 1962.

Hirst, R.J., *The Problems of Perception*, George Allen and Unwin, London, 1959.

Hornsby, J., *Actions*, RKP, London, 1980.

Jackson, F., *Perception*, CUP, Cambridge, U.K., 1977.

————, 'The Existence of Mental Objects', in *Perceptual Knowledge*, ed. J. Dancy, Oxford, 1988.

Jespersen, O., *The Philosophy of Grammar*, George Allen and Unwin, London, 1924.

Johnson, A.R., *The Vitality of the Individual in the Thought of Ancient Israel*, 2nd ed., University of Wales Press, Cardiff, 1964.

Kenny, A., *Action, Emotion, and Will*, Routledge, London, 1963.

————, 'Intellect and Imagination in Aquinas' in *Aquinas: A Collection of Critical Essays*, ed. A. Kenny, Macmillan, London, 1970.

————, 'Freedom and Determinism' in *Will, Freedom and Power*, Blackwell, Oxford, 1975.

Kleene, S.C., *Mathematical Logic*, Wiley, New York, 1967.

Kripke, S., *Wittgenstein on Rules and Private Language*, Blackwell, Oxford, 1982.

Lloyd, A.C., 'The Self in Berkeley's Philosophy', in *Essays on Berkeley*, ed. J. Foster and H. Robinson, OUP, Oxford, 1985.

Lonergan, B., *Verbum*, Darton, Longman, and Todd, London, 1967.

Lucas, J., 'Mind, Machines and Gödel', in *Philosophy* (1961), London.

Lyons, J., *Semantics*, CUP, Cambridge, 1977.

Mackie, J.L., *Problems from Locke*, OUP, Oxford, 1976.

Malcolm, N., 'Wittgenstein's Philosophical Investigations', in *Knowledge and Certainty*, Prentice-Hall, New Jersey, 1964.

———, *Ludwig Wittgenstein: A Memoir*, OUP, Oxford, 1967.

———, *Problems of Mind*, Allen and Unwin, London, 1972.

Merleau-Ponty, M., *The Structure of Behaviour*, Methuen, London, 1965.

———, *The Phenomenology of Perception*, RKP, London, 1962.

Mitchell, B., *Justification of Religious Belief*, Macmillan, London, 1973.

Moore, G.E., *Ethics*, OUP, Oxford, 1912.

———, *Some Main Problems of Philosophy*, George Allen and Unwin, London, 1953.

Nagel, T., 'Physicalism', *Philosophical Review* 74, 1965.

———, 'What is it like to be a bat?' in *Mortal Questions*, CUP, Cambridge, 1979.

———, 'The Limits of Objectivity' in *The Tanner Lectures on Human Values 1980*, I, CUP, Cambridge, 1980.

Nowell-Smith, P.H., *Ethics*, Penguin, Harmondsworth, U.K., 1954.

O'Shaughnessy, B., *The Will: A Dual Aspect Theory*, CUP, Cambridge, 1980.

Paris, J., and Harrington, L., 'A Mathematical Incompleteness in Peano Arithmetic', in *Handbook of Mathematical Logic*, ed. J. Barwise, North-Holland, Amsterdam, 1977.

Passingham, R.E., *The Human Primate*, Freeman, New York, 1982.

Peacocke, C., *Holistic Explanation: Action, Space, Interpretation*, OUP, Oxford, 1979.

Plantinga, A., *God and Other Minds*, Cornell, Ithaca, New York, 1967.

Polanyi, M., *Personal Knowledge*, RKP, London, 1958.

Price, H.H., *Perception*, Methuen, London, 1932.

———, *Hume's Theory of the External World*, OUP, Oxford, 1940.

Quine, W.O. von, 'On What Exists', in *From a Logical Point of View*, reprinted Harper and Row, New York, 1963.

———, 'Homage to Rudolf Carnap' in *Boston Studies in the Philosophy of Science*, VIII (1970), Reidel, Dordrecht, 1971.

Rahner, K., *Theological Investigations*, vol. 1, Darton, Longman, and Todd, London, 1961.

Ramsey, F.P., *Foundations of Mathematics and other Logical Essays*, RKP, London, 1931.

Riet, G. van, *Problemes d'Epistemologie*, Publications Universitaire, Louvain, London, 1960.

Robinson, Howard, 'The General Form of the Argument for Berkeleian Idealism', in *Essays on Berkeley*, ed. J. Foster and H. Robinson, OUP, Oxford, 1985.

Robinson, H.W., 'Hebrew Psychology' in *The People and the Book*, ed. A.S. Peake, OUP, Oxford, 1925.

———, *The Christian Doctrine of Man*, 3rd ed., T.& T. Clark, Edinburgh, 1926.

Russell, B., 'On Denoting', *Mind*, 1905.

Ryan, C.P., O.P., 'The Theory of Substance as developed by Aquinas considered with reference to later philosophy', 1948, MS D. Phil. CO21–2, Bodleian Library, Oxford.

Ryle, G., *The Concept of Mind* (Hutchinson, London, 1949), Penguin, Harmondsworth, 1963.

——, *Collected Papers*, Hutchinson, London, 1971.

——, 'Mowgli in Babel', in *On Thinking*, Blackwell, Oxford, 1979.

Schopenhauer, A., *The World as Will and Idea*, trans. R.B. Haldane and J. Kemp, Kegan Paul, Trench, Grabner, London, 1883.

Searle, J., *Intentionality*, CUP, Cambridge, 1983.

——, *Minds, Brains and Science*, BBC, London, 1984.

Shoemaker, S., *Self-Knowledge and Self-Identity*, Cornell, New York, 1962.

Sperber, D., and Wilson, D., *Relevance*, Blackwell, Oxford, 1986.

Strawson, P.F., 'On Referring', reprinted in *Logico-Linguistic Papers*, Methuen, London, 1971.

——, *Individuals*, Methuen, London, 1959.

——, 'Perception and Its Objects', reprinted in *Perceptual Knowledge*, ed. J. Dancy, OUP, Oxford, 1988.

Swinburne, R., *The Evolution of the Soul*, OUP, Oxford, 1986.

Taylor, C., *The Explanation of Behaviour*, RKP, London, 1964.

Thomas Aquinas, *Summa Theologica, Prima Pars* (cited as *S. Th. Ia*); English trans. English Dominican Fathers (2nd ed.; Burns and Oates, London, 1941), vols. i-v; Parallel Latin and English edition, English Dominican Fathers (Blackfriars, London, 1961–70), vols. i-xv.

——, *Summa Contra Gentes* (cited as *SCG*); trans. Fathers of the English Dominican Province, Burns and Oates, London, 1929, and more recently, trans. A.C. Pegis, Notre Dame UP, Notre Dame, 1975, 5 vols.

——, *Commentary on Aristotle's De Anima* (cited as *Comm. De An.*); Moerbeke's translation of Aristotle's *De Anima* and Aquinas' commentary, trans. K. Foster and S. Humphries, RKP, London, 1951.

——, *Quaestiones Disputatae De Anima* (cited as *Q. D. De An.*); English trans., *The Soul*, trans. J.P. Rowan, Herder and Herder, New York, 1949.

——, *Quaestiones Disputatae De Potentia Dei* (cited as *De Potentia*); English trans., *On the Power of God*, trans. English Dominican Fathers, Burns and Oates, London, 1932–34.

Turing, A.M., 'Systems of Logic based on Ordinals', *London Mathematical Society*, vol. 45 (1939), London.

Whitehead, A.N., *Science and the Modern World*, Cambridge University Press, New York, 1926.

Wiggins, D., *Sameness and Substance*, Blackwell, Oxford, 1980.

——, 'Towards a Reasonable Libertarianism', in *Needs, Values, Truth: Essays in the Philosophy of Value*, Blackwell, Oxford, 1987.

Wittgenstein, L., *Tractatus*, trans. D.F. Pears and B.F. McGuiness, RKP, London, 1961.

——, *Philosophical Grammar*, trans. A.J.P. Kenny, Blackwell, Oxford, 1974.

——, *Philosophical Investigations*, trans. G.E.M. Anscombe, Blackwell, Oxford, 1953.

——, *Remarks on the Philosophy of Psychology*, trans. G.E.M. Anscombe, Blackwell, Oxford, 1980.

Wojtyla, K., *Love and Responsibility* (1960), trans. H.T. Willetts, Collins, London, and Farrar, Straus, and Giroux, New York, 1981.

Woodger, J.H., *Biology and Language*, CUP, Cambridge, 1952.

Wooldridge, D., *The Machinery of the Brain*, McGraw Hill, New York, 1963.

Wright, C., *Realism, Meaning and Truth*, Blackwell, Oxford, 1987.

Index of Names